NOTE

MOST OF THE ESSAYS in this volume are reprinted from earlier books: From *Primitivism and Decadence* (Arrow Editions, 1937) The Morality of Poetry, The Experimental School, Poetic Convention, Primitivism and Decadence, and The Influence of Meter on Poetic Convention; from *Maule's Curse* (New Directions, 1938) Maule's Curse, Fenimore Cooper, Herman Melville, Edgar Allan Poe, Jones Very and R. W. Emerson, Emily Dickinson, and Maule's Well; from *The Anatomy of Nonsense* (New Directions, 1943) Preliminary Problems, Henry Adams, Wallace Stevens, T. S. Eliot, John Crowe Ransom, and Post Scripta.

Acknowledgment should be made also to the following magazines, in which some of this material appeared originally: The Hound and Horn, Poetry, American Literature, The American Review, and The Kenyon Review.

IN DEFENSE OF
REASON

PRIMITIVISM AND DECADENCE:
A Study of American Experimental Poetry

MAULE'S CURSE:
Seven Studies in the History of American Obscurantism

THE ANATOMY OF NONSENSE

THE SIGNIFICANCE OF *THE BRIDGE* by Hart Crane,
or What Are We to Think of Professor X?

BY

Yvor Winters

ROUTLEDGE & KEGAN PAUL LTD
Broadway House, 68-74 Carter Lane
London, E.C.4

CONTENTS

IN DEFENSE OF REASON

A FOREWORD

THE ESSAYS NOW REPRINTED in this volume are the work of more than fifteen years. Although this collection, like any collection of essays, suffers from its miscellaneous character, there is a single theory of literature developed throughout and a single theory of the history of literature since the Renaissance. These theories are developed mainly with reference to American literature. It may be of some service to the reader if I recapitulate briefly.

There have been various ideas regarding the nature and function of literature during the twenty-five hundred years or so that literature has been seriously discussed. One might think, offhand, that the possibilities were limitless; but they are actually limited and even narrowly limited—the ideas are all classifiable under a fairly small number of headings. I shall not attempt an historical survey but shall merely attempt a brief classificatory survey. The theories in question can all be classified, I believe, under three headings: the didactic, the hedonistic, and the romantic. I am not in sympathy with any of these, but with a fourth, which for lack of a better term I call the moralistic. This concept of literature has not been adequately defined in the past so far as my limited knowledge extends, but I believe that it has been loosely implicit in the inexact theorizing which has led to the most durable judgments in the history of criticism.

The didactic theory of literature is simple; it is this: that literature offers us useful precepts and explicit moral instruction. If the theory is sound, then literature is useful; but the question arises as to whether there may not be other fields of study, such

3

as religion or ethics, which may accomplish the same end more efficiently. The question is usually met by the Horatian formula, which combines the didactic with the hedonistic, telling us that the function of literature is to provide instruction (or profit) in conjunction with pleasure, to make instruction palatable. Of this I shall say more later. There arises another question in connection with the didactic theory: can one say, as someone—I believe it was Kenneth Burke—has remarked, that *Hamlet* was written to prove that procrastination is the thief of time, or to prove something comparably simple? Or is there more than that to *Hamlet*? And if there is more, is it worth anything? It seems obvious to me that there is more and that it is worth a great deal, that the paraphrasable content of the work is never equal to the work, and that our theory of literature must account not only for the paraphrasable content but for the work itself. The didactic theory of literature fails to do this.

The hedonist sees pleasure as the end of life, and literature either as a heightener of pleasure or as the purveyor of a particular and more or less esoteric variety of pleasure. The term *pleasure* is applied indiscriminately to widely varying experiences: we say, for example, that we derive pleasure from a glass of good whisky and that we derive pleasure from reading *Hamlet*. The word is thus misleading, for it designates two experiences here which have little relationship to each other. There is a great range in the kinds of pleasure advocated in various hedonistic philosophies, but in general one might remark this defect which is common to nearly all, perhaps to all, such systems: pleasure is treated as an end in itself, not as a by-product of something else. If we recognize that certain feelings which are loosely classifiable as forms of pleasure result from our recognition of various kinds of truth and from the proper functioning of our natures in the process of this recognition, we then have a principle which may enable us to distinguish these pleasures from pleasures less important or less desirable, such as the pleasures or satisfactions which we derive from the gratification of physical appetites or from the excitement of stimulants, and a principle which may even enable us to evaluate relatively to each other the

4

higher pleasures themselves. But pleasure then becomes incidental and not primary, and our system can no longer be classified as properly hedonistic. Furthermore, there is this distinction at least between hedonistic ethics and hedonistic aesthetics: hedonistic ethics, as in the philosophy of Epicurus, may take on a somewhat passive or negativistic character; that is pleasure may come to be more or less nearly identified simply with the avoidance of pain. But one cannot praise a poem or a picture merely by saying that it gives no pain: the experience of the poem or of the picture must be strongly positive. Hedonistic theories of literature tend in the main, and this is especially true in the past two hundred years, to take one of two forms.

The first might be connected with the name of Walter Pater. According to this view there is a close relation between hedonistic ethics and hedonistic aesthetics. Pleasure is the aim of life. Pleasure consists in intensity of experience; that is in the cultivation of the feelings for their own sake, as a good in themselves. And literature, or at any rate the arts in general, can provide a finer technique of such cultivation than can any other mode of activity. We meet here the first difficulty which I mentioned in connection with hedonistic doctrines; namely, that unless we have illicit relations with some non-hedonistic ethical theory, we have no way of distinguishing among the many and diverse excitements that are commonly described as pleasurable. And we shall discover, as a matter of human nature which is recorded in the history of literature and the other arts, that this search for intensity of experience leads inevitably to an endless pursuit either of increasing degrees of violence of emotion or of increasingly elusive and more nearly meaningless nuances, and ultimately to disillusionment with art and with life. It is possible, of course, that art and life are really worthless, but on the other hand it is possible that they are valuable. And until we have made sure that our hedonistic theory offers a true description of human experience, that no better description is possible, we should be unwise to commit ourselves to it, for the ultimate consequences appear both certain and unfortunate.

The second form of hedonistic theory tends to dissociate the

5

artistic experience sharply from all other experience. T. S. Eliot, for example, tells us that the human experience about which the poem appears to be written has been transmuted in the aesthetic process into something new which is different in kind from all other experience. The poem is not then, as it superficially appears, a statement about a human experience, but is a thing in itself. The beginnings of this notion are to be found in Poe and are developed further by the French Symbolists, notably by Mallarmé. The aim of the poem so conceived is again pleasure, pleasure conceived as intensity of emotion; but the emotion is of an absolutely special sort. Some such notion of the artistic experience is the essential concept of Santayana's aesthetics; in fact, it is essential to almost any treatment of "aesthetics" as a branch of philosophy, and one will find it everywhere in the work of the academic aestheticians of the past half-century. The nature of the "aesthetic" experience as conceived in these terms has never been clearly defined; we commonly meet here a kind of pseudo-mysticism. The chief advantage of this kind of hedonism over the Paterian variety is that one can adhere to it without adhering to a doctrine of ethical hedonism, for art and life are absolutely severed from each other. Eliot, for example, considers himself a Christian. The chief disadvantage is that it renders intelligible discussion of art impossible, and it relegates art to the position of an esoteric indulgence, possibly though not certainly harmless, but hardly of sufficient importance to merit a high position among other human activities. Art, however, has always been accorded a high position, and a true theory of art should be able to account for this fact.

Certain theorists who have been aware that art is more than moral precept on the one hand and more than a search for cultivated excitement on the other have tried to account for its complexity by combining the didactic and the hedonistic theories: this gives us the Horatian formula, that art combines profit with pleasure. When this formula occurs, as it often does, in the writing of a great poet or of some other person who takes his poetry seriously, it apparently represents a somewhat rough and ready recognition of the fact that poetry has intellectual content and

6

something more; that its power is real and cannot be accounted for too easily. But if one regard the doctrine itself, and regard it as pure theory, it is unsatisfactory; or at any rate it relegates art to an unsatisfactory position. For the didactic element in art so conceived will be no more efficient as didacticism than we have seen it to be before: that is, the serious moralist may quite reasonably argue that he prefers to get his teaching in a more direct and compact form; and the pleasure is still in the unhappy predicament in which we found it in the purely hedonistic theory.

The Romantic theory of literature takes account more seriously than the theories which I have thus far mentioned of the power which literature seems to exert over human nature, and to that extent offers a more realistic view of literature. I am concerned with literature which may be loosely described as artistic: that is, with literature which communicates not only thought but also emotion. I do not like the expression *imaginative literature*, for in its colloquial acceptation the phrase excludes too much: it excludes the persuasive and hortatory, for example, the sermon and the political tract; and *imagination* as a term of sophisticated criticism has been used so variously and so elusively, especially during the past hundred and fifty years, that I am not quite sure what it means. But the power of artistic literature is real: if we consider such writers as Plato, Augustine, Dante, Shakespeare, Rousseau, Voltaire, Emerson, and Hitler, to go no further, we must be aware that such literature has been directly and indirectly one of the greatest forces in human history. The Gospels gave a new direction to half the world; *Mein Kampf* very nearly reversed that direction. The influence of Rimbaud and of Mallarmé is quite as real but has operated more slowly and with less of obvious violence. It behooves us to discover the nature of artistic literature, what it does, how it does it, and how one may evaluate it. It is one of the facts of life, and quite as important a fact as atomic fission. In our universities at present, for example, one or another of the hedonistic views of literature will be found to dominate, although often colored by Romantic ideas, with the result that the professors of literature, who for the most part are genteel but mediocre men, can make but a poor defence of their profession, and the professors of science, who are frequently men of great intelligence but of limited interests and education, feel a politely disguised contempt for it; and thus the study of one of the most pervasive and powerful influences on human life is traduced and neglected.

The Romantics, however, although they offer a relatively realistic view of the power of literature, offer a fallacious and dangerous view of the nature both of literature and of man. The Romantic theory assumes that literature is mainly or even purely an emotional experience, that man is naturally good, that man's impulses are trustworthy, that the rational faculty is unreliable to the point of being dangerous or possibly evil. The Romantic theory of human nature teaches that if man will rely upon his impulses, he will achieve the good life. When this notion is combined, as it frequently is, with a pantheistic philosophy or religion, it commonly teaches that through surrender to impulse man will not only achieve the good life but will achieve also a kind of mystical union with the Divinity: this, for example, is the doctrine of Emerson. Literature thus becomes a form of what is known popularly as self-expression. It is not the business of man to understand and improve himself, for such an effort is superfluous: he is good as he is, if he will only let himself alone, or, as we might say, let himself go. The poem is valuable because it enables us to share the experience of a man who has let himself go, who has expressed his feelings, without hindrance, as he has found them at a given moment. The ultimate ideal at which such a theory aims is automatism. There is nothing in the theory to provide a check on such automatism; if the individual man is restrained by some streak of personal but unformulated common sense, by some framework of habit derived from a contrary doctrine, such as Christian doctrine, or by something in his biological inheritance, that is merely his good fortune—the Romantic doctrine itself will not restrain him. The Romantic doctrine itself will urge him toward automatism. And the study of history seems to show that if any doctrine is widely accepted for a long period of time, it tends more and more strongly

8

to exact conformity from human nature, to alter human nature. The Romantic theory of literature and of human nature has been the dominant theory in western civilization for about two and a half centuries. Its influence is obviously disastrous in literature and is already dangerous in other departments of human life.

There are certain other general notions of human nature and of values which are related to the notions which I have been discussing, but which are not exactly correlative with them. I shall refer to them rather baldly as determinism, relativism, and absolutism.

Determinism is that theory of the universe which holds that the whole is a single organism, pursuing a single and undeviating course which has been predestined by God or determined by its own nature. It sees the human being simply as a part of this organism, with no independent force of his own. One must distinguish sharply between a deterministic theory and a theory which recognizes the real existence of influences outside of the individual, whether those influences be historical, biological, or other. One may even take a pessimistic view of such influences without being a determinist. If one admits that man may understand in some measure the conditions of his existence, that as a result of such understanding he may choose a mode of action, that as a result of such choice he may persevere in the mode of action chosen, and that as a result of his perseverance he may in some measure alter the conditions of his existence, then one is not a determinist. Few people who profess deterministic doctrines are willing to envisage clearly their implications, however. As a result, one will find all three of the views of poetry which I have mentioned held by determinists.

It is natural that deterministic and Romantic theories should coincide, for Romanticism teaches the infinite desirability of automatism, and determinism teaches the inevitability of automatism. Determinism is Romanticism in a disillusioned mood; Henry Adams is little more than the obverse side of Emerson, the dark side of the moon. And since hedonism is, like determinism, an anti-intellectualistic philosophy and is somewhat vague in all its tenets, it is not surprising that determinists should

9

sometimes appear as hedonists: since they cannot control in any measure the courses of their lives, the determinists sometimes find solace in seeking pleasure along the way, without stopping to consider that such a search is a willful activity involving at least limited consideration and choice. It is curious that the didactic view of literature should so often be adopted by determinists, however, for the determinist really has no right to the didactic method. Yet the most vigorous, one might say the most religious, of the various species of determinist, such for example as the Calvinists of the past and the Marxists of the present, are commonly the most didactic of men, both in their literature and in their behavior.

The absolutist believes in the existence of absolute truths and values. Unless he is very foolish, he does not believe that he personally has free access to these absolutes and that his own judgments are final; but he does believe that such absolutes exist and that it is the duty of every man and of every society to endeavor as far as may be to approximate them. The relativist, on the other hand, believes that there are no absolute truths, that the judgment of every man is right for himself. I am aware that many persons believe that they have arrived at some kind of compromise between these two positions, but actually no compromise is possible. Any such attempt at compromise, if closely examined, will exhibit an ultimate allegiance to one position or the other or else will exhibit simple confusion. It is popular at present to profess relativism and yet in important matters to act as if we were absolutists. Our ideas of justice, which we endeavor to define by law and for which wars are often fought, can be defended only by invoking moral absolutism. Our universities, in which relativistic doctrines are widely taught, can justify their existence only in terms of a doctrine of absolute truth. The professor of English Literature, who believes that taste is relative, yet who endeavors to convince his students that *Hamlet* is more worthy of their attention than some currently popular novel, is in a serious predicament, a predicament which is moral, intellectual, and in the narrowest sense professional, though he commonly has not the wit to realize the fact.

The Romantic is almost inescapably a relativist, for if all men follow their impulses there will be a wide disparity of judgments and of actions and the fact enforces recognition. The Emersonian formula is the perfect one: that is right for me which is after my constitution; that is right for you which is after yours; the common divinity will guide each of us in the way which is best for him. The hedonist is usually a relativist and should logically be one, but there is often an illicit and veiled recognition of absolutism in his attempts to classify the various pleasures as more or less valuable, not for himself alone but in general. The defender of the didactic view of literature has been traditionally an absolutist, but he is not invariably so: didacticism is a method, and when one sees literature only as didacticism one sees it as a method, and the method may be used, as Emerson used it, to disseminate relativistic doctrine.

The theory of literature which I defend in these essays is absolutist. I believe that the work of literature, in so far as it is valuable, approximates a real apprehension and communication of a particular kind of objective truth. The form of literature with which I am for the most part concerned is the poem; but since the poem exhausts more fully than any other literary form the inherent possibilities of language, what I say about poetry can be extended to include other literary forms with relatively unimportant qualifications, and in point of fact I devote considerable space to other literary forms. The poem is a statement in words about a human experience. Words are primarily conceptual, but through use and because human experience is not purely conceptual, they have acquired connotations of feeling. The poet makes his statement in such a way as to employ both concept and connotation as efficiently as possible. The poem is good in so far as it makes a defensible rational statement about a given human experience (the experience need not be real but must be in some sense possible) and at the same time communicates the emotion which ought to be motivated by that rational understanding of that experience. This notion of poetry, whatever its defects, will account both for the power of poetry and of artistic literature in general on its readers and for the seriousness with which the great poets have taken their art. Milton, for example, did not write *Paradise Lost* to give pleasure to Professor So-and-So, nor did he write it to give free rein to his emotions; he wrote it in order to justify the ways of God to men, and the justification involved not merely a statement of theory but a conformity of the emotional nature of man with the theory.

Poetry, and in a less definite fashion all artistic literature, involves not only the two aspects of language which I have just mentioned, but also the rhythmic and the formal. Rhythm, for reasons which I do not wholly understand, has the power of communicating emotion; and as a part of the poem it has the power of qualifying the total emotion. What we speak of loosely as the "form" of a poem is probably, at least for the most part, two-fold: we have on the one hand the rational structure of the poem, the orderly arrangement and progression of thought; and we have on the other a kind of rhythm broader and less easily measurable than the rhythm of the line—the poem exists in time, the mind proceeds through it in time, and if the poet is a good one he takes advantage of this fact and makes the progression rhythmical. These aspects of the poem will be efficient in so far as the poet subordinates them to the total aim of the poem.

One criticism which has been made of me repeatedly is this: that I wish to discard every poem to which I make objections. This is not true. Probably no poem is perfect in the eye of God. So far as I am concerned, a good many poems approach so nearly to perfection that I find them satisfactory. But there are many poems which seem to me obviously imperfect and even very seriously imperfect, which I have no wish to discard. Some of these I have analyzed both in respect to their virtues and to their defects; others, because of the nature of my discussion, mainly with reference to their defects; but I have dealt with few works which do not seem to me to have discernible virtues, for to do otherwise would seem to me a waste of time. If we were all to emulate Hart Crane, the result would be disastrous to literature and to civilization; it is necessary to understand the limitations of Hart Crane, which are of the utmost seriousness; but when we understand those limitations, we are in a position to profit by his virtues with impunity, and his virtues are sometimes very great. If we are not aware of his limitations but are sufficiently sensitive to guess in some fashion at his virtues, he may easily take possession of us wholly. This difficulty indicates the function of criticism.

Certain poetry of the sixteenth and seventeenth centuries approximates most closely the qualities which seem to me the best. It seems to me, as it has seemed to many others, that there has been a general deterioration of the quality of poetry since the opening of the eighteenth century. Like many others, I have endeavored to account for this deterioration. It would surprise no one if I stated that Collins' *Ode to Evening* was an imperfect and secondary poem if judged in comparison with all English poetry; but it arouses antagonism when I give reasons, partly because there is a general dislike for reasons, and partly because my reasons are not complimentary to the orthodoxies of our time. I regret the antagonism, but since I believe my reasons to be sound and the matter in general serious, I must maintain my position and take the consequences. These essays, then, endeavor not only to defend a theory of poetry and to judge certain writers with reference to that theory, but to outline as far as this kind of writing permits certain historical tendencies and the reasons for them. I do this in the hope that my efforts may in some small measure contribute to the alteration of these tendencies; our literary culture (to mention nothing more) appears to me to be breaking up, and the rescue of it appears to me a matter of greater moment than the private feelings of some minor poet or scholar.

I should perhaps call attention to one other matter in connection with my aims. It seems to me impossible to judge the value of any idea in a vacuum. That is, the hedonistic view of literature may conceivably appear sound, or the relativistic view of literature and morals may appear sound, if the idea is circumscribed by a few words. But either idea implies a fairly complete description of a large range of human experience, and if the description does not agree with the facts as we are forced to recognize them, then something is wrong. I am acquainted, for example, with the arguments which prove that the wall is not there, but if I try to step through the wall, I find that the wall is there notwithstanding the arguments. During the past century or so, the number of poets who have endeavored to conform their practice to the ideas which seem to me unsound has been rather large, and we can judge the ideas more or less clearly in the light of these experiments. A large part of this book is devoted to the analysis of such experiments.

Finally, I am aware that my absolutism implies a theistic position, unfortunate as this admission may be. If experience appears to indicate that absolute truths exist, that we are able to work toward an approximate apprehension of them, but that they are antecedent to our apprehension and that our apprehension is seldom and perhaps never perfect, then there is only one place in which those truths may be located, and I see no way to escape this conclusion. I merely wish to point out that my critical and moral notions are derived from the observation of literature and of life, and that my theism is derived from my critical and moral notions. I did not proceed from the opposite direction.

All of the concepts outlined briefly and incompletely in this foreword, with the exception of that mentioned in the last paragraph, will be found more fully explained at various points in the present volume. These remarks are not offered as a complete statement, but are offered merely as a guide and an introduction.

Primitivism and

Decadence:

A STUDY OF AMERICAN

EXPERIMENTAL POETRY

THE MORALITY OF POETRY

BEFORE ATTEMPTING TO ELUCIDATE or to criticize a poetry so difficult and evasive as that of the best moderns, it would appear wise to summarize as clearly as possible those qualities for which one looks in a poem. We may say that a poem in the first place should offer us new perceptions, not only of the exterior universe, but of human experience as well; it should add, in other words, to what we have already seen. This is the elementary function for the reader. The corresponding function for the poet is a sharpening and training of his sensibilities; the very exigencies of the medium as he employs it in the act of perception should force him to the discovery of values which he never would have found without the convening of all the conditions of that particular act, conditions one or more of which will be the necessity of solving some particular difficulty such as the location of a rhyme or the perfection of a cadence without disturbance to the remainder of the poem. The poet who suffers from such difficulties instead of profiting by them is only in a rather rough sense a poet at all.

If, however, the difficulties of versification are a stimulant merely to the *poet*, the reader may argue that he finds them a hindrance to himself and that he prefers some writer of prose who appears to offer him as much with less trouble to all concerned. The answer to such a reader is that the appearance of equal richness in the writer of prose is necessarily deceptive.

For language is a kind of abstraction, even at its most concrete; such a word as "cat," for instance, is generic and not particular. Such a word becomes particular only in so far as it gets into some kind of experiential complex, which qualifies it and limits it,

17

which gives it, in short, a local habitation as well as a name. Such a complex is the poetic line or other unit, which, in turn, should be a functioning part of the larger complex, or poem. This is, I imagine, what Mallarmé should have had in mind when he demanded that the poetic line be a new word, not found in any dictionary, and partaking of the nature of incantation (that is, having the power to materialize, or perhaps it would be more accurate to say, *being*, a new experience.)[1]

The poem, to be perfect, should likewise be a new word in the

[1] Stéphane Mallarmé: *Avant-Dire* du *Traité du Verbe*, par René Ghil. Giraud, 18 Rue Drouot, Paris. 1886. Actually, Mallarmé seems to have had more in mind, though he should have had no more, in my opinion. The margin of difference is the margin in which post-romantic theory has flourished and from which post-romantic poetry has sprung. I quote the entire curious passage:

"Un désir indéniable à l'époque est de séparer comme en vue d'attributions différentes, le double état de la parole, brut ou immédiate ici, là essentiel.

"Narrer, enseigner, même décrire, cela va et encore qu'à chacun suffirait peut-être, pour échanger toute pensée humaine, de prendre ou de mettre dans la main d'autrui en silence une pièce de monnaie, l'emploi élémentaire du discours dessert l'universel reportage dont, la Littérature exceptée, participe tout, entre les genres d'écrits contemporains.

"A quoi bon la merveille de transposer un fait de nature en sa presque disparition vibratoire selon le jeu de la parole cependant, si ce n'est pour qu'on émane, sans la gêne d'un proche ou concret rappel, la notion pure?

"Je dis: une fleur! et, hors de l'oubli où ma voix relègue aucun contour, en tant que quelque chose d'autre que les calices sus, musicalement se lève, idée rieuse ou altière, l'absente de tous bouquets.

"Au contraire d'une fonction de numéraire facile et représentatif, comme le traite d'abord la foule, le parler qui est, après tout, rêve et chant, retrouve chez le poète, par nécessité constitutive d'un art consacré aux fictions, sa virtualité.

"Le vers qui de plusieurs vocables refait un mot total, neuf, étranger à la langue et comme incantatoire, achève cet isolement de la parole: niant, d'un trait souverain, le hasard demeuré aux termes malgré l'artifice de leur retrempe alternée en le sens et la sonorité, et vous cause cette surprise de n'avoir ouï jamais tel fragment ordinaire d'élocution, en même temps que la réminiscence de l'objet nommé baigne dans une clairvoyante atmosphère."

This is in some respects an admirable summary, and is certainly important historically. The entire tendency of the passage is to encourage the elimination of the rational from poetry. One should observe the sequence: "narrer, enseigner, *même* decrire," as if description were more nearly poetic than the other activities. The word *essentiel*, at the end of the first paragraph is the crux of the whole passage. The critic says that words have an obvious (that is, a rational) meaning, and a fringe of feeling, which he chooses to call essential: if only one kind of content is essential, we are naturally inclined to try to eliminate the other, and we have in this confusion, which reappears spontaneously, and without any discernible indebtedness to Mallarmé, in each successive generation of post-romantic poets, the real basis for post-romantic obscurantism. The sound idea that a poem is more than its rational content is thus perverted and distorted.

same sense, a word of which the line, as we have defined it, is merely a syllable. Such a word is, of course, composed of much more than the sum of its words (as one normally uses the term) and its syntax. It is composed of an almost fluid complex, if the adjective and the noun are not too nearly contradictory, of relationships between words (in the normal sense of the term), a relationship involving rational content, cadences, rhymes, juxtapositions, literary and other connotations, inversions, and so on, almost indefinitely. These relationships, it should be obvious, extend the poet's vocabulary incalculably. They partake of the fluidity and unpredictability of experience and so provide a means of treating experience with precision and freedom. If the poet does not wish, as, actually, he seldom does, to reproduce a given experience with approximate exactitude, he can employ the experience as a basis for a new experience that will be just as real, in the sense of being particular, and perhaps more valuable.

Now verse is more valuable than prose in this process for the simple reasons that its rhythms are faster and more highly organized than are those of prose, and so lend themselves to a greater complexity and compression of relationship, and that the intensity of this convention renders possible a greater intensity of other desirable conventions, such as poetic language and devices of rhetoric. The writer of prose must substitute bulk for this kind of intensity; he must define his experience ordinarily by giving all of its past history, the narrative logic leading up to it, whereas the experiential relations given in a good lyric poem, though particular in themselves, are applicable without alteration to a good many past histories. In this sense, the lyric is general as well as particular; in fact, this quality of transferable or generalized experience might be regarded as the defining quality of lyrical poetry.

What I have just said should make plain the difficulty of comprehending a poem exactly and fully; its total intention may be very different from its paraphrasable, or purely logical content. If one take, for example, Mr. Allen Tate's sonnet, *The Subway*, and translate it into good scholarly prose, using nothing but the rational content of the poem as a reference, one will find the author saying that as a result of his ideas and of his metropolitan environment, he is going mad. Now as a matter of fact, the poem says nothing of the sort:

> *Dark accurate plunger down the successive knell*
> *Of arch on arch, where ogives burst a red*
> *Reverberance of hail upon the dead*
> *Thunder, like an exploding crucible!*
> *Harshly articulate, musical steel shell*
> *Of angry worship, hurled religiously*
> *Upon your business of humility*
> *Into the iron forestries of hell!*
>
> *Till broken in the shift of quieter*
> *Dense altitudes tangential of your steel,*
> *I am become geometries—and glut*
> *Expansions like a blind astronomer*
> *Dazed, while the worldless heavens bulge and reel*
> *In the cold revery of an idiot.*

The sonnet indicates that the author has faced and defined the possibility of the madness that I have mentioned (a possibility from the consideration of which others as well as himself may have found it impossible to escape) and has arrived at a moral attitude toward it, an attitude which is at once defined and communicated by the poem. This attitude is defined only by the entire poem, not by the logical content alone; it is a matter not only of logical content, but of feeling as well. The feeling is particular and unparaphrasable, but one may indicate the nature of it briefly by saying that it is a feeling of dignity and of self-control in the face of a situation of major difficulty, a difficulty which the poet fully apprehends. This feeling is inseparable from what we call poetic form, or unity, for the creation of a form is nothing more nor less than the act of evaluating and shaping (that is, controlling) a given experience. It should be obvious that any attempt to reduce the rational content of such a poem would

20

tend to confuse or even to eliminate the feeling: the poem consists in the relationship between the two.

To reënforce my point, I shall take the liberty of quoting another poem, this one by Mr. Howard Baker, in which something comparable occurs. The title is *Pont Neuf*:

> *Henry the Fourth rides in bronze,*
> *His shoulders curved and pensive, thrust*
> *Enormously into electric*
> *Blazonments of a Christmas trust.*
>
> *Children pass him aghast and pleased,*
> *Reflective of the flickerings*
> *Of jerky bears and clowns. Alone,*
> *Astute to all the bickerings*
>
> *Of age and death rides Henry the Grand.*
> *A lean tug shudders in the Seine;*
> *And Notre Dame is black, a relic*
> *Of the blood of other men.*
>
> *Peace to the other men! And peace*
> *To the mind that has no century,*
> *And sees the savage pull the statue down,*
> *And down the bear and clown.*

The spiritual control in a poem, then, is simply a manifestation of the spiritual control within the poet, and, as I have already indicated, it may have been an important means by which the poet arrived at a realization of spiritual control. This conception must not be confused with the conception of the poem as a safety valve, by which feeling is diverted from action, by which the writer escapes from an attitude by pouring it into his work and leaving it behind him. The conception which I am trying to define is a conception of poetry as a technique of contemplation, of comprehension, a technique which does not eliminate the need of philosophy or of religion, but which, rather, completes and enriches them.

One feels, whether rightly or wrongly, a correlation between the control evinced within a poem and the control within the poet behind it. The laxity of the one ordinarily appears to involve laxity in the other. The rather limp versification of Mr. Eliot and of Mr. MacLeish is inseparable from the spiritual limpness that one feels behind the poems, as the fragmentary, ejaculatory, and over-excited quality of a great many of the poems of Hart Crane is inseparable from the intellectual confusion upon which these particular poems seem to rest (for examples, *The Dance, Cape Hatteras,* and *Atlantis*). Crane possessed great energy, but his faculties functioned clearly only within a limited range of experience (*Repose of Rivers, Voyages II, Faustus and Helen II*). Outside of that range he was either numb (*My Grandmother's Love-letters* and *Harbor Dawn*) or unsure of himself and hence uncertain in his detail (as in *The River,* a very powerful poem in spite of its poor construction and its quantities of bad writing) or both (see *Indiana,* probably one of the worst poems in modern literature). Many of the poems of Mr. Eliot and of Mr. Mac-Leish could be reduced by paraphrase to about the same thing as my paraphrase of Mr. Tate's sonnet; the difference between them and Mr. Tate in this connection is that, as the form of nearly all of their poems is much looser to start with, the process of paraphrasing would constitute a much slighter act of betrayal. And we must not forget that this quality, form, is not something outside the poet, something "æsthetic," and superimposed upon his moral content; it is essentially a part, in fact it may be the decisive part, of the moral content, even though the poet may be arriving at the final perfection of the condition he is communicating while he communicates it and in a large measure as a result of the act and technique of communication. For the communication is first of all with himself: it is, as I have said, the last refinement of contemplation.

I should pause here to remark that many writers have sought to seize the fluidity of experience by breaking down the limits of form, but that in so doing, they defeat their own ends. For, as I have shown, writing, as it approaches the looseness of prose and departs from the strictness of verse, tends to lose the capacity for fluid or highly complex relationships between words; language, in short, reapproaches its original stiffness and generality; and one is forced to recognize the truth of what appears a paradox, that the greatest fluidity of statement is possible where the greatest clarity of form prevails. It is hard to see how the existence of such a work as Mr. Joyce's latest creation[2] can be anything but precarious, in spite of its multitudes of incidental felicities; for it departs from the primary condition of prose—coherent and cumulative logic or narrative—without, since it is, finally, prose, achieving the formal precision of verse. These remarks should not be construed, however, as an argument against free verse, though, with proper qualification, they could be brought to bear in such an argument. The free verse that is really verse—the best, that is, of W. C. Williams, H. D., Miss Moore, Wallace Stevens, and Ezra Pound—is, in its peculiar fashion, the antithesis of free, and the evaluation of this verse is a difficult problem in itself.

Thus we see that the poet, in striving toward an ideal of poetic form at which he has arrived through the study of other poets, is actually striving to perfect a moral attitude toward that range of experience of which he is aware. Such moral attitudes are contagious from poet to poet, and, within the life of a single poet, from poem to poem. The presence of Hardy and Arnold, let us say, in so far as their successful works offer us models and their failures warnings or unfulfilled suggestions, should make it easier to write good poetry; they should not only aid us, by providing standards of sound feeling, to test the soundness of our own poems, but, since their range of experience is very wide, they should aid us, as we are able to enter and share their experience, to grow into regions that we had not previously mastered or perhaps even discovered. The discipline of imitation is thus valuable if it leads to understanding and assimilation. Too often a minor poet or other reader will recognize in such a master the validity of only that part of the master's experience which corresponds to

[2] Entitled at this writing (1935) *Work in Progress.* (Ultimately published as *Finnegans Wake.*)

23

his own limited range, and will rule out the poetry to which he is consequently numb as sentimental or otherwise imperfect. Inflexibility of critical opinion in such matters is not particularly conducive to growth.

Random experiment may have a related value: one may hit on a form (perhaps the rough idea or draft of a form) which induces some new state or states of mind. I regard as fallacious the notion that form is determined by a precedent attitude or a precedent subject matter, at least invariably: the form (that is, the general idea of a certain type of form) *may* precede, and the attitude, in any case, is never definite till the form is achieved.[3] It does not follow that any attitude resulting from random experiment is intrinsically desirable; undesirable attitudes, like desirable, are contagious and may spread widely; it is here that criticism becomes necessary. A failure, however, to achieve something valuable may offer a valuable suggestion to someone else. The poet who has succeeded once or twice in mastering difficult and central emotions and in recording his mastery for future reference should find it easier to succeed again.

I am not endeavoring in the two foregoing paragraphs to establish poetry as a substitute for philosophy or for religion. Religion is highly desirable if it is really available to the individual; the study of philosophy is always available and is of incalculable value as a preliminary and as a check to activities as a poet and as a critic (that is, as an intelligent reader). I am, then, merely attempting to define a few of the things which poetry does.

It would perhaps be wise to add another caution: I suffer from no illusion that any man who can write a good poem has a naturally sweet moral temper or that the man who has written three good poems is a candidate for canonization. Literary history is packed with sickening biographies. But it is worth noting that the poetry of such a man, say, as Rochester (who in this is typical of his age) displays a mastery of an extremely narrow range of

[3] As a single example, consider the manner in which the Petrarchan experimenters in England, most of them feeble poets and the best of them given to empty and inflated reasoning, worked out the technique of reasoning elaborately in graceful lyrical verse and bequeathed that technique to the 17th century: the form preceded the matter.

experience, and that his moral brutality falls almost wholly in those regions (nearly every region save that of worldly manners, if we except some few poems, notably *Upon Nothing, Absent from Thee*, and, possibly, *A Song of a Young Lady to Her Ancient Lover*, in which last there is a curious blending of the erotic with deep moral feeling) with which his poetry fails to deal or with which it deals badly.

This statement requires elucidation. Rochester frequently writes of his debauchery, and sometimes writes well of it, but in the best poems on the subject, in such poems as *The Maim'd Debauchee* and *Upon Drinking in a Bowl*, he writes, as do his contemporaries in the comedy, as a witty and satirical gentleman: the wit inspired by the material is mastered, and other aspects of the material are ignored. In the worst poems on more or less similar material (for examples, the numerous lampoons upon Charles II and upon Nell Gwyn) we have a grossness of feeling comparable to that of his worst actions. All of this, however, detracts not in the least from the quality of Rochester's best poetry, which is remarkably fine; Rochester seldom extends the standards which he recognizes into fields to which they are inapplicable, and hence he is seldom guilty of false evaluation. In reading him, one is aware that he is a sound and beautiful poet, and that there are greater poets. That is all of which one has a right to be aware.[4]

If a poem, in so far as it is good, represents the comprehension on a moral plane of a given experience, it is only fair to add that some experiences offer very slight difficulties and some very great, and that the poem will be the most valuable, which, granted it achieves formal perfection, represents the most difficult victory. In the great tragic poets, such as Racine or Shakespeare, one feels that a victory has been won over life itself, so much is implicated in the subject matter; that feeling is the source of their power over us, whereas a slighter poet will absorb very little of our experience and leave the rest untouched.

This requisite seems to be ignored in a large measure by a good

[4] *The Collected Poems of John Wilmot, Earl of Rochester*, edited by John Hayward. The Nonesuch Press, 16 Great James St., London, W.C. 1926.

many contemporary poets of more or less mystical tendencies, who avoid the difficult task of mastering the more complex forms of experience by setting up a theoretic escape from them and by then accepting that escape with a good deal of lyrical enthusiasm. Such an escape is offered us, I fear, by Hart Crane, in one of the most extraordinary sections of his volume, *The Bridge*,[5] in the poem called *The Dance*, and such escapes are often employed by Mr. Yeats. In the religious poets of the past, one encounters this vice very seldom; the older religions are fully aware that the heart, to borrow the terms of a poem by Janet Lewis, is untranslatable, whatever may be true of the soul, and that one can escape from the claims of the world only by understanding those claims and by thus accustoming oneself to the thought of eventually putting them by. This necessity is explicitly the subject of one of Sidney's greatest sonnets, *Leave me, O Love, which reachest but to dust*, and of the greatest poem by George Herbert, *Church Monuments*; one can find it elsewhere. The attitude is humane, and does not belittle nor evade the magnitude of the task; it is essentially a tragic attitude.

For this reason, the religious fervor of Gerard Hopkins, of John Donne, or of George Herbert should weaken but little the force of most of their poems for the non-believer, just as the deterministic doctrines, whatever their nature and extent, to be found in Hardy, should not weaken for us those poems which do not deal too pugnaciously with the doctrines, and for the same reason. Though a belief in any form of determinism should, if the belief is pushed to its logical ends, eliminate the belief in, and consequently the functioning of, whatever it is that we call the will, yet there is no trace of any kind of disintegration in Hardy's poetic style, in his sense of form, which we have seen to be, so far as writing is concerned, identical with the will or the ability to control and shape one's experience. The tragic necessity of putting by the claims of the world without the abandonment of self-control, without loss of the ability to go on living, for the present, intelligently and well, is just as definitely the subject of Hardy's poetry as of Herbert's. We have in both poets

[5] *The Bridge*, by Hart Crane, Horace Liveright: N. Y.: 1930.

a common moral territory which is far greater than are the theological regions which they do not share; for, on the one hand, the fundamental concepts of morality are common to intelligent men regardless of theological orientation, except in so far as morality may be simply denied or ignored, and, on the other hand, the Absolute is in its nature inscrutable and offers little material for speculation, except in so far as it is a stimulus to moral speculation. It would be difficult, I think, to find a devotional poem of which most of the implications were not moral and universal. So with Hardy: his determinism was mythic and animistic and tended to dramatize the human struggle, whereas a genuinely rational and coherent determinism would have eliminated the human struggle. He was thrown back upon traditional literary and folk wisdom in working out moral situations, and for these situations his mythology provided a new setting, sometimes magnificent, sometimes melodramatic, but, thanks to its rational incompleteness, not really destructive of a working morality. Like many another man who has been unable to think clearly, he was saved by the inability to think coherently: had he been coherent, he would probably have been about as interesting as Godwin; as it is, his professed beliefs and his working beliefs have only a little in common, and the former damage his work only in a fragmentary way, as when satires of circumstance are dragged into a novel or isolated in a poem to prove a point (and they can prove nothing, of course) and usually to the detriment of coherent feeling and understanding.

Crane's attitude, on the other hand, often suggests a kind of theoretic rejection of all human endeavor in favor of some vaguely apprehended but ecstatically asserted existence of a superior sort. As the exact nature of the superior experience is uncertain, it forms a rather uncertain and infertile source of material for exact poetry; one can write poetry about it only by utilizing in some way more or less metaphorical the realm of experience from which one is trying to escape; but as one *is* endeavoring to escape from this realm, not to master it and understand it, one's feelings about it are certain to be confused, and one's imagery drawn from it is bound to be largely formulary and devoid of meaning. That is, in so far as one endeavors to deal with the Absolute, not as a means of ordering one's moral perception but as the subject itself of perception, one will tend to say nothing, despite the multiplication of words. In *The Dance* there seems to be an effort to apply to each of two mutually exlusive fields the terms of the other. This is a vice of which Rochester was not guilty.

Crane's best work, such as *Repose of Rivers* and *Voyages II*, is not confused, but one feels that the experience is curiously limited and uncomplicated: it is between the author, isolated from most human complications, and Eternity. Crane becomes in such poems a universal symbol of the human mind in a particular situation, a fact which is the source of his power, but of the human mind in very nearly the simplest form of that situation, a fact which is the source of his limitation.

Objective proof of this assertion cannot be found in the poems, any more than proof of the opposite quality can be found in Hardy; it is in each poet a matter of feeling invading the poetry mainly by way of the non-paraphrasable content: one feels the fragility of Crane's finest work, just as one feels the richness of Hardy's. Hardy is able to utilize, for example, great ranges of literary, historical, and other connotations in words and cadences; one feels behind each word the history of the word and the generations of men who embodied that history; Hardy gets somehow at the wealth of the race. It should be observed again how the moral discipline is involved in the literary discipline, how it becomes, at times, almost a matter of living philology. From the greater part of this wealth Crane appears to be isolated and content to remain isolated. His isolation, like Hardy's immersion, was in part social and unavoidable, but a clearer mind and a more fixed intention might have overcome much of the handicap.

I should like to forestall one possible objection to the theory of poetry which I am trying to elucidate. Poetry, as a moral discipline, should not be regarded as one more means of escape. That is, moral responsibility should not be transferred from action to paper in the face of a particular situation. Poetry, if pursued either by the poet or by the reader, in the manner which

I have suggested, should offer a means of enriching one's awareness of human experience and of so rendering greater the possibility of intelligence in the course of future action; and it
should offer likewise a means of inducing certain more or less
constant habits of feeling, which should render greater the possibility of one's acting, in a future situation, in accordance witl
the findings of one's improved intelligence. It should, in othe.
words, increase the intelligence and strengthen the moral temper;
these effects should naturally be carried over into action, if,
through constant discipline, they are made permanent acquisitions. If the poetic discipline is to have steadiness and direction,
it requires an antecedent discipline of ethical thinking and of at
least some ethical feeling, which may be in whole or in part the
gift of religion or of a social tradition, or which may be largely the
result of individual acquisition by way of study. The poetic discipline includes the antecedent discipline and more: it is the
richest and most perfect technique of contemplation.

This view of poetry in its general outline is not original, but is
a restatement of ideas that have been current in English criticism
since the time of Sidney, that have appeared again in most of
the famous apologists for poetry since Sidney, especially in
Arnold and in Newman. In summarizing these ideas, I have
merely endeavored to illuminate a few of the more obscure relationships and to dispose of them in such a way as to prepare
the reader for various analyses of poetic method which I intend,
in other essays, to undertake. Poetic morality and poetic feeling
are inseparable; feeling and technique, or structure, are inseparable. Technique has laws which govern poetic (and perhaps
more general) morality more widely than is commonly recognized. It is my intention to examine them.

THE EXPERIMENTAL SCHOOL
IN AMERICAN POETRY

An Analytical Survey of Its Structural Methods,
Exclusive of Meter

DURING THE SECOND and third decades of the twentieth century, the chief poetic talent of the United States took certain new directions, directions that appear to me in the main regrettable. The writers between Robinson and Frost, on the one hand, and Allen Tate and Howard Baker on the other, who remained relatively traditional in manner were with few exceptions minor or negligible;·.the more interesting writers, as I shall endeavor to show in these pages, were misguided, and in discussing them I shall have little to say of their talents, their ineliminable virtues, but shall rather take these for granted.

In order that I may evaluate the new structural methods, I shall have first to describe at least briefly the old. Inasmuch as a wider range of construction is possible in the short poem than in any of the longer literary forms, I shall deal with principles that are fundamental to all literary composition, and shall here and there have recourse to illustrations drawn from the novel or perhaps from the drama. The virtues of the traditional modes of construction will be indicated chiefly in connection with my discussion of the defects of the recent experimental modes.

Type I: THE METHOD OF REPETITION

KENNETH BURKE HAS NAMED and described this method without evaluating it.[1] It is the simplest and most primitive method pos-

[1] In *Counterstatement* (Harcourt, Brace and Co.: 1932).

sible, and is still in common use; if limited to a short lyrical form, it may still be highly effective. It consists in a restatement in successive stanzas of a single theme, the terms, or images, being altered in each restatement. Two of the finest poems in the form are Nashe's poem on the plague (*Adieu! Farewell earth's bliss*) and Raleigh's poem entitled *The Lie*. In such a poem there is no rational necessity for any order of sequence, the order being determined wholly by the author's feeling about the graduation of importance or intensity. Nevertheless, such a poem rests on a formulable logic, however simple; that is, the theme can be paraphrased in general terms. Such a paraphrase, of course, is not the equivalent of a poem: a poem is more than its paraphrasable content. But, as we shall eventually see, many poems cannot be paraphrased and are therefore defective.

The method of repetition is essentially the same today as it has always been, if we confine our attention to the short poem. Of recent years, however, there has been a tendency to extend it into longer forms, with unfortunate results. Such extension is the chief method of Whitman, and results in a form both lax and diffuse. Such extension occurs even in many modern attempts at narrative, both in prose and in verse. To illustrate what I say, I shall venture to summarize the structural defects of the narrative poetry of Robinson Jeffers:

Mr. Jeffers is theologically some kind of monist. He envisages, as did Wordsworth, nature as Deity; but his Nature is the Nature of the text-book in physics and not that of the rambling botanist —Mr. Jeffers seems to have taken the terminology of modern physics more literally than it is meant by its creators. Nature, or God, is thus a kind of self-sufficient mechanism, of which man is a product, but from which man is cut off by his humanity (just what gave rise to this humanity, which is absolutely severed from all communication with God, is left for others to decide): as there is no mode of communication with God or from God, God is praised adequately only by the screaming demons that make up the atom. Man, if he accepts this dilemma as necessary, can choose between two modes of action: he may renounce God and rely upon his humanity, or he may renounce his humanity and rely upon God.

In the narratives preceding *Cawdor*[2] and in most of the lyrics, Mr. Jeffers preaches the second choice. In *Cawdor* and in *Thurso's Landing*,[3] he has attempted a compromise: that is, while the tragic characters recognize that the second choice would be the more reasonable, they make the first in a kind of half-hearted stubbornness. They insist on living, but without knowing why, and without any good to which to look forward save the final extinction in God, when it comes in God's time. Their stubbornness is meaningless.

Life as such is incest, an insidious and destructive evil. So much, says Mr. Jeffers by implication, for Greek and Christian ethics. Now the mysticism of such a man as San Juan de la Cruz offers at least the semblance of a spiritual, a human, discipline as a preliminary to union with Divinity; but for Mr. Jeffers a simple and mechanical device lies always ready; namely, suicide, a device to which he has, I believe, never resorted.

In refusing to take this step, however, Mr. Jeffers illustrates one of a very interesting series of romantic compromises. The romantic of the ecstatically pantheistic type denies life yet goes on living;[4] nearly all romantics decry the intellect and philosophy, yet they offer justifications, necessarily incoherent but none the less rational in intention, of their attitude, they are prone to belittle literary technique, yet they write, and too often with small efficiency; they preach, in the main, the doctrine of moral equivalence, yet their every action, whether private or literary, since it rests on a choice, is a denial of the doctrine. Not all romantics are guilty of all these forms of confusion, but the romantic who is guilty of all is more consistent than is he who is guilty only of some, for all inhere in each from a rational standpoint. And Mr. Jeffers, having decried human life, and having denied the worth of the rules of the game, endeavors to

[2] *Cawdor and Other Poems,* by Robinson Jeffers. Horace Liveright, New York, 1928.

[3] *Thurso's Landing,* same. Liveright Inc., New York, 1932.

[4] Hart Crane, unlike Mr. Jeffers, demonstrated the seriousness of his conviction, but the demonstration did nothing to clarify his concepts.

write narrative and dramatic poems, poems, in other words, dealing with people who are playing the game. Jesus, the hero of *Dear Judas*,[5] speaking apparently for Mr. Jeffers, says that the secret reason for the doctrine of forgiveness is that all men are driven to act as they do, by the mechanism-God, that they are entirely helpless; yet he adds in the next breath that this secret must be guarded, for if it were given out, men would run amuck—they would begin acting differently.[6]

The Women at Point Sur[7] is a perfect laboratory of Mr. Jeffers' philosophy and a perfect example of his narrative method. Barclay, an insane divine, preaches Mr. Jeffers' religion, and his disciples, acting upon it, become emotional mechanisms, lewd and twitching conglomerations of plexuses, their humanity annulled. Human experience in these circumstances, having necessarily and according to the doctrine, no meaning, there can be no necessary sequence of events: every act is equivalent to every other; every act is devoid of consequence and occurs in a perfect vacuum; most of the incidents could be shuffled about into different sequences without violating anything save Mr. Jeffers' sense of their relative intensity.

Since the poem is his, of course, this sense may appear a legitimate criterion; the point is, that this is not a narrative nor a dramatic but is a lyrical criterion. A successful lyrical poem of one hundred and seventy-five pages is unlikely, for the essence of lyrical expression is concentration; but it is at least hypothetically possible. The difficulty here is that the lyric achieves its effect by the generalization of experience (that is, the motivation of the lyric is stated or implied in a summary form, and is ordinarily not given in detailed narrative) and by the concentration of expression; lyrical poetry tends to be expository. Narrative can survive fairly well without distinction of style, provided the narrative logic is complete and compelling, as in the works

---

[5] *Dear Judas* (Horace Liveright: 1929).

[6] This dilemma is not new in American literature. In the eighteenth century, Jonathan Edwards accomplished a revival in the Puritan Church, that is, induced large numbers of sinners to repent and enter the church, by preaching the doctrine of election and the inability to repent.

[7] *The Women at Point Sur* (Boni and Liveright: 1927).

of Balzac, though this occurs most often in prose. Now Mr. Jeffers, as I have pointed out, has abandoned narrative logic with the theory of ethics, and he has never, in addition, achieved a distinguished style: his writing, line by line, is pretentious trash. There are a few good phrases, but they are very few, and none is first-rate.

Mr. Jeffers has no method of sustaining his lyric, then, other than the employment of an accidental (that is, a non-narrative and repetitious) series of anecdotes (that is, of details that are lyrically impure, details clogged with too much information to be able to function properly as lyrical details); his philosophical doctrine and his artistic dilemma alike decree that these shall be at an hysterical pitch of feeling. By this method, Mr. Jeffers continually *lays claim* to extreme feeling, which has no support whether of structure or of detail and which is therefore simply unmastered and self-inflicted hysteria.

Cawdor contains a plot which in its rough outlines might be sound, and *Cawdor* likewise contains his best poetry: the lines describing the seals at dawn, especially, are very good. But the plot is blurred for lack of style and for lack of moral intelligence on the part of the author. As in *Thurso's Landing*, of which the writing is much worse, the protagonists desire to live as the result of a perfectly unreasoning and meaningless stubbornness, and their actions are correspondingly obscure. Mr. Jeffers will not even admit the comprehensible motive of cowardice. In *The Tower beyond Tragedy*,[8] Mr. Jeffers takes one of the very best of ready-made plots, the Orestes-Clytemnestra situation, the peculiar strength of which lies in the fact that Orestes is forced to choose between two crimes, the murder of his mother and the failure to avenge his father. But at the very last moment, in Mr. Jeffers' version, Orestes is converted to Mr. Jeffers' religion and goes off explaining to Electra (who has just tried to seduce him) that though men may think he is fleeing from the furies, he is really doing no more than drift up to the mountains to meditate on the stars. And the preceding action is, of course, rendered meaningless.

[8] In the volume called *The Women at Point Sur*, previously mentioned.

34

Dear Judas is a kind of dilution of *The Women at Point Sur*, with Jesus as Barclay, and with a less detailed background. *The Loving Shepherdess*[9] deals with a girl who knows herself doomed to die at a certain time in child-birth, and who wanders over the countryside caring for a small and diminishing flock of sheep in an anguish of devotion. The events here also are anecdotal and reversible, and the feeling is lyrical or nothing. The heroine is turned cruelly from door to door, and the sheep fall one by one before the reader's eyes, the sheep and the doors constituting the matter of the narrative; until finally the girl dies in a ditch in an impossible effort to give birth to her child.

Type II: THE LOGICAL METHOD

BY THE LOGICAL METHOD of composition, I mean simply explicitly rational progression from one detail to another: the poem has a clearly evident expository structure. Marvell's poem *To His Coy Mistress,* as Mr. T. S. Eliot has said, has something of the structure of a syllogism, if the relationships only of the three paragraphs to each other be considered:[10] within each paragraph the structure is repetitive. The logical method is a late and sophisticated procedure that in Europe is most widespread in the sixteenth and seventeenth centuries, though it appears earlier and continues later. It was exploited, mastered, and frequently debauched by the English Metaphysical School, for example, though it was not invariably employed by them.

Sometimes in the Metaphysical poets, frequently in the dramatists contemporary with them, and far too often in the poetry of the twentieth century, the logical structure becomes a shell empty of logic but exploiting certain elusive types of feeling. The forms of pseudo-logic I shall reserve for treatment under another heading.

By stretching our category a trifle we may include under this heading poems *implicitly* rational, provided the implications of rationality are at all points clear. William Carlos Williams' poem,

[9] In the volume entitled *Dear Judas.*
[10] *Selected Essays,* by T. S. Eliot. Harcourt, Brace and Co., New York: 1932.

On the Road to the Contagious Hospital, may serve as an example.[11] On the other hand, Rimbaud's *Larme*, a poem which, like that of Dr. Williams, describes a landscape, is unformulable: it is an example of what Kenneth Burke has called qualitative progression, a type of procedure that I shall consider later. The poem by Williams, though its subject is simple, is a poem of directed meditation; the poem by Rimbaud is one of non-rational and hallucinatory terror.

Type III: NARRATIVE

NARRATIVE ACHIEVES coherence largely through a feeling that the events of a sequence are necessary parts of a causative chain, or plausible interferences with a natural causative chain. In this it is similar to logic. The hero, being what he is and in a given situation, seems to act naturally or unnaturally; if his action seems natural, and is in addition reasonably interesting and, from an ethical point of view, important, the narrative is in the main successful. To this extent, Mr. Kenneth Burke is wrong, I believe, in censuring nineteenth century fiction for its concern with what he calls the psychology of the hero as opposed to the concern with the psychology of the audience:[12] by the former, he means the plausibility of the portrait; by the latter the concern with those rhetorical devices which please and surprise the reader, devices, for example, of the type of which Fielding was a consummate master. Mr. Burke overlooks the facts that rhetoric cannot exist without a subject matter, and that the subject matter of fiction is narration, that, in short, the author's most important instrument for controlling the attitude of the audience is precisely the psychology of the hero. Mr. Burke is right, however, in that there are other, less important but necessary means of controlling the attitude of the audience, and that most of the standard fiction of the nineteenth century, sometimes for neglecting them, sometimes for utilizing them badly, suffers considerably.

Mr. Burke, in his own compositions, with a precocious security

[11] *Spring and All*, by William Carlos Williams. Contact Editions, Paris. The poem is quoted in full in the essay on *Poetic Convention*, in this book.
[12] In the volume called *Counterstatement*, already mentioned.

36

that is discouraging, reverses the Victorian formula: in his novel, *Towards a Better Life*,[13] he concentrates on the sentence, or occasionally on the paragraph, that is, on the incidental. He has attained what appears to be his chief end: he has made himself quotable. His book contains some good aphorisms and many bad; it contains some excellent interludes, such as the fable of the scholar with the face like a vegetable, or the paragraph on Voltaire. Any of these felicities may be removed from their context with perfect impunity, for there really is no context: *Towards a Better Life*, as a whole, is duller than Thackeray. On the other hand, such writers as Jane Austen and Edith Wharton are likely to be wittier than Mr. Burke; but their wit, like that of Molière, is not often separable from their context, since it is primarily a context that they are creating.

Short sketches in prose often deal with the revelation of a situation instead of with the development of one. The result is static, but if the prose is skillful and does not run to excessive length, it may be successful: Cunninghame Graham's *At Dalmary*[14] is a fine example. Other things being equal, however (which, of course, they never are), action should lend power. In a short narrative poem it matters little whether the situation be revealed or developed: the force of the poetic language can raise the statement to great impressiveness either way; in fact, the process of revelation itself may take on in a short poem a quality profoundly dramatic.[15] The famous English Ballad, *Edward*, Mr. E. A. Robinson's *Luke Havergal*,[16] *Her Going*[17] by Agnes Lee, are all examples of revelation at a high level of excellence. Mr. Robinson's *Eros Turannos*[16] is a fine example of development within a short form.

[13] *Towards a Better Life*, by Kenneth Burke. Harcourt, Brace and Co.: New York: 1932.

[14] *Hope*, by Cunninghame Graham. Duckeworth, London.

[15] It is curious that this procedure if employed in a long form, such as the novel or the play, tends to degenerate into bald melodrama; it is the essential, for example, of detective fiction. On the other hand, it is in a large part the form of *The Ambassadors*, the revelation in this, however, motivating further development.

[16] *Collected Poems*, by E. A. Robinson: Macmillan.

[17] *Faces and Open Doors*, by Agnes Lee. R. F. Seymour, Chicago, 1932.

The coherence of character may be demonstrated, as in the novels of Henry James, in a closed, or dramatic plot, in which personage acts upon personage, and in which accident and mechanical change play little part; or the personage may prove himself coherent in a struggle with pure accident, as in Defoe, who pits Moll Flanders against the wilderness of London, or as in Melville, who pits Ahab against the complex wilderness of the sea, of brute nature, and of moral evil; or there may be, as in Mrs. Wharton, a merging of the two extremes: in Mrs. Wharton, the impersonal adversary is usually represented by a human being such as Undine Spragg or the elder Raycie, who is morally or intellectually undeveloped, so that the protagonist is unable to cope with him in human terms. The novel is not the drama, and to demand of it dramatic plot appears to me unreasonable. The form permits the treatment of a great deal of material impossible in the drama, and the material, since it is important in human life, ought to be treated. It is certain, however, that narrative requires coherence of character, and coherence necessitates change. Fielding is dull in bulk because his characters do not develop and because his incidents are without meaning except as anecdotal excuses for the exercise of style. Defoe's rhetoric is less agile, but his conception is more solid.

In addition to having greater range, the novel of accident may have advantages over the dramatic novel which are perhaps too seldom considered. The author is less likely to be restricted to the exact contents of the minds of his characters, and so he may have greater opportunity to exhibit, directly or indirectly, his own attitudes, which, in most cases, may be more complex than the attitudes of his characters. Fielding, for example, would have been seriously embarrassed to treat Tom Jones from the point of view of Tom Jones. Melville accomplishes even more with his personal freedom than does Fielding. The superstition that the author should write wholly from within the minds of his characters appears to have grown up largely as a reaction to the degeneration of Fieldingese among the Victorians, notably Thackeray and Dickens, and perhaps Meredith, and perhaps in part as a result of the achievements in the newer mode by Flaubert and by Henry

James. Flaubert is misleading, however, in that the perfection and subtlety of his style introduces an important element from without the consciousness of the character in a manner that may be overlooked; and James is misleading not only in this respect but because his characters are usually almost as highly developed as the author himself, so that the two are frequently all but indistinguishable. The superstition is reduced to absurdity in some of Mr. Hemingway's short stories about prize-fighters and bull-fighters, whose views of their own experience are about as valuable as the views of the Sunbonnet Babies or of Little Black Sambo.

Theoretically, that fictional convention should be most desirable which should allow the author to deal with a character from a position formally outside the mind of the character, and which should allow him to analyze, summarize, and arrange material, as author, and without regard to the way in which the character might be supposed to have perceived the material originally. This procedure should permit the greatest possibility of rhetorical range; should permit the direct play of the intelligence of the author, over and above the intelligence and limitations of the character; it should permit the greatest possible attention to what Mr. Kenneth Burke has called the psychology of the audience in so far as it is separable from what he calls the psychology of the hero: Mr. Burke, in fact, in his own novel, *Towards a Better Life*, employs a modified stream-of-consciousness convention, thus limiting the rhetorical range very narrowly, and confining himself to a very narrow aspect of the psychology of the hero, so far as the construction of his work as a whole is concerned, and in a large measure as regards all relationships beyond those within the individual sentence. The convention which I should recommend is that of the first-rate biography or history (Johnson's *Lives*, for example, or Hume, or Macaulay) instead of the various post-Joycean conventions now prevalent. Exposition may be made an art; so may historical summary; in fact, the greatest prose in existence is that of the greatest expository writers. The novel should not forego these sources of strength. If it be argued that the first aim of the novelist is to reach a public from whom the great ex-

39

positors are isolated by their very virtues, then the novelist is in exactly that measure unworthy of serious discussion. My recommendation is not made wholly in the absence of examples, however: allowances made for individual limitations of scope and defects of procedure, Jane Austen, Melville, Hawthorne, Henry James, Fielding, and Defoe may be called to serve; Edith Wharton at her best, in such performances as *Bunner Sisters* and *False Dawn*, as *The Valley of Decision* and *The Age of Innocence*, is nearly the perfect example.

Type IV: PSEUDO-REFERENCE

EVERY LINE or passage of good poetry, every good poetic phrase, communicates a certain quality of feeling as well as a certain paraphrasable content. It would be possible to write a poem unimpeachable as to rational sequence, yet wholly inconsecutive in feeling or even devoid of feeling. Meredith and Browning often display both defects. Chapman's *Hero and Leander* is a rational continuation of Marlowe's beginning, but the break in feeling is notorious.

Suppose that we imagine the reversal of this formula, retaining in our language coherence of feeling, but as far as possible reducing rational coherence. The reduction may be accomplished in either of two ways: (1) we may retain the syntactic forms and much of the vocabulary of rational coherence, thus aiming to exploit the feeling of rational coherence in its absence or at least in excess of its presence; or (2) we may abandon all pretence of rational coherence. The first of these methods I have called *pseudo-reference* and shall treat in this section. The second I shall reserve for the next section.

Pseudo-reference takes a good many forms. I shall list as many forms as I have observed. My list will probably not be complete, but it will be nearly enough complete to illustrate the principle and to provide a basis of further observation.

1. *Grammatical coherence in excess of, or in the absence of, rational coherence.* This may mean no more than a slight excess

of grammatical machinery, a minor redundancy. Thus Miss Moore, in *Black Earth*:

> *I do these*
> *things which I do, which please*
> *no one but myself.*[18]

The words which I have set in Roman are redundant. Again, in *Reinforcements*,[18] Miss Moore writes:

> *the future of time is determined by*
> *the power of volition*

when she means:

> *volition determines the future.*

Miss Moore is usually ironic when writing thus, but not always; and I confess that it appears to me a somewhat facile and diffuse kind of irony, for the instrument of irony (the poetry) is weakened in the interests of irony. It is an example of what I shall have repeated occasion to refer to as the fallacy of expressive, or imitative, form; the procedure in which the form succumbs to the raw material of the poem. It is as if Dryden had descended to imitating Shadwell's style in his efforts to turn it to ridicule.

Closely related to this procedure, but much more audacious, is the maintenance of grammatical coherence when there is no coherence of thought or very little. Hart Crane, for example, has placed at the beginning of his poem, *For the Marriage of Faustus and Helen*,[19] the following quotation from Ben Jonson's play, *The Alchemist*:

> *And so we may arrive by Talmud skill*
> *And profane Greek to raise the building up*

[18] *Observations*, by Marianne Moore. The Dial Press: N. Y. 1924.
[19] *White Buildings*, by Hart Crane. Boni and Liveright: 1926.

Of Helen's house against the Ismaelite,
King of Thogarma, and his habergeons
Brimstony, blue and fiery; and the force
Of King Abaddon, and the beast of Cittim;
Which Rabbi David Kimchi; Onkelos,
And Aben Ezra do interpret Rome.[20]

This is one of the numerous passages in the play, in which the characters speak nonsense purporting to contain deep alchemical secrets or to express a feignedly distraught state of mind: this particular passage serves both functions at once. The nonsense is necessary to Jonson's plot; the reader recognizes the necessity and can make no objection, so that he is forced to accept with unalloyed pleasure whatever elusive but apparently real poetic implications there may be in such a passage, since he receives these implications absolutely gratis. The technique of expressive form, to which I have alluded, is here forced upon Jonson in a measure by the dramatic medium, for the characters must be represented in their own persons; this may or may not indicate a defect in the medium itself, as compared to other methods of satire, but at any rate there is no misuse of the medium. Jonson appears, then, to have been wholly aware of this procedure, which is usually regarded as a Mallarmean or Rimbaldian innovation, and Crane appears to have found at least one of his chief models for this kind of writing in Jonson. Jonson differs from Crane in that he does not employ the method when writing in his own name, but merely employs it to characterize his cozeners.

The two sections in blank verse of *Faustus and Helen* resemble Jonson's nonsense very closely. For example:

The mind is brushed by sparrow wings;
Numbers, rebuffed by asphalt, crowd
The margins of the day, accent the curbs,
Conveying divers dawns on every corner
To druggist, barber, and tobacconist,
Until the graduate opacities of evening

[20] Act IV: 3. Regarding this discussion, see Foreword on p. 153.

> *Take them away as suddenly to somewhere*
> *Virginal, perhaps, less fragmentary, cool.*

This is perfectly grammatical, and if not examined too carefully may appear more or less comprehensible. But the activities of the numbers, if the entire sentence is surveyed, appear wholly obscure. If one suppose *numbers* to be a synonym for *numbers of persons*, for *crowds*, one or two points are cleared up, but no more. If one suppose the numbers to be the mathematical abstractions of modern life, structural, temporal, financial, and others similar, there is greater clarity; but the first five lines are so precious and indirect as to be somewhat obscure, and the last three lines are perfectly obscure.

There is a pleasanter example of the same kind of writing in a shorter poem by Crane, and from the same volume, the poem called *Sunday Morning Apples:*

> *A boy runs with a dog before the sun, straddling*
> *Spontaneities that form their independent orbits,*
> *Their own perennials of light*
> *In the valley where you live*
> > *(called Brandywine.)*

The second line, taken in conjunction with the first, conveys the action of the boy, but it does so indirectly and by suggestion. What it says, if we consider rational content alone, is really indecipherable. One can, of course, make a rational paraphrase, but one can do it, not by seeking the rational content of the lines, but by seeking suggestions as to the boy's behavior, and by then making a rational statement regarding it. The line has a certain loveliness and conveys what it sets out to convey: the objection which I should make to it is that it goes through certain motions that are only half effective. A greater poet would have made the rational formula count rationally, at the same time that he was utilizing suggestion; he would thus have achieved a more concentrated poetry.

2. *Transference of Values from one field of experience to an-*

other and unrelated field. I shall illustrate this procedure with passages from Crane's poem, *The Dance.*[21] The poem opens with the description of a journey first by canoe down the Hudson, then on foot into the mountains. As the protagonist, or narrator, proceeds on his way, he appears to proceed likewise into the past, until he arrives at the scene of an Indian dance, at which a chieftain, Maquokeeta, is being burned at the stake. The poem from this point on deals with the death and apotheosis of Maquokeeta, the apotheosis taking the form of a union with Pocahontas, who has been introduced in this poem and in the poem preceding, *The River,* as a kind of mythic deity representing the American soil. The following passage is the climax and the most striking moment in the poem:

> *O, like the lizard in the furious noon,*
> *That drops his legs and colors in the sun,*
> *—And laughs, pure serpent, Time itself, and moon*
> *Of his own fate, I saw thy change begun!*
>
> *And saw thee dive to kiss that destiny*
> *Like one white meteor, sacrosanct and blent*
> *At last with all that's consummate and free*
> *There where the first and last gods keep thy tent.*

The remainder of the poem develops the same theme and the same mood. The following phrases are typical:

> *Thy freedom is her largesse, Prince . . .*
> *And are her perfect brows to thine? . . .*

The difficulty resides in the meaning of the union. It may be regarded in either of two ways: as the simple annihilation and dissolution in the soil of Maquokeeta, or as the entrance into another and superior mode of life. There is no possible compromise.

If we select the former alternative, the language of mystical

[21] From *The Bridge,* by Hart Crane. Horace Liveright, N. Y.: 1930.

and physical union has no relationship to the event: it is language carried over, with all or a good deal of its connotation, from two entirely different realms of experience. The passage is thus parasitic for its effect upon feelings unrelated to its theme. The words *consummate and free*, for example, carry the connotations common to them, but their rational meaning in this context is *terminated and dissipated. Sacrosanct*, similarly, while carrying certain feelings from its religious past, would mean *devoid of human meaning*, or, more concisely, *devoid of meaning*. Similarly, *perfect*, in the last line quoted, carries feelings from love poetry, but it would actually signify *meaningless*. In other words, extinction is beatitude. But this is nonsense: extinction is extinction. If there is a state of beatitude, it is a state; that is, it is not extinction.

If we accept the second alternative and assume that some really mystical experience is implied, there is nothing in the poem or elsewhere in Crane's work to give us a clue to the nature of the experience. The only possible conclusion is that he was confused as to his own feelings and did not bother to find out what he was really talking about. That odd bits of this obscurity can be glossed I am fully aware; but it cannot be cleaned up to an extent even moderately satisfactory. There is a wide margin of obscurity and of meaningless excitement, despite a certain splendor of language which may at times move one to forget, or to try to forget, what the poem lacks.

Further, there seems actually little doubt that Crane did confuse in some way the ideas of extinction and of beatitude, and that he was an enthusiastic pantheistical mystic. The mere fact that beatitude is represented in this poem by the union with Pocahontas, who stands for the soil of America, is evidence in itself; and further evidence may be found in *The River* and in some of the shorter poems. But one does not create a religion and a conception of immortality simply by naming the soil Pocahontas and by then writing love poetry to the Indian girl who bore that name. Crane repeatedly refers to an idea which he cannot define and which probably never had even potential existence.

A similar difficulty occurs in *Atlantis*, the final section of *The Bridge*, the sequence of which *The Dance* and *The River* are central parts. The Brooklyn Bridge is seen in a kind of vision or hallucination as the new Atlantis, the future America. The language is ecstatic; at certain moments and in certain ways it comes near to being the most brilliant language in Crane's work:

> *Like hails, farewells—up planet-sequined heights*
> *Some trillion whispering hammers glimmer Tyre:*
> *Serenely, sharply up the long anvil cry*
> *Of inchling æons silence rivets Troy . . .*

But the only poetic embodiment of the future, the only source of the ecstacy, is a quantitative vision of bigger cities with higher buildings. One can read a certain amount of allegory into this, but in so far as one makes the allegory definite or comprehensible, one will depart from the text; the enthusiasm again is obscure.

3. *Reference to a non-existent plot.* This is most easily illustrated by selections from T. S. Eliot. I quote from *Gerontion:*[22]

> *To be eaten, to be divided, to be drunk*
> *Among whispers; by Mr. Silvero*
> *With caressing hands, at Limoges*
> *Who walked all night in the next room;*
> *By Hakagawa, bowing among the Titians;*
> *By Madame de Tornquist, in the dark room*
> *Shifting the candles; Fräulein von Kulp*
> *Who turned in the hall, one hand on the door.*

Each one of these persons is denoted in the performance of an act, and each act, save possibly that of Hakagawa, implies an anterior situation, is a link in a chain of action; even that of Hakagawa implies an anterior and unexplained personality. Yet we have no hint of the nature of the history implied. A feeling is claimed by the poet, the motivation, or meaning, of which is with-held, and of which in all likelihood he has no clearer notion

---

* *Poems 1909-1925*, by T. S. Eliot.

than his readers can have. I do not wish to seem to insist that Mr. Eliot should have recounted the past histories in order to perfect this particular poem. Given the convention, the modus operandi, the obscurity is inevitable, and compared to the obscurity which we have just seen in Crane, it is relatively innocent. But obscurity it is: discreetly modulated diffuseness. A more direct and economical convention seems to me preferable.

Mr. Eliot does much the same thing, but less skillfully, elsewhere. The following passage is from *Burbank with a Baedecker; Bleistein with a Cigar:*[23]

> *Burbank crossed a little bridge,*
> *Descending at a small hotel;*
> *Princess Volupine arrived,*
> *They were together, and he fell.*

What is the significance of the facts in the first two lines? They have no real value as perception: the notation is too perfunctory. They must have some value as information, as such details might have value, for example, in a detective story, if they are to have any value at all. Yet they have no bearing on what follows; in fact, most of what follows is obscure in exactly the same way. They are not even necessary to what occurs in the next two lines, for Princess Volupine might just as well have encountered him anywhere else and after any other transit.

4. *Explicit Reference to a non-existent symbolic value.* The following lines are taken from a poem entitled *Museum,*[24] by Mr. Alan Porter:

> *The day was empty. Very pale with dust,*
> *A chalk road set its finger at the moors.*
> *The drab, damp air so blanketed the town*
> *Never an oak swung leather leaf. The chimneys*

---

[23] *Poems 1909-1925,* by T. S. Eliot.
[24] *Signature of Pain,* by Alan Porter. The John Day Company: New York: 1931.

Pushed up their pillars at the loose-hung sky;
And through the haze, along the ragstone houses,
Red lichens dulled to a rotten-apple brown.

. . . . .

Suddenly turning a byeway corner, a cripple,
Bloodless with age, lumbered along the road.
The motes of dust whirled at his iron-shod crutches
And quickly settled. A dog whined. The old
Cripple looked round, and, seeing no man, gave
A quick, small piping chuckle, swung a pace,
And stopped to look about and laugh again.
"That," said a girl in a flat voice, "is God."
Her mother made no answer; she remembered,
"I knew an old lame beggar who went mad."
He lumbered along the road and turned a corner.
His tapping faded and the day was death.

This poem is ably written and has an unusually fine texture; in fact, it is the texture of the entire work which provides the effective setting for the factitious comment on the beggar, and the comment is introduced with great skill. The landscape is intense and mysterious, as if with meaning withheld. In such a setting, the likening of the beggar to God appears, for an instant, portentous, but only for an instant, for there is no discernible basis for the likening. The beggar is treated as if he were symbolic of something, whereas he is really symbolic of nothing that one can discover. The introduction of the beggar appears to be a very skillful piece of sleight-of-hand; yet it is not an incidental detail of the description, but is rather the climax of the description, the theme of the poem. We have, in other words, a rather fine poem about nothing.

5. *Implicit Reference to a non-existent symbolic value.* It may be difficult at times to distinguish this type of pseudo-reference from the last or from the type which I have designated under the

heading of transferred value. I shall merely endeavor to select examples as obvious as possible.

There is, in the first place, such a thing as implicit reference to a genuine symbolic value. The second sonnet in Heredia's *Trophées*, the sonnet entitled *Némée*, describes the slaying of the Nemean lion by Hercules. Hercules is the typical hero; the slaying of the lion is the heroic task; the fleeing peasant is the common mortal for whom the task is performed. It is nakedly and obviously allegorical, yet there is no statement within the poem of the allegorical intention: it is our familiarity with the myth and with other similar myths which makes us recognize the poem as allegory. Similarly, there is no statement of allegorical intention within Blake's poem, *The Tiger*: the recognition of the intention is due to Blake's having been fairly explicit in other works.

Further, it is possible to describe an item with no past history in such a way that it will have a significance fairly general. This is the procedure of a handful of the best poems of the Imagist movement; for example, of Dr. Williams' poem, *On the road to the contagious hospital*. Thus Miss Moore describes a parakeet, in the poem entitled *My Apish Cousins*:

> the parakeet,
> trivial and humdrum on examination,
> destroying
> bark and portions of the food it could not eat.

There is also the legitimate field of purely descriptive poetry, with no general significance and no claim to any. For examples, one could cite many passages from *The Seasons*, or from Crabbe. There is no attempt in such poetry to communicate any feeling save the author's interest in visible beauties. Such poetry can scarcely rise to the greatest heights, but within its field it is sound, and it can, as in some of Crabbe's descriptions, especially of the sea, achieve surprising power. There is a good deal of this sort of thing scattered through English literature.

49

Growing out of these two types of poetry (that which refers to a genuine symbolic value, but implicitly, and the purely descriptive), there is a sentimental and more or less spurious variety, a good deal of which was recently fostered by the Imagist movement, but which actually antedates the Imagist movement by more than a century.

This poetry describes landscape or other material, sometimes very ably, but assumes a quality or intensity of feeling of which the source is largely obscure. Thus in Collins' *Ode to Evening* we find a melancholy which at moments, as in the description of the bat, verges on disorder, and which at all times is far too profound to arise from an evening landscape alone. Collins' bat differs from Miss Moore's parakeet in this: that the parakeet is a genuine example of the way in which the exotic may become humdrum with familiarity—there is, in other words, a real perception of the bird involved, which does not exceed the order of experience which the bird may reasonably represent; whereas Collins' bat is not mad nor a sufficient motive for madness, but is used to express a state of mind irrelevant to him. It is as if a man should murder his mother, and then, to express his feelings, write an *Ode to Thunder*. Or rather, it is as if a man should murder his mother with no consciousness of the act, but with all of the consequent suffering, and should then so express himself. A symbol is used to embody a feeling neither relevant to the symbol nor relevant to anything else of which the poet is conscious: the poet expresses his feeling as best he is able without understanding it. Collins in this poem, and in his odes to the disembodied passions, is perhaps the first purely romantic poet and one of the best. He does not, like Gray, retain amid his melancholy any of the classical gift for generalization, and he has provided the language with no familiar quotations. Shelley's *Ode to the West Wind*, and in a measure Keats' *Ode to the Nightingale*, are examples of the same procedure; namely, of expressing a feeling, not as among the traditional poets in terms of its motive, but in terms of something irrelevant or largely so, commonly landscape. No landscape, in itself, is an adequate motive for the feelings expressed in such poems as these; an appropriate landscape merely brings to mind

50

certain feelings and is used as a symbol for their communication. The procedure can be defended on the grounds that the feeling may be universal and that the individual reader is at liberty to supply his own motive; but the procedure nevertheless does not make for so concentrated a poetry as the earlier method, and as an act of moral contemplation the poem is incomplete and may even be misleading and dangerous.

H. D. employs a formula nearly identical with that of Collins in most of her poems. In describing a Greek landscape, she frequently writes as if it had some intrinsic virtue automatically evoked by a perception of its qualities as landscape but more important than these qualities in themselves. It is not Greek history or civilization with which she is concerned, or most often it is not: the material is simple and more or less ideally bucolic. Frequently the ecstasy (the quality of feeling assumed is nearly identical in most of her poems) is evoked merely by rocks, sea, and islands. But it would not be evoked by any rock, sea, or islands: they must be Greek. But why must they be Greek? Because of Athenian civilization? If so, why the to-do about material irrelevant to Athenian civilization? There is some wholly obscure attachment on the poet's part to anything Greek, regardless of its value: the mention of anything Greek is sufficient to release her very intense feeling. But since the relationship between the feeling and the Greek landscape has no comprehensible source and is very strong, one must call it sentimental.

This is not to say that all her poetry is spoiled by it: much of it is spoiled and nearly all is tainted, but the taint is sometimes very slight; and the description, in addition, is sometimes very fine. Exotic landscapes of one kind or another have been employed in exactly this fashion for about a century, and, in America, the American landscape has been so employed by such writers as Whitman, Sandburg, Crane, and Williams.

6. *Explicit Reference to a non-existent or obscure principle of motivation*. This may at times be hard to distinguish from almost any of the types of obscurity which I have described, but there are to be found occasionally passages of pseudo-reference which will fit into scarcely any other category. Bearing in mind the

51

fundamental obscurity of *The Dance,* by Hart Crane, an obscurity which I have already discussed at some length, let us consider these two lines from it:

> *Mythical brows we saw retiring—loth,*
> *Disturbed, and destined, into denser green.*

This passage depends for its effect wholly upon the feeling of motivation.

The mythical has rational content for the believer in myths or for him who can find an idea embodied in the myth. The major Greek divinities exist for us chiefly as allegorical embodiments of more or less Platonic ideas. What myths have we in mind here? None. Or none unless it be the myth of Pocahontas, which, as we have seen, is irreducible to any idea. There is merely a feeling of mythicalness.

Loth, disturbed, destined are words of motivation; that is, each one implies a motive. But the nature of the motive is not given in the poem, nor is it deducible from the poem nor from the body of Crane's work. In fact, it is much easier to read some sort of general meaning into these lines in isolation than in their context, which has already been discussed.

Such terms give, then, a feeling of reasonable motivation unreasonably obscured. The poet speaks as if he had knowledge incommunicable to us, but of which he is able to communicate the resultant feelings. There is a feeling of mystery back of an emotion which the poet endeavors to render with precision. It is a skillful indulgence in irresponsibility. The skill is admirable, but not the irresponsibility. The poetry has a ghostly quality, as if it were only half there.

7. *Reference to a purely private symbolic value.* A poet, sometimes because of the limitations of his education, and sometimes for other reasons, may center his feelings in symbols shared with no one, or perhaps only with a small group. The private symbol may or may not refer to a clear concept or understanding. If it does so refer and the poetry is otherwise good, readers are likely eventually to familiarize themselves with the symbols; in fact

brilliant writing alone will suffice to this end, as witness the efforts that have been made to clarify the essentially obscure concepts of Blake and of Yeats. A certain amount of this kind of thing, in fact, is probably inevitable in any poet, and sometimes, as in the references to private experience in the sonnets of Shakespeare, the obscurity, as a result of the accidents of history, can never be penetrated.

I have illustrated one extreme type of pseudo-reference with a passage from Ben Jonson; I might have utilized also the "mad songs" of the sixteenth and seventeenth centuries, such as were written by Shakespeare, Fletcher, and Herrick. Samuel Johnson wrote thus in his *Life of Dryden*: "Dryden delighted to tread upon the brink of meaning, where light and darkness mingle. . . . This inclination sometimes produced nonsense, which he knew; and sometimes it issued in absurdity, of which perhaps he was not conscious." The method appears, then, to have been for a long time one of the recognized potentialities of poetic writing, but to have been more or less checked by the widespread command of rational subject matter.

It should naturally have been released, as it appears to have been, by a period of amateur mysticism, of inspiration for its own sake, by a tendency such as that which we have for some years past observed, to an increasingly great preoccupation with the fringe of consciousness, to an increasing emphasis on the concept of continuous experience, a tendency to identify, under the influence, perhaps, of scientific or of romantic monism, subconscious stimuli and reactions with occult inspiration, to confuse the divine and the visceral, and to employ in writing from such attitudes as this confusion might provide, a language previously reserved to the religious mystics. Such a change would involve along its way such indefinable philosophies as Bergsonism[25] and Transcendentalism,[26] such half-metaphorical sciences

[25] *Le Bergsonisme*, by Julien Benda. Mercure de France: 1926. Also *Flux and Blur in Contemporary Art*, by John Crowe Ransom in the Sewanee Review, July, 1929.

[26] H. B. Parkes on Emerson, in the Hound and Horn, Summer, 1932; included in *The Pragmatic Test*, by H. B. Parkes, The Colt Press, San Francisco, 1942.

as psychoanalysis, and especially the popular myths and superstitions which they and the more reputable sciences have engendered. In such an intellectual milieu, semi-automatic writing begins to appear a legitimate and even a superior method.

Emerson, in *Merlin*, for example, gives this account of the bard's activity:

> *He shall not his brain encumber*
> *With the coil of rhythm and number;*
> *But, leaving rule and pale forethought,*
> *He shall aye climb*
> *For his rhyme.*
> *"Pass in, pass in," the angels say,*
> *"In to the upper doors,*
> *Nor count compartments of the floors,*
> *But mount to paradise*
> *By the stairway of surprise."*

Just how much Emerson meant by this passage it would be hard to say; it is always hard to say just how much Emerson meant, and perhaps would have been hardest for Emerson. Mr. Tate reduces Emerson's Transcendentalism[27] to this formula: ". . . In Emerson, man is greater than any idea, and being the Over-Soul is potentially perfect; there is no struggle because—I state the Emersonian doctrine, which is very slippery, in its extreme terms—because there is no possibility of error. There is no drama in human character, because there is no tragic fault."

To continue with extreme terms—which will give us, if not what Emerson desired, the results which his doctrine and others similar have encouraged—we arrive at these conclusions: If there is no possibility of error, the revision of judgment is meaningless; immediate inspiration is correct; but immediate inspiration amounts to the same thing as unrevised reactions to stimuli; unrevised reactions are mechanical; man in a state of perfection is

---

[27] *New England Culture and Emily Dickinson*, by Allen Tate: The Symposium, April, 1932. Reprinted in a somewhat revised form in *Reactionary Essays on Poetry and Ideas*, by Allen Tate, Scribners, 1936.

an automaton; an automatic man is insane. Hence, Emerson's perfect man is a madman.

The important thing about all this is not Emerson's originality, but his complete lack of any: exactly the same conclusions are deducible from the *Essay on Man,* and the convictions which lead to them one meets everywhere in the eighteenth, nineteenth, and twentieth centuries.

Dr. W. C. Williams, for example, who, like Emerson, does not practice unreservedly what he preaches, but who more perhaps than any writer living encourages in his juniors a profound conviction of their natural rightness, a sentimental debauchery of self-indulgence, is able to write as follows: "It is the same thing you'll see in a brigand, a criminal of the grade of Gerald Chapman, some of the major industrial leaders, old-fashioned kings, the Norsemen, drunkards and the best poets. . . . Poetry is imposed on an age by men intent on something else, whose primary cleanliness of mind makes them automatically first-rate." [28]

A few months later Dr. Williams writes of and to his young admirers somewhat querulously:[29] "Instead of that—Lord how serious it sounds—let's play tiddly-winks with the syllables. . . . Experiment we must have, but it seems to me that a number of the younger writers has forgotten that writing doesn't mean just inventing new ways to say 'So's your Old Man.' I swear I myself can't make out for the life of me what many of them are talking about, and I have a will to understand them that they will not find in many another." He demands substance, not realizing that his own teachings have done their very respectable bit toward cutting the young men off from any.

The Emersonian and allied doctrines differ in their moral implications very little from any form of Quietism or even from the more respectable and Catholic forms of mysticism. If we add to the doctrine the belief in pantheism—that is, the belief that the Over-Soul is the Universe, that body and soul are one—we have

---

[28] Blues (published by C. H. Ford, at Columbus, Miss.) for May, 1929.

[29] Blues for Autumn of 1930. The reference to the game of tiddly-winks will be clear only to those persons familiar with the imitators of Mr. James Joyce's fourth prose work, exclusive of *Exiles,* entitled *Finnegans Wake.*

the basis for the more or less Freudian mysticism of the surreal-
ists and such of their disciples as Eugene Jolas; we have also—
probably—a rough notion of Hart Crane's mysticism. There is
the danger for the Quietist that the promptings of the Devil or
of the viscera may be mistaken for the promptings of God. The
pantheistic mystic identifies God, Devil, and viscera as a point
of doctrine: he is more interested in the promptings of the "sub-
conscious" mind than of the conscious, in the half-grasped intention, in the fleeting relationship, than in that which is wholly
understood. He is interested in getting just as far off in the direction of the uncontrolled, the meaningless, as he can possibly get
and still have the pleasure of talking about it. He is frequently
more interested in the psychology of sleeping than in the psychology of waking;[30] he would if he could devote himself to
exploring that realm of experience which he shares with sea-
anemones, cabbages, and onions, in preference to exploring the
realm of experience shared specifically with men.

So far as my own perceptions are able to guide me, it appears
that the writers employing such methods are writing a little too
much as Jonson's alchemists spoke, with a philosophical background insusceptible of definition, despite their apparently careful references to it, but as their own dupes, not to dupe others.
They have revised Baudelaire's dictum that the poet should be
the hypnotist and somnambulist combined; he should now be the
cozener and the cozened. Crane, despite his genius, and the same
is true of Mr. James Joyce, appears to answer Ben Jonson's
scoundrels across the centuries, and in their own language, but
like a somnambulist under their control.

This kind of writing is not a "new kind of poetry," as it has
been called perennially since Verlaine discovered it in Rimbaud.
It is the old kind of poetry with half the meaning removed. Its
strangeness comes from its thinness. Indubitable genius has been
expended upon poetry of this type, and much of the poetry so
written will more than likely have a long life, and quite justly,
but the nature of the poetry should be recognized: it can do us

[30] Cf. Mr. James Joyce's *Finnegans Wake,* and the voluminous works by
Mr. Joyce's apologists and imitators.

no good to be the dupes of men who do not understand themselves.

Type V: QUALITATIVE PROGRESSION

THE TERM *qualitative progression* I am borrowing from Mr.
Kenneth Burke's volume of criticism, *Counterstatement,* to which
I have already had several occasions to refer. This method arises
from the same attitudes as the last, and it resembles the last except that it makes no attempt whatever at a rational progression.
Mr. Pound's *Cantos*[31] are the perfect example of the form; they
make no unfulfilled claims to matter not in the poetry, or at any
rate relatively few and slight claims. Mr. Pound proceeds from
image to image wholly through the coherence of feeling: his sole
principle of unity is mood, carefully established and varied. That
is, each statement he makes is reasonable in itself, but the progression from statement to statement is not reasonable: it is the
progression either of random conversation or of revery. This kind
of progression might be based upon an implicit rationality; in
such a case the rationality of the progression becomes clearly
evident before the poem has gone very far and is never thereafter lost sight of; in a poem of any length such implicit rationality would have to be supported by explicit exposition. But in Mr.
Pound's poem I can find few implicit themes of any great clarity,
and fewer still that are explicit.[32]

[31] *A Draft of XXX Cantos,* by Ezra Pound. Hours Press: 15 rue Guénégaud:
Paris: 1930.
[32] Mr. Pound, writing in The New English Weekly, Vol. III, No. 4, of remarks similar to the above which I published in The Hound and Horn for the
Spring of 1933, states: "I am convinced that one should not as a general rule
reply to critics or defend works in process of being written. On the other hand,
if one prints fragments of a work one perhaps owes the benevolent reader
enough explanation to prevent his wasting time in unnecessary misunderstanding.
"The nadir of solemn and elaborate imbecility is reached by Mr. Winters in
an American publication where he deplores my 'abandonment of logic in the
Cantos,' presumably because he has never read my prose criticism and has never
heard of the ideographic method, and thinks logic is limited to a few 'forms of
logic' which better minds were already finding inadequate to the mental needs
of the XIIIth century."
As to the particular defects of scholarship which Mr. Pound attributes to

The principle of selection being less definite, the selection of details is presumably less rigid, though many of the details display a fine quality. The symbolic range is therefore reduced, since the form reduces the importance of selectiveness, or self-directed action. The movement is proportionately slow and wavering—indeed is frequently shuffling and undistinguished—and the range of material handled is limited: I do not mean that the poetry cannot refer to a great many types of actions and persons, but that it can find in them little variety of value—it refers to them all in the same way, that is, casually. Mr. Pound resembles a village loafer who sees much and understands little.

The following passage, however, the opening of the fourth *Canto*, illustrates this kind of poetry at its best:

Palace in smoky light,
Troy but a heap of smouldering boundary stones,
ANAXIFORMINGES! Aurunculeia!
Hear me, Cadmus of Golden Prows!
The silver mirrors catch the bright stones and flare,
Dawn, to our waking, drifts in the cool green light;
Dew-haze blurs, in the grass, pale ankles moving.
Beat, beat, whirr, thud, in the soft turf under the apple-trees,
Choros nympharum, goat-foot, with the pale foot alternate;
Crescent of blue-shot waters, green-gold in the shallows,
A black cock crows in the sea-foam;
And by the curved, carved foot of the couch, claw-foot and
                              lion-head, an old man seated
Speaking in the low drone. . . . :
                              Ityn
Et ter flebiliter, Ityn, Ityn!
And she went toward the window and cast her down

---

me, he is, alas, mistaken. For the rest, one may only say that civilization rests on the recognition that language possesses both connotative and denotative powers; that the abandonment of one in a poem impoverishes the poem to that extent; and that the abandonment of the denotative, or rational, in particular, and in a pure state, results in one's losing the only means available for checking up on the qualitative or "ideographic" sequences to see if they really are coherent in more than vague feeling. Mr. Pound, in other words, has no way of knowing whether he can think or not.

> *"And the while, the while swallows crying:*
>
> Ityn!
>
> *"It is Cabestan's heart in the dish."*
> *"It is Cabestan's heart in the dish?*
> *"No other taste shall change this."*

The loveliness of such poetry appears to me indubitable, but it is merely a blur of revery: its tenuity becomes apparent if one compares it, for example, to the poetry of Paul Valéry, which achieves effects of imagery, particularly of atmospheric imagery, quite as extraordinary, along with precision, depth of meaning, and the power that comes of close and inalterable organization, and, though Mr. Pound's admirers have given him a great name as a metrist, with incomparably finer effects of sound.

Mr. Kenneth Burke defines the qualitative progression[33] by means of a very fine analysis of the preparation for the ghost in *Hamlet* and by reference to the porter scene in *Macbeth*, and then proceeds to the public house scene in *The Waste Land*[34] as if it were equally valid. Actually, the qualitative progression in Shakespeare is peripheral, the central movement of each play being dependent upon what Mr. Burke calls the psychology of the hero, or narrative logic, and so firmly dependent that occasional excursions into the rationally irrelevant can be managed with no loss of force, whereas in *The Waste Land* the qualitative progression is central: it is as if we should have a dislocated series of scenes from *Hamlet* without the prince himself, or with too slight an account of his history for his presence to be helpful. The difference between Mr. Eliot and Mr. Pound is this: that in *The Waste Land*, the prince is briefly introduced in the footnotes, whereas it is to be doubted that Mr. Pound could manage such an introduction were he so inclined. And the allegorical interpretation, or the germ of one, which Mr. Eliot has provided helps very little in the organization of the poem itself. To guess that the rain has a certain allegorical meaning when the rain is so indifferently described, or to guess at the allegorical relation-

[33] *Counterstatement:* page 38 and thereafter.
[34] *Poems 1909-25*, by T. S. Eliot.

ships as a scholar might guess at the connections between a dozen odd pages recovered from a lost folio, is of very small aid to ourselves or to the poet.

If Mr. Eliot and Mr. Pound have employed conventions that can be likened to revery or to random conversation, Rimbaud and Mr. Joyce have gone farther. I quote Rimbaud's *Larme*:

> *Loin des oiseaux, des troupeaux, des villageoises,*
> *Je buvais accroupi dans quelque bruyère*
> *Entourée de tendres bois de noisetiers,*
> *Par un brouillard d'après-midi tiède et vert.*
>
> *Que pouvais-je boire dans cette jeune Oise,*
> *Ormeaux sans voix, gazon sans fleurs, ciel couvert:*
> *Que tirais-je à la gourde de colocase?*
> *Quelque liqueur d'or, fade et qui fait suer.*
>
> *Tel, j'eusse été mauvaise enseigne d'auberge.*
> *Puis l'orage changea le ciel jusqu' au soir.*
> *Ce furent des pays noirs, des lacs, des perches,*
> *Des colonnades sous la nuit bleue, des gares.*
>
> *L'eau des bois se perdait sur les sables vierges.*
> *Le vent, du ciel, jetait des glaçons aux mares . . .*
> *Or! tel qu'un pêcheur d'or ou de coquillages,*
> *Dire que je n'ai pas eu souci de boire!*

The feelings of this poem are perhaps those attendant upon dream, delirium, or insanity. The coming of night and the storm is an intensification of the mood; the protagonist is suddenly sucked deeper in the direction of complete unconsciousness, and the terror becomes more profound.

In *Finnegans Wake*, by James Joyce, the dream convention is unmistakable. It penetrates the entire texture of the work, not only the syntax but the words themselves, which are broken down and recombined in surprising ways.

This unbalance of the reasonable and the non-reasonable, whether the non-reason be of the type which I am now discussing or of the pseudo-referent type, is a vice wherever it occurs, and in the experimental writers who have worked very far in this direction, it is, along with Laforguian irony, which I shall discuss separately, one of the two most significant vices of style now flourishing. The reasons have already been mentioned here and there, but I shall summarize them.

Since only one aspect of language, the connotative, is being utilized, less can be said in a given number of words than if the denotative aspect were being fully utilized at the same time. The convention thus tends to diffuseness. Further, when the denotative power of language is impaired, the connotative becomes proportionately parasitic upon denotations in previous contexts, for words cannot have associations without meanings; and if the denotative power of language could be wholly eliminated, the connotative would be eliminated at the same stroke, for it is the nature of associations that they are associated with something. This means that non-rational writing, far from requiring greater literary independence than the traditional modes, encourages a quality of writing that is relatively derivative and insecure.

Since one of the means to coherence, or form, is impaired, form itself is enfeebled. In so far as form is enfeebled, precision of detail is enfeebled, for details receive precision from the structure in which they function just as they may be employed to give that structure precision; to say that detail is enfeebled is to say that the power of discrimination is enfeebled. Mr. Joyce's new prose has sensitivity, for Mr. Joyce is a man of genius, but it is the sensitivity of a plasmodium, in which every cell squirms independently though much like every other. This statement is a very slight exaggeration if certain chapters are considered, notably the chapter entitled *Anna Livia Plurabelle,* but for the greater part it is no exaggeration.

The procedure leads to indiscriminateness at every turn. Mr. Joyce endeavors to express disintegration by breaking down his form, by experiencing disintegration before our very eyes, but this destroys much of his power of expression. Of course he controls the extent to which he impairs his form, but this merely means that he is willing to sacrifice just so much power of expression—in an effort to express something—and no more. He is like Whitman trying to express a loose America by writing loose poetry. This fallacy, the fallacy of expressive, or imitative, form, recurs constantly in modern literature.

Anna Livia Plurabelle is in a sense a modern equivalent of Gray's *Elegy*, one in which the form is expressive of the theme to an unfortunate extent; it blurs the values of all experience in the fact of change, and is unable, because of its inability to deal with rational experience, to distinguish between village Cromwells and the real article, between Othello on the one hand and on the other hand Shem and Shaun. It leads to the unlimited subdivision of feelings into sensory details till perception is lost, instead of to the summary and ordering of perception; it leads to disorganization and unintelligence. In Mr. Joyce we may observe the decay of genius. To the form of decay his genius lends a beguiling iridescence, and to his genius the decay lends a quality of novelty, which endanger the literature of our time by rendering decay attractive.

Mr. T. S. Eliot, in his introduction to the *Anabase* of St. Jean Perse,[35] has written: "There is a logic of the imagination as well as a logic of concepts. People who do not appreciate poetry always find it difficult to distinguish between order and chaos in the arrangement of images." Later in the same essay he says: "I believe that this is a piece of writing of the same importance as the later work of Mr. James Joyce, as valuable as *Anna Livia Plurabelle*. And this is a high estimate indeed."

The logic in the arrangement of images of which Mr. Eliot speaks either is formulable, is not formulable, or is formulated. If it is neither formulated nor formulable (and he admits that it is not formulated), the word *logic* is used figuratively, to indicate qualitative progression, and the figure is one which it is hard to pardon a professed classicist for using at the present time. If the logic is formulable, there is no need for an apology and there is

---

[35] *Anabasis*, a poem by St. Jean Perse, with translation and Preface by T. S. Eliot. Faber and Faber, London: 1930.

no excuse for the reference to *Anna Livia Plurabelle;* and there is reason to wonder why no formulation is given or suggested by the critic. Mr. Eliot has reference obviously, merely to the type of graduated progression of feeling that we have been discussing, and the poem shares the weakness of other works already discussed.

Mr. Eliot's remarks are typical of the evasive dallying practiced by the greater number of even the most lucid and reactionary critics of our time when dealing with a practical problem of criticism. It is well enough to defend Christian morality and to speak of tradition, but forms must be defined and recognized or the darkness remains. A classicist may admire the sensibilities of Joyce and Perse with perfect consistency (though beyond a certain point not with perfect taste), but he cannot with consistency justify the forms which those sensibilities have taken.

If the reader is curious to compare with the *Anabase* a prose work of comparable length and subject in the traditional manner, he will find a specimen of the highest merit in *The Destruction of Tenochtitlan*[30] by William Carlos Williams, which, like the *Anabase,* deals with the military conquest of an exotic nation, but which utilizes not only qualitative progression but every other mode proper to narrative and in a masterly way. The form is exact; the rhetoric is varied and powerful; the details, unlike those of the *Anabase,* are exact both as description and, where symbolic force is intended, as symbols. Displaying fullness and precision of meaning, it is in no wise "strange" and has been ignored. But its heroic prose is superior to the prose of *Anabase* and of *Anna Livia Plurabelle,* is superior in all likelihood to nearly any other prose of our time and to most of the verse.

The so-called stream-of-consciousness convention of the contemporary novel is a form of qualitative progression. It may or may not be used to reveal a plot, but at best the revelation can be fragmentary since the convention excludes certain important functions of prose—summary, whether narrative or expository,

---

[30] *In the American Grain,* by W. C. Williams. A. and C. Boni, New York, 1925.

being the chief. It approximates the manner of the chain of thought as it might be imagined in the mind of the protagonist: that is, it tends away from the reconsidered, the revised, and tends toward the fallacy of imitative form, which I have remarked in the work of Joyce and of Whitman.[37] It emphasizes, wittingly or not, abject imitation at the expense of art; it is technically naturalism; it emphasizes to the last degree the psychology of the hero, but the least interesting aspect of it, the accidental. Mr. Kenneth Burke, in his novel, *Toward a Better Life*[38] thus falls into the very pit which he has labored most diligently to avoid: he expends his entire rhetorical energy on his sentences, but lets his story run loosely through the mind of his hero. The quality of the detail is expository and aphoristic; the structure is not expository but is qualitative. One feels a discrepancy between the detail and the form; the detail appears labored, the form careless and confused.

The convention of reminiscence, a form of the stream-of-consciousness technique, which is employed by Mr. Burke and by others, has a defect peculiar to itself alone. It commonly involves the assumption, at the beginning of a story, of the state of feeling proper to the conclusion; then by means of revelation, detail by detail, the feeling is justified. In other words, the initial situations are befogged by unexplained feeling, and the feeling does not develop in a clean relationship to the events. The result is usually a kind of diffuse lyricism.

Type VI: THE ALTERNATION OF METHOD

TWO OR MORE METHODS may be used in formal arrangements. In a play or novel, where there is plenty of room for change, a great

---

[37] This law of literary æsthetics has never that I know been stated explicitly. It might be thus formulated: Form is expressive invariably of the state of mind of the author; a state of formlessness is legitimate subject matter for literature, and in fact all subject matter, as such, is relatively formless; but the author must endeavor to give form, or meaning, to the formless—in so far as he endeavors that his own state of mind may imitate or approximate the condition of the matter, he is surrendering to the matter instead of mastering it. Form, in so far as it endeavors to imitate the formless, destroys itself.

[38] Op. cit.

many modes of procedure may be employed. In a lyrical poem there will seldom be more than two. In Marvell's *To His Coy Mistress*, for example, the progression from stanza to stanza is logical, but within each stanza the progression is repetitive.

Mallarmé's *L'Après-Midi d'un Faune* illustrates a method toward which various writers have tended; namely to shift out of the logical into the pseudo-referent or qualitative, back into the logical, and so on, but at irregular intervals. The appearance of shifting may be due, of course, to my own inability to follow the argument, but it appears to be a real shifting. The faun recounts his adventure, trying to philosophize concerning it: hence narrative alternates with what should be exposition, but actually both narrative and exposition move in a more or less dreamy fashion at times, so that the cleavage in method does not coincide with the cleavage in subject matter.

Type VII: THE DOUBLE MOOD

A SHORT POEM or passage may be composed of alternating passages of two distinct and more or less opposed types of feeling, or of two types of feeling combined and without discernible alternation. A long poem may involve many types of feeling, but where two types alone are involved, one of them is usually ironic: it is with this situation in particular that I am here concerned. Byron, for example, commonly builds up a somewhat grandiloquent effect only to demolish it by ridicule or by ludicrous anticlimax. His effects are crude in the main, the poems being ill-written, but he was the first poet to embody on a pretentious scale, and to popularize, this common modern attitude.

The particular form which his method has taken in modern poetry is closely related to the poetry of Jules Laforgue, though Laforgue is not in every case an influence. I quote Laforgue's *Complainte du Printemps:*

> *Permettez, ô sirène,*
> *Voici que votre haleine*
> *Embaume la verveine;*
> *C'est le printemps qui s'amène!*

—Ce système, en effet, ramène le printemps,
Avec son impudent cortège d'excitants.

    Otez donc ces mitaines;
    Et n'ayez, inhumaine,
    Que mes soupirs pour traine:
    Ous'qu'il y a de la gêne . . .

—Ah! yeux bleus méditant sur l'ennui de leur art!
Et vous, jeunes divins, aux soirs crus de hasard!

    Du géant à la naine,
    Vois, tout bon sire entraine
    Quelque contemporaine,
    Prendre l'air, par hygiène . . .

—Mais vous saignez ainsi pour l'amour de l'exil!
Pour l'amour de l'Amour! D'ailleurs, ainsi soit-il . . .

    T'ai-je fait de la peine?
    Oh! viens vers les fontaines
    Où tournent les phalènes
    Des nuits Elyséennes!

—Pimbèche aux yeux vaincus, bellâtre aux beaux jarrets,
Donnez votre fumier à la fleur du Regret.

    Voilà que son haleine
    N'embaum' plus la verveine!
    Drôle de phénomène . . .
    Hein, à l'année prochaine?

Vierges d'hier, ce soir traineuses de fœtus,
A genoux! voici l'heure où se plaint l'Angélus.

    Nous n'irons plus au bois,
    Les pins sont éternels,

Les cors ont des appels! . . .
Neiges des pâles mois,
Vous serez mon missel!
—Jusqu'au jour du dégel.

The opposition and cancellation of the two moods is so obvious as to need no particular comment: there is romantic nostalgia (romantic because it has no discernible object, is a form of unmotivated feeling) canceled by an immature irony (immature because it depends upon the obviously but insignificantly ridiculous, as in the third quatrain, or upon a kind of physical detail which is likely to cause pain to the adolescent but which is not likely to interest the mature, as in couplets four and five). The application of the irony, in turn, deepens the nostalgia, as in the fourth quatrain and the conclusion. It is the formula for adolescent disillusionment: the unhappily "cynical" reaction to the loss of a feeling not worth having.

A few years earlier than Laforgue, Tristan Corbière had employed the same procedure in a few poems, most vigorously in *Un Jeune Qui S'en Va*, but from his greatest work (*La Rapsode Foraine* and *Cris d'Aveugle*, two poems which are probably superior to any French verse of the nineteenth century save the best of Baudelaire), it is either absent or has lost itself amid an extremely complex cluster of feelings.

Previously to Corbière, Gautier had written in much the same fashion, but usually of very different subjects. His *Nostalgies des Obélisques* are examples. They consist of two poems, monologues spoken by two Egyptian obelisks, one of which has been transported to Paris and compares the Parisian and Egyptian scenes, lamenting the loss of the latter, the other of which remains behind, only to make the same comparison but to long for Paris. The alternations are almost mathematically balanced, though occasionally both moods will rest on a single image, as when an Egyptian animal performs a grotesquely ludicrous action in magnificent language. There is not, in Gautier, the adolescent mood of Laforgue, for Gautier was a vastly abler rhetorician and was too astute to give way to such a mood, but there is no meaning to his experience, as it appears in such poems, outside of the contrast, and the contrast is painfully precise. Gautier resembles a child fascinated by the task of separating and arranging exactly, blocks of exactly two colors. The moral sense of such a poet is too simple to hold the interest for many readings. Mr. Eliot in his quatrains employed the same formula; in fact several of his most striking lines are translated or imitated from *Emaux et Camées*.[39]

Similar to Laforgue's use of this kind of irony is Mr. Pound's use of it in *Hugh Selwyn Mauberly*.[40] The two attitudes at variance in this sequence are a nostalgic longing of which the visible object is the society of the Pre-Raphaelites and of the related poets of the nineties, and a compensatory irony which admits the mediocrity of that society or which at least ridicules its mediocre aspects. Even in the midst of the most biting comment, the yearning is unabated:

> *The Burne-Jones cartons*
> *Have preserved her eyes;*
> *Still, at the Tate, they teach*
> *Cophetua to rhapsodize;*
>
> *Thin, like brook-water,*
> *With a vacant gaze.*
> *The English Rubaiyat was still-born*
> *In those days.*[41]

And again, to quote an entire poem:

> *Among the pickled foetuses and bottled bones*
> *Engaged in perfecting the catalogue,*
> *I found the last scion of the*
> *Senatorial families of Strassbourg, Monsieur Verog.*

[39] Poems 1909-25, by T. S. Eliot: the series of poems in octosyllabic quatrains, of which the most successful is *Sweeney among the Nightingales*.

[40] *Hugh Selwyn Mauberly*, by Ezra Pound. Included in *Personæ*, by Ezra Pound. Boni and Liveright. New York. 1926.

[41] *Yeux Glauqes*, from *Mauberly*.

For two hours he talked of Gallifet;
Of Dowson; Of the Rhymers' Club;
Told me how Johnson (Lionel) died
By falling from a high stool in a pub . . .

But showed no trace of alcohol
At the autopsy, privately performed—
Tissues preserved—the pure mind
Arose toward Newman as the whiskey warmed.

Dowson found harlots cheaper than hotels;
Headlam for uplift; Image impartially imbued
With raptures for Bacchus, Terpsichore, and the Church
So spoke the author of "The Dorian Mood,"

M. Verog, out of step with the decade,
Detached from his contemporaries,
Neglected by the young,
Because of these reveries.[42]

As so often happens when this kind of irony occurs, the poem is guilty of a certain amount both of doggerel and of verbosity. It is not without virtues, however; and it is not the best poem in the sequence. It is worth noting that the two moods are not precisely separable here, as in so much of Eliot and of Gautier, but are usually coincident. This likewise is true of the irony of Wallace Stevens.

Mr. Stevens' commonest method of ironic comment is to parody his own style, with respect to its slight affectation of elegance; or perhaps it were more accurate to say that this affectation itself is a parody, however slight, of the purity of his style in its best moments. The parody frequently involves an excess of alliteration, as in the opening lines of the poem entitled *Of the Manner of Addressing Clouds:*[43]

---

[42] *"Siena Mi Fe': Disfecemi Maremma."* The same.
[43] This poem and others by the same author may be found in: *Harmonium,* by Wallace Stevens, Alfred A. Knopf, New York, 1931.

> *Gloomy grammarians in golden gowns,*
> *Meekly you keep the mortal rendezvous. . . .*

The same device is more obviously employed in *The Comedian as the Letter C,* in which appears an explicit statement of the source of the irony, his inability to justify the practice of his art, his own lack of respect for what he is doing, and in which the irony frequently descends to the tawdry. In some poems he is entirely free of the quality, as, for examples, in *Sunday Morning, Death of a Soldier, Of Heaven Considered as a Tomb.* In such work, and in those poems such as that last quoted and, to choose a more ambitious example, *Le Monocle de Mon Oncle,* in which the admixture is very slight, he is probably the greatest poet of his generation.

The double mood is not strictly post-romantic, either in English or in French, nor is ironic poetry, but both are perhaps more frequently so, and in pre-romantic poetry neither is employed for the purpose which I have been describing. For instance, in Dryden's *MacFlecknoe,* the combination of the heroic style and the satirical intention constitutes a kind of double mood, but there is no mutual cancellation; the same is true of Pope's *Dunciad,* of *La Pucelle* by Voltaire, and of a good many other poems. Churchill's *Dedication to Warburton,* in its semblance of eulogy actually covering a very bitter attack, employs both irony (as distinct from satire) and something that might be called a double mood. But in all of these examples, the poet is perfectly secure in his own feelings; he is attacking something or someone else from a point of view which he regards as tenable. The essence of romantic irony, on the other hand, is this: that the poet ridicules himself for a kind or degree of feeling which he can neither approve nor control; so that the irony is simply the act of confessing a state of moral insecurity which the poet sees no way to improve.[44]

A twentieth century ironist who resembles the earlier ironists instead of her contemporaries is Miss Marianne Moore. If one

[44] The relationship and partial indebtedness of this technical analysis of romantic irony to Irving Babbitt's more general treatment of the same subject in *Rousseau and Romanticism* will be evident to anyone familiar with the latter.

can trust the evidence of her earlier and shorter poems, she stems from the early Elizabethan epigrammatists. Turberville, a few years before Spenser and Sidney, writes *To One of Little Wit:*

> *I thee advise*
> *If thou be wise*
> *To keep thy wit*
> *Though it be small.*
> *'Tis hard to get*
> *And far to fet—*
> *'Twas ever yet*
> *Dear'st ware of all.*

Miss Moore writes *To an Intramural Rat:*[45]

> *You make me think of many men*
> *Once met, to be forgot again,*
> *Or merely resurrected*
> *In a parenthesis of wit*
> *That found them hastening through it*
> *Too brisk to be inspected.*

In Miss Moore's later work, the same quality is developed through a very elaborate structure, in which the magnificent and the curious are combined with the ironical and the ludicrous: I have in mind in particular such poems as *My Apish Cousins* (later entitled *The Monkeys*), *New York*, *A Grave*, and *Black Earth*. These poems illustrate perfectly Miss Moore's virtues: unshakable certainty of intention, a diction at once magnificent and ironic (her cat, for example, in *My Apish Cousins*, raises Gautier's formula for fantastic zoölogy into the realm of high art), and the fairly consistent control of an elaborate rhetoric. They suggest her weaknesses, which are more evident in other poems: a tendency to a rhetoric more complex than her matter, a tendency to be led astray by opportunities for description, and a tendency to base her security on a view of manners instead of morals.

[45] *Observations*, by Marianne Moore, The Dial Press, New York, 1924.

The romantic antithesis of moods is the central theme of Joyce's *Ulysses*, which, at the same time, is rendered diffuse by a stream-of-consciousness technique and by the fallacy of imitative form.[46] The book has great virtues, which its admirers have long since fully enumerated, but it lacks final precision both of form and of feeling. It is adolescent as Laforgue is adolescent; it is ironic about feelings which are not worth the irony.

Mr. Kenneth Burke's novel, *Towards a Better Life*, displays the same kind of irony, which adds to the confusion coming from other sources which I have already mentioned. Mr. Burke, instead of giving us the progression of a narrative, endeavors, as I have said, to give us a progression of pure feeling. Frequently there is not even progression; we have merely a repetitious series of Laforguian antitheses.

Mr. Burke, in his volume of criticism, *Counterstatement*, offers the best defense with which I am familiar, of the attitudes to which I am now objecting.[47] He writes: "The ironist is essentially *impure*, even in the chemical sense of purity, since he is divided. He must deprecate his own enthusiasms, and distrust his own resentments. He will unite waveringly, as the components of his attitude, 'dignity, repugnance, the problematical, and art.' To the slogan-minded, the ralliers about a flag, the marchers who convert a simple idea into a simple action, he is an 'outsider.' Yet he must observe them with nostalgia, he must feel a kind of awe for their fertile assurance, even while remaining on the alert to stifle it with irony each time he discovers it growing in unsuspected quarters within himself."

In admitting no distinction save that between the ironist and the slogan-minded, Mr. Burke himself verges upon a dangerous enthusiasm, perhaps even upon a slogan. The whole issue comes down to the question of how carefully one is willing to scrutinize his feelings and correct them. Miss Rowena Lockett once remarked to me that Laforgue resembles a person who speaks with undue harshness and then apologizes; whereas he should have made the necessary subtractions before speaking. The objection

---

[46] *Ulysses*, by James Joyce, Shakespeare and Co., Paris.
[47] In the essay on *Thomas Mann and André Gide*, pages 116 and following.

implies an attitude more sceptical and cautious than that of Mr. Burke; instead of irony as the remedy for the unsatisfactory feeling, it recommends the waste-basket and a new beginning. And this recommendation has its basis not only in morality but in æsthetics: the romantic ironists whom I have cited write imperfectly in proportion to their irony; their attitude, which is a corruption of feeling, entails a corruption of style—that is, the irony is an admission of careless feeling, which is to say careless writing, and the stylist is weak in proportion to the grounds for his irony. To see this, one has only to compare the best work of these writers to the best of Churchill, Pope, Gay, Marot, or Voltaire.

Mr. Burke states elsewhere:[48] "The 'sum total of art' relieves the artist of the need of seeing life steadily and seeing it whole. He will presumably desire to be as comprehensive as he can, but what he lacks in adjustability can be supplied by another artist affirming some other pattern with equal conviction."

Except for the likelihood that two opposite excesses may not be equivalent to something intelligent, Mr. Burke's statement may up to a certain point be well enough for Society (whatever the word may mean in this connection), but from the standpoint of the individual seeking to train himself, it is not very helpful.

Mr. Burke does give the artist a morality, however: he bases it upon what he believes Society needs: "Alignment of forces. On the side of the practical: efficiency, prosperity, material acquisitions, increased consumption, 'new needs,' expansion, higher standards of living, progressive rather than regressive evolutions, in short ubiquitous optimism. . . . On the side of the æsthetic (the Bohemian): inefficiency, indolence, dissipation, vacillation, mockery, distrust, 'hypochondria,' non-conformity, bad sportsmanship, in short, negativism. We have here a summary of the basic notion of all of Mr. Burke's writings, the doctrine of balanced excesses. Perhaps they will balance each other, and perhaps not, but suppose a man should desire to be intelligent with regard to himself alone; suppose, in other words, a particular artist should lack entirely the high altruism which Mr. Burke demands of him—of what value will he find Mr. Burke's morality? Mr.

---

[48] *Counterstatement:* the chapter called *Lexicon Rhetoricæ:* page 231.

73

Burke's doctrine, in the realms of art and of morality, is really the least sceptical, the most self-confident possible: no point of view is tenable and hence no feeling is adequately motivated; all feeling is thus seen to be excessive, and neither more nor less excessive than any other, for there is no standard of measurement; any excess can be canceled by an opposite excess, which is automatically equal, and careful evaluation, as it is impossible, is likewise unnecessary.

I have stated the matter very baldly, but quite fairly. Any artist holding Mr. Burke's views, in so far as he is an artist, will be restrained more or less by his natural feeling for rightness of expression; but as the theory does not, if pushed to its conclusions, admit the existence of rightness, the theory encourages shoddy writing and shoddy living. The hero of Mr. Burke's novel goes mad, for the reason that, the need of judgment having been removed by his (and Mr. Burke's) theories, the power of judgment atrophies; yet Mr. Burke continues to preach the doctrine which brought him to this end.

The perfect embodiment of Mr. Burke's doctrines, whether as an individual man, or as an allegorical representation of Society, is that Shan O'Neale who flourished in Ireland in the sixteenth century, and whose character David Hume has described as follows in his *History of England:* "He was a man equally noted for his pride, his violence, his debaucheries, and his hatred of the English nation. He is said to have put some of his followers to death because they endeavored to introduce the use of bread after the English fashion. Though so violent an enemy to luxury, he was extremely addicted to riot; and was accustomed, after his intemperance had thrown him into a fever, to plunge his body into the mire, that he might allay the flame which he had raised by former excesses."

POETIC CONVENTION

I SHALL ENDEAVOR to define a concept which is fundamental to any discussion of poetry, and shall employ to indicate the concept the terms *convention* and *conventional*. In popular speech, these terms are frequently synonymous with *banality* and *banal*; in discussions of literary technique, the term *convention* frequently signifies *a fixed and generally accepted device for the simplified representation of some particular kind of truth*, as: the pastoral convention, the convention of the dramatic unities, the convention of the dramatic chorus. The sense in which I shall use the term is not unrelated to these, but it is none the less distinct from them. It is a sense which is perhaps more difficult to grasp, which also is frequently vaguely implicit in the use of the word for both of the above meanings.

It should be remembered in connection with this and other definitions that a critical term ordinarily indicates a quality, and not an objectively demonstrable entity, yet that every term in criticism is an abstraction, that is, in a sense, is statistical or quantitative in its own nature. This means that no critical term can possibly be more than a very general indication of the nature of a perception. Philosophy labors under the same difficulty, since all generalization is made from perception, or from experience inextricably involved in perception. There is nothing revolutionary about such a statement, but it needs to be kept in mind. Much of the Socratic hair-splitting of some of the more recent critics arises from a failure to observe in particular instances that any critical definition is merely an indication of a unique experience which cannot be exactly represented by any formula, though it may be roughly mapped out; and it is frequently of greater importance to discover something of the nature of the experience than to reduce the more or less expert formula to something simpler and still less veracious and then to demolish it.

When one speaks of standards of critical judgment, one does not ordinarily think of weights and measures. One has in mind certain feelings of rightness and completeness, which have been formed in some measure, refined in a large measure, through a study of the masters. The terms that one will use as a critic will stand for those feelings. Definitions of such terms can never be exact beyond misconstruction, but by dint of careful description and the use of good examples, one may succeed in communicating standards with reasonable accuracy—to those, at least, to whom it is important that communication should be made. For if values cannot be measured, they can be judged; and the bare existence of both art and criticism shows the persistence of the conviction that accuracy of judgment is at least ideally possible, and that the best critics, despite the inevitable margin of difference, and despite their inevitable duller moments, approximate accuracy fairly closely: by that, I mean that great men tend to agree with each other, and the fact is worth taking seriously. I am more or less aware of the extent of the catalogue of disagreements that might be drawn up in reply to such a statement, but it is far less astounding than, let us say, the unanimity of the best minds on the subject of Homer and Vergil, particularly if we accept the doctrine of relativism with any great seriousness.

The two paragraphs foregoing are not to be regarded as a plea for intellectual amateurism or for any kind of impressionism. Definition should be as exact as possible, as professional as possible. It is through the definition of others that we learn of realms of perception that we have overlooked, and are brought to a position in which we may attempt judgment and perhaps arrive at approbation. But there are limits to language, and the failure to remember this fact, even though one may grant it readily as a formal proposition, can lead to nothing save incomprehension on the part of a reader and obscurantism on the part of a writer.

Keeping these warnings in mind, the reader is now requested

to examine carefully the two poems following. The first is entitled *Eros*[1] and is by Robert Bridges; the second [2] has no title,
and is by William Carlos Williams.

Why hast thou nothing in thy face?
Thou idol of the human race,
Thou tyrant of the human heart,
The flower of lovely youth that art;
Yea, and that standest in thy youth
An image of eternal truth,
With thy exuberant flesh so fair,
That only Pheidias might compare,
Ere from his chaste marmoreal form
Time had decayed the colors warm;
Like to his gods in thy proud dress
Thy starry sheen of nakedness.

Surely thy body is thy mind,
For in thy face is nought to find,
Only thy soft unchristened smile,
That shadows neither love nor guile,
But shameless will and power immense,
In secret sensuous innocence.

O king of joy, what is thy thought?
I dream thou knowest it is nought,
And wouldst in darkness come, but thou
Makest the light where'er thou go.
Ah, yet no victim of thy grace,
None who ere longed for thy embrace,
Hath cared to look upon thy face.

[1] *Shorter Poems*, by Robert Bridges. Oxford Press, 1931.
[2] *Spring and All*, by William Carlos Williams, Contact Publishing Company,
Paris, 1923.

By the road to the contagious hospital
under the surge of the blue
mottled clouds driven from the
northeast—a cold wind. Beyond, the
waste of broad muddy fields
brown with dried weeds, standing and fallen

patches of standing water
the scattering of tall trees

All along the road the reddish
purplish, forked, upstanding, twiggy
stuff of bushes and small trees
with dead, brown leaves under them
leafless vines—

Lifeless in appearance, sluggish
dazed spring approaches—

They enter the new world naked,
cold, uncertain of all
save that they enter. All about them
the cold familiar wind—

Now the grass, tomorrow
the stiff curl of wildcarrot leaf

One by one objects are defined—
It quickens: clarity, outline of leaf

But now the stark dignity of
entrance—Still, the profound change
has come upon them: rooted they
grip down and begin to awaken.

A scutiny of these poems will show that most of the poetic power is concentrated in less than half the number of the lines; in the first poem, the greatest power is reached in the middle paragraph, and in the second poem it is reached in the eight lines beginning *Lifeless in appearance*. The remaining lines in each poem vary in power; the chief virtue of many of the lines in each poem may seem at first glance to reside in the plain conveyance of necessary information.

And yet the first glance, if it has led to this conclusion, is illusory. The passages of the greatest power lose much of their power in isolation: therefore one is justified in saying that something essentially poetic suffuses the entire structure.

This "something" I shall name the *convention* of the poem: I shall use the term *convention* to indicate the initial assumption of feeling, or value, to which the poem is laying claim. It is not equivalent to the term *style*, though style is necessary to the establishment and maintenance of convention. Again, convention is distinct from any set of technical devices, though technical devices will be employed in the establishment of any convention. The convention of a poem is not, finally, a part or ingredient of a poem, for a poem is a unit, and the dissection of it is artificial, though frequently valuable if one recognize the nature of the process. Convention is an aspect of poetry that can best be explained by illustration.

Consider the opening lines of the poem by Williams. The nervous meter, words like "surge," "mottled," "driven," suggest an intensity of feeling not justified by the actual perceptions in the lines. These words are therefore conventional. The content of the passage is factual to a greater degree than it is perceptual, and in itself has extremely little interest. In thus describing the lines, I employ the terms *perception* and *perceptual* solely with reference to the awareness of the author of fine relationships between facts observed (or perceived directly) and language, or the medium of judgment and communication. More feeling is *assumed*, or *claimed*, by the poet, in a passage such as that under discussion, than is justified by his language: he claims more than he is able to communicate, or more, perhaps, than he chooses to communicate. At first glance a passage of this sort appears a trifle strained, to use a common but somewhat vague epithet. But in the present poem, the strain is deliberately sought and exactly rendered. The tempo established in these lines, the whole quality of the feeling, the information conveyed, are all necessary to, in fact are a part of, the effect of the eight central lines. With the line beginning "lifeless in appearance" the intensity claimed by the opening is at once justified and increased by the quality of the perception: the initial assumption prepares one for the exact increase which occurs, and the preparation is necessary. The feeling of the last two of the eight central lines (*Now the grass,* etc.) differs widely from the feeling in the preceding six, but is dependent largely upon the feeling already established in the preceding six for its existence. The feeling is one of pathos, aroused by the small and familiar in austere and unfriendly surroundings. It is related to the feeling of *Animula Vagula.* The last six lines of Williams' poem revert to the conventional level, but carry with them, if read in their context, an echo of the precedent intensity.

My analysis of the poem has been oversimplified for the sake of momentary convenience. The conventional passages are not devoid of perceptual value: the skill with which the details of the landscape are placed in juxtaposition in the opening lines is in itself an act of perception. The beat, also, in lines nine, ten, and eleven, taken in conjunction with the material described, has perceptual value, and one could point out other details. The details are not of a uniform level of intensity: no two details can be so. The important thing for the moment is that the intensity claimed by the passage is on the whole in excess of the justification within the passage, and that the intensity assumed is indicated with the greatest of firmness, with the result that departures from it can be made with equal firmness.

For example, I have said that the beat in lines nine, ten, and eleven has perceptual value, as indicating the "twiggy" appearance of the landscape. Yet the meaning-content (as distinct from the sound-content) of every adjective contributing to this perception is a little vague: "reddish," "purplish," for instance, are by definition uncertain in their import. But the vagueness is willed and controlled: one has a definite measure of vagueness set against the definite intensity of the meter. To make these perceptions more precise would lessen the impact of the central lines. This mastery of emphases and of the conventional is one of the marks, and probably the most important mark, of the great stylist: without this mastery poetry degenerates into slipshod sentiment at worst, and at best, as in much of Crane, into brilliant, but disconnected, epithets and ejaculations.

Conventional language, then, is not in itself stereotyped language, though a strongly defined convention may safely carry a little stereotyped language: in fact stereotyped language may often be used deliberately to establish a convention. Conventional language is not dead language, but rather is very subtly living, if well employed. In so far as any passage is purely conventional, that is, conventional as distinct from perceptual, it does not represent a perception of its own content, the feeling it assumes is not justified within the passage in question. When I speak of *conventional language,* I shall mean language in which the perceptual content is slight or negligible. A conventional passage, the adjective *conventional* being employed in this sense, is poetic, however, in so far as it is essential to the entire poetic intention, that is, in so far as its effects reach forward or backward within the poem.

Let me resume my definitions briefly, that I may add a little more before proceeding. Poetic convention is the initial, or basic, assumption of feeling in any poem, from which all departures acquire their significance. The convention of a poem is present, or at least discernible as the norm of feeling, throughout the entire poem, so that in a sense all the language of a poem is conventional; but when I use the term *conventional language* I shall commonly be speaking of passages in which the perceptual justification of the feeling is slight. I shall likewise use the term conventional in a generic sense, to indicate a type of convention, as: the Laforguian convention, the pseudo-referent convention. The context will ordinarily render my intention perfectly clear.

But I am concerned for the moment with the subject of particular convention, primarily. The conventional intensity in the poem by Williams was somewhat in excess of the perceptual value of many lines in the poem; it would, as I said, appear slightly strained to many readers. This feeling of strain is not necessarily concomitant with convention; in the poem by Bridges there is no such strain. The movement of Bridges' poem is quiet; the language, like that of Williams, is plain, but it verges more nearly on the stereotyped than does the language of Williams in the poem quoted. The intensity assumed is at a more familiar level of initial assumption and so appears never to be in excess of the least important fact conveyed: that is, the convention is nearer to the matter-of-fact tone of prose than is the convention employed by Williams. Strangely enough, a convention of such a type can serve, as on this occasion, with perfect effectiveness in a poem of the most powerful feeling.

I shall now give a brief account of a few general terms deducible from these ideas regarding convention:

I. *Traditional poetry* is poetry which endeavors to utilize the greatest possible amount of the knowledge and wisdom, both technical and moral, but technical only in so far as it does not obstruct the moral, to be found in precedent poetry. It assumes the ideal existence of a normal quality of feeling, a normal convention, to which the convention of any particular poem should more or less conform. Actually, the conformity of any poem, even though the traditional norm could be exactly defined or could be found embodied in a single work (Lady Winchilsea's flawlessly beautiful and eminently traditional poems *The Tree* or *The Change*, or George Herbert's *Church Monuments*), would be impossible, since every poem, good or bad, is unique. But if we cannot lay a finger precisely upon the norm, we can recognize the more or less normal. If the reader does not follow me, let me point out that it is easy to recognize the Laforguian convention in Apollinaire, in the early Eliot, and in Pound's *Mauberly*, or the Miltonic convention, even though indifferently managed, in Thomson and in Wordsworth. The traditional norm is less obviously discernible, for it embraces a wider variety of essential qualities, and no one of them receives so marked an emphasis. One might describe it negatively as that type of poetry which displays at one and the same time the greatest possible distinction with the fewest possible characteristics recognizable as the marks of any particular school, period, or man; as, in brief, that type of poetry which displays the greatest polish of style and the smallest trace of mannerism. One may describe traditional poetry positively by saying that it possesses these closely related qualities: (1) equivalence of motivation and feeling; (2) a form that permits a wide range of feeling; (3) a conventional norm of feeling which makes for a minimum of "strain"; (4) a form and a convention which permit the extraction from every unit of language of its maximum content, both of connotation and of denotation; that is, a form and a convention which are in the highest degree economical, or efficient.

II. *Experimental poetry* endeavors to widen the racial experience, or to alter it, or to get away from it, by establishing abnormal conventions. In one sense or another Spenser, Donne, Milton, Hopkins, Laforgue, and Rimbaud are experimental poets of a very marked kind. The most striking example in English of a convention of heightened intensity (that is, of what the unsympathetic might call poetic strain) is to be found in *Paradise Lost*. When the poem does not achieve grandeur, it is grandiloquent; yet the quality of the grandiloquence could have been achieved only by a master of the highest order, and without it the poem could hardly have been accomplished. As an act of invention, of daring experiment, the creation of Miltonic blank verse, both meter and rhetoric, is not equaled in English poetry; in fact one is tempted to wonder if it is equaled in any other. The perils amid which Milton ventured and which he avoided with perfect equanimity are best estimated by a consideration of his disciples. Yet in spite of his mastery, the emphatic and violent rhetoric which he created limits his range, as compared to the range of Shakespeare, a man of comparable genius but working in a series of conventions which are relatively traditional. The same relationship holds between the sonnets of the two men, and is the more readily discernible, perhaps, because of the smaller form. Milton is the more complex rhetorician, but the simpler moralist and a man of far less subtle perception. Milton is the nobler, but Milton's nobility is in part, and as compared to Shakespeare, the over-emphasis of imperception.

An experimental poet may be traditional in many aspects. Thus Crashaw, who carries certain experimental qualities of diction and image found in Donne much farther from the norm than even Donne ventured, is nevertheless traditional in that he utilizes by means of discreet suggestion the more emphatic and experimental metrical forms of the sixteenth century to suggest complexities of feeling not possible in those metrical forms as the poets of the sixteenth century used them. He suggests the songbooks in his devotional poetry, as he therein utilizes the common imagery of the Petrarchan love lyric. Dr. W. C. Williams, an experimental poet by virtue of his meter, is in other qualities of his language one of the most richly traditional poets of the past hundred and fifty years; in fact, making allowances for his somewhat narrow intellectual scope, one would be tempted to compare him, in this respect, to such poets as Hardy and Bridges. No two experimental conventions will have similar poetic results; one cannot predicate a great deal that is important of experimental poetry in general; but, as one might suspect, some forms of experimental poetry have had dire results, and of individual types of convention one can frequently say a great deal.

III. *Pseudo-traditional or "literary" poetry* is the work of writers insufficiently aware of what they have stylistically and morally in common with the best poetry of the race to master this common element (I am referring, of course, to a common distinction, skill, and moral intelligence, that which one may find in Campion, Jonson, and Herrick) and in a manner of speaking to take it for granted. The literary poet, cut off from his tradition by education, for he usually occurs in the late eighteenth, the nineteenth, or the twentieth century, regards the tradition as something exotic, and employs it accordingly. He imitates the idioms of the traditional poet, but they are no longer for him familiar and exact; they are foreign and decorative; they degenerate into mannerism. He comes to regard certain words, phrases, or rhythms, as intrinsically poetic, rather than as instruments of perception or as the clues to generative ideas. His imitation is thus crude, as we can see by comparing the pseudo-Elizabethan meters of Beddoes to the meters of Campion, the meters of Chatterton to the meters of the best lyrics of the thirteenth century, the meters of Swinburne to the meters of Sidney, from which they are frequently derived.

When, as in the traditional poet, the wisdom and expression of the past are both a basic part of the individual, when they are at once taken casually for granted and thoroughly understood, the individual contribution to the poem can be made with force and precision. But if the combiner of two elements understands only one of them, the combination will hardly be satisfactory; and in this instance it is unlikely that the comprehension of only one element is possible: it is both or nothing. A purely literary poet can very likely never exist; the literary quality rather invades the work in a greater or smaller measure. Swinburne is one of the best examples I know of a poet of a fairly high order of talent whose work is pretty evenly corrupted by "literary" habits. Mr. T. S. Eliot's essay on Swinburne defines the quality admirably. Symons, Wilde, and Dowson carry farther what Swinburne began: their poetry is almost devoid of meaning.

As one approaches a norm, one's variations from that norm take on more significance. If the convention of a poem is badly defined, the poetry is vague. This is one of the many things wrong with most of Shelley, Byron, Hugo, De Musset, Lamartine, and the other typical romantics. The same weakness inheres in some measure in Swinburne, though Swinburne's vagueness is commonly of a more consistent quality.

The "literary," of course, is what commonly appears traditional to the popular and even the academic taste: Swinburne is preferred to Landor, and Housman to Bridges. The traditional is ordinarily thrust aside as merely literary; or else, in such poets as Crashaw or Williams, it is completely overlooked because the reader is nonplussed by experimental elements. We have nothing but Arnold's touchstones to guide us in this difficulty, and our own hard work to make us worthy of guidance; that, and the Grace of God. It is an obscure procedure, but Landor is surely greater than Swinburne and Bridges than Housman.

IV. *Pseudo-experimental poetry* is the work of a poet who confuses tradition with convention, and who, desiring to experiment, sees no way to escape from or alter tradition save by the abandonment of convention: it means the abandonment of form and of poetry. Mr. E. E. Cummings is a good example of this type of poet. When Mr. Cummings ceases to experiment, and essays the traditional, he becomes painfully literary. Either way he shows little comprehension of poetry.

To what extent can the principles herein defined be brought to the defense of the methods employed by the experimental poets of twentieth century America and of the French Symbolist School, methods to which I have elsewhere objected? Any answer must be prefaced with the warning that what is true of one type of convention need not be true of another. What is true even of one sub-type need not be true of another sub-type of the same group: consider, for example, the number and variety of the forms of pseudo-reference.

The convention of heightened intensity is sound procedure in Williams' poem *On the road to the contagious hospital*, which I have discussed at length, because there is poetic justification, a genuine motivation, for the conventional language, and the conventional language is graduated to the wholly poetic with great skill and energy. Were there no such justification, however, the poem would belong, with many of H. D.'s poems on Greek landscape, in the class of implicit reference to a non-existent symbolic value. Much of Wordsworth's more or less Miltonic grandiloquence belongs in the same class: the grandeur never emerges or emerges too seldom. Bryant is sometimes similar, when he applies a tone of moral grandeur to material that is purely physical and unable to support such a tone.

The pseudo-reference of T. S. Eliot's *Gerontion*, partly a matter of reference to non-existent plots, partly a matter of purely grammatical logic, seems in some ways to resemble the heightened intensity employed by Dr. Williams in *On the road to the contagious hospital*. That is, while Dr. Williams, in certain passages, assumes more feeling than he perceives, Mr. Eliot, in certain passages, assumes more reasonableness than he perceives. Dr. Williams works up to passages in which his claims are supported by perception; so does Mr. Eliot; and in each poem these passages represent the core of the poem, not only as regards feeling, but as regards rational theme. The climax of Mr. Eliot's poem, the passage beginning: "I that was near your heart was removed therefrom," justly one of the most famous passages in recent poetry, is probably greater than anything in the poem by Dr. Williams, though perhaps not so much greater as Mr. Eliot's admirers (who commonly fail to understand Dr. Williams altogether) might be ready to believe.

On the other hand, Dr. Williams' poem is far more solidly written. The fine passages in *Gerontion*, though frequently of a magnificent precision in themselves, arise from a mass of carefully veiled imprecisions, which, on first glance, appear to have more meaning than they really have. The success of conventional language of this kind depends very largely on the reader's being more or less deluded: the procedure in Dr. Williams' poem is at once more in the open and more definite, and one knows what is happening at every instant. There are moments in Mr. Eliot's poem at which no one can be really sure of what is going on, and as a result one feels, or I cannot escape feeling, a degree of uncertainty in the very essence of the poem. One has again, perhaps, the fallacy of imitative form: the attempt to express a state of uncertainty by uncertainty of expression; whereas the sound procedure would be to make a lucid and controlled statement regarding the condition of uncertainty, a procedure, however, which would require that the poet understand the nature of uncertainty, not that he be uncertain. *Gerontion*, at any rate, is the most skillful modern poem in English to employ any large measure of pseudo-reference; the superiority of its pseudo-reference to most of that of Crane and of Yeats probably derives from the fact that it is deliberate, whereas theirs is commonly in a large part unintentional—in *Gerontion* it is mystification instead of confusion, or at least is employed willfully and deliberately as a means of bringing certain recognized, and, for the author, irreducible confusion, under a little control.

To cite another example of pseudo-reference, Hart Crane's poem *The Dance* reverses the order of conventional and poetic language employed by Williams. That is, Williams' language is largely conventional in the early part of the poem, and then takes on poetic fullness at the climax. Crane's poem, on the other hand, displays most of its fully poetic content (the purely but brilliantly descriptive writing) scattered through the first half, approximately, of the poem, and then breaks into a complete disjunction of feeling and meaning at the climax.

The purely grammatical logic of much of *Faustus and Helen*, parts I and III, might be in a measure defensible on the same grounds as the pseudo-reference of *Gerontion*, or to the same extent, except that there is a much greater proportion of pseudo-reference in the poem by Crane and that there is much less clarity as to the general theme, so that the moments of coherence are never sufficient to give any perceptible support to the conglomeration of conventional language.

But we may probably say for any kind of pseudo-reference that it goes through the forms of reasonable statement and hence may be a preparation for reasonable statement, or a stop-gap between passages of reasonable statement, and that, if it does not occur in great excess and is distributed in small enough bits, if, in short, it is not too obtrusive and is not too seriously involved in the very conception of the poem, it may do relatively little harm and so be accepted at times as an apparently inevitable evil.

Laforguian irony, however, is not a preparation for anything else, is not an unfulfilled form, but is merely a slipshod attitude, final in itself, and invariably a vice of feeling. Qualitative progression, likewise, is not a preparation for anything else; it offers no unfulfilled claims or half-utilized machinery. If it is central to the structure of the work—that is, if the theme is really unformulable and merely a mood—it is a vice for the reasons which I have given elsewhere. It is legitimate only when used occasionally and in an impure way, as Mr. Burke has shown it in use on the periphery of *Hamlet*.

We may say in general, then, that some kinds of experimental convention are more dangerous than others, and the more recent types appear to be the most dangerous, perhaps because they have been used more boldly—or rather, more rashly—than experimental conventions have ever been used before. Secondly and finally, traditional poetry is the most economically and firmly constructed variety possible. To see this, one has only to compare Bridges' *The southwind strengthens to a gale* to *Gerontion* or to *The Dance*.

PRIMITIVISM AND DECADENCE

THE DICHOTOMY of major and minor poetry is obviously unsatisfactory, nor is the reason for this the one so often given, that general descriptive terms have no meaning. They can at least be given meaning. If Ben Jonson is a major poet and Campion a minor poet, it is patently outrageous to apply either epithet to Byron; yet Byron for the present has a place in our literature, and, though it seems incredible that he should be read as long as Jonson or as Campion, it is probable that he will be read for a long time. Of Jonson and Campion we may say that both are masters; few men have lived to write as well; it is unlikely that many men have lived to appreciate them fully. Their difference is mainly a difference of scope; the achievement of Campion cannot be dimmed by comparison with the achievement of the greatest poets, for within its scope it is unimpeachable. The achievement of Byron, on the other hand, suffers by comparison with the work of any of the minor masters, even with that of Googe or Turberville; in a superficial sense he attempted as much as did Jonson, but he understood with precision nothing that he touched, and his art he understood least of all.

The more important poets might be placed in four groups: the second-rate, those whose gift for language is inadequate to their task, poets such as Byron, D. H. Lawrence, or Poe, and regardless of their other virtues or failings; the major, those who possess all of the virtues, both of form and of range; the primitive, those who utilize all of the means necessary to the most vigorous form, but whose range of material is limited; and the decadent, those who display a fine sensitivity to language and who may have a very wide scope, but whose work is incomplete formally (in the manner of the pseudo-referent and qualitative poets) or is somewhat but not too seriously weakened by a vice of feeling (in the manner of the better post-romantic ironists). The second type of decadent poets may differ from the second-rate only in degree of weakness. In this essay I shall endeavor to discover some of the implications of the terms *decadent* and *primitive* as used in this way. The nature of major poetry and of the second-rate should be reasonably obvious, even though there might be disagreement over examples.

It will be seen that most experimental poetry, particularly experimental poetry of the types developed in the late nineteenth and early twentieth centuries, appears to issue either in primitivism or in decadence, if it issues in nothing worse. The term *primitivism*, however, may be allowed to include traditional minor poetry as well.

If we compare *The Dance,* by Hart Crane, to one of the better poems of Jonson or of George Herbert, it is decadent in the sense in which I have just defined the term: it is incomplete poetry. Historically, however, Crane's poetry is related not only to Jonson, but to the romantics, especially to Whitman, much of whose doctrine Crane adopts. Whitman's doctrine is illusory: like all of the anti-rational doctrines of the past two centuries, it vanishes if pursued by definition. Whitman, as a second-rate poet, however, was equipped to write of it, after a fashion, without rendering its nature immediately evident. His poetic language was as vague as his expository; he had no capacity for any feeling save of the cloudiest and most general kind. Crane's poetic gift is finer than Whitman's, and the precision of his language forces one to recognize the inadequacy of his reference. If he is decadent in comparison to Jonson, he yet marks an advance in relationship to Whitman. It would probably be easier to convince most readers at present that something is wrong with Crane than that something is wrong with Whitman. The reason for this is simple: one observes rather quickly that something is wrong with Crane, because something is right, and one is thus able to get one's bearings. From one point of view his language is frequently that of a master. Nowhere in Whitman can one find such splendor or even such precision of language as in *The Dance* or as in *The River*. And if one proceeds from these to his most finished performances, *Repose of Rivers, Faustus and Helen II,* and *Voyages II,* one has poems in which the trace of decadence is scarcely discernible.[1] It would not have been impossible, then, for Crane to decrease the amount of pseudo-reference in his poems; as a decadent poet, he was not bound to deteriorate; nor does his poetry indicate that contemporary literature is in a state of deterioration.

Mr. Pound's *Cantos* are decadent in relation to *Paradise Lost,* since their structure is purely qualitative. But, historically, there is probably another relationship to Whitman here, in which Mr. Pound shows not decay but growth. It is not a relationship of

---

[1] Of *Repose of Rivers* one may say that the individual images are miraculous, but that their order is not invariably necessary; this fact, combined with the lack of rhythmical conviction as the poet proceeds from one image to the next, results in a frail, almost tentative structure. *Faustus and Helen II* is purely descriptive and hence offers no temptations to sin; the fantastic subject matter, combined with the relative safety of the approach, enabled Crane to utilize his entire talent for rhetorical ingenuity without risk of its betraying him. In *Voyages II,* which seems to me his greatest poem, he disciplined this talent to meet a more dangerous and exacting theme, and achieved greater solidity than in *Repose of Rivers.*

It will be observed that my selections do not coincide with those of Mr. Allen Tate. Mr. Tate speaks of *The River* as Crane's "most complex and sustained performance, a masterpiece of æsthetic form," and of *Praise for an Urn* as "the finest elegy in American poetry" (Hound and Horn: Summer, 1932). This seems to me sheer nonsense. The latter poem is metrically a very stiff and inexpert free verse; except for the two striking lines about the clock and half a dozen other passable lines, it is sentimental and affected. "The slant moon on the slanting hill," "Delicate riders of the storm," "The everlasting eyes of Pierrot/ and of Gargantua the laughter," are sentimental clichés of the twenties, and their quality pervades the whole poem. As to *The River,* it is as ineptly put together as any romantic poem I have read: the poem should begin with the passage about the cannery works, and everything previous should be discarded; about half the lines from the cannery works to the Pullman breakfasters should be revised, the eyeless fish, the old gods of the rain, and much of the rest of it being the shoddiest of decoration, not even skillful charlatanry; and in the last part of the poem, which is the finest and which is very powerful, there are still bad lines, for examples, "Throb past the city storied of three thrones," "All fades but one thin skyline 'round. . . . Ahead," and the two final lines of the poem: The defects of *The River* are not due to the theme, but merely to carelessness, and could easily have been revised away. The pantheism which wrecks *The Dance* appears in *The River* in a fairly harmless form, and merely lends pathos to certain lines, particularly to those describing the end of Dan Midland.

theme, as in Crane's poetry, but one of form. Mr. Pound's long line is in part a refinement of Whitman's line; his progression from image to image resembles Whitman's in everything save Whitman's lack of skill. The *Cantos* are structurally Whitmanian songs, dealing with non-Whitmanian matter, and displaying at their best great suavity and beauty. As Crane shifts out of pseudo-reference into rational reference in *Voyages II,* so Mr. Pound in his versions of Propertius, using the same form as in the *Cantos,* produces coherent comment on formulable themes, or does so part of the time. The change may be due to the genius of Propertius, but it is possible in Mr. Pound's form. The form, however, would not permit of any very rapid or compact reasoning.

I have elsewhere suggested that post-romantic irony represents an advance over the uncritical emotionalism of such poets as Hugo or Shelley, in so far as it represents the first step in a diagnosis.

The primitive poet is the major poet on a smaller scale. The decadent poet is the major, or primitive, poet with some important faculty absent from the texture of all his work. Dr. Williams is a good example of the type of poet whom I should call the contemporary primitive. His best poems display no trace of the formal inadequacies which I have mentioned as the signs of decadence. Such poems as *The Widow's Lament* or *To Waken an Old Lady* are fully realized; the form is complete and perfect; the feeling is sound. Dr. Williams has a surer feeling for language than any other poet of his generation, save, perhaps, Stevens at his best. But he is wholly incapable of coherent thought and he had not the good fortune to receive a coherent system as his birthright. His expository writing is largely incomprehensible; his novel, *A Voyage to Pagany,* displays an almost ludicrous inability to motivate a long narrative. His experience is disconnected and fragmentary, but sometimes a fragment is wrought to great beauty. His widest range has been reached in a single piece of prose, *The Destruction of Tenochtitlan,* in which he found his material more or less ready for treatment in the form of history: in treating it, he achieved one of the few great prose styles of our time.[2]

Dr. Williams bears a certain resemblance to the best lyric poets of the thirteenth century: there is in both an extreme sophistication of style, a naïve limitation of theme (Dr. Williams has a wider range than the early poets, however) and a fresh enthusiasm for the theme. It was out of such poetry as *Alisoun* that English poetry little by little grew. Sidney represents a resurgence of the same quality at a later date, but touched with Petrarchan decadence.[3] Decadent poetry, as I have defined it, would have been impossible in thirteenth century England: it requires a mature poetry as a background.

A decadent poet such as Crane may, as I have said, if considered historically, represent a gain and not a loss. As a matter of fact, he may embody the most economical method of recovery for an old and rich tradition in a state of collapse, for he offers all of the machinery of a mature and complicated poetry. Both decadent and primitive lack an understanding and correlation of their experience: the primitive accepts his limitations through wisdom or ignorance; the decadent endeavors to conceal them, or, like some primitives, may never discover them; the primitive, however, treats of what he understands and the decadent of more than he understands. For either to achieve major poetry there is necessary an intellectual clarification of some kind. But to attain major poetry from the position of a primitive poet such as Dr. Williams might necessitate the creation of a good deal of technical machinery as well; whereas the pseudo-referent poet has most of his machinery made and already partly in action.

[2] In connection with the fragmentariness, the primitivism, of this piece, it is worth noting that the rhetoric, perhaps merely because of the perfection to which it raises traditional heroic prose, resembles closely that of Macaulay's *History*, the passage in Macaulay describing the formation and character of Cromwell's army, offering especially striking similarity. Macaulay *chose* to write a five volume work, one of the supreme English masterpieces, in this style. Dr. Williams *happened* to write a twelve-page masterpiece in the style, or so one is forced to conclude from the quality of most of his prose.

[3] In connection with this statement and others regarding the lyrics of the sixteenth century, see my review of the *Oxford Book of 16th Century Verse*, edited by E. K. Chambers, in the Hound and Horn, Volume VI, Number 4.

94

There is probably the same relationship between the Petrarchan rhetoric of the sixteenth century, with its decorative and more or less pseudo-referent conceit, and the best Metaphysical verse of the seventeenth century. In Shakespeare's sonnets the rhetoric is Petrarchan, yet the Petrarchan conceit is given a weight of meaning new to it; something similar occurs in the poetry of Fulke Greville. The gap between the sonnets of Shakespeare and the sonnets of Donne is not extremely great. Yet the best thirteenth century lyrics, like the best early Tudor lyrics, those by such men as Vaux, Googe, Gascoigne, and Turberville, are better poetry than the work of Daniel or of Drayton, in spite of the fact that they would have been less immediately useful in certain ways to Donne. So with our contemporaries: Dr. Williams is more consistently excellent than Crane, and at his best is possibly better. Crane's machinery, convenient as it might at any moment prove, remains, so long as it is not utilized, a source of confusion.

The decadent poetry of Mr. Pound does not appear to me to provide so many opportunities for filling out as does that of Crane, partly because of the meter, which presents a problem too elaborate in itself for discussion here, and partly because all, or nearly all, superfluous machinery in the way of pseudo-referent forms has been avoided. That is, the difficulty of extending the usefulness of a convention may often bear a direct relationship to the perfection with which the convention accomplishes the aims for which it was created.

A perfect primitive poet is not of necessity better than a decadent poet, though he may be; in fact a decadent poet may seem of greater value than a poet whom one might call major. Some major poets are greater than others, and a poem by Mr. Stevens, technically decadent because tinged with his vice—*Of the Manner of Addressing Clouds*, for example—may suffer extremely little from its decadence and be in other respects a poem of tremendous power.

The poetry of Mr. Paul Valéry demonstrates that decadence may be a very economical mode of recovery. Mr. Valéry was formed in the influence of the Symbolists, poets decadent, frequently, in the same way as the Americans of the second and third decades of the twentieth century. The poet who illustrates this point more clearly than any other in English is Mr. T. Sturge Moore, who shares in a considerable measure the background of Mr. Valéry.

Mr. J. V. Cunningham, in the Commonweal for July 27, 1932, describes Mr. Moore's favorite theme as that "spiritual pride which would overreach natural limits . . . the effort to violate human relationships by imposing one's identity on others," together with criticism of such spiritual pride. Mr. Cunningham cites the excellent poem *On Four Poplars* as an instance of the subject matter, and other poems could be cited. The theme, however, is not limited to the ethical sphere in Mr. Moore, but has its religious counterpart, in a mysticism related to that of poets so diverse as Hart Crane and Robinson Jeffers, which leads to the attempt to violate our relationship with God, or with whatever myth we put in his place, even with Nothingness, and which leads concurrently to the minimizing of moral distinctions, that is, of the careful perception of strictly human experience. Mr. Moore differs from the Romantic mystics in defining this temptation without succumbing; in defining not only the temptation but its legitimate uses, and its dangers. His repeated poems on the subject of Silence, and his repeated references to Semele, are among the more obvious indications of his interest in the subject. His great lyric *To Silence* may be taken as an allegorical summary of this theme and of his own relationship to romantic tradition, the tradition of rejuvenation through immersion in pure feeling, or sensation, the immersion which is the mystical communion of the romantic, and which occurs in its most perfect literary examples among the devotees of imitative form to be found in the French Symbolist and American Experimental schools.

Mr. Moore's immersion has actually led to rejuvenation, to an inexhaustibly fascinating freshness of perception: the immersion of other poets has too often led to disintegration. I quote the entire text of the poem *To Silence*:

O deep and clear as is the sky,
A soul is as a bird in thee
That travels on and on; so I,
Like a snared linnet, now break free,
Who sought thee once with leisured grace
As hale youth seeks the sea's warm bays.

And as a floating nereid sleeps
In the deep-billowed ocean-stream;
And by some goat-herd on lone rock
Is thought a corpse, though she may dream
And profit by both health and ease
Nursed on those high green rolling seas,—

Long once I drifted in thy tide,
Appearing dead to those I passed;
Yet lived in thee, and dreamed, and waked
Twice what I had been. Now, I cast
Me broken on thy buoyant deep
And dreamless in thy calm would sleep.

Silence, I almost now believe
Thou art the speech on lips divine,
Their greatest kindness to their child.
Yet I, who for all wisdom pine,
Seek thee but as a bather swims
To refresh and not dissolve his limbs:—

Though these be thine, who asked and had,
And asked and had again, again,
Yet always found they wanted more
Till craving grew to be a pain;
And they at last to silence fled,
Glad to lose all for which they pled.

O pure and wide as is the sky
Heal me, yet give me back to life!

Though thou foresee the day when I,
Sated with failure, dead to strife,
Shall seek in thee my being's end,
Still be to my fond hope a friend.

The structure of the poem is logical and the reference is exact, but the feeling is very strange. There is a remarkable freshness of sensitivity, yet it is a different freshness from that of a primitive, such as Dr. Williams. It might almost be characterized as the hypersensitivity of convalescence: the poet is minutely sensitive to dangers and meanings past but imminent, to which Dr. Williams is not only insensitive but of the very existence of which he is unaware.

If we can imagine that human experience is portrayable geometrically as a continuous circle on which there are equally spaced points, A, C, E, and G, and that classical poetry has been written with these as its chief points of reference, we can then imagine a breakdown, a period of confusion, in which these points are lost, but after which a new set of points, B, D, F, and H, also spaced equally but not the same points, are established. These new points would give a comparable balance, or intelligence, perhaps, but an altered view of the detail, that is, an altered quality of perception, of feeling. Or it might be that the old points would merely be regained after the breakdown, the quality of the perception being then affected by the past experience of the breakdown.

It is as if we extended the allegory of the poem just quoted, thus: Silence is equal to pure quality, unclassified sensation (a purely hypothetical infinity, which, however, we can approach indefinitely),[4] and the immersion in sensation (or confusion)

[4] Cf. Morris Cohen, *Reason and Nature*, page 37: "Avenarius wishes to purify our world-view by returning to the natural view of experience as it existed before it was vitiated by the sophistications of thought (in the form of introjection). But the empiricist's uncritical use of the category of the *given*, and the nominalistic dogma that relations are created rather than discovered by thought, lead Avenarius to banish not only animism and other myths, but also the categories, substance, causality, etc., as inventions of the mind. In doing this he runs afoul of the great insight of Kant that without concepts or categories percepts are blind." Also Allen Tate, *The Fallacy of Humanism*, in *The*

amounts to the dissolution of one's previous standards in order to obtain a fresh sensibility. This is what the romantic movement amounted to, the degree of dissolution varying with each poet, regardless of whether the dissolution was necessary. Mr. Moore states explicitly, however, in this poem and in others, not only the value of the immersion, but its peril, and the need of the return. This does not mean that Mr. Moore at any point in his career has performed experiments like those of Rimbaud or of Joyce; he has not done so publicly, and there is no reason to suppose that he has done so privately. But his sensibility was profoundly affected by those who did perform them; he is a part of the tradition that had at an earlier point in its history subjected itself to the immersion; his private history as a poet begins at the point in the history of the tradition at which recovery has begun, and his talents enable him to bring that recovery to its highest pitch of development; but he remembers and understands what preceded him, and his sensibility bears witness to the fact. He thus resembles Paul Valéry, though of the two poets his relationship to the Symbolist tradition is perhaps the more obvious. The feeling of strangeness and freshness is still upon Mr. Moore's poetry, as upon one who has just emerged from the sea. One should examine in particular the following poems: *To Silence*, *To Slow Music*, *From Titian's Bacchanal*, the first half of the double sonnet *Silence*, *Love's First Communion*, *An Aged Beauty's Prayer*, *The Deeper Desire*, the sonnets on Sappho, *Semele*, *Io*, *Suggested by the Representation on a Grecian Amphora*, *The Song of Chiron*, *Tragic Fates*, *To a Child Listening to a Repeater*, and, among his longer works, *Daimonassa* (perhaps his greatest single achievement), *Mariamne*, *The Sea Is Kind*, *The Centaur's Booty*, and *The Rout of the Amazons*.

The term *decadence* is frequently used to denote or connote personal immorality, yet even in this sense the historical defense is sometimes effective. There is no doubt that Verlaine was per-

---

Critique of Humanism (Brewer and Warren: 1930): "Pure Quality is nature itself because it is the source of experience. . . . Pure Quality would be pure evil, and it is only through the means of our recovery from a lasting immersion in it . . . that any man survives the present hour; Pure Quality is pure disintegration."

sonally childish, sentimental, and debauched. He was in some ways one of the most muddled souls of a muddled century: his life was pseudo-referent even though his poetry was frequently not, and, like his poetry, was too often governed wholly by mood. He was not, as Baudelaire was, morally intelligent among whatever sins he may have committed, and was never much the wiser for his sins or wrote better poetry because of them. The greater part of his life was simply confusion; yet a narrow margin of it he evaluated with precision; to that extent he was superior to such formless predecessors as Lamartine or de Musset, who smeared everything with a consistent texture of falsity. As a poet, Verlaine at his best was rather a primitive than a decadent, for his poetry is not ambitious; his best art was as natural and proper, if we consider his situation in time and space, and potentially as valuable to his successors, as was the art of the author of *Alisoun*.

I do not mean that Verlaine's limitations were inevitable, however. In offering an historical excuse for decadence, formal or personal, I do not mean to imply that there is ever an historical necessity for either, but merely that life is painful if one expects more than two or three men in a century to behave as rational animals, and that for a good many men there are mitigating circumstances. Baudelaire ran through romanticism early in his career, to achieve the most remarkable balance of powers in French literature after Racine; he had no need of several generations of graduated decadence; his recovery was accomplished at a bound. He was determined by his period only to this extent: that he dealt with the problem of evil in the terms in which he had met it, the terms of the romantic view of life; and it was because of these terms that he was able to embody the universal principles of evil in the experience of his own age and evaluate that experience.

Our own position may be similar. If we doubt the value of the romantic communion, if we cannot see that the poet who has survived it is a better poet for it, we may at least say this: that the communion, as we have experienced it historically, if not personally, has extended our knowledge of evil and so made us wiser; for the moral intelligence is merely the knowledge and evaluation of evil; and the moral intelligence is the measure of the man and of the poet alike. It may seem a hard thing to say of that troubled and magnificent spirit, Hart Crane, that we shall remember him chiefly for his having shown us a new mode of damnation, yet it is for this that we remember Orestes, and Crane has in addition the glory of being, if not his own Æschylus, perhaps, in some fragmentary manner, his own Euripides.

Again, we should remember that there is no certitude that several generations of graduated decadence will lead to recovery; they may lead merely to a general condition of hypochondria. Crane's first book was better than his second, and the work of his last few years displays utter collapse. T. S. Eliot abandoned Laforguian irony not to correct his feelings, but to remain satisfied with them: his career since has been largely a career of what one might call psychic impressionism, a formless curiosity concerning queer feelings which are related to odds and ends of more or less profound thought. There is current at present a very general opinion that it is impossible in our time to write good poetry in the mode, let us say, of Bridges, either because of the kind of poetry that has been written since ("the stylistic advances of Eliot and of Pound"), or because of social conditions ("the chaos of modern thought"), or because of both, or because of something else. I believe this to be a form of group hypochondria. The simple fact of the matter is, that it is harder to imitate Bridges than to imitate Pound or Eliot, as it is harder to appreciate him, because Bridges is a finer poet and a saner man; he knows more than they, and to meet him on his own ground we must know more than to meet them.

Many experimental poets, by limiting themselves to an abnormal convention, limit themselves in range or in approach: that is, become primitives or decadents of necessity; and they lack the energy or ability to break free of the elaborate and mechanical habits which they have, in perfecting, imposed upon themselves. Miss Moore, Dr. Williams, Gerard Hopkins, and Ezra Pound might all serve as examples. In other words, the selection of a convention is a very serious matter; and the poet who sets out to widen his tradition may often succeed only in narrowing or sterilizing himself. Crashaw's experimenting at its wildest gets wholly out of hand and becomes pseudo-referent decadence. Nevertheless, the experimenting of Donne and of Crashaw is subject to the check of a comprehensible philosophy, as the experimentalism of Pound and of Crane is not. The experimentalism of Milton was subject to such a check and was, I think one may say, necessitated by the unprecedented scope of his plan and by the unprecedented violence and magnificence of his mind, but this is not to say that he was the greatest of poets, though he was, of course, one of the greatest.

The relationship between experimentalism, decadence, and primitivism is thus seen to be intimate, though it would be rash to formulate many laws of the relationship.

Decadent poetry may be valuable as a point of departure, either to its authors or to others, exactly in so far as its deficiencies are recognized and are susceptible of correction. Not all types of decadent poetry need be equally valuable in this respect, though the understanding of one may equal in value the understanding of another as a form of moral knowledge. Unless the deficiencies of a decadent convention are recognized, there is little likelihood that the convention will be improved; there is great likelihood that it will deteriorate; for it is the nature of man to deteriorate unless he recognizes the tendency and the source of the deterioration and expends actual effort to reduce them.

THE INFLUENCE OF METER ON
POETIC CONVENTION

Section I: FOREWORD

I HAVE ENDEAVORED to show in other essays that the morality of
poetry is inextricably involved in its form, and in a particular
essay that it is closely related to the *convention,* or norm of feeling, of any particular poem, and to certain general types of convention. As the norm of a poem will set certain limits upon the
range and procedure and quality of feeling possible within the
poem, we may say that a convention, whether we take the term
in the particular or in the generic sense, has a life of its own to
which the poet is largely subjected once he has adopted it. I have
tried to indicate, in discussing the idea of convention, that meter
plays an important part in the establishment of convention. I shall
now endeavor to draw certain general conclusions regarding the
poetic effectiveness of a few basic types of meter.

This essay will be divided into five sections, as follows:

The first section comprises the present descriptive foreword.

The second section contains a brief sketch of the theory of
traditional English meter on which my scansion of experimental
meter and my theories regarding the relationship of meter to
poetic convention are based.

The third section is a study of the scansion of free verse and of
the influence of free verse rhythms upon poetic convention. I
have begun this analysis with specimens of my own free verse because I can speak of my own intentions with a certain amount of
authority. I have proceeded thence to the poets from whose
practice I derived my own. I am not sure, however, that my own

poems offer the clearest illustrations available with which to introduce the medium to the reader unfamiliar with its principles. The deliberate effort which I made in most of these poems to introduce a substructure, iambic as to beat, but not pentameter, as a kind of counterpoint to the free-verse beat, probably renders much of my free-verse too difficult for the beginner to scan and may even ruin much of it entirely. The specimens from Dr. Williams, H. D., and Mr. Wallace Stevens, however, though they possess great finish and variety of movement, probably keep the metrical norm a little more obviously in view. If the reader finds the meter of my own poems obscure, therefore, he may fairly reserve his incredulity regarding the system of scansion until after he shall have studied the specimens of scansion from the other writers.

Even so, I have little hope that many readers will understand the scansion that I propose for free verse, chiefly because an understanding of it requires a very thorough knowledge of all the best poems employing the medium in the second and third decades of our century, a sensitive and conscientious study of several years in dŭration, the immersion of the student in a particular way of feeling, the acquisition of a new and difficult set of habits of hearing and of audible reading. This discipline is arduous and on the face of it is not particularly tempting: there are so many other things that one can do instead. In the few years past, the discipline has been almost wholly abandoned save by the few poets of the Experimental Generation[1] whose sensibilities were

---

[1] For the sake of a few loose but usable terms, I offer the following classification of 20th century poetry in English: I. The Generation of Forerunners: Hardy, Bridges, Yeats, T. Sturge Moore, and Alice Meynell; II. The Generation of Transition: Robinson, Frost, and Agnes Lee; III. The Experimental Generation: Stevens, Williams, Miss Moore, Miss Loy, Joyce (whose prose is related in important ways to the verse of his contemporaries), Adelaide Crapsey, Pound, Eliot, H. D., and Lawrence; IV. The Reactionary Generation: Crane (a member of this group, instead of the last, solely by virtue of his dates, personal affiliations, and inability to write or understand free verse), Tate, Baker, Blackmur, Clayton Stafford, Louise Bogan, Grant Code, J. V. Cunningham, Don Stanford, Barbara Gibbs. Mr. J. C. Ranson is a kind of ambiguous and unhappy though sometimes distinguished connective between this group and the last. The direction and significance of this group are clearest in Howard Baker, in a little of Tate, and in the writing, very small in bulk at present, of Stafford, Stanford, Cunningham, and perhaps Miss Gibbs. Such a classifica-

largely formed in this discipline. The most distinguished poets of the Reactionary Generation[1] who have attempted free verse—Hart Crane and Louise Bogan, for example—have been wholly unsuccessful in their brief and rare excursions into the medium. The Experimental poets who mastered the medium, it is worth observing, were those who for some years were more or less fanatical on the subject and gave themselves over to it wholly or almost wholly: Wallace Stevens is perhaps the only poet living who has practiced the new and the old meters simultaneously and at a high level of excellence. Very few readers, even professionally literary and academic readers, will give the subject the attention necessary for even a preliminary perception of it, but I am certain of the soundness of my scansion and wish to set it on record, for it will be of value to students here and there as time goes on.

For the present, suffice it to say that my *objections* to free verse do not depend upon the scansion of free verse, whether the verse be mine or that of any other; the objections are more cogent if the verse cannot be scanned. My system of scansion is offered by way of a preliminary defense of the medium, to show what it really has accomplished, and to limit as far as possible my objections, which, in my opinion, have only a narrow, though a quite definite, margin of relevancy. The objections are closely related to objections which I have made elsewhere to the other aspects of the recent experimental conventions.

The fourth section will deal with the relationship of experimental to traditional meters, the examples being drawn mainly from the sixteenth and seventeenth centuries, and will endeavor to show that the relationships are more fruitful of good within the old framework of accentual-syllabic meters than within, or in connection with, the framework of free verse.

The fifth section will give a brief summary of the history and principles of the heroic couplet, and of its effect upon poetic convention in the past, and a brief comparison of the powers of the

---

tion omits good poets here and there: de la Mare and Viola Meynell cannot quite be included; the most important omission is Elizabeth Daryush, the finest British poet since T. Sturge Moore.

heroic couplet (one of the most thoroughly traditional of all forms) with the powers of the forms that have been used in recent years to take something resembling its place: Websterian verse, the long free-verse line, stemming from Whitman and brought to its greatest perfection by Pound and by Miss Moore, and the syllabic meters of Robert Bridges.

Although this essay does not cover every known form of meter, it should be kept in mind that it does cover the following fields: the chief types of modern experimental meter in their relationship to convention (that is, the common varieties of lyrical free verse, and of semi-didactic free verse, Websterian verse, and the accentual and syllabic systems of Hopkins and of Bridges), the principles of traditional meter in its relationship to convention, and the principles of the relationships between traditional and experimental meters. That, as nearly as I can discover, is the entire bearing of the subject of meter on my present studies.

Section II: GENERAL PRINCIPLES OF METER

THE POETIC LINE, as I understand the subject, has at one time or another been constructed according to four different systems of measurement: the quantitative, or classical system, according to which a given type of line has a given number of feet, the feet being of certain recognized types and being constructed on the basis of the lengths of the component syllables; the accentual, or Anglo-Saxon, system, according to which the line possesses a certain number of accents, the remainder of the line not being measured, a system of which free verse is a recent and especially complex subdivision; the syllabic, or French, system, according to which a line is measured solely by the number of syllables which it contains; and the accentual-syllabic, or English, system, which in reality is identical with the classical system in its most general principles, except that accented and unaccented syllables displace long and short as the basis of constructing the foot, and that pyrrhic and spondaic feet seldom occur and might in fact be regarded as ideally impossible because of the way in which accent is determined, a matter which I shall presently discuss.

Mechanically perfect meter, were it possible, would be lifeless; meter of which the variation is purely accidental is, like all other manifestations of pure accident, awkward and without character. There are in English accentual-syllabic meter the following principles of variation, if no others:

(1) *Substitution:* That is, an inverted or trisyllabic or other foot may be substituted for an iambic foot in an iambic line, or similar alterations may be introduced into other lines. The method of substitution varies with writers and with periods. In the blank verse of Ben Jonson, there is a taut regularity, the result of the very careful manipulation of iambic and trochaic feet; and then occasionally there occurs a trisyllabic substitution, which effects a nervous leap, as suddenly stilled as it was undertaken:

> *Thou vermin, have I ta'en thee out of dung,*
> *So poor, so wretched, when no living thing*
> *Would keep thee company but a spider or worse?*

The device of trisyllabic and even of quatrosyllabic substitution is practiced by Webster to such an extent that the verse norm almost disappears, and certain passages are interpreted by some editors as prose and by others as verse, with about an equal show of reason. Milton, on the other hand, is extremely cautious in the use of trisyllabic feet—his extra syllables are all but lost in elision—but he goes very far in the use of trochaic feet and of trochaic words in iambic feet. To illustrate the use of the trochaic word in the iambic foot, we may employ the first line of Jonson's lyric, *Drink to me only with thine eyes.* Here we have a trochee for the first foot and iambs for the remainder; but the word *only* is itself trochaic and echoes the trochaic foot with which the line opens and at the same time functions in two iambic feet.

(2) *Quantity.* Quantity is an element of poetic rhythm in every language, regardless of whether the measure is based upon it. In French, a relatively unaccented language of which the verse is purely syllabic, quantity and phrase-stress, which are governed by no set rules, provide the chief sources of variation; in English, quantity provides one major source of variation.

In an iambic foot, for example, the unaccented syllable may be short and the accented syllable long (there is no strict dividing point, of course, between short and long, no two syllables being of identical length, and no arbitrary categories being necessary where the measure is not based upon quantity): such a foot will seem to be very heavily marked. On the other hand, it is quite possible for the unaccented syllable to be very long and the accented syllable very short—consider, for example, the first foot, a strictly iambic one, in this line of *The Nightingales*, by Robert Bridges:

Nay, barren are those mountains and spent the streams.

The variations resulting from this principle can be very finely shaded; so much so, in fact, as to obscure the accent on some occasions.

(3) *Varying Degrees of Accent.* Accent, like quantity, is unlimited in its variations. In practice, the manner of distinguishing between an accented and an unaccented syllable is superior, I believe, to the manner of distinguishing in classical verse between a long syllable and a short. In English verse, a syllable is accented or unaccented wholly in relation to the other syllables in the same foot, whereas in classical verse each syllable is arbitrarily classified by rule, and its length is in a very small measure dependent upon the context. This makes for a greater fluidity and sensitivity in English, I suspect, and with no loss of precision, perhaps with a gain in precision. It also renders the spondaic and pyrrhic feet theoretically impossible, as I have said, though they may sometimes be approximated; a close approximation of a pyrrhic is usually followed by a close approximation of a spondaic as in the following line:

Through rest or motion the noon walks the same.[2]

The latter half of the word *motion* and the article following form a fair pyrrhic, the two subsequent words a spondaic.

[2] From *Noon at Neebish*, by Don Stanford, Hound and Horn, VII-4.

If we take Ben Jonson's line, "Drink to me only with thine eyes," we find that *with* is accented in relation to the syllable preceding it, but that it is more lightly accented than the unaccented syllable of the subsequent foot. One has, in other words, a mounting series of four accents, which can be formally divided into two iambic feet, and which is in addition emphasized by an almost equally progressive quantitative series. A very slight shift of emphasis in each of these two feet would have made them resemble the two in the line previously quoted, the pyrrhic followed by the spondaic; yet the pyrrhic-spondaic combination appears strikingly abnormal as one reads it, and the sequence by Jonson glides by almost imperceptibly.

This rule in regard to the variation of accent is normally overlooked by metrists; it is wholly overlooked, for example, by Robert Bridges. The oversight results in Bridges' refusal to differentiate, so far as terminology is concerned—though he differentiates sharply in actual practice—between what I have called accentual-syllabic and syllabic meters: Bridges applies the term syllabic indiscriminately to both, and this confusion vitiates in a serious manner, I believe, the general conclusions of his work on Milton's prosody: he scans Milton incorrectly, it appears to me, for this reason, and more particularly Milton's later work, which merely represents learned variation to an extreme degree from a perfectly perceptible accentual-syllabic norm, variation expressive of very violent feeling.

(4) *Sprung Meter.* Sprung meter is loosely described by Hopkins in his preface to his poems. It consists essentially of the juxtaposition of heavily and more or less equally accented syllables by other means than normal metrical inversion; it is thus a normal and characteristic phenomenon of English syllabic meter, as written by Robert Bridges and by Elizabeth Daryush, meter in which accents may be combined at will, since they have no part in the measure, and it is equally characteristic of purely accentual meter, in which the measure is based on the number of accents and on nothing else, so that monosyllabic feet may easily occur in sequence. When sprung meter occurs as a variant of normal accentual-syllabic meter, it represents, actually, the abandonment,

for the moment, of the accentual-syllabic norm in favor either of the syllabic or of an accentual norm.

Wyatt employs the accentual variety of sprung rhythm, that in which an unaccented syllable is dropped from between two accented, so that a monosyllabic foot occurs, as in the second line below:

> *They flee from me, that sometimes did me seek*
> *With naked foot, stalking in my chamber.*[3]

Robert Green, whom Hopkins names as the last English poet to use sprung meter, employs the same species as a variant on his seven-syllable-couplets:

> *Up I start, forth went I,*
> *With her face to feed mine eye.*[4]

The norm of this line is iambic tetrameter, with the initial unaccented syllable omitted; in the first line above, an additional unaccented syllable is dropped between the second and third accented. Green often writes a line of this kind, but with the initial unaccented syllable returned to its place, so that the syllable count is undisturbed:

> *That when I woke, I 'gan swear,*
> *Phyllis' beauty palm did bear.*[5]

A more normal, perhaps a more true, example of syllabic sprung rhythm within an accentual-syllabic poem, is the following line from a poem by Barnabe Googe, *Of Money:*[6]

> *Fair face show friends when riches do abound.*

Here the accentual weight of the first and third places is increased to equal approximately the weight of the second and fourth; we

---

[3] and [4] and [5] *Oxford Book of 16th Century Verse*, pages 51, 382, and 381.
[6] Arber's *English Reprints*.

might describe the first two feet as spondaic, except that, as there is no compensatory pair of pyrrhics, two extra accents are introduced into the line, with the result that the accentual measure is abandoned and we have no measure left save the purely syllabic.

Robert Bridges' poem, *A Passerby*, whatever may have been the intention of the author, can be scanned as a poem in iambic pentameter, with certain normal substitutions, and with examples at irregular intervals of both kinds of sprung meter.

The first of the two lines below, written by the present author, contains both kinds of sprung meter within a single line:

> *Warm mind, warm heart, beam, bolt, and lock,*
> *You hold the love you took, and now at length. . . .*[7]

The first four syllables are modeled on the first four in the line by Googe; the next two shift to accentual meter, for each represents a single foot; the last two syllables are a perfect iambic foot. The line is a variant within a sonnet in iambic pentameter; it contains, according to the scansion just given, eight syllables, five feet, seven accented syllables (six of them being in unbroken sequence), and one unaccented syllable. Variants so extraordinary as this are seldom wholly admirable, and this one is offered primarily as an example and a curiosity.

The reader will find a particularly fine example of sprung meter in a poem wholly syllabic, in *Still-Life,* by Elizabeth Daryush;[8] of sprung meter in a poem wholly accentual in *Inversnaid,* by Gerard Hopkins.

[7] In a pamphlet called *Before Disaster,* published by Tryon Pamphlets, Tryon, N. C.
[8] This poem appears in full near the end of this essay, and is quoted from *The Last Man, and Other Poems,* by Elizabeth Daryush, Oxford Press, England. Mrs. Daryush has published four other books of importance: *Verses: First to Fourth Books* inclusive. She is one of the few first-rate poets living, and is all but unknown.

Section III: THE SCANSION OF FREE VERSE

I SHALL BEGIN the description of my system for the scansion of free verse with an account of two poems of my own and of what I endeavored to accomplish in them. The foot which I have used consists of one heavily accented syllable, an unlimited number of unaccented syllables, and an unlimited number of syllables of secondary accent. This resembles the accentual meter of Hopkins, except that Hopkins employed rhyme He appears to have had the secondary accent, or subordinate and extra-metrical "foot," in mind, when he spoke of "hangers" and "outrides."

Accents, as I have already pointed out, cannot be placed in a definite number of arbitrary categories; language is fluid, and a syllable is accented in a certain way only in relation to the rest of the foot. The secondary accent is discernible as a type if the poet makes it so. A dozen types of accent are possible in theory, but in practice no more than two can be kept distinct in the mind; in fact it is not always easy to keep two.

Ambiguity of accent will be more common in such verse as I am describing than in the older verse, but up to a certain point this is not a defect, this kind of ambiguity being one of the chief beauties of Milton's verse, for example. The poet must be permitted to use his judgment in dubious instances, and the critic must do his best to perceive the reason for any decision. Quantity will obviously complicate this type of foot more than it will the foot of the more familiar meters.

I shall mark and discuss two poems of my own, and shall then proceed to specimens of free verse from some of the chief poets of the Experimental generation, upon whose work my own ear for this medium was trained. Since a line which is complete metrically may for the sake of emphasis be printed as two lines, I shall place a cross-bar (/) at the end of each complete line. I shall number the lines which are so marked, for ease in reference. Lines which are incomplete metrically, but which are independent and not parts of complete lines, will likewise be marked and numbered, and these lines will also be marked with an asterisk

(*). I shall mark each primary stress with double points (″) and each secondary stress with a single point (′).

"Quod Tegit Omnia"

1 Earth därkens and is beáded/
2 with a swéat of búshes and/
3 the béar comes forth:
   the mind stored with/
4 magnificence proceëds into/
5 the mýstery of Time, nów/
6 cértain óf its chóice of/
7 pässion but úncértain óf the/
8 pássion's end.

          Whën/
9 Pláto témporizes on the näture/
10 of the plümage óf the sóul, the/
11 wind hums in the féathers ás/
12 acróss a córd impéccable in/
13 taütness bút of nó mind:/
                Time,
14 the sine-póndere, móst/
15 impertürbable of ëlements,/
16 assümes its ówn propórtions/
17 śilentlý, of its ówn próperties—/
18 an ëxcellence at which óne
    sighs./

19   Advënturer in
    living fäct, the póet/
20 móunts intó the spring/
21 upón his tóngue the täste of/
22 áir becóming bódy: is/
23 Embëdded in this crýstalline/
24 precípitáte of Time./

There are no incomplete lines in the preceding poem, though a few lines are broken in two for the sake of emphasis. The next poem is more difficult. I shall mark it as if it contained two feet to the line, and as if most of the lines were printed in two parts. The imperfect lines (unassimilable half-lines) are marked with a single asterisk (*). Unbroken lines are marked with a double asterisk (**).

The Bitter Moon

1   Dry snŏw runs búrning
    on the grŏund like fíre—/
2   the quíck of Héll spin ón
    the wind. Should Í belíeve/
3   in thĭs your bódy, táke it
    at its wŏrd? I háve belíeved/
4   in nóthing. Eárth burns with a
    shádow thát has héld my/
5   flésh; the ëye is a shádow
    that consümes the mínd/
6 * Scréam into äir! The vóices/
7 ** Of the dëad still víbrate—/
8   théy will fínd them, thréading
    áll the pást with twínging/
9 ** wíres alíve like häir in cóld./
10 * Thése are the nërves/
11 ** of déath. Í am its bräin./

12 ** Yóu are the wäy, the óath/
13   I táke. I hóld to thĭs—
    I bént and thwárted by a wíll/
14 ** to líve amóng the líving déad/
15 ** instéad of the dead líving; Í/
16 * becóme a vóice to soünd for./
17 ** Can you féel through Spáce,/
18 ** imágine beyond Tíme?
                            The/

114

19   *snów alíve with möonlight*
        licks aboút my änkles./
20   ** *Can you fïnd this eñd?/*

This poem is marked, as I have said, as if it contained two feet to the line. It is possible, however, to regard the poem as having a one-foot line, in which case the lines marked with the single asterisk and those unmarked are regular, and those marked with the double asterisk are irregular. The two-foot hypothesis involves the smaller number of irregular lines, and it would eliminate for this poem a difficulty in the matter of theory; to wit the question of whether a one-foot line is a practical possibility. Consider, for example, the possibility of a poem in iambic lines of one foot each. The poem will be, if unrhymed, equal to an indefinite progression of iambic prose. But in reply, one may object that except for iambic pentameter, and except for occasional imitations of classical verse, no unrhymed verse has ever been successful in English in the past, and that Herrick, at any rate, composed one excellent poem in lines each of one iambic foot ("Thus I / Pass by / To Die," etc.) I believe that this discussion will show that the secondary accent makes possible the use of unrhymed lines of any length, from one foot up to as many as can be managed in any other form of meter whether rhymed or not.

In the poem preceding the last, there was very little difficulty in distinguishing between the primary and the secondary accents; the trouble lay in distinguishing between secondary accents and unaccented syllables. But when, as here, it is the two types of stress that are hard to separate, we stand in danger of losing entirely our system of measurement. Now, if the meter is successful, there are in this poem two meters running concurrently and providing a kind of counterpoint: one is the free-verse meter, marked by the heavy beats, and the other is an iambic meter, marked by all the beats, whether heavy or light. The poem cannot be arranged in blank verse, however, for the iambic passages are incomplete, are fragments laid in here and there to provide musical complication and for the sake of their connotative value. If the heavy beats cannot be heard as distinct from the light, then the free verse scheme vanishes and one has left only a fragmentary blank verse, badly arranged.

Mr. William Rose Benét, in the Saturday Review of Literature (New York) for September 6, 1930, objected to the structure of my own free verse, at the same time offering realignments of two passages, which he regarded as superior to my own alignments. A few weeks later, he published a letter from myself, which stated, and for the first time in public, the general principles which I am now discussing. One of his revisions was of the opening lines of the poem which I have just quoted. He heard only the incomplete blank verse and rearranged the passage accordingly, some of the available fragments of blank verse, however, being broken in ways that were to myself inexplicable.

My own free verse was very often balanced on this particular tight-rope. During the period in which I was composing it, I was much interested in the possibility of making the stanza and wherever possible the poem a single rhythmic unit, of which the line was a part not sharply separate. This effect I endeavored to achieve by the use of run-over lines, a device I took over from Dr. Williams, Miss Moore, and Hopkins, and by the extreme use of a continuous iambic undercurrent, so arranged that it could not be written successfully as blank verse and that it would smooth over the gap from one line of free verse to the next.

In the standard meters, the run-over line tends to be awkward because of the heavy rhythmic pause at the end of each line: Milton alone, perhaps, has been highly and uniformly successful in the employment of the device, and he has been so by virtue of the greatest example of the grand manner in literature, a convention so heightened as to enable him to employ this device, which in most poets is destructively violent, as a basis for sensitive modulations of rhetoric. Even in Websterian verse the line-end is too heavily marked for the run-over to be pleasing. But if the *rhythm* can be made to run on rapidly, the meaning can be allowed to do so with impunity: hence the terminations in articles, adjectives, and similar words so common in free verse of this type, and even the frequent terminations in mid-word to be observed in Hopkins and in Miss Moore, this last liberty, of course, being common also in classical verse, in which, as in much free verse, the line-end pause is frequently extremely slight. Of the dangers of this type of free verse I shall have more to say later.

In the poem last quoted, much of the metrical ambiguity arises from the use of an unusually long foot, which allows quantity an opportunity somewhat greater than usual to obscure the accent. In the line, "at its word? I have believed," *word* receives the primary accent, but *believed*, which receives a secondary accent, is longer and may seem more heavily accented to the unwary. In the line "flesh; the eye is a shadow," the heavy accent goes to *eye*, but *flesh*, because of its position at the beginning of the line and before the semi-colon, receives more length than it would receive in most other places, and may seem for the moment to receive the main accent. In most cases, the reader will find that the ambiguity is one of alternatives; that is, he will naturally place a heavy accent on one word or on the other, so that the pattern will not be damaged. Ambiguities of this sort, and within the limits just mentioned, may be a source of value; they are, as I have said, one of the principle beauties of Milton's versification. If the ambiguity, in free verse, however, ceases to be a hesitation between alternatives, and becomes more general, the metrical norm is destroyed.

The poets from whom I learned to write free verse are probably better subjects than myself for a demonstration of the theory. The poem quoted below, which is by Dr. Williams, contains two lines of double length, each of which I have marked with an asterisk:

To Waken an Old Lady

1	Old áge is
2	a flíght of smáll
3	chéeping bírds
4	skímming
5	bare trées
6	abóve a snów glaze.
7	* Gaíning and faíling,

8   théy are búffeted
9   by a dárk wind—
10   but whát?
11   Ón the hársh weëdstalks
12   the flóck has résted—
13   the snŏw
14   is cóvered with bróken
15   seëd-husks,
16   and the wind témpered
17   with a shríll
18   * píping of plénty.

It will be observed that free verse requires a good deal of variation from line to line if the poem is to keep moving, and that as the one-foot line permits only a limited amount of variation if the foot is not to be stretched out to the danger-point, the poet must choose between a very short poem and a good sprinkling of irregular lines.

H. D.'s `Orchard` is one of the principal masterpieces of the free-verse movement. It employs a one-foot line, with fourteen lines of double length out of a total of thirty lines:

1   I sáw the first péar
2   As it féll.
3   * The hóney-séeking, gólden-bánded,
4   The yĕllow swárm
5   Was nót more fléet than Í
6   * (Spăre us fróm lóvelinéss!)
7   And I féll próstrate,
8   Crÿing
9   * "Yóu have fláyed us with your blóssoms;
10   * Spăre us the bĕauty
11   Of frŭit-trees!"

12   The hóney-séeking
13   Páused not;

14   * *The áir thǘndered their sŏ́ng*
15   * *And Ĭ alŏ́ne was prŏ́strate.*

16   *O rŏ́ugh-héwn*
17   *Gŏ́d of the ŏ́rchard*
18   * *I bríng yóu an ŏ́ffering;*
19   *Do yóu alóne unbéautiful*
20   *Sŏ́n of the gŏ́d*
21   * *Spä̆re us from lŏ́veliness!*

22   *These fállen hä̆zel-nuts*
23   * *Stripped lä̆te of their grë̆en sheaths;*
24   * *Grä̆pes, red-pü̆rple,*
25   *Their bë̆rries*
26   * *Drípping with wíne;*
27   * *Pómegrä̆nates alréady brŏ́ken*
28   *And shrúnken fĭ́gs*
29   * *And quínces untŏ́uched*
30   * *I bríng you as ŏ́ffering.*

Some of the details of this poem should be mentioned. Where there is a long foot, the heavily accented syllable usually appears to receive much less weight than in a short foot, the crowd of minor syllables absorbing emphasis from the major syllable. This absorption is sometimes, though not invariably, facilitated by the placing of two long feet in a single line. Line three is an example of this rule; line nine is an exception to it. The position of the accent in these lines is relevant to their respective effects: in line three, the accent is at the beginning of each foot, with the secondary accent and the unaccented syllables following in a rapid flicker, an arrangement which makes for speed; in line nine, the accent falls near the end of the foot, an arrangement which makes for a heavy stop; in both lines the second foot repeats the arrangement of the first foot, except for the very light syllable before the first heavy accent in line three, an arrangement which makes for clarity and emphasis of rhythm.

If the reader will examine again some of the preceding poems, he will find that this device of occasional repetition, either within the line or from line to line, may be used effectively for another purpose: it may provide the poet with a kind of pause, or moment of balance, between different movements, both of them rapid, a pause which is roughly analogous to a pause at the end of a line in the older meters.

Miss Marianne Moore has carried the method of continuity, of unbroken rush, farther than anyone, not even excepting Hopkins. The following lines are from her poem, *A Grave*. Since an extremely long foot is employed, in an extremely long line, I have placed a cross-bar at the end of each foot:

1 *mén lower néts,/ uncónscious óf the fáct/ that théy are désecráting/ a gráve,/*

2 *and row qúickly/ awáy/ the bládes/ of the óars/*

3 *móving togéther líke the/ féet of wáter-spíders/ as íf there wére no such thíng/ as déath./*

4 *The wrínkles progréss/ upón themsélves in a phálanx,/ beáutiful/ únder nétworks of fóam,/*

5 *and fáde bréathlessly/ while the séa rústles/ in and óut of/ the séaweed./*

Most of the generalizations drawn from the poem by H. D. could be as well illustrated by examples taken from this passage.

I have spoken of the remarkably continuous movement in Miss Moore's verse; but Miss Moore is seldom wholly at one with her meter. There may be, as in this passage, brilliant onomatopoetic effects, but the breathlessness of the movement is usually in contrast to the minuteness of the details, and this contrast frequently strengthens the half-ominous, half-ironic quality of the details, at the same time that it is drawing them rather forcibly into a single pattern. This is not a defect, at least in the shorter poems: it is a means of saying something that could have been said in no other way; and what is said is valuable. But the instrument is highly specialized and has a very narrow range of effectiveness.

A further danger inherent in the instrument becomes apparent in Miss Moore's longer poems, such as *Marriage* and *The Octopus*. These poems are at once satiric and didactic, but the satiric and didactic forms require of their very nature a coherent rational frame. The poems have no such frame, but are essentially fragmentary and disconnected. The meter, however, is emphatically continuous, and creates a kind of temporary illusion of complete continuity: it is a conventional continuity which never receives its justification. Despite the brilliance of much of the detail, this unsupported convention is as disappointing as the Miltonic convention in Thomson; it is a meaningless shell. In the shorter poems, the stated theme often correlates the details rationally.

Dr. W. C. Williams once remarked to me in a letter that free verse was to him a means of obtaining widely varying speeds within a given type of foot. I believe that this describes what we have seen taking place in the examples of free verse which I have analyzed. But if the secondary accent becomes negligible for many lines in sequence, if, in other words, the speed from foot to foot does not vary widely, the poem becomes one of two things: if the accentuation is regular, the poem is unrhymed metrical verse of the old sort; or if the accentuation is irregular, the poem may be a loose unrhymed doggerel but will probably be prose. Or there may be an uneven mixture of regularity and of irregularity, which is the possibility least to be desired.

The opening of Richard Aldington's *Choricos* illustrates the mixture of free and regular verse:

1   *The ancient songs*
2   *Pass deathward mournfully.*

3   *Cold lips that sing no more, and withered wreaths,*
4   *Regretful eyes, and drooping breasts and wings—*
5   *Symbols of ancient songs*
6   *Mournfully passing*
7   *Down to the great white surges. . . .*

The first four lines comprise three perfect lines of blank verse

Elsewhere in the same poem, we may find free verse abandoned for prose, the line-endings serving only as a kind of punctuation:

1   *And silently,*
2   *And with slow feet approaching,*
3   *And with bowed head and unlit eyes*
4   *We kneel before thee,*
5   *And thou, leaning toward us,*
6   *Caressingly layest upon us*
7   *Flowers from thy thin cold hands;*
8   *And, smiling as a chaste woman*
9   *Knowing love in her heart,*
10 *Thou sealest our eyes.*
11 *And the illimitable quietude*
12 *Comes gently upon us.*

The first three lines of this passage might pass for free verse of the same kind that Mr. Aldington has used elsewhere in the same poem, but line four, in spite of the fact that it can be given two major accents, does not continue the movement previously established. Line eight is similarly troublesome, and the remaining lines are uncertain. The difficulty is not mathematical but rhythmic: the movement of the lines in the context is awkward and breaks down the context.

This passage raises and answers a rather troublesome question. It is possible that any passage of prose—even the prose that I am now writing—might be marked off into more or less discernible feet of the kind that I have described, each foot having a heavy accent and one or more or perhaps no light accents, and a varying number of relatively unaccented syllables. These feet could then be written one or two or three to a line. Would the result be free verse? I believe not.

We are supposing in the first place that the writer of prose will instinctively choose syllables that fall naturally into three clearly discernible classes; whereas this classification of syllables in free verse is, in the long run, the result of a deliberate choice, even though the poet may be guided only by ear and not by theory. But let us for the sake of argument neglect this objection.

The accented syllables are necessary to free verse, but more is necessary: the remaining syllables must be disposed in such a way as to establish an harmonious and continuous movement. But can the laws of this harmonious and continuous movement be defined? That is, can one define every possible type of free verse foot and can one then establish all of the combinations possible and rule out all the unsatisfactory combinations? I have never gone into this subject experimentally, but I believe that one can demonstrate rationally that the compilation of such laws is impossible.

The free verse foot is very long, or is likely to be. No two feet composed of different words can ever have exactly the same values either of accent or of quantity. If one will mark off the passage quoted from Mr. Aldington, for example, one will get certain combinations which are unsuccessful; but one cannot say that the duplication of the same series of accent marks in a different group of words will be unsuccessful, because the duplication of accent marks will not mean the duplication of the exact weights and lengths of the original passage. The free verse foot is simply too long and too complicated to be handled in this way. If the reader feels that this proves free verse to be no verse at all, I have two answers: first, that he will have the same difficulty with any other purely accentual verse, from the Anglo-Saxon to Hopkins and with any purely syllabic; secondly, that if the rhythms which I have described can be *perceived* in a fairly large number of poems, and if the failure to establish such rhythms can be perceived in other poems, one has a rhythmic system distinguishable from prose and frequently of poetic intensity, and it matters very little what name it goes by. What is really important is the extent of its usefulness, its effect upon poetic convention.

I do not wish to claim that the poets of whom I write in this essay had my system of scansion in mind when writing their poems. Probably none of them had it. What I wish to claim is this: that the really good free verse of the movement can be scanned in this way, and that the nature of our language and the difficulties of abandoning the old forms led inevitably to this system, though frequently by way of a good deal of uncertain experimenting.

Mr. Aldington's *Choricos* is an attempt to combine certain traditional meters, English and classical, and a little biblical prose, in a single poem, just as Hugo, for example, employed different meters in a single poem, but this procedure, whether employed by Hugo or by Richard Aldington, is inevitably too loose to be satisfactory. Other poets have quite deliberately employed simple prose rhythms. Sometimes the prose is very good, as in *One City Only*, by Alice Corbin, or as in a few poems by Mina Loy. But it is not verse, and it is not often a satisfactory medium for poetic writing.

The masters of free verse of the Experimental Generation are William Carlos Williams, Ezra Pound, Marianne Moore, Wallace Stevens, H. D., and perhaps Mina Loy in a few poems, though the movement of Mina Loy's verse is usually so simplified, so denuded of secondary accent, as to be indistinguishable from prose. Mr. Eliot never got beyond Websterian verse, a bastard variety, though in *Gerontion*, he handled it with great skill—with far greater skill than Webster usually expends upon it. Mr. T. Sturge Moore, at the very beginning of the twentieth century, published a very brilliant and very curious specimen of experimental meter, in *The Rout of the Amazons*, which, like the neo-Websterian verse of Mr. Eliot and of others, employs blank verse as its norm, but departs farther from the norm than the neo-Websterian poets have been able to depart, and, unlike the neo-Websterian verse, never seems to approach prose, but rather approaches a firm and controlled free verse as its extreme limit.

Free verse has been all but abandoned by the next generation: a few good specimens are to be found in minor poems by Glenway Wescott, Grant Code, and the late Kathleen Tankersley Young; but Messrs. Wescott and Code have written their best poems in other forms, and so have all of their ablest contemporaries.

A major objection to free verse as it has been written by H. D., Dr. Williams, and perhaps others, and the objection can be raised against much of Hopkins as well, is this: that it tends to a rapid run-over line, so that the poem, or in the case of a fairly long poem, the stanza or paragraph, is likely to be the most important rhythmic unit, the lines being secondary. Hopkins was aware of this tendency in his poems, but apparently not of its danger. In his own preface to his poems, he writes: ". . . it is natural . . . for the lines to be *rove over*, that is, for the scanning of each line immediately to take up that of the one before, so that if the first has one or more syllables at its end the other must have as many the less at its beginning; and in fact the scanning runs on without break from the beginning, say, of a stanza to the end and all the stanza is one long strain, though written in lines asunder." The result is a kind of breathless rush, which may very well be exciting, but which tends to exclude or to falsify all save a certain kind of feeling, by enforcing what I have called, in my essay on Poetic Convention, a convention of heightened intensity.

Hopkins meets the difficulty by excluding from his poetry nearly all feeling that is not ecstatic; Dr. Williams meets it by allowing and utilizing a great deal of language that is largely conventional. But if a poem is written wholly in conventional language, it becomes, when the convention is of this type, merely melodramatic and violent, and, when the convention is of some other type, weak in some other and corresponding manner. Dr. Williams has thrown away much good material thus; so has H. D. done; and so have others.

The extremely abnormal convention is seldom necessary, I believe, to the expression of powerful feeling. Shakespeare can be just as mad in a sonnet as can Hopkins, and he can be at the same time a great many other things which Hopkins cannot be. He has a more limber medium and is able to deal with more complex feelings. I mean by this, that if no one quality receives extreme emphasis, many diverse qualities may be controlled simultaneously, but that if one single quality (the ecstasy of the thirteenth century lyric, *Alisoun*, for example) does receive extreme emphasis, it crowds other qualities out of the poem. The meter, the entire tone, of *Alisoun,* render impossible the overtone of grief which would have been present had Hardy dealt with the same material, and which would'have given the poem greater scope, greater universality. One may state it as a general law, moral as well as metrical, that an increase in complexity commonly results in a decrease in emphasis: extreme emphasis, with the resultant limitation of scope, is a form of unbalance. Sexual experience is over-emphasized in the works of D. H. Lawrence, because Lawrence understood so little else—and consequently understood sexual experience so ill. In a very few poems, notably in the sonnet *To R. B.,* Hopkins avoids his usual tone in a considerable measure, by reverting toward standard meter. His rhymes and his consequent independence of the secondary accent enable him to do this, but a similar reversion is impossible in free verse, a medium in which the reversion would simply result in a break-down of form. It is difficult to achieve in free verse the freedom of movement and the range of material offered one by the older forms.

A few poems appear to indicate that a greater variety of feeling is possible in free verse, however, than one might be led to suspect by the poems thus far quoted. One of the best is *The Snow Man,* by Wallace Stevens:

1   * Óne must háve a mínd of wínter
2   To regárd the fróst and the bóughs
3   Of the píne-trees crústed with snów;

4   And háve been cóld a lóng tíme
5   * Tó behóld the júnipers shágged with íce,
6   The sprúces róugh in the dístant glíiter

7   Óf the Jánuáry sún; and nót to thínk
8   Of ány míserý in the sóund of the wínd,
9   In the sóund of a féw léaves,

10 * Which is the sóund of the lánd
11   Fúll of the sáme wínd
12   Thát is blówing in the sáme báre pláce

13 For the listener, who listens in the snow,
14 And, nothing himself, beholds
15 * Nothing that is not there and the nothing that is.

The norm is of three beats, and there are four irregular lines, the first and third having two beats each, the second and fourth having four. Each line in this poem ends on a very heavy pause, provides, that is, a long moment of balance before the next movement begins. The manner in which the secondary accents are disposed in the fifth, sixth, and seventh lines, in order to level and accelerate the line, is remarkably fine, as is also the manner in which the beat becomes slow and heavy in the next few lines and the way in which the two movements are resolved at the close. There is complete repose between the lines, great speed and great slowness within the line, and all in a very short poem. Dr. Williams has got comparable effects here and there. The following poem by Dr. Williams is called *The Widow's Lament in Springtime:*

1 Sorrow is my own yard
2 Where the new grass
3 Flames as it has flamed
4 often before, but not
5 with the cold fire
6 that closes round me this year.
7 Thirty-five years
8 I lived with my husband.
9 The plum-tree is white today
10 with masses of flowers.
11 Masses of flowers
12 load the cherry branches
13 and color some bushes
14 yellow and some red,
15 but the grief in my heart
16 is stronger than they;
17 for though they were my joy
18 formerly, today I notice them

19   *and túrn awáy forgétting.*
20   *Todáy my són tóld me*
21   * *Thát in the méadow*
22   *at the édge of the héavy wóods*
23   *in the dístance, he sáw*
24   *trées of whíte flówers.*
25   *I féel that Í would líke*
26   * *to gó there*
27   *and fáll into those flówers*
28   * *and sínk into the märsh néar them.*

The slow heavy movement of this poem of two-foot lines is ac-
centuated by the periodic swift lines (four, six, nine, thirteen
and fourteen, seventeen and eighteen and nineteen, twenty-two,
along with a few more or less intermediate lines, like one, ten,
eleven, twelve, and twenty-eight) out of which the slow lines
fall with greater emphasis. A poem of much greater length which
displays a remarkable range of feeling is Mr. T. Sturge Moore's
play (or, to be more exact, Eclogue) entitled *The Rout of the
Amazons.* Mr. Pound's *Cantos* offer a slow and deliberative
movement, but are as bound to it as is H. D. to her ecstasy.

There are at least two additional objections which I should
mention in connection with the tyranny of free-verse movements,
objections perhaps inclusive or causative of those already made;
namely, that two of the principles of variation—substitution and
immeasurably variable degrees of accent—which are open to the
poet employing the old meters, are not open to the poet employing free verse, for, as regards substitution, there is no normal foot
from which to depart, and, as regards accent, there is no foot to
indicate which syllables are to be considered accented, but the
accented syllable must identify itself in relation to the entire line,
the result being that accents are of fairly fixed degrees, and certain ranges of possible accent are necessarily represented by gaps.
In free verse the only norm, so far as the structure of the foot is
concerned, is perpetual variation, and the only principle governing the selection of any foot is a feeling of rhythmical continuity;
and on the other hand the norm of the line, a certain number of

128

accents of recognizably constant intensity, and in spite of the presence of the relatively variable secondary accents, inevitably results in the species of inflexibility which we have seen equally in the fast meters of Williams and in the slow meters of Pound. The free-verse poet, however, achieves effects roughly comparable to those of substitution in the old meters in two ways: first by the use of lines of irregular length, a device which he employs much more commonly than does the poet of the old meters and with an effect quite foreign to the effect of too few or of extra feet in the old meters; and, secondly, since the norm is perpetual variation, by the approximate repetition of a foot or of a series of feet. It is a question whether such effects can be employed with a subtlety equal to that of fine substitution. Personally I am convinced that they cannot be; for in traditional verse, each variation, no matter how slight, is exactly perceptible and as a result can be given exact meaning as an act of moral perception. Exactness of language is always a great advantage, and the deficiencies of free verse in this respect will be more evident after an examination of some of the traditional meters.

Section IV: EXPERIMENTAL AND TRADITIONAL METERS

IN DESCRIBING THE CONSEQUENCES of the swifter forms of free verse and of the meters of Hopkins, I have indicated a general principle which accounts for a definite and often-regretted tendency in the history of English meter—the tendency of successive generations of poets to level their meters more and more toward the iambic, that is, toward the normal meter of the language, and at the same time to simplify their rhyme schemes, to depart, at least, from those schemes, which, like that of *Alisoun*, contribute to a swift and lilting music or to some other highly specialized effect. Without assuming the truth of any theories of evolution, of progress, or of continuous development in poetry, we may recognize the facts that within limited historical patterns, early poetry is simple and later poetry is likely to be relatively complex, these two adjectives being understood as relating to the content of the poetry, the moral consciousness of the art; that, as the complex poetry deadens, or, the commoner phenomenon, as the critical sensibility to it deadens and the fashion begins to change, there are likely to be new outbreaks of emphatic and relatively simple, but nevertheless fresh, feeling, which eventually may reinvigorate the older tradition.

How, then, can one reconcile in theory this tendency to increasing complexity of feeling with the tendency to increasing simplicity of means? The answer, I believe, is fairly simple. The nearer a norm a writer hovers, the more able is he to vary his feelings in opposite or even in many directions, and the more significant will be his variations. I have observed elsewhere that variations of any kind are more important in proportion as they are habitually less pronounced: a man who speaks habitually at the top of his voice cannot raise his voice, but a man who speaks quietly commands attention by means of a minute inflection. So elaborately and emphatically joyous a poem as *Alisoun*, for example, can be only and exclusively joyous; but Hardy, in the more level and calmer song, *During Wind and Rain*, can define a joy fully as profound, indeed more profound, at the same time that he is dealing primarily with a tragic theme. To extend the comparison to free verse, H. D.'s *Orchard* is purely ecstatic; it is as limited in its theme as is *Alisoun*, and as specialized in its meter. But Dr. Williams' poem, *The Widow's Lament*, is at once simpler and calmer in meter and more profound in feeling. The difference between these two poems, of course, is due wholly to a difference in temperament, and not to the passage of centuries. That a specimen of free verse can be found displaying a complexity and a profundity comparable to those of such poems as Hardy's *During Wind and Rain* and Bridges' *Love not too much*, I do not believe; nor do I believe that such a poem can ever be composed. For reasons that will become increasingly clear as this discussion progresses, I believe that the nature of free verse is a permanent obstacle to such a composition.

It is worth noting that the songs of Shakespeare are, for the most part, the most varied and brilliant exhibitions of minutely skillful writing which we possess, as well as the most song-like of songs. They are likewise nearly as frail, nearly as minor, as any wholly successful poetry could be. The sonnets, on the other hand, remain, I suppose, our standard of the greatest possible poetry; they are written in the normal line of our poetry and in the simplest form of the sonnet.

The lilting movement of the sixteenth century lyrical meters, of Sidney, of *England's Helicon*, disappears from the work of the great masters of the seventeenth century. Even Herrick suggests the old feeling ever so slightly, though quite deliberately—his line has a stony solidity utterly foreign to the lyrics of fifty years earlier. Donne employs at times movements which suggest the earlier movements, as, for example, in the songs, *Sweetest love I do not go*, and *Go and catch a falling star*, but his bony step is wholly different from the light pausing and shifting of Sidney; it is a grimly serious parody. George Herbert's *Church Monuments*, perhaps the most polished and urbane poem of the Metaphysical School and one of the half dozen most profound, is written in an iambic pentameter line so carefully modulated, and with its rhymes so carefully concealed at different and unexpected points in the syntax, that the poem suggests something of the quiet plainness of excellent prose without losing the organization and variety of verse.

Crashaw, in his most beautiful devotional poetry, employs cadences and imagery suggestive of earlier love poetry and drinking songs. Thus, in his paraphrase of the *Twenty-third Psalm*, he writes:

> *When my wayward breath is flying,*
> *He calls home my soul from dying.*

This passage corresponds closely to a passage in a translation made by Crashaw from an Italian love song, a fact which might lead one to suspect that he sought deliberately for relationships between disparate modes of experience and that the correspondences—and there are many of them—in his other poems are not accidental:

> *When my dying*
> *Life is flying,*

Those sweet airs, that often slew me
Shall revive me,
Or reprive me,
And to many deaths renew me.

The reader should observe that there is here not only a resemblance between the first couplet of the translated stanza and the couplet of the psalm, but that the traditional image of physical love, as it appears in the translated stanza, serves as a basis for the image of salvation in the psalm; something similar occurs at the climax of the famous poem to Saint Theresa; similar also is the use, in his various references to the Virgin, of imagery borrowed from Petrarchan love-poetry; similar also is his application of Petrarchan wit to sacred subjects, as if he were, like some celestial tumbler, displaying his finest training and ingenuity for the greater glory, and out of the purest love, of God—in fact, it is in Crashaw that the relationship between the Petrarchan conceit and the Metaphysical conceit is perhaps most obvious. The paraphrase of the psalm, which is the more complex and profound of the two poems just mentioned, is written in couplets and exhibits very few feminine rhymes. The sudden shift into the feminine rhyme in this particular couplet gives an unexpected and swiftly dissipated feeling of an earlier, more emphatic, and more naïve lyricism.

In the following couplet, likewise from the paraphrase of the psalm, there is both in the meter and in the imagery a strong suggestion of the poetry of conviviality:

How my head in ointment swims!
How my cup o'erlooks her brims!

The head, of course, is not swimming with drink, and the cup is the cup of bliss, but the instant of delirium is deliberately sought and impeccably fixed. The meter contributes to this effect in two ways: through the approximate coincidence of length and accent, with the resultant swift and simplified movement, and through the almost exact metrical similarity of the two lines. The spiritualization, if one may employ such a term, of the convivial image is partly, of course, the work of the context, but it is also, in a large measure, the work of the startling word *o'erlooks,* which takes the place of the commoner and purely physical *o'erflows:* the word not only implies animation, but suggests a trembling balance. The last couplet of the same poem recalls the earlier love-lyrics in a similar manner:

> *And thence my ripe soul will I breath*
> *Warm into the Arms of Death.*

One can find many other passages in Crashaw's devotional verse to illustrate this practice. Crashaw does not, in passages like these, quote or borrow from earlier poetry; he does not ordinarily even suggest a particular passage or line from an earlier poet. Rather, by fleeting nuances of language, he suggests an anterior mode of poetic expression and hence of experience, and in a context which is new to it. More commonly than not, he suggests in this manner not what is most striking in an earlier body of poetry but what is most commonplace: an earlier poetic convention becomes the material of his perception, and contributes, along with other, apparently disparate, and non-literary material, the material of an extremely complex poetic structure. It is in ways such as this that Crashaw is traditional; he is experimental in the ways in which he pushes metaphor beyond the bounds of custom and frequently even of reason. Crashaw is noted for his experiments; the large amount of poetry in which the traditional predominates and the experimental is under full control is too seldom appreciated.

This illusion of simplicity, this retreat toward the norm, of which I have been speaking, can, however, be achieved only by those writers who have mastered the more emphatic and athletic exercises; it is inconceivable that a poet insensitive to the fresh and skillful enthusiasm of Sidney should achieve the subdued complexity of Crashaw, Jonson, or Herrick. The beauty of the later masters resides in a good measure in what they suggest and refrain from doing, not in that of which they are ignorant or incapable. Within the pattern of free verse, this kind of suggestion is impossible: to depart from a given movement is to abandon it; the absence of a metrical frame accounting for the agreement or variation of every syllable, heavy or light, and allowing immeasurable variation of accent, makes exact and subtle variation and suggestion impossible. Similarly, there is no manner in which the rhythms of a poem in free verse, such as H. D.'s *Orchard,* could be utilized or suggested in a poem in accentual-syllabic meter, for the two systems are unrelated and mutually destructive. In so far, however, as the difficulties of maintaining rhythm in new and structurally unsatisfactory patterns, may have forced poets and their readers to strain the attention upon certain fine shades of accent and quantity, it is possible that the free-verse poets may have eventually a beneficial effect upon poets writing in accentual-syllabic verse; in so far as free verse has encouraged careless substitution in the older meter, has encouraged an approximation of the movement of accentual-syllabic verse to that of purely accentual, its effect has quite perceptibly been undesirable. Eliot, Tate, and MacLeish exemplify the latter influence.

Section V: THE HEROIC COUPLET
AND ITS RECENT RIVALS

A BRIEF STUDY of the heroic couplet and a comparison of the couplet with certain forms that have been used for more or less the same purposes as those which encouraged the couplet may throw a little more light on our subject.

The chief masters of the heroic couplet during the period in which it was the most widely used and the most widely useful poetic instrument are: Dryden, Pope, Gay, Johnson, and Churchill. In Goldsmith and in Crabbe alike the instrument is relaxed and the poem is diluted either with facile sentiment or with plodding exposition, although much admirable poetry may be found in these writers.

Dryden used the couplet for a wide variety of purposes. In his *Æneid,* it is an adequate epic instrument, only a little inferior to

Milton's blank verse, the inferiority being so slight as to be fairly attributable to the men and not to their instruments. As an example of the grandeur to which Dryden is able to raise this form, we may turn to the descent of Æneas into Hell in the sixth book, a passage quoted by Saintsbury, and as fine in its way as the original of Vergil.

Dryden employs the couplet as a powerful satirical instrument, as the meter for some of our greatest didactic poetry, and, in the opening lines of *Religio Laici*, as the medium for meditative lyricism of a very high order.

By changing to feminine rhymes, by placing the cesura regularly after the third foot, and by using an internal rhyme at this point in the first two lines, Dryden transforms the couplet into a song meter:

> *No, no poor suff'ring heart, no change endeavor;*
> *Choose to sustain the smart, rather than leave her:*
> *My ravished eyes behold such charms about her,*
> *I can die with her but not live without her;*
> *One tender sigh of hers to see me languish,*
> *Will more than pay the price of my past anguish.*
> *Beware, O cruel fair, how you smile on me;*
> *'Twas a kind look of yours that has undone me.*
>
> *Love has in store for me one happy minute.*
> *And she will end my pain who did begin it:*
> *Then no day void of bliss or pleasure leaving,*
> *Ages shall slide away without perceiving;*
> *Cupid shall guard the door, the more to please us,*
> *And keep out time and Death, when they would seize us.*
> *Time and Death shall depart, and say in flying,*
> *Love has found out a way to live by dying.*

The double meaning of the word *dying* and the compact wit recall slightly the Metaphysical School, as the former recalls also the song-books; the subject also recalls the song-books, and so does the careful suggestion of song-rhythm. Yet the poem has the sophisticated plainness of Herrick. These suggestions of earlier, simpler, and more emphatic modes are real, and they give a real profundity to the poem, a profundity fixed in the pun on the last word. It is a profundity of feeling, not of thought. The poem is one of the best examples that I know of what can be accomplished by means of meticulous variations from a rigid norm.

Pope restricted the couplet more rigidly than did Dryden. In fact, Pope, and his friend and disciple, Gay, represent the closest approximation to what we now recognize as the normal form of the instrument. Earlier poets appear to be converging consciously toward Pope and Gay, who are, in turn, the norm from which later poets consciously and carefully depart. Pope in particular is crucial to the history of the form, partly by virtue of his very deficiencies.

Pope, for example, had no talent for purely lyrical composition: his efforts in that direction resulted in the genteel ineptitude of A Dying Christian to His Soul, Eloisa to Abelard, and the Elegy to the Memory of an Unfortunate Lady. But his inability so to express himself was compensated by, and may even have caused, a greater complexity of attitude and of subject matter in his satirical and didactic poems than Dryden ever achieved in any single work. This additional complication appears to be roughly of three sorts: the illustration of the general with a deeply personal allusion, such as occurs in the fine couplets on Gay in the Epistle to Dr. Arbuthnot; the intensification of the heroic aspect of the mock-heroic passage, till it takes on, as does the close of The Dunciad, a kind of metaphysical magnificence, an intensity of terror which renders the satire all the more savage and destructive; and the statement in language at once general, concentrated, dignified, and pathetic of a truth both tragic and so universal as to be wholly impersonal.

The first of these sources of complication, the introduction of the pathos of private loss or of self-justification, is roughly the subject matter of Churchill's greatest work, though Churchill's approach differs profoundly from that of Pope, and in exploring this particular field more fully than did Pope, Churchill in one poem all but equals Pope's brilliance and range. The magnifi-
136

cence of the mock-heroic is to be found before Pope, in *Mac-Flecknoe*, especially in the passage which parodies Cowley's great description of the underwaters of the sea, which occurs near the opening of his *Davideis*, but the mock-heroic in Dryden is primarily in the interests of hilarity. Gay, in *The Birth of the Squire*, comes closer to Pope in this respect than does anyone else, but with this difference: Gay has wit but no malice, and almost invariably sympathizes with his victim and at moments appears wholly charmed by him, with the result that his pathos is humorous and particular rather than bare and universal. The last source of complication, or perhaps one should say the last mode in which Pope forces the didactic-satiric poem to invade lyrical territory, represents nearly the sole mode in which Johnson attains poetic greatness, and the mode in which Goldsmith achieved what is perhaps his only moment of great poetry.

I have illustrated the first and second of these classes by reference to familiar passages. Let me illustrate the last by quotation. Pope writes in *An Essay on Man:*

> *Heav'n forming each on other to depend,*
> *A master, or a servant, or a friend,*
> *Bids each on other for assistance call,*
> *Till one man's weakness grows the strength of all.*
> *Wants, frailties, passions, closer still ally*
> *The common int'rest, or endear the tie.*
> *To these we owe true friendship, love sincere,*
> *Each home-felt joy that life inherits here;*
> *Yet from the same we learn, in its decline,*
> *Those joys, those loves, those int'rests to resign;*
> *Taught half by Reason, half by mere decay,*
> *To welcome Death, and calmly pass away.*

It is this kind of pathos in isolation and perhaps more profoundly felt which renders memorable *The Vanity of Human Wishes* and more particularly Johnson's two great prologues, to *Comus* and to *A Word to the Wise*. It is this kind of pathos to which Goldsmith builds in a few brief climactic passages in *The De-*

serted *Village*, but especially in the following couplets, more famous, perhaps, in our own age for what may appear their democratic morality than for their rhetorical grandeur:

> *Ill fares the land, to hastening ills a prey,*
> *Where wealth accumulates and men decay;*
> *Princes and lords may flourish, or may fade;*
> *A breath can make them, as a breath has made;*
> *But a bold peasantry, their country's pride,*
> *When once destroyed can never be supplied.*

We might summarize these distinctions thus: Dryden touches successfully upon a wider range of experience than does Pope, and employs the couplet successfully in a greater variety of styles; but Pope through the concentration of his entire forces upon a single method achieves a greater range in certain individual poems than Dryden ever achieves in a single poem; Pope contains the germs of all the masters of the couplet to follow him in his century save Crabbe, and all of them save Crabbe achieve greatness by developing some one aspect of feeling to be found in Pope; Johnson, nevertheless, attains a greatness, even a universality, in a few poems, which appears scarcely inferior to Pope, chiefly by virtue of the way in which the dignity and grandeur of his character, his curious combination of private bitterness, public generosity, and Christian humility qualify his apprehension of relatively simple themes. It should be noted also, that if Dryden employs the couplet for a wide diversity of ends, by means of small variations, Pope, in combining a comparable diversity into a single complexity, varies the couplet noticeably less than does Dryden; yet he is successful, to the reader familiar with his sensibility he is one of the most exquisitely finished, as well as one of the most profoundly moving, poets in English. Churchill I reserve for detailed treatment. He is the most radical innovator in the history of the couplet, and by means of his innovations he uncovered a range of feeling, and created a poetry, as complex in their way, perhaps, as those of Pope, though he lived to master his discoveries in one poem only.

Churchill's early work contributes nothing of importance to the development of heroic verse: it is frequently good—the mannerisms described in *The Rosciad* are amusing, though little more—but it attempts nothing that Dryden had not already accomplished with greater brilliancy.

The Candidate, however, introduces a new procedure and a new quality of feeling into satirical verse, and the very structure of the poem forces one to study the innovation if one is not to remain, as a reader of it, suspended in ambiguity. The poem is directed against Lord Sandwich, who sought the Highstewardship of Cambridge, in spite of his notoriously licentious and unscholarly career. The poem, after various preliminaries, gives us a portrait of Lothario, a kind of ideal rake, whose identity is not given, but who is really Sandwich in disguise. At the conclusion of this portrait, the poet informs us that Nature, aghast at having created such a monster, by way of atonement gave us Sandwich, too. There follows a long account of Sandwich under his own name, an account which has at the outset all the appearance of the warmest eulogy; as one proceeds, one gradually begins to feel the undertone of irony, an undertone which becomes more and more evident, until, after several pages, Sandwich and his friends are being openly pilloried. This sort of thing, to the best of my knowledge, had never been done before; and to the best of my knowledge no one has ever pointed out that Churchill did it; Churchill, like Gascoigne at an earlier period and like Johnson in his own, was a great master obscured by history, that is, by the mummification, for purposes of immortal exhibition, of a current fashion—Gray and Collins, slighter poets in spite of all their virtues, were of the party that produced the style of the next century and they have come to be regarded, for this reason, as the best poets of their period. We have not in *The Candidate* the mock-heroic convention of *MacFlecknoe* or of *Hudibras*, which, though it involves feigned praise, is frank burlesque. It is closer to a quality of Pope, to which I have already referred, but it is ironical rather than epigrammatical; it is more evasive, less didactic or illustrative of the general, more personal, closer to the sophisticated lyrical tradition of such writers as Gascoigne,

Ben Jonson, and Donne. Churchill, in his ambiguous territory between irony and eulogy, awakened a number of feelings belonging neither to irony nor to eulogy, but capable of joining with both, and the most perfect example of the junction may be found in his greatest poem, the posthumous *Dedication to Warburton*. The poem opens thus:

> *Health to great Glo'ster!—from a man unknown,*
> *Who holds thy health as dearly as his own,*
> *Accept this greeting—nor let modest fear*
> *Call up one maiden blush—I mean not here*
> *To wound with flattery; 'tis a villain's art,*
> *And suits not with the frankness of my heart.*
> *Truth best becomes an orthodox divine,*
> *And, spite of Hell, that character is mine:*
> *To speak e'en bitter truths I cannot fear;*
> *But truth, my lord, is panegyric here.*
>   *Health to great Glo'ster!—nor, through love of ease,*
> *Which all priests love, let this address displease.*
> *I ask no favor, not one note I crave,*
> *And when this busy brain rests in the grave,*
> *(For till that time it never can have rest)*
> *I will not trouble you with one bequest.*
> *Some humbler friend, my mortal journey done,*
> *More near in blood, a nephew or a son,*
> *In that dread hour executor I'll leave,*
> *For I, alas! have many to receive;*
> *To give, but little.—To great Glo'ster health!*
> *Nor let thy true and proper love of wealth*
> *Here take a false alarm—in purse though poor,*
> *In spirit I'm right proud, nor can endure*
> *The mention of a bribe—thy pocket's free.*

The feeling, and, as I have said, it is a new kind of feeling, is deeply involved in the rhythms, especially in the relationship of syntax to versification. The long and involved sentence, with its numerous parenthetical interruptions, hesitations, and afterthoughts, is foreign to the other masters of the couplet. It appears in Churchill's earlier work in a crude form, but here it carries as high a polish as anything in Pope. The style is more different from Dryden, Pope, Gay, or Johnson than they are from each other, and it is probably a more complex style than any one of them ever achieved, though all of them are sufficiently complex, Pope and Johnson especially so; Churchill does not, as did Dryden, vary the epigrammatic norm of the familiar couplet, but he established a different norm, from which he can, by means of suggestion, utilize the norm of Pope much as Dryden and Crashaw utilized the song-books, at the same time that he is engaged in arriving at a very different end. His poetry is one of profound and bitter innuendo.

The heroic couplet must have certain qualities which enable the poet employing it to pass easily from description, to lyricism, to didacticism, to satire, and so on, or even at times to combine several of these qualities at a single stroke. It is doubtful whether so much freedom is possible in blank verse; the only satirical poet who has employed blank verse with major success is Ben Jonson, and much of his satire depends upon significance derived from the structure of the play—the details from line to line are usually variations upon an anterior theme rather than autonomous summaries. Ben Jonson himself employed the heroic couplet in some of his shorter poems, when he wished to indulge in a more direct and concentrated attack, and with remarkable vigor, in spite of the roughness of his versification. As a didactic instrument, blank verse is comparatively heavy and comparatively incapable of epigrammatic point; as a lyrical instrument, the range of blank verse, though wide, tends to be more closely limited to the grandiloquent and is less capable (in spite of charming passages in Fletcher and of *Tears Idle Tears*) of approaching the flexibility and variety of song. The heroic couplet, all things considered, appears to be the most flexible of forms: it can suggest by discreet imitation, the effects of nearly any other technique conceivable; it can contain all of these effects, if need be, in a single poem.

What, then, makes the couplet so flexible? The answer can be given briefly: its seeming inflexibility. That is, the identity of the line is stronger in rhymed verse than in unrhymed, because a bell is rung at the end of every second line; the identity of the line will be stronger in the couplet than in any other stanza because the couplet is the simplest and most obvious form of stanza possible. This mathematical and almost mechanical recurrence of line and stanza provides an obvious substructure and core of connotation over which poetic variations may move, from which they derive an exact identity. There is, in addition, a norm within the norm, at least in the case of every master save Churchill, the norm of the Popian couplet; and even Churchill can refer to this norm from a distance.

In spite of this regularity of basic scheme, there is no confinement of variation. The secondary rhythmic relationships of the couplet are unhampered by the rigidity of the primary, and the resultant set of relationships (the tertiary) between the constant element and the varying element, will be therefore unlimited, at the same time, however, that the constant element is providing a permanent point of reference, or feeling of cohesion, for the whole. The poet may move in any direction whatever, and his movement will be almost automatically graduated by the metronomic undercurrent of regularity; and if he chooses at certain times to devote himself to prosaic explanation, the metronome and the Popian balance, emerging naked, are capable of giving his prose an incisiveness possible in no other form, and of maintaining the relationship of the didacticism to the rest of the poem —the relationship in regard to feeling, I mean, for a didactic passage would of necessity represent by explicit statement the rational relationships within the poem.

A longer stanza is likely to be tyrannical. Within a single Spenserian stanza, for example, one cannot gracefully abandon a thought and take up another, nor can one let a thought run over a large number of stanzas. In the couplet we may have an entirely free play of thought over a rigid metrical substructure; in the longer stanza, thought and stanzaic structure must, very largely, coincide. To state it otherwise, in the long stanza the varying and constant elements which have already been mentioned in connection with heroic verse tend to fuse in a single movement, which, if protracted, becomes monotonous; whereas the poet employing couplets and employing at the same time a sufficiently comprehensive plot or frame, could move at will through all the complexities of Churchill and through all the pure and isolated moods to be found in Dryden—it would be largely a matter of timing.

Such a form, it seems to me, is the desideratum of those poets, who, following more or less in the wake of Mr. Eliot, have endeavored to employ a more or less Websterian verse as a carry-all meter. Websterian verse is much looser than good free verse: by Websterian verse, I mean that kind of blank verse which has been so named in our time, the loose blank verse of the speeches of Bosola, of Mr. T. S. Eliot's Gerontion, and of Mr. Archibald MacLeish. In nearly all verse of this kind, the sense of the blank verse norm is feeble; the substitution of feet becomes meaningless because there is so much of it; there is no care for the distribution of secondary accents or lesser syllables; and there is no basic regularity which can be made to support didactic or other linking passages when they are necessary, for the Websterian poet simply does not dare to revert over the long distance to formal blank verse, for fear of destroying the cohesion of his poem.

This last weakness means that necessary connecting links are evaded, and the evasion has at least two consequences of its own: first, the poetry, in so far as it needs logical linking, tends to break down into lyrical fragments, as in *The Waste Land*,[9] and, second, the didacticism, not being properly accounted for, is likely to edge into passages where it does not belong, and in a fragmentary and unsatisfactory form, frequently in the evasive and indeterminable form which I have described at length in another essay under the name of pseudo-reference. This fragmentary didacticism is unsatisfactory, because the poems I have in mind—*The Waste Land*, and Allen Tate's *Causerie*,[10] and *Retroduction to American History*[11]—are fundamentally exposi-

[9] *Poems 1909-25*, by T. S. Eliot, Faber and Gwyon, London.
[10] *Poems 1928-31*, by Allen Tate, Scribners, 1932.
[11] *Mr. Pope and Other Poems*, by Allen Tate, Minton Balch, N. Y., 1928.

tory poems, akin to the expository poems of Pope and Dryden, in that they endeavor to give a summary of a contemporary view of life and a criticism of such a view.

To say that a poet is justified in employing a disintegrating form in order to express a feeling of disintegration, is merely a sophistical justification of bad poetry, akin to the Whitmanian notion that one must write loose and sprawling poetry to "express" the loose and sprawling American continent. In fact, all feeling, if one gives oneself (that is, one's form) up to it, is a way of disintegration; poetic form is by definition a means to arrest the disintegration and order the feeling; and in so far as any poetry tends toward the formless, it fails to be expressive of anything.

Mr. Tate's *Causerie* embodies social criticism and moral indignation, two traditionally didactic-satiric themes:

> *The essential wreckage of your age is different,*
> *The accident the same; the Annabella*
> *Of proper incest, no longer incestuous;*
> *In an age of abstract experience, fornication*
> *Is self-expression, adjunct to Christian euphoria,*
> *And whores become delinquents; delinquents, patients;*
> *Patients, wards of society. Whores, by that rule,*
> *Are precious.*

> *Was it for this that Lucius*
> *Became the ass of Thessaly? For this did Kyd*
> *Unlock the lion of passion on his stage?*
> *To litter a race of politic pimps? To glut*
> *The Capitol with the progeny of ostlers,*
> *Where now the antique courtesy of your myths*
> *Goes in to sleep under a still shadow?*

Compared to any modern satirical or ironical verse, the passage is vigorous; compared to the passage from Churchill, it wants finish. Yet it is in a sense more serious than Churchill, for it has wider implications and rests upon wider and more careful thought.

The poet who has made the most ambitious attempt of our century to create a carry-all form is Ezra Pound, but his free verse, though the best of it is better meter than any of the neo-Websterian verse, remains in spite of his efforts a lyrical instrument which is improperly used for other than lyrical effects.

As in all free verse, and as in Websterian verse, we have in Mr. Pound's verse no normal foot, nothing to take the place of the couplet's basic regularity, no substructure insisting steadily on the identity of the poem, regardless of whither it wander. The meter, as in nearly all free verse, is wholly at one with the mood, and if the mood undergoes a marked change, the whole poem goes off with it and becomes incoherent. Purely didactic poetry is impossible in the form, because of the chanting, emotional quality of the rhythms, from which there is no escape, even momentarily: the rhythm implies a limited lyrical mood.

Unlike the Websterians, Mr. Pound in his best *Cantos* does not muddy his verse with secondary and uncontrolled didacticism: he is usually didactic, if at all, by implication only, but implication is inadequate, in the long run, as a didactic instrument. In the best *Cantos*,[12] at least, Mr. Pound is successful, whether in fragments or on the whole, but he presents merely a psychological progression or flux, the convention being sometimes that of wandering revery, sometimes that of wandering conversation. The range of such a convention is narrowly limited, not only as regards formulable content, but as regards feeling. The feelings attendant upon revery and amiable conversation tend to great similarity notwithstanding the subject matter, and they simply are not the most vigorous or important feelings of which the human being is capable.

The method, when employed in satirical portraiture, lacks the incisiveness of the eighteenth century masters:

So we léft him at lást in Chiấsso
Alóng with the old wóman from Kánsas,

[12] *A Draft of Thirty Cantos,* by Ezra Pound. Hours Press: Paris: 1932.

Sólid Kánsas, her dáughter had márried that Swíss
Who képt the Buffét in Chiásso.
Did it sháke her? It díd not sháke her.

She sát thére in the wáiting róom, sólid Kánsas,
* *Stíff as a cigár store Índian from the Bówery*
Súch as óne sáw in the níneties,
First sód of bléeding Kánsas
That had prodúced this lígneous sólidness.
* *If thóu wilt gó to Chiásso wilt find that indestrúctible fémale*
As if wáiting for the tráin to Topéka.

The passage is amusing in a way, but is soft and diffuse. Even *The Rosciad* affords more successful portraits. Notwithstanding the concreteness of the material, the meter is already outside the range in which it functions most effectively—the range, that is, of the fourth or of the seventh Canto. The meter is naturally elegiac, and the handling of it in such a passage as this is bound to be arbitrary and insensitive: the secondary accents fall accidentally, are hard to identify, and are neither perceptive nor intrinsically pleasing as sound, and so little attention is paid to shadings of quantity as to render the passage very awkward of movement. These defects in general are the defects of Mr. Pound's style, though in many passages they are far less evident than here. Like Swinburne, he has acquired an undeserved reputation for metrical mastery, largely as a result of a fairly suave manipulation of certain insistently recurring mannerisms, which, to the half-trained or the half-alert, appear signs of finish and control rather than what they are, the signs of a measure of incertitude and of insensitivity.

Mr. Pound has come no closer than Mr. Tate to creating a carry-all meter, but in his efforts he has sometimes created a purer poetry than has Mr. Tate while indulging in strictly similar efforts, chiefly, perhaps, because Mr. Pound has not been aware of comparably difficult material.

The Testament of Beauty, by Robert Bridges, offers one other experiment toward a carry-all form, which I should like, but am unable, to admire. The form is unrhymed duodecasyllabics, de-

146

pendent for their existence as such upon a definite and reasonably workable system of elision, a form which Bridges calls syllabic hexameter or Alexandrin verse. The form, as I understand it, evolved roughly in this fashion: through Bridges' failure to recognize the principle of varying accent and the law of the identification of accent, as I gave them early in this essay, Bridges came to regard standard English verse as fundamentally syllabic, but hampered by certain other half-observed rules; the details of this notion he worked out in his metrical study entitled *Milton's Prosody*. In *Samson Agonistes*, he found certain twelve-syllable lines, which in nearly every case I should be inclined to read as violent aberrations from iambic pentameter, but which Bridges, since he had a predisposition in favor of the syllable-count as the basis of the measure, read as Alexandrins. On the basis of these violent and impassioned lines, lines whose metrical force, as far as I can feel them, resides in a terrible struggle with the iambic pentameter norm, a struggle comparable at moments to the struggle of Samson with the pillars, save that in this instance the pillars do not, I believe, quite yield, Bridges constructed an unrhymed syllabic hexameter, in which the accents follow no law save that of variation, and employed it in a long expository poem conceived, like most didactic poetry, at a low and calm level of feeling. The Miltonic struggle was eliminated, and had it remained it would have been highly improper in conjunction with the subject-matter; but so also was the Miltonic form eliminated. The meter suffers from one of the two basic defects of free verse: there is not, as there is in free verse, a limit to the variability of accent, but there is, as in free verse, no norm as the basis of variation, so that syllables within the line are loose and shuffling, though usually, by means of a little arbitrary classification one can scan the lines accentually. The result is a meter as invariably monotonous as that of Orm, and the reason for the monotony is the same: regardless whether one attempts to scan the line accentually, or whether one follows Bridges and scans it syllabically (by all odds the preferable procedure), it successfully avoids the accentual-syllabic, avoids, that is, any pattern or norm underlying every syllable, so that, though one has constant change of movement from moment to moment, one has no variation, no precision of intention. It has certain advantages, possibly, for the purpose to which it is put in the *Testament of Beauty* over the heavily accented meter of Pound: its very monotony gives it a certain coherence, the coherence, however, merely of undefined intention, yet its freedom from the constant recurrence of the heavy measuring accent does not commit it so closely to a particular range of feeling; but if Pound's best *Cantos*, the first six or seven, are considered, the meter of Bridges is far less interesting in itself. This is curious, for Bridges, in general, is incomparably the better poet and the better metrist.

Bridges' syllabics, as employed by himself and by his daughter, Elizabeth Daryush, resemble free verse in certain other respects: they are more amenable to treatment if rhymed than if unrhymed, just as the double-accentual poems of Hopkins are firmer metrically than any of the unrhymed free verse of the Americans; and they are more likely to succeed in a short poem than in a long, for in the former the possibilities inherent in the various dispositions of accent can be more or less nearly exhausted without being repeated. Mrs. Daryush has been more successful, in my estimation, in writing syllabics, than was her father, though her greatest work, like that of her father, has been in the traditional meters. The following sonnet, entitled *Still-Life*, is one of her finest syllabic experiments:

> *Through the open French window the warm sun*
> *lights up the polished breakfast-table, laid*
> *round a bowl of crimson roses, for one—*
> *a service of Worcester porcelain, arrayed*
> *near it a melon, peaches, figs, small hot*
> *rolls in a napkin, fairy rack of toast,*
> *butter in ice, high silver coffee-pot,*
> *and, heaped on a salver, the morning's post.*
> *She comes over the lawn, the young heiress,*
> *from her early walk in her garden-wood,*
> *feeling that life's a table set to bless*
> *her delicate desires with all that's good,*

that even the unopened future lies
like a love-letter, full of sweet surprise.

One imagines that the medium could not be used with greater beauty than in this poem; there is certainly nothing in the work of the American masters of free verse to surpass it, and there is little to equal it. Yet like the best free verse, it lacks the final precision and power, the flexibility of suggestion, of the best work in accentual-syllabics, in which every syllable stands in relationship to a definite norm.

But I must now summarize my position in general terms. The sum total of the metrical virtues is necessary to didactic verse or to any sort of long poem, and is a profound advantage even to the shortest lyric. The sum total may be described briefly as follows: coherence of movement, variety of movement, and fine perceptivity. These virtues can occur in conjunction only in a system in which every detail is accounted for. That is, if the system is based (as English verse is normally based) on accent, then every syllable must be recognizably in or out of place whether stressed or not, and if out of place in a classifiable way; the degree of accent must vary perceptibly though immeasurably from a perceptible though immeasurable norm; quantity should be used consciously to qualify these conditions; in brief, the full sound-value of every syllable must be willed for a particular end, and must be precise in the attainment of that end. As language has other values than those of sound, this ideal will be always forced into some measure of compromise with the other values; nevertheless, the essence of art, I take it, is that no compromise should be very marked, and the perfection of art, though rare and difficult, is not unattainable. In a system such as English syllabics, or as free verse, most or all of the individual syllables can have no definite relationship to the pattern; so that there is no exact basis for judging them, and they are, when chosen, relatively without meaning.

Traditional meter, then, like the other aspects of traditional convention which I have discussed in other essays, tends to exploit the full possibilities of language; experimental meter, like other aspects of experimental convention, is incomplete. To push the analogy farther, experimental conventions in general tend to abandon comprehensible motive, to resort to unguided feeling; similarly experimental meter loses the rational frame which alone gives its variations the precision of true perception. Or to put it another way: as traditional poetry in general aims to adjust feeling rightly to motive, it needs the most precise instrument possible for the rendering of feeling, and so far as meter is concerned, this instrument will be traditional meter. Further, as traditional poetry tends to enrich itself with past wisdom, with an acquired sense of what is just, so the traditional meters, owing to their very subtle adjustibility and suggestibility, are frequently very complex in their effects, whereas the looser meters tend to be over-emphatic and over-simple.

It will be seen that what I desire of a poem is a clear understanding of motive, and a just evaluation of feeling; the justice of the evaluation persisting even into the sound of the least important syllable. Such a poem is a perfect and complete act of the spirit; it calls upon the full life of the spirit; it is difficult of attainment, but I am aware of no good reason to be contented with less.

Maule's Curse

SEVEN STUDIES IN THE
HISTORY OF
AMERICAN OBSCURANTISM

FOREWORD

DURING THE YEAR 1937, I published through the Arrow Editions in New York City a volume of criticism entitled *Primitivism and Decadence;* this book is a study of the technical forms taken by American Experimental Poetry during the twentieth century—it is a study very largely of the forms of unconscious and of conscious obscurantism which are the ultimate development of Romantic aesthetic principles qualified to a greater or smaller extent by certain aspects of American history. Had I required any further proof of the essential confusion of the literary mind of our period, the reception met by this book would have more than satisfied me. Its contents were described with placid and painstaking inaccuracy by many reviewers, with bitterly excited inaccuracy by others; it was attacked for opinions which it did not maintain or even suggest. But above all, it was attacked because it pointed to the dangers inherent in obscurantism, and because it found obscurity where the reviewer found none.

The subject of my reception by certain reviewers is not one of great general interest, but one series of incidents in connection with these reviews perhaps transcends that subject and has a certain theoretic interest. In discussing a passage quoted from the opening of Hart Crane's poem, *For the Marriage of Faustus and Helen,* I complained of the obscurity of the lines beginning, "Numbers rebuffed by asphalt," and said that the numbers might refer to numbers of people or to the mathematical abstractions of modern life, but that either interpretation left the passage imperfectly comprehensible. Now I was wrong, and in justice to Crane, I ought to correct the error. The numbers in question refer to the sparrows' wings in the preceding line, and by extension, to the sparrows, and with this understanding the passage is perfectly clear. Crane is in a good measure to blame for the difficulty, for the grammatical reference here and throughout the poem is of the loosest, and as one of my reviewers, to whom I shall refer in a moment, pointed out, there are elements in the passage that actively support the second interpretation and that would no doubt be a sufficient justification of the second interpretation if that interpretation clarified the passage within itself. My error does not, I believe, invalidate my general criticism of Crane, for the type of obscurity which I mistakenly found in this passage is certainly to be found elsewhere in Crane, though commonly in shorter fragments, and I see no reason to believe that I was mistaken in regard to other passages which I found obscure.

So much, however, for justice to Crane and to myself; it is something else that concerns me primarily. A well-known reviewer for a certain journal of advanced political and economic theory, who attacked my book, or rather who attacked me personally, in terms the most irresponsible and scurrilous, and who even ventured· to accuse me of insanity because I objected up to a certain point to incoherent poetry, stated in private to one of my friends, Mr. Don Stanford, that the numbers in question were numbers of people, and that the passage was perfectly clear; he did not, however, risk any interpretation of this passage or of any other in print, and thus displayed a caution common to practically all of my critics. On the other hand, a more friendly reviewer, in the *Southern Review,* displayed something of my own naïveté, and exposed himself lamentably. He asserted that this passage was sufficiently clear, and that the numbers were the mathematical abstractions of modern life, and that the lines a little preceding, which deal with baseball scores, stock quotations, and similar items support this interpretation; and that they do support the interpretation I believe to be true, but they do not clarify it. He then rather curiously and not quite coherently added a defense of the kind of obscurity to be found in this passage.· The defense in itself was ingenious and admirable; it was borrowed without acknowledgment from the last three pages of the third essay in my book under review, pages in which the reader who is curious may find likewise an even more valuable answer to the defense.

But here were two writers who found the passage clear enough for each of them, and who were even a trifle contemptuous about the whole matter, yet who disagreed with each other as to what the passage meant. One of them must be wrong, and if the disinterested reader will consider the passage in the light of the new interpretation which I have offered, I think he will agree that both are wrong. The passage, then, is unquestionably on record as exactly the sort of obscurantism which I asserted it to represent, although it is not Crane, in this particular passage, who is guilty, but two of his admirers. Crane obviously will gain little from the sort of defense which they offered him, nor will literature in general profit from the state of mind which led to it.

The present volume is an attempt to trace some of the earlier aspects of this state of mind in America, to suggest at least a part of the outline of a history of this state of mind. In so far as this history is merely a history of the international romantic movement, it is probably fairly well understood, at least in general terms; in so far as it is merely a history of American religious and other ideas and attitudes, it has been well treated by other writers, to many of whom I shall refer in the essays to follow. The relationship of the history of ideas to the history of literary forms, however, or conversely, the intellectual and moral significance of literary forms, has not been adequately studied; yet this subject is the very core of literary criticism and of the understanding of the history of literature. In my previous book, I described and endeavored to evaluate forms, primarily, and used writers merely to illustrate them. In the present volume I have examined individual writers, a procedure which enables me to examine subject matter more fully and to relate subject matter more fully to form.

Stanford University, 1938

MAULE'S CURSE

or Hawthorne and the Problem of Allegory

"At the moment of execution—with the halter about his neck and while Colonel Pyncheon sat on horseback, grimly gazing at the scene—Maule had addressed him from the scaffold, and uttered a prophecy, of which history as well as fireside tradition, has preserved the very words. 'God,' said the dying man, pointing his finger, with a ghastly look, at the undismayed countenance of his enemy, 'God will give him blood to drink!'"
—The House of the Seven Gables

OF HAWTHORNE'S THREE most important long works—*The Scarlet Letter, The House of the Seven Gables,* and *The Marble Faun*—the first is pure allegory, and the other two are impure novels, or novels with unassimilated allegorical elements. The first is faultless, in scheme and in detail; it is one of the chief masterpieces of English prose. The second and third are interesting, the third in particular, but both are failures, and neither would suffice to give the author a very high place in the history of prose fiction. Hawthorne's sketches and short stories, at best, are slight performances; either they lack meaning, as in the case of *Mr. Higginbotham's Catastrophe,* or they lack reality of embodiment, as in the case of *The Birthmark,* or, having a measure of both, as does *The Minister's Black Veil,* they yet seem incapable of justifying the intensity of the method, their very brevity and attendant simplification, perhaps, working against them; the best of them, probably, is *Young Goodman Brown.* In his later romances, *Septimius Felton, Dr. Grimshaw's Secret, The Ancestral Footstep,* and *The Dolliver Romance,* and in much of *The Blithedale Romance* as well, Hawthorne struggles unsuccessfully with the problem of allegory, but he is still obsessed with it.

Hawthorne is, then, essentially an allegorist; had he followed the advice of Poe and other well-wishers, contemporary with himself and posthumous, and thrown his allegorizing out the window, it is certain that nothing essential to his genius would have remained. He appears to have had none of the personal qualifications of a novelist, for one thing: the sombre youth who lived in solitude and in contemplation in Salem, for a dozen years or more, before succumbing to the charms and propinquity of Miss Sophia Peabody and making the spasmodic and only moderately successful efforts to accustom himself to daylight which were to vex the remainder of his life, was one far more likely to concern himself with the theory of mankind than with the chaos, trivial, brutal, and exhausting, of the actuality. Furthermore, as we shall see more fully, the Puritan view of life was allegorical, and the allegorical vision seems to have been strongly impressed upon the New England literary mind. It is fairly obvious in much of the poetry of Emerson, Emily Dickinson, Byrant, Holmes, and even Very—Whittier, a Quaker and a peasant, alone of the more interesting poets escaping; Melville, relatively an outsider, shows the impact of New England upon his own genius as much through his use of allegory as through his use of New England character; and the only important novelist purely a New Englander, aside from Hawthorne, that is, O. W. Holmes, was primarily concerned with the Puritan tendency to allegory, as its one considerable satirist, yet was himself more or less addicted to it.

These matters are speculative. That New England predisposed Hawthorne to allegory cannot be shown; yet the disposition in both is obvious. And it can easily be shown that New England provided the perfect material for one great allegory, and that, in all likelihood, she was largely to blame for the later failures.

The Puritan theology rested primarily upon the doctrine of predestination and the inefficaciousness of good works; it separated men sharply and certainly into two groups, the saved and the damned, and, technically, at least, was not concerned with any subtler shadings. This in itself represents a long step toward the allegorization of experience, for a very broad abstraction is substituted for the patient study of the minutiae of moral behavior long encouraged by Catholic tradition. Another step was necessary, however, and this step was taken in Massachusetts almost at the beginning of the settlement, and in the expulsion of Anne Hutchinson became the basis of governmental action: whereas the wholly Calvinistic Puritan denied the value of the evidence of character and behavior as signs of salvation, and so precluded the possibility of their becoming allegorical symbols— for the orthodox Calvinist, such as Mrs. Hutchinson would appear to have been, trusted to no witness save that of the Inner Light—it became customary in Massachusetts to regard as evidence of salvation the decision of the individual to enter the Church and lead a moral life. "The Puritans," says Parkes, "were plain blunt men with little taste for mysticism and no talent for speculation. A new conception was formulated by English theologians, of whom William Ames was the most influential. The sign of election was not an inner assurance; it was a sober decision to trust in Christ and obey God's law. Those who made this sober decision might feel reasonably confident that they had received God's grace; but the surest proof of it was its fruit in conduct; complete assurance was impossible. It was assumed that all was the work of grace; it was God, without human coöperation, who caused the sober decision to be made. But in actual practice this doctrine had the effect of unduly magnifying man's ability to save himself, as much as Calvin's conception had unduly minimized it; conversion was merely a choice to obey a certain code of rules, and did not imply any emotional change, any love for God, or for holiness, or any genuine religious experience; religion in other words was reduced to mere morality." [1] Objective evidence thus took the place of inner assurance, and the behavior of the individual took on symbolic value. That is, any sin was evidence of damnation; or, in other words, any sin represented all sin. When Hester Prynne committed adultery, she committed an act as purely representative of complete corruption as the act of Faustus in signing a contract with Satan. This view of the matter is certainly not Catholic and is little short of appalling; it derives

---

[1] *The Puritan Heresy*, by H. B. Parkes, The Hound and Horn V-2, Jan.-March 1932, pages 173-4. See also *The Pragmatic Test* by H. B. Parkes, The Colt Press, San Francisco.

from the fact, that although, as Parkes states in the passage just quoted, there occurred an exaggeration of the will in the matter of practical existence, this same will was still denied in the matter of doctrine, for according to doctrine that which man willed had been previously willed by God.

The belief that the judgment of a man is predestined by God, and the corollary that the judgment of a good man, since all men are either good or bad, purely and simply, is the judgment of God, may lead in the natural course of events to extraordinary drama; and this the more readily if the actors in the drama are isolated from the rest of the world and believe that the drama in which they take part is of cosmic importance and central in human destiny. Andrews writes: "The belief that God had selected New England as the chosen land was profoundly held by the Puritans who went there. Winthrop himself in 1640 wrote to Lord Saye and Sele of 'this good land which God hath found and given to his people,' adding that 'God had chosen this country to plant his people in.' Cotton in his sermon, *God's Promise to His Plantation* (London, 1634), devotes much space to the same idea—'This place is appointed me of God.'" [2] And Schneider writes on the same subject: "No one can live long in a Holy Commonwealth without becoming sensitive, irritable, losing his sense of values and ultimately his balance. All acts are acts either of God or of the devil; all issues are matters of religious faith; and all conflicts are holy wars. No matter how trivial an opinion might appear from a secular point of view, it became vital when promulgated as a theological dogma; no matter how harmless a fool might be, he was intolerable if he did not fit into the Covenant of Grace; no matter how slight an offense might be, it was a sin against Almighty God and hence infinite. Differences of opinion became differences of faith. Critics became blasphemers, and innovators, heretics." [3] And again: ". . . the mind of the Puritan was singularly unified and his imagination thoroughly moralized. The clergy were, of course, the pro-

---

[2] *The Colonial Period of American History*, by Charles M. Andrews; Yale University Press, 1934. Vol. I, page 386, note 2.
[3] *The Puritan Mind*, by H. W. Schneider; Henry Holt, 1930, pages 51-2.

fessional moral scientists, but the laymen were no less dominated by such mental habits. The common man and illiterate shared with the expert this interest in divining God's purposes in the course of events. No event was merely natural; it was an act of God and was hence charged with that 'numinous' quality which gives birth to both prophetic insight and mystic illumination." [4] And again: "Nature was instructive to them only in so far as it suggested the hidden mysterious operations of designing agents. God and devil were both active, scheming, hidden powers, each pursuing his own ends by various ministrations, and natural events were therefore to be understood only in so far as they showed evidence of some divine or diabolical plot." [5]

Now according to the doctrine of predestination, if we interpret it reasonably, Hester merely gave evidence, in committing adultery, that she had always been one of the damned. This point of view, if really understood, could never have led to the chain of events which Hawthorne described in *The Scarlet Letter*; neither could it have led to the events of the actual history of New England. It is at this point that we must consider that fluid element, history, in connection with dogma, for Hester, like the witches who so occupied the Mathers, was treated as if she had wilfully abandoned the ways of God for the ways of Satan. This final illogicality introduces the element of drama into the allegory of *The Scarlet Letter* and into the allegorical morality of the Puritans.

The English Puritans who settled Massachusetts were socially the product of centuries of the type of ethical discipline fostered by the Catholic and Anglo-Catholic Churches. They may have denied the freedom of the will and the efficaciousness of good works by lip, but by habit, and without really grasping the fact, they believed in them and acted upon them. Edwards exhorts sinners to repent while preaching the doctrine of the inability to repent; the Mathers wrestled with demons physically and in broad daylight, and quite obviously felt virtuous for having done so; in fact, to such a pass did Puritanism come, that Melville's Ahab, who wilfully embarks upon the Sea of Unpredictability

[4] Ibid., page 48.   [5] Ibid., pages 42-3.

in order to overtake and slay the Spirit of Evil—an effort in which he is predestined and at the end of which he is predestined to destruction—appears to us merely the heroic projection of a common Puritan type. The Puritan may be said to have conceived the Manicheistic struggle between Absolute Good and Absolute Evil, which he derived through the processes of simplification and misunderstanding which have already been enumerated, as a kind of preordained or mechanical, yet also holy combat, in which his own part was a part at once intense and holy and yet immutably regulated.

There were at least two motives in the new environment which tended to intensify the effect of habit in this connection: one was the inevitable impulse given to the will by the exaltation attendant upon a new religious movement; the other was the impulse given by the supremely difficult physical surroundings in which the new colonies found themselves. Foster writes on these points: "The first Puritans, sure in their own hearts that they were the elect of God, found the doctrine necessary to sustain them in the tremendous struggle through which they passed. . . . Hence the doctrine nerved to greater activity; and it produced a similar effect during the first period of the promulgation of Calvinism, among every nation which accepted the system." [6] The force of the will was strengthened at the beginning, then, at the same time that its existence was denied and that reliance upon its manner of functioning (that is, upon good works) was, from a doctrinal standpoint, regarded as sin. The will, highly stimulated, but no longer studied and guided by the flexible and sensitive ethical scholarship of the Roman tradition, might easily result in dangerous action.

Andrews speaks of this subject as follows: "The dynamic agency . . . the driving force which overrode all opposition, legal and otherwise, was the profound conviction of the Puritan leaders that they were doing the Lord's work. They looked upon themselves as instruments in the divine hand for the carrying out of a great religious mission, the object of which was the rebuild-

* A Genetic History of the New England Theology, by Frank Hugh Foster; University of Chicago Press, 1907; page 29.

ing of God's church in a land—the undefiled land of America—divinely set apart as the scene of a holy experiment that should renovate the church at large, everywhere corrupt and falling into ruins. This new and purified community was to be the home of a saving remnant delivered from the wrath to come and was to serve as an example to the mother church of a regenerated form of faith and worship. It was also to become a proselyting center for the conversion of the heathen and the extension of the true gospel among those who knew it not. In the fulfillment of this mission the Puritans counted obstacles, moral and physical, of no moment. Theirs was a religious duty to frustrate their enemies, to eradicate all inimical opinions, religious and political, and to extend the field of their influence as widely as possible. Once they had determined on their rules of polity and conduct, as laid down in the Bible and interpreted by the clergy, they had no doubts of the justness and rightness of their course. The means employed might savor of harshness and inequity, but at all costs and under all circumstances, error, sin, and idolatry, in whatever form appearing and as determined by themselves, must be destroyed. In the process, as events were to prove, a great many very human motives played an important part in interpreting the law of God, and personal likes and dislikes, hypocrisy, prejudice, and passion got badly mixed with the higher and more spiritual impulses that were actively at work purging the church of its errors." [7]

Over a long period, however, the doctrine of predestination would naturally lead to religious apathy, for it offered no explicit motive to action; and this is precisely that to which it led, for after the Great Awakening of the middle of the eighteenth century, itself a reaction to previous decay in the Church, the Church lost power rapidly, and by the opening of the nineteenth century was succumbing on every hand to Unitarianism, a mildly moralistic creed, in which the element of supernaturalism was minimized, and which, in turn, yielded rapidly among the relatively intellectual classes to Romantic ethical theory, especially as propounded by the Transcendentalists. "It has never been a good

[7] Charles M. Andrews, op. cit., Vol. I, pages 430-1.

way to induce men to repent," says Foster, "to tell them that they cannot." [8] Or at least the method has never been highly successful except when employed by a rhetorician of the power of Edwards, or by an orator of the effectiveness of Whitefield; and the effect can scarcely be expected long to outlive the immediate presence of the speaker. The Unitarians, in depriving the ethical life of the more impressive aspects of its supernatural sanction, and in offering nothing to take the place of that sanction, all but extinguished intensity of moral conviction, although their own conviction—we may see it portrayed, for example, in *The Europeans*, by Henry James, and exemplified in the lucid and classical prose of W. E. Channing—was a conviction, at least for a period, of the greatest firmness and dignity. Emerson eliminated the need of moral conviction and of moral understanding alike, by promulgating the allied doctrines of equivalence and of inevitable virtue. In an Emersonian universe there is equally no need and no possibility of judgment; it is a universe of amiable but of perfectly unconscious imbeciles; it is likewise a universe in which the art of the fictionist—or for that matter, any other art—can scarcely be expected to flourish. A fictionist who has been in any considerable measure affected by Emersonian or allied concepts, or even who is the product of the historical sequence which gave rise to Emerson, is likely to find himself gravely confused and may even find himself paralyzed; and we have only to read such a document, to cite a single example, as *The New Adam and Eve*, to realize that Hawthorne's own moral ideas, in spite of his intense but conflicting moral sentiments, and in spite of his professed dislike for Emerson's philosophy, were much closer to the ideas of Emerson than to those of Edwards.

Now in examining Hawthorne, we are concerned with two historical centers: that of the first generation of Puritans in New England, in which occurs the action of *The Scarlet Letter*; and that of the post-Unitarian and Romantic intellectuals, in which was passed the life of Hawthorne.

Hawthorne, by nature an allegorist, and a man with a strong moral instinct, regardless of the condition of his ideas, found in

[8] Frank Hugh Foster, op. cit., page 29.

the early history of his own people and region the perfect material for a masterpiece. By selecting sexual sin as the type of all sin, he was true alike to the exigencies of drama and of history. In the setting which he chose, allegory was realism, the idea was life itself; and his prose, always remarkable for its polish and flexibility, and stripped, for once, of all superfluity, was reduced to the living idea, it intensified pure exposition to a quality comparable in its way to that of great poetry.

The compactness and complexity of the allegory will escape all save the most watchful readers. Let us consider the following passage as a representative example. Hester has learned that the magistrates and clergy are considering whether or not she ought to be separated from her child, and she waits upon Governor Bellingham in order to plead with him:

"On the wall hung a row of portraits, representing the forefathers of the Bellingham lineage, some with armor on their breasts, and others with stately ruffs and robes of peace. All were characterized by the sternness and severity which old portraits so invariably put on; as if they were the ghosts, rather than the pictures, of departed worthies, and were gazing with harsh and intolerant criticism at the pursuits and enjoyments of living men.

"At about the center of the oaken panels, that lined the hall, was suspended a suit of mail, not, like the pictures, an ancestral relic, but of the most modern date; for it had been manufactured by a skillful armorer in London, the same year in which Governor Bellingham came over to New England. There was a steel head-piece, a cuirass, a gorget, and greaves, with a pair of gauntlets and a sword hanging beneath; all, especially the helmet and breast-plate, so highly burnished as to glow with white radiance, and scatter an illumination everywhere about the floor. This bright panoply was not meant for mere idle show, but had been worn by the Governor on many a solemn muster and training field, and had glittered, moreover, at the head of a regiment in the Pequot war. For, though bred a lawyer, and accustomed to speak of Bacon, Coke, Noye, and Finch as his professional associates, the exigencies of this new country had transformed Governor Bellingham into a soldier as well as a statesman and ruler.

"Little Pearl—who was as greatly pleased with the gleaming armor as she had been with the glittering frontispiece of the house—spent some time looking into the polished mirror of the breast-plate.

" 'Mother,' cried she, 'I see you here. Look! Look!'

"Hester looked, by way of humoring the child; and she saw that, owing to the peculiar effect of the convex mirror, the scarlet letter was represented in gigantic and exaggerated proportions, so as to be greatly the most prominent feature of her appearance. In truth, she seemed absolutely hidden behind it. Pearl pointed upward, also, at a similar picture in the head-piece; smiling at her mother with the elfish intelligence that was so familiar an expression on her small physiognomy. That look of naughty merriment was likewise reflected in the mirror, with so much breadth and intensity of effect, that it made Hester Prynne feel as if it could not be the image of her own child, but of an imp who was seeking to mold itself into Pearl's shape."

The portraits are obviously intended as an apology for the static portraits in the book, as an illustration of the principle of simplification by distance and by generalization; the new armor, on the other hand, is the new faith which brought the Puritans to New England, and which not only shone with piety—"especially the helmet and breast-plate," the covering of the head and heart—but supported them in their practical struggles with physical adversaries, and which in addition altered their view of the life about them to dogmatic essentials, so that Hester was obliterated behind the fact of her sin, and Pearl transformed in view of her origin. Governor Bellingham, in his combination of legal training with military prowess, is representative of his fellow colonists, who displayed in a remarkable degree a capacity to act with great strength and with absolutely simple directness upon principles so generalized as scarcely to be applicable to any particular moral problem, which mastered moral difficulties not by understanding them, but by crushing them out.

Historically and relatively considered, Richard Bellingham might conceivably have been spared this function in the story, for of his group he was one of the two or three most humane and liberal; but the qualities represented were the qualities of the group of .which he was a leader, and were extremely evident in most of the actions of the colony. Perhaps the best—or in another sense, the worst—embodiment of these qualities is to be found in John Endecott, of whom Andrews gives the following characterization: "Endecott had few lovable qualities. He was stern, unyielding, and on some subjects a zealot. Johnson apostrophizes him as 'strong, valiant John,' whom Christ had called to be his soldier, but the Old Planters, most if not all of whom were Anglicans and demanded service according to the Book of Common Prayer, deemed themselves slaves and took in very bad part his determination to suppress the Church of England in the colony. They preferred Roger Conant, who though a less forcible man was one much easier to get along with. Endecott's later career discloses his attitude toward those who differed with him —the heathen Indian, the Quaker, the prisoner before him for judgment, and the Brownes and other upholders of the Anglican service who were disaffected with the Puritan government. It also shows his dislike of forms and devices that offended him— the Book of Common Prayer, the cross of St. George, and the Maypole. He was hard, intolerant, and at times cruel. Even the Massachusetts government caused him 'to be sadly admonished for his offense' in mutilating the flag at Salem in 1635, charging him with 'rashness, uncharitableness, indiscretion, and exceeding the limits of his calling'; and again in the same year 'committed' him for losing his temper. Endecott once apologized to Winthrop for striking 'goodman Dexter,' acknowledging that he was rash, but saying that Dexter's conduct 'would have provoked a very patient man.' The best that can be said of him has been said by Chapple ('The Public Service of John Endecott,' Historical Collections, Essex Institute), an essay in the best Palfrey manner. It is odd that Endecott should have chosen for his seal a skull and cross-bones." [9] It is interesting to observe in such a passage, as in many others, that the Puritans cannot be discussed, nor can they discuss each other, without the language employed exceeding the limits proper to predestinarians and invoking the traditional mo-

[9] Charles M. Andrews, op. cit., Vol. I, page 361, note 3.

rality of the older churches; yet the attempt to ignore this traditional morality as far as might be, and, in the matter of formal doctrine, to repudiate it, unquestionably had much to do with the formation of such characters as Professor Andrews here describes and as Hawthorne in the last passage quoted from him symbolizes. The imperceptive, unwavering brutality of many of the actions committed in the name of piety in the Massachusetts colonies more than justified the curse and prophecy uttered by Matthew Maule, that God would give these Puritans blood to drink; in the name of God, they had violently cut themselves off from human nature; in the end, that is in Hawthorne's generation and in the generation following, more than one of them drank his own heart's blood, as Hawthorne himself must have done in his ultimate and frustrated solitude, and more than one of them shed it.

It is noteworthy that in this passage from *The Scarlet Letter* Hawthorne turns his instrument of allegory, the gift of the Puritans, against the Puritans themselves, in order to indicate the limits of their intelligence; it is noteworthy also that this act of criticism, though both clear and sound, is negative, that he nowhere except in the very general notion of regeneration through repentance establishes the nature of the intelligence which might exceed the intelligence of the Puritans, but rather hints at the ideal existence of a richer and more detailed understanding than the Puritan scheme of life is able to contain. The strength of *The Scarlet Letter* is in part safe-guarded by the refusal to explore this understanding; the man who was able in the same lifetime to write *The New Adam and Eve*, to conceive the art-colony described in *The Marble Faun*, and to be shocked at the nude statues of antiquity, was scarcely the man to cast a clear and steady light upon the finer details of the soul.

The conception of the book in general is as cleanly allegorical as is the conception of the passage quoted. Hester represents the repentant sinner, Dimmesdale the half-repentant sinner, and Chillingworth the unrepentant sinner. The fact that Chillingworth's sin is the passion for revenge is significant only to the extent that this is perhaps the one passion which most completely isolates man from normal human sympathies and which therefore is most properly used to represent an unregenerate condition.

The method of allegorization is that of the Puritans themselves; the substance of the allegory remained in a crude form a part of their practical Christianity in spite of their Calvinism, just as it remained in their non-theological linguistic forms, just as we can see it in the language of the best poems of so purely and mystically Calvinistic a writer as Jones Very, a living language related to a living experience, but overflowing the limits of Calvinistic dogma; Hawthorne's point of view was naturally more enlightened than that of the Puritans themselves, yet it was insufficiently so to enable him to recover the traditional Christian ethics except in the most general terms and by way of historical sympathy, for had a more complete recovery been possible, he would not have been so narrowly bound to the method of allegory and the frustration of the later romances would scarcely have been so complete.

Once Hawthorne had reduced the problem of sin to terms as general as these, and had brought his allegory to perfect literary form, he had, properly speaking, dealt with sin once and for all; there was nothing further to be said about it. It would not serve to write another allegory with a new set of characters and a different sin as the motive; for the particular sin is not particular in function, but is merely representative of sin in general, as the characters, whatever their names and conditions may be, are merely representative of the major stages of sin—there is no escape from the generality so long as one adheres to the method. There was nothing further, then, to be done in this direction, save the composition of a few footnotes to the subject in the form of sketches.

The only alternative remaining was to move away from the allegorical extreme of narrative toward the specific, that is, toward the art of the novelist. The attempt was made, but fell short of success. In *The House of the Seven Gables* and in *The Marble Faun* alike the moral understanding of the action—and there is a serious attempt at such understanding, at least in *The Marble Faun*—is corrupted by a provincial sentimentalism ethically far inferior to the Manicheism of the Puritans, which was plain and comprehensive, however brutal. And Hawthorne had small gift for the creation of human beings, a defect allied to his other defects and virtues: even the figures in *The Scarlet Letter* are unsatisfactory if one comes to the book expecting to find a novel, for they draw their life not from simple and familiar human characteristics, as do the figures of Henry James, but from the precision and intensity with which they render their respective ideas; the very development of the story is neither narrative nor dramatic, but expository. When, as in *The Marble Faun* or *The House of the Seven Gables*, there is no idea governing the human figure, or when the idea is an incomplete or unsatisfactory equivalent of the figure, the figure is likely to be a disappointing spectacle, for he is seldom if ever a convincing human being and is likely to verge on the ludicrous. Hawthorne had not the rich and profound awareness of immediacy which might have saved a writer such as Melville in a similar predicament.

His effort to master the novelist's procedure, however, was not sustained, for his heart was not in it. In *The Blithedale Romance*, he began as a novelist, but lost himself toward the close in an unsuccessful effort to achieve allegory; the four unfinished romances represent similar efforts throughout.

His procedure in the last works was startlingly simple; so much so, that no one whom I can recollect has run the risk of defining it.

In *The Scarlet Letter* there occurs a formula which one might name the formula of alternative possibilities. In the ninth chapter, for example, there occurs the following passage: "The people, in the case of which we speak, could justify its prejudice against Roger Chillingworth by no fact or argument worthy of serious refutation. There was an aged handicraftsman, it is true, who had been a citizen of London at the period of Sir Thomas Overbury's murder, now some thirty years agone; he testified to having seen the physician, under some other name, which the narrator of the story had now forgotten, in company with Dr. Forman, the famous old conjuror, who was implicated in the affair of Overbury. Two or three individuals hinted, that the man of skill, during his Indian captivity, had enlarged his medical attainments by joining in the incantations of the savage priests; who were universally acknowledged to be powerful enchanters, often performing seemingly miraculous cures by their skill in the black art. A large number—many of them were persons of such sober sense and practical observation that their opinions would have been valuable in other matters—affirmed that Roger Chillingworth's aspect had undergone a remarkable change while he had dwelt in the town, and especially since his abode with Dimmesdale. At first, his expression had been calm, meditative, scholar-like. Now, there was something ugly and evil in his face, which they had not previously noticed, and which grew still more obvious to sight the oftener they looked upon him. According to the vulgar idea, the fire in his laboratory had been brought from the lower regions, and was fed with infernal fuel; and so, as might be expected, his visage was getting sooty with smoke."

In such a passage as this, the idea conveyed is clear enough, but the embodiment of the idea appears far-fetched, and Hawthorne offers it whimsically and apologetically, professing to let you take it or leave it. Another example occurs in the eighteenth chapter; Dimmesdale and Hester are sitting in the forest, planning the flight which ultimately is never to take place, and Pearl, the symbolic offspring of the untamed elements of human nature, and hence akin to the forest, which, in the Puritan mind, was ruled by Satan in person, plays apart: "A fox, startled from his sleep by her light footstep on the leaves, looked inquisitively at Pearl, as doubting whether it were better to steal off or renew his nap on the same spot. A wolf, it is said—but here the tale has surely lapsed into the improbable—came up and smelt of Pearl's robe, and offered his savage head to be patted by her hand. The truth seems to be, however, that the mother-forest, and these wild things which it nourished, all recognized a kindred wildness in the human child." Similarly, in *The Marble Faun*, one never learns whether Donatello had or had not the pointed ears which serve throughout the book as the physical symbol of his moral nature; the book ends with the question being put to Kenyon, who has had opportunities to observe, and with his refusing to reply.

This device, though it becomes a minor cause of irritation through constant recurrence, is relatively harmless, and at times is even used with good effect. If we reverse the formula, however, so as to make the physical representation perfectly clear but the meaning uncertain, we have a very serious situation; and this is precisely what occurs, in some measure toward the close of *The Blithedale Romance*, and without mitigation throughout the four unfinished romances. We have in the last all of the machinery and all of the mannerisms of the allegorist, but we cannot discover the substance of his communication, nor is he himself aware of it so far as we can judge. We have the symbolic footprint, the symbolic spider, the symbolic elixirs and poisons, but we have not that of which they are symbolic; we have the hushed, the tense and confidential manner, on the part of the narrator, of one who imparts a grave secret, but the words are inaudible. Yet we have not, on the other hand, anything approaching realistic fiction, for the events are improbable or even impossible, and the characters lack all reality. The technique neither of the novelist nor of the allegorist was available to Hawthorne when he approached the conditions of his own experience: he had looked for signals in nature so long and so intently, and his ancestors before him had done so for so many generations, that, like a man hypnotized, or like a man corroded with madness, he saw them; but he no longer had any way of determining their significance, and he had small talent for rendering their physical presence with intensity.

Percy Boynton,[10] in quoting the following passages from *Septimius Felton*, refers to it as a self-portrait: "As for Septimius, let him alone a moment or two, and then they would see him, with his head bent down, brooding, brooding, his eyes fixed on some chip, some stone, some common plant, any commonest

[10] *Literature and American Life*, by Percy H. Boynton; Ginn and Co., 1936; page 518.

thing, as if it were the clew and index to some mystery; and when, by chance startled out of these meditations, he lifted his eyes, there would be a kind of perplexity, a dissatisfied, foiled look in them, as if of his speculations he found no end."

It is in this generation and the next that we see most clearly and bitterly the realization of Maule's prophecy. These men were cut off from their heritage, from their source of significance, and were abnormally sensitive to the influence of European Romanticism. In Emerson[11] the terms of New England mysticism and of Romantic amoralism were fused and confused so inextricably that we have not yet worked ourselves free of them. In Poe, a man born without a background, New England or any other, Romantic doctrine was introduced directly, in a form free of theological terminology, but in a form none the less which would tend in the long run to support the influence of Emerson. In Melville, the greatest man of his era and of his nation, we find a writer superior at certain points in his career—in books such as *Moby Dick* and *Benito Cereno,* for example—to the confusion and apparently understanding it; at other points—in books like *Mardi* and *Pierre,*—succumbing to the confusion; at all points in his career made to suffer for the confusion of contemporary literary taste; and at the end, settling himself in silence, a figure more difficult to face than the later Hawthorne— more difficult, because more conscious, more controlled, and more nearly indifferent.

In Henry Adams we see the curse at work most clearly: intellectual but inconsecutive, unable to justify any principle of action, yet with a character of the highest, a character which demanded not only just action but its justification, he was damned to a kind of restless torment; in which, though an historian of great learning and of high academic distinction, he transformed the Middle Ages by a process of subtle falsification, into a symbol of his own latter-day New England longing; in which, though a stylist of great power and precision, he propounded the aes-

[11] This subject is fully discussed by H. B. Parkes, The Hound and Horn, V-4, July-Sept. 1932, pages 581-601, and *The Pragmatic Test.*

thetic theory that modern art must be confused to express confusion;[12] in which, though a philosopher of a sort, he created one of the most unphilosophical theories of history imaginable, as a poetic symbol of his own despair. In the suicide of Henry Adams' wife it is conceivable that we see the logical outcome of his own dilemma, an outcome in his own case prevented by the inheritance of character, which, like the inheritance of confusion, was bequeathed him by early New England.[13]

In *The Scarlet Letter*, then, Hawthorne composed a great allegory; or, if we look first at the allegorical view of life upon which early Puritan society was based, we might almost say that he composed a great historical novel. History, which by placing him in an anti-intellectual age had cut him off from the ideas which might have enabled him to deal with his own period, in part made up for the injustice by facilitating his entrance, for a brief time, into an age more congenial to his nature. Had he possessed the capacity for criticizing and organizing conceptions as well as for dramatizing them, he might have risen superior to his disadvantages, but like many other men of major genius he lacked this capacity. In turning his back upon the excessively simplified conceptions of his Puritan ancestors, he abandoned the only orderly concepts, whatever their limitations, to which he had access, and in his last work he is restless and dissatisfied. The four last romances are unfinished, and in each successive one he sought to incorporate and perfect elements from those preceding; the last, *The Dolliver Romance*, which he had sought to make the best, had he lived, is a mere fragment, but on the face of it is the most preposterous of all. His dilemma, the choice between abstractions inadequate or irrelevant to experience on the one hand, and experience on the other as far as practicable unilluminated by understanding, is tragically characteristic of the history of this country and of its literature; only a few scattered individuals, at the cost of inordinate labor, and often impermanently, have achieved the permeation of human

[12] See the last three or four pages of *Mont Saint-Michel and Chartres*.
[13] This idea is very ably defended by Katherine Simonds, the New England Quarterly, December, 1936.

experience by a consistent moral understanding which results in wisdom and in great art. If art is to be measured by the greatness of the difficulties overcome—and the measure is not wholly unreasonable, for there can scarcely be virtue without a comprehension of sin, and the wider and more careful the comprehension the richer the virtue—then these few writers are very great indeed. Hawthorne, when he reversed his formula of alternative possibilities, and sought to grope his way blindly to significance, made the choice of the later Romantics; and his groping was met wherever he moved by the smooth and impassive surface of the intense inane.

FENIMORE COOPER

or The Ruins of Time

"From this point the northern side of the bay is a confused mass of villages, villas, ruins, palaces, and vines, until we reach its extremity; a low promontory, like its opposite neighbor. A small island comes next, a sort of natural sentinel; then the coast sweeps northward into another and smaller bay, rich to satiety with relics of the past, terminating at a point some miles farther seaward, with a high, reddish, sandy bluff, which almost claims to be a mountain."

—Wing-and-Wing

SINCE THE PUBLICATION of Robert Spiller's admirable work on Cooper,[1] his importance as a social critic has been generally recognized; his literary virtues have had in the past their distinguished admirers, though today his reputation as a literary artist is very much in eclipse. Of these virtues Mr. Spiller, who has done more for him than has any other critic of our period, says relatively little, and it may be profitable to attempt a redefinition of them in part in the light of Mr. Spiller's examination of the social theories.

Cooper believed in democratic government; and, as an aggressively patriotic American, he was capable, among the enemies of democratic theory, of going to considerable length in its defense; but he distrusted the common and uneducated man—that is, he feared irrational mob action; he feared that the idea of democracy might easily be degraded into the dogma that whatever a majority decides is right. Such a degradation would result naturally in the immediate subversion of law and of civilization; and it would open the way for all kinds of illegal individual action, which might in turn lead to the acquisition by a few

[1] *Fenimore Cooper, Critic of His Times,* by Robert E. Spiller; Minton Balch and Co., 1931.

176

uneducated and unscrupulous men of great power, either by way of finance or by way of demagoguery—that is, he saw that it might be only a short step from irrational democracy to unscrupulous oligarchy. In such works as *The Redskins, Home as Found,* and *The Ways of the Hour*—extremely bad novels, all of them, but extremely acute criticism of his period and of ours —he portrays and more particularly he comments directly upon the incipient symptoms of the disease which he intensely feared, even though he did not and could scarcely have been expected to foresee the rapidity and extent of its development. In *The Bravo,* in so far as the book is to be regarded merely as a social novel, he depicts the evils of oligarchy; within a decade of his death, the oligarchy of which he had discerned the first symptoms was developing with astonishing rapidity, and within two decades of his death it had as regards practical results rendered the legal government very largely null, and the nation was adrift in the administration of U. S. Grant.

The nature of this development he understood well enough; with characteristically heavy but accurate irony, he described it in the pages of his neglected satirical allegory, *The Monikins,* a work which contains much of his ablest prose: "I found . . . that the wisest and best of the species, or, what is much the same thing, the most responsible, uniformly maintain that he who has the largest stake in society is, in the nature of things, the most qualified to administer its affairs. By a stake in society is meant, agreeable to universal convention, a multiplication of those interests which occupy us in our daily concerns—or what is vulgarly called property. This principle works by exciting us to do right through those heavy investments of our own which would inevitably suffer were we to do wrong. The proposition is now clear, nor can the premises readily be mistaken. Happiness is the aim of society; and property, or a vested interest in society, is the best pledge of our disinterestedness and justice, and the best qualification for its proper control. It follows as a legitimate corollary, that a multiplication of those interests will increase the stake, and render us more and more worthy of the trust by elevating us as near as may be to the pure and ethereal condition of the angels." This may fairly be taken as a prophecy of the approach, if not of the imminence, of celestial luminaries of the quality of Vanderbilt, Sage, Drew, and Gould.

As a check to the social danger, he envisaged two defenses, both of which were more or less in effect at the time of his writing, and both of which crumbled at the first impact of the enemy in the actual event: abstract principle, as embodied in law, especially in the courts; and the extension into other parts of the country, and the perpetuation, of an hereditary landed aristocracy such as that of New York—of a class wealthy enough to enjoy leisure for study and for self-cultivation, yet not wealthy enough, and too cultivated to desire, to obtain inordinate power for its own sake. This aristocracy should serve as a guide, a model, and a stabilizing force; it was the class of which his American Gentleman was the type. In the Littlepage trilogy he made his most ambitious and successful effort to portray this aristocracy as it had existed in New York and to define its social function.

In connection with this check to the danger, he seems to have been guilty of certain errors. He failed to see that because of technological and industrial growth and because of the westward expansion which was receiving only at the time of his death the rapid acceleration which was to effect in three decades the greatest migration in the annals, whether written or reconstructed, of man, a new financial oligarchy was bound to arise so rapidly as to render his landed aristocracy negligible and casually to feed upon and absorb it. Further, he apparently believed it possible to establish in actual social institutions a close relationship between worth and ability on the one hand, and, on the other hand, wealth, family, and political influence, whereas all history indicates this to be impossible. At the end of his life, he still preferred democratic government to any other, but he had little hope for democracy. Spiller quotes the following passage from a posthumous fragment:[2] "Nevertheless the community will live on, suffer, and be deluded; it may even fancy itself almost within reach of perfection, but it will live on to be dis-

[2] Ibid., pages 315-6.

appointed. There is no such thing on earth—and the only real question for the American statesman is, to measure the results of different defective systems for the government of the human race. We are far from saying that our own, with all its flagrant and obvious defects, will be the worst, more especially when considered solely in connection with whole numbers; though we cannot deny, nor do we wish to conceal, the bitterness of the wrongs that are so frequently inflicted by the many on the few. This is, perhaps, the worst species of tyranny. He who suffers under the arbitrary power of a single despot, or by the selfish exactions of a privileged few, is certain to be sustained by the sympathies of the masses. But he who is crushed by the masses themselves must look beyond the limits of his earthly being for consolation and support. The wrongs committed by democracies are of the most cruel character; and though wanting in that apparent violence and sternness that mark the course of law in the hands of narrower governments, for it has no need of this severity, they carry with them in their course all the feelings that render injustice and oppression intolerable."

Of these wrongs he himself had suffered more than the common portion. Out of love for his country and the desire to perpetuate her institutions, he had criticized such of her vices as appeared to imperil her life, and he had been met with hatred. His criticism being unanswerable, and the hatred therefore intense, he had been libelled in the press, and though for fifteen years he had won suit after suit in the courts and had silenced his detractors, the press had won the sympathy of the multitude and Cooper had lost his public. He had defined for posterity the dangers which threatened; and he had established in legal precedent that was to endure until late in the century the laws of libel and the public rights of the private gentleman; but he knew at the end that he could not stay or turn the enchanneled torrent of human stupidity, which, when eventually we regard it behind us, we know as history. His concern was primarily for public morality; it was the concern of the statesman, or of the historian, first, and of the artist but secondarily; this concern was already obsolescent in America, and Henry Adams found it a generation after Cooper's death to be obsolete. Its disappearance, no less than the disappearance of the theological dogmas supporting private morality, contributed in some measure to the later difficulties of Henry James.

II

The Littlepage novels—*Satanstoe, The Chainbearer,* and *The Redskins*—were written to illustrate a thesis: the justice of the property-rights of the landed proprietors. But underlying this is a more general thesis: the social function of an aristocracy, a concept based on the old but dying social organization of New York. To illustrate this thesis, he was forced to contrast the virtues of the aristocracy with the defects of the vulgar; that this contrast represented not his own complete view of the two social classes thus roughly divided but an arbitrary isolation of qualities in each class for purposes of expository effectiveness, we may see readily enough in his other novels: in his novels of adventure, his favorite characters are drawn from the lower classes, and in *The Bravo,* another thesis novel, this one written to exhibit the dangers of oligarchy, his heroic figures are drawn from the lower classes and his corrupt from the upper.

Like most novelists of class-struggle, he separated his characters pretty sharply into the more or less Calvinistical categories of the socially saved and the socially damned. The only American novel of class-struggle of any importance, and so far as my reading extends, to surpass this formula, is *The Octopus,* by Frank Norris; a novel in which the social struggle sets in motion and complicates certain dramas of private morality, so that we get a novel of a very impressive kind in spite of the illiteracy of two thirds of the writing, and in spite of the plunge into Emersonian mysticism at the close, in which the author endeavors to cancel the drama that he has constructed. Since Cooper is dealing primarily with manners and not with morals—that is, with society as such, and not with the salvation of the soul—his figures must of necessity be offered as representative social types and not as moral abstractions like the figures in Hawthorne.

They are types of manners, and not types of morality; they are thus closer to the surface of life, to the daily reality which we perceive superficially about us; and we are tempted—or more truly, we are forced—to regard them as human beings primarily, not as dramatized ideas. But as human beings they are unduly simplified, and in their purity of type inheres a certain quality, very slight in a few cases, very great in a few, and moderately obvious in most, of priggishness or of unreality. Furthermore, the dichotomy of Good and Evil in Hawthorne is essentially so serious that the extreme concentration upon it which is implicit in allegorical simplification appears justified. The corresponding concepts in the field of manners, however,—the Genteel and the Vulgar—appear at a considerable remove from the spiritual seriousness of the Good and the Evil; we can demonstrate certain imperfect relationships between the two pairs of concepts easily enough in a rational fashion, but the second pair is derivative and therefore inferior, and it is bound to be felt as inferior when perceived in action; so that a concentration by Cooper upon the second pair of abstractions comparable, though far less intense, to the concentration upon the first pair by Hawthorne, is certain in itself to create in some degree an atmosphere of priggishness. The vigor with which Cooper realizes at least a few characters and patterns of action, and the sense with which he leaves us when the books have long been read and laid away, of a rich and varied way of life, are sufficient evidence of the reality of his genius, for these ends are achieved in the face of obstacles.

This effect of priggishness is sure to be intensified in an era like our own, in which the concept of a traditional aristocracy is obsolete and even as an historical phenomenon is seldom understood. For the modern American who has let himself be seduced by any of the absolute categories of our own period—more especially, in this case, of the radical labor movement, since these categories are diametrically opposed to those of Cooper—an understanding of Cooper, and I mean an understanding of Cooper merely as an artist portraying in some measure a life which he knew, may prove difficult or even impossible. Cooper's dichotomy of the Genteel and the Vulgar may appear to correspond precisely to the later dichotomy of the Parasitic and the Productive, the emphasis having been shifted from intrinsic qualities to what is conceived as material effectiveness. For any modern American, an act of sympathetic historical imagination is necessary to understand Cooper; for the American whose perceptions are governed by a scheme as simple as Cooper's, but the exact reverse of it, this act will presumably be impossible.

Because of the simplification, the central figures of the Littlepage novels—the Littlepages and their respective loves—were doomed to be uninteresting, even if Cooper had not had an unqualified penchant for conventional sentimental romance as the structural principle in plot. The secondary figures, even when employed more or less obviously for illustrative purposes, are frequently more successful. The best single creation of the Littlepage novels—a creation rivalling Natty Bumppo—is Jason Newcome, the devious and moralizing New Englander. In *Satanstoe*, the secondary and tragic love affair of Guert Ten Eyck and of Mary Wallace is moving and suggests complexity and fullness of character not found in any other love story in Cooper. Guert, Mary Wallace, the loping dominie, Andries Coejemans, and in a smaller measure the somewhat melodramatic but still effective Aaron Thousandacres, are memorable creations.

In the first two novels, especially, of the Littlepage trilogy, Cooper endeavored to underline certain aspects of New York society which he believed deserving of preservation and extension; and in the third of the series, *The Redskins*, he sought primarily to demonstrate the opposing evil, the evil of confusing the whim of the mob with the principle of democracy, a subject with which he dealt in other late novels: in *The Crater*, in *Home as Found*, and especially in *The Ways of the Hour*, a novel in which is portrayed in a manner of the greatest accuracy so far as the social phenomena are concerned, though profoundly unsatisfactory as art, the way in which criminal justice may be subverted by unrestrained popular meddling. In *The Redskins*, *Home as Found*, and *The Ways of the Hour* Cooper is nearly at his worst as a novelist—his worst, absolutely considered, is the initial effort, *Precaution*, and its nearest rival, perhaps, is *Mer-*

cedes of Castille—for in these three works, he is not displaying a way of life, but is demonstrating assorted vices and his tendency to overemphasis becomes so extreme as to destroy both plot and character. The criticism offered in these books, however, is both just and penetrating, and the reader with taste and patience can cull from them if he so desires a collection of epigrams as sound, as biting, and as numerous as he is likely to find in any other three volumes in English. *The Monikins*, a satirical allegory on the subject of various social systems, though tiresome in the main, offers the same fragmentary rewards, and perhaps in a larger measure, in addition to the remarkable summary of the life and death of the elder Goldencalf, with which the work begins.

The Monikins has commonly been regarded as one of the worst of Cooper's efforts, and even those who have found it in one manner or another interesting have objected to the narrator's account of his pedigree and of his childhood, but there is something horrible in the account, which, brief and fragmentary as the passage may be, is unrivalled in its particular fashion in English prose. "I have generally considered myself on a level with the most ancient gentlemen of Europe, on the score of descent," says the narrator, "few families being more clearly traced into the mist of time than that of which I am a member. My descent from my father is undeniably established by the parish register as well as by the will of that person himself, and I believe no man could more directly prove the truth of the whole career of his family than it is in my power to show that of my ancestor up to the hour when he was found, in the second year of his age, crying with cold and hunger in the parish of St. Giles, in the city of Westminster, and in the United Kingdom of Great Britain." In the same tone of precise and unwavering respect, the career of the elder Goldencalf, financial and domestic, and fearful in its intense inhumanity, is carried to its close: "The difficult breathing, haggard countenance, and broken utterance of my father struck me with awe. This was the first death-bed by which I had ever stood; and the admonishing picture of time passing into eternity was indelibly stamped on my memory. It was not only a death-bed scene, but it was a family death-bed scene. I know not how it was, but I thought my ancestor looked more like the Goldencalfs than I had ever seen him look before." Thomas Goldencalf is literally on the brink of eternity throughout the short narrative; for, as his son, the supposed narrator, informs us, he rose directly and with no antecedents from the obscurity of time, and his life was reduced so purely to a single passion, one might say to a single perception, that he existed but as a silhouette upon the void and sank as directly into the void as he had arisen from it. The cold and formal irony of the prose achieves at times a metaphysical violence which puts one in mind of Pope.

The Bravo, one of the most important of the novels of social criticism, suffers in certain respects by comparison with the first two novels of the Littlepage trilogy: no single Italian character is realized with the same effect of intimacy as that achieved in the best American characters, although no major character, perhaps, is quite so simplified as are the representatives of the Littlepage family itself, for the conception of The Bravo does not enforce such simplification. The protagonist is a more or less normal man, endeavoring to maintain his integrity in a struggle with a variety of hidden evils. He is essentially active and individual, and not a social type, although the subtleties of his surface are not rendered with any such perception as that displayed in the creation of Jason Newcome and of Guert Ten Eyck. The manner in which the aristocrats themselves are corrupted by their fears of each other—the subtle inter-relation and inter-propagation among such vices as avarice, desire for power, and fear—offers a moral portrait worthy of Hawthorne.

The stylistic tone of The Bravo is of the slightly sentimental variety at the time regarded as indispensable to historical romance; this is no doubt a defect, but the tone is at least consistently maintained, so that once one has become familiar with it, one can in a measure forget it, and can appreciate subtleties of perception much as in any other style. The fifteenth chapter, for example, describing the murder of Antonio, is very impressive as one comes to it in the actual narrative, but is much less impressive if one reads it in isolation. Coming to it from the beginning of the story, one is not only familiar with the style, but one is acutely aware of the symbolic value of the moonlit water, and of fragments of action discernible upon it, in this narrative of secret and evasive evil. In isolation the passage appears to display something of the over-wrought affectation of Poe; in its context, the tone is supported, as it is never supported in Poe, by a comprehensible theme, so that the details, melodramatic, perhaps, if read alone, are sustained by a genuinely dramatic significance. The two companion pieces of *The Bravo*, *The Heidenmauer* and *The Headsman*, are less remarkable, though *The Heidenmauer* contains a fairly memorable character in the Abbot of Limburg.

III

In the Leatherstocking Series, as in the other novels of American history and of frontier adventure, and as in the sea stories (except *The Crater*), we have nothing whatever to do with social criticism, or at least nothing of importance. One of the Leatherstocking Series, however, *The Pioneers*, the fourth in the series but the first to be written, should be mentioned in connection with *Satanstoe* and *The Chainbearer* as one of Cooper's three most interesting novels of manners; like the first two Littlepage novels, it is a portrait of life on the frontier, but in a considerable measure of the semi-aristocratic frontiersman. These three works should be regarded as a prelude to such works by Mrs. Wharton as the four novelettes of the Old New York Series and *The Age of Innocence*; in spite of great defects they have great vigor, and as regards the portrayal of their particular place and period they have no rivals and must always remain as a part of our historical literature if as nothing more.

The inferiority of plot in Cooper to the incidental is tacitly recognized by him in the fact that the one figure who unifies all five of the Leatherstocking novels is a secondary figure in all of them; in each novel he is the practical abettor of the loves of the pair about whom the conventional plot is constructed, although in *The Pathfinder* he appears for a time as a rival in love to his friend.

These novels are familiar to every reader, and comment upon them may appear superfluous; nevertheless, familiarity appears to have bred in this case a good deal of contempt, and certain things, perhaps, need to be stated briefly.

It is the isolated adventures of Natty, and the continuity of his character, that bring the novels to life; although there are other excellent characterizations, especially of the residents of the frontier village of *The Pioneers,* and of the Indians Mahtoree and Hardheart, and of the emigrant family of *The Prairie.* And here we begin to encounter some of the strange paradoxes of Cooper's achievement; for if Natty is his greatest single achievement— and great he is, a great national myth, with a life over and above the life of the books in which he appears, a reality surpassing that even of an historical figure such as Daniel Boone—yet only two of these novels, *The Pioneers* and conceivably *The Prairie,* could rank among Cooper's half dozen best individual novels. Furthermore, the best single passage of prose in Cooper is probably the seventh chapter of *The Deerslayer,* a book which displays few other serious merits, and which even as a story purely of adventure is far inferior in plot and in movement to half a dozen other stories by Cooper. The next best prose in the series, and perhaps in Cooper, though this is doubtful, is probably to be found in the first and last chapters of *The Prairie,* heavily dramatic as they may conceivably be. The best single plot of adventure in Cooper is beyond a doubt that of *The Last of the Mohicans,* but the style in this work is so consistently florid and redundant that in spite of the action, in spite of the magnificent timing of many scenes, in spite of a certain amount of fairly respectable characterization, the book nowhere rises to a level of seriousness. It is curious that the tone of conventional romance which vitiates a great part of his effort should have accumulated so unfortunately here, for there are passages in other books in the series which are not only beautiful but beautiful in a restrained and classical fashion, and which display great richness of moral substance.

The seventh chapter of *The Deerslayer*, or more properly its first incident, Natty's encounter with the Indian whom he is forced to kill, is probably as great an achievement of its length as one will find in American fiction outside of Melville. The prose is plain and factual, yet by rendering with a kind of bare precision the drifting of the canoes, the motion of the water, and the caution with which Natty views the edge of the forest, Cooper communicates with a power that has rarely been equalled the tremendous and impersonal quiet of the virgin American wilderness: "The air, for wind it could scarcely be called, was still light, it is true, but it had increased a little in the course of the night, and as the canoes were mere feathers on the water, they had drifted twice the expected distance; and, what was still more dangerous, had approached so near the base of the mountain that here rose precipitously from the eastern shore as to render the carols of the birds plainly audible. This was not the worst. The third canoe had taken the same direction, and was slowly drifting toward a point where it must inevitably touch, unless turned aside by a shift of wind or human hands. In other respects nothing presented itself to attract attention or to awaken alarm."

One of the canoes goes aground, and Natty must rescue it, in spite of the danger to himself, in order to insure the safety of his friends. "If anyone had been lying in wait for the arrival of the waif, he must be seen, and the utmost caution in approaching the shore became indispensable; if no one was in ambush, hurry was unnecessary. The point being nearly diagonally opposite the Indian encampment, he hoped the last, though the former was not only possible but probable; for the savages were prompt in adopting all the expedients of their particular modes of warfare, and quite likely had many scouts searching the shores for crafts to carry them off to the castle. As a glance at the lake from any height or projection would expose the smallest object on its surface, there was little hope that either of the canoes could pass unseen; and Indian sagacity needed no instruction to tell which way a boat or a log would drift when the direction of the wind was known. As Deerslayer drew nearer and nearer to the land, the stroke of his paddle grew slower, his eye became more watchful, and his ears and nostrils almost dilated with the effort to detect any lurking danger. 'Twas a trying moment for a novice, nor was there the encouragement which even the timid sometimes feel when conscious of being observed and commended. He was entirely alone, thrown on his own resources, and was cheered by no friendly eye, emboldened by no encouraging voice. Notwithstanding all these circumstances, the most experienced veteran in forest warfare could not have behaved better. Equally free from recklessness and hesitation, his advance was marked by a sort of philosophical prudence that appeared to render him superior to all motives but those which were best calculated to effect his purpose. Such was the commencement of a career in forest exploits that afterward rendered this man, in his way, and under the limits of his habits and opportunities, as renowned as many a hero whose name has adorned the pages of works more celebrated than legends simple as ours can ever become." The explicit comment of the historian at the close of this passage is one of the greatest triumphs of Cooper's rhetoric; the quietness of the prose and of the scene is not impaired, but the prose suddenly takes on a quality of universality and of grandeur such as to prepare one for the metaphysical quality of the action shortly to follow.

The Indian in ambush fires and misses, attacks, and then, being outwitted by Deerslayer but allowed to escape, retreats to cover; Deerslayer is quickly on shore and behind a tree. Then commences the series of hesitations on the part of Deerslayer to kill this man, hesitations which arouse the wonder and then the contempt of the Indian. Deerslayer has never killed a man, yet he has embarked upon the career of a professional scout, and this Indian is his enemy. His wonder, his hesitation, the infallibility of his instincts and muscular reactions, the immense passivity of the morning wilderness, give the scene something of the tenderness and wonder of idyllic first love. But this is first death, and not first love; and the act must be committed in solitude and with deliberation. Deerslayer's consciousness of the significance of the act which he momently withholds, and the pure spiritual isolation of the consciousness, the quiet clarity with which the whole is rendered, constitute, surely, one of the most remarkable passages in our literature.

After some maneuvering, Deerslayer persuades the Indian to give up the canoes without bloodshed, or he believes that he persuades him, and then, after a momentary suspicion of treachery, he pushes off from shore: "This distrust, however, seemed to be altogether uncalled for, and, as if ashamed to have entertained it, the young man averted his look, and stepped carelessly up to his boat. Here he began to push the canoe from the shore, and to make his other preparations for departing. He might have been thus employed a minute, when, happening to turn his face toward the land, his quick and certain eye told him at a glance, the imminent jeopardy in which his life was placed. The black, ferocious eyes of the savage were glancing on him, like those of the crouching tiger, through a small opening in the bushes, and the muzzle of his rifle seemed already to be opening in a line with his own body.

"Then, indeed, the long practice of Deerslayer as a hunter did him good service. Accustomed to fire with the deer on the bound, and often when the precise position of the animal's body had in a manner to be guessed at, he used the same expedients here. To cock and poise his rifle were the acts of a single moment and a single motion; then, aiming almost without sighting, he fired into the bushes where he knew a body ought to be in order to sustain the appalling countenance which alone was visible. There was not time to raise the piece any higher or to take a more deliberate aim. So rapid were his movements that both parties discharged their pieces at the same instant, the concussions mingling in one report. The mountains, indeed, gave back but a single echo. Deerslayer dropped his piece, and stood, with head erect, steady as one of the pines in the calm of a June morning, watching the result, while the savage gave the yell that has become historical for its appalling influence, leaped through the bushes, and came bounding across the open ground, flourishing a tomahawk. Still Deerslayer moved not, but stood with his unloaded rifle fallen against his shoulders, while, with a hunter's

189

habits, his hands were mechanically feeling for the powder-horn and charger. When about forty feet from his enemy, the savage hurled his keen weapon; but it was with an eye so vacant, and a hand so unsteady and feeble, that the young man caught it as it was flying past him. At that instant the Indian staggered and fell his whole length on the ground." We have thus the instantaneous coincidence of intuition and determinant action, and the quick rush and ebbing of life, as symbolized by the ease with which the hatchet falls into the hand of Deerslayer; and thereafter a brief passage in which the Indian dies in Deerslayer's arms at the edge of the lake, a passage in which the quiet of the morning is reëstablished. One should mention also Deerslayer's perception of the opening of the rifle muzzle, a fine detail, by means of which his perception of the Indian's aim is communicated.

The skill of this backwoodsman, and the skill as well as other characteristics attributed by Cooper to the Indians, are frequently derided, but probably with small justice. In any environment certain particular skills will be generally developed, which are foreign to other environments, and the skills required in the wilderness are now far away from us and of their nature we can have but very small understanding. Yet the feats performed in Cooper's novels with the canoe are of no greater moment than the feats performed daily on our highways with much more dangerous engines, sometimes disastrously, often with success; they are as nothing compared to the daily feats of the army flyer. We should remember, moreover, that if any particular way of life long exists, or even if any particular exercise is long practiced with assiduity, there will inevitably arise, once or twice or occasionally more often in a generation, an individual of a skill such as far to surpass the powers of credible description. The boxer of genius, or even the billiard-player of genius, may perform feats which if recounted in detail would seem far less plausible than the most extraordinary feats of Leatherstocking.

Furthermore, as to feats of woodmanship, the historic feats of the partisan leader, Rogers, as described by the meticulous Parkman in *Montcalm and Wolfe,* surpass anything imagined by Cooper. And Parkman, who objects to Cooper's treatment of Indian character, especially in regard to the capacity delineated for heroic action and for love at a higher level than that of physical passion, yet recounts in *The Conspiracy of Pontiac* the case of a young Indian who followed his white mistress back to the edge of the settlements when she had been captured by a marauding band of whites, in order to be with her as long as possible and to hunt for her; and his account of Pontiac himself establishes that remarkable Ottawa not only as a man of genius but as thoroughly capable of heroic action. Our historic knowledge of Tecumseh, of King Philip, of Massassoit, of the humane and heroic Canonchet, should justify Cooper beyond all question at least as regards the general outlines of his characterization. That such characters were exceptional among the Indians goes without saying, but they would have been exceptional anywhere; and that there were aspects of Indian life on which Cooper seldom dwells is equally certain, but it is also true that the houses of Shakespeare's London were in general, drafty, smoky, dirty, infected with disease, and full of vermin, and Shakespeare is not in general blamed for dealing primarily with the spiritual problems of such men as Macbeth and Coriolanus.

Anyone who will take the trouble to acquaint himself with the works of Parkman—and anyone who will not is to be commiserated in general and distrusted in particular as a commentator on certain aspects of American literature and history—or anyone who will read a dozen odd journals of life in the wilderness, will scarcely, I imagine, object very seriously to this aspect of Cooper on purely factual grounds. Cooper errs not in the plausibility of his facts, but in relying so heavily for the maintenance of interest on so limited a range of facts, and frequently in the sentimental and inflated redundancy with which the facts are rendered; and so far as the Indians are concerned, this redundancy is not without its verisimilitude, whatever we may think of its absolute merits as style, for the eloquence of the Indians in their more formal and heroic moments, as we find it recorded by those who

191

knew them intimately and in their primitive condition, is not as remote from the redundant passages of Cooper as one might at first glance suppose.

This particular defect of style damages white and Indian character about equally, so far as its effect on the modern reader is concerned—and indeed, though the Indian, historically considered, may actually have employed a roughly similar style on certain occasions, one may reasonably protest that in the interests of true eloquence he should not have done so—but in some of the novels, in which the style is not pushed to the appalling limits reached in *The Last of the Mohicans,* one becomes, as I have said in discussing *The Bravo,* more or less accustomed to it, and forgets it. This is largely true of *The Wept of Wish-ton-Wish,* a novel containing three of Cooper's best Indian Characters, all of them based on historic Indians: Uncas, the Pequot or Mohegan, who betrayed his chieftain, Sassacus, sold himself to the English, and helped in the destruction of his own people, first in the Pequot War, and later, as an old man, in King Philip's War; Philip, or Metacom, the Wampanoag; and Canonchet, the Narraganset. One of the better scenes in Cooper, in spite of the sentimental rhetoric is that in which Uncas, who feels himself to be judged a traitor by his captive Canonchet, whose father, Miantonomo, he had murdered years before, endeavors to break the moral character of Canonchet by subtle spiritual torture before murdering him. The conception of Canonchet's white wife, who recovers only at the moment before death her memory of childhood and her childish fear of the forest and of the Indian as the symbols of darkness and of evil, is a conception which deserved a more successful rendering, but which is rendered with sufficient success to merit more appreciation than it has received.[3] This novel is notable also for certain passages of historical exposition, especially in the earlier chapters; passages in which Cooper appears as one of the last representatives of the great tradition of formal historical narrative, of which Hume, Gibbon, and Macaulay are the masters. The passages are brief and scat-

[3] Parkman recounts in *Pontiac,* Chapter XXVIII, an historical incident closely though incompletely resembling this.

tered; they show the tradition in a state of decay, and corroded by sentiment; but they are still in the great tradition, and as prose they probably surpass most passages of comparable length to be found in Prescott or even in Parkman; they are a moving, if melancholy, spectacle.

One other novel of frontier adventure, *The Oak Openings*, deserves particular attention, if only because of its extraordinary difference from the other novels on similar subjects. As a story of simple adventure, it is one of Cooper's best; as a portrait of the Indian in his more familiar and less heroic moments, it is both convincing and amusing and has no parallel in Cooper or elsewhere in our literature. The scenes in which the assembled chieftains discuss the anthropological theories of the errant clergyman and conclude that the Indians are not descended from the lost tribes of Israel are especially admirable. "I am a Pottawattamie," says Crowsfeather. "My brothers know that tribe. It is not a tribe of Jews, but a tribe of Injins. It is a great tribe. It never was *lost*. It *cannot* be lost. No tribe better knows all the paths, and all the best routes to every point where it wishes to go. It is foolish to say you can lose a Pottawattamie. A duck would be as likely to lose itself as a Pottawattamie. I do not speak for the Ottawas; I speak for the Pottawattamies. . . . We are not lost; we are not Jews. I have done."

IV

In addition to the novels which I have mentioned and a few others of similar nature, there remain a somewhat miscellaneous lot of novels superficially of a class in that they are all novels of adventure and all save two, *The Spy* and *Lionel Lincoln*, of adventure at sea.

The Spy, a very early and fairly popular work, is a second rate novel of adventure, as are also *Homeward Bound*, *The Pilot*, and *The Two Admirals*. *The Red Rover*, a sea story, is probably the best tale of adventure, questions of style aside, to be found in Cooper except for *The Last of the Mohicans*, but like *The Last of the Mohicans* it has few other merits. *Afloat and Ashore*, and its sequel, *Miles Wallingford*, combine fair sea-adventure, one of the best incidents being based on an actual occurrence recounted by Irving in his *Astoria*, with a fairly pleasant and moderately sentimental portrait of early New York manners. *Jack Tier* is a novel of sentimental adventure at sea which is chiefly remarkable for the portrait of the extraordinary figure from whom the book takes its title; among the sea stories, it has something of the casual charm displayed by *The Oak Openings* among the novels of the wilderness. *The Sea Lions*, though diffuse and full of irrelevancies, offers a portrait of Yankee avarice in a struggle with death in the antarctic circle, which deserved a more careful treatment.

Three other stories—*Lionel Lincoln*, *Wing-and-Wing*, and especially *The Water-Witch*—are remarkable for their rhetorical experiments, and display Cooper in a capacity in which he has never been seriously studied or even regarded.

In *Lionel Lincoln*, the character in connection with whom the experimental rhetoric is most often successful, is Polwarth, a British officer stationed in Boston, a gentleman by birth and courageous by nature, but stout, overfond of eating, and somewhat talkative. Polwarth must beyond any question be the prototype of W. G. Simms' Porgy, and though Cooper makes less use of Polwarth than Simms makes of his southerner, Cooper's portrait is in some ways the more effective. Polwarth speaks a species of semi-Elizabethan prose which is not without its wit and its poetry, and of which the very affectation has a real stylistic charm. The following passage, taken from the ninth chapter, is descriptive of the removal of the British troops from Boston the night before the battle of Lexington:

"Polwarth had established himself by the side of Lionel, much to the ease of his limbs, and as they moved slowly into the light, all those misgivings which had so naturally accompanied his musings on the difficulties of a partisan irruption, vanished before the loveliness of the time, and possibly before the quietude of the action.

" 'There are moments when I could fancy the life of a sailor,' he said, leaning indolently back, and playing with one hand in the water. 'This pulling about in boats is easy work, and must be capital assistance for a heavy digestion, inasmuch as it furnishes air with as little violent exercise as may be. Your marine should lead a merry life of it!'

" 'They are said to murmur at the clashing of their duties with those of the sea-officers,' said Lionel; 'and I have often heard them complain of a want of room to make use of their legs.'

" 'Humph!' ejaculated Polwarth; 'the leg is a part of a man for which I see less actual necessity than for any other portion of his frame. I often think there has been a sad mistake in the formation of the animal; as, for instance, one can be a very good waterman, as you see, without legs—a good fiddler, a first-rate tailor, a lawyer, a doctor, a parson, a very tolerable cook, and in short, anything but a dancing-master. I see no use in a leg unless it be to have the gout—at any rate, a leg of twelve inches is as good as one a mile long, and the saving might be appropriated to the nobler parts of the animal; such as the brain and the stomach.'

" 'You forget the officer of light-infantry,' said Lionel, laughing.

" 'You might give him a couple of inches more; though as everything in this wicked world is excellent only by comparison, it would amount to the same thing, and on my system a man would be just as fit for the light-infantry without, as with legs; and he would get rid of a good deal of troublesome manoeuvering, especially of this new exercise. It would then become a delightful service, Leo; for it may be said to monopolize all the poetry of military life, as you may see. Neither the imagination nor the body can require more than we enjoy at this moment, and of what use, I would ask, are our legs? if anything, they are incumbrances in this boat. Here we have a soft moon, and softer seats—smooth water, and a stimulating air—on one side fine country, which, though but faintly seen, is known to be fertile and rich to abundance; and on the other a picturesque town, stored with condiments of every climate—even those rascally privates look mellowed by the moonbeams, with their scarlet coats and glittering arms! . . . Where now are your companies of the lines; your artillery and dragoons; your engineers and staff! night-capped and snoring to a man, while we enjoy here the very dessert of existence— I wish I could hear a nightingale!' "

This is obviously less excellent than Falstaff, but on the other hand it does not really endeavor to compete with Falstaff, and, having a minor excellence of its own, should survive the comparison. I should like to insist that here, as in other scattered passages of Cooper, there is a prose possessing at once an authentic poetic perception and a rhetorical procedure both ingenious and controlled; that these scattered passages are frequently of sufficient length to be impressive; that among them there is considerable variety as regards the kind of prose employed; and that they display a stylist superior to any other in America—and I do not except Hawthorne—before Melville, one who in some respects foreshadows Melville, and one who can still be examined with pleasure and with profit.

In *Wing-and-Wing*, Cooper writes a story of his favorite type of sailing vessel, a light and elusive fugitive from authority; and he places the vessel in the marine setting which of all he regarded as the most beautiful and the most ethereal, the Mediterranean. The plot, as in nearly all of his tales of adventure, is one of pursuit and flight, but in these conditions the pursuit and flight acquire an air of illusion which at a few moments, especially in the discussion of solipsistic philosophy which takes place between the vice-governor of Elba and his podesta while halfway down the ship's ladder of a British cruiser, all but evaporates into madness.

Wing-and-Wing, though occasionally amusing or even beautiful, is less certain of its intention than the earlier novel of a somewhat similar kind, *The Water-Witch*. The action of *The Water-Witch* is extremely unreal, and the unreality, not to say the impossibility of much of it, would be preposterous did Cooper not utilize this very quality. It has the plot, entrances, exits, abductions, and mysteries of a comic opera; and the style is adjusted to the plot in a manner at once brilliant and meticulous. Plot and character alike have the unreality, but the consistency within themselves, of the plot and character, let us say, of *Volpone*; and

196

Cooper endeavors to achieve a style not dissimilar, so far as the limits of prose permit, to the style of Jonson's dramatic verse. This novel, though imperfect artistically, is imperfect in minor ways; questions of scope aside, it is probably Cooper's ablest piece of work, as it is certainly one of the most brilliant, if scarcely one of the most profound, masterpieces of American prose.

The numerous quotations from Shakespeare employed in this work give a clue to the Elizabethan models for the prose; and if they did not, there would be clues sufficiently obvious scattered throughout the prose itself. The following commentary, for example is spoken by the incredible Thomas Tiller: " 'Every craft has its allotted time, like a mortal,' continued the inexplicable mariner of the India-shawl. 'If she is to die a sudden death, there is your beam-end and stern-way, which takes her into the grave without funeral service or parish prayers; your dropsy is being water-logged; gout and rheumatism kill like a broken back and loose joints; indigestion is a shifting cargo, with guns adrift; the gallows is a bottomry-bond, with lawyers' fees; while fire, drowning, death by religious melancholy, and suicide, are a careless gunner, sunken rocks, false lights, and a lubberly captain.' "

The best prose, however, is to be found where the imitation of rhetorical forms is not so close, but where the intention of schematization is equally marked. The two most successful characters, from the point of view of one who seeks this particular quality, are the loquacious Dutch Alderman, Van Beverout, and his taciturn and aristocratic young friend, Oloff Van Staats, the Patroon of Kinderhook, the former as a commentator on the action and on life at large, and the latter as one providing much food for comment. To the reader who does not find a certain pleasure in the texture of the prose in which the meditations of the Alderman are couched, the Alderman must needs be very tiresome; but his reveries and his commercial imagery possess a hard and clear, if somewhat baroque and elaborate, beauty, which, though it does not lend itself convincingly to brief quotation, is fairly impressive in the text.

The essential difficulty in connection with these rhetorical excursions resides simply in the fact that the subject is never adequate to permit the extraction from the rhetoric its full possibilities, so that we have a species of lyricism, which, though real enough, is frequently all but verbal or even syntactical; we have something approaching pure rhetoric. Cooper conceived a comic-opera plot to provide the motive for his poetry; in *Moby Dick*, on the other hand, the plot is the plot of an epic, and not only are the possibilities of the rhetoric exhausted, but the rhetoric has greater possibilities.

V

If we except *The Water-Witch*, a minor but original master-piece, not flawless, perhaps, but still a unit, we find Cooper to be essentially a man of fragments; it is likely that the best part of him is in the fragments, moreover, and not in *The Water-Witch*. He embodies a social ideal that in his own lifetime was so far gone in decay that his defense of it cost him his reputation, and that it may scarcely be said to have survived him to the extent of two decades. He displays at his best a rhetorical grandeur of a kind cognate with his social ideals, but habitual rather than understood, and commonly collapsing for lack of support from his action; that is, he displays a great traditional moral sense corroded by the formulary romantic sentiment of his own period, and apparently with no realization that the two are incompatible. On a few occasions he displays great vigor of conception, as in the creation of such plots as *The Sea Lions* and *The Wept of Wish-ton-Wish*, as in the creation of such characters as Leatherstocking and Jason Newcome, as in the residual feeling of intimacy with which he leaves one, from perhaps a half-dozen of novels, with life in frontier and provincial New York. This is a vigor which has little to do with rhetoric, or at least has to do with it but seldom, and which frequently survives a great deal of bad rhetoric: the figure of Leatherstocking emerges from the débris of the five novels in which he was created, independent, authentic, and unforgettable. For the American who desires a polite education in his own literature, the five novels of the Leatherstocking series are indispensable, as are the first two Littlepage novels, *The Bravo,* and *The Water-Witch.* For the American who desires an education historical as well as literary, and richly literary instead of superficially, the entire work should be exhumed. It is a mass of fragments, no doubt; but the fragments are those of a civilization.

HERMAN MELVILLE

and The Problems of Moral Navigation

"The ribs and terrors of the whale
Arched over me a dismal gloom. . . ."
Father Mapple's hymn, *in* MOBY DICK

IN *Pierre,* Melville remarks: "Fortunately for the felicity of the Dilettante in Literature, the horrible allegorical meanings of the *Inferno* lie not on the surface." We naturally desire to shelter the dilettante as far as possible; but when he obscures a writer of Melville's dimensions for three quarters of a century, we begin to find him an obstacle in our own paths. The field of Melville criticism is far more heartening than it was thirty years ago, for there is much activity; the activity, unfortunately, is for the greater part desperately confused. If one is bent on an understanding of Melville, his greatest work, *Moby Dick,* is the most complete statement of his subject;[1] two unsuccessful works, *Pierre* and *The Confidence Man,* come next in this particular respect. I shall therefore begin with *Moby Dick.*

The symbolism of *Moby Dick* is based on the antithesis of the sea and the land: the land represents the known, the mastered, in human experience; the sea, the half-known, the obscure region of instinct, uncritical feeling, danger, and terror.

"Yea, foolish mortals, Noah's flood is not yet subsided; two thirds of the fair world it yet covers.

"Wherein differ the sea and the land, that a miracle upon one

---

[1] In my remarks on the symbolism of *Moby Dick,* I am indebted for a good many details to an unpublished thesis by Achilles Holt, done at Stanford University. Mr. Holt examines the subject very minutely, and I have used only a small part of his material; his thesis ought to be published. On the other hand, I have added a good deal of my own, and I differ radically with Mr. Holt as to his interpretation of the central theme, that is, in regard to the significance of Ahab's character and actions.

is not a miracle upon the other? Preternatural terrors rested upon the Hebrews, when under the feet of Korah and his company the live ground opened and swallowed them up for ever; yet not a modern sun ever sets, but in precisely the same manner the live sea swallows up ships and crews.

"But not only is the sea such a foe to man who is alien to it, but it is also a fiend to its own offspring; worse than the Persian host who murdered his own guests; sparing not the creatures which itself hath spawned. Like a savage tigress that overlays her own cubs, so the sea dashes even the mightiest whales against the rocks, and leaves them there side by side with the split wrecks of ships. No mercy, no power but its own controls it. Panting and snorting like a mad battle steed that has lost its rider, the masterless ocean overruns the globe.

"Consider the subtleness of the sea; how its most dreaded creatures glide under the water, unapparent for the most part, and treacherously hidden beneath the loveliest tints of azure. Consider also the devilish brilliance and beauty of many of its most remorseless tribes, as the dainty embellished shape of many species of sharks. Consider once more the universal cannibalism of the sea, all whose creatures prey upon each other, carrying on eternal war since the world began.

"Consider all this; and then turn to this green, gentle, and most docile earth. Consider them both, the sea and the land; and do you not find a strange analogy to something in yourself? For as this appalling ocean surrounds the verdant land, so in the soul of man there lies one insular Tahiti, full of peace and joy, but encompassed by all the horrors of the half known life. God help thee! Push not off from that isle, thou canst never return!"

The ocean is the home of demons and symbols of evil too numerous to mention. It is the home especially of Moby Dick, the white whale, the chief symbol and spirit of evil; it is also the home of the great white squid, chaotic and formless, the symbol of chance in life: "A vast pulpy mass, furlongs in length and breadth, of a glancing cream-color, lay floating on the water; innumerable long arms radiating from its center, and curling and twisting like a nest of anacondas, as if blindly to catch at any hapless object within reach. No perceptible face or front did it have; no conceivable token of either sensation or instinct; but undulated there on the billows, an unearthly, formless, chance-like apparition of life."

Pip, the little negro boy, falls overboard from a whale boat; that is, he is immersed in the sea. As a result, and after his rescue, he is mad. In the chapter entitled The Mast-head, Ishmael speaks of his own contemplation of the sea from aloft, where he had been sent as a look-out: ". . . lulled into such an opium-like list-lessness of vacant unconscious revery is this absent-minded youth by the blending cadence of waves with thoughts, that at last he loses his identity; takes the mystic ocean at his feet for the visible image of that deep, blue, bottomless soul, pervading mankind and nature; and every strange, half-seen, gliding beautiful thing that eludes him; every dimly discovered, uprising fin of some undiscernible form, seems to him the embodiment of those elusive thoughts that only people the soul by continuously flitting through it. In this enchanted mood thy spirit ebbs away to whence it came; becomes diffused through time and space; like Cranmer's sprinkled Pantheistic ashes, forming at last a part of every shore the round globe over.

"There is no life in thee now, except that rocking life imparted by a gentle rolling ship; by her, borrowed from the sea; by the sea from the inscrutable tides of God. But while this sleep, this dream, is on ye, move your foot or hand an inch; slip your hold at all; and your identity comes back in horror. Over Descartian vortices you hover. And perhaps, at midday, in the fairest weather, with one half-throttled shriek you drop through that transparent air into the summer sea, no more to rise for ever. Heed it well, ye Pantheists!"

The relationship of man to the known and to the half known, however, is not a simple and static one; he cannot merely stay on land, or he will perish of imperception, but must venture on the sea, without losing his relationship to the land; we have, in brief, the relationship of principle to perception, or, in other words, the problem of judgment. This is made clear in the invocation to Bulkington, a helmsman even more memorable than

Palinurus, in the chapter entitled The Lee Shore: "When on that shivering winter's night, the Pequod thrust her vindictive bows into the cold malicious waves, whom should I see standing at her helm but Bulkington! I looked with sympathetic awe and fearfulness upon the man, who in mid-winter just landed from a four years' dangerous voyage, could so unrestingly push off again for still another tempestuous term. The land seemed scorching to his feet. Wonderfullest things are ever the unmentionable; deep memories yield no epitaphs; this six-inch chapter is the stoneless grave of Bulkington. Let me only say that it fared with him as with the storm-tossed ship that miserably drives along the leeward land. The port would fain give succor; the port is pitiful; in the port is safety, comfort, hearthstone, supper, warm blankets, friends, all that's kind to our mortalities. But in that gale, the port, the land, is that ship's direst jeopardy; she must fly all hospitality; one touch of land, though it but graze the keel, would make her shudder through and through. With all her might she crowds all sail off shore; in so doing fights 'gainst the very winds that fain would blow her homeward; seeks all the lashed seas' landlessness again; for refuge's sake forlornly rushing into peril; her only friend her bitterest foe!

"Know ye, now, Bulkington? Glimpses do ye seem to see of that mortally intolerable truth; that all deep, earnest thinking is but the intrepid effort of the soul to keep the open independence of her sea; while the wildest winds of heaven and earth conspire to cast her on the treacherous, slavish shore?

"But as in landlessness alone resides the highest truth, shoreless, indefinite as God—so, better is it to perish in that howling infinite, than be ingloriously dashed upon the lee, even if that were safety! For worm-like, then, oh! who would craven crawl to land! Terrors of the terrible! is all this agony so vain? Take heart, take heart, O Bulkington! Bear thee grimly, demigod! Up from the spray of thy ocean-perishing—straight up leaps thy apotheosis!"

It should be observed that this passage is addressed to a helmsman, governed by the laws of his calling, and obeying the commands of a navigator, one who guides the ship with reference to the position of the land. Symbolically, the passage represents the process of living by judgment; that is by perception of individual, shifting, and chaotic phenomena, but by perception trained in principle, in abstraction, to the point where it is able to find its way amid the chaos of the particular. Ahab is ultimately betrayed to his end by the white whale, who is the spirit of evil, in the farthest Pacific, after destroying his quadrant (the instrument which gives him his mathematical position upon the ocean), after having his compass needle reversed by a storm (a warning that he should turn about and retrace his way), after the snapping of his log-line (which enabled him to gauge his position roughly), and after the sinking of the life-buoy and the caulking of Queequeg's coffin to take its place.

With these basic ideas, and these few illustrative passages clearly in mind, we may follow the details of the book with great facility.

Ishmael, having decided to go to sea, notes the attraction which the sea possesses for landsmen: "Circumambulate the city of a dreamy Sabbath afternoon. Go from Corlears Hook to Coenties Slip, and from there by Whitehall, northward. What do you see?—Posted like silent sentinels all around the town, stand thousands upon thousands of mortal men fixed in ocean reveries. Some leaning against the spiles; some seated upon the pier-heads; some looking over the bulwarks of ships from China; some high aloft in the rigging, as if striving to get a still better seaward peep. But these are all landsmen; of week-days pent up in lath and plaster—tied to counters, nailed to benches, clinched to desks. How then is this? Are the green fields gone? What do they here?

"But look! here come more crowds, pacing straight for the water, and seemingly bound for a dive. Strange! Nothing will content them but the extremest limit of the land; loitering under the shady lee of yonder warehouses will not suffice. No. They must get just as nigh the water as they possibly can without falling in. . . ."

Ishmael leaves New York for New Bedford, arrives at night, and seeks an inn. Since he is low in funds, he seeks the cheapest inns, which are nearest the water-front, and his approach to water is represented as an approach to chaos, death, and hell. Ishmael proceeds through dismal streets, stumbles into a negro church, and then comes to The Spouter Inn, kept by Peter Coffin, a juxtaposition of names which gives us our first explicit hint of one of the two major symbolisms of the whale: death and evil. And in the third chapter, we are given a clue to both meanings, for the sailors' bar is over-arched by the jawbone of a whale; the symbolism of this passage is clear, and the description is horribly vivid:

"Entering that gable-ended Spouter Inn, you found yourself in a wide, low, straggling entry with old-fashioned wainscots, reminding one of the bulwarks of some condemned old craft. . . .

"The opposite wall of this entry was hung all over with a heathenish array of monstrous clubs and spears. Some were thickly set with glittering teeth resembling ivory saws; others were tufted with knots of human hair; and one was sickle-shaped, with a vast handle sweeping round like the segment made in the new-mown grass by a long-armed mower. You shuddered as you gazed, and wondered what monstrous cannibal and savage could ever have gone a death-harvesting with such a hacking, horrifying implement. Mixed with these were rusty old whaling lances and harpoons all broken and deformed. . . .

"Crossing this dusty entry, and on through yon low-arched way—cut through what in old times must have been a great central chimney with fire-places all round—you enter the public room. A still duskier place is this, with such low ponderous beams above, and such old wrinkled planks beneath, that you would almost fancy you trod some old craft's cockpits, especially of such a howling night, when this corner-anchored old ark rocked so furiously. On one side stood a long, low, shelf-like table covered with cracked glass cases, filled with dusty rarities gathered from this wide world's remotest nooks. Projecting from the farther angle of the room stands a dark-looking den—the bar—a rude attempt at a right whale's head. Be that how it may, there stands the vast arched bone of the whale's jaw, so wide a coach might almost drive beneath it. Within are shabby shelves, ranged round with old decanters, bottles, flasks; and in those jaws of swift destruction, like another cursed Jonah (by which name indeed they call him) bustles a little withered old man, who, for their money, dearly sells the sailors deliriums and death."

It is at this inn that Ishmael meets his future boon-companion, Queequeg, a tattooed cannibal, whose head, in the half-light, resembles a mildewed skull. The harpooneers on the voyage all turn out to be savages: the first three, Queequeg, the Pacific islander, Daggoo, the African negro, and Tashtego the Gay Head Indian, represent the basic pagan virtues of strength and accuracy, both muscular and instinctive, and of absolute fidelity, but below the level of reason, so that they are governed unquestioningly by the damned Ahab and do his bidding to the end: when the ship finally sinks to perdition, Tashtego is nailing a sky-hawk, a piece of heaven, to the mast, to carry it down with him.

After a few minor adventures, Ishmael finds his way to Father Mapple's church, inspects the memorial tablets for whalemen lost at sea, and speculates on the horrible implications of death, especially upon the universal and ineradicable feeling among men that death is essentially and profoundly evil. The reasoning implied here is the same as that developed fully in the great chapter on the whiteness of the whale; namely, that this instinctive knowledge of evil and demonism is trustworthy and is embedded in the race as a remnant of an earlier and fuller knowledge: "In what eternal, unstirring paralysis, and deadly, hopeless trance, yet lies antique Adam who died sixty round centuries ago; how is it that we still refuse to be comforted for those who we nevertheless maintain are dwelling in unspeakable bliss; why all the living so strive to hush all the dead; wherefore but the rumor of the knocking of a tomb will terrify a whole city. All these things are not without their meanings."

Father Mapple preaches on Jonah, and the whale is the symbol of hell and death. The hymn contains the essence of the sermon:

> *The ribs and terrors of the whale,*
> *Arched over me a dismal gloom,*
> *While all God's sunlit waves rolled by,*
> *And left me deepening down to doom.*

I saw the opening maw of hell,
  With endless pains and sorrows there;
Which none but they that feel can tell—
  Oh, I was plunging to despair.

In black distress, I called my God,
  When I could scarce believe him mine,
He bowed his ear to my complaints—
  No more the whale did me confine.

With speed he flew to my relief,
  As on a radiant dolphin borne;
Awful, yet bright as lightning, shone
  The face of my Deliverer God.

My song forever shall record
  That terrible that joyful hour;
I give the glory to my God,
  His all the mercy and the power.

Jonah, having sinned, is given a foretaste of hell, and then he repents, and God delivers him; "and Jonah, bruised and beaten —his ears, like two seashells, still multitudinously murmuring of the ocean—Jonah did the Almighty's bidding." But so Ahab did not, and Ahab was damned.

They proceed a little farther to sea; that is, to the island of Nantucket, from which they plan to ship. Nantucket is represented as the very essence of the New England sea-coast, the fishiest of fishing towns. Ishmael is excited with his coming adventure, and the cod and clam chowders of Mistress Hussey render him momentarily delirious: "But look, Queequeg, ain't that a live eel in your bowl? Where's your harpoon?" Even the landlord's cow appears a trifle tipsy: "I saw Hosea's brindled cow feeding on fish remnants, and marching along the sand with each foot in a cod's decapitated head, looking very slipshod, I assure ye."

Ishmael and Queequeg sign to ship on the Pequod, a Nantucket whaler commanded by Captain Ahab, and of which the retired captains Peleg and Bildad are part owners. Queequeg's island divinity, whom he carries about with him, had communicated to Queequeg that Ishmael was fated to choose the boat on which they were fated to sail, and thus was the matter done. Immediately after signing, they receive a warning from Bildad: "Meanwhile Captain Bildad sat earnestly and steadfastly eyeing Queequeg, and at last rising solemnly and fumbling in the huge pockets of his broad-skirted drab coat, took out a bundle of tracts, and selecting one entitled, 'The Latter Day Coming; or No Time to Lose,' placed it in Queequeg's hands, and then grasping them and the book in both his, looked earnestly into his eyes, and said, 'Son of darkness, I must do my duty by thee; I am part owner of this ship and feel concerned for the souls of all its crew; if thou still clingest to thy pagan ways, which I sadly fear, I beseech thee, remain not for aye a Belial bondsman. Spurn the idol Bell, and the hideous dragon; turn from the wrath to come; mind thine eye, I say; oh! goodness gracious! steer clear of the fiery pit!'" The grotesque combination of the familiar and the terrible in this passage is due to the fact that a common and somewhat ludicrous man and action are utilized to recall symbolic meanings of which the actors are unaware but which the reader supposedly has fathomed. The ominous humor of other scenes in the early parts of the book, especially that relating to the two inns and the first meeting with Queequeg, is of the same kind. Bildad's outburst, like Father Mapple's sermon, is one of the many unheeded warnings with which the progress of the book is marked.

After they set sail, the mates are introduced and described. They represent various levels of normal human attitudes toward physical and spiritual danger, the highest being that of Starbuck, the first mate, who represents the critical intelligence: "Starbuck was no crusader after perils; in him courage was not a sentiment; but a thing simply useful to him, and always at hand upon all mortally practical occasions. . . . For, thought Starbuck, I am here in this critical ocean to kill whales for my living, and not to be killed by them for theirs; and that hundreds of men had been so killed Starbuck well knew. What doom was his own father's?

Where in the bottomless deeps could he find the torn limbs of his brother?" Starbuck's desperate effort to turn Ahab from his purpose, and, after his failure, his submission to Ahab, is thus a major crisis in the book; it represents the unsuccessful rebellion of sanity and morality against a dominant madness.

Ahab himself has lost a leg to Moby Dick, the white whale, on a previous voyage, and has set out on this voyage with the secret intention of vengeance, in spite of the fact that he owes a primary allegiance to the interests of his owners. As the whale represents death and evil, Ahab's ivory leg represents the death that has become a part of the living man as a result of his struggle with evil; it is the numb wisdom which is the fruit of experience. Stubb displeases Ahab and dreams that Ahab kicks him with the ivory leg; Stubb meditates vengeance, but he eventually concludes that it is an honor to be kicked by the ivory leg of a great man. When Ahab meets another captain at sea who has an ivory right arm as a result of a similar accident, and when the captain in question extends his dead arm in greeting, Ahab hoists his ivory leg and crosses the arm with it.

Although these Nantucket sea-officers are nominally Quakers, they have more of the Calvinist in their make-up than of the Friend, and Melville treats them in more or less Calvinistic terms; they are, says Melville, "Quakers with a vengeance." The Calvinist, though he believes that every phenomenon in the universe is decreed by God, though he believes that good works are of no value toward salvation, yet believes, sometimes as a theologian, sometimes merely as a practitioner of traditional modes of speech who is too uncritical to be aware of discrepancies, that man is morally responsible to God; and, if he is wise enough not to attempt to resolve this contradiction, having once discovered it, consigns it to the plane of Absolute Understanding, eternally unattainable by man. Jonathan Edwards elaborates this somewhat by separating, in effect, the predestined and sinning will from the understanding soul; so that the soul, conceived for the moment as pure understanding, may observe its own actions, which it cannot avoid committing, and approve its own damnation. It is in some such terms as these that Ahab is conceived. There are many passages in the book indicating the theme of predestination; the most striking occur in the forty-ninth chapter:

". . . it almost seemed that while he himself was marking out lines and courses on the wrinkled charts, some invisible pencil was also tracing lines and courses upon the deeply marked chart of his forehead. . . .

"Often, when forced from his hammock by exhausting and intolerably vivid dreams of the night, which, resuming his own intense thoughts through the day, carried them on amid a clashing of phrensies, and whirled them round and round in his blazing brain, till the very throbbing of his life-spot became insufferable anguish; and when, as was sometimes the case, these spiritual throes in him heaved its being up from its base, and a chasm seemed opening in him, from which forked flames and lightnings shot up, and accursed fiends beckoned him to leap down among them; when this hell in himself yawned beneath him, a wild cry would be heard through the ship; and with glaring eyes Ahab would burst from his stateroom, as though escaping from a bed that was on fire. Yet these, perhaps, instead of being the insuppressible symptoms of some latent weakness, or fright at his own resolve, were but the plainest tokens of its intensity. For at such times, crazy Ahab, the scheming, unappeasedly steadfast hunter of the White Whale; this Ahab that had gone to his hammock, was not the agent that so caused him to burst from it in horror again. The latter was the eternal, living principle or soul in him; and in sleep, being for the time dissociated from the characterizing mind, which at other times employed it for its outer vehicle or agent, it spontaneously sought escape from the scorching contiguity of the frantic thing, of which, for the time, it was no longer an integral. But as the mind does not exist, unless leagued with the soul, therefore it must have been that, in Ahab's case, yielding up all his thoughts and fancies to his one supreme purpose; that purpose by its own sheer inveteracy of will forced itself against gods and devils into a kind of self-assumed, independent being of its own. Nay, could grimly live and burn, while the common vitality to which it was conjoined, fled horror-stricken from the unbidden and unfathered birth. Therefore, the tormented spirit that glared out of bodily eyes, when what seemed Ahab rushed from his room, was for the time but a vacated thing, a formless somnambulistic being, a ray of living light, to be sure, but without an object to color, and therefore a blankness in itself. God help thee, old man, thy thoughts have created a creature in thee; and he whose intense thinking thus makes him a Prometheus; a vulture feeds upon his heart forever; that vulture the very creature he creates."

Considered in this light, Fedallah, Ahab's harpooneer, who guides and advises him in the direction of his undoing, and who, according to Melville's own suggestion, may be some kind of emanation from Ahab himself, is perhaps the sinning mind as it shows itself distinct from the whole man. Fedallah and his boat-crew are smuggled on board and concealed until the ship is in mid-ocean and Ahab's intention is disclosed; they are seen in Nantucket only as ghostly figures hurrying toward the ship in the dawn, at a time when there are the vaguest of rumors afloat about Ahab; Fedallah is destined to die before Ahab; it is Fedallah, moreover, who sights the spirit-spout, which guides the ship into the Pacific. The crew regard Fedallah as the devil in disguise, and he appears in general to be offered as a manifestation of pure evil. His relationship to Ahab is underlined at the end of the seventy-third chapter: "Meantime Fedallah was calmly eyeing the right whale's head, and ever and anon glancing from the deep wrinkles there to the lines in his own hand. And Ahab chanced so to stand, that the Parsee occupied his shadow; while if the Parsee's shadow was there at all, it seemed only to blend with and lengthen Ahab's. As the crew toiled on, Laplandish speculations were bandied among them, concerning all these passing things."

But predestined or otherwise, it is with Ahab the sinner that the book is concerned; his sin, in the minor sense, is monomaniac vengeance; in the major, the will to destroy the spirit of evil itself, an intention blasphemous because beyond human powers and infringing upon the purposes of God. After Starbuck tries and fails to turn Ahab aside, we have a series of chapters illus-

trating the effect of this action on the voyage. The first is a monologue spoken by Ahab:

"Dry heat upon my brow? Oh! time was, when as the sunrise
nobly spurred me, so the sunset soothed. No more. This lovely
light, it lights not me; all loveliness is anguish to me, since I
can ne'er enjoy. Gifted with the high perception, I lack the low,
enjoying power; damned, most subtly and most malignantly!
damned in the midst of Paradise! Good night—good night!

" 'Twas not so hard a task. I thought to find one stubborn at
the least; but my one cogged circle fits into all their various
wheels, and they revolve. . . . They think me mad—Starbuck
does; but I'm demoniac, I am madness maddened! The wild
madness that's only calm to comprehend itself!"

The next monologue is spoken by Starbuck: "My soul is more
than matched; she's overmanned; and by a madman! Insufferable sting that sanity should ground arms on such a field! But
he drilled deep down and blasted all my reason out of me! . . .
Oh God! to sail with such a heathen crew that have small touch
of human mothers in them! Whelped somewhere by the sharkish
sea. The White Whale is their demigorgon. Hark! the infernal
orgies!"

There follows a brief monologue by Stubb, the imperceptive,
the porter at the gate, and then comes the scene of the "infernal
orgies" in the forecastle, in which, as a result of the defeat of
Starbuck, who represents reason, the brutal instincts of the crew
are progressively loosened, until, on the brink of catastrophe,
they are brought to order by the need of coping with a physical
adversary, a rising storm. From this time forward, however, the
ship is in Ahab's hands; he ultimately destroys his nautical instruments and sails by instinct until he finds the whale in the
remote Pacific and is destroyed.

The symbolism of the whale is part of the symbolism of the
sea. The sea is the realm of the half-known, at once of perception and of peril; it is infested by subtle and malignant creatures,
bent on destruction; it is governed by tremendous, destructive,
and unpredictable forces, the storms, calms, currents, tides,
depths, and distances, amid which one can preserve oneself by

virtue only of the greatest skill, and then but precariously and from moment to moment. Of all the creatures in the sea, the whale is the greatest, the most intelligent, and the most dangerous. It is for whalemen the chief object in life upon the sea; it lures them to sea; it brings them frequently to death; they are of necessity much impressed with its dangers and its power. It is thus naturally, in a general way, the symbol of evil and of death, and this symbolism is developed from beginning to end of the book carefully and elaborately; it is especially explicit in the description of the skeleton whale which Ishmael once saw in a bower in the Arsacides. The description of the skeleton follows a great many other chapters in which the anatomy of the whale is treated part by part: one is familiarized in great detail with the structure, size, and functions of the animal, as well as with his habits, and with the stupendous medium in which he moves. Probably no other book exists which so impresses us at once with the vastness of the physical universe and with the vastness of the idea of the universe. The allegory is incalculably strengthened by this sense of vastness and power, and by the detailed reality through which it is established. Ultimately we are shown the extent of time which the whale inhabits, as well as of space; we meet the fossil whale; and we see how the idea of the whale is imbedded in all nature, for his physical form is repeatedly suggested in rocks, in mountains, and in stars.

This general symbolism is concentrated in Moby Dick, the White Whale, who is especially intelligent, malignant, and powerful; who has destroyed or seriously injured every whaler who has sought to kill him, and who has become among whalemen a more or less legendary figure. In an earlier encounter, he had bitten off Ahab's leg; Ahab is bent on vengeance. This intense desire for revenge is a sin; and in Ahab's case the sin is heightened by the conviction that a power greater and more malignant than any proper to mere animal nature is acting in or through the whale: he is convinced of the true existence of the "demonism of the world." He thus endeavors to step outside of the limitations of man and revenge himself upon the permanent order of the universe; as Melville says, in a passage already quoted, he is Promethean, in that he defies the gods; but he goes beyond Prometheus in his fury, for he seeks to destroy a god. He represents, essentially, the ultimate distillation of the Calvinistic temperament.

" 'Vengeance on a dumb brute!' cried Starbuck, 'that simply smote thee from blindest instinct! Madness! To be enraged with a dumb thing, Captain Ahab, seems blasphemous.'

" 'Hark ye yet again—the little lower layer. All visible objects, man, are but as pasteboard masks. But in each event—in the living act, the undoubted deed—there, some unknown but still reasoning thing puts forth the mouldings of its features from behind the unreasoning mask. If man will strike, strike through the mask! How can the prisoner reach outside except by thrusting through the wall? To me the white whale is that wall, shoved near to me. Sometimes I think there's naught beyond. But 'tis enough. He tasks me; he heaps me; I see in him outrageous strength, with an inscrutable malice sinewing it. That inscrutable thing is chiefly what I hate; and be the white whale agent, or be the white whale principal, I will wreak that hate upon him. Talk not to me of blasphemy, man; I'd strike the sun if it insulted me.' "

The most extensive elucidation and defense of the notion of the demonism of Moby Dick, as well as of "the demonism of the world," occurs in the chapter on the whiteness of the whale, equally one of the most astonishing pieces of rhetoric and one of the most appalling specimens of metaphysical argument in all literature:

"Tell me why this strong young colt, foaled in some peaceful valley of Vermont, far removed from all beasts of prey—why is it that upon the sunniest day, if you but shake a fresh buffalo robe behind him, so that he cannot even see it, but only smells its wild animal muskiness—why will he start, snort, and with bursting eyes paw the ground in phrensies of affright? There is no remembrance in him of any gorings of wild creatures in his green northern home, so that the strange muskiness he smells cannot recall to him anything associated with the experience of former perils; for what knows he, this New England colt, of the black bisons of distant Oregon?

"No: but here thou beholdest even in a dumb brute, the instinct of the knowledge of the demonism of the world. Though thousands of miles from Oregon, still when he smells that savage musk, the rending, goring bison herds are as present as to the deserted wild foal of the prairies, which this instant they may be trampling into dust.

"Thus, then, the muffled rollings of the milky sea; the bleak rustlings of the festooned frosts of mountains; the desolate shiftings of the windrowed snows of prairies; all these, to Ishmael, are as the shaking of that buffalo robe to the frightened colt!

"Though neither knows where lie the nameless things of which the mystic sign gives forth such hints; yet with me, as with the colt, somewhere those things must exist. Though in many of its aspects, this visible world seems formed in love, the invisible spheres were formed in fright.

"But not yet have we solved the incantation of this whiteness, and learned why it appeals with such power to the soul; and more strange and far more portentous—why, as we have seen, it is at once the most meaning symbol of spiritual things, nay, the very veil of the Christian's Deity; and yet should be as it is, the intensifying agent in things the most appalling to mankind.

"Is it that by its indefiniteness it shadows forth the heartless voids and immensities of the universe, and thus stabs us from behind with the thought of annihilation, when beholding the depths of the milky way? Or is it that in essence whiteness is not so much a color as the visible absence of color, and at the same time the concrete of all colors; is it for these reasons that there is such a dumb blankness, full of meaning, in a wide landscape of snows—a colorless all-color of atheism from which we shrink? And when we consider that other theory of the natural philosophers, that all other earthly hues—every stately or lovely emblazoning—the sweet tinges of sunset skies and woods; yea, and the gilded velvets of butterflies, and the butterfly cheeks of young girls; all these are but subtle deceits, not actually inherent in substances, but only laid on from without; so that all deified nature absolutely paints like the harlot, whose allurements cover nothing but the charnel-house within; and when we proceed further, and consider that the mystical cosmetic which produces every one of her hues, the great principle of light, for ever remains white or colorless in itself, and if operating without medium upon matter, would touch all objects, even tulips and roses, with its own blank tinge—pondering all this, the palsied universe lies before us a leper; and like wilfull travellers in Lapland, who refuse to wear colored and coloring glasses upon their eyes, so the wretched infidel gazes himself blind at the monumental white shroud that wraps all the prospect around him. And of all these things the Albino whale was the symbol. Wonder ye then at the fiery hunt?"

Through elaborate and magnificent physical description we are made to realize the tremendousness of the whale and of his medium; through exposition of this nature, we are shown his spiritual significance. It is not that one object stands for another, as a bare allegorical formula; the relationship is more fully and subtly developed in the book than one can develop it in summary. The possibility that the physical and the spiritual are one and the same, according to the terms employed, is established; and one is convinced, with Ahab, for the time being, of the probability in this instance. Or if one is not, one is brought to an understanding of Ahab's conviction; so that his entire course of action becomes, in its spiritual effect, what it was for him in literal fact, a defiance of the divine order.

The union of the physical and the spiritual is at all times impressive in this narrative; it reaches, in two descriptions of Moby Dick himself, a sublimity and terror probably never surpassed in literature, and but seldom equalled. The first, and slighter, is the description of the spirit-spout, which lured Ahab into the far Pacific:

"It was while gliding through these latter waters that one serene and moonlight night, when all the waves rolled by like scrolls of silver; and, by their soft suffusing seethings, made what seemed a silvery silence, not a solitude: on such a silent night a

216

silvery jet was seen far in advance of the white bubbles at the bow. Lit up by the moon, it looked celestial; seemed some plumed and glittering god uprising from the sea. Fedallah first descried this jet. For of these moonlit nights, it was his wont to mount to the mainmast head, and stand a look-out there, with the same precision as if it had been day. And yet, though herds of whales were seen by night, not one whaleman in a hundred would venture a lowering for them. You may think with what emotions, then, the seamen beheld this Oriental perched aloft at such unusual hours; his turban and the moon, companions in one sky. But when, after spending his uniform interval there for several successive nights without uttering a single sound; when, after all this silence, his unearthly voice was heard announcing that silvery moonlit jet, every reclining mariner started to his feet as if some winged spirit had lighted in the rigging, and hailed the mortal crew."

The second is the description of Moby Dick near the close of the book, when he is actually sighted by daylight for the first time:

"Like noiseless nautilus shells, their light prows sped through the sea; but only slowly they neared the foe. As they neared him, the ocean grew still more smooth; seemed drawing a carpet over its waves; seemed a noon-meadow, so serenely it spread. At length the breathless hunter came so nigh his seemingly unsuspecting prey, that his entire dazzling hump was distinctly visible, sliding along the sea as if an isolated thing, and continually set in a revolving ring of finest, fleecy, greenish foam. He saw the vast, involved wrinkles of the slightly projecting head beyond. Before it, far out on the soft Turkish-rugged waters, went the glistening white shadow from his broad, milky forehead, a musical rippling playfully accompanying the shade; and behind, the blue waters interchangeably flowed over into the moving valley of his steady wake; and on either hand bright bubbles rose and danced by his side. But these were broken again by the light toes of hundreds of gay fowls softly feathering the sea, alternate with their fitful flight; and like to some flag-staff rising from the painted hull of an argosy, the tall but shattered pole of a recent lance projected from the White Whale's back; and at intervals one of the cloud of soft-toed fowls hovering, and to and fro skimming like a canopy over the fish, silently perched and rocked on this pole, the long tail-feathers streaming like pennons.

"A gentle joyousness, a mighty mildness of repose in swiftness, invested the gliding whale. Not the white bull Jupiter swimming away with ravished Europa clinging to his graceful horns; his lovely leering eyes sideways intent upon the maid; with smooth bewitching fleetness, rippling straight for the nuptial bower in Crete; not Jove, not that mighty majesty Supreme! did surpass the glorified White Whale as he so divinely swam.

"On each soft side—coincident with the parted swell, that but once leaving him, then flowed so wide away—on each bright side, the whale shed off enticings. No wonder there had been some among the hunters who namelessly transported and allured by all this serenity, had ventured to assail it; but had fatally found that quietude but the vesture of tornadoes. Yet calm, enticing calm, oh whale! thou glidest on, to all who for the first time eye thee, no matter how many in that same way thou may'st have bejuggled and destroyed before.

"And thus, through the serene tranquillities of the tropical sea, among waves whose handclappings were suspended by exceeding rapture, Moby Dick moved on, still withholding from sight the full terrors of his submerged trunk, entirely hiding the wrenched hideousness of his jaw. But soon the fore part of him slowly rose from the water; for an instant his whole marbleized body formed a high arch, like Virginia's Natural Bridge, and warningly waving his bannered flukes in the air, the grand god revealed himself, sounded, and went out of sight. Hoveringly halting, and dipping on the wing, the white sea-fowls longingly lingered over the agitated pool that he left."

We have now the main outline of the plot and symbolism of the book; with these in mind, the reader can readily distinguish the significance of the smaller details.

The book has more or less defied classification, yet chiefly because it fuses categories in the matter of structure, so as to produce a new structure, and because it is long and complex and has been imperfectly studied: it is beyond a cavil one of the most carefully and successfully constructed of all the major works of literature; to find it careless, redundant, or in any sense romantic, as even its professed admirers are prone to do, is merely to misread the book and to be ignorant of the history leading up to it.

The book is less a novel than an epic poem. The plot is too immediately interpenetrated with idea to lend itself easily to the manner of the novelist. The language in which it is written is closer to the poetry of *Paradise Lost* or of *Hamlet* than it is to the prose of the realistic novelist. The extremes of prosaic and of poetic language, each at a high level of excellence, might be illustrated by the prose of *The Age of Innocence*, on the one hand, and by one of the best sonnets of Shakespeare on the other: the extreme of prose is the recounting of individual facts; the extreme of poetry is the lyrical, in the best sense; that is, the expository concentration of a motivating concept, in language such that motivating concept and motivated feeling are expressed simultaneously and in brief space. Between these extremes, but a little nearer to the sonnet than to Mrs. Wharton, is the language of the great epic or dramatic poem: in *Macbeth*, or in *Paradise Lost*, the individual passage is never self-sustaining in the same measure as the poetry of the great sonnet by either author; even the greatest passages are dependent upon the structure and upon the total theme for their greatness, and must be read in their context if they are not to seem inferior in quality to the shorter poems. This does not mean that they are an inferior kind of poetry; it means that they are a different kind of poetry. In the prose of *Moby Dick*, this difference in texture is carried a little farther, but only a very little. The prose, of *Moby Dick*, though mechanically it is prose and not verse—except for those passages where it occasionally falls fragmentarily into iambic pentameter—is by virtue of its elaborate rhythms and heightened rhetoric closer in its aesthetic result to the poetry of *Paradise Lost* than to the prose of Mrs. Wharton. The instrument, as an invention, and even when we are familiar with the great prose of the seventeenth century as its background, is essentially as original and powerful an invention as the blank verse of Milton. On the whole, we may fairly regard the work as essentially a poetic performance.

If we so regard it, however—that is, if we regard it as an epic poem—we must mark another exception. Except in *Paradise Lost*, that other great masterpiece of more or less Calvinistic literature—the epic hero is normally a successful figure, and not a tragical one; Ahab, on the other hand, obeys the traditional law of tragedy, and destroys himself through allowing himself to be dominated by an heroic vice: he is another Coriolanus, but in dimensions epical, in the quality of his mind and of his sin metaphysical, and in his motivating ideas Calvinistical. One should note that Melville, in writing a tragic instead of a traditionally heroic epic, displayed a thorough understanding of his material: the Calvinistic view led to sin and catastrophe, not to triumph, although at times to sin and catastrophe on an inspired and heroic scale; Ahab is the magnificent fruition of Maule's curse. Melville, on the other hand, escaped the curse by comprehending it.

The book, then, partakes in some measure of the qualities of a novel and of a tragic drama; but essentially it is an epic poem. Form and subject are mastered with a success equal to that observable in Milton, Vergil, or Shakespeare.

The book is not only a great epic; it is profoundly an American epic. It is easy to exaggerate the importance of nationalism in literature, but in this particular case, the nationalism is the historical element, and not to perceive it is to fail to understand the very subject of the book. In its physical events, *Moby Dick* is a narration of exploration and heroic adventure; it is thus typical of the United States of the nineteenth century, by land as well as by sea: "They may celebrate as they will the heroes of Exploring Expeditions, your Cookes, your Krusensterns; but I say that scores of anonymous captains have sailed out of Nantucket, that were as great and greater than your Cooke and your Krusenstern. For in their succorless empty-handedness, they, in the heathenish sharked waters, and by the beaches of unrecorded javelin islands, battled with virgin wonders and terrors that Cooke with all his marines and muskets would not have willingly dared."

The adventure, in its physical aspects, is of New England and hence by sea; the original New Englanders, indeed, two centuries earlier, had adventured by sea into a virgin wilderness, believing themselves led by God, and there had wrestled with the Wonders of the Invisible World. The fusion of the physical with the spiritual in New England is older than Melville; the New Englanders of whom Melville wrote were descended from the Mathers and their townsmen, from the contemporaries of the more recent Jonathan Edwards, men who saw chimneys suddenly leap into flame in the midst of a revival sermon, upon whom a church might fall, immediately following a preacher's prophecy of doom. With physical and spiritual adventure alike, and with the two interpenetrative, the New Englanders were familiar from childhood, had even been familiar for generations, so that Melville but spoke the literal truth of his representative New Englanders, those of Nantucket, when he spoke with double meaning of their adventures at sea: "The Nantucketer, he alone resides and riots on the sea; he alone, in Bible language, goes down to it in ships; to and fro ploughing it as his own special plantation. *There* is his home; *there* lies his business, which a Noah's flood would not interrupt, though it overwhelmed all the millions in China. He lives on the sea, as prairie cocks in the prairie; he hides among the waves, he climbs them as chamois hunters climb the Alps. For years he knows not the land; so that when he comes to it at last, it smells like another world, more strangely than the moon would to an Earthsman. With the landless gull, that at sunset folds her wings and is rocked to sleep between billows; so at nightfall, the Nantucketer, out of sight of land, furls his sails, and lays him to rest, while under his very pillow rush herds of walruses and whales."

II

The greatest works of Melville, aside from *Moby Dick*, and contrary to the popular view, are among those which follow, not among those which precede it. They are *Benito Cereno*, *The*

Encantadas, and *Billy Budd.* These works, in the matter of style, are essentially prose; *The Encantadas* contains traces of the style of *Moby Dick,* along with traces of its subject-matter, but the rhetoric is subdued in structure and in feeling. In *Benito Cereno,* and in the other later works, there is scarcely a trace of the style of *Moby Dick;* we have the style of a novelist, and in *Benito Cereno* especially this style occurs in a form both classical and austere.

The subject matter of the first two of the later masterpieces may be briefly defined: In *Benito Cereno,* the Spanish sea-captain of that name takes insufficient precautions in the transporting of a ship-load of negro slaves belonging to a friend; the slaves mutiny, kill most of the crew, and enslave the remainder, including the captain. When Cereno is finally rescued by Captain Delano, he is broken in spirit, and says that he can return home but to die. When Captain Delano inquires what has cast such a shadow upon him, he answers: "The negro." His reply in Spanish would have signified not only the negro, or the black man, but by metaphorical extension the basic evil in human nature. The morality of slavery is not an issue in this story; the issue is this, that through a series of acts of performance and of negligence, the fundamental evil of a group of men, evil which normally should have been kept in abeyance, was freed to act. The story is a portrait of that evil in action, as shown in the negroes, and of the effect of the action, as shown in Cereno. It is appalling in its completeness, in its subtle horror, and in its silky quiet.

In *The Encantadas,* we have a series of ten sketches, descriptive of the Galápagos Islands. These islands, as described by Melville, are more of the sea, as the sea appears in *Moby Dick,* than is any other land. In the first place they are so surrounded by treacherous calms and ocean currents, that for many years their exact location was wrongly charted, two groups of islands at a considerable distance apart having been charted instead of one: it was this mysterious quality which gave them their early name, *The Enchanted Islands.* Further, of all land they are the most barren, according to Melville, and the most hostile to human life:

they are inhabited only by reptiles and by seabirds, and one or two of them by the most desperate and debased of human renegades.

Melville's descriptive power in this series is at its best; the islands in all their barren and archaic horror are realized unforgettably. The climax of the series is the account of Hunilla, the Chola, who went to the islands with her husband and her brother to gather turtle oil, much as the Nantucketers went to sea for the oil of the whale. Her husband and her brother were drowned while fishing. The ship that left them did not return. She was ravished by the boat-crews of two whalers and left behind by them, and was ultimately rescued and returned to Peru by the ship of which Melville was one of the seamen. She was thus a victim of the sea; that is, of brute chance and brutal malice, forces over which she had no control, and in the face of which the only supporting virtues were absolute humility and absolute fortitude: "The last seen of the lone Hunilla she was passing into Payta town, riding upon a small gray ass; and before her on the ass's shoulders, she eyed the jointed workings of the beast's armorial cross."

The subject of *Billy Budd* may best be considered after a short account of *Pierre* and *The Confidence Man*, the two works which in reality, though unsuccessful, do more to clarify Melville's total work than any book save *Moby Dick*, and which have above all others left his critics in the most abysmal confusion.

The plot of *Pierre, or The Ambiguities* may be summarized briefly thus: Pierre Glendinning, the son of a wealthy and aristocratic New York family, discovers that he has an illegitimate half-sister the daughter of his father and of a young French girl. This is a severe shock, for he had revered his father's memory deeply. The sister, Isabel, is without friends or funds. Pierre feels morally bound to help her in some manner, and also in some way to acknowledge her, to unite his life to hers, yet he knows that to acknowledge her as a sister will blight his mother's life. Hence, though he is engaged to marry Lucy Tartan, he announces to Lucy and his mother that he and Isabel have been secretly married, and he takes Isabel to New York, and tries to support himself by his pen. His mother disowns and disinherits him. Lucy is prostrated, but recovers and follows Pierre to New York, where she joins the household under the guise of a cousin. She is pursued by her brother and by Pierre's cousin, who has supplanted Pierre as the Glendinning heir. Pierre kills the cousin; Lucy dies of shock and Pierre and Isabel commit suicide in Pierre's prison cell.

Now despite the difference in plot and in subject matter, the idea of this book is the same as that governing *Moby Dick*, but with a shift in emphasis: it is the relationship of principle to perception, and the difficulty of adjusting principle to perception in such a manner as to permit a judgment which shall be a valid motive to action. In *Moby Dick*, Melville assumed that such judgment, though difficult, was possible; Ahab sinned by disregarding the counsel of Starbuck (the critical intellect), by destroying his nautical instruments, with the aid of which he maintained his position while at sea (that is, in the half-known) with relation to the land (the known), and by committing himself to his own unaided instincts. In *Pierre* and in *The Confidence Man* alike it is assumed that valid judgment is impossible, for every event, every fact, every person, is too fluid, too unbounded to be known:

"If among the deeper significances of its pervading indefiniteness," he says in *Pierre*, "which significances are wisely hidden from all but the rarest adepts, the pregnant tragedy of Hamlet convey any one particular moral at all fitted to the ordinary uses of man, it is this:—that all meditation is worthless, unless it prompt to action; that it is not for man to stand shilly-shallying amid the conflicting invasions of surrounding impulses; that in the earliest instant of conviction, the roused man must strike, and, if possible, with the precision and force of the lightning bolt."

This is obviously the counsel of the despairing moralist; briefly, it may be reduced to this advice: act quickly, for if you give yourself time to reconsider, you will be unable to act. Pierre acts—he surely cannot be accused of moral paralysis—but he acts hastily and on unsound principles; he is convinced that the world is one of moral confusion, and he proceeds in confusion; intellectually, if not emotionally, he is satisfied with confusion; and for the time being his author is at one with him in this respect. The following passage from *Pierre* recalls, in its governing idea, the invocation to Bulkington, but again with the change of emphasis characteristic of the later work:

"As the vine flourishes, as the grape empurples, close up to the very walls and muzzles of cannoned Ehrenbreitstein; so do the sweetest joys of life grow in the very jaws of its perils.

"But is life, indeed, a thing for all infidel levities, and we, its misdeemed beneficiaries, so utterly fools and infatuate, that what we take to be our strongest tower of delight, only stands at the caprice of the minutest event—the falling of a leaf, the hearing of a voice, or the receipt of one little bit of paper scratched over with a few small characters by a sharpened feather?"

The substance of this passage is this: that our safety is momentary and precarious; but that there is no trustworthy precaution that we can take against evil. It thus resembles the invocation to Bulkington in its general proposition, but differs from it, in that the present passage would imply that Bulkington's efforts were unavailing.

Isabel, similarly, after telling how she gradually regained a normal attitude after being removed from the madhouse at the age of nine or ten, and being placed with a friendly family, remarks: "I cannot speak coherently here; but somehow I felt that all good harmless men and women were human things, placed at cross-purposes, in a world of snakes and lightnings, in a world of horrible and inscrutable inhumanities."

There are in the plot of *Pierre*, two situations in particular, the two central issues of the book, which are intended to illustrate the ambiguity of all supposed morality. One is the double image of his father: that of the father remembered and represented by the portrait painted after his marriage; and that of the young rake who begot Isabel, whose existence was suddenly disclosed to Pierre, and who is represented by the portrait painted when he was visiting Isabel's mother. Between the extremes of the two portraits Pierre's judgment of his father blurs and shifts and cannot be fixed; it is this difficulty that disturbed Pierre to the extent that he precipitately projected himself into the relationship with Isabel. This relationship provides the second ambiguity, for though at the time of his action Pierre believed that he was acting wholly for moral and generous reasons, he discovered immediately after acting that he was the victim of an incestuous passion for Isabel, so that he learns to distrust his own motives. At the conclusion of the book, the author confronts the reader with a final ambiguity, the problem of judging Pierre: " 'All's over and ye know him not!' came gasping from the wall; and from the fingers of Isabel dropped an empty vial—as it had been a run-out sand-glass—and shivered upon the floor; and her whole form sloped sideways, and she fell upon Pierre's heart, and her long hair ran over him and arbored him in ebon vines."

The lecture of Plotinus Plinlimmon on clocks and chronometers, which falls into Pierre's hands as a kind of warning, teaches that we should establish a working compromise between absolute and worldly truth, if we are not to destroy ourselves. This also is the moral of Moby Dick: the need of recognizing not only man's aspirations, but his limitations. Pierre, however, like Ahab, lacks humility; unlike Ahab, he is not seen by his author in perspective—that is, Melville agrees with him: "In those Hyperborean regions, to which enthusiastic Truth, and Earnestness, and Independence, will invariably lead a mind fitted by nature for profound and fearless thoughts, all objects are seen in a dubious, uncertain, and refracting light. Viewed through that rarified atmosphere the most immemorially admitted maxims of men begin to slide and fluctuate, and finally become wholly inverted; the very heavens themselves being not innocent of producing this confounding effect, since it is mostly in the heavens themselves that these wonderful mirages are exhibited.

"But the example of many minds forever lost, like undiscoverable arctic explorers, amid those treacherous regions, warns us entirely away from them; and we learn that it is not for man to follow the trail of truth too far, since by so doing he entirely loses the directing compass of his mind; for arrived at the Pole, to whose barrenness only it points, there, the needle indifferently respects all points of the horizon alike."

226

This morality is that of the book: that the final truth is absolute ambiguity, and that nothing can be judged. It frustrates all action, including that of the artist and that of the critic. We are explicitly informed that we cannot judge Pierre; the essence of Pierre is that he can judge nothing and that all his actions derive from confusion and end in it. It is small wonder that a book composed in this temporary twilight should have been so unsatisfactory as a whole and in detail; for a work of art, like each detail comprising it, is by definition a judgment. The prose of Pierre is excited and inflated; it contains brilliant passages, but in the main is a bad compromise between the prose of *Moby Dick* and the prose of the novelist.

The theme of *The Confidence Man* is identical; the details of the action are very different. The action takes place on a Mississippi River steamer, aboard which a confidence man, a scoundrel of metaphysical abilities and curiosity, operates partly for profit and partly for malicious enjoyment. He appears in various disguises: as the deaf mute in cream-colored clothes; as the negro cripple; as the man in mourning; as the man in the gray coat and the white tie; as the President of the Black Rapids Coal Company; as the herb doctor; as "the man with the brass plate," or the representative of the Philosophical Intelligence Office; and as the cosmopolitan.

In each avatar, the Confidence Man tries to beguile his fellow-travelers into feeling enough confidence in him to give him money; that is, to form a judgment on which they are willing to act. It should be noted, of course, that if they do so, they are hoodwinked. The word *confidence* recurs repeatedly, and is the key-word of the allegory.

In the third chapter, after the man with the wooden leg (a major disseminator of distrust) has nearly started a riot against the crippled negro, the Methodist Minister moves to the center of things, gives the man with the wooden leg a beating, and addresses the crowd:

"Oh friends, oh beloved, how are we admonished by the melancholy spectacle of this raver. Let us profit by the lesson; and is it not this: that if, next to mistrusting Providence, there be

227

ought that a man should pray against, it is against mistrusting his fellow-man. I have been in mad-houses full of tragic mopers, and seen there the end of suspicion: the cynic, in the moody madness muttering in the corner; for years a barren fixture there; head lopped over, gnawing his own lip, vulture of himself; while by fits and starts from the opposite corner came the grimaces of the idiot at him."

This sounds well, till we remember the context; the minister, in avoiding the madhouse, becomes a dupe. This antithesis alone, or the escape into deliberate hypocrisy, is all that Melville will allow in this book; the possibility of the reasonable skepticism of the cautious and critical man, as a prelude to a judgment at least practically usable, he will not admit.

The man in the gray coat and the white tie is trying to restore the confidence of the young minister (not the Methodist Minister) in the old negro, when they encounter the man with the wooden leg, who laughs insanely and tells an anecdote casting ridicule on confidence. The man with the wooden leg claims that the negro is a·white imposter. The man with the gray coat and the white tie says:

" 'Tell me, sir, do you really think that a white could look the negro so? For one, I should call it pretty good acting.'

" 'Not much better than any other man acts.'

" 'How? Does all the world act? Am I, for instance, an actor? Is my reverend friend here, too, a performer?'

" 'Yes, don't you both perform acts? To do is to act; so all doers are actors.' "

The effect of this passage is as follows: to perform an action is to have confidence in the motivating judgment. But no man save a hypocrite can profess to have such confidence. Hence a "doer" is an "actor."

The most amusing illustration of the theme is the story of the Indian hater, with its attendant and philosophical theory of Indian-hating. The Indian, in this legend, represents the man or fact to be judged and so trusted or suspected; if trusted, he is necessarily untrustworthy, in accordance with the doctrine, for it is impossible to obtain knowledge adequate for a sound judg-

228

ment. The Indian-hater is one who trusts no Indian, but spends his life in the woods killing every Indian he meets. But most Indian-haters are imperfect; sometimes one will unaccountably become lonely and trust an Indian at random and so meet his end; others take frequent vacations and return to their families. Of these last, the narrator says: "For the diluted Indian hater, although the vacations he permits himself impair the keeping of his character, yet, it should not be overlooked that this is the man who, by his very infirmity, enables us to form surmises, however inadequate, of what Indian-hating in its perfection is." Henry Adams, I should imagine, is the most distinguished example of the diluted Indian-hater in our literature.

The Confidence Man is unsatisfactory as philosophy and is tediously repetitious as narrative; but the prose, unlike that of *Pierre,* is crisp and hard, and in a few passages the comment is brilliant. The incident of the mystic, Mark Winsome, and of his disciple, the wealthy young merchant, who turns the mystical doctrine to practical ends, is a very biting commentary on Emerson and on the practical implications of Emersonian philosophy.

Melville was in a kind of moral limbo when he wrote these books, however, and they are essentially unsatisfactory, though they display greater intellectual activity than such works as *White Jacket, Typee,* and *Omoo,* works which within their limits are successful. His failure in the two, however, is in a sense a proof of the seriousness with which he took his central problem of moral navigation; he considered the problem in all its possibilities, and with sufficient imaginative intensity to leave a fairly complete record of his consideration behind him. The notion advanced by Mumford and others, that these books come out of a period of insanity, is as absurd as the notion of Weaver that *Pierre,* if psychoanalyzed in the proper spirit, is autobiographical. Both theories, of course, may be correct, but there is no evidence to support either that would be admitted in court by a disinterested criminal judge; and furthermore, it is the relationship of these books to his work that we must understand if we desire to profit by his work—their relationship to his life is as unprofitable as it is unfathomable.

Hawthorne finished his career in much the same limbo; Henry Adams passed his entire career there, but not so far in. There is more madness in *The Sense of the Past*, by Henry James, than in either book, and far more in the poetry of T. S. Eliot. Yet none of these writers is insane; as a result, rather, of being involved in historical processes beyond their own powers to understand the processes and extricate themselves, they are guilty of forms of literary procedure which isolate certain aspects of the consciousness from the rest, thus producing, within the literary form, an imperfect intelligence; which, however, if mistaken for a perfect portrait and used as a model for imitation, may be a step toward personal disintegration.

In the final masterpiece, *Billy Budd*, the most profound of the later works, if not the best written—the prose, unfortunately, shows a little structural awkwardness, the result of thirty years of disuse—the problem posed in *Pierre* and *The Confidence Man* received its answer. The plot is as follows: Billy Budd, a handsome young sailor on a British frigate, is accused to the captain of conspiracy; the accuser, Claggart, is constitutionally a malicious and dishonest man, who perjures himself to gratify an irrational dislike. Billy is called before the captain to meet the accusation; he is young, strong, and a man of quick feeling, and he is handicapped by an innocent mind and a bad stutter. His muscles move quicker than his tongue; he strikes Claggart in the head and kills him; he is tried and hanged.

The captain, Vere, is able to fathom the situation; from the standpoint of purely private morality, he sympathizes with Billy. But Billy, in striking Claggart under these conditions committed a capital crime, and in killing him committed another, facts which Billy knew perfectly; to free him would establish at least a precedent for freeing the whole matter of criminal justice in the navy to the caprices of private judgment; the men would be likely to take advantage of it, to the damage of discipline. There had, moreover, been serious riots in the navy but a short time before. Vere can see only one solution to the situation: to act according to established principle, which supports public order, and, for the margin of difference between established principle and the facts of the particular situation, to accept it as private tragedy.

The solution, with certain modifications, is the solution of Mrs. Wharton for the same moral problem as it was later posed by Henry James; the moral principle, in the better works of Mrs. Wharton, however, is usually incarnate in a code of manners, and at times appears less defensible than in Billy Budd, because of the tendency observable in codes of manners to become externalized and superficial, to become insulated from the principles informing them with life. The solution, in terms as bald and absolute as the terms of Melville, was likewise the solution of Socrates. It is not every situation, of course, which admits of a solution by virtue of so certain a reference to the "known": there may be cases, as Henry James was later to demonstrate almost to his own undoing, and as Melville asserted in *Moby Dick*, in which the problem of moral navigation, though not insoluble, is a subtler one, in which the exact relevance of any single principle is harder to establish, and in which there may appear to be the claims of conflicting principles. The solution, however, in the case of this story, and as a matter of general principle, is at once unanswerable, dignified, and profound; the characterization of Vere and of Claggart represents an insight worthy to be the final achievement of so long and so great a life.

III

The other works which deserve discussion may now be considered very briefly. The first two, *Typee* and *Omoo*, are anecdotal narratives of personal adventure in the south seas. There is no guiding theme; the prose has a freshness and loveliness that at times put one inexplicably in mind of the verse of the early Marlowe, but its virtues are minor and fragmentary. The next work, *Mardi*, is a long allegorical narrative, with what purports to be a south Pacific setting; it is the most ambitious work in length and scope, aside from *Moby Dick*, and though scarcely unified is extremely powerful.

Mardi falls into four parts; the opening chapters, in which the protagonist tells of his life on a Pacific whaler; the subsequent chapters, following his desertion, with a comrade, Jarl, in which he describes the ocean as seen from an open boat, chapters rivalling in their description all save the finest descriptive passages in *Moby Dick;* the chapters describing their life for some weeks on a small island schooner which they overtake, manned only by a native islander and his wife, this section containing the sharpest and most amusing characterization of island temperament that Melville ever achieved; and the remainder and chief part of the book, which deals with the imaginary and allegorical region of Mardi. The allegory of the last part deals with the search for the maiden Yillah, who appears to represent earthly happiness; the narrator and searcher is pursued by Queen Hautia, who appears to represent sensual corruption, and who is inescapably related in some mysterious fashion to Yillah, and by the sons of a priest whom he slew early in the narrative to obtain temporary possession of Yillah. We appear to have, then, the pursuit for something approaching romantic love, with the flight at once from romantic disillusionment (Hautia) and from the consequences of one's own sins committed in the name of love. In the search, the narrator and his companions visit all the realms of Mardi, and observe every possible mode of life and government, but they fail to find Yillah. The only one of the party who finds happiness is the half-mad and embittered philosopher, Babbalanja, who is converted to Christianity on the way, and who thereupon renounces the world.

The theme is immature and romantic, and many of the parts are of small interest; yet many of the parts, within the limits of their subject, possess extraordinary beauty, and had Melville never developed beyond this point, it would have been necessary to accord him one of the very highest places in romantic literature. The most extraordinary portion of the book is the series of chapters, numbers seventy-one to eighty-five, inclusive, dealing with the stay in Willamilla; they constitute the richest, and from a rhetorical point of view the most powerfully moving, rhapsody on romantic sensuousness with which I am acquainted. The supper of Abrazza, toward the close, and the conversion of Babbalanja, though briefer, are at moments nearly as excellent. In these passages, and elsewhere in the book, notably in the great invocation to Kamehameha, in chapter sixty-eight, the epic prose of *Moby Dick* is already highly developed.

In *White-Jacket* we have another anecdotal journal, of which the high points are the account of Dr. Cuticle and his operation, and the brief chapter entitled The Bay of All Beauties; in this work, the romanticism has already begun to wane. *Redburn*, published in the same year, and dealing with Melville's first voyage, has similar virtues and limitations, and is perhaps more consistently of interest. *Israel Potter*, the life of an American patriot of the Revolutionary War, is one of the few great novels of pure adventure in English; it comes after *Moby Dick* in point of time, and probably surpasses all the works preceding *Moby Dick* save, possibly, *Mardi*.

EDGAR ALLAN POE

A Crisis in the History of American Obscurantism

("Men have called me mad; but the question is not yet settled, whether madness is or is not the loftiest intelligence)—whether much that is glorious—whether all that is profound—does not spring from disease of thought—from moods of mind exalted at the expense of the general intellect."

—Eleanora

I AM ABOUT TO promulgate a heresy; namely, that E. A. Poe, although he achieved, as his admirers have claimed, a remarkable agreement between his theory and his practice, is exceptionally bad in both. I am somewhat startled, moreover, to awaken to the fact that this is a heresy, that those who object to Poe would do well to establish their position now if ever. Poe has long passed casually with me and with most of my friends as a bad writer accidentally and temporarily popular; the fact of the matter is, of course, that he has been pretty effectually established as a great writer while we have been sleeping. The menace lies not, primarily, in his impressionistic admirers among literary people, of whom he still has some, even in England and in America, where a familiarity with his language ought to render his crudity obvious, for these individuals in the main do not make themselves permanently very effective; it lies rather in the impressive body of scholarship, beginning, perhaps, with Harrison, Woodberry, and Stedman, and continuing down to such writers as Campbell, Stovall, and Una Pope-Hennessy. Much of this scholarship is primarily biographical, historical, and textual; but when a writer is supported by a sufficient body of such scholarship, a very little philosophical elucidation will suffice to establish him in the scholarly world as a writer whose greatness is self-evident. This fact is made especially evident in the work of the two critics who come closest to taking the position which I shall take: W. C. Brownell [1] and especially Norman Foerster.[2] Both approach the essential issue; neither is able, or it may be that because of its absurdity neither is willing, to define it; and both maintain the traditional reverence for Poe as a stylist, a reverence which I believe to be at once unjustified and a source of error in dealing with his theory.

My consternation became acute upon the examination of a recent edition of selections from Poe, prepared, it is true, merely as a classroom text, but prepared with great competence, by a respectable Poe scholar, the late Margaret Alterton, and by an exceptionally distinguished scholar in the field of the English Renaissance, Professor Hardin Craig.[3] The Introduction to this text, the first and second parts of which were written by Miss Alterton and after her death revised by Professor Craig, the third part of which was written wholly by Professor Craig, offers the best general defense of Poe with which I am acquainted; it is careful and thorough, and it makes as good a case for Poe, I imagine, as can be made. And when one has finished it, one has a perfectly clear idea of why it is wrong.

The problem is a simple one. Most of Poe's essential theory is summarized in three essays: *The Poetic Principle*, *The Philosophy of Composition*, and *The Rationale of Verse*. Important statements can be found elsewhere, and I shall draw upon other essays, but these essays contain most of the essential ideas. Furthermore the essential statements recur repeatedly in other essays, frequently almost verbatim. By confining oneself largely to these essays, by selecting the crucial statements, by showing as briefly as possible their obvious relations one to another, one can reduce Poe's aesthetic to a very brief and a perfectly accurate

[1] W. C. Brownell, *American Prose Masters* (New York, 1909).
[2] Norman Foerster, *American Criticism* (Boston and New York, 1928). I should like, if I had time, to examine Professor Foerster's essay on Poe at length, partly because of the similarities and the differences between his position and my own, and partly because of a matter largely irrelevant but none the less astonishing—that is, Professor Foerster's view of the nature and history of music, subjects of which he displays an ignorance nothing less than sweeping.
[3] *Edgar Allan Poe*, edited by Craig and Alterton (New York, 1935).

statement. In doing this, I shall endeavor in every case to inter-pret what he says directly, not with the aid of other writers whose theories may have influenced him and by aid of whose theories one may conceivably be able to gloss over some of his confusion; and I shall endeavor to show that this direct approach is fully justified by his own artistic practice.

The passages which I shall quote have all been quoted many times before; I shall have to beg indulgence on that score and ask the reader to examine once and for all their obvious significance.

Any study of Poe should begin with a statement made in con-nection with Elizabeth Barrett's *A Drama of Exile*. He says: "This is emphatically the thinking age; indeed it may very well be questioned whether man ever substantially thought before." [4] This sentence displays an ignorance at once of thought and of the history of thought so comprehensive as to preclude the pos-sibility of our surprise at any further disclosures. It helps to ex-plain, furthermore, Poe's extraordinary inability to understand even the poetry of ages previous to his own, as well as his sub-servience in matters of taste to the vulgar sentimentalism which dominated the more popular poets of his period, such poets as Moore, Hood, and Willis, to mention no others. One seldom en-counters a writer so thoroughly at the mercy of contemporaneity. Professor Foerster writes of him: "Of this sustaining power of the past, it must be admitted, Poe himself had but a dim understand-ing." And he quotes Professor Woodberry (*Life*, I, 132) as fol-lows: "He had, in the narrowest sense, a contemporaneous mind, the instincts of the journalist, the magazine writer." [5]

II

One cannot better introduce the question of Poe's aesthetics than by his well-known remarks about Tennyson, in *The Poetic Prin-ciple:* "In perfect sincerity, I regard him as the noblest poet that

---

[4] All quotations in this essay are from the edition of Stedman and Wood-berry. Quotations from the criticism only are given footnotes. This quotation is from Vol. I, page 294, of the three volumes of criticism.

[5] Foerster, op. cit., pages 1 and 2.

ever lived. . . . I call him and *think* him, the noblest of poets, not because the impressions he produces are at *all* times the most profound, not because the poetical excitement which he induces is at *all* times the most intense, but because it *is*, at all times the most ethereal,—in other words, the most elevating and the most pure. No poet is so little of the earth, earthy." [6] The italics, of course, here and elsewhere are Poe's; it is seldom necessary to improve upon Poe in this respect. Our task will be primarily to find out what this passage means. I believe that I shall be able to show that it means this: that the poet should not deal with human, that is, moral, experience; that the subject-matter of poetry is of an order essentially supra-human; that the poet has no way of understanding his subject-matter. There will appear certain qualifications to this summary, but they are of very little importance.

In the same essay Poe states: "I hold that a long poem does not exist. I maintain that the phrase, 'a long poem,' is a flat contradiction of terms." [7] And again, thus connecting the last statement with the statement regarding Tennyson: "A poem deserves its title only inasmuch as it elevates by exciting the soul. . . . But all excitements are, through a psychal necessity, transient." "After the lapse of half an hour at the utmost, it [the excitement] flags—fails—a revulsion ensues—and then the poem is in effect, and in fact, no longer such." [8] "This great work [*Paradise Lost*], in fact, is to be regarded as poetical, only when, losing sight of that vital requisite of all works of Art, Unity, we view it merely as a series of minor poems. If, to preserve its Unity,—its totality of effect or impression—we read it (as would be necessary) at a single sitting, the result is but a constant alternation of excitement and depression. . . . It follows from all this that the ultimate, aggregate, or absolute effect of even the best epic under the sun is a nullity:—and this is precisely the fact." [9]

From these passages it follows: first, that Poe's very conception of poetic unity is one of mood, or emotion; and second, that

[6] Stedman and Woodberry, op. cit., I, 27.
[7] Ibid., I, 3
[8] Ibid., I,
[9] Ibid., I, 4.

he regards the existence of mood to be governed by narrow mechanical rules—in other words, exaltation of spirit is merely a form of nervous excitement. The word *effect* is used here as elsewhere as a synonym for *impression;* artistic unity is described specifically as totality of effect. There appears to be no awareness whatever of that comprehensive act of the spirit, in part intellectual, whereby we understand and remember *Paradise Lost* as a whole, seize the whole intention with intellect and with memory, and, plunging into any passage, experience that passage in relationship to the whole, an act in which the emotional element, since it is involved in and supported by the rational understanding, rises superior to mechanical necessity.

We should observe further that in these passages Poe begins that process of systematic exclusion, in the course of which he eliminates from the field of English poetry nearly all of the greatest acknowledged masters, reserving the field very largely to Coleridge, Tennyson, Thomas Moore, himself, and R. H. Horne. As we shall see, this process of elimination is not a mere accident of temperament, is not merely a series of accidents of judgment, but is the necessary corollary, in the field of particular judgments, of the general theory which we are now considering.

Poe continues: "On the other hand, it is clear that a poem may be improperly brief. Undue brevity degenerates into mere epigrammatism. A *very* short poem, while now and then producing a brilliant or vivid, never produces a profound or enduring effect." [10] He cites *The Indian Serenade,* by Shelley, a poem of twenty-four lines, as unduly brief. He regarded one hundred lines as approximately the most effective number for a poem; the length of the lines themselves, he appears never to have considered, though if we compare two of his own poems of nearly the same number of lines, *Ulalume* and *The Raven,* the former, in fact and in effect, is much the shorter.

We may observe in the preceding quotation once more the obliviousness to the function of intellectual content in poetry, and an act of exclusion which deals very shortly, not only with the epigrammatists, but also with every sonneteer in the lan-

[10] Ibid., I, 6.

guage, including Shakespeare and Milton, and with all the masters of the short lyric, including so wide a diversity of poets as Herbert, Herrick, Donne, and Landor.

By a further act of exclusion, he eliminates the great satirical and didactic masters. In his essay on Bryant, he says: "A satire is, of course, no poem." [11] And in *The Poetic Principle*: "We find it [the 'epic mania'] succeeded by a heresy too palpably false to be long tolerated. . . . I allude to the heresy of *The Didactic*. It has long been assumed that the end of all poetry is Truth. Every poem, it is said, should inculcate a moral; and by this moral is the poetical merit of the work to be adjudged. We Americans, especially, have patronized this happy idea; and we Bostonians, very especially, have developed it in full. We have taken it into our heads to write a poem simply for the poem's sake, and to acknowledge such to have been our design would be to confess ourselves radically wanting in true poetic dignity and force; but the simple fact is, that, would we but permit ourselves to look into our own souls, we should immediately there discover that under the sun there neither exists nor *can* exist any work more thoroughly dignified, more supremely noble, than this very poem—this poem *per se*—this poem which is a poem and nothing more—this poem written solely for the poem's sake." [12]

Now if Poe had merely intended to exclude some of the unsatisfactory didactic poetry, let us say, of Longfellow or of Lowell, we should have very little complaint to make; however, these poets are bad not because they are didactic, but because they write badly, and because their didacticism is frequently unsound in conception, and because the lesson which they endeavor to teach is frequently connected only arbitrarily with their subjects. The didactic close of Byrant's great lyric, *To a Waterfowl*, on the other hand, is merely an explicit statement, and a fine statement, of the idea governing the poem, an idea inherent, but insufficiently obvious, in what has gone before, and it is foolish to object to it; and in the poetry of Samuel Johnson, of Dryden,

[11] Ibid., I, 111.
[12] Ibid., I, 8.

and of Pope, as in Milton's sonnets, we have yet another form of didacticism, the loss of which would leave us vastly impoverished.[13]

Poe appears never to have grasped the simple and traditional distinction between matter (truth) and manner (beauty); he does not see that beauty is a quality of style instead of its subject-matter, that it is merely the most complete communication possible, through connotation as well as denotation, of the poet's personal realization of a moral (or human) truth, whether that truth be of very great importance or very little, a truth that must be understood primarily in conceptual terms, regardless of whether the poem ultimately embodies it in the form of description, of narration, or of exposition. A sound attitude toward a major problem, communicated with adequacy of detail, is what we ordinarily mean by sublimity. It is through the neglect of these fundamental ideas that Poe runs into difficulty.

"With as deep a reverence for the True as ever inspired the bosom of man," he continues, "I would, nevertheless, limit its modes of inculcation. I would limit to enforce them. I would not enfeeble them by dissipation. The demands of Truth are severe; she has no sympathy with the myrtles. All *that* which is so indispensable in Song, is precisely all *that* with which *she* has nothing whatever to do. . . . In enforcing a truth . . . we must be in that mood which, as nearly as possible, is the exact converse of the poetical." [14]

Poe appears oblivious to the possibility that we may come to a truth with an attitude other than that of the advocate; that we may, in brief, contemplate, with Dante, rather than enforce, with Aquinas. It follows that he would not recognize the more complex procedure of contemplating the enforcement of truth, the procedure which results, for example, in the didacticism of Pope and of Dryden; nor yet the contemplation of the need of the

---

[13] It is instructive to compare *To a Waterfowl* with *The Chambered Nautilus*. Both follow the same rhetorical formula, but in Bryant's poem the "moral" is implicit throughout; in the poem by Holmes, it is a rhetorical imposition. The poem by Holmes is impressively written, notwithstanding; but it illustrates the more vulgar procedure.

[14] Stedman and Woodberry, op. cit., I, 9.

enforcement of truth, the procedure which results in the satirical poetry of the same writers; nor the contemplation of a discrepancy between personal experience and a standard truth, a procedure which results in much of the poetry of Donne. Yet these are all major human experiences; they all require individual perception and moral adjustment; according to the traditional view, they are thus legitimate material for poetry.

Poe sees truly enough that the enforcement of truth, in itself, does not constitute poetry, and on the basis of that elementary observation he falls into the common romantic error, which may be stated briefly as follows: truth is not poetry; truth should therefore be eliminated from poetry, in the interests of a purer poetry. He would, in short, advise us to retain the attitude, but to discard the object of the attitude. The correct formula, on the other hand, is this: truth is not poetry; poetry is truth and something more. It is the completeness of the poetic experience which makes it valuable. How thoroughly Poe would rob us of all subject matter, how thoroughly he would reduce poetry, from its traditional position, at least when ideally considered, as the act of complete comprehension, to a position of triviality and of charlatanism, we shall presently see.

Poe's passion for exclusion, and the certitude that he has no conception of moral sublimity in poetry, appear very clearly in the essay on Horne's *Orion:* "We shall now be fully understood. If, with Coleridge, who, however erring at times, was precisely the mind fitted to decide such a question as this—if, with him, we reject passion from the true, from the pure poetry—if we reject even passion—if we discard as feeble, as unworthy of the high spirituality of the theme (which has its origin in the Godhead)—if we dismiss even the nearly divine emotion of human *love,* that emotion which merely to name causes the pen to tremble,—with how much greater reason shall we dismiss all else?" [15]

The dismissal appears to be inclusive enough, by this time, in all conscience. There would appear to be some confusion in Poe's mind between a passionate or violent style, which (in spite of the

[15] Ibid., I, 268.

magnificence of *King Lear*) he might reasonably regard as inferior to a style more serene, regardless of subject, as if the poet were to rise superior to his passions in his contemplation of them, and passion as subject-matter. It is his fundamental confusion of matter and manner, to which I have already alluded.

In the same essay, and on the same subject, he writes: "Although we argue, for example, with Coleridge, that poetry and passion are discordant, yet we are willing to permit Tennyson to bring, to the intense passion which prompted his *Locksley Hall,* the aid of that terseness and pungency which are derivable from rhythm and from rhyme. The effect he produces, however, is purely passionate, and not, unless in detached passages of this magnificent philippic, a properly poetic effect. His *Oenone*, on the other hand, exalts the soul not into passion, but into a conception of pure *beauty,* which in its elevation, its calm and intense rapture, has in it a foreshadowing of the future and spiritual life, and as far transcends earthly passion as the holy radiance of the sun does the glimmering and feeble phosphorescence of the glow-worm. His *Morte-d'Arthur* is in the same majestic vein. *The Sensitive Plant* of Shelley is in the same sublime spirit . . . Readers do exist . . . and always will exist, who, to hearts of maddening fervor, unite in perfection, the sentiment of the beautiful—that divine sixth sense which is yet so faintly understood, that sense which phrenology has attempted to embody in its organ of *ideality*,[16] that sense which speaks of God through His purest, if not His *sole* attribute, which proves, and which alone proves his existence . . . the origin of poetry lies in a thirst for a wilder beauty than earth supplies. . . . Poetry itself is the imperfect effort to quench this immortal thirst by novel combinations of beautiful forms. . . ."[17]

In the remarks on *Oenone*, we may seem at first glance to have the hint that Poe has approached the concept of moral sublimity, but the last sentence quoted brings us back abruptly to the trivial; the exaltation is not a moral exaltation, not the result of

---

[16] See Edward Hungerford, *Poe and Phrenology*, American Literature, II, 209-31 (Nov., 1930).

[17] Stedman and Woodberry, op. cit., I, 267-8.

the exercise of the intelligence and of character, but is the result of manipulation and of trickery. And were we to allow ourselves the luxury of worrying about Poe's minor obscurities, his use of the word *beautiful* in the last sentence would complicate our problem inextricably: that is, it appears that we achieve the beautiful by new combinations of items which are already beautiful; we have again his helpless inability to separate matter from manner, the poem from its subject.

It is obvious, then, that poetry is not, for Poe, a refined and enriched technique of moral comprehension. It can be of no aid to us in understanding ourselves or in ordering our lives, for most of our experience is irrelevant to it. If, indeed, certain human experiences are admitted as legitimate subjects, they are admitted, as we shall see, because the poet cannot write without writing about something—even the most irresponsible use of language involves an inescapable minimum of statement, however incomplete or dismembered; and those experiences are admitted which seem to involve the minimum of complexity. They are admitted, moreover, not as something valuable in themselves, not as something to be understood, but as ingredients in a formula by means of which something outside our experience may be suggested. If Poe moves us most to indignation when defining his exclusions, he perplexes us most profoundly when he endeavors to approximate a definition of what he would include.

He writes in *The Poetic Principle:* "An immortal instinct, deep within the spirit of man, is thus, plainly, a sense of the Beautiful. . . . This thirst belongs to the immortality of man. It is at once a consequence and an indication of his perennial existence. It is the desire of the moth for the star. It is no mere appreciation of the Beauty before us, but a wild effort to reach the Beauty above. Inspired by an ecstatic Prescience of the glories beyond the grave, we struggle by multiform combinations among the things and thoughts of Time to attain a portion of that Loveliness whose very elements, perhaps, appertain to eternity alone. And thus when by Poetry—or when by Music, the most entrancing of the Poetic moods—we find ourselves melted into tears, we weep then, not as the Abbate Gravia supposes through excess of pleasure, but through a certain petulant, impatient sorrow at our inability to grasp now, wholly, here on earth, at once and forever, those divine and rapturous joys, of which *through* the poem, or *through* the music, we attain to but brief and indeterminate glimpses." [18]

Briefly, Poe implies something like this: the proper subject-matter of poetry is Beauty, but since true Beauty exists only in eternity, the poet cannot experience it and is deprived of his subject-matter; by manipulating the materials of our present life, we may *suggest that Beauty exists elsewhere,* and this is the best that we can do.

This is not the same thing as the mysticism of such a writer as Very, for Very sought to define what he considered a truth, the experience of mystical beatitude, and the experience of human longing for it; the former experience, though inexpressible, he strove to express clearly; the latter experience, since it was clearly expressible, he expressed clearly. Very, moreover, as a Christian, believed in moral judgment, in poetry and out, in spite of the fact that as a Calvinist he seems to have believed that his moral judgments were actually dictated by God. Nor is it the same thing as the awareness on the part of Emily Dickinson of the abyss between the human and the supra-human or the extra-human, for she merely defines the tragic experience of confronting the abyss and communicates her own moral adjustment to the experience, or at least she does no more than this in her better poems. Both poets seek to understand and both are as far as may be successful; Poe seeks a justification for refusing to understand. Poe is no more a mystic than a moralist; he is an excited sentimentalist.

As we may discover from other passages, especially in *The Philosophy of Composition,* Poe had certain definite ideas in regard to which forms of human experience lent themselves best to this procedure, and also in regard to the rules of the procedure. Having decided, in an astonishing passage to which I shall presently return, that a melancholy tone most greatly facilitated his purpose, he wrote: " 'Of all melancholy topics, what,

[18] Ibid., 10-11.

244

according to the universal understanding of mankind is the *most* melancholy?' Death—was the obvious reply. 'And when,' I said, 'is this most melancholy of topics most poetical?' From what I have already explained at some length, the answer here also is obvious—'When it most closely allies itself to Beauty; the death, then, of a beautiful woman is, unquestionably, the most poetical topic in the world. . . .'" [19] In other words, we are not concerned to understand human experience; we are seeking, rather, the isolated elements, or fragments, of experience which may best serve as the ingredients of a formula for the production of a kind of emotional delusion, and our final decision in the matter is determined again by our inability to distinguish between the subject and the style of poetry, by the conviction that beauty is the subject of poetry.

The reader should note carefully what this means; perhaps he will pardon me for restating it: the subject-matter of poetry, properly considered, is by definition incomprehensible and unattainable; the poet, in dealing with something else, toward which he has no intellectual or moral responsibilities whatever ("Unless incidentally," says Poe, "poetry has no concern whatever either with Duty or with Truth" [20]), should merely endeavor to *suggest that a higher meaning exists*—in other words, should endeavor to suggest the presence of a meaning when he is aware of none. The poet has only to write a good description of something physically impressive, with an air of mystery, an air of meaning concealed.

An air of mystery, of strangeness, will then be of necessity, not an adjunct of poetic style, but the very essence of poetic style. In *Ligeia* there occurs the well-known passage which it is now necessary to quote: " 'There is no exquisite beauty,' says Bacon, Lord Verulam, speaking truly of all the forms and genera of beauty, 'without some *strangeness* in the proportion.' " But in Poe's terms, strangeness and beauty, from the standpoint of the practical poet, are identical. Related to this concept is his concept of originality, which I shall take up later and separately.

[19] Ibid., I, 39.
[20] Ibid., I, 12.

Poe is, in brief, an explicit obscurantist. Hawthorne, in his four last and unfinished romances, gives us the physical embodiment of allegory without the meaning to be embodied, but he appears to hope for a meaning, to be, somehow, pathetically and unsuccessfully in search of one. Henry James, in many stories, as in *The Spoils of Poynton*, to choose an obvious example, gives us a sequence of facts without being able to pass judgment upon them, so that the stories remain almost as inconclusive as Stockton's trivial *tour de force, The Lady or the Tiger?* Both men frequently write in advance of their understanding, the one as an allegorist, the other as a novelist. But in Poe, obscurantism has ceased to be merely an accident of inadequate understanding; it has become the explicit aim of writing and has begun the generation of a method. Poe's aesthetic is an aesthetic of obscurantism. We have that willful dislocation of feeling from understanding, which, growing out of the uncertainty regarding the nature of moral truth in general and its identity in particular situations which produced such writers as Hawthorne and James, was later to result through the exploitation of special techniques in the violent aberrations of the Experimental School of the twentieth century, culminating in the catastrophe of Hart Crane.[21]

Poe speaks a great deal of the need of originality. This quality, as he understands it, appears to be a fairly simple mechanical device, first, for fixing the attention, and second, for heightening the effect of strangeness. We may obtain a fair idea of his concept of originality of theme from his comment on a poem by Amelia Welby, quoted in the series of brief notes entitled *Minor Contemporaries:* "The subject has *nothing* of originality:—A widower muses by the grave of his wife. Here then is a great demerit; for originality of theme, if not absolutely first sought, should be among the first. Nothing is more clear than this proposition, although denied by the chlorine critics (the grass-green). The desire of the new is an element of the soul. The most exquisite pleasures grow dull in repetition. A strain of music enchants. Heard a second time, it pleases. Heard a tenth, it does

[21] For a detailed study of these techniques, see pages 30 to 101 of this volume.

not displease. We hear it a twentieth, and ask ourselves why we admired. At the fiftieth it produces ennui, at the hundredth disgust." [22]

Now I do not know what music most delighted Poe, unless perchance it may have been the melodies of Thomas Moore, but if I may be permitted to use exact numbers in the same figurative sense in which I conceive that Poe here used them, I am bound to say that my own experience with music differs profoundly. The trouble again is traceable to Poe's failure to understand the moral basis of art, to his view of art as a kind of stimulant, ingeniously concocted, which may, if one is lucky, raise one to a moment of divine delusion. A Bach fugue or a Byrd mass moves us not primarily because of any originality it may display, but because of its sublimity as I have already defined the term. Rehearing can do no more than give us a fuller and more secure awareness of this quality. The same is true of *Paradise Lost*. Poe fails to see that the originality of a poem lies not in the newness of the general theme—for if it did, the possibilities of poetry would have been exhausted long before the time of Poe—but in the quality of the personal intelligence, as that intelligence appears in the minutiae of style, in the defining limits of thought and of feeling, brought to the subject by the poet who writes of it. The originality, from Poe's point of view, of the subjects of such poems as *The Raven*, *The Sleeper*, and *Ulalume* would reside in the fantastic dramatic and scenic effects by means of which the subject of simple regret is concealed, diffused, and rendered ludicrous. From the same point of view, *Rose Aylmer* would necessarily be lacking in originality.

In *The Philosophy of Composition* Poe gives us a hint as to his conception of originality of style. After a brief discourse on originality of versification, and the unaccountable way in which it has been neglected, he states that he lays no claim to originality as regards the meter or the rhythm of *The Raven*, but only as regards the stanza: "nothing even remotely approaching this combination has ever been attempted." [23] Again we see Poe's tend-

[22] Stedman and Woodberry, op. cit., III, 284.
[23] Ibid., I, 42.

ency to rely upon the mechanically startling, in preference to the inimitable. This fact, coupled with his extraordinary theories of meter, which I shall examine separately, bears a close relationship to the clumsiness and insensitivity of his verse. Read three times, his rhythms disgust, because they are untrained and insensitive and have no individual life within their surprising mechanical frames.

Before turning to the principal poems for a brief examination of them, we should observe at least one remark on the subject of melancholy. In *The Philosophy of Composition*, after stating that, in planning *The Raven*, he had decided upon Beauty as the province of the poem, Poe writes as follows: "Regarding, then, Beauty as my province, my next question referred to the tone of its highest manifestation—and all experience has shown that this tone is one of *sadness*. Beauty, of whatever kind, in its supreme development, invariably excites the sensitive soul to tears. Melancholy is thus the most legitimate of all the poetical tones." [24]

Now if the reader will keep in mind the principles that we have already deduced; namely, that Beauty is unattainable, that the poet can merely suggest its existence, that this suggestion depends upon the ingenious manipulation of the least obstructive elements of normal experience—it will at once be obvious that Poe is here suggesting a reversal of motivation. That is, since Beauty excites to tears (let us assume with Poe, for the moment, that it does), if we begin with tears, we may believe ourselves moved for a moment by Beauty. This interpretation is supported solidly by the last two sentences quoted, particularly when we regard their order.

The Philosophy of Composition thus appears after all to be a singularly shocking document. Were it an examination of the means by which a poet might communicate a comprehensible judgment, were it a plea that such communication be carefully planned in advance, we could do no less than approve. But it is not that; it is rather an effort to establish the rules for a species of incantation, of witchcraft; rules, whereby, through the ma-

[24] Ibid., I, 36.

nipulation of certain substances in certain arbitrary ways, it may be possible to invoke, more or less accidentally, something that appears more or less to be a divine emanation. It is not surprising that Poe expressed more than once a very qualified appreciation of Milton.

We may fairly conclude this phase of the discussion by a passage from *The Poetic Principle,* a passage quoted also by Miss Alterton: "It may be, indeed, that here this sublime end is, now and then, attained in fact. We are often made to feel, with a shivering delight, that from an earthly harp are stricken notes which *cannot* have been unfamiliar to the angels." [25] It should now be clear what Poe had in mind when he referred to Tennyson as the most elevating and the most pure of the poets; what Tennyson might have thought of the attribution is beside the point.

III

Before turning to the poems themselves, we should examine very briefly Poe's general theory of meter, as it appears primarily in *The Rationale of Verse*. And before doing this we should recall to mind in very general terms the common methods of scansion. They are: first, the classical, in which the measure is based upon quantity, or length of syllable, and in which accent is a source merely of variation and of complication; second, the French, or syllabic, in which the measure is a matter wholly of the number of syllables in the line, and in which the primary source of variation is quantity, if the language be one, like French, which lacks mechanical stress; third, the Anglo-Saxon, or accentual, in which the measure is based purely upon the number of accents, variation being derived from every other source possible; and fourth, the English, or accentual-syllabic, which resembles the classical system in its types of feet, but in which the foot and measure are determined by accent instead of by quantity.

Since it is with English verse, primarily, that we are dealing,

[25] Ibid., I, 12.

we should note one or two other points in connection with it. First, the language is not divided into accented and unaccented syllables; within certain limits, there is an almost infinite variation of accent, and no two syllables are ever accented in exactly the same way. Consequently, for metrical purposes, a syllable is considered accented or unaccented only in relationship to the other syllables in the same foot. For example, let us take Ben Jonson's line:

Drink to/ me on/ly with/ thine eyes.

The accentuation of the first foot is inverted; in each of the other feet the accent falls on the second syllable. Yet the word *with*, which even in normal prose receives more accent than the last syllable of *only*, is less heavily accented than the word *thine*; so that in the last two feet we have a mounting series of four degrees of accent. This variety of accent is one form of variation in English meter; another is quantity; another is the normal procedure of substitution.

We may observe the obvious opposition of quantity to accent in the first foot, a normal iambic one, of this line from Robert Bridges:

Nay, barren are the mountains, and spent the streams.

The first syllable of the foot, *Nay*, is long and unaccented; the second and final syllable, *bar-*, is short and accented. On the other hand, length and accent may be brought to coincide; or there may be immeasurably subtle variations between the two extremes. These sources of variation, when understood and mastered, provide the fluid sensitivity to be found in the best English verse, within even the most rigid of patterns.

But to all this Poe appears oblivious. He says: "Accented syllables are of course always long." [26] This initial confusion is obviously related to Poe's preference for meters dependent upon a heavy, unvaried, and mechanical beat. He makes little use of

[26] Ibid., I, 60.

quantity except as a reinforcement of accent; where it does not reinforce the accent, the failure is an accident and usually results in a clumsy variant rather than a pleasing one.

In *The Rationale of Verse*, Poe offers a new system for marking scansion, based in part upon the heresy which I have just mentioned, in part upon the equally gross concept that all syllables can be grouped into general classes, each class having a fixed and recognizable degree of accent. He is even so rash as to attempt the scansion of Horace on this basis, and to state that French verse is without music because the language is without accent. Poe had an ear for only the crudest of distinctions.

IV

The poems on which Poe's reputation as an important poet must rest are the following: *The City in the Sea, The Haunted Palace, The Conqueror Worm, Ulalume, The Raven,* and *The Sleeper.* These are the ambitious efforts; the others, even if one grant them a high measure of success, are minor. *The City in the Sea* is generally, and I believe rightly, regarded as Poe's best performance. After the first five lines, which are bad enough to have been written by Kipling, the poem displays few gross lapses and some excellent passages. There is admirable description, and there is throughout an intense feeling of meaning withheld. We have, in brief, all of the paraphernalia of allegory except the significance. The poem falls short of being one of the romantic masterpieces of obscure emotionalism chiefly because of weak phrases: it remains Poe's most startling and talented failure.

In *The Haunted Palace*, the physical material has allegorical significance which is perfectly definite. The palace of the monarch Thought is the head; the windows are the eyes; the door is the mouth; the spirits are the thoughts, which issue as words. This, however, is not the real explanation of the poem, for the subject is the change from sanity to insanity. The change occurs in the fifth stanza, suddenly, and without motivation: we have feeling divorced completely from understanding; the change itself is mad, for it is inexplicable.

Ulalume contains very much the same problems as the other poems not yet considered. In examining this poem, we must confine ourselves strictly to what Poe offered us, namely, the poem, and refrain from biographical entanglements, which are both gratuitous and uncertain. If the poem is not self-sufficient, it is obscure; and, as critics of art, we are bound to rest with the assumption that the obscurity was satisfactory to Poe.

The poem opens with allusions to unidentified places, places with dark but unexplained histories: Weir, Auber, ghoul-haunted woodlands; we have, in other words, a good deal of ready-made Gothic mystery. The items are introduced to evoke emotion at small cost: they are familiar romantic devices, but they are none the less deliberately obscure. In the passage opening with the alley Titanic, and ending with Mount Yaanek and the Boreal Pole, we have an explicit reference to a period of violent feeling in the history of the protagonist: the cause and nature of the feeling are alike unexplained at the time, and even the loss of Ulalume, which is a very general sort of datum, is an inadequate account of feelings so grotesquely violent. In lines twenty to twenty-nine, there are dark references to a past event, references which are ultimately cleared up when we learn of the burial of Ulalume, but which, as we come to them, have the effect of gratuitous emotionalizing. Lines thirty to forty are the best in the poem: they hint of the strangeness of the nocturnal turning toward dawn, and then describe the appearance of Astarte, as the rising moon; if this strangeness has any spiritual significance, however, we are given no clue to it. The protagonist wishes to accept Astarte as a guide; Psyche distrusts her; they argue at length but darkly—darkly, in that the purpose of the protagonist and the fears of Psyche alike are not given us, so that the argument is like one in a dream. Psyche yields, but as she does so, they are led by Astarte to the door of the tomb, which brings the protagonist up shortly, with a cold realization of his loss. Lines ninety-five to one hundred and four, omitted by Griswold and by most of the cheap popular editions, but important, it would seem, to the poem, state the possibility that Astarte may have been conjured up to prevent their further irresponsible wandering in the haunted woodlands (which I take to represent the loose feelings through which they have been moving) by recalling them to a sense of definite tragedy.

In other words, the subject of grief is employed as a very general excuse for a good deal of obscure and only vaguely related emotion. This subject is used exactly as we should expect to find it used after examining Poe's aesthetic theory. The poem is as surely an excursion into the incoherencies of dream-consciousness as is the *Larme* of Rimbaud; yet it lacks wholly the fine surface of that poem.

In *The Raven*, that attenuated exercise for elocutionists, and in *The Sleeper*, the general procedure is identical, but the meter in the former and the writing in both are so thoroughly bad that other considerations appear unnecessary. *The Sleeper* is a kind of Gothic parody of Henry King's imperfect but none the less great *Exequy*: a comparison of the two poems will show the difference between moral grandeur and the sensationalism of a poet devoid of moral intelligence. It is noteworthy that King is commonly and justly regarded as one of the smaller poets of his period.

In *The Conqueror Worm*, the desire for inexpensive feeling has led to a piece of writing that is, phrase by phrase, solidly bromidic.

V

In his criticism of Hawthorne's *Tales,* Poe outlines his theory of the short story. He defends the tale, as preferable to the novel, on the same grounds as those on which he defends the short poem in preference to the long. He states the necessity of careful planning and of economy of means.

He says: ". . . having conceived with deliberate care, a certain unique or single *effect* to be wrought out, he [the skillful literary artist] then invents such incidents—he then combines such events as may best aid him in establishing this preconceived effect." [27] Now the word *effect,* here as elsewhere in Poe, means

[27] Ibid., II, 31.

impression, or mood; it is a word that connotes emotion purely and simply. So that we see the story-teller, like the poet, interested primarily in the creation of an emotion for its own sake, not in the understanding of an experience. It is significant in this connection that most of his heroes are mad or on the verge of madness; a datum which settles his action firmly in the realm of inexplicable feeling from the outset.

Morella begins thus: "With a feeling of deep yet most singular affection I regarded my friend Morella. Thrown by accident into her society many years ago, my soul, from our first meeting, burned with fires it had never before known; but the fires were not of Eros, and bitter and tormenting to my spirit was the gradual conviction that I could in no manner define their unusual meaning or regulate their vague intensity." And *Ligeia*: "I cannot, for my soul, remember how, when, or even precisely where, I first became acquainted with the Lady Ligeia. Long years have since elapsed, and my memory is feeble through much suffering." *The Assignation*: "Ill-fated and mysterious man!—bewildered in the brilliancy of thine own imagination, and fallen in the flames of thine own youth." *The Tell-Tale Heart*: "True! —nervous—very, very dreadfully nervous I had been and am! but why *will* you say that I am. mad?" *Berenice*: ". . . it *is* wonderful what a stagnation there fell upon the springs of my life— wonderful how total an inversion took place in the character of my commonest thought." *Eleanora*: "I am come of a race noted for vigor of fancy and ardor of passion. Men have called me mad; but the question is not yet settled, whether madness is or is not the loftiest intelligence—whether much that is glorious— whether all that is profound—does not spring from disease of thought—from *moods* of mind exalted at the expense of the general intellect." Roderick Usher, in addition, is mad; *The Black Cat* is a study in madness; *The Masque of the Red Death* is a study in hallucinatory terror. They are all studies in hysteria; they are written for the sake of the hysteria.

In discussing Hawthorne,. however, Poe suggests other possibilities: "We have said that the tale has a point of superiority even over the poem. In fact, while the rhythm of this latter is an essential aid in the development of the poem's highest idea—the idea of the Beautiful—the artificialities of this rhythm are an inseparable bar to the development of all points of thought or expression which have their basis in *Truth.* But Truth is often, and in very great degree, the aim of the tale. Some of the finest tales are tales of ratiocination. Thus the field of this species of composition, if not in so elevated a region on the mountain of the Mind, is a tableland of far vaster extent than the domain of the mere poem. Its products are never so rich, but infinitely more numerous, and infinitely more appreciable by the mass of mankind. The writer of the prose tale, in short, may bring to his theme a vast variety of modes of inflection of thought and expression (the ratiocinative, for example, the sarcastic, or the humorous) which are not only antagonistic to the nature of the poem, but absolutely forbidden by one of its most peculiar and indispensable adjuncts; we allude, of course, to rhythm. It may be added here, par parenthèse, that the author who aims at the purely beautiful in a prose tale is laboring at a great disadvantage. For Beauty can be better treated in the poem. Not so with terror, or passion, or horror, or a multitude of other such points." [28]

Poe speaks in this passage, not only of the tale of effect, to which allusion has already been made, but of the tale of ratiocination, that is, of the detective story, such as *The Gold Bug* or *The Murders in the Rue Morgue.* It is noteworthy that this is the only example which he gives of the invasion of the field of fiction by Truth; in other words, his primary conception of intellectual activity in fiction appears to be in the contrivance of a puzzle. Between this childish view of intellectuality, on the one hand, and the unoriented emotionalism of the tale of effect on the other, we have that vast and solid region inhabited by the major literary figures of the world, the region in which human experience is understood in moral terms and emotion is the result of that understanding, or is seen in relationship to that understanding and so judged. This region appears to have been closed to

[28] Ibid., II, 31.

Poe; if we except the highly schematized and crudely melodramatic allegory of *William Wilson*, we have no basis for believing that he ever discovered it.

VI

If Poe's chief work is confined to the communication of feeling, what can we say of the quality of that communication? Poe rests his case for art on taste, and though we may disagree with him, yet we are bound to examine his own taste, for if he has no taste, he has nothing. It is my belief that he has little or none.

Every literary critic has a right to a good many errors of judgment; or at least every critic makes a good many. But if we survey Poe's critical opinions we can scarcely fail to be astonished by them. He understood little or nothing that was written before his own age, and though he was not unaware of the virtues, apparently, of some of the better stylists of his period, as for example Coleridge, he at one time or another praised such writers as R. H. Horne, N. P. Willis, Thomas Hood, and Thomas Moore as highly or more highly; in fact, he placed Horne and Moore among the greatest geniuses of all time. He praised Bryant above his American contemporaries, but he based his praise upon poems which did not deserve it. He was able to discover numerous grammatical errors in one of the lesser novels of Cooper, but he was unable to avoid making such errors in large numbers in his own prose; and the faultless, limpid, and unforgettable prose of the seventh chapter of *The Deerslayer*, the profundity of conception of *The Bravo*, the characterization of *Satanstoe* and *The Chainbearer*, were as far beyond his powers of comprehension as beyond his powers of creation.

If we neglect for a moment the underlying defect in all of Poe's work, the absence of theme, and scrutinize carefully the manner in which he communicates feeling, in which alone he is interested, we can scarcely avoid the observation that his work is compounded almost wholly of stereotyped expressions, most of them of a very melodramatic cast. Now one cannot object to a man wholly on the basis of stereotyped expression. There is a measure of stereotyped expression, apparently inadvertent, in many poems and works of prose which sustain themselves notwithstanding by virtue of a fundamental vigor of conception: W. H. Hudson is a writer of prose who sins extensively in this respect, but survives; Henry King is such a poet. On the other hand, the most finished masters of style, and this is perhaps especially true of the poets, have all, in some measure, employed the formulary phrase deliberately to achieve various but precise results: Crashaw, Milton, and Blake are familiar examples of the procedure. Indeed, if we imagine a very precise and solid substructure of theme, as in Crashaw's paraphrase of the *Twenty-third Psalm*, it is possible to see how a passage deliberately stereotyped in a certain measure, yet with a slight but precise admixture of personal perception, may at once define a traditional concept and the relationship of that concept to a personal perception, in fact the entire relationship of personal to traditional feeling—and the perception of such a relationship is in itself and as a whole a profoundly personal or original perception—in a manner more successful than any other conceivable; this procedure, however, presupposes a theme, a sense of history, or tradition, and a recognition of the poetic art as a technique of judgment, and it necessitates incidentally a masterly understanding and control of meter. Poe, on the other hand endeavors as far as may be to escape from a paraphrasable theme; he recognizes no obligation to understand the minimum of theme from which he cannot escape—in fact, he seems to recognize an obligation not to understand it; his historical training and understanding amounted nearly to nothing; so that there is nothing in his work either to justify his formulary expression and to give it content and precision of meaning, on the one hand, or, on the other, to give his work as a whole sufficient force and substance to make us forget the formulary expression—we merely have melodramatic stereotypes in a vacuum. The last instrument which, if well employed, might to some extent have alleviated his phrasing, and which did, in fact, alleviate it in part in a few fragments to which I shall presently allude, the instrument of meter, he was unable to control except occasionally and accidentally. His theory of meter was false. Whether the theory arose from imperception or led to imperception is immaterial, but the fact remains that his meter is almost invariably clumsy and mechanical in a measure perhaps never equalled by another poet who has enjoyed a comparable reputation. His favorite stanzaic and structural device, the device of mechanical repetition, is perhaps equally the result of his untrained and insensitive taste and of his feeling no responsibility to say anything accurately—when there is nothing in particular to be said, every technique is a technique of diffusion, for a technique of concise definition would reduce the poem to nothing.

To illustrate the weakness of detail in his poems and stories is an easy matter; to illustrate the extent of that weakness is impossible, for his work is composed of it. In his poems, one may enumerate the following passages as fairly well executed, if one grants him temporarily his fundamental assumptions about art: *Ulalume*, lines thirty to thirty-eight, provided one can endure the meter; *The City in the Sea*, lines six to eleven, lines twenty-four to the end; *To One in Paradise*, the first stanza and perhaps the last; the early poem *To Helen*, especially the first three or four lines; *The Spirits of the Dead*, lines five to ten. Perhaps the only passage of his prose which displays comparable ability is the opening of *The Assignation*: the conception is merely that of the typically Byronic man of mystery, and the detail, in its rough identity, is comparably typical, but there is a certain life in the language, especially in the rhythm of the language, that renders the passage memorable.

For the rest, we encounter prose such as the following: "As if in the superhuman energy of his utterance there had been found the potency of a spell, the huge antique panels to which the speaker pointed threw slowly back, upon the instant, their ponderous and ebony jaws." "It was a voluptuous scene, that masquerade. But first let me tell of the rooms in which it was held. They were seven—an imperial suite." "Where were the souls of the haughty family of the bride, when, through thirst of gold, they permitted to pass the threshold of an apartment *so* bedecked, a maiden and a daughter so beloved?" "Morella's erudition was

258

profound. As I hope to live, her talents were of no common order
—her powers of mind were gigantic."

We are met on every page of his poetry with resounding puerilities such as "the pallid bust of Pallas," and "the viol, the violet, and the vine." The poetry, in fact, is composed almost wholly of such items as these:

Ah, broken is the golden bowl!—the spirit flown forever!
Let the bell toll! a saintly soul floats on the Stygian river:—
And, Guy de Vere, hast thou no tear?—weep now or never more!
See! on yon drear and rigid bier low lies thy love, Lenore!

> *At midnight in the month of June,*
> *I stand beneath the mystic moon.*

> *For alas! alas! with me*
> *   The light of Life is o'er!*
> *No more—no more—no more—*
> *   (Such language holds the solemn sea*
> *To the sands upon the shore)*
> *   Shall bloom the thunder-blasted tree,*
> *Or the stricken eagle soar!*

> *That motley drama—oh, be sure*
> *   It shall not be forgot!*
> *With its Phantom chased forevermore,*
> *   By a crowd that seize it not,*
> *Through a circle that ever returneth in*
> *   To the self-same spot,*
> *And much of Madness, and more of Sin,*
> *   And horror the soul of the plot.*

And the silken, sad, uncertain rustling of each purple curtain
Thrilled me—filled me with fantastic terrors never felt before.

This is an art to delight the soul of a servant girl; it is a matter for astonishment that mature men can be found to take this kind of thing seriously. It is small wonder that the claims of Chivers have been seriously advanced of late years in the face of such an achievement; they have been fairly advanced, for Chivers is nearly as admirable a poet. If one is in need of a standard, one should have recourse to Bridges' *Eros*, to Hardy's *During Wind and Rain*, or to Arnold's *Dover Beach*. And in making one's final estimate of the quality of Poe's taste, one should not fail to consider the style of his critical prose, of which the excerpts quoted in the present essay are fair, and indeed, as specimens of taste, are random examples.

VII

On what grounds, if any, can we then defend Poe? We can obviously defend his taste as long as we honestly like it. The present writer is willing to leave it, after these few remarks, to its admirers. As to his critical theory, however, and the structural defects of his work, it appears to me certain that the difficulty which I have raised is the central problem in Poe criticism; yet not only has it never been met, but, so far as one can judge, it has scarcely been recognized.

The attempt to justify Poe on the basis of his place in history can arise only from a confusion of processes: to explain a man's place in history is not the same thing as to judge his value. Poe was largely formed by the same influences which formed other men, both better and worse, Coleridge as well as Chivers; his particular nature resulted in his pushing certain essential romantic notions very nearly as far as they could go. It is unlikely, on the other hand, that the course of romantic literature would have been very different except (perhaps) in America, had Poe never been born; in any event, his influence could only have been a bad one, and to assert that he exerted an influence is not to praise him. His clinical value resides in the fact that as a specimen of late romantic theory and practice he is at once extreme and typical. To understand the nature of his confusion is to come nearer to an understanding not only of his American contemporaries, but of French Symbolism and of American Experimentalism as well.

There are, I believe, two general lines of argument or procedure that may be used more or less in support of Poe's position; one is that of the Alterton-Craig Introduction, the other (if I may cite another eminent example) is that of Professor Floyd Stovall.

The argument of the Introduction appears to be roughly that Poe is an intellectual poet, because: first, he worked out in *Eureka* a theory of cosmic harmony and unity; second, related to this, he held a theory of the harmony and unity of the parts of the poem; and third, he devoted a certain amount of rational effort to working out the rules by which this harmony and unity could be attained.

But this intellectuality, if that is the name for it, is all anterior to the poem, not in the poem; it resides merely in the rules for the practice of the obscurantism which I have defined. The Introduction cites as evidence of Poe's recognition of the intellectual element in poetry, his essay on Drake and Halleck, yet the intellectuality in question here is plainly of the sort which I have just described. As a result, Professor Craig's comparison of Poe to Donne, Dryden, and Aquinas, is, to the present writer at least, profoundly shocking.

The only alternative is that of Professor Stovall, as well as of a good many others: to accept Poe's theory of Beauty as if it were clearly understood and then to examine minor points of Poe criticism with lucidity and with learning. But Poe's theory of Beauty is not understood, and no casual allusion to Plato will ever clarify it.

JONES VERY AND R. W. EMERSON

Aspects of New England Mysticism

But thou art far away among Time's toys. . . .

IN THE PAST TWO DECADES two major American writers have been rediscovered and established securely in their rightful places in literary history. I refer to Emily Dickinson and to Herman Melville. I am proposing the establishment of a third, who is no doubt the least of the three but who is nevertheless a writer of impressive qualities.[1]

Jones Very was born at Salem, Massachusetts, on August 28th, 1813, and died there on May 8th, 1880. In 1839 a collection of his essays and poems, selected at least in part by R. W. Emerson, was published at Boston by Little and Brown, in the third year of that firm's existence. In 1883 an incomplete but on the whole a very judicious collection of his poems alone, with William P. Andrews as editor and memorialist, was issued at Boston by Houghton Mifflin. And in 1886 the same firm issued a "Complete and Revised Edition" of *Poems and Essays*, by Jones Very, with a brief but admirable biographical sketch by James Freeman Clarke, and a wholly superfluous preface by C. A. Bartol. This edition, in spite of its containing a few excellent poems lacking in the previous edition, and in spite of its offering a few prefer-

---

[1] One should mention also Frederick Goddard Tuckerman, a selection of whose poems was issued in 1931 by Knopf; the rediscoverer, editor, and memorialist being Mr. Witter Bynner. Tuckerman is unquestionably a distinguished poet: he is, however, romantic in the essential sense; he divorces feeling from motive as far as possible. The beautifully executed sonnet beginning "An upper chamber in a darkened house" is a perfect example of the procedure: a man is imagined in a tragic, but impenetrable, setting, to serve as the symbol of a feeling with which he has no connection and the source of which we are not given. Tuckerman is much like the Hawthorne of the last romances, except that he writes better. [After these remarks were written, Professor Thomas H. Johnson, of Yale, announced a major and now famous discovery: that of Edward Taylor.]

able, as well as a few less excellent, variants, may have been responsible for the death of Very's nascent reputation, for it carries an enormous amount of dead material. If there are further editions, they have not fallen into my hands.[2] The volume of 1886 contains as a frontispiece a photograph of the author, showing a long and narrow New England face, extremely sensitive yet equally ascetic, immaculate alike in flesh and in spirit, surely the face of a saint, and a face worthy of one of the finest of poets.

Very was about ten years younger than Emerson and about four years older than Thoreau. He preached at times in the Unitarian pulpit; he is commonly listed as one of the minor Transcendentalists; yet both facts are misleading. He was a mystic, primarily, whose theological and spiritual affiliations were with the earlier Puritans and Quakers rather than with the Unitarians or with the friends of Emerson; and if a minor writer, he was at least not one in relationship to the Transcendentalists.

He was a Unitarian only by virtue of the historical connection between the Unitarian and Puritan Churches and by virtue of the wide hospitality of the Unitarians. He was not a Transcendentalist at all, but a Christian, and a dogmatic one; his only point of contact with Emerson was in regard to the surrender of the will, that is, the submission of oneself to the direct guidance of the Spirit. He differed from Emerson in that Emerson was a pantheist and a moral relativist, so that Emerson's guiding Spirit was, in effect, instinct and personal whim, which, in his terms, became identical with the Divine Imperative, but which, in practice, amounted to a kind of benevolent if not invariably beneficent sentimentalism. The religious experience for Emerson was a kind of good-natured self-indulgence; for Very it was a sublime exaltation, which appears to have endured until his death. Very was beyond question a saintly man, and we hesitate to doubt a

[2] When I first published this essay, in the American Review, for May, 1936, I stated that I had not seen the edition of 1839. I was promptly, and, considering its rarity, munificently, presented with a copy by the Reverend Charles Morris Addison, of Cambridge, Mass. A comparison of the three texts makes it obvious that a critical edition of Very is much to be desired.

saint when he states that he is a mystic. Very's poems bear witness unanswerably that he had the experience which Emerson merely recommends.

Very's spiritual life was passed on that minute island of being, which is occupied in common by the more exalted of the Friends and of the Puritans. Whereas the Friend taught the importance of the submission to the Divine Will, the Puritan taught the inevitability of the submission; the private will, either way, is stricken from the conscious life of the intensely devout; and when the Holy Spirit bears witness to the beatitude of the Puritan, as it bore witness in the heart of Jonathan Edwards, that Puritan lives much as does an exalted member of the Society of Friends. The reader might be led to believe that Very's connections with the Friends were more obvious than his connections with the Puritans, for he recommended the submission of the will in many poems, and in only one—*Justification by Faith,* which appears only in the edition of 1886—spoke of the inevitability of the submission; but as a Unitarian, his background was Puritan, and it is characteristic of the Puritan, as of every other kind of determinist, to recommend on moral grounds that which he professes to believe inevitable as a matter of cosmology, to confess by implication to a belief in that power of choice which he explicitly denies; indeed the familiar and daily literature of the Puritans—the literature of sermons, memoirs, and similar documents—displays repeatedly the same recommendation that we find in Very, and the novels of O. W. Holmes, if we feel that we need their testimony, bear witness to the recurrence of the recommendation in Calvinistic conversation.

The perfect dogmatic definition of Very's position as a New England mystic occurs in the sonnet entitled *The Hand and Foot:*

> *The hand and foot that stir not, they shall find*
> *Sooner than all the rightful place to go:*
> *Now in their motion free as roving wind,*
> *Though first no snail so limited and slow;*
> *I mark them full of labor all the day,*

Each active motion made in perfect rest;
They cannot from their path mistaken stray,
Though 'tis not theirs, yet in it they are blest;
The bird has not their hidden track found out,
The cunning fox though full of art he be;
It is the way unseen, the perfect rout,
Wherever bound, yet thou art ever free;
The path of Him, whose perfect law of love
Bids spheres and atoms in just order move.

The first two lines of the poem imply an initial choice, and thus might be considered to be in agreement not only with colloquial Calvinism, but also with the Friends and with Emerson. The last three lines, however, are deterministic, and put the orthodox stamp on the statement; the twelfth line is in effect a paraphrase of various passages to be found in certain earlier Puritan theologians. Thus John Norton wrote in 1654: "The liberty of man, though subordinate to God's decree, freely willeth the very same thing and no other than that which it would have willed if (upon a supposition of impossibility) there had been no decree." And again: "Man acts freely as if there were no decree; yet as infallibly as if there were no liberty." [3] And Isaac Chauncey, writing in 1694, says that God's decree "maintains the liberty of the creature's will, that all free agents act as freely according to the decree as agents of necessity do act necessarily." [4] It is curious to observe that the resolution of the two discordant concepts of free choice and of predestination, as it appears in the theologians, is purely verbal; it was the result of the inability of the Puritans to establish a genuine resolution that their Church declined; yet in the poem, while one is reading the poem, the resolution is experienced, or to put it otherwise the conviction felt by the poet is communicated. I should not like to leave this poem without calling attention to the haunting precision with which feeling as

[3] *The Orthodox Evangelist* by John Norton; quoted from *History of New England Theology*, by Frank Hugh Foster (University of Chicago Press, 1909), first chapter.
[4] *The Doctrine Which Is According to Godliness*, by Isaac Chauncey, 1694; from Foster, first chapter.

well as dogma is rendered; lines nine to twelve are exceptionally beautiful.

Very saw in the surrender to God of the will not only the means of salvation, but the sole act of the will acceptable as an act of devotion. Similarly, Edwards, from the more strictly Calvinistic point of view, saw in the doctrine of predestination the only doctrine that tended adequately to the glory of God: "Hence these doctrines and schemes of divinity that are in any respect opposite to such an absolute and universal dependence upon God, derogate from his glory, and thwart the design of our redemption. And such are those schemes that . . . own an entire dependence upon God for some things, but not for others; they own that we depend on God for the Gift and Acceptance of a Redeemer, but deny so absolute a dependence on him for the obtaining an interest in the Redeemer. . . . They own a dependence on God for the means of Grace, but not so absolutely for the success." [5]

Edwards seems to be guilty of the heresy which he is attacking; that is, "trust in a covenant of works"; for were the dependence absolute, no doctrine could thwart our redemption, and no theologian need come to aid us. It was in the same spirit that Edwards brought about a revival in the Puritan Church, that is, induced large numbers of sinners to repent, by preaching in language of almost unequalled magnificence and terror the doctrine of predestination and of the inability to repent. It was in the same spirit that the Mathers took it upon themselves to rid New England of witches. For the exercise of the will, the sense of the moral drama, was not at first weakened by the impact of Calvinistic dogma, but was excited by the new exaltation of spirit, and as the will was excited, so was the study of its proper use neglected by a doctrine which denied it and which relegated a belief in the efficaciousness of good works to the category of sin, and this discrepancy led at times to intense and mystical piety on the one hand, and frequently to brutal bigotry on the other, the two often existing in a single man, as in Cotton Mather.

[5] *God Glorified in Man's Redemption*, by Jonathan Edwards, 1731; from Foster, Chapter II; Edwards' *Works*, Dwight's Edition, Vol. VII, page 149.

In Emerson the exercise of the will is as active as ever, and his moral judgments are frequently made with force and with accuracy; but his central doctrine is that of submission to emotion, which for the pantheist is a kind of divine instigation: an inadmissible doctrine, for it eliminates at a stroke both choice and the values that serve as a basis for choice, it substitutes for a doctrine of values a doctrine of equivalence, thus rendering man an automaton and paralyzing all genuine action, so that Emerson's acceptable acts of expression are accidental poems or epigrams drawing their only nutriment from the fringe or from beyond the fringe of his doctrine. To understand the difference between Very and Emerson at this point, we are forced to engage at least tentatively in that most precarious of pastimes, psychological analysis. Very believed that he had surrended himself to God, but it was to the God of Christianity, who disapproved of surrender to emotion and whose moral standards had been revealed; so that Very, if we assume for the moment that there was an element of self-delusion in his mysticism, must have engaged in a good deal of rapid, efficient, and scarcely conscious criticism and selection of his own impulses, and on the basis of traditional Christian morality; or if we assume that Very's faith in his experience was justified, then it was the same God of Christianity who guided him in fact, and presumably on the same basis. Emerson, on the other hand, believed that flesh and spirit were one, that the universe was divine, and that all impulses were of divine origin. Emerson's personal acts, like those of Very, were qualified by tradition, for he was the descendent of a line of clergymen, and his character had been formed by the society which they and their kind had formed, so that his impulses were no doubt virtuous; but his doctrine abandoned the last connection with Christianity and the last support for personal dignity, and the difference, though it does not appear in his life as a man, is already apparent in the whimsical facility of feeling to be discerned equally in his prose and in his verse, a feeling very different from the austere purity of Very. Emerson could write such a poem as *Mithridates*, for example, with enough rhetorical vigor to make it an important part of our literary heritage, but with no realization of its implications; it required Rimbaud, who probably never heard of the poem, or Hart Crane, who probably derived the Emersonian influence indirectly, and in some part through Emerson's chief disciple, Whitman, to realize the implications of such an attitude in life and in art.

Emerson was the most influential preacher to appear in America after Edwards, for the lecture platform was merely the ultimate step in the secularization of the pulpit, a step that was inevitable after Unitarianism had displaced Calvinism, and Emerson, moreover, succeeded in focussing upon his romantic amoralism a national religious energy which had been generated by a doctrine and by circumstances now equally remote. And he was the most widely read and most pungent aphorist to appear in America since that other limb of the Devil, Benjamin Franklin. The Church, and the spirit which had maintained it, were in ruins; and the acceptance of Emerson's doctrine produced a new spirit, foreign even to his own, or at least acting in regions beyond his comprehension and in ways that would surely have troubled him.[6] In Emerson's day, the practical, if illogical, Cal-

---

[6] This fact has been pointed out by H. B. Parkes (*Emerson*, Hound and Horn V-4), a writer to whom I am more deeply indebted than I can indicate in any series of footnotes, not only in respect to Emerson, but in respect to other aspects of American thought. Parkes quotes Emerson as saying: "Success consists in close appliance to the laws of the world and since those laws are intellectual and moral, an intellectual and moral obedience;" and: "Money . . . is, in its effects and laws, as beautiful as roses. Property keeps the accounts of the world, and is always moral . . ." and: "An eternal, beneficent necessity is always bringing things right." As Parkes adds of this notion, "Among the Yankee farmers of Concord it had a little plausibility. But its effect was to justify new forces, which were soon to destroy the society in which Emerson lived." As an example of the justification to which Parkes refers, one might mention that curious novel by Frank Norris, *The Octopus*. In spite of being couched in an illiterate style the book has extraordinary force: the plot displays a series of related personal tragedies resulting from the impact upon individual lives of a corrupt financial power. The financial magnate responsible justifies his actions in Emersonian terms, and the author's representative in the story, Presley, enlarges upon this justification in extensive passages that might have been plagiarized from the Essays. Norris, however, was so little a literary scholar that one is inclined to believe it more likely that he got these passages from the philosophical atmosphere of his period than from Emerson's text. There is likewise an episode in Melville's work entitled *The Confidence Man*, which appears to reflect this aspect of Emerson, but consciously and satirically:

vinism, which, as an historical fact, had enabled Hawthorne to produce *The Scarlet Letter,* existed only in a few rapidly crumbling islands of culture, such as that to which we owe Emily Dickinson; and the mystical Puritanism which had lived in Anne Hutchinson and in Jonathan Edwards existed nowhere that we can determine save in the spirit of Jones Very.

That Very should so long have been neglected, that he should be left, a century after the production of most of his best poetry, to the best defense that one, like myself, at every turn unsympathetic with his position, is able to offer, is one of the anomalies of literary history. Of the sincerity of his profession, we can hold no doubt. His best poems are as convincing, and within their limits as excellent, as are the poems of Blake, or Traherne, or George Herbert. His contemporaries, those who regarded him not only in the spirit, but in the flesh, paid his sincerity the highest tribute that men can pay to that of any man: they adjudged him insane. He voluntarily spent a short time under observation, but was discharged. "At the McLean Asylum," says Emerson, "the patients severally thanked him when he came away, and told him that he had been of great service to them." It was during his stay at the asylum that he finished his three essays in literary criticism, which, whatever their faults, are beautifully written and display great penetration and perfect presence of mind.

The attitude of the Transcendentalists toward Very is instructive and amusing, and it proves beyond cavil how remote he was from them. In respect to the doctrine of the submission of the will, he agreed with them in principle; but whereas they recommended the submission, he practiced it, and they regarded him with amazement. It is worthy of repetition in this connection, that had Emerson accomplished the particular surrender which, as a pantheist, he directly or indirectly recommended, he would have been mad, that is, an automaton guided by instinct; that the surrender recommended by Emerson when carried no farther than it was commonly carried by his disciples, that is, to an uncritical exaggeration of the importance of temperament, led to the pas-

the episode of the mystic, Mark Winsome, and of his disciple, The India Merchant.

toral idiosyncrasies of Thoreau, who valued a packing box as highly as a house and a scrap of newspaper as highly as Homer, or led to the mild idiocy of Alcott, who refused to eat root vegetables because they grew downward instead of aspiring upward; whereas surrender in Very's terms—and we who have never practiced Very's surrender may reasonably refrain from offering any doubts or other views as to the absolute truth of the terms—meant an experience of a wholly different order.

James Freeman Clarke, in his biographical sketch of Very, has thus described an encounter between Very and Channing: "I was one day at Dr. Channing's house, when he had just received a visit from Jones Very. Dr. Channing, like Emerson, was always looking for any symptoms of a new birth of spiritual life in the land. Having heard of Mr. Very, he invited him to come and see him, and inquired what were his views on religious subjects. Having listened attentively, he asked him whether it was in consequence of his invitation or in obedience to the Spirit that he came to Boston that morning. Mr. Very answered, 'I was directed to accept your invitation.' Then Dr. Channing said, 'I observed that during our conversation you left your chair and went while speaking to the fireplace, and rested your arm on the mantel. Did you do that of your own accord, or in obedience to the Spirit?' Very replied, 'In obedience to the Spirit.' And indeed, if it has become a habit of the soul to be led in all things, great and small, why not in this, too? Only, I suppose, that most of us would not think it worth while to consult the Spirit in such a purely automatic action as this."

That the gulf between Emerson and Very, if not wide, was yet immeasurably profound, we may observe from one of Emerson's notes: "When Jones Very was in Concord, he had said to me: 'I always felt when I heard you speak, or read your writings, that you saw the truth better than others; yet I felt that your spirit was not quite right. It was as if a vein of colder air blew across me.' He seemed to expect from me—once especially in Walden Wood—a full acknowledgment of his mission, and a participation in the same. Seeing this, I asked him if he did not see that my thoughts and my position were constitutional, and that it would be false and impossible for me to say his things or try to occupy his ground as for him to usurp mine? After some time and full explanation he conceded this. When I met him afterwards, one evening at my lecture in Boston, I invited him to go home to Mr. A's with me to sleep; which he did. He slept in the room adjoining mine. Early next day, in the gray dawn, he came into my room and talked while I dressed. He said: 'When I was in Concord I tried to say you were also right; but the Spirit said you were not right. It is just as if I should say, It is not morning, but the Morning says it is the Morning.'"

Surely no misunderstanding could have been more complete: Emerson tried to explain to Very that truth is relative, and Very tried to point out to Emerson that truth is absolute. Very had been subjected to an overwhelming experience, and he was certain of what he had lived; Emerson had had no such experience, but by trusting implicitly to the whimsical turns of his thought he had arrived at certain beliefs regarding it. Emerson, who was interested primarily in thought about the mystical experience, and whose attitude toward thought was self-indulgent, could not think clearly or coherently; and Very, whose thought was precise, if limited, whose attitude toward thought was ascetic, who regarded thought as sin, save as directed by the Spirit, accomplished a life of nearly perfect intuition.

The absolute strangeness of Very to Emerson's group of friends may best be shown by another passage from Emerson: "When he is in the room with other persons, speech stops, as if there were a corpse in the apartment."

In the poem entitled *Yourself*, that is, addressed to the reader, Very indicates his awareness of the difficulty that the outsider will have in understanding the nature of his communion with the Spirit:

> *But now you hear us talk as strangers, met*
> *Above the room wherein you lie abed;*
> *A word perhaps loud spoken you may get,*

Or hear our feet when heavily we tread;
But he who speaks, or him who's spoken to,
Must both remain as strangers still to you.

We may accept Very's explanation of the imperfect audibility, since he has every appearance of deep conviction; yet to us in the lower room, he none the less remains imperfectly audible, and if our life is to be passed in the lower room, we must concern ourselves primarily with its conditions, lest, in the dark, we break our heads against a door or a cabinet. But while recognizing that Very's mystical poetry is imperfectly relevant to us, we may get what we can from it, and since that which we can obtain is frequently of great value, we can scarcely be losers in the relationship.

To the fine anguish which Very suffered from his sense of defilement in a sinful world, and to the strange conflict which must have lived within him between this feeling—which, indeed, is the only approach in his poems to a state of mind that might be suspected of a quality of insanity—and the real humility which appears in many of his poems, we may obtain a clue in the extraordinary poem entitled *Thy Brother's Blood:*

I have no brother. They who meet me now
Offer a hand with their own wills defiled,
And, while they wear a smooth unwrinkled brow,
Know not that Truth can never be beguiled.
Go wash the hand that still betrays thy guilt;—
Before the Spirit's gaze what stain can hide?
Abel's red blood upon the earth is spilt,
And by thy tongue it cannot be denied.
I hear not with the ear,—the heart doth tell
Its secret deeds to me untold before;
Go, all its hidden plunder quickly sell,
Then shalt thou cleanse thee from thy brother's gore,
Then will I take thy gift;—that bloody stain
Shall not be seen upon thy hand again.

272

That this sonnet embodies a personal experience, as we might surmise from its tone of rapt obsession, and is not an idealized statement, an address delivered dramatically, as it were, by the Divine Spirit to fallen man, we may gather from Emerson, who reports of Very's conversation as follows: "He says it is with him a day of hate: that he discerns the bad element in every person whom he meets, which repels him: he even shrinks a little to give the hand, that sign of receiving." [7] The word *wills* in the second line represents a kind of theological pun: in the terminology of traditional Christianity, it would mean *willful sin*; in the strict sense of Very's mysticism, it would mean the *exercise of the will*. If we disregard this second meaning, the poem is in no sense bound to Very's theology, but is comprehensible in traditional terms; it is abnormal not in its thoughts but only in the intense egocentricity of its feeling. This feeling might or might not verge on insanity; it is, however, comprehensible as one extreme of religious experience; and it is here rendered with a purity, directness, and intensity but seldom equalled in English devotional poetry.

The following poem, *The Garden*, is restrained and precise in its imagery, and may conceivably find few admirers; an appreciation of its beauty depends upon a realization of the mystical significance, or some part of it, back of the description. Though my own sympathy with the author's religious views is largely one of a kind of hypothetical acquiescence, the poem nevertheless seems very fine to me. Regardless of the intrinsic merits of the piece, however, it is valuable as an introduction to certain other poems in which the rapt contemplation of natural landscape is in some measure offered as the equivalent, or at least as the best available poetic substitute, for the contemplation of God achieved by the mystic.

I saw the spot where our first parents dwelt;
And yet it wore to me no face of change.

[7] This passage and all others quoted herein from Emerson appear in his Journals and are quoted by Andrews in his memoir of 1883.

And while amid its fields and groves, I felt
As if I had not sinned, nor thought it strange;
My eye seemed but a part of every sight,
My ear heard music in each sound that rose;
Each sense forever found a new delight,
Such as the spirit's vision only knows;
Each act some new and ever-varying joy
Did by my Father's love for me prepare;
To dress the spot my ever fresh employ,
And in the glorious whole with Him to share;
No more without the flaming gate to stray,
No more for sin's dark stain the debt of death to pay.

The next poem, *The Lost*, is one of the author's four or five most beautiful; it appears to go close to the heart of the mystical experience, and in spite of the obscurity resulting is unforgettable. The use of natural landscape in this poem and in one or two others might seem to lend some support to the idea that Emerson had drawn Very toward pantheism, but the argument is a weak one. First of all, mystical poets have always found themselves forced to employ analogy in dealing with the mystical experience: St. John of the Cross, as well as Crashaw in his great poem on Saint Theresa, employed the analogy of sexual love, a common analogy in Catholic tradition. Edwards, in telling of his religious experience, tells of the intense pleasure that he received from the contemplation of natural landscape: he exulted in this physical beauty as the workmanship of God, but the feeling is so intense that he appears at moments to see God in his works; the attitude is something between the attitude of Very when he writes in *The Garden*, "And in the glorious whole with Him to share," and Very in the more rapt and perhaps more confused condition of *The Lost*, in which God and His Garden are scarcely distinguished. The mystical experience is by definition incommunicable; to the lay mind it may appear a form of self-delusion. In any event, the inevitable technique of approximating it by analogy, if one is to deal with it at all, leads of necessity to a measure of falsification in one way or another; this procedure is part of the tradition of Christian poetry, and the fact that Very's analogy led him in the direction of pantheistic imagery in a few poems is insufficient to convict him of pantheism, in the lack of additional evidence, and in the face of the vast bulk of his explicitly Christian statement.

The subject of the poem is identity with God, and hence with all time and place, of the divine life in the unchanging present of eternity; or rather, the subject is the comparison of that life with the life of man, "the lost." The nature of the state of beatitude is of necessity communicated but very imperfectly; the core of the poem is a radiant and concentrated cloud of obscurity. The longing for beatitude, however, is a normal and comprehensible human experience, and though it is communicated largely by indirect means in this poem, it is communicated with extraordinary power. The obscurity, the imperfection, of the poem is as slight as the treatment of the mystical theme permits; few mystical poems, on the other hand, have expressed as wide a margin of comprehensible experience, and few have been written with such luminous directness and power. The mysterious and subdued longing expressed in the poem culminates, perhaps in lines five and six, and again in lines nine and ten, and the reader may possibly work his way into the poem best by concentrating for a moment on these lines:

> *The fairest day that ever yet has shone,*
> *Will be when thou the day within shalt see;*
> *The fairest rose that ever yet has blown,*
> *When thou the flower thou lookest on shalt be;*
> *But thou art far away among Time's toys;*
> *Thyself the day thou lookest for in them,*
> *Thyself the flower that now thine eye enjoys,*
> *But wilted now thou hang'st upon thy stem.*
> *The bird thou hearest on the budding tree,*
> *Thou hast made sing with thy forgotten voice;*
> *But when it swells again to melody,*

The song is thine in which thou wilt rejoice;
And thou new risen midst these wonders live
That now to them dost all thy substance give.

The same subject and imagery recur in the poem entitled *Today*,
a lovely but less finished performance:

I live but in the present,—where art thou?
Hast thou a home in some past, future year?
I call to thee from every leafy bough,
But thou art far away and canst not hear.

Each flower lifts up its red or yellow head,
And nods to thee as thou art passing by:
Hurry not on, but stay thine anxious tread,
And thou shalt live with me, for there am I.

The stream that murmurs by thee,—heed its voice,
Nor stop thine ear; 'tis I that bid it flow;
And thou with its glad waters shalt rejoice,
And of the life I live within them know.

And hill, and grove, and flowers, and running stream,
When thou dost live with them shall look more fair;
And thou awake as from a cheating dream,
The life today with me and mine to share.

The New Man, a companion-piece to *The Lost*, which appears
only in the edition of 1886, like *The Hand and Foot*, the first
poem quoted in this essay, treats the converse of this theme, or
the experience of achieving salvation:

The hands must touch and handle many things,
The eyes long waste their glances all in vain;
The feet course still in idle, mazy rings,
Ere man himself, the lost, shall back regain
The hand that ever moves, the eyes that see,

While day holds out his shining lamp on high,
And, strait as flies the honey-seeking bee,
Direct the feet to unseen flowers they spy;
These, when they come, the man revealed from heaven,
Shall labor all the day in quiet rest
And find at eve the covert duly given,
Where with the bird they find sweet sleep and rest,
That shall their wasted strength to health restore,
And bid them seek with morn the hills and fields once more.

Much of Very's Nature poetry, especially of his later work, is merely dull; the best of it resembles that of Blake, but is less excellent. Nature, as in Blake, is seen through a daze of beatitude and with only occasional clarity of outline. Nevertheless, there are lovely passages. The following lines are from the sonnet entitled *To the Pure All Things Are Pure:*

Nature shall seem another house of thine,
When he who formed thee bids thee live and play,
And in thy rambles, e'en the creeping vine
Shall keep with thee a jocund holiday.

This passage is from *The Song:*

I plunge me in the river's cooling wave,
Or on the embroidered bank admiring lean,
Now some endangered insect life to save,
Now watch the pictured flowers and grasses green;
Forever playing where a boy I played,
By hill and grove, by field and stream delayed.

Equally lovely are *The Wild Rose of Plymouth, The Fair Morning* (as it appears in the edition of 1886), and *The Lament of the Flowers* (which appears only in the edition of 1886), a curiously haunting poem, too long to quote in full and too elusive to quote in part. In *Autumn Flowers*, the natural description becomes a firm moral allegory; the poem is nearly one of the best.

Yet was there not some excuse for the disturbed clergymen of New England, who, when Very called upon them in their studies and exhorted them to a more devout life, believed him a madman? The clergymen did not represent civilization and the moral life, exactly, but they represented what was left of civilization and the moral life in New England—they were at least the ruined dust of tradition—and Very, though a living spirit, was primarily representative of something else. He was not mad, but he existed in a state resembling madness from a strictly moralistic point of view; he denied the existence, so far as practical behavior was concerned, of the whole world of judgment and of choice; he was like Parmenides, who, having proven the universe by logic to be a perfect and motionless sphere, and having observed about him a universe which did not conform to the definition, pronounced the latter an illusion and turned his back upon it forever.

But in that illusion we live from day to day; and in that life of illusion we govern ourselves by judgment and by choice; and should we deny or lose control of these, the illusion would become a horror. A Very, a Traherne, or a Blake, is a luxury which we can well afford so long as he refrains from making converts. Should he convert us all, he would certainly be destroyed along with us, or so, to us, in our darkness, it must needs appear. But secure and unimpeded in our universe, which he deplores, he expresses one limited aspect of our spiritual life, an aspect which, to express well, he must live fully. The Roman Church has canonized individual mystics, but has suppressed or excommunicated the mystical sects.

But Very seldom preached, like Emerson; rather, he gave us his life: he is a mystic, not a sectary and a reformer. It is true that he argued with Emerson in the woods and with the clergymen in their studies, but the efforts were rare, brief, and private; he had no access, such as Emerson had, to the general public, and he sought for none. His poems sometimes employ the rhetorical forms of exhortation, but the substance is the substance of personal experience: he expressed his own experience of beatitude, or his longing for the experience, or his pity for us, the lost, the dead. Emerson, if he was to concern himself with mysticism at all, could do no other than reform, for he had no mystical life to give: if we are to judge him by his writing, he never experienced that which he recommended, and judged in his own terms he was a failure. His poetry deals not with the experience, but with his own theory of the experience; it is not mystical poetry but gnomic or didactic, poetry, and as the ideas expounded will not stand inspection, the poetry is ultimately poor in spite of a good deal of vigorous phrasing. Or to put it another way, Very speaks with the authority of experience—and this holds true, even if we feel less certain than Very as to the origin of the experience—whereas Emerson claims to speak with the authority of thought, but he lacks that authority.

Yet the measure of Emerson's failure may seem at times the measure of the superiority of at least a little of his poetry to the work of Very, at any rate to those of us who inhabit the lower room, the chamber of illusions, and endeavor to keep it in order that the mystic on the floor above us may suffer as little inconvenient disturbance as possible. For Emerson's failure drove him to examine at odd moments the broken shards and tablets buried in his character from an earlier culture. He was by accident and on certain occasions a moral poet, and he was by natural talent a poet of a good deal of power. When we come from the more purely mystical works of Very to *The Concord Hymn*, or to *Days*, we may feel that we are entering a world of three dimensions, of solid obstacles, and of comprehensible nobility.

But we have not done with Very so easily. Emerson at the core is a fraud and a sentimentalist, and his fraudulence impinges at least lightly upon everything he wrote: when it disappears from the subject, it lingers in the tone; even when he brings his very real talent to bear upon a thoroughly sound subject, he does so with a manner at once condescending and casual, a manner of which the justification, such as it is, may be found in his essays, but of which the consequence is a subtle degradation of the poetic art. Very at the core is a saint; though he is no more often successful than is many another poet, yet he invariably gives the impression of a conscientious effort to render exactly that which

279

he has to say. Very believed that his poems, like his actions, were dictated by a higher power; but, as I have already shown, the power was not the same as that to which Emerson owed allegiance. Very's poetry, like his life, was founded on a belief in Absolute Truth; and either Very (without perhaps wholly realizing it), or the Power that directed him, displayed the conscience, the seriousness, of the artist.

When he brings his character to bear upon matters that we can understand, we find ourselves, for all our doubts, in the presence of one of the finest devotional poets in English. The following poem, *The Created*, is probably the best single poem that Very composed:

> *There is naught for thee by thy haste to gain;*
> *'Tis not the swift with me that win the race;*
> *Through long endurance of delaying pain,*
> *Thine opened eye shall see thy Father's face;*
> *Nor here nor there, where now thy feet would turn,*
> *Thou wilt find Him who ever waits for thee;*
> *But let obedience quench desires that burn,*
> *And where thou art thy Father too will be.*
> *Behold! as day by day the spirit grows,*
> *Thou see'st by inward light things hid before;*
> *Till what God is, thyself, His image shows;*
> *And thou wilt wear the robe that first thou wore,*
> *When bright with radiance from his forming hand,*
> *He saw the lord of all His creatures stand.*

We have here perfection of structure, perfection and power of phrase, great moral scope, at least by way of generality of implication, and sublimity of conception. The intention of this poem must have been purely Calvinistic; yet the second quatrain, in which the Calvinism is most explicit, is stated in terms so general that it might equally well be interpreted as a traditional recommendation of humility and endurance; the term, "inward light," though it is a more or less technical term of Calvinism and of Quietism, has figuratively a very wide applicability; the third line of the poem, though it is in the tradition of Calvinistic exhortation, exceeds any rigorous and literal interpretation of Calvinistic dogma, for it recommends a course of action as a means to salvation. In this poem, then, we see the religious experience expressed fully and richly, unhampered by the heretical dogmas of the author.

Nor is the vision of the resurrection an obstacle to the nonbeliever, for it may, as in so much devotional but non-mystical poetry, be accepted merely as an allegorical representation of a moral state—of the condition of Socrates just before drinking the hemlock instead of a few hours later.

Equally perfect, but of less power, is a hymn entitled *The Visit*; nearly as perfect is a song, *The Call*, of which the last stanza is missing from the edition of 1883; less perfect still, and less compact, but of a magnificence at moments comparable to that of Henry Vaughan, is a hymn entitled *The Coming of the Lord*. There are other poems, which, because of imperfections or limitations of scope, are of secondary importance, but which are still worthy of examination: *The Presence, The Still-Born* (which appears only in the edition of 1886), *The Son, In Him We Live, The Earth, The New Birth, The New World, The Morning Watch, The Dead, The Prison, Enoch,* and *The Cottage;* and there are doubtless others.

I might endeavor to illustrate Very's genius further by the quotation of a good many fine lines from the poems I have just mentioned, but the procedure would be largely unjust, for Very is not a poet of separable moments; his poems are reasoned and coherent, and the full force of a passage will be evident only when one meets it in the context.[8] Further, there is a quality of intense personal conviction in Very, a kind of saturation with his subject and his feeling, which one tends to lose in a brief passage; it is a conviction so extraordinary that in some of his secondary achievements it is able to carry a considerable weight of sterotyped language without the destruction of the poem. To appreciate the finer shades of his statement one should be familiar,

[8] See page 344.

moreover, with his work as a whole, for he is essentially a theological poet, and his references to doctrine are on the one hand fleeting and subtle, and on the other hand of the utmost importance to a perception of his beauty; and in addition, his finest effects are the result of fine variations in tone, the appreciation of which must of necessity depend in a large measure upon a consciousness of the norm from which the variations occur.

Very numbered among his admirers the elder W. E. Channing, Emerson, Clarke, Andrews, Norton, Hawthorne, Bryant, and other persons of distinction; his contemporaries repeatedly compared him to George Herbert, and it would appear with at least a show of reason. Yet for fifty years he has rested in oblivion, except as a name, incorrectly described, in the academic summaries of his period. It is now fifty-seven years since his death, and a hundred years since he first entered upon his full poetic power; we are now very close to the centenary of his confinement to the asylum at Somerville. In this last, at least, it should be possible to find some significance that will justify our recalling him to memory. Perhaps the moral is merely this: that it is nearly time that we paid him the apology long due him and established him clearly and permanently in his rightful place in the history of our literature.

EMILY DICKINSON
and The Limits of Judgment

Antiquest felt at noon
When August, burning low,
Calls forth this spectral canticle,
Repose to typify.

WHEN THE POEMS of Emily Dickinson first began to appear, in the years shortly following her death, she enjoyed a period of notoriety and of semi-popularity that endured for perhaps ten years; after about ten years of semi-obscurity, her reputation was revived with the publication of *The Single Hound,* and has lasted unabated to the present day, though with occasional signs that it may soon commence to diminish. A good many critics have resented her reputation, and it has not been hard for them to justify their resentment; probably no poet of comparable reputation has been guilty of so much unpardonable writing. On the other hand, one cannot shake off the uncomfortable feeling that her popularity has been mainly due to her vices; her worst poems are certainly her most commonly praised, and as a general matter, great lyric poetry is not widely read or admired.

The problem of judging her better poems is much of the time a subtle one. Her meter, at its worst—that is, most of the time—is a kind of stiff sing-song; her diction, at its worst, is a kind of poetic nursery jargon; and there is a remarkable continuity of manner, of a kind nearly indescribable, between her worst and her best poems. The following poem will illustrate the defects in perfection:

I like to see it lap the miles,
And lick the valleys up,

And stop to feed itself at tanks;
And then, prodigious, step

Around a pile of mountains,
And, supercilious, peer
In shanties by the sides of roads;
And then a quarry pare

To fit its sides, and crawl between,
Complaining all the while
In horrid, hooting stanza;
Then chase itself down hill

And neigh like Boanerges;
Then, punctual as a star,
Stop—docile and omnipotent—
At its own stable door.

The poem is abominable; and the quality of silly playfulness which renders it abominable is diffused more or less perceptibly throughout most of her work, and this diffusion is facilitated by the limited range of her metrical schemes.

The difficulty is this: that even in her most nearly perfect poems, even in those poems in which the defects do not intrude momentarily in a crudely obvious form, one is likely to feel a fine trace of her countrified eccentricity; there is nearly always a margin of ambiguity in our final estimate of even her most extraordinary work, and though the margin may appear to diminish or disappear in a given reading of a favorite poem, one feels no certainty that it will not reappear more obviously with the next reading. Her best poems, quite unlike the best poems of Ben Jonson, of George Herbert, or of Thomas Hardy, can never be isolated certainly and defensibly from her defects; yet she is a poetic genius of the highest order, and this ambiguity in one's feeling about her is profoundly disturbing. The following poem is a fairly obvious illustration; we shall later see less obvious:

I started early, took my dog,
And visited the sea;
The mermaids in the basement
Came out to look at me,

And frigates in the upper floor
Extended hempen hands,
Presuming me to be a mouse
Aground, upon the sands.

But no man moved me till the tide
Went past my simple shoe,
And past my apron and my belt,
And past my bodice too,

And made as he would eat me up
As wholly as a dew
Upon a dandelion's sleeve—
And then I started too.

And he—he followed close behind;
I felt his silver heel
Upon my ankle,—then my shoes
Would overflow with pearl.

Until we met the solid town,
No man he seemed to know;
And bowing with a mighty look
At me, the sea withdrew.

The mannerisms are nearly as marked as in the first poem, but whereas the first poem was purely descriptive, this poem is allegorical and contains beneath the more or less mannered surface an ominously serious theme, so that the manner appears in a new light and is somewhat altered in effect. The sea is here the traditional symbol of death; that is, of all the forces and qualities in nature and in human nature which tend toward the dissolution of human character and consciousness. The playful protagonist, the simple village maiden, though she speaks again in the first person, is dramatized, as if seen from without, and her playfulness is somewhat restrained and formalized. Does this formalization, this dramatization, combined with a major symbolism, suffice effectually to transmute in this poem the quality discerned in the first poem, or does that quality linger as a fine defect? The poem is a poem of power; it may even be a great poem; but this is not to answer the question. I have never been able to answer the question.

Her poetic subject matter might be subdivided roughly as follows: natural description; the definition of moral experience, including the definition of difficulties of comprehension; and mystical experience, or the definition of the experience of "immortality," to use a favorite word, or of beatitude. The second subdivision includes a great deal, and her best work falls within it; I shall consider it last. Her descriptive poems contain here and there brilliant strokes, but she had the hard and uncompromising approach to experience of the early New England Calvinists; lacking all subtlety, she displays the heavy hand of one unaccustomed to fragile objects; her efforts at lightness are distressing. Occasionally, instead of endeavoring to treat the small subject in terms appropriate to it, she endeavors to treat it in terms appropriate to her own temperament, and we have what appears a deliberate excursion into obscurity, the subject being inadequate to the rhetoric, as in the last stanza of the poem beginning, "At half-past three a single bird":

> At half-past seven, element
> Nor implement was seen,
> And place was where the presence was,
> Circumference between.

The stanza probably means, roughly, that bird and song alike have disappeared, but the word "circumference," a resonant and impressive one, is pure nonsense.

286

This unpredictable boldness in plunging into obscurity, a boldness in part, perhaps, inherited from the earlier New Englanders whose sense of divine guidance was so highly developed, whose humility of spirit was commonly so small; a boldness dramatized by Melville in the character of Ahab; this congenital boldness may have led her to attempt the rendering of purely theoretic experience, the experience of life after death. There are numerous poems which attempt to express the experience of posthumous beatitude, as if she were already familiar with it; the poetic terms of the expression are terms, either abstract or concrete, of human life, but suddenly fixed, or approaching fixation, as if at the cessation of time in eternity, as if to the dead the living world appeared as immobile as the dead person appears to the living, and the fixation frequently involves an element of horror:

> Great streets of silence led away
> To neighborhoods of pause;
> Here was no notice, no dissent,
> No universe, no laws.
>
> By clocks 'twas morning, and for night
> The bells at distance called;
> But epoch had no basis here,
> For period exhaled.

The device here employed is to select a number of terms representing familiar abstractions or perceptions, some of a commonplace nature, some relatively grandiose or metaphysical, and one by one to negate these terms; a number of statements, from a grammatical point of view, have been made, yet actually no concrete image emerges, and the idea of the poem—the idea of the absolute dissidence of the eternal from the temporal—is stated indirectly, and, in spite of the brevity of the poem and the gnomic manner, with extraordinary redundancy. We come painfully close in this poem to the irresponsible playfulness of the poem about the railway train; we have gone beyond the irresponsible obscurity of the poem about the bird.

This is technically a mystical poem: that is, it endeavors to render an experience—the rapt contemplation, eternal and immovable, which Aquinas describes as the condition of beatitude —which is by definition foreign to all human experience, yet to render it in terms of a modified human experience. Yet there is no particular reason to believe that Emily Dickinson was a mystic, or thought she was a mystic. The poems of this variety, and there are many of them, appear rather to be efforts to dramatize an idea of salvation, intensely felt, but as an idea, not as something experienced, and as an idea essentially inexpressible. She deliberately utilizes imagery irrelevant to the state with which she is concerned, because she cannot do otherwise; yet the attitude toward the material, the attitude of rapt contemplation, is the attitude which she presumably expects to achieve toward something that she has never experienced. The poems are invariably forced and somewhat theoretical; they are briskly clever, and lack the obscure but impassioned conviction of the mystical poems of Very; they lack the tragic finality, the haunting sense of human isolation in a foreign universe, to be found in her greatest poems, of which the explicit theme is a denial of this mystical trance, is a statement of the limits of judgment.

There are a few curious and remarkable poems representing a mixed theme, of which the following is perhaps the finest example:

> Because I could not stop for Death,
> He kindly stopped for me;
> The carriage held but just ourselves
> And Immortality.
>
> We slowly drove, he knew no haste,
> And I had put away
> My labor, and my leisure too,
> For his civility.
>
> We passed the school where children played
> At wrestling in a ring;

We passed the fields of gazing grain,
We passed the setting sun.

We paused before a house that seemed
A swelling of the ground;
The roof was scarcely visible,
The cornice but a mound.

Since then 'tis centuries; but each
Feels shorter than the day
I first surmised the horses' heads
Were toward eternity.

In the fourth line we find the familiar device of using a major abstraction in a somewhat loose and indefinable manner; in the last stanza there is the semi-playful pretence of familiarity with the posthumous experience of eternity, so that the poem ends unconvincingly though gracefully, with a formulary gesture very roughly comparable to that of the concluding couplet of many an Elizabethan sonnet of love; for the rest the poem is a remarkably beautiful poem on the subject of the daily realization of the imminence of death—it is a poem of departure from life, an intensely conscious leave-taking. In so far as it concentrates on the life that is being left behind, it is wholly successful; in so far as it attempts to experience the death to come, it is fraudulent, however exquisitely, and in this it falls below her finest achievement. Allen Tate, who appears to be unconcerned with this fraudulent element, praises the poem in the highest terms; he appears almost to praise it for its defects:[1] "The sharp *gazing* before *grain* instils into nature a kind of cold vitality of which the qualitative richness has infinite depth. The content of death in the poem eludes forever any explicit definition . . . she has presented a typical Christian theme in all its final irresolution, without making any final statement about it." The poem ends in irresolution in the sense that it ends in a statement that is not offered seriously; to praise the

[1] *Reactionary Essays on Poetry and Ideas,* by Allen Tate. Scribners, 1936. The essay on Emily Dickinson.

poem for this is unsound criticism, however. It is possible to solve any problem of insoluble experience by retreating a step and defining the boundary at which comprehension ceases, and by then making the necessary moral adjustments to that boundary; this in itself is an experience both final and serious, and it is the experience on which our author's finest work is based.

Let me illustrate by citation. The following poem defines the subject which the mystical poems endeavor to conceal: the soul is taken to the brink of the incomprehensible, and is left there, for retreat is impossible, and advance is impossible without a transmutation of the soul's very nature. The third and fourth lines display the playful redundancy of her weaker poems, but the intrusion of the quality here is the result of habit, and is a minor defect; there is nothing in the conception of the poem demanding a compromise. There is great power in the phrasing of the remainder of the poem, especially in the middle stanza:

> *Our journey had advanced;*
> *Our feet were almost come*
> *To that odd fork in Being's road,*
> *Eternity by term.*
>
> *Our pace took sudden awe,*
> *Our feet reluctant led.*
> *Before were cities, but between*
> *The forest of the dead.*
>
> *Retreat was out of hope,—*
> *Behind, a sealëd route,*
> *Eternity's white flag before,*
> *And God at every gate.*

She is constantly defining the absolute cleavage between the living and the dead. In the following poem the definition is made more powerfully, and in other terms:

> *'Twas warm at first, like us,*
> *Until there crept thereon*

> A chill, like frost upon a glass,
> Till all the scene be gone.
>
> The forehead copied stone,
> The fingers grew too cold
> To ache, and like a skater's brook
> The busy eyes congealed.
>
> It straightened—that was all—
> It crowded cold to cold—
> It multiplied indifference
> As Pride were all it could.
>
> And even when with cords
> 'Twas lowered like a freight,
> It made no signal, nor demurred,
> But dropped like adamant.

The stiffness of phrasing, as in the barbarously constructed fourth and twelfth lines, is allied to her habitual carelessness, yet in this poem there is at least no triviality, and the imagery of the third stanza in particular has tremendous power.

The poem beginning, "The last night that she lived," treats the same theme in more personal terms; the observer watches the death of a friend, that is follows the friend to the brink of the comprehensible, sees her pass the brink, and faces the loss. The poem contains a badly mixed figure and at least two major grammatical blunders, in addition to a little awkward inversion of an indefensible variety, yet there is in the poem an immediate seizing of terrible fact, which makes it, at least fragmentarily, very great poetry:

> And we, we placed the hair,
> And drew the head erect;
> And then an awful leisure was,
> Our faith to regulate.

Her inability to take Christian mysticism seriously did not, however, drive her to the opposite extreme of the pantheistic mysticism which was seducing her contemporaries. The following lines, though not remarkable poetry, are a clear statement of a position consistently held:

> *But nature is a stranger yet;*
>   *The ones that cite her most*
> *Have never passed her haunted house,*
>   *Nor simplified her ghost.*
>
> *To pity those that know her not*
>   *Is helped by the regret*
> *That those who know her, know her less*
>   *The nearer her they get.*

Nature as a symbol, as Allen Tate has pointed out in the essay to which I have already referred, remains immitigably the symbol of all the elements which corrupt, dissolve, and destroy human character and consciousness; to approach nature is to depart from the fullness öf human life, and to join nature is to leave human life. Nature may thus be a symbol of death, representing much the same idea as the corpse in the poem beginning " 'Twas warm at first, like us," but involving a more complex range of association.

In the following poem, we are shown the essential cleavage between man, as represented by the author-reader, and nature, as represented by the insects in the late summer grass; the subject is the plight of man, the willing and freely moving entity, in a universe in which he is by virtue of his essential qualities a foreigner. The intense nostalgia of the poem is the nostalgia of man for the mode of being which he perceives imperfectly and in which he cannot share. The change described in the last two lines is the change in the appearance of nature and in the feeling of the observer which results from a recognition of the cleavage:

> *Farther in summer than the birds,*
> *Pathetic from the grass,*

A minor nation celebrates
Its unobtrusive mass.

No ordinance is seen,
So gradual the grace,
A pensive custom it becomes,
Enlarging loneliness.

Antiquest felt at noon
When August, burning low,
Calls forth this spectral canticle,
Repose to typify.

Remit as yet no grace,
No furrow on the glow,
Yet a druidic difference
Enhances nature now.

The first two lines of the last stanza are written in the author's personal grammatical short-hand; they are no doubt defective in this respect, but the defect is minor. They mean: There is as yet no diminution of beauty, no mark of change on the brightness. The twelfth line employs a meaningless inversion. On the other hand, the false rhymes are employed with unusually fine modulation; the first rhyme is perfect, the second and third represent successive stages of departure, and the last a return to what is roughly the stage of the second. These effects are complicated by the rhyming, both perfect and imperfect, from stanza to stanza. The intense strangeness of this poem could not have been achieved with standard rhyming. The poem, though not quite one of her most nearly perfect, is probably one of her five or six greatest, and is one of the most deeply moving and most unforgettable poems in my own experience; I have the feeling of having lived in its immediate presence for many years.

The three poems which combine her greatest power with her finest execution are strangely on much the same theme, both as regards the idea embodied and as regards the allegorical embodiment. They deal with the inexplicable fact of change, of the absolute cleavage between successive states of being, and it is not unnatural that in two of the poems this theme should be related to the theme of death. In each poem, seasonal change is employed as the concrete symbol of the moral change. This is not the same thing as the so-called pathetic fallacy of the romantics, the imposition of a personal emotion upon a physical object incapable either of feeling such an emotion or of motivating it in a human being. It is rather a legitimate and traditional form of allegory, in which the relationships between the items described resemble exactly the relationships between certain moral ideas or experiences; the identity of relationship evoking simultaneously and identifying with each other the feelings attendant upon both series as they appear separately. Here are the three poems, in the order of the seasons employed, and in the order of increasing complexity both of theme and of technique:

1

A light exists in spring
Not present in the year
At any other period.
When March is scarcely here

A color stands abroad
On solitary hills
That science cannot overtake,
But human nature feels.

It waits upon the lawn;
It shows the furthest tree
Upon the furthest slope we know;
It almost speaks to me.

Then, as horizons step,
Or noons report away,

Without the formula of sound,
It passes, and we stay:

A quality of loss
Affecting our content,
As trade had suddenly encroached
Upon a sacrament.

2

As imperceptibly as grief
The Summer lapsed away,—
Too imperceptible, at last,
To seem like perfidy.

A quietness distilled,
As twilight long begun,
Or Nature, spending with herself
Sequestered afternoon.

The dusk drew earlier in,
The morning foreign shone,—
A courteous, yet harrowing grace,
As guest who would be gone.

And thus, without a wing,
Or service of a keel,
Our summer made her light escape
Into the beautiful.

3

There's a certain slant of light,
On winter afternoons,

That oppresses, like the weight
Of cathedral tunes.

Heavenly hurt it gives us;
We can find no scar,
But internal difference
Where the meanings are.

None may teach it anything,
'Tis the seal, despair,—
An imperial affliction
Sent us of the air.

When it comes, the landscape listens,
Shadows hold their breath;
When it goes, 'tis like the distance
On the look of death.

In the seventh, eighth, and twelfth lines of the first poem, and, it is barely possible, in the seventh and eighth of the third, there is a very slight echo of the brisk facility of her poorer work; the last line of the second poem, perhaps, verges ever so slightly on an easy prettiness of diction, though scarcely of substance. These defects are shadowy, however; had the poems been written by another writer, it is possible that we should not observe them. On the other hand, the directness, dignity, and power with which these major subjects are met, the quality of the phrasing, at once clairvoyant and absolute, raise the poems to the highest level of English lyric poetry.

The meter of these poems is worth careful scrutiny. The basis of all three is the so-called Poulter's Measure, first employed, if I remember aright, by Surrey, and after the time of Sidney in disrepute. It is the measure, however, not only of the great elegy on Sidney commonly attributed to Fulke Greville, but of some of the best poetry between Surrey and Sidney, including the fine poem by Vaux on contentment and the great poem by Gascoigne in praise of a gentlewoman of dark complexion. The English poets commonly though not invariably wrote the poem in two long lines instead of four short ones, and the lines so conceived were the basis of their rhetoric. In the first of the three poems just quoted, the measure is employed without alteration, but the short line is the basis of the rhetoric; an arrangement which permits of more varied adjustment of sentence to line than if the long line were the basis. In the second poem, the first stanza is composed not in the basic measure, but in lines of eight, six, eight, and six syllables; the shift into the normal six, six, eight, and six in the second stanza, as in the second stanza of the poem beginning, "Farther in summer," results in a subtle and beautiful muting both of meter and of tone. This shift she employs elsewhere, but especially in poems of four stanzas, to which it appears to have a natural relationship; it is a brilliant technical invention.

In the third poem she varies her simple base with the ingenuity and mastery of a virtuoso. In the first stanza, the two long lines are reduced to seven syllables each, by the dropping of the initial unaccented syllable; the second short line is reduced to five syllables in the same manner. In the second stanza, the first line, which ought now to be of six syllables, has but five metrical syllables, unless we violate normal usage and count the second and infinitely light syllable of *Heaven,* with an extrametrical syllable at the end, the syllable dropped being again the initial one; the second line, which ought to have six syllables, has likewise lost its initial syllable, but the extrametrical *us* of the preceding line, being unaccented, is in rhythmical effect the first syllable of the second line, so that this syllable serves a double and ambiguous function—it maintains the syllable-count of the first line, in spite of an altered rhythm, and it maintains the rhythm of the second line in spite of the altered syllable-count. The third and fourth lines of the second stanza are shortened to seven and five. In the third stanza the first and second lines are constructed like the third and fourth of the second stanza; the third and fourth lines like the first and second of the second stanza, except that in the third line the initial unaccented position is filled and we have a light anapest; that is, the third stanza repeats the construction of the second, but in reverse order. The final stanza is a triumphant resolution of the three preceding: the first and third lines, like the second and fourth, are metrically identical; the first and third contain seven syllables each, with an additional extrametrical syllable at the end which takes the place of the missing syllable at the beginning of each subsequent short line, at the same time that the extrametrical syllable functions in the line in which it is written as part of a two-syllable rhyme. The elaborate structure of this poem results in the balanced hesitations and rapid resolutions which one hears in reading it. This is metrical artistry at about as high a level as one is likely to find it.

Emily Dickinson was a product of the New England tradition of moral Calvinism; her dissatisfaction with her tradition led to her questioning most of its theology and discarding much of it, and led to her reinterpreting some of it, one would gather, in the direction of a more nearly Catholic Christianity. Her acceptance of Christian moral concepts was unimpaired, and the moral tone of her character remained immitigably Calvinistic in its hard and direct simplicity. As a result of this Calvinistic temper, she lacked the lightness and grace which might have enabled her to master minor themes; she sometimes stepped without hesitation into obscurantism, both verbal and metaphysical. But also as a result of it, her best poetry represents a moral adjustment to certain major problems which are carefully defined; it is curious in the light of this fact, and in the light of the discussion which they have received, that her love poems never equal her highest achievement—her best work is on themes more generalized and inclusive.

Emily Dickinson differed from every other major New England writer of the nineteenth century, and from every major American writer of the century save Melville, of those affected by New England, in this: that her New England heritage, though it made her life a moral drama, did not leave her life in moral confusion. It impoverished her in one respect, however: of all great poets, she is the most lacking in taste; there are innumerable beautiful lines and passages wasted in the desert of her crudities; her defects, more than those of any other great poet that I have read, are constantly at the brink, or pushing beyond the brink, of her best poems. This stylistic character is the natural product of the New England which produced the barren little meeting houses; of the New England founded by the harsh and intrepid pioneers, who in order to attain salvation trampled brutally through a world which they were too proud and too impatient to understand. In this respect, she differs from Melville, whose taste was rich and cultivated. But except by Melville, she is surpassed by no writer that this country has produced; she is one of the greatest lyric poets of all time.

MAULE'S WELL

or Henry James and the Relation of Morals
to Manners

"Be careful not to drink at Maule's well!" said he. "Neither drink nor bathe your face in it!"
"Maule's well!" answered Phoebe. "Is that it with the rim of mossy stones? I have no thought of drinking there—but why not?"
"Oh," rejoined the daguerreotypist, "because, like an old lady's cup of tea, it is water bewitched!"
— The House of the Seven Gables

THE MOTIVATING IDEAS of most of the novels of Henry James might be summarized very briefly, and perhaps a trifle crudely, as follows: that there is a moral sense, a sense of decency, inherent in human character at its best; that this sense of decency, being only a sense, exists precariously, and may become confused and even hysterical in a crisis; that it may be enriched and cultivated through association with certain environments; that such association may, also, be carried so far as to extinguish the moral sense. This last relationship, that of the moral sense to an environment which may up to a certain point enrich it and beyond that point dissolve it, resembles the ordinary relationship of intellect to experience, of character to sensibility.

If we carry these generalizations a little farther into the special terms of his novels, we find, however: that the moral sense as James conceives it is essentially American or at least appears to James most clearly in American character; that it can be cultivated by association with European civilization and manners; that it may be weakened or in some other manner betrayed by an excess of such association.

Superficially this description seems to omit the novels of the

300

brief middle period, in which most of the characters were British and in which none were American; but actually these novels are in nearly every case constructed in much the same terms, for the "American" characteristics are given to certain personages, and the "European" to certain others. This formula will be somewhat qualified as we proceed, but I believe that it is essentially sound.

Now this particular kind of moral sense may have existed in Europe as well as in America, but so far as James was concerned, it was essentially an American phenomenon: in the first place, I believe that I shall be able to show how a degree of intensity of this moral sense was an actual and historical development in the American context; in the second place, we have in James the ultimate and rarefied development of the spiritual antagonism which had existed for centuries between the rising provincial civilization and the richer civilization from which it had broken away, an antagonism in which the provincial civilization met the obviously superior cultivation of the parent with a more or less typically provincial assertion of moral superiority. The same theme obsesses Fenimore Cooper for a large portion of his career, though conceived in terms less subtle; it is the same antagonism which, from pre-Revolutionary days to the present, has resulted in the attempt, unhealthy in its self-consciousness and in its neurotic intensity, to create a literature which shall be utterly independent of that of England; it is the same antagonism which has led many of the compatriots of Henry James to disown him as a foreigner because of his long residence abroad, and which led his western contemporaries of the intellectual stamp of Clemens to despise James in turn for his cultivation and artistry. There is further evidence that James conceived this moral sense to be essentially American, moreover, in the fact that the moral phenomenon and its attendant dramatic formula alike were first defined in the early American period of his art, and that they were most fully and richly developed in his last great masterpieces, *The Ambassadors, The Wings of the Dove,* and *The Golden Bowl.*

The origin of this moral sense may be given briefly and with fair certainty, though James himself nowhere defines it: it was the product of generations of discipline in the ethical systems of the Roman Catholic and Anglo-Catholic Churches, a product which subsisted as a traditional way of feeling and of acting after the ideas which had formed it, and which, especially in Europe and before the settlement of America, had long supported it, had ceased to be understood, or, as ideas, valued. The Anglo-Catholic Church in New York and farther south, even before the Revolutionary War, tended to rely upon society for its support, rather than to support society; it was the external sign of the respectability of a class, and was scarcely an evangelizing or an invigorating force. This phenomenon can be observed in the social novels of Cooper, who views it benignantly; and it is mentioned specifically by Mrs. Wharton, whose approval is tempered with comprehension, in the opening pages of *The Old Maid*. In this condensed novel, Mrs. Wharton writes as follows: "The Ralstons were of middle-class English stock. They had not come to the colonies to die for a creed but to live for a bank account. The result had been beyond their hopes, and their religion was tinged by their success. An edulcorated Church of England which, under the conciliatory name of the 'Episcopal Church of the United States of America,' left out the coarser allusions in the Marriage Service, slid over the comminatory passages in the Athanasian Creed, and thought it more respectful to say 'Our Father *Who*' than '*Which*' in the Lord's Prayer, was exactly suited to the spirit of compromise whereon the Ralstons had built themselves up. There was in all the tribe the same instinctive recoil from new religions as from unaccounted-for people. Institutional to the core, they represented the conservative element that holds new societies together as sea-plants bind the seashore." And a little farther on she writes as follows: "The fourth generation of Ralstons had nothing left in the way of convictions save an acute sense of honor in private and business matters; on the life of the community and the state they took their daily views from the newspapers, and the newspapers they already despised."

The moral sense in question, however, might have been a

much weaker motive, and certainly would not have been an essentially American motive, had it not been intensified through the influence of New England. In New England, the Calvinistic theology denied the freedom of the will and the efficaciousness of good works—that is, it denied the importance of the whole subject of morality, at least in formal doctrine—but at the same time, as a result of its inner inconsistencies and of the practical struggles of the Puritans, as I have shown in discussing Hawthorne, it dramatized and intensified the moral struggle in an extraordinary manner. Throughout a relatively brief period, perhaps for less than a century, the moral sense of New England as a whole, and throughout a much longer period the moral sense of large segments of New England, was both simplified and intensified by Calvinistic ideas, at the same time that these ideas, because of their inner contradictions, and as they worked, under the emotional pressure of the period, in the minds of the subtler theologians, were literally proving self-destructive. By 1730 the ideas were become so widely ineffective as to alarm the surviving faithful. The preachers of the Great Awakening gave them a renewed energy, in part intellectual, but primarily emotional, but the new energy, being factitious, the result of the impact of a new rhetoric rather than of a new clarification, was short-lived. Edwards gave them a new and powerful intellectual adjustment, but the adjustment was among the ideas themselves, and scarcely clarified the increasingly obvious discrepancies between the ideas and daily life, so that daily life moved on and left them. The ideas killed themselves off, except as they existed, half-understood, in the remoter village congregations; but the emotional energy, the New England conscience, was longer in dying. It gave the Unitarian Church its principal claim to dignity; it persisted even in Emerson, as a private citizen, at the same time that Emerson was preaching pantheism, equivalence, and surrender to instinct.

Now except for the Mormon community of Utah, New England was the only part of America in which a church ever exercised a formative and governing influence upon society, so that for certain periods in American history the adjectives *Puritan* and *New England* are practically interchangeable. Further, New England until well into the nineteenth century provided the schoolmasters for most of the United States. Van Wyck Brooks comments upon this fact in *The Flowering of New England;*[1] he says: "Edward Everett Hale relates that a certain French investigator, sent by Napoleon III to study American education, found that virtually every teacher in the West and South had come from one small corner of the couhtry, either Connecticut or Massachusetts. He asked Hale to explain this fact, which he said was unique in history. Hale, to settle the question, enquired of a leading citizen of Massachusetts how many young people of his town, when they left school, began as teachers. 'He heard me,' says Hale, 'with some impatience, and then said, "Why all of them, of course." ' " Brooks cites Emerson, in addition, as advising "his fellow-townsmen to manufacture school-teachers and make them the best in the world." If one has ever read *Satanstoe,* by Fenimore Cooper, one will scarcely forget Jason Newcome, the New England schoolmaster who settled in New York, nor the inabillty of Corny Littlepage, the New Yorker, to understand Jason's belief that the calling of the schoolmaster was both respectable and enviable; this in spite of the fact that Jason represented the New England conscience in a degraded form, that of the caution of the hypocrite.

Further, New England until the middle of the nineteenth century not only produced at least a fair proportion of the political talent of the nation, but she produced nearly all of the major literary talent. If we except Poe, a Southerner, whose literary merit appears to the present writer to be a very frail delusion; if we except Irving, a charming writer, but a minor writer at best; if we except Cooper, a great writer, and a New Yorker without mitigation; we have but two great New York talents after Freneau and preceding the Civil War: W. C. Bryant, a New Englander in origin, who wrote most of his best work before leaving New England; and Herman Melville, whose father and grandfather were born in New England, whose mother came of an old

---

[1] *The Flowering of New England,* by Van Wyck Brooks, Dutton, 1936; page 252.

New York family, who was himself born and raised in New York, yet all of whose work was profoundly colored by New England, and whose greatest work was an allegorical epic of New England. The influence of New England upon the spiritual life of the nation till about 1850 or 1860 may thus be conceded to have been extremely great; as a matter of fact it continued much later, though with diminishing force. The most remarkable evidence of its later continuance is the work of Henry James, another New Yorker; and of this continuance there is ample objective evidence, in such characters as Lambert Strether, in that unforgettable legend of New England, *The Europeans*, perhaps the most beautiful of James's minor works, and omitted from the definitive edition for reasons that must always remain obscure to me, and even in *The Bostonians*—for had he not been as familiar with the New England conscience as with his own, he could scarcely have written such a work—and without recourse to the historical summary and ethical analysis of which this essay will consist.

For practical purposes, the New England moral sense was merely an intensification of that of New York; like that of New York it derived ultimately from the pre-American Catholic discipline, but unlike that of New York, or at least of English New York, it had experienced a Calvinistic interlude, which intensified it, notwithstanding the fact that such an interlude, rationally considered, ought to have destroyed it at the time, and notwithstanding the additional fact that the interlude, historically considered, ultimately did destroy it, but long afterward, by severing its connection with the one and only source of its nourishment, the Aristotelian ethical tradition, as embodied in the Catholic Church. The New England moral sense, then, might readily enough be imposed in some measure upon the New Yorker, and though it often appeared both obnoxious and ludicrous to him, because of the very intensification in question, as we see it appearing in *Satanstoe*, in *The Chainbearer*, and in *The Bostonians*, it none the less influenced and strengthened him in the long run, or at least until it began to die in both environments. Its death came through the increase of the temporal separation from its source, through the corrupting influence of the anti-moral philosophy of Emersonian and other romantics, through dilution with the post-war inundation of uprooted immigrants, through the reversion of influence from the uprooted Americans who in tremendous numbers had broken with their traditions and moved west, through the inundation of new and imperfectly digested scientific knowledge, and through the influence of the new financial aristocracy which had arisen after the Civil War with great rapidity and by methods in most cases not only immoral and illegal and hence corrupting by way of example, but causing a tremendous drain upon the spiritual life of the nation through the material impoverishment of great multitudes.

This moral sense, as it existed about equally in James and in his characters, then, was a fine, but a very delicate perception, unsupported by any clear set of ideas, and functioning, not only in minds of very subtle construction, but at the very crisis in history at which it was doomed not only to be almost infinitely rarefied but finally to be dissolved in air. Since James conceived the art of the novel primarily in terms of plot, and plot almost wholly in terms of ethical choice and of its consequences; since he raised the plotting of the novel to a level of seriousness which it had never before attained in English; since all intelligent criticism of James is resolved inevitably into a discussion of plot; this moral sense, this crisis in history, will prove, I believe, to be the source of the essential problem of James's art.

II

James displays in all of his more serious work an unmistakable desire to allow his characters unrestricted freedom of choice and to develop his plots out of such choice and out of consequent acts of choice to which the initial acts may lead. Now absolutely considered, no human complex is ever free from a great many elements which are without the control and even the understanding of the human participants. We may discover this fact very simply if we consider for a moment *A Portrait of a Lady*.

We may fairly say that it is chance which brings Madame

Merle into the life of Isabel Archer: at any rate, the entrance of Madame Merle is a fact in itself of absolutely no ethical antecedents or significance. On the other hand, we may say that the actions of Isabel Archer are in certain respects and up to a certain point determined: she is first of all human, and is subject to the fundamental necessities of humanity; being a normal young woman, she is fairly certain to marry, for example. And if she marries, she will in the matter of choice be limited by chance—that is, she will have to choose from among the men whom she happens to know, even if we suppose it to be within her power to attract any man whom she desires. Her choice within these limits may in a sense be said to be determined—as perhaps it actually was—by a temperamental bent of her own which she fails to understand and consider, or by the facts of her personal history, which result in certain forms of knowledge and certain forms of ignorance, and which may consequently lead her to judge a situation on the basis of imperfect knowledge. The initial tragic error of Hyacinth Robinson, of *The Princess Casamassima*, for example, is conceived as a free choice made in ignorance of the essential knowledge which would have prevented it; similarly, Mrs. Wharton's finest short work, *Bunner Sisters*, is conceived as a sequence of steps taken by the two protagonists into tragic knowledge, each step being made freely and apparently wisely on the basis of the imperfect knowledge held at the time it is taken.

Elements of this sort are what we call the given facts of the plot: they are the ineliminable facts of character and of initial situation. We have a certain group of particularized individuals in juxtaposition; the particularity is destiny, the juxtaposition chance. But the understanding and the will may rise in some measure superior to destiny and to chance, and when they do so, we have human victory; or they may make the effort and fail, in which case we have tragedy; or the failure having occurred, there may be a comprehension of the failure and a willed adjustment to it, in which case we have the combination of tragedy and victory. It is this combination, the representation of which Henry James especially strives to achieve.

Some novelists—Defoe, for example, or Hardy—make a conscious effort to give the human participant the smallest possible freedom of play; James endeavors to give him the greatest possible freedom, and he is so successful in the effort that in reading one of his better novels one is conscious almost exclusively of the problem of ethical choice.

Now the norm of human experience, in the matter of unhampered choice, is probably somewhere between the extremes of Moll Flanders and of Isabel Archer, and the novelist who goes to one extreme or the other simply refuses to consider intelligently certain aspects of human life. There is possibly greater educative value—there are wider ethical implications—in suffering the consequences of an ill-judged but unhampered choice than in any other department of experience; on the other hand, the person whose choice is normally unhampered may often appear to have an abominably facile existence in the eyes of him whose life is an unbroken and unavailing endurance of necessity, whose primary virtue must of necessity be fortitude.

James sought in so far as possible, it would seem, to create the illusion of unhampered choice, he sought to study the ethical judgment of his time and nation in the purest essence to which he could distill it. This I believe to have been a limitation, but of the two alternative limitations, if one is to choose one or the other extreme, distinctly the lesser evil. Of the limitation as such, I shall have nothing further to say; but it was also the source of obscurity, and the nature of this obscurity, and the nature of James's struggle to master it, will be the subject of this examination.

James was abetted in his effort to isolate the moral problem by the defects of his own knowledge: although he possessed the most refined ethical sensibility of his period, and the sensibility the most profoundly American, his education and background were such that he knew very little of American life and manners. With the American abroad he was familiar; with the travelled American on his return, he was not unfamiliar; and one could extend the catalogue to a few other particulars. But he knew nothing of American economic life, a fact which he recognized and deplored; and he knew next to nothing of the daily detail, of the manners, of any single and reasonably representative American class in its native environment, a fact which will become abundantly obvious if one compares any of his novels whatever to *The Age of Innocence*, by Mrs. Wharton. His own childhood, under the guidance of his elegantly bohemian father, familiarized him with an intellectual class, but with a class consistent only in its intellectuality, and composed of individuals largely detached, as he saw them, from their social backgrounds—his social experience was essentially amorphous.

In one of his letters,[2] he addresses a correspondent as follows: "I sympathize even less with your protest against the idea that it takes an old civilization to set a novelist in motion—a proposition that seems to me so true as to be a truism. It is on manners, customs, usages, habits, forms, upon all these things matured and established, that a novelist lives—they are the very stuff his work is made of." James was no doubt right in the general proposition, for a novel requires bulk, and the bulk can be composed only of a scrutiny of the daily detail of life; but the notion that America did not offer any body of manners worth examining was false, as the work of Mrs. Wharton, again, to go no further, amply shows—James was simply insufficiently familiar with his country or insufficiently observant of it.

In such a book as *The Age of Innocence*, Mrs. Wharton shows us a group of characters whose actions are governed according to the same ethical history and principles which I have mentioned in connection with James. But the characters are living in a society cognate and coterminous with those principles; the society with its customs and usages, is the external form of the principles. Now the customs and usages may become unduly externalized, and when they appear so to become, Mrs. Wharton satirizes them; but in the main they represent the concrete aspect of the abstract principles of behavior. Thus when Newland Archer and the Countess Olenska are on the point of eloping, one of the strongest incentives to their withdrawal is the fact that they will be forced into a mode of life of a bohemian and

[2] Letters, edited by Percy Lubbock, Vol. I, page 72.

disorderly sort which must inevitably degrade their love in their own eyes; and this incentive is essentially serious, for the usages which they are unwilling to abandon are the embodiment of serious principles; whereas the usages which they are unwilling to adopt represent a weak falling away from those principles. In this way Mrs. Wharton gives greater precision to her moral issues than James is able to achieve, for James endeavors, as I have said, to isolate from the manners which might have given it concreteness a moral sense which is already isolated by history from the ideas which gave rise to it. Ellen Glasgow, in such novels as *They Stooped to Folly* and *Virginia*, carries the procedure of Mrs. Wharton a step farther, and by the measure of that step loses in seriousness: she shows her characters so dominated by a system of manners, or so emotionally, so automatically, in rebellion against a system of manners, as to be essentially unconscious of their motives and so determined. She does not give an untrue picture of life, for there are more people in the world resembling Virginia and her husband than resembling Newland Archer; but she gives a less complete picture of human nature, for Newland Archer is a man of intelligence as well as of sensibility.

In comparison with a Jamesian character, however, Archer and Ellen Olenska are governed by circumstance; the Jamesian character has greater freedom, in part because James couldn't help it, and in part because he would no doubt have wished it anyway. The moral issue, then, since it is primarily an American affair, is freed in most of the Jamesian novels, and in all of the greatest, from the compulsion of a code of manners.

The moral issue is also freed from economic necessity. Money is never an impelling motive in a Jamesian novel: that is, no one is forced to choose, as Moll Flanders was forced to choose, between crime and starvation. On the other hand, a lack of sufficient funds to live in luxury is a frequent motive to baseness among the corrupt characters; Lambert Strether, in *The Ambassadors*, surmounts this temptation among others. The lack of money may be sufficiently great to be a temptation; but it is never sufficiently great to be compelling. Isabel Archer is benevolently provided with funds after her story opens, with the express purpose that her action shall thereafter be unhampered.

This necessity, in the Jamesian art, of seeing to it that the leading characters shall be well-heeled, leads to some curious paradoxes. Christopher Newman, of *The American,* for example, is a perfect embodiment of the Jamesian conscience, yet he is a man of fabulous wealth, which he has acquired himself and in a very few years, immediately following the Civil War, and very largely in western railroads, and he is, in addition, a citizen of San Francisco—he is, in brief, a colleague of Leland Stanford and of Collis P. Huntington. James conceives nearly all of his American financiers in the same terms, until he comes to write *The Ivory Tower,* a book in which an intense suspicion, never supported by exact knowledge, of the evil of American financial life, of its actually corrupting effect on the characters of the participants, is the explicit theme.

If we demand of a novelist that he portray a society accurately as regards all its externals, this contradiction in Jamesian character would be all but fatal to his art. We could justify it to a certain extent by saying that there were in the eastern United States individuals of moderate wealth either inherited or otherwise honestly acquired; that James erred only in the unnecessary exaggeration of the wealth of his characters, in attributing to a man of the character, let us say, of an Adams or a Phillips, the wealth of a Sage or a Vanderbilt, in a period in which it is notorious that such wealth could not be decently accumulated. We might justify him to a certain extent by pleading the indisputable fact that many men who are notoriously unscrupulous in matters of finance or of politics preserve the domestic virtues intact; though such an apology in the background of *The Golden Bowl* would necessarily mitigate our sense of the tragedy of Adam Verver.

Such apologies would up to a certain point be sound, although they would certainly be insufficient. The real objection to them, however, is that they would be irrelevant; they would be offered in defense of a misconception of the Jamesian art. For James is definitely not examining the whole of a society; he is examining the mathematical center of a society—the ethical consciousness of a society—and he is examining nothing more. For the rest, so far as his Americans are concerned, he is employing a fictive convention, the convention of fabulous wealth fabulously acquired and resulting in the freedom of the possessor from necessity, in order to isolate the ethical consciousness in question more perfectly than it is to be found isolated in life. In this respect, his art approaches that of the allegorist, of the symbolic poet: it is an art not of inclusion, but of representative and essential selection.

We find, then, that James succeeded to a remarkable degree in separating the problem of ethical choice from the influence of ethical habit and of social pressure as they appear in the guise of manners or of economic necessity. The consequences of this success remain to be seen.

III

James, then, was unequipped to deal adequately with any major aspect of American manners, yet he was a novelist of manners by natural gift and by his own admission; he was furthermore profoundly American in character. The problem was solved naturally by the facts of his personal history: he dealt with the American, uprooted from his native usages, and confronted with the alien usages of a subtle and ancient society.

In the early works and in some of the minor works of later years, the confrontation leads to curious results. Christopher Newman may serve again as the illustration: there is not only the paradox of his possessing a virgin New England conscience along with a fortune acquired in western railroads, but there is the additional paradox of his possessing the gentle flexibility of a New England or New York aristocrat at his best, along with a social naïveté that irritates the Bellegardes. James in his effort to indicate a part of the basis for this irritation writes certain scenes in which Newman converses with a rural and moralizing garrulity that puts one strongly in mind of Natty Bumppo.

In the more mature works, the relationship is, of course, stated far more subtly. The Ververs are gentle and cultivated people, who are circumvented by persons a shade less gentle and a shade more cultivated, the fine degrees of difference, however, being firmly indicative of an essential cleavage in character. Lambert Strether is from the outset of *The Ambassadors* a person of great astuteness of perception as well as of unusual character; Chad Newsome, the character in this particular novel most profoundly affected by the contact with Europe, starts out as a crude and unformed boy, his crudity being largely accounted for by his age. The difference is most obvious, perhaps, in the case of Isabel Archer: she is, from the beginning, the social equal of any person whom she encounters; but she is inexperienced, and her exposure to Europe is an exposure to an unexpectedly rich and extraordinary experience, which confuses her.

Nevertheless, from the beginning to the end of James, certain major relationships are apparent.

There is the American who is subjected to the European influence and enriched by it; as examples, we may cite Ralph Touchett of the *Portrait,* and Strether and Maria Gostrey of *The Ambassadors.* There is the American who in the process of becoming so enriched, suffers a dissolution of his moral nature, and who becomes merely a more or less conscious scoundrel: as extreme examples of this type, we may cite Osmund and Mme. Merle of the *Portrait;* as an example of a less conscious type of corruption, we may cite Christina Light, especially as she appears in *Roderick Hudson,* less obviously as she appears in *The Princess Casamassima;* Strether appears of this type to the Newsomes in Massachusetts; Chad Newsome appears of this type at the outset of *The Ambassadors,* later appears of the admirable type of Touchett, and at the end remains ambiguous and unresolved, a question for the future, in the eyes of the reader and of Strether alike. There is the American who, in the process of acquiring this valuable experience, is betrayed by another character, whether American or native European, who has too much of it, or conversely and proportionately too little moral sense: such characters are Maggie Verver and her father in *The Golden Bowl,* Milly Theale in *The Wings of the Dove,* Isabel Archer in the *Portrait,* and (if we suspect a trifle the worst of Chad

Newsome) Lambert Strether in *The Ambassadors*. This formula of betrayal is the tragic formula in the Jamesian novel: in a subplot of *The Ambassadors*, there is (but only, again, if we suspect the worst of Chad Newsome) a curious variation of it, in which Chad, who has been enriched and so (perhaps) corrupted through his experience with Mme. de Vionnet, appears (perhaps) likely at the end of the book to betray Mme. de Vionnet, who, though she is a European and though she has displayed certain comprehensible human weaknesses, is a sympathetic character. There are the Americans who are essentially too provincial, and who are frequently too coarse, to be subject either to the benefits or to the dangers of the European experience: these individuals are sometimes merely dull vulgarians, like Jim Pocock of *The Ambassadors*; they are sometimes comic but sympathetic figures like Waymarsh of *The Ambassadors*, or like Henrietta Stackpole of the *Portrait*; they are sometimes admirable in a very limited sense, but invidious in the long run to the decencies, through their very limitations and a kind of neurotic intensity, like Mrs. Newsome and her daughter, of *The Ambassadors*; more rarely, like Caspar Goodwood, of the *Portrait*, they have a kind of tragic simplicity of directness in a world essentially fluid, evasive, and incomprehensible, at least as regards human motive. Goodwood is tragic because, though imperceptive, he has high character and high intelligence, and because he unfailingly and in spite of constant disappointment expects human beings to act intelligently; Henrietta Stackpole has the same expectation, but lacking so fine an intelligence or so high a character (though of course she is a very good soul in her fashion) she is necessarily comic. The character immune to European influence is never central to the Jamesian plot, and seldom alters or develops to any serious degree in the course of the book, though things may happen to him.

In the British novels of the middle period, the same precarious balance between character and sensibility is studied, and from the same hypersensitive American point of view, in spite of there being no American characters. In *The Tragic Muse*, the solid qualities and limitations of the British upper class replace the narrower and more intense moral qualities of the American heritage; Dormer and Sherringham attempt to build a richer life on this foundation, Sherringham to fail, Dormer presumably to succeed—the book, though it offers a handful of unforgettable characters, collapses structurally as a result of its double plot, so that one's recollection of the manners, or the medium in which the characters move, is likely to be more clear than the morality, or the form of their motion. In *The Awkward Age*, to select another example, Nanda, Mitchy, and Mr. Longdon, the only characters possessing sufficient moral quality to rely in some measure upon it, are all more or less the victims of persons unable to distinguish between morals and manners, of persons so externalized as to be essentially corrupt. In the British novels in general, I should say, and especially in *The Spoils of Poynton*, this antithesis of morals and manners appears less clearly than in *The American*; in fact, in *The Spoils of Poynton*, the morality is largely an isolated question, and stands only in the vaguest sense in the usual relationship to manners.

Toward the end of his life, in *The Ivory Tower*, James reversed the formula. He appeared to be troubled by the corrupting influence of American financial life on those who were not subjected to a civilizing influence. In this book, he employs as hero a Europeanized American, Graham Fielder, a man of the same admirable type as Ralph Touchett, but of much less force of character. Fielder had been raised in Europe, apart from the financial life in America; he was thus the heir in some measure and perhaps in a diluted form of the earlier American moral sense as well as of European cultivation. James brings him into contact with the corrupt financial life of America early in the twentieth century, shows him defeated in the realm of action by an exemplar of this life, but rising superior to his adversary morally. This form of corruption had, of course, been thriving throughout James's career, and James had shown little suspicion of its existence; even in *The Ivory Tower* he does not know exactly what form the corruption takes, but merely feels its presence, as a kind of social atmosphere. However, the same corruption in the background of *The Ambassadors*—the same stupid corruption which was sufficient to drive Henry Adams out of political life—lends a certain seriousness to the choice which confronts Chad Newsome, the choice between the life of a businessman in America and (since he lacks both the genius and the character of a Henry Adams) the life of a cultivated idler in Europe.

In general, however, the subject of the characteristic Jamesian novel is the influence of the cultivation of sensibility (in other words, the experience of contact with European manners) upon moral character in a pure or isolated form (that is, upon the American moral sense, divorced from any body of American manners). The implications of this relationship of morality to sensibility are of the most profound and the most general sort, in spite of the fact that the concrete terms giving rise to the implications are relatively limited. It is obvious, then, that James is much more than a mere portrayer of the American abroad; his work partakes in a considerable measure of the allegorical character of the work of Hawthorne. The principal dangers inherent in the subject and in the method we shall now examine.

IV

Edmund Wilson in an essay in The Hound and Horn[3] has defended the theory that *The Turn of the Screw* should be regarded not as a ghost story but as a study of hallucination. The story is told by the governess, who is to be regarded either as the victim of the hallucinations or as the observer of the ghosts and their machinations. If we assume that the children did not see the ghosts—and we have only the word of the governess that they did see them—their every action becomes innocent and commonplace except, toward the end, as they are terrified by the unbalanced behavior of the governess. There are a few small

[3] The Ambiguity of Henry James, by Edmund Wilson; The Hound and Horn, VII-3, April-June, 1934. A greatly extended version of this essay, which I had not read till the present volume was ready for the printer, appears in *The Triple Thinkers*, by Edmund Wilson, Harcourt, Brace and Co., 1938. My essay and the enlarged essay of Mr. Wilson deal with many of the same problems, but from very different points of view.

difficulties of interpretation either way, but Mr. Wilson's hypothesis strikes the present writer as more plausible than the popular one. As Mr. Wilson points out, the story is not published among the ghost stories in the collected edition; there is another story, *The Marriages*, which resembles it in method if we assume the truth of his theory; resembles it in the fact that this story is likewise told from the point of view of an unbalanced girl, except that in this case the clue to the interpretation is given explicitly at the end.

For the purposes of this essay, Mr. Wilson's interpretation need not be granted, though I personally agree with it. But the story if so interpreted—even if so interpreted only for a moment—has great illustrative value. For in the story so interpreted, the governess constructs out of a series of innocent and unrelated acts, a consistent and coherent theory of corrupt action and a very intense emotional reaction to the theory. The gap between rational motive and resulting state of mind is so wide as to include every item in the story: for this reason, the governess must be insane. There is more than one other Jamesian effort, however, in which the margin of unmotivated, or obscure, feeling is nearly as wide, and apparently without James's realizing it; there is almost invariably at least a narrow margin of obscurity; and the entire drama of the typical Jamesian novel is the effort of some character or group of characters to reduce this margin, to understand what is going on.

Joseph Warren Beach[4] describes *The Sacred Fount* in the following passage: "It consists of a series of discussions at a week-end party concerning the sentimental relationships of certain men and women present. Not a single incident is brought into the narrative more important than the intimate look of two persons observed together in an arbor, a gentleman's appearance of age, or the waxing and waning of a lady's wit. The discussions are held largely between 'me' and 'Mrs. Briss'; and the climax of the story is found simply in the most extended of our debates, late at night in the hospitable drawing-room. Each one of us has

* *The Method of Henry James*, by Joseph Warren Beach; Yale University Press, 1918, pages 43-4.

developed an elaborate hypothesis to account for certain social phenomena,—phenomena whose actuality may itself be brought in question, being so much an affair of the interpretation (if not the imaginative invention) of appearance. 'I' hold that the present wit and competence of Percy Long—heretofore a dull and unskillful member of society—have had to be paid for by the woman who loves him; and that this accounts for the nervous manner and peculiar tactics of Mae Server, who has lost her former cleverness and is trying to conceal the fact. On the same grounds I explain to myself the blooming of Mrs. Brissenden—my opponent in this debate—at the expense of 'poor Briss,' who daily presents an older face to the world. 'Poor Briss,' like Mae Server, has had to tap the 'sacred fount' the limited source of vital energy, in order to give abundant life to the one he loves. Following this clue, it appears to me that Percy Long and 'Mrs. Briss,' conscious of the similarity of their position, have formed a tacit league for concealment and the defense of their common interest. And again 'poor Briss' and Mae Server seem to have been drawn together by a sense of their community and a common need for sympathy. It was Mrs. Briss in the first place who helped me to my theory. But it is obvious that, when she comes to realize how far I may carry its application, she must deny these facts and make her own independent interpretation of the facts she acknowledges. And Mrs. Briss is a most ingenious and plausible debater. So that 'I' am obliged to hurry away from her neighborhood in order to maintain my own view of the facts. And so, in the end, the reader is left provided with two complete sets of interpretations of a group of more or less hypothetical relations. . . ."

This is, I believe, a fair summary; it comes from one of the most enthusiastic admirers of James, and, so far as my knowledge of Jamesian criticism extends, from his ablest critic, albeit from a critic with whom I frequently disagree. Yet we have here a summary of a state of mind that verges on madness, and the novel was not ultimately included by the author in the definitive edition of his works.

Similarly, one may fairly ask whether Fleba Vetch, of *The*

Spoils of Poynton, does not do something similar to what the governess does in *The Turn of the Screw*, though in the case of Fleda, of course, it would be moral hysteria, if such a phrase may be used, rather than madness. Fleda has it in her power to break the engagement to marry another woman of the man whom she loves and who loves her; the rival does not appear to be so much in love with him as with his perquisites—in fact, it is the rival herself who threatens to break if certain demands are not granted within a limited time, and her attitude appears to be one primarily of bad-tempered selfishness. Fleda, notwithstanding, constructs a moral obligation out of this situation, constructs it so deviously and subtly that it would be utterly lost in summary and is sufficiently elusive in the text, enforces the compliance, and assures the marriage, thereby, presumably, ruining her own life, her lover's, and that of her lover's mother. The attitude of the lover, Owen Gereth, never becomes clear: Mrs. Gereth appears to assume that it is, like Fleda's, one of unwholesome moral refinement; when Owen discusses the situation with Fleda, nevertheless, he appears primarily hurt and bewildered, so that the reader is free to wonder whether he simply performed a quixotic act to win Fleda's esteem in default of her hand; Fleda, however, in a passage which is analytical rather than emotional, deduces that he was repelled by his somewhat spoiled fiancée, when, as the result of a check, her action became vulgar and unpleasant, and so imagined himself in love with Fleda, but that when the check was removed and her charm automatically returned, he was again moved to admire her and forget Fleda—an hypothesis which would render Fleda's tragedy a waste of passion in a vulgar cause, though of this Fleda, as well as James, appears to be unaware. In any event, Owen remains at the end of the story an unresolved figure, a group of at least three mutually repellent hypotheses; the value of Fleda's action is unjudged—Fleda herself was ready to surrender and in fact tried to surrender when it was already too late and Owen was married, but then apparently returned later to her original view of the situation—so that Fleda represents a pair of alternative hypotheses. The result of this uncertainty is that we do not have a tragic moral victory, in which the protagonist judges, makes a sacrifice, and saves her soul; nor do we have a tragic defeat, in which she makes an unjustified choice and is judged by the author—that is, suffers the consequences. We have rather an intense situation, developed with the utmost care, so far as the succeeding facts and states of mind are concerned, but remaining at nearly all times and certainly at the end uncertain as to significance. Fleda's attitude is never resolved; nor is ours; but the experience has been intense, and as we have not understood it, we cannot but feel it to be essentially neurotic and somewhat beyond the margin of the intelligible.

The Awkward Age is another novel which very clearly illustrates the difficulty. This novel is usually one of the first attacked by those who dislike the author, and it is in subject and in treatment alike unquestionably one of the most tenuous. I personally find it, as I find *The Spoils of Poynton,* and for reasons to which later I shall allude briefly, both moving and amusing in spite of the defects which I am considering, but that fact for the moment is beside the point.

The book centers on Mrs. Brookenham, the guiding spirit of a clever social group, and her daughter, Nanda, who as the book opens, arrives at that age of formal and recognized maturity at which she is permitted to "come down stairs," or be one of her mother's guests. The circle in question is witty, moderately intellectual, and accustomed to perfect freedom of discussion. The question then arises whether conversation shall be sacrificed to the young girl, or the young girl to conversation. The latter, in a sense, occurs: that is, Nanda takes part in conversations, from which, according to dying but not yet dead traditions, a young girl should be guarded. Nanda is in love with Vanderbank, a contemporary and apparently an old admirer of her mother. Vanderbank is attracted to Nanda, but gradually comes to feel that she is in some way spoiled by this exposure, and turns away from her. Mr. Longdon, who had been in love with Nanda's grandmother, to whom Nanda bears an exact physical resemblance, is necessarily attracted to Nanda, and tells Vanderbank that he will provide Nanda with a considerable dowry, in the hope of moving Vanderbank to marry her. This, however, fails. Mitchett, a wealthy young man of no family and of no looks, but of a character both fine and charming, loves Nanda, but unsuccessfully; at her request, and as a kind of pledge of his love for her, he marries her friend, Aggie, a young girl who had been conventionally reared, and who after her marriage becomes a lewd and vulgar little trollop; after the marriage, one suspects also that Nanda suspects that perhaps she had loved Mitchett without knowing it. Finally she goes off with Mr. Longdon, either to be adopted by him, or to marry him, presumably the latter. The situation is that of *Daisy Miller* infinitely rarefied: a young girl of moral integrity and of more or less "natural" manner, though she is not in this case an American, violates a code of manners and is penalized very severely.

The situation turns purely on a point, and a very subtle one, of manners; Nanda is delicate and sophisticated and a person of the finest social perception, so that her sins are of the most nearly imperceptible kind. It is a tragedy of manners, in which no genuine moral issue is involved, but in which vague depths of moral ugliness, especially in Vanderbank, are elusively but unforgettably suggested. Vanderbank is a creature through whose tranquil and pellucid character there arises at the slightest disturbance of his surface a fine cloud of silt, of ugly feeling far too subtle to be called suspicion, but darkening his entire nature and determining his action. The tragedy far outweighs the motive, and the relations between character and character are frequently so subtle as to be indefinable. The endeavor to make the motive serve in such a case no doubt accounts in part for the excessive subtlety with which the characters scrutinize each other and the whole situation; they continually try to find more in it all than is really there, in the effort to understand their own feelings, or rather to justify them. They remind one—and James, since his plight for the moment is their own, likewise reminds one—of Hawthorne scrutinizing Dr. Grimshaw's spiders with insanse intensity, but with no illumination.

Mrs. Brookenham says: " 'The thing is, don't you think?'—she appealed to Mitchy—'for us not to be so awfully clever as to make it believed that we can never be simple. We mustn't see *too* tremendous things—even in each other.' She quite lost patience with the danger she glanced at. 'We *can* be simple!'

'We can, by God!' Mitchy laughed.

'Well, we are now—and it's a great comfort to have it settled,' said Vanderbank.

'Then you see,' Mrs. Brook returned, 'what a mistake you'd make to see abysses of subtlety in my having been merely natural.' "

And on another occasion Vanderbank says to Nanda: "You're too much one of us all. We've tremendous perceptions."

It is a remarkable evidence of the genius of James that though most of the important actions in the story are either flatly incredible or else are rendered so subtly as to be indeterminable, yet the resultant attitudes and states of mind of the actors are rendered with extraordinary poignancy: the obscure, slow, and ugly withdrawal of Vanderbank, the final scene between Mitchy and Nanda, the final departure of Nanda and Mr. Longdon (even though one is none too certain of the exact nature of the relationship to which they are departing) are, for myself, among the most haunting memories which I retain from my fragmentary experience as a reader of novels. Yet few memorable novels are less satisfactory.

In order to indicate sharply the nature of the Jamesian obscurity, I am purposely citing the most extreme examples of it, before examining the manner in which it invades the more important works. I wish to conclude this phase of the discussion, with an account of the most extraordinary plunge into pure incoherence which James ever made, the posthumous and unfinished book entitled *The Sense of the Past*. Though the work is unfinished, we possess the author's notes for the unfinished portion, so that we have a very good idea of what would have happened.

The story deals with Ralph Pendrel, a young man of about thirty years and some wealth, who has been prevented from visiting Europe because of various personal obligations. Death, having eliminated the last of these obligations, he goes. He is a kind of amateur historical scholar, and he has published a monograph on a theory of the historical approach. A distant relative in England has read this monograph and admired it, and, dying just before the visit to Europe, has bequeathed the young man a house in London, which had been built early in the eighteenth century. Pendrel visits the house immediately upon arriving, and spends an afternoon and evening in the examination of it; an examination in which he observes among other items the portrait of a young man of the early nineteenth century, that is, of about a hundred years before the initial action, which arouses his curiosity: the portrait is a three-quarters rear view of the head, so that the features are not shown. Late in the evening the young man of the portrait steps down, and the two meet and strike a bargain: the young man of the portrait had always had great curiosity about the future, just as Pendrel has had about the past, and they exchange periods, the agreement being that either will come to the aid of the other if the going becomes difficult.

The next morning Pendrel pays a visit to the American ambassador, tells him what has happened, takes him to the house, bids him goodbye, and steps into the doorway, thereupon entering the past. He finds a young woman within, Miss Molly Midmore, a distant relative, whom, it appears, he has just come from America to marry. The remainder of the book as far as written and apparently as far as planned deals with a conversation between these two and others, the conversation running through the remainder of the day and evening. The other persons are Molly's sister, Nan, who appears on the scene late, and with whom Pendrel gradually falls in love, Molly's mother, Molly's brother, and Nan's suitor.

The plot is something like this: as a result of the protracted conversation, Pendrel and his hosts gradually become aware of fine differences of social tone; differences which make Pendrel feel an alien to the point of arousing his terror, and which on the other hand cause the Midmores to feel a suspicion of Pendrel which becomes in the long run almost equally intense. These differences are first a greater sophistication on the part of the British than on the part of the American, and second a greater brutality in regard to the essentially moral or humane values on the part of the nineteenth century than on the part of the twentieth. It is this latter difference which gradually becomes the more obvious and which arouses Pendrel's terror.

Now the original young man of the nineteenth century had really married Molly; but Pendrel gradually comes to find her vaguely gross and repulsive, and he falls in love with Nan, who is less characteristic of her period, and who falls in love with him. Pendrel thus betrays his bargain; the other young man appears to him from time to time to threaten him, and finally decides to abandon him to the nineteenth century and his own devices, from which he is ultimately rescued by the self-sacrifice of Nan.

In the course of the conversation, Pendrel finds himself from the beginning provided with information about his situation, and about the entire Midmore family, as the need arises, like a man in a dream. At one point he even finds himself provided with a miniature painting of Molly: he extracts it from his vest pocket, in spite of the fact that a moment before he had had no inkling of its existence.

The conversation is devoted in a large measure, so far as subject matter is concerned, to establishing through this dream-procedure, the antecedent relationships between the Pendrels and the Midmores; so far as tone and effect are concerned, it is devoted to establishing the differences already mentioned. It is often difficult if not impossible to grasp these differences, they are so nearly imperceptible: the result of the difficulty is in a large measure the feeling that James is nearly as hallucinated as Pendrel; it is a kind of pushing of James's passion for subtle distinctions of manner to something resembling madness. James, like the characters in *The Awkward Age*, becomes so watchful for symptoms that he appears to become self-hypnotized; in this again he resembles the later Hawthorne.

To illustrate the difficulty, let me quote from the description of Mrs. Midmore: "However, she was herself an apparition of such force that the question of his own luck missed application and he but stared at her lost, and yet again lost, in that reflection that yes, absolutely yes, no approach to such a quality of tone as

324

she dealt in had ever in his own country greeted his ear. Yes, again and yet again, it spoke of ten thousand things that he could guess at now in her presence, and that he had even dreamed of, beforehand, through faint echoes and in other stray lights; things he could see she didn't in the least think of at the moment either, all possessed as she was with the allowance she had in her hospitality already made for him. Every fact of her appearance contributed somehow to this grand and generous air, the something-or-other suggesting to him that he had never yet seen manner at home at that pitch, any more than he had veritably heard utterance. When or where, in any case, had his eye, alert as he might feel it naturally was, been caught by such happy pomp as that of the disposed dark veil or mantilla which, attached to her head, framed in hoodlike looseness this seat of her high character and, gathering about her shoulders, crossed itself as a pair of long ends that depended in lacelike fashion almost to her feet? He had apprehended after a few more seconds that here was 'costume' beheld of him in the very fact and giving by its effect all the joy of recognition—since he had hitherto had but to suppose and to conceive it, though without being in the effort, as his own person might testify, too awkwardly far out. Yes, take him for what she would, she might see that he too was dressed—which tempered his barbarism perhaps only too much and referred itself back at all events, he might surely pretend, to a prime and after all not uncommendable intuition of the matter. If he had always been, as he would have allowed, overdressed for New York, where this was a distinct injury to character and credit, business credit at least, which he had none the less braced, so he had already found he was no more than quite right for London, and for Mansfield Square in especial; though at the same time he didn't aspire, and wouldn't for the world, to correspond with such hints as Mrs. Midmore threw off. She threw it off to a mere glance that she represented by the aid of dress the absolute value and use of presence as presence, apart from any other office—a pretension unencountered in that experience of his own which he had yet up to now tended to figure as lively. Absolutely again, as he could recover, he had never understood presence without use to play a recognized part; which would but come back indeed to the question of what use—great ambiguous question-begging term!—might on occasion consist of. He was not to go into that for some time yet, but even on the spot it none the less shone at him for the instant that he was apparently now to see ornament itself frankly recognized as use; and not only that, but boldly contented, unassailably satisfied, with a vagueness so portentous—which it somehow gave a promise to his very eyes of the moment that he should find convincingly asserted and extended. All this conspired toward offering him in this wondrous lady a figure that made ladies hitherto displayed to him, and among whom had been several beauties, though doubtless none so great as splendid Molly, lose at a stroke their lustre for memory, positively vitiated as they thus seemed by the obscurity, not to say the flat humility, of their employed and applied and their proportionately admired state."

One should note in connection with a passage like this one, that concentration so intense and so exclusive on so trivial an aspect of character amounts to madness, and that Pendrel's intense excitement is vastly disproportionate to any actual perception that one can disentangle, as it is likewise later in the story when his attention begins to focus on what he conceives to be the difference between the two periods, so that Pendrel, like other characters mentioned, strongly resembles Mr. Wilson's version of the governess in *The Turn of the Screw*. Further, in the story as a whole, one perception is only indicated or suggested before it suggests another and is consequently dropped; Pendrel's (that is, James's) feelings and interpretations of events are essentially similar in their emergence and progression to the information on which they are based, which emerges and proceeds as in a dream. This passage endeavors to make a marginal aspect of experience ("tone") carry vastly more significance than is proper to it, and it is, in addition, uncertain and incoherent in its import. It is a striking fore-runner of the Experimental poetry of the twentieth century, even of the extreme forms of such poetry, and indicates more clearly than anything else could do the historical continuity between the earlier American culture and the more

326

recent literature; for this phenomenon in James is distinctly, and nothing more than, an extreme development of a difficulty inherent in all his work and in the society which gave rise to his work, a difficulty of which he was in a considerable measure aware, but of which he was insufficiently aware to correct it. The obscurity of the moral problem, the development of the feeling in excess of the motive, is a familiar phenomenon of the romantic period, that is, of the period extending roughly from about 1750 to the present. The conscientious concentration upon this obscurity—conscientious almost to hallucination, and almost to hallucination because so seldom intellectual in spite of the conscientiousness—is the residue of the New England heritage, as I have endeavored to show, even when that concentration is imputed to an English character, such as Fleda Vetch.

I should like to consider briefly the margin of similar difficulty inhering in some of the more successful novels.

Roderick Hudson is a portrait of a certain type of romantic genius in disintegration. Hudson, the genius, is taken to Rome by a wealthy compatriot, Mallett, and there rapidly matures as an artist, but in the process of so doing loses control of himself morally, sinks into a condition of mental and moral lethargy, and eventually dies in a storm in the Alps, perhaps by suicide, probably by accident, after a brief but brilliant career in which he has managed to outrage most of the human decencies and apparently with very small consciousness of what he is doing. James in his preface to this work remarks: "My mistake on Roderick's behalf —and not in the least of conception, but of composition and expression—is that, at the rate at which he falls to pieces, he seems to place himself beyond our understanding and our sympathy. These are not our rates, we say; we ourselves certainly, under like pressure,—for what is it, after all?—would make more of a fight. We conceive going to pieces—nothing is easier, since we see people do it, one way or another, all round us; but this young man must either have had less of the principle of development to have had so much of the principle of collapse, or less of the principle of collapse to have had so much of the principle of development. 'On the basis of so great a weakness,' one hears the reader say, 'where was the idea of your interest? On the basis of so great an interest, where is the provision for so much weakness?' One feels indeed, in the light of this challenge, on how much too scantily projected and suggested a field poor Roderick and his large capacity for ruin are made to turn round. It has all begun too soon, as I say, and too simply, and the determinant function attributed to Christina Light, the character of well-nigh sole agent of his catastrophe that this young woman has forced upon her, fails to commend itself to our sense of truth and proportion."

We have here the objection of the experienced novelist in his old age to a work of his youth; and he seems to miss the point as a result of concentrating so acutely upon the problems of the construction of novels in general as to forget the subject of the novel in hand. The subject in hand is a particular type of irrational genius fairly common since the third quarter of the eighteenth century; and anyone who has ever played in a modest way the role of a Mallett or even of a more remote observer of a creature like Hudson, or anyone who has ever seriously considered the life and letters, let us say, of Shelley, can scarcely fail to be struck by the verisimilitude. From the point of view of the Jamesian novelist, the work is not properly a novel, and for the reasons which James assigns—it contains too little of the element of struggle to be dramatic—but as a full-length and objective portrait of an uncommon but still recognizable type, the book is in its fashion superb.

It is the subject, then, and not the method, which justifies the younger James against the older; but if the same objections can be raised against the treatment of individuals presumably more normal, the situation becomes more serious.

In *The American,* an early novel to which I have repeatedly referred in the earlier sections of this essay, Christopher Newman, the American who gives the book its title, becomes engaged to marry Mme. de Cintré, a beautiful and aristocratic young French widow, of the family Bellegarde; then her mother and her older brother break off the engagement, on the grounds that, on second thought, an alliance with so rank a barbarian is a more painful experience than they can endure. Newman has disliked

328

these two from the outset, and has suspected them of an evil past; the suspicion hovers over the entire book. Mme. de Cintré, in taking leave of Newman, in her mother's presence, says she is doing it because she is afraid of her mother. The younger brother, who has become Newman's friend, and who feels the family to have been disgraced by this perfidy on the part of his brother and mother, tells Newman on his deathbed that he is sure that his mother and brother between them killed his father and that a certain family servant knows the details. From this servant, Newman obtains a note written by the elder marquis just before his death and given her as he was dying, which says that his wife has killed him, but with no explanation. The servant hazards the guess that when the marquise was with the marquis alone, she may have poured his medicine on the ground when he called for it, in an attack of pain, and at the same time have given him a look so full of hatred that he wished to die. At any rate, after a long illness, and shortly after he had begun to recover, he lapsed into a coma after his wife had spent some hours alone with him, and recovered only long enough to write this note and give it to the servant.

The details of the evil in the Bellegardes are very uncertain; yet the effect in the form of their social presence, their emotional effect upon Newman, is very definite. Also, the fear felt by the heroine of her mother, the nature of the power wielded by the mother over her, is largely obscure, though it may in part be explained by social usage and by consequently ingrained habit, beginning in childhood.

James is fairly severe on this work in his preface. He writes: "The only *general* attribute of projected romance that I can see, the only one that fits all its cases, is the fact of the kind of experience with which it deals—experience liberated, so to speak; experience disengaged, disembroiled, disencumbered, exempt from the conditions that we usually know to attach to it and, if we wish so to put the matter, drag upon it, and operating in a medium which relieves it, in a particular interest, of the inconvenience of a *related*, a measurable state, a state subject to all our vulgar communities. The greatest intensity may so be arrived at

329

evidently—when the sacrifice of community, of the 'related' sides of situations, has not been too rash. It must to this end not flagrantly betray itself; we must even be kept if possible, for our illusion, from suspecting any sacrifice at all. The balloon of experience is in fact of course tied to the earth, and under that necessity we swing, thanks to a rope of remarkable length, in the more or less commodious car of the imagination; but it is by the rope we know where we are, and from the moment that cable is cut we are at large and unrelated: we only swing apart from the globe—though remaining as exhilarated, naturally, as we like, especially when all goes well. The art of the romancer is, 'for the fun of it,' insidiously to cut the cable, to cut it without our detecting him. What I have recognized then in 'The American,' much to my surprise and after long years, is that the experience here represented is the disconnected and uncontrolled experience— uncontrolled by our general sense of 'the way things happen'— which romance alone more or less successfully palms off on us."

James in discussing the defects of this plot in the preface states that the Bellegardes, had they been real French people of their class and type, would not have treated Newman as in the novel; that they would have got hold of him and kept him as quietly as possible and have fed their self-esteem and sense of security on the profit. This, of course, is conjecture, and in actual life it is at least conceivable that they might have acted either way. But he gets closer to the heart of the difficulty in discussing Mme. de Cintré, her fear of her mother, and the obscure influence wielded over her by her mother. He says: "It is as difficult, I said above, to trace the dividing line between the real and the romantic as to plant a mile-stone between north and south; but I am not sure an infallible sign of the latter is not this rank vegetation of the 'power' of bad people that good get into, or vice-versa. It is so rarely, alas, into *our* power that anyone gets!"

Now it so happens that this formula is applicable, not only to *The American,* but to a good deal of James: this particular rank vegetation is the specific form that the Jamesian moral obscurity frequently takes. Christina Light exercises some such power over Roderick Hudson, but, as I have already pointed out, the power, like the other aspects of Hudson's behavior, becomes comprehensible on the understanding that Hudson is essentially an incomprehensible type; in *The Turn of the Screw*, the ghosts exercise such a power over the children, but they again are immune to ordinary standards of criticism, for either they are ghosts, and so supernatural, or else they are the products of an insane mind and so legitimately romantic. The power of Muniment and of the Princess Casamassima (formerly Christina Light) over Hyacinth Robinson verges on this phenomenon, but perhaps less clearly. The power of Osmund over his wife and his daughter in *The Portrait of a Lady*, is a particularly clear example; and to this I shall return in a moment.

James writes further in the preface to *The American*: "Nothing here is in truth 'offered'—everything is evaded, and the effect of this, I recognize, is of the oddest. His relation to Mme. de Cintré takes a great stride, but the author appears to view that but as a signal for letting it severely alone." And again, of Mme. de Cintré: "With this lady, altogether, I recognize, a light plank, too light a plank, is laid for the reader over a dark 'psychological' abyss. The delicate clue to her conduct is never definitely placed in his hand: I must have liked to think verily it *was* delicate and to flatter myself that it was to be felt with the finger-tips rather than heavily tugged at." Much of the obscurity of this plot, then, became evident to James, and the obscurity as described in his own terms is of much the same sort as that which he found in Roderick Hudson; but we cannot find in the subject of *The American* the justification for the obscurity which we can find in the subject of the other book. There is a marked tendency in this book on the part of James and of his characters alike to read into situations more than can be justified by the facts as given, to build up intense states of feeling, on the basis of such reading, and to judge or act as a result of that feeling. This is what we found Fleda Vetch doing in *The Spoils of Poynton*, and above all it is what we found the governess doing in *The Turn of the Screw*, so intensely, in fact, that the story may well be taken to serve, if we accept the psychopathic interpretation, as a very acute and devastating self-parody.

In *The Portrait of a Lady* the chief difficulty resides in the feelings inspired by Osmund in the latter part of the book, and in Isabel's final decision; the margin of obscurity here is slight, and to the average American admirer of James will no doubt appear negligible, but the margin is genuine notwithstanding and is worth examining if we wish to get a broad view of the man. Osmund is a kind of neurotic aesthete, self-centered, unscrupulous within the limits of safety, and thoroughly unpleasant, but the species of terror which Isabel comes to feel in regard to him is absolutely unexplained by any of his actions or by any characteristic described. He betrayed Isabel in regard to his marriage with her, but this betrayal is scarcely a motive for the particular feeling which Isabel comes to experience. Furthermore, the same feeling is experienced by the daughter, Pansy, who was presumably unaware of the deception: Pansy is confined in a convent to break off her attachment to her young and unsuitable admirer; the convent is the one in which she went to school throughout childhood and is wholly familiar, and the nuns are devoted and kind; but Pansy after a brief period there can endure no more and surrenders abjectly and in fear. The influence of Osmund here is of the same obscure type as the influence of the Bellegardes. And at the end, though Isabel returns to her husband because of an intense moral sense, generically of the same type as that of Fleda Vetch, James seems to fear the inadequacy of this sense as a sole motive, and bolsters it up by her desire and promise to stand by Pansy in the trials ahead of her. The power and influence thus obscurely wielded by Osmund provide the dramatic crisis of the book.

In *The Princess Casamassima* a similar power is exerted over Hyacinth Robinson by Paul Muniment and by the Princess; in fact, the entire effect of Muniment's character is unexplained, and that of the Princess is but partly explained. Muniment is a member of a secret revolutionary and terroristic group, and his entire value in the novel derives from this fact; he is the moral agent of a hidden and malign power; the impressiveness of his character is the perceptible token of this fact; his influence over Hyacinth is the power in action. But on the actual stage of the novel he does little or nothing; of the views, purposes, and activities of his group we know next to nothing and we suspect that James knew less; we see Muniment enter a dark doorway occasionally, accompanied by the Princess, a doorway behind which we suspect that a meeting is in progress; we hear the last, ominous, but uninformative conversational exchange between the two immediately prior to their separating after a discussion of some kind; and for the rest we observe Muniment at tea-parties, conversing very little but tremendously impressing all present. In *The Ivory Tower* the *effect* of the American financial career is portrayed in much the same manner, but the real action producing the effect, the essential evil, is not described, for of that, James, as he admitted, knew nothing. The remarkable thing about both of these plots is the degree of realism that James manages to extract from them, when they are, essentially, so inane.

Joseph Warren Beach remarks of *The Princess Casamassima*:[5] "As for the revolutionary movement, the very vagueness of its presentation was a part of James's scheme. 'My scheme,' he says, 'called for the suggested nearness (to all our apparently ordered life) of some sinister anarchic underworld, heaving in its pain, its power and its hate; a presentation not of sharp particulars, but of loose appearances, vague motions and sounds and symptoms, just perceptible presences and general looming possibilities.'" The trouble appears to the present writer to be that as a motivating force for a two-volume novel, especially a novel which purports to spread so vast a canvas for the representation of various levels of society, these "vague motions, sounds, and symptoms" have little more force or dignity than a small boy under a sheet on Hallowe'en; they repeatedly approach the ludicrous: the adult in broad daylight, that is the reader of a Jamesian novel, is unlikely to experience terror without admitting good reason. Beach a little later remarks of the Princess herself:[6] "But she is also, for Hyacinth and for us, the mystery of a character not thoroughly understood . . . what we are never sure of is how far she is human." Beach prefers her representation in this novel to her rep-

[5] J. W. Beach, op. cit., page 213.
[6] Ibid., page 215.

resentation in *Roderick Hudson,* and regards this book as one of the greater ones. But in *Roderick Hudson* we are fairly certain as to how far she is human and how far not, and the exact degree is rendered not only clearly but compactly, and in terms of definite action; she appears there in a clear light, a figure of inimitable beauty and perversity. *The Princess Casamassima* as a novel suffers in its actual form from the obscure background of all save three of its characters—Anastasius Vetch, Miss Pynsent, and in a measure Hyacinth—and so many and such long scenes are devoted to the representation of obscure characters that the novel appears to have little form; we are most of the time in a kind of stagnant water.

If we proceed from these latter works to the latest, and consider the book which for James was his most satisfactory, *The Ambassadors,* we have at least three sources of difficulty, of possible dissatisfaction. In the first place, it is only by stretching a point that we can bring ourselves to consider Chad Newsome at best a bone worth quite so much contention, worth the expenditure of quite so much moral heroism as Strether expends upon him. We can understand Chad's hesitation to return to the American business life of his period, but his alternative—that of a young man about Paris, however cultivated,—is scarcely the alternative of a Henry Adams. The central issue does not quite support the dramatics, as does, on the other hand, the central issue of each of the other late masterpieces, *The Golden Bowl* and *The Wings of the Dove.* Furthermore, our final attitude toward Chad is unresolved, and thus resembles our final attitude toward Owen Gereth in *The Spoils of Poynton;* this may not be untrue to life, but it is untrue to art, for a work of art is an evaluation, a judgment, of an experience, and only in so far as it is that is it anything; and James in this one respect does not even judge the state of uncertainty, but as in *The Spoils of Poynton,* he merely leaves us uncertain. Shakespeare left us in no uncertainty about Coriolanus; Melville in none about Ahab or Benito Cereno; nor did either author lack subtlety. And finally, Strether's ultimate scruple—to give up Maria Gostrey, so that he may not seem in Woollett to have got anything for himself from a situation in which he will seem to his friends in Woollett to have betrayed his trust, and in spite of the fact that Miss Gostrey could scarcely have been regarded as in any sense a bribe—this scruple, I say, impresses me very strongly as a sacrifice of morality to appearances: there might, conceivably, have been more Christian humility in considering the feelings of Maria Gostrey and in letting his reputation in Woollett go by the board. The moral choice, here, appears to be of the same strained and unjustifiable type as that of Fleda Vetch, or as that of Isabel Archer.

Joseph Warren Beach[7] in his chapter on the ethics of James asserts that no one save an American, or conceivably an Englishman, will ever understand James and admire him as he deserves, because the Jamesian morality will be incomprehensible; and he adds that the morality is essentially the morality of the New England of Emerson and Thoreau. Beach does not enlarge upon these ideas; they stand in his text very much as impressions; but they would seem to be fairly sound. I have endeavored to define the Jamesian morality as closely as possible and to show its background in history. It does not seem to me possible that an American, even a provincial American like myself, can be wholly sympathetic with James if he examines him closely and in his historical context. Mr. Beach, though he does not examine that context, though he appears to be almost as helplessly in it and of it as James himself—I should add, perhaps, that my admiration for Mr. Beach, like my admiration for James, is very great—is aware, though imperfectly, of the difficulty, or at least perceives a good many individual representations of the difficulty. And James is almost more perceptive in this respect than is Mr. Beach, in spite of his having been the primary sinner. I have already cited a number of examples of his self-criticism; I might cite a passage from a novel, *The Bostonians,* which satirizes the very social context from which he arose, and which would seem to have been largely responsible for his difficulty. James describes Mrs. Tarrant, the wife of the faith-healer and charlatan-at-large, in terms that might also serve as an exaggerated description of James himself at his worst: "When she talked and wished to insist, and she was al-

Ibid., page 131.

335

ways insisting, she puckered and distorted her face, with an effort to express the inexpressible, which turned out, after all, to be nothing." Of this woman's husband, he wrote: "Tarrant was a moralist without a moral sense." But in this Tarrant did not resemble James, but was rather the representative of another aspect of New England, the aspect best represented in literature, perhaps, by Cooper's Jason Newcome, and best promoted in life by Benjamin Franklin, though Franklin personally had little enough in common or at the very worst a great deal that was not in common with Tarrant and Newcome. James, however, had too much moral sense, but was insufficiently a moralist.

V

The foregoing pages might lead the careless reader to assume that my opinion of James is low; the fact of the matter is, that if I were permitted a definition of the novel which should exclude among other works *Moby Dick, Mardi, The Encantadas,* and the autobiographical works of Melville—and such a definition would be neither difficult nor illegitimate—I should be inclined to consider James as the greatest novelist in English, as he is certainly one of the five or six greatest writers of any variety to be produced in North America, though the estimate would proceed from a view of the history and form of the novel that would in all likelihood be pleasing to few devotees of that art.

The fact of the matter is, that in reading most of the English and American novelists preceding James who are commonly conceded to be great, our estimate of the writers' genius is formed very largely on the quality of the incidentals of the works under consideration, and not on the quality of what in a drama or an epic would be the essentials. Jane Austen, who is inescapably one of the best, hangs her remarkably brilliant comment and characterization on frames of action so conventional as to be all but trivial; the same is true of Trollope; it is more obviously true of Scott. It is less true of such a writer as Dickens, but a plot by Dickens, and usually half of the attendant characters, will ordinarily be so corrupted by insufferable sentimentalism, that one turns hither and yonder infallibly to reap what profit one may from the details. The plotting of Meredith and of George Eliot is far more serious, but both writers fall very much below James in characterization and in the quality of their prose. The prose of James is sometimes obscure, and as a result of the obscurity it may sometimes be found diffuse, but it is always sensitive and honest; the prose of George Eliot is laborious, and the prose of Meredith is worse—it is laboriously clever.

If we come to James as we come to Dickens or to Trollope, with the initial assumption that the plot can be taken or left according to the mood of the reader, the wealth of incidental felicities which we are likely to find will scarcely be equalled by any other novelist in English. Many writers have commented upon the unforgettable vividness of James's characterization; I personally have a far sharper recollection of the characteristics and attitudes, even of the external appearance, of many characters from James, and I have such a recollection of more characters, than I have from all the rest of English fiction, and certainly far more than I have from my own life. Consider, for a moment, an incomplete enumeration such as the following: Roderick Hudson, Rowland Mallett, Christina Light, and Mary Garland, from *Roderick Hudson*, not to mention minor characters so charming as Sam Singleton; Isabel Archer, Ralph Touchett, Mme. Merle, Gilbert Osmund, Caspar Goodwood, Henrietta Stackpole, and Lord Warburton, of *The Portrait of a Lady*; Hyacinth Robinson, Miss Pynsent, and Anastasius Vetch (one of the most moving of all the minor figures) of *The Princess Casamassima*; from *The Tragic Muse*, Sherringham, Dormer, Lady Julia, Dormer's mother, Mr. Carteret, and Gabriel Nash, a figure more perverse and astonishing than any other save Christina Light or possibly her poodle; Nanda, Mitchy, and Mr. Longdon of *The Awkward Age*; Strether, Maria Gostrey, the Newsomes and Pococks, Waymarsh, Mme. de Vionnet, of *The Ambassadors*; Kate Croy, Merton Densher, and Milly Theale, of *The Wings of the Dove*; Maggie Verver, her father, the Prince, and Charlotte Stant, of *The Golden Bowl*; Fleda Vetch and Mrs. Gereth, of *The Spoils of Poynton*; the legendary but beautiful figures, all but static in their remote perfection, of *The Europeans;* these are only a few of the creatures of James whom, if one once has met them, one can never forget. They are not great caricatures, like Sir Pitt Crawley, whom one remembers carrying Becky Sharp's trunk into the house, or like the old laird of *Kidnapped,* whose nightcapped head one remembers projecting from the window, but they are created with a restraint such that there is no exaggeration, yet with an awareness so rich that every essential detail is realized; after the lapse of years they are remembered not like portraits from a book but like persons one has known, yet they are remembered more clearly, for the observation of James is finer than our own would have been.

Further, the margin of imperfection in many of the works is not of the utmost seriousness aesthetically. Many of the minor works—*The Europeans* is nearly the best example—are perfect within their limits; the margin of difficulty in such major efforts as *The Portrait of a Lady* and *The Ambassadors* is not great in proportion to the wealth offered us; *The Wings of the Dove* and *The Golden Bowl,* though both books display undue clairvoyance on the part of certain characters, are both in their central plotting, it seems to me, perfectly sound.

Finally, his very virtues, in the semi-successful works, and in the successful as well, are closely related to his defects. His defects arise from the effort on the part of the novelist and of his characters to understand ethical problems in a pure state, and to understand them absolutely, to examine the marginal, the semi-obscure, the fine and definitive boundary of experience; the purely moral—that is, the moral divorced from all problems of manners and of compulsion, as it appears in the case of Fleda Vetch—can probably be defined but very rarely, and more or less as the result of good fortune in regard to the given facts of the situation, with the precision which James appears to seek, so that the effort in all save a few occasional and perfect situations must necessarily lead to more or less supersubtlety, and if the supersubtlety is pushed far enough, as it sometimes is, to an obsurantism amounting in effect to hallucination. On the other hand, the effort unquestionably results in a degree of very genuine subtlety, not only of central moral perception, but of incidental perception of character, that no other novelist has equalled. An additional reason for the memorableness of the Jamesian characters is the seriousness with which they take themselves and each other: we feel that we are somehow on essential ground with them, even if the essentiality of the ground results in its shifting like quicksand; we may disapprove of Fleda Vetch as a person for her errors and as a creation for the errors of James; but the integrity with which the errors are made, their fidelity to the historical context of which they are an essential part, and in spite of the fact that a great artist properly considered ought to have a better understanding than James displayed of the defects and dangers of his own historical context, this integrity and this fidelity in themselves are unforgettable; we do not have great tragedy, but we at least share a real experience, and the reality is of a quality that we shall find but rarely if at all in other novelists. And finally, we have only the loosest conception of the successful works and elements of James, if we do not fully understand his kind and degree of failure, for the failure represents the particular problem with which he was struggling to deal—one could almost regard it as his subject-matter.

As Mr. Beach points out, James's technical development is a development steadily in the direction of identifying the author's point of view with that of some particular character, toward the elimination of the function of the omniscient author. One might imagine that the obscurity in many of the novels resulted from the elimination of the author as commentator, from his resigning himself to the point of view of his character, except for two reasons: first, the character chosen to provide the point of view is usually very close to James himself in the quality of his intelligence, and second, the obscurity is as obvious in the early novels, in which the omniscient author is plainly discernible, as it is in the later, from which he has evaporated. This technical aim, however, seems to me unquestionably to result in a certain vitiation of the prose as prose: explicit and compact exposition or description of any kind is eliminated from the later novels, the matter that would ordinarily go into such prose being broken up and diffused in minutely discernible fragments through conversations and the miscellaneous perceptions of daily life; the attempt is made to introduce the material that would ordinarily be conveyed in such prose in a manner closely resembling the manner in which it entered the experience, and perhaps hovered there, of the character in question, so that we tend strongly in the later novels, so far as the prose itself is concerned, toward the fallacy of expressive form. The prose of *The Age of Innocence* or of *The Valley of Decision* is certainly superior to the prose of James; the prose of Melville in such a passage as that describing Dr. Cuticle and his operation, in *White Jacket,* in compactness, richness of implication, clarity of detail, and rhetorical variety and mastery, surpasses James incomparably. Mr. Beach[8] cites the following passage from *Roderick Hudson* as an example of the sort of traditional prose which James mercifully outgrew in the later novels: "Rowland's second guest was also an artist, but of a very different type. His friends called him Sam Singleton; he was an American, and he had been in Rome a couple of years. He painted small landscapes, chiefly in water-color; Rowland had seen one of them in a shop window, had liked it extremely and, ascertaining his address, had gone to see him and found him established in a very humble studio near the Piazza Barberini, where apparently fame and fortune had not yet come his way. Rowland, treating him as a discovery, had bought several of his pictures; Singleton made few speeches, but was intensely grateful. Rowland heard afterwards that when he first came to Rome he painted worthless daubs and gave no promise of talent. Improvement had come, however, hand in hand with patient industry, and his talent, though of a slender and delicate order, was now incontestable. It was as yet but scantly recognized and he had hard work to hold out. Rowland hung his little water-colors on the library wall, and found that as he lived with them he grew very fond of them. Singleton, short and spare, was made as if for sitting on very small camp-stools and eating the tiniest luncheons. He had a transparent brown regard, a perpetual smile, an extraordinary expression of modesty and pa-

[8] Ibid., page 192.

tience. He listened much more willingly than he talked, with a little fixed grateful grin; he blushed when he spoke, and always offered his ideas as if he were handing you useful objects of your own that you had unconsciously dropped; so that his credit could be at most for honesty. He was so perfect an example of the little noiseless devoted worker whom chance, in the person of a moneyed patron, has never taken by the hand, that Rowland would have liked to befriend him by stealth."

This is not great prose, but it is fine prose and fine perception. Neither as prose nor as characterization will it suffer by comparison with the portrait of Mrs. Midmore cited earlier in these pages. One could find better sketches of the same type in the early novels, and even as late as the *Portrait*; this type of prose can be developed very far indeed, as one can readily discover by reading Melville. It does not sacrifice reality, and it can be made to possess both sinew and form. The mere fact that this type of sketch is a traditional device is irrelevant to its virtues; James's later method is equally a device, and more obtrusively so, since we are forced to concentrate upon it, and as a device it is in our own day no longer new.

It would be easy to say that the virtues which I have described are inseparable from the methods of style which I deplore, but I doubt it; the virtues are already strongly marked in the early works, in which the later technique is not employed, so that one has some justification for feeling that a certain maturity of outlook and richness of observation increased, as a result of age and experience, concomitantly with a defective procedure in style, the result of an error in theory. It is only a step, in the matter of style, from *The Golden Bowl* to Dorothy Richardson and Proust, from them to the iridescent trifling of Mrs. Woolf, and from her to the latest Joyce; in fact James travelled the greater part of this distance when he wrote *The Sense of the Past*. I do not deny the genius of these writers—if I did not feel it, I should not consider it profitable to cite them—but they are all, even Proust by at least a perceptible margin, inferior to James, and they represent a progressive decay, an increase in diffusion, a decrease in detailed effectiveness, in the matter of style. Mr. Beach, on the other hand, believes that James's technical development was toward perfection; but if the prose must be weakened in order to perfect the novel, then something is radically wrong with the novel as a form of art.

It is likely that one can find an isolated novel here and there to surpass any by James; one might argue with considerable reason that *The Age of Innocence,* partly because it corrects, as I have shown, a serious defect in the Jamesian conception of the novel, partly because of its finer prose, is the finest single flower of the Jamesian art; one which James fertilized but would have been unable to bring to maturity. *The Valley of Decision,* a novel of a very different cast, might also be defended as superior to any single work by James, as might also *Billy Budd* and *Benito Cereno,* which unlike most of the work of Melville are true novels. But neither Mrs. Wharton nor Melville can equal James in the vast crowd of unforgettable human beings whom he created; Melville, moreover, except in *Billy Budd, Benito Cereno,* and *Israel Potter,* is scarcely a novelist, and Mrs. Wharton, except in the two novels mentioned, in *The Custom of the Country,* and in a small group of novelettes, is mediocre when she is not worse.

It is James himself, as I have abundantly indicated, who holds our attention so constantly on his defects of conception. As I have shown, he was so obsessed with the problem of moral judgment in its relation to character, that he not only constructed his plots so that they turned almost wholly on problems of ethical choice, but he sought to isolate the ethical problem as far as possible from all determining or qualifying elements, an effort which in any period would have led to difficulty, and which in his period would have been sufficient to dissolve in complete obscurity any talent save one of the greatest. As a result of this effort at isolation, he accomplished two secondary ends which have no bearing upon the value of his art as such: he focussed attention forever upon the problems of serious plotting, and in this respect he probably brought about the greatest single change in the practice of the novel ever effected by one man; and in addition he fixed imperishably the finest quality of American life of his period. In connection with this second accomplishment, it should be added that he himself appears to have had but an imperfect understanding of that quality, so that he not only fixed the defects as well as the virtues of the quality, but did so without the comprehension of the defects, or with a very imperfect comprehension, did so partly by representing them, but also, and unfortunately almost more clearly by embodying them. Regarded only for the kind and degree of its failure, but regarded patiently and intelligently, his art is a social phenomenon equalled in its interest by few others in the history of our nation, and equalled, I should imagine, by no other in the history of our literature; it is a phenomenon as representative intensively and extensively as the career, let us say, of John D. Rockefeller, in another realm of action. To understand him, we must understand the history of which he is the culmination; and when we understand him, we have the key to most of the literature and to much else that has followed and is likely to follow.

A Brief Selection of the Poems of
JONES VERY

The Coming of the Lord

Come suddenly, O Lord, or slowly come:
I wait thy will; thy servant ready is:
Thou hast prepared thy follower a home,—
The heaven in which Thou dwellest, too, is his.

Come in the morn, at noon, or midnight deep;
Come, for thy servant still doth watch and pray:
E'en when the world around is sunk in sleep.
I wake and long to see thy glorious day.

I would not fix the time, the day, nor hour,
When Thou with all thine angels shalt appear;
When in thy kingdom Thou shalt come with power,—
E'en now, perhaps, the promised day is near!

For though in slumber deep the world may lie,
And e'en thy Church forget thy great command;
Still, year by year, thy coming draweth nigh,
And in its power thy kingdom is at hand.

Not in some future world alone 'twill be,
Beyond the grave, beyond the bounds of time;
But on the earth thy glory we shall see,
And share thy triumph, peaceful, pure, sublime.

Lord, help me that I faint not, weary grow,
Nor at thy coming slumber, too, and sleep;
For Thou hast promised, and full well I know
Thou wilt to us thy word of promise keep.

THE SON

Father, I wait thy word. The sun doth stand
Beneath the mingling line of night and day,
A listening servant, waiting thy command
To roll rejoicing on its silent way;
The tongue of time abides the appointed hour,
Till on our ears its solemn warnings fall;
The heavy cloud withholds the pelting shower,
Then every drop speeds onward at thy call;
The bird reposes on the yielding bough,
With breast unswollen by the tide of song;
So does my spirit wait thy presence now
To pour thy praise in quickening life along,
Chiding with voice divine man's lengthened sleep,
While round the Unuttered Word and Love their vigils keep.

THE NEW BIRTH

'Tis a new life;—thoughts move not as they did,
With slow uncertain steps across my mind;
In thronging haste fast pressing on they bid
The portals open to the viewless wind,
That comes not save when in the dust is laid
The crown of pride that guilds each mortal brow,
And from before man's vision melting fade
The heavens and earth; their walls are falling now.
Fast crowding on, each thought asks utterance strong;
Storm-lifted waves swift rushing to the shore,
On from the sea they send their shouts along,
Back through the cave-worn rocks their thunders roar;
And I, a Child of God by Christ made free,
Start from death's slumbers to eternity.

THE NEW WORLD

The night that has no star lit up by God,
The day that round men shines who still are blind,
The earth their grave-turned feet for ages trod,
And sea swept over by His mighty wind,—
All these have passed away; the melting dream
That flitted o'er the sleepers' half-shut eye,
When touched by morning's golden-darting beam;
And he beholds around the earth and sky
What ever real stands; the rolling spheres,
And heaving billows of the boundless main,
That show, though time is past, no trace of years,
And earth restored he sees as his again,
The earth that fades not, and the heavens that stand,
Their strong foundations laid by God's right hand!

THE EARTH

I would lie low—the ground on which men tread—
Swept by thy Spirit like the wind of heaven;
An earth, where gushing springs and corn for bread
By me at every season should be given;
Yet not the water or the bread that now
Supplies their tables with its daily food,
But they should gather fruit from every bough,
Such as Thou givest me, and call it good;
And water from the stream of life should flow,
By every dwelling that thy love has built,
Whose taste the ransomed of thy Son shall know,
Whose robes are washed from every stain of guilt;
And men would own it was thy hand that blest,
And from my bosom find a surer rest.

THE PRESENCE

I sit within my room, and joy to find
That Thou, who always lov'st, art with me here;
That I am never left by Thee behind,
But by Thyself Thou keep'st me ever near.
The fire burns brighter when with Thee I look,
And seems a kinder servant sent to me;
With gladder heart I read thy holy book,
Because Thou art the eyes by which I see;
This aged chair, that table, watch, and door
Around in ready service ever wait;
Nor can I ask of Thee a menial more
To fill the measure of my large estate,
For Thou thyself, with all a Father's care
Where'er I turn, art ever with me there.

THE SONG

When I would sing of crooked streams and fields,
On, on from me they stretch too far and wide,
And at their look my song all powerless yields,
And down the river bears me with its tide.
Amid the fields I am a child again,
The spots that then I loved I love the more,
My fingers drop the strangely scrawling pen,
And I remember nought but Nature's lore.
I plunge me in the river's cooling wave,
Or on the embroidered bank admiring lean,
Now some endangered insect life to save,
Now watch the pictured flowers and grasses green;
Forever playing where a boy I played,
By hill and grove, by field and stream delayed.

347

To the Pure All Things Are Pure

The flowers I pass have eyes that look at me,
The birds have ears that hear my spirit's voice,
And I am glad the leaping brook to see,
Because it does at my light step rejoice.
Come, brothers, all who tread the grassy hill,
Or wander thoughtless o'er the blooming fields,
Come learn the sweet obedience of the will;
Thence every sight and sound new pleasure yields.
Nature shall seem another house of thine,
When He who formed thee, bids it live and play,
And in thy rambles e'en the creeping vine
Shall keep with thee a jocund holiday,
And every plant, and bird, and insect be
Thine own companions born for harmony.

The Fair Morning

(as in the edition of 1886)

The clear bright morning, with its scented air
And gaily waving flowers, is here again;
Man's heart is lifted with the voice of prayer,
And peace descends, as falls the gentle rain;
The tuneful birds, that all the night have slept,
Take up at dawn the evening's dying lay,
When sleep upon their eyelids gently crept
And stole with gentle craft their song away.
High overhead the forest's swaying boughs
Sprinkle with drops the traveller on his way;
He hears far off the tinkling bells of cows
Driven to pasture at the break of day;
With vigorous step he passes swift along,
Making the woods reëcho with his song.

THE CALL

Why art thou not awake, my son?
The morning breaks I formed for thee;
And I thus early by thee stand,
Thy new-awakening life to see.

Why are thou not awake, my son?
The birds upon the bough rejoice;
And I thus early by thee stand,
To hear with theirs thy tuneful voice.

Why sleep'st thou still? The laborers all
Are in my vineyard: hear them toil,—
As for the poor, with harvest song
They treasure up the wine and oil.

I come to wake thee; haste, arise,
Or thou no share with Me can find;
Thy sandals seize, gird on thy clothes,
Or I must leave thee far behind.

THE PRAYER

Wilt Thou not visit me?
The plant beside me feels thy gentle dew,
  And every blade of grass I see
From thy deep earth its quickening moisture drew.

  Wilt Thou not visit me?
Thy morning calls on me with cheering tone;
  And every hill and tree
Lend but one voice,—the voice of Thee alone.

  Come, for I need thy love,
More than the flower the dew or grass the rain;

Come gently as thy holy dove;
And let me in thy sight rejoice to live again.

I will not hide from them
When thy storms come, though fierce may be their wrath,
But bow with leafy stem,
And strengthened follow on thy chosen path.

Yes, Thou wilt visit me:
Nor plant nor tree thine eye delights so well,
As, when from sin set free,
My spirit loves with thine in peace to dwell.

THE COTTAGE

The house my earthly parent left
My heavenly parent still throws down,
For 'tis of air and sun bereft,
Nor stars its roof with beauty crown.

He gave it me, yet gave it not
As one whose gifts are wise and good;
'Twas but a poor and clay-built cot,
And for a time the storms withstood.

But lengthening years and frequent rain
O'ercame its strength: it tottered, fell,
And left me homeless here again,—
And where to go I could not tell.

But soon the light and open air
Received me as a wandering child,
And I soon thought their house more fair,
And all my grief their love beguiled.

Mine was the grove, the pleasant field
Where dwelt the flowers I daily trod;

And there beside them, too, I kneeled
And called their friend, my Father, God.

Autumn Flowers

Still blooming on, when Summer flowers all fade,
The golden-rods and asters fill the glade;
The tokens they of an Exhaustless Love
That ever to the end doth constant prove.

To one fair tribe another still succeeds,
As still the heart new forms of beauty needs;
Till these bright children of the waning year,
Its latest born, have come our souls to cheer.

They glance upon us from their fringëd eyes,
And to their look our own in love replies;
Within our hearts we find for them a place,
As for the flowers which early spring-time grace.

Despond not, traveler! On life's lengthened way,
When all thy early friends have passed away;
Say not, "No more the beautiful doth live,
And to the earth a bloom and fragrance give."

To every season has our Father given
Some tokens of his love to us from heaven;
Nor leaves us here, uncheered, to walk alone,
When all we loved and prized in youth have gone.

Let but thy heart go forth to all around,
Still by thy side the beautiful is found;
Along thy path the autumn flowers shall smile,
And to its close life's pilgrimage beguile.

The Lament of the Flowers

I looked to find Spring's early flowers,
    In spots where they were wont to bloom;
But they had perished in their bowers;
    The haunts they loved had proved their tomb!

The alder, and the laurel green,
    Which sheltered them, had shared their fate;
And but the blackened ground was seen,
    Where hid their swelling buds of late.

From the bewildered, homeless bird,
    Whose half-built nest the flame destroys,
A low complaint of wrong I heard,
    Against the thoughtless, ruthless boys.

Sadly I heard its notes complain,
    And ask the young its haunts to spare;
Prophetic seemed the sorrowing strain,
    Sung o'er its home, but late so fair!

"No more with hues like ocean shell
    The delicate wind-flower here shall blow;
The spot that loved its form so well
    Shall ne'er again its beauty know.

"Or, if it bloom, like some pale ghost
    'Twill haunt the black and shadeless dell,
Where once it bloomed a numerous host,
    Of its once pleasant bowers to tell.

"And coming years no more shall find
    The laurel green upon the hills;
The frequent fire leaves naught behind,
    But e'en the very roots it kills.

"No more upon the turnpike's side
    The rose shall shed its sweet perfume;
The traveler's joy, the summer's pride,
    Will share with them a common doom.

"No more shall these returning fling
    Round childhood's home a heavenly charm,
With song of bird in early spring,
    To glad the heart and save from harm."

THE STILL-BORN

I saw one born, yet he was of the dead;
    Long since the spirit ceased to give us birth;
For lust to sin, and sin to death, had led,
    And now its children people o'er the earth.

And yet he thought he lived, and as he grew
    Looked round upon the world and called it fair;
For of the heaven he lost he never knew,
    Though oft he pined in spirit to be there.

And he lived on, the earth became his home,
    Nor learnt he aught of those who came before;
For they had ceased to wish from thence to roam,
    And for the better land could not deplore.

Time passed, and he was buried; lo! the dust
    From which he first was taken him received;
Yet in his dying hour ne'er ceased his trust,
    And still his soul for something heavenly grieved.

And we will hope that there is One who gave
    The rest he sighed for, but the world denied;
That yet his voice is heard beyond the grave,
    That he yet lives who to our vision died.

THE WILD ROSE OF PLYMOUTH

Upon the Plymouth shore the wild rose blooms,
As when the Pilgrims lived beside the bay,
And scents the morning air with sweet perfumes;
Though new this hour, more ancient far than they;
More ancient than the wild, yet friendly race,
That roved the land before the Pilgrims came,
And here for ages found a dwelling-place,
Of whom our histories tell us but a name!
Though new this hour, out from the past it springs,
Telling this summer morning of earth's prime;
And happy visions of the future brings,
That reach beyond, e'en to the verge of time;
Wreathing earth's children in one flowery chain
Of love and beauty, ever to remain.

THE ORIGIN OF MAN

Man has forgot his origin; in vain
He searches for the record of his race
In ancient books, or seeks with toil to gain
From the deep cave, or rocks, some primal trace.
And some have fancied, from a higher sphere,
Forgetful of his origin, he came,
To dwell awhile a wandering exile here,
Subject to sense, another, yet the same.
With mind bewildered, weak, how should he know
The Source Divine from whom his being springs?
The darkened spirit does its shadow throw
On written record and on outward things,
That else might plainly to his thought reveal
The wondrous truths which now they but conceal.

The Morning Watch

'Tis near the morning watch: the dim lamp burns,
But scarcely shows how dark the slumbering street;
No sound of life the silent mart returns;
No friends from house to house their neighbors greet.
It is the sleep of death,—a deeper sleep
Than e'er before on mortal eyelids fell;
No stars above the gloom their places keep;
No faithful watchmen of the morning tell;
Yet still they slumber on, though rising day
Hath through their windows poured the awakening light;
Or, turning in their sluggard trances, say,—
"There yet are many hours to fill the night."
They rise not yet; while on the Bridegroom goes
Till He the day's bright gates forever on them close.

The Prison

The prison-house is full; there is no cell
But hath its prisoner laden with his chains;
And yet they live as though their life was well,
Nor of its burdening sin the soul complains;
Thou dost not see where thou hast lived so long,—
The place is called the skull where thou dost tread.
Why laugh'st thou, then, why sing the sportive song,
As if thou livest, and know'st not thou art dead.
Yes, thou art dead, the morn breaks o'er thee now,—
Where is thy Father, He who gave thee birth?
Thou art a severed limb, a barren bough,
Thou sleepest in deep caverns in the earth.
Awake! thou hast a glorious race to run;
Put on thy strength, thou hast not yet begun.

YOURSELF

'Tis to yourself I speak; you cannot know
Him whom I call in speaking such a one,
For you beneath the earth lie buried low,
Which he alone as living walks upon:
You may at times have heard him speak to you,
And often wished perchance that you were he;
And I must ever wish that it were true,
And then you could hold fellowship with me:
But now you hear us talk as strangers, met
Above the room wherein you lie abed;
A word perhaps loud spoken you may get,
Or hear our feet when heavily they tread;
But he who speaks, or him who's spoken to,
Must both remain as strangers still to you.

THY FATHER'S HOUSE

Thou art not yet at home; perhaps thy feet
Are on the threshold of thy Father's door,
But still thy journey is not there complete,
If thou canst add to it but one step more;
'Tis not thy house which thou with feet can reach,
'Tis where when wearied they will enter not,
But step beneath an earthly roof, where each
May for a time find comfort in his lot;
Then called to wander soon again must mourn
That such frail shelter they should call relief;
And onward seek again that distant bourne,
The home of all the family of grief,
Whose doors by day and night stand open wide,
For all who enter there shall evermore abide.

THE CUP

The bitterness of death is on me now,
Before me stands its dark unclosing door;
Yet to Thy will submissive still I bow,
And follow Him who for me went before;
The tomb cannot contain me though I die,
For His strong love awakes its sleeping dead,
And bids them through Himself ascend on high
To Him who is of all the living Head;
I gladly enter through the gloomy walls,
Where they have passed who loved their Master here;
The voice they heard, to me it onward calls,
And can when faint my sinking spirit cheer;
And from the joy on earth it now has given
Lead on to joy eternal in the heaven.

The Anatomy of

Nonsense

PRELIMINARY PROBLEMS

FIRST PROBLEM

Is it possible to say that Poem A (one of Donne's *Holy Sonnets,* or one of the poems of Jonson or of Shakespeare) is better than Poem B (Collins' *Ode to Evening*) or vice versa?

If not, is it possible to say that either of these is better than Poem C (*The Cremation of Sam Magee,* or something comparable)?

If the answer is no in both cases, then any poem is as good as any other. If this is true, then all poetry is worthless; but this obviously is not true, for it is contrary to all our experience.

If the answer is yes in both cases, then there follows the question of whether the answer implies merely that one poem is better than another for the speaker, or whether it means that one poem is intrinsically better than another. If the former, then we are impressionists, which is to say relativists; and are either mystics of the type of Emerson, or hedonists of the type of Stevens and Ransom. If the latter, then we assume that constant principles govern the poetic experience, and that the poem (as likewise the judge) must be judged in relationship to those principles. It is important, therefore, to discover the consequences of assuming each of these positions.

If our answer to the first question is no and to the second yes, then we are asserting that we can distinguish between those poems which are of the canon and those which are not, but that within the canon all judgment is impossible. This view, if adopted, will require serious elucidation, for on the face of it, it appears inexplicable. On the other hand, one cannot deny that within the canon judgment will become more difficult, for the nearer two poems may be to the highest degrees of excellence, the harder it will be to choose between them. Two poems, in fact, might be so excellent that there would be small profit in endeavoring to say that one was better, but one could arrive at this conclusion only after a careful examination of both.

SECOND PROBLEM

If we accept the view that one poem can be regarded as better than another, the question then arises whether this judgment is a matter of inexplicable intuition, or whether it is a question of intuition that can be explained, and consequently guided and improved by rational elucidation.

If we accept the view that the judgment in question is inexplicable, then we are again forced to confess ourselves impressionists and relativists, unless we can show that the intuitions of all men agree at all times, or that the intuitions of one man are invariably right and those of all others wrong whenever they differ. We obviously can demonstrate neither of these propositions.

If we start, then, with the proposition that one poem may be intrinsically superior to another, we are forced to account for differences of opinion regarding it. If two critics differ, it is possible that one is right and the other wrong, more likely that both are partly right and partly wrong, but in different respects: neither the native gifts nor the education of any man have ever been wholly adequate to many of the critical problems he will encounter, and no two men are ever the same in these respects or in any others. On the other hand, although the critic should display reasonable humility and caution, it is only fair to add that few men possess either the talent or the education to justify their being taken very seriously, even of those who are nominally professional students of these matters.

But if it is possible by rational elucidation to give a more or less clear account of what one finds in a poem and why one approves or disapproves, then communication between two critics, though no doubt imperfect, becomes possible, and it becomes possible that they may in some measure correct each other's errors and so come more near to a true judgment of the poem.

THIRD PROBLEM

If rational communication about poetry is to take place, it is necessary first to determine what we mean by a poem.

A poem is first of all a statement in words.

But it differs from all such statements of a purely philosophical or theoretical nature, in that it has by intention a controlled content of feeling. In this respect, it does not differ from many works written in prose, however.

A poem differs from a work written in prose by virtue of its being composed in verse. The rhythm of verse permits the expression of more powerful feeling than is possible in prose when such feeling is needed, and it permits at all times the expression of finer shades of feeling.

A poem, then, is a statement in words in which special pains are taken with the expression of feeling. This description is merely intended to distinguish the poem from other kinds of writing; it is not offered as a complete description.

FOURTH PROBLEM

What, however, are words?

They are audible sounds, or their visual symbols, invented by man to communicate his thoughts and feelings. Each word has a conceptual content, however slight; each word, exclusive, perhaps, of the particles, communicates vague associations of feeling.

The word *fire* communicates a concept; it also connotes very vaguely certain feelings, depending on the context in which we happen to place it—depending, for example, on whether we happen to think of a fire on a hearth, in a furnace, or in a forest.

363

These feelings may be rendered more and more precise as we render the context more and more precise; as we come more and more near to completing and perfecting our poem.

FIFTH PROBLEM

But if the poem, as compared to prose, pays especial attention to feeling, are we to assume that the rational content of the poem is unimportant to its success?

The rational content cannot be eliminated from words; consequently the rational content cannot be eliminated from poetry. It is there. If it is unsatisfactory in itself, a part of the poem is unsatisfactory; the poem is thus damaged beyond argument. If we deny this, we must surely explain ourselves very fully.

If we admit this, we are faced with another problem: is it conceivable that rational content and feeling-content may both be perfect, and yet that they may be unrelated to each other, or imperfectly related? To me this is inconceivable, because the emotional content of words is generated by our experience with the conceptual content, so that a relationship is necessary.

This fact of the necessity of such relationship may fairly return us for a moment to the original question: whether imperfection of rational content damages the entire poem. If there is a necessary relationship between concept and feeling, and concept is unsatisfactory, then feeling must be damaged by way of the relationship.

SIXTH PROBLEM

If there is a relationship between concept and feeling, what is the nature of that relationship?

To answer this, let us return to the basic unit, the word. The concept represented by the word, motivates the feeling which the word communicates. It is the concept of fire which generates the feelings communicated by the word, though the sound of the word may modify these feelings very subtly, as may other accidental qualities, especially if the word be used skillfully in a given context. The accidental qualities of a word, however, such as its literary history, for example, can only modify, cannot essentially change, for these will be governed ultimately by the concept; that is, *fire* will seldom be used to signify *plum-blossom*, and so will have few opportunities to gather connotations from the concept, *plum-blossom*. The relationship, in the poem, between rational statement and feeling, is thus seen to be that of motive to emotion.

SEVENTH PROBLEM

But has not this reasoning brought us back to the proposition that all poems are equally good? For if each word motivates its own feeling, because of its intrinsic nature, will not any rational statement, since it is composed of words, motivate the feeling exactly proper to it?

This is not true, for a good many reasons, of which I shall enumerate only a few of the more obvious. In making a rational statement, in purely theoretical prose, we find that our statement may be loose or exact, depending upon the relationships of the words to each other. The precision of a word depends to some extent upon its surroundings. This is true likewise with respect to the connotations of words. Two words, each of which has several usably close rational synonyms, may reinforce and clarify each other with respect to their connotations or they may not do so.

Let me illustrate with a simple example from Browning's *Serenade at the Villa:*

> So wore night; the East was gray,
> White the broad-faced hemlock flowers.

The lines are marred by a crowding of long syllables and difficult consonants, but they have great beauty in spite of the fault. What I wish to point out, for the sake of my argument, is the relationship between the words *wore* and *gray*. The verb *wore* means literally that the night passed, but it carries with it connotations of exhaustion and attrition which belong to the condition of the protagonist; and grayness is a color which we associate with such a condition. If we change the phrase to read: "Thus night passed," we shall have the same rational meaning, and a meter quite as respectable, but no trace of the power of the line: the connotation of *wore* will be lost, and the connotation of *gray* will remain merely in a state of ineffective potentiality. The protagonist in seeing his feeling mirrored in the landscape is not guilty of motivating his feeling falsely, for we know his general motive from the poem as a whole; he is expressing a portion of the feeling motivated by the total situation through a more or less common psychological phenomenon. If the poem were such, however, that we did not know why the night *wore* instead of *passed*, we should have just cause for complaint; in fact, most of the strength of the word would probably be lost. The second line contains other fine effects, immediately with reference to the first line, ultimately with reference to the theme; I leave the reader to analyze them for himself, but he will scarcely succeed without the whole poem before him.

Concepts, as represented by particular words, are affected by connotations due to various and curious accidents. A word may gather connotations from its use in folk-poetry, in formal poetry, in vulgar speech, or in technical prose: a single concept might easily be represented by four words with these distinct histories; and any one of the words might prove to be proper in a given poetic context. Words gain connotation from etymological accidents. Something of this may be seen in the English word *outrage*, in which is commonly felt, in all likelihood, something associated with *rage*, although there is no rage whatever in the original word. Similarly the word *urchin*, in modern English, seldom connotes anything related to hedgehogs, or to the familiars of the witches, by whose intervention the word arrived at its modern meaning and feeling. Yet the connotation proper to any stage in the history of such a word might be resuscitated, or a blend of connotations effected, by skillful use. Further, the connotation of a word may be modified very strongly by its function

366

in the metrical structure, a matter which I shall discuss at length in connection with the theories of Ransom.

This is enough to show that exact motivation of feeling by concept is not inherent in any rational statement. Any rational statement will govern the general possibilities of feeling derivable from it, but the task of the poet is to adjust feeling to motive precisely. He has to select words containing not only the right relationships within themselves, but the right relationships to each other. The task is very difficult; and this is no doubt the reason why the great poetry of a great poet is likely to be very small in bulk.

EIGHTH PROBLEM

Is it not possible, however, to escape from this relationship of motive to emotion by confining ourselves very largely to those words which denote emotion: love, envy, anger, and the like?

This is not possible, for these words, like others, represent concepts. If we should confine ourselves strictly to such a vocabulary, we should merely write didactic poetry: poetry about love in general, or about anger in general. The emotion communicated would result from our apprehension of the ideas in question. Such poetry is perfectly legitimate, but it is only one kind of poetry, and it is scarcely the kind which the Romantic theorist is endeavoring to define.

Such poetry has frequently been rendered particular by the use of allegory. The playful allegorizing of minor amoristic themes which one encounters in the Renaissance and which is possibly descended from certain neo-Platonic elements in medieval poetry may serve as illustration. Let us consider these and the subsequent lines by Thomas Lodge:

> Love in my bosom like a bee
>   Doth suck his sweet;
> Now with his wings he plays with me,
>   Now with his feet.

Love itself is a very general idea and might include many kinds of experience; the idea is limited by this allegory to the sentimental and sensual, but we still have an idea, the subdivision of the original idea, and the feeling must be appropriate to the concept. The concept is rendered concrete by the image of Cupid, whose actions, in turn, are rendered visible by comparison to the bee: it is these actions which make the poem a kind of anticipatory meditation on more or less sensual love, a meditation which by its mere tone of expression keeps the subject in its proper place as a very minor one. Sometimes the emphasis is on the mere description of the bee, sometimes on the description of Cupid, sometimes on the lover's feeling; but the feeling motivated in any passage is governed by this emphasis. The elements, once they are united in the poem, are never really separated, of course. In so far as the poet departs from his substantial theme in the direction of mere bees and flowers, he will achieve what Ransom calls irrelevance; but if there is much of this the poem will be weakened. Whether he so departs or not, the relation of motive to emotion must remain the same, within each passage. I have discussed this problem in my essay on Ransom.

A common romantic practice is to use words denoting emotions, but to use them loosely and violently, as if the very carelessness expressed emotion. Another is to make a general statement, but seem to refer it to a particular occasion, which, however, is never indicated: the poet thus seems to avoid the didactic, yet he is not forced to understand the particular motive. Both these faults may be seen in these lines from Shelley:

> Out of the day and night
> A joy has taken flight;
>   Fresh spring, and summer, and winter hoar,
> Move my faint heart with grief, but with delight
>   No more—oh, never more.

The poet's intention is so vague, however, that he achieves nothing but stereotypes of a very crude kind.

The Romantics often tried other devices. For example, it would be possible to write a poem on fear in general, but to avoid in some measure the effect of the purely didactic by illustrating the emotion along the way with various experiences which might motivate fear. There is a danger here, though it is merely a danger, that the general idea may not dominate the poem, and that the poem may thus fall apart into a group of poems on particular experiences. There is the alternative danger, that the particular quality of the experiences may be so subordinated to the illustrative function of the experiences, that within each illustration there is merely a stereotyped and not a real relationship of motive to feeling: this occurs in Collins' *Ode to Fear*, though a few lines in the Epode come surprisingly to life. But the methods which I have just described really offer no semblance of an escape from the theory of motivation which I am defending.

Another Romantic device, if it is conscious enough to be called a device, is to offer instead of a defensible motive a false one, usually culled from landscape. This kind of writing represents a tacit admission of the principle of motivation which I am defending, but a bad application of the principle. It results in the kind of writing which I have called pseudo-reference in my volume, *Primitivism and Decadence*. One cannot believe, for example, that Wordsworth's passions were charmed away by a look at the daffodils, or that Shelley's were aroused by the sight of the leaves blown about in the autumn wind. A motive is offered, and the poet wants us to accept it, but we recognize it as inadequate. In such a poem there may be fragments of good description, which motivate a feeling more or less purely appropriate to the objects described, and these fragments may sustain our liking for the poem: this happens in Collins' *Ode to Evening;* but one will find also an account of some kind of emotion essentially irrelevant to the objects described, along with the attempt, more or less explicit, to deduce the emotion from the object.

There remains the method of the Post-Romantics, whether French Symbolists or American Experimentalists: the method of trying to extinguish the rational content of language while retaining the content of association. This method I have discussed in *Primitivism and Decadence,* and I shall discuss it again in this book.

The relationship in the poem of rational meaning to feeling we have seen to be that of motive to emotion; and we have seen that this must be a satisfactory relationship. How do we determine whether such a relationship is satisfactory? We determine it by an act of moral judgment. The question then arises whether moral judgments can be made, whether the concept of morality is or is not an illusion.

If morality can be considered real, if a theory of morality can be said to derive from reality, it is because it guides us toward the greatest happiness which the accidents of life permit: that is, toward the fullest realization of our nature, in the Aristotelian or Thomistic sense. But is there such a thing, abstractly considered, as full realization of our nature?

To avoid discussion of too great length, let us consider the opposite question: is there such a thing as obviously unfulfilled human nature? Obviously there is. We need only turn to the feeble-minded, who cannot think and so cannot perceive or feel with any clarity; or to the insane, who sometimes perceive and feel with great intensity, but whose feelings and perceptions are so improperly motivated that they are classed as illusions. At slightly higher levels, the criminal, the dissolute, the unscrupulously selfish, and various types of neurotics are likely to arouse but little disagreement as examples.

Now if we are able to recognize the fact of insanity—if in fact we are forced to recognize it—that is, the fact of the obvious maladjustment of feeling to motive, we are forced to admit the possibility of more accurate adjustment, and, by necessary sequence, of absolutely accurate adjustment, even though we admit the likelihood that most people will attain to a final adjustment but very seldom indeed. We can guide ourselves toward such an adjustment in life, as in art, by means of theory and the critical examination of special instances; but the final act of judgment is in both life and art a unique act—it is a relationship between two elements, the rational understanding and the feeling, of which only one is classificatory and of which the other has infinite possibilities of variation.

TENTH PROBLEM

If the final act of adjustment is a unique act of judgment, can we say that it is more or less right, provided it is demonstrably within the general limits prescribed by the theory of morality which has led to it? The answer to this question is implicit in what has preceded; in fact the answer resembles exactly that reached at the end of the first problem examined. We can say that it is more or less nearly right. If extreme deviation from right judgment is obvious, then there is such a thing as right judgment. The mere fact that life may be conducted in a fairly satisfactory manner, by means of inaccurate judgment within certain limits, and that few people ever bother to refine their judgment beyond the stage which enables them to remain largely within those limits, does not mean that accurate judgment has no reality. Implicit in all that has preceded is the concept that in any moral situation, there is a right judgment as an ultimate possibility; that the human judge, or actor, will approximate it more or less nearly; that the closeness of his approximation will depend upon the accuracy of his rational understanding and of his intuition, and upon the accuracy of their interaction upon each other.

ELEVENTH PROBLEM

Nothing has thus far been said about human action, yet morality is supposed to guide human action. And if art is moral, there should be a relationship between art and human action.

The moral judgment, whether good, bad, or indifferent, is commonly the prelude and instigation to action. Hastily or care-

371

fully, intelligently or otherwise, one arrives at some kind of general idea of a situation calling for action, and one's idea motivates one's feeling: the act results. The part played by will, or the lack of it, between judgment and act, the possibility that action may be frustrated by some constitutional or habitual weakness or tendency, such as cowardice or a tendency to anger, in a person of a fine speculative or poetic judgment, are subjects for a treatise on ethics or psychology; a treatise on poetry stops with the consideration of the speculative judgment, which reaches its best form and expression in poetry. In the situations of daily life, one does not, as a rule, write a poem before acting: one makes a more rapid and simple judgment. But if the poem does not individually lead to a particular act, it does not prevent action. It gives us a better way of judging representative acts than we should otherwise have. It is thus a civilizing influence: it trains our power of judgment, and should, I imagine, affect the quality of daily judgments and actions.

TWELFTH PROBLEM

What, then, is the nature of the critical process?

It will consist (1) of the statement of such historical or biographical knowledge as may be necessary in order to understand the mind and method of the writer; (2) of such analysis of his literary theories as we may need to understand and evaluate what he is doing; (3) of a rational critique of the paraphrasable content (roughly, the motive) of the poem; (4) of a rational critique of the feeling motivated—that is, of the details of style, as seen in language and technique; and (5) of the final act of judgment, a unique act, the general nature of which can be indicated, but which cannot be communicated precisely, since it consists in receiving from the poet his own final and unique judgment of his matter and in judging that judgment. It should be noted that the purpose of the first four processes is to limit as narrowly as possible the region in which the final unique act is to occur.

In the actual writing of criticism, a given task may not require all of these processes, or may not require that all be given equal emphasis; or it may be that in connection with a certain writer, whether because of the nature of the writer or because of the way in which other critics have treated him previously, one or two of these processes must be given so much emphasis that others must be neglected for lack of space. These are practical matters to be settled as the occasions arise.

HENRY ADAMS

or The Creation of Confusion

I. THE HISTORICAL BACKGROUND

HENRY ADAMS saw modern history as a progress from unified understanding, or the illusion of such, in the century following the year 1150, toward the dispersion of understanding and force in the twentieth century; and he saw himself as the product of an earlier New England. In regard to himself he was correct; and as for modern history, his view of it, though scarcely defensible, provides a clue to certain historical processes of which the history of New England is perhaps the most dramatic single illustration.

The history immediately relevant to an understanding of Adams' mind might be said to begin with the first great theological critics of Aquinas, especially with Ockham. Aquinas endeavored as far as possible to establish a separation between philosophy and theology; philosophy was guided by natural reason, theology was derived from Revelation. But he believed that philosophical knowledge was possible, and in his pursuit of it, he composed the most complete and lucid critique of previous philosophy that had been made, and the most thorough and defensible moral and philosophical system, in all likelihood, that the world has known.

Ockham, the most profound of the medieval nominalists, struck at the very heart of this philosophy by attacking the reality of universals, by endeavoring to show the illusory nature of all ideas whatsoever. Etienne Gilson has described the immediate results as follows:[1]

Thus blended together, Empiricism and theologism made a most explosive combination. At the top of the world, a God whose absolute power knew no limits, not even those of a stable nature endowed with a necessity and an intelligibility of its own. Between His will and the countless individuals that co-exist in space or succeed each other and glide away in time, there was strictly nothing. Having expelled from the mind of God the intelligible world of Plato, Ockham was satisfied that no intelligibility could be found in any one of God's works. How could there be order in nature, when there is no nature? And how could there be a nature when each singular being, thing, or event, can claim no other justification for its existence than that of being one among the elect of an all-powerful God? That was not the God of theology, but of theologism; for though the living God of theology be infinitely more than the "Author of Nature," He is at least that, whereas Ockham's God was not even that. Instead of being an eternal source of that concrete order of intelligibility and beauty, which we call nature, Ockham's God was expressly intended to relieve the world of the necessity of having any meaning of its own. The God of theology always vouches for nature; the jealous God of theologism usually prefers to abolish it.

The universe of Ockham here described bears a precise resemblance, as we shall eventually see, to the universe of Henry Adams, with this exception: that in the universe of Henry Adams there is no God. In the universe of Ockham, all morality and moral knowledge, or what we call such, are independent of nature, and depend directly from the arbitrary will of God; and had that will chanced to be otherwise, they would then have been otherwise. We have no way of obtaining knowledge of man through the study of man; we are the recipients of arbitrary instructions which we disobey at our peril. In the universe of Aquinas, which resembles in many important respects that of his great predecessor, Aristotle, we can learn a great deal by the light

[1] *The Unity of Philosophical Experience,* by Etienne Gilson, Scribners, 1937. P. 85.

of natural reason. The universe was created by God, it is true; but it was so created as to pursue its own laws, and those laws, including many which govern the nature of man, can be discovered with reasonable accuracy after careful examination of the data before us. The risk which Ockham ran is clearly stated by Gilson:[2]

Different as they may be, owing to the various times, places and civilizations in which they were conceived, these doctrines resemble each other at least in this, that all of them are thoroughly intoxicated with a definite religious feeling which I beg leave to call, for simplicity's sake, the feeling of the Glory of God. Needless to say, there is no true religion without that feeling. The deeper it is, the better it is; but it is one thing to experience a certain feeling deeply, and another thing to allow it to dictate, uncontrolled by reason, a completely rounded interpretation of the world. When and where piety is permitted to inundate the philosophical field, the usual outcome is that, the better to extol the Glory of God, pious-minded theologians proceed joyfully to annihilate God's own creation. God is great and high and almighty; what better proof could be given of these truths than that nature and man are essentially insignificant, low and utterly powerless creatures? A very dangerous method indeed, for in the long run it is bound to hurt both philosophy and religion. In such a case the sequence of doctrines too often runs in the following way: with the best intentions in the world, some theologian suggests, as a philosophically established truth, that God is and does everything, while nature and man are and do nothing; then comes a philosopher who grants the theologian's success in proving that nature is powerless, but emphasizes his failure to prove that there is a God. Hence the logical conclusion that nature is wholly deprived of reality and intelligibility. This is scepticism, and it cannot be avoided in such cases. Now one can afford to live on philosophical scepticism, so long as it is backed by a positive religious faith; yet, even while our faith is there, one still remains a sceptic in philosophy, and were faith ever to go, what would be left of us but an absolute sceptic?

Once a more or less Ockhamist position is taken, there are various ways by which faith may be lost, as one can discover by examining the history of European thought from the time of

[2] Ibid. pp. 37-8.

Ockham to the present. Moreover, Ockham was by no means the inventor of the general religious position which he took; he was merely the last of its great defenders, and as a logician the greatest of them. The type of Christianity to place faith, which results from an act of the will made possible by Divine Grace, above understanding, has its first great exponent in Augustine, but is older than Augustine. This type of Christianity, the fideistic, or voluntaristic, derives all knowledge from faith and Revelation, and refuses to take the natural reason seriously; and although some voluntarists are willing to argue rationally from Revelation, their theology leads commonly and rapidly to a daily dependence upon Grace and distrust of reason—that is, to extreme mysticism. Aquinas was a sane enough man to wish to make the most of all his faculties, and a good enough Christian to believe that God had given him his faculties for use.

The voluntaristic tradition seems to have grown upon Christianity of all kinds since the fifteenth century, but especially upon the western churches severed from Rome. Voluntarism is an easy form of Christianity for those who are not vigorous intellectually but who are slow to give up old habits, and it may for this reason have gained upon the Church of England and upon the Episcopal Church in the United States, churches in which faith seems to have died so slowly and gently that its demise is only half suspected today.[3] It was in Calvinism, however, that voluntarism received its logical expression, and it was in New England that Calvinism was able to work out its own natural development with less interference or outside influence than was possible anywhere in Europe.

The Calvinistic doctrines were all doctrines that should have followed naturally from the position taken by Ockham: the doctrine of predestination, or the arbitrary separation from all eternity of the few to be saved from the many to be damned; the doctrine of God's Decrees, or the predestination from all eternity of every event, to the falling of the last leaf; the doctrine of justi-

[3] One of the many amusing comments which I have heard attributed to the late David Starr Jordan goes somewhat as follows: "The Episcopal Church is so constituted that its members can really believe anything; but of course almost none of them do."

fication by faith alone; the doctrine, closely allied to the last, of the inefficaciousness of good works; and the doctrine of Grace as an experience essentially mystical and almost melodramatic in its violence.

Yet the Christians of the Reformation, in spite of their anti-moral theology, were extremely moral people; and the Reformation itself was in a large measure a protest against the abuses which had grown up in the Roman Church during a period of decadence. One needed courage, both physical and moral, to go with Luther and Calvin; and of those who believed with the reformers in England, perhaps the most convinced, the most indomitably moral, were those who went into the wilderness rather than compromise their convictions.

But their morality remained fideistic. Good works were good, not because of their intrinsic worth, but because God had arbitrarily termed them so; good works were the fruits of faith, but could accomplish nothing in themselves; and faith was the arbitrary gift of God, which only a few would receive. Works apparently good, but performed by those not of the elect, were a delusion. And yet in most Calvinistic systems, and by nearly all Calvinistic preachers, man was held morally responsible to God for his behavior. The Calvinists, in refusing to distinguish, with Aquinas, between the ideas of Divine prescience and Divine predestination, which was purely a philosophical matter, found themselves confronted with the very practical conflict between the ideas of predestination and of man's moral responsibility for his acts. The wiser Calvinistic writers have admitted that the ideas are logically incompatible with each other and have said that the conflict is a mystery understood by God alone; but the New England Calvinists, in the isolation of their new community, endeavored all too often to argue their way free; and the result was the destruction of theology. Since the philosophic understanding of morality was essentially lost in their tradition, the source of it having been renounced, the death of theology, which alone could give authority for moral principles or behavior, was a very serious matter; and it was the more serious because New

England Calvinism had generated in its adherents very intense moral habits.

These habits, as I have indicated, must have been very strong in the founders of Massachusetts, and the continuation of them may have been in part merely the biological inheritance of a constitutional tendency; but the situation in Massachusetts must have done much to perpetuate and strengthen them. The New Englanders, as predestinarians, believed that they had been sent into a new land to found a pure church; not only were they the elect of God, but they represented the ultimate and predestined culmination of Christian history, which in turn was the predestined triumph of all preceding human history: these simple men in a struggle for life against the wilderness represented the dramatic victory of religion, toward which God had ordained the progress of the world. This view was seriously taken, and it was seriously expressed at the time by many writers; the reader may examine it in its completeness in Cotton Mather's Introduction to the *Magnalia Christi Americana*, an Introduction of which the opening recalls the opening of the *Aeneid*, and which sets out to summarize the matter of the Christian epic:

> I write the *Wonders* of the Christian Religion, flying from the depravations of *Europe*, to the *American Strand*: and, assisted by the Holy Author of that *Religion*, I do, with all conscience of *Truth*, required therein by Him, who is the *Truth* itself, report the *wonderful displays* of His infinite Power, Wisdom, Goodness, and Faithfulness, wherewith His Divine Providence hath *irradiated* an *Indian Wilderness*.

The morality of these men may have been in fact merely habitual, but in theory it was predestined and arbitrary, as I have said. It did not derive, theoretically, from an understanding of human nature and a desire to improve human nature by careful and enlightened modification. It derived from the arbitrary will of God: God had given a few simple commands for behavior, and they were to be obeyed simply and literally. The theology employed by the 17th century church in New

England modified original Calvinism in certain important respects; the most important being with reference to the signs of election. The importance of the mystical experience was minimized; in its place was encouraged the belief that a man might know himself one of the elect when he decided to enter the church and conform to its principles. The doctrine of predestination was not altered by this belief, for the decision, apparently an act of the private will, had been predestined.

Every human act thus became a sign in an allegory, as did every event in nature. If a man sinned, it was fairly obvious that he was an evil man and one of the damned, in spite of the theoretic but negligible possibility that he might be predestined to a later repentance and ultimate salvation. The most insignificant events were predetermined by God in accordance with His eternal plan: by a cast of the dice one might discover God's will, for the fall of the dice was predestined; though it is hard in these later days to understand why confirmed predestinarians should ever have required the intervention of the dice, when they had renounced with abhorrence the intervention of the Church of Rome.

Further, until the time of Andros, the church ruled the state; and it was not until the charter of 1692 that there was any real relaxation of the theory that the church had a right to do so, and the relaxation, when it came, was merely the slow beginning of a long process. The result was the fixing of certain social and mental habits, stronger, in all probability, than any others which have ever permeated a society at all its levels. Morality was strong, simple, and arbitrary; and under the influence of the doctrine of predestination, it transformed the human mind into an allegorical machine. One can open the diary of Cotton Mather almost at random and verify this assertion: people encountered casually on the street, the vicissitudes of private experience, a dog urinating at a wall, were signs which Mather read for their divine meaning. And one can verify the assertion in innumerable minor documents of the time. This allegorism was not a literary movement or device, such as one meets among the neo-Platonists in various periods; nor was it the property of an academic class, like the medieval realism which expressed itself in a somewhat less allegorical allegory than that of the Puritans, for example in that of Dante; nor was it a pedagogic device for instructing the illiterate, such as one meets at the lower levels of medieval literature, doubtless as a result of the influence of the realists; it was a form of the mind in daily life, a way of seeing the universe, which appears to have been common to an entire society, and it persisted well into the nineteenth century, after the ideas which had given rise to it had long since passed away. The works of Hawthorne, Melville, Henry James, and Henry Adams are its belated fruits in literature; in fact the diary of Cotton Mather and the *Education* of Henry Adams offer one of the most curious cases of similar temperaments that one is ever likely to find in two literary periods so far apart.

By the end of the 17th century, New England Calvinism was disintegrating, especially along the Massachusetts seaboard; and about 1733 there began in the parish of Jonathan Edwards a revival of Calvinism, which, under the influence of several powerful, though but vaguely Calvinistical field-preachers, was to sweep New England within the next few years. The excitement of this movement resulted in the breaking off of many small and strangely inspired sects from the main Calvinistic body; but it resulted also in the establishment of a revised and renewed Calvinism, under the guidance of Edwardian theology.

Edwardian theology abandoned the early New England modifications of Calvinism; it taught an undisguised determinism and a purely mystical doctrine of Grace. New England mystical tendencies had by no means been suppressed by the earlier doctrine: there had been doctrinal heretics, and even among the orthodox, such as Increase and Cotton Mather, there had been mystical trances, ecstasies, and visions, Cotton Mather, in fact, having been visited by an angel during one of the sunlit mornings of his youth. But Edwards revived and encouraged this tendency by explicit doctrine; and the New Englander's capacity for mystical belief and feeling was thus carried over to the period when Emerson should redescribe the mystical experience, em-

ploying the ideas of Romantic pantheism recently imported from
the literary movements of Europe, and as far as might be the
language of Edwardian Calvinism, so that Romantic doctrine
was offered in a language carrying most of the emotional im
plications of the New England religious tradition in its most
intense aspects. Mind and matter, God and Creation were one;
the inundation of the mind by instinct and emotion was Divine
Grace; and surrender to whim was surrender to the Spirit. Whitman restated this doctrine in a vulgar style, and increased its
popularity; William James did much to give it academic respectability; and it reached its final and dramatic fulfillment in
the life and work of Hart Crane. The mystical tradition would
appear to have had little influence upon Adams at the beginning,
but as we shall ultimately see, he drew very near to it in the
later years of his life.

But Edwards had little influence along the seaboard: the
churches there continued their process of breaking down the
17th century theology which they had long since begun. The
moral sense proved stronger than the belief in predestination,
and with the disappearance of the doctrine of predestination
went most of what was precise and strong in Calvinistic theology. Certainly the doctrine of predestination was the essential
element in Calvinism; and when that went, theology was gone,
for the ancient and habitual antagonism to Romanism, Angli-
canism and Arminianism remained when the doctrinal justification for it was dead: there were a few apostates to Anglican-
ism, such as the American Samuel Johnson, but in general the
New Englander was incapable even of thinking of a Christianity
antecedent to Calvin. Whatever the intellectual troubles of the
New Englander, he was the creature of the strongest habits that
the world had ever seen.

The result was Unitarianism. Among the Unitarian and related churches of the early nineteenth century there was a good
deal of variation in doctrine, but the tendency was toward a
belief in a benevolent God, in place of the angry God of the
fathers; in Christ as a moral teacher, and not as the son of God;

in freedom of the will; in the complete efficaciousness of good works. And there was an increasing tendency toward disbelief in eternal damnation. Unitarianism placed man's responsibility for his acts and his salvation wholly within himself, but the acts of a well-bred man conformed almost inevitably to the strong customs of the society which had been generated by the earlier ideas; so that between the ease with which one might be moral and the gentlemanly attitude of God, salvation appeared a fairly simple matter. This period produced a type of mind which we may still observe in the poetry of Bryant, and in the prose of Prescott and of the first Charles Francis Adams: able, dignified, and at times distinguished; governed easily by firm convictions; uncritical of accepted principles; and tending to substitute general stereotypes for precise perceptions and ideas. Men of this type adopted easily and turned to their own purposes the literary style produced by English deism, a style composed of somewhat vaguely general ideas, of an easy and well-constructed period, and of the highly generalized statement which tended at its best toward the aphorism, at its weakest toward the cliché. *Thanatopsis* is a sound poem and a serious and moving one; and rhetorically it is a masterpiece. But as compared even to so simple a piece as Herbert's *Church Monuments*, it displays a very simple and generalized grasp of its subject; and the same comments may be made upon Byrant's best work throughout— *To a Waterfowl, The Battlefield, The Grave,* and *The Tides.*

It was the Unitarians who provided the immediate background of Henry Adams, and he described their mentality on many occasions, and always with bewilderment. In the history he writes:[4]

No more was heard of the Westminster doctrine that man had lost all ability of will to any spiritual good accompanying salvation, but was dead in sin. So strong was the reaction against old dogmas that for thirty years society seemed less likely to resume the ancient faith in the Christian Trinity, than to establish a new Trinity in which a deified humanity should have a place. Under the influence

[4] *History of the United States during the Administrations of Jefferson and Madison,* by Henry Adams. Albert and Charles Boni, 1930. Vol. IX, pp. 182-3.

of Channing and his friends, human nature was adorned with virtues hardly suspected before, and with hopes of perfection on earth altogether strange to theology. The Church then charmed. The worth of man became under Channing's teachings a source of pride and joy, with such insistence as to cause his hearers at last to recall, almost with a sense of relief, that the Saviour himself had been content to regard them only as of more value than many sparrows.

And a few lines below, he adds of the doctrine of Hosea Ballou:

This new doctrine, which took the name of Universalism, held as an article of faith "that there is one God, whose nature is love, revealed in one Lord Jesus Christ, by one Holy Spirit of Grace, who will finally restore the whole family of mankind to holiness and happiness." In former times anyone who had publicly professed belief in universal salvation would not have been regarded as a Christian. . . . Yet the Universalists steadily grew in numbers and respectability, spreading from State to State under Ballou's guidance. . . .

It is their bland security that most puzzles Adams, as it may well puzzle us today. In the *Education* he writes:[5]

Nothing quieted doubt so completely as the mental calm of the Unitarian clergy. In uniform excellence of life and character, moral and intellectual, the score of Unitarian clergymen about Boston, who controlled society and Harvard College, were never excelled. They proclaimed as their merit that they insisted on no doctrine, but taught, or tried to teach, the means of leading a virtuous, useful, unselfish life, which they held to be sufficient for salvation. For them difficulties might be ignored; doubts were waste of thought; nothing exacted solution. Boston had solved the universe; or had offered and realized the best solution yet tried. The problem was worked out.

And in the *History* he quotes a passage from Channing which illustrates this view, and comments upon it:[6]

[5] *The Education of Henry Adams,* by Henry Adams, Modern Library Edition, p. 34.
[6] Op. cit. Vol. IX, pp. 181-2.

"We lay it down as a great and indisputable opinion, clear as the sun at noon-day, that the great end for which Christian truth is revealed is the sanctification of the soul, the formation of the Christian character; and wherever we see the marks of this character displayed in a professed disciple of Jesus, we hope and rejoice to hope, that he has received all the truth which is necessary to his salvation." The hope might help to soothe anxiety and distress, but it defied conclusions reached by the most anxious and often renewed labors of churchmen for eighteen hundred years. Something more than a hope was necessary as the foundation of a faith.

This was, however, the last step possible to a voluntaristic Christianity which should remain non-mystical. Dogmas were ignored as misleading and vicious; theology was so simplified that one could scarcely identify the God in whom one believed. But belief remained, and one's entire theory of human nature, or rather of human conduct, depended arbitrarily but historically and helplessly from that belief. As long as the belief remained, the spiritual result was a kind of placid security; but the New Englander retained his need for security, and wherever the belief departed and the evidence is still available for examination, we commonly find a kind of willed confusion and religious horror, best represented in literature by Melville's *Pierre* and *The Confidence Man* and by the later work of Henry Adams.

The strength of the voluntaristic tradition may be observed in a New Englander of our own period, the late Irving Babbitt. Babbitt found that human nature functioned at three levels, to use his own figure: the naturalistic, which was the level of the emotions and instincts, and which had been exploited by the writers of the Romantic movement; the humanistic, or critical, at which we are able to examine the lower level, understand it, and control it; and the religious, which is above criticism. In his most valuable book, *Rousseau and Romanticism,* he devotes himself primarily to the criticism of Romantic principles from what he calls a humanistic position, and he refers to himself as an Aristotelian. The book is marred by his reference to the "Inner Check," or conscience, a feeling which functions at the religious level; but I believe that this element can be dissected out with no great damage to the criticism of the Romantic movement.

In his later work, however, his religious doctrines become more important, and in the book entitled *On Being Creative*, he asserts the absolute primacy of the will: man must will to submit his private will to the higher will, in which he must believe, and from that act understanding can follow; and the Inner Check, or Conscience, the feeling superior to reason and which guides us in emergencies, is identified with Divine Grace. This is Augustinism without the Christianity: we must believe in that which is superior to reason and which we therefore cannot define, much less examine critically; and in that which is divorced from any particular historical tradition such as that which still, I suppose, supports the belief of the Christian. And we have as our ultimate guide an emotional experience which is above rational criticism: the practical question therefore arises as to how we shall distinguish between an experience which is above criticism and one which is fairly subject to it, if we cannot bring criticism properly to bear on the first. Babbitt's final position seems to be little better than a starting point for a short-cut back to Emersonian mysticism.

Babbitt believed the Inner Check to be a psychological fact, observable and therefore a fit beginning for discussion. But the question remains as to the exact nature of the fact. The feeling which is called conscience in Protestant and post-Protestant society is presumably real; but when Aquinas comes to define conscience, he identifies it with reason, and he discusses the moral consequences of the identification at great length. From a Thomistic position, there would always remain the possibility of divine intervention in a particular instance; but the Catholic Christian, whether Thomistic or other, would be protected against error by the supervision of the Church, a supervision which Babbitt did not enjoy: and this supervision is, in theory, the supervision of the disinterested reason.

But Aquinas would be forced, I believe, by his definition of conscience and by his use of the Aristotelian doctrine of

386

habit, to identify Babbitt's Inner Check in most of its individual occurrences as an habitual way of feeling about certain kinds of acts; the habit having been generated by training in a particular kind of society, which in turn had grown up originally in conformity with certain kinds of ideas. There is nothing in Babbitt to make one relinquish this interpretation, or even to make one believe that he suspected the possibility of this interpretation; and if the interpretation is true, it follows, as various critics have suggested, that the Inner Check will become progressively weaker as the generating ideas tend less and less to acceptance and the society in consequence alters its nature. Babbitt's doctrine of the Inner Check appears to be a late expression of the voluntaristic belief that morality is arbitrary and incomprehensible; the exact reverse of the Aristotelian doctrine, by which Babbitt appears to be mainly influenced in his early work, that morality is a fair subject for philosophical and psychological investigation, and that its principles can be discovered in a large measure through the use of the natural reason in the study of nature.

I should like also to cite the instance of Henry James, for his connections with Adams are immediate and important. In my essay on James,[7] I have shown that the character in the Jamesian novel is guided by a moral sense, or habit, which, though very intense, has lost its connections with its origins, so that it is never adequately guided by any critical apparatus, and that a good deal of obscurity results directly from this situation in many of the novels. The interesting thing about James as a critic is that he appears to be in precisely the same predicament as the characters in his novels. He objects to various continental writers for their lack of moral sense, and he criticizes many of his own books for the obscurity of their motivation, an obscurity which, though he realizes the fact imperfectly, results from the confusion of his own moral sense; but when he discusses the general principles of fiction,[8] he derides the

---

[7] See page 300 of this volume.
[8] The references are to *The Art of Fiction*, in *Partial Portraits*. It is early, but characteristic.

idea that morality has anything to do with fiction, yet he insists that fiction "must take itself seriously," is obliged "really to represent life"; he takes it for granted "that some incidents are intrinsically much more important than others," although a few lines further, he is willing to grant the artist any subject and judge him only by what he does with it.

His terms, when he goes behind the terms relating to the technical structure of the novel, are extremely confused; but he insists that the novel shall be interesting. And when we have read a great deal of his criticism, we discover that he means that it must be interesting to Henry James; and to discover the meaning of this interest, we must first come to understand Henry James, which we can best do through the study of his novels. Ultimately he demands that the novel display (in a very finished form, naturally) the particular moral sense, or feeling for human motivation, which he himself possesses. This moral sense is the product of New England and of a very special section of history; and it has lost all connection with its intellectual sources, merely existing, more and more precariously, in vacuo; but James assumes it to be, if not universal, at least a standard universally applicable, so that he is in about the same situation as the later Babbitt.

Adams possessed the same moral sense, in a very exasperated form. He knew that he had it, and he knew that it closely resembled that of James; but unlike James, he felt that it needed justification, either philosophical or religious, and he convinced himself that neither was possible. Before proceeding to an examination of Adams' thought and art, I wish to cite a few of his references to James, for they will illuminate a great deal of that which is to follow.

In 1903 Adams wrote to James after reading James's life of Story:[9]

More than ever, after devouring your William Story, I feel how difficult a job was imposed on you. It is a *tour de force*, of course,

* *Letters of Henry Adams 1892-1918*, edited by W. C. Ford. Houghton Mifflin, 1938, p. 414.

but that you knew from the first. Whether you have succeeded or not, I cannot say, because it all spreads itself out as though I had written it, and I feel where you are walking on firm ground, and where you are on thin ice, as though I were in your place. Verily I believe I wrote it. Except your specialty of style, it is me.

The painful truth is that all of my New England generation, counting the half-century, 1820-1870, were in actual fact only one mind and nature; the individual was a facet of Boston. We knew each other to the last nervous center, and feared each other's knowledge. We looked through each other like microscopes. There was absolutely nothing in us that we did not understand merely by looking in the eye.[10] There was hardly a difference even in depth, for Harvard College and Unitarianism kept us all shallow. We knew nothing—no! but really nothing! of the world. One cannot exaggerate the profundity of ignorance of Story in becoming a sculptor, or Sumner in becoming a Statesman, or Emerson in becoming a philosopher. Story and Sumner, Emerson and Alcott, Lowell and Longfellow, Hillard, Winthrop, Motley, Prescott, and all the rest, were the same mind,—and so, poor worm!—was I!

Type bourgeois-bostonien! A type quite as good as another, but more uniform. What you say of Story is at bottom exactly what you would say of Lowell, Motley, and Sumner, barring degrees of egotism. You cannot help smiling at them, but you smile at us all equally. God knows that we knew our want of knowledge! the self-distrust became introspection—nervous self-consciousness—irritable dislike of America, and antipathy to Boston. *Auch ich war in Arcadien geboren!*

So you have written not Story's life, but your own and mine—pure autobiography—the more keen for what is beneath, implied, intelligible only to me, and half a dozen other people still living; like Frank Boott: who knew our Boston, London, and Rome in the fifties and sixties. You make me curl up like a trodden-on worm. Improvised Europeans we were, and—Lord God!—how thin! No, but it is too cruel! Long ago,—at least thirty years ago,—I discovered it, and have painfully held my tongue about it. You strip us gently and kindly, like a surgeon, and I feel your knife in my ribs.

[10] It is amusing to compare this statement with the statement of Dallas Archer to his father, near the end of *The Age of Innocence*: "You never did ask each other anything, did you? And you never told each other anything. You just sat and watched each other, and guessed at what was going on underneath. A deaf-and-dumb asylum, in fact! Well, I back your generation for knowing more about each other's thoughts than we ever have time to find out about our own."

In 1901 he had written to Elizabeth Cameron:[11]

Harry James has upset me. John Hay has been greatly troubled by Harry's last volume, *The Sacred Fount*. He cannot resist the suspicion that it is very close on extravagance. His alarm made me read it, and I recognized at once that Harry and I had the same disease, the obsession of *idée fixe*. . . .

In 1908 he wrote to William James of his own *Education*:[12]

As for the volume, it interests me chiefly as a literary experiment, hitherto, as far as I know, never tried or never successful. Your brother Harry tries such experiments in literary art daily, and would know instantly what I mean; but I doubt whether a dozen people in America—except architects or decorators—would know or care.

And in 1916, on learning of the death of this friend and alterego, he wrote to Elizabeth Cameron:[13]

Today the death of Harry James makes me feel the need of a let-up; I must speak to some one, and here I have no one Jamesian to talk to, except Wendell Holmes, and I never see him, for he is like me in avoiding contemporaries. Harry's death hits me harder than any stroke since my brother Charles' death a year ago. Not only was he a friend of mine for more than forty years, but he also belonged to the circle of my wife's set long before I knew him or her, and you know how I have clung to all that belonged to my wife. Swallow, sister! sweet sister swallow! indeed and indeed, we were really happy then.

II. THE THEORY OF HISTORY

Adams' theory of history is really a philosophy and a theory of human nature; it is wholly indefensible and perverse, and we should be hard pressed to understand how a man of genius could conceive it if we had not some understanding of the history

[11] *Letters of Henry Adams*, op. cit., p. 333.
[12] Ibid. p. 490.
[13] Ibid. p. 638.

which is largely responsible for his state of mind. Briefly, he possessed the acute moral sense of New England to which I have already referred and the New Englander's need to read the significance of every event which he saw. But he was of the Ockhamist tradition; and as for the Mathers, so for him, the significance could not reside within the event but must reside back of it. He would scarcely have put it this way, and he might have denied the paternity of Ockham; but he belonged to a moral tradition which had taken its morality wholly on faith for so long that it had lost the particular kind of intelligence and perception necessary to read the universe for what it is; and had developed instead a passion to read the universe for what it means, as a system of divine shorthand or hieroglyphic, as a statement of ultimate intentions.

He had no faith, however, and hence he could not believe that there was anything back of the event: the event was merely isolated and impenetrable. Yet he possessed the kind of mind which drove him to read every event with a kind of allegorical precision; and since every event was isolated and impenetrable, he read in each new event the meaning that the universe is meaningless. Meaning had been a function of faith; and faith had been faith not only in God and his decalogue but in a complete cosmology and chronology, that is, in all of Revelation; and if any part of this system was injured, every part was destroyed. The discoveries of geologists and astronomers caused him indescribable suffering and made it utterly impossible that he should examine dispassionately the moral nature of man.

I shall deal later with Adams' view of the Middle Ages, thus reversing his chronology. He saw the twentieth century as an age of multiplicity or chaos, in which man was forced to recognize the confusion of his own understanding; the twentieth century was thus a falling away from the late twelfth century, in which man had enjoyed the illusion of a unified mind, society, and cosmology.

It is simplest, perhaps, to begin with his way of looking at human character; and that particular topic immediately indicates something of his relationship to James. In the *Education* he wrote:[14]

Henry James had not yet taught the world to read a volume for the pleasure of seeing the lights of his burning-glass turned on alternate sides of the same figure.

I have shown in writing of James, how the Jamesian burning-glass thus employed resulted very commonly in the reader's being left with two or more versions of both character and action and with no way of making any selection; how it resulted, briefly, in an ambiguity which might in certain novels amount to a perfect opacity. It is a question, as a rule, to what extent James realized and intended this opacity, to what extent he may have succeeded in mystifying himself as well as his reader, but so far as Adams is concerned, such opacity is a virtue, for it renders the only perceptible truth in experience. Character after character in the *Education* is described as incomprehensible; Adams appears to make the discovery in each instance as if it were cause for astonishment; but eventually one notes that the discovery with regard to nearly every person encountered is inevitable, that it proceeds from a fixed habit of mind and results in a literary mannerism. Of Garibaldi he wrote:[15]

Adams had the chance to look this sphinx in the eyes, and, for five minutes, to watch him like a wild animal, at the moment of his greatest achievement and most splendid action. One saw a quiet-featured, quiet-voiced man in a red flannel shirt; absolutely impervious; a type of which Adams knew nothing. Sympathetic it was, and one felt that it was simple; one suspected even that it might be childlike, but could form no guess of its intelligence. In his own eyes Garibaldi might be a Napoleon or a Spartacus; in the eyes of Cavour he might become a Condottiere; in the eyes of history he might, like the rest of the world, be only the vigorous player in the game he did not understand. The student was none the wiser.

This compound nature of patriot and pirate had illumined Italian

14 Op. cit., p. 163.
15 Ibid., pp. 94-5.

history from the beginning, and was no more intelligible to itself than to a young American who had no experience in double natures. In the end, if the "Autobiography" tells truth, Garibaldi saw and said that he did not understand his own acts; that he had been an instrument; that he had served the purposes of the class he least wanted to help; yet in 1860 he thought himself the revolution anarchic, Napoleonic, and his ambition was unbounded. What should a young Bostonian have made of a character like this, internally alive with childlike fancies, and externally, quiet, simple, and almost innocent; uttering with apparent conviction the usual commonplaces of popular politics that all politicians use as the small change of their intercourse with the public; but never betraying a thought?

Precisely this class of mind was to be the toughest problem of Adams's practical life, but he could never make anything of it. The lesson of Garibaldi, as education, seemed to teach the extreme complexity of extreme simplicity; but one could have learned this from a glow-worm. One did not need the recollection of the low-voiced, simple-mannered seafaring captain of Genoese adventurers and Sicilian brigands, supping in the July heat and Sicilian dirt and revolutionary clamor, among the barricaded streets of insurgent Palermo, merely in order to remember that simplicity is complex.

One might at first consideration decide that Garibaldi was incomprehensible to Adams merely because he was an extremely foreign type; but Adams was convinced that Garibaldi could understand nothing of himself; and Adams could do no better with Seward, who was surely a native American product:[10]

A slouching, slender figure; a head like a wise macaw; a beaked nose; shaggy eyebrows; unorderly hair and clothes; hoarse voice; offhand manner; free talk and perpetual cigar, offered a new type —of western New York—to fathom; a type in one way simple because it was only double—political and personal; but complex because the political had become nature, and no one could tell which was the mask and which was the features. At table, among friends, Mr. Seward threw off restraint, or seemed to throw it off, in reality, while in the world he threw it off, like a politician, for effect. In both cases, he chose to appear as a free talker, who loathed pomposity and enjoyed a joke; but how much was nature and how much was mask, he was himself too simple a nature to know.

[10] Ibid. p. 104.

And if one is to trust the testimony of the chapter entitled *Eccentricity*, he found the entire English nation so impenetrably obscure that they provided him with material for little save satirical bewilderment.

And he found the same obscurity in events, whether major or minor:[17]

That Sumner and Hoare, the two New Englanders in great position who happened to be the two persons most necessary for his success at Washington, should be the first victims of Grant's lax rule, must have had some meaning for Adams's education, if Adams could only have understood what it was. He studied, but failed.

And since he was sure of the impossibility of understanding anything, he was sure above all of the impossibility of understanding his function as a teacher at Harvard:[18]

He never knew whether his colleagues shared his doubts about their own utility. Unlike himself, they knew more or less their business. He could not tell his scholars that history glowed with social virtue; the professor of Chemistry cared not a chemical atom whether society was virtuous or not. Adams could not pretend that medieval society proved evolution; the Professor of Physics smiled at evolution. Adams was glad to dwell on the virtues of the Church and the triumphs of its art: the Professor of Political Economy had to treat them as a waste of force. They knew what they had to teach; he did not. They might perhaps be frauds without knowing it; but he knew certainly nothing else of himself. He could teach his students nothing; he was only educating himself at their cost.

The mere sequence of these quotations should indicate the extent to which this state of mind had become a mechanical affair, habitual and unquestioned. The passages in question are not quoted from passages of argument which clarify them in the text; they are essentially as unexplained in the original text as in that of the present essay. Nowhere does Adams, for example, so much as look at the reasons traditionally offered for teaching history, to say nothing of trying to find any new ones;

[17] Ibid. p. 279.
[18] Ibid. p. 306.

394

he merely asserts that it is fraudulent to pretend to teach history. Nowhere does he examine the validity of the view of art attributed to the Professor of Economics; he merely opposes it to his own interest in art, as if by virtue of its existence it were indiscutable. One feels that if he had gone to the zoo, he would have returned in all philosophical seriousness with the report: "I saw a giraffe: but the farmer beside me denied the existence of such an animal." His discussion never gets very far beyond this kind of statement.

He finds the problem of judging works of art equally incomprehensible, and in the chapter of the *Education* entitled *Dilettantism*, he tells a story which is supposed to demonstrate his thesis. He tells of going to an auction and buying a drawing, which F. T. Palgrave had recommended to him as surely by Rafael and as having a good deal of intrinsic excellence. After buying the drawing, he submitted it to various other experts and found them in wide disagreement as to its authenticity and as to its virtues. The moral is, that one cannot form any valid judgments about a work of art.

The story is amusingly told, and makes excellent gossip, but the purpose to which it is put betrays an almost childish mentality. The sketch was, in the first place, a working draft of a fragment of a picture, probably done in a moment and the next day discarded. It was not a finished work of art, and the impossibility of identifying the workmanship to a certainty would be manifest. Further, the question of authorship and the question of excellence are quite distinct from each other. Adams' discovery that two critics can disagree about the value of a work of art—let us assume that we have a finished work—is surely nothing to astonish us. We may assume that a given masterpiece—let us say *Macbeth*—has a certain absolute value and perhaps certain real flaws as well, and that critics will differ in their approximation of a true judgment of the work in proportion to their own imperfections of native ability, education, and capacity for effort; or we may assume that every man's judgment is right for himself, and that all judgments are relative, as Adams repeatedly states. The first theory will account for the persistence of great reputations as well as for difference of opinion; the second will offer an alternative explanation for difference of opinion but for nothing more. Throughout *Mont Saint-Michel and Chartres* he insists that the judgment of art is wholly relative, at the same time that the insistence causes him deep regret. He prefers the older tower of Chartres cathedral to the later, and as far as one can judge from the photographs the preference is certainly sound; but he cannot defend the preference. He apologizes, and says that after all the later tower was better for the people who made it and may be better for his reader: a position which is defensible, needless to say, only if one is willing to push it to its unmistakable conclusion, and assert that the latest roadside horror is better for its builders than either tower and may be better for the reader. There is no defensible compromise in this matter between a thorough relativism and a thorough absolutism.

Adams appears to have felt that modern science had destroyed the last possibility of human understanding, and his later writing is largely the record of an effort to bring scientific ideas to bear upon his problem. He found, first, that modern science made for confusion; and later he tried to find in scientific principles an exact formulation of the reasons why we are moving into greater confusion and of the rate of movement.

He sought in the findings of the 19th century geologists and in the theories of Darwin a new cosmology, to replace the old cosmology which these findings and others had destroyed. His discussion of his geological and evolutionary adventures is as amusing as his account of the investigation of the drawing; but it is incoherent, an assertion and exhibition of confusion, rather than explanation of it; and it is notable mainly for the anguish underlying the wit. In this department of his experience, as in others, his frustrated passion for precise understanding drove him toward the dogmatic certainty, to be achieved at any sacrifice of rationality, that no understanding of any kind was possible:[19]

[19] Ibid., p. 225

396

He was ready to become anything but quiet. As though the world had not been enough upset in his time, he was eager to see it upset more. He had his wish, but he lost his hold on the results by trying to understand them.

His method, in general, is to leap nervously into the midst of a science of which he has no particular knowledge and worry a few details with a kind of irritated persistence:[20]

Objections fatal to one mind are futile to another, and as far as concerned the article, the matter ended there, although the glacial epoch remained a misty region in the young man's Darwinism. Had it been the only one, he would not have fretted about it; but uniformity often worked queerly and sometimes did not work as Natural Selection at all. Finding himself at a loss for some single figure to illustrate the Law of Natural Selection, Adams asked Sir Charles for the simplest case of uniformity on record. Much to his surprise Sir Charles told him that certain forms, like Terebratula, appeared to be identical from the beginning to the end of geological time. Since this was altogether too much uniformity and much too little selection, Adams gave up the attempt to begin at the beginning and tried starting at the end—himself. Taking for granted that the vertebrates would serve his purpose, he asked Sir Charles to introduce him to the first vertebrate. Infinitely to his bewilderment, Sir Charles informed him that the first vertebrate was a very respectable fish, among the earliest of all fossils, which had lived, and whose bones were still reposing, under Adams' own favorite Abbey on Wenlock Edge . . . *Pteraspis*, a cousin of the sturgeon, and whose kingdom, according to Sir Roderick Murchison, was called Siluria. Life began and ended there. Behind that horizon lay only the Cambrian, without vertebrates or any other organism except a few shell-fish. On the further verge of the Cambrian rose the crystalline rocks from which every trace of organic existence had been erased.

Now whatever the virtues or defects of the doctrine of Natural Selection, Lyell's statement regarding Terebratula would scarcely damage it; an elementary knowledge of biology is sufficient to give a theoretic explanation of such a phenomenon. And when Adams was in search of his earliest vertebrate ancestor, and was

[20] Ibid., p. 227.

397

assuming that one would be shown to him, there was no particular justification for his being infinitely bewildered when a particular ancestor was indicated. Nor was there cause for astonishment in the ancestor's being a fish; for the fish are the lowest vertebrates. Nor is a cousin to a sturgeon a perfectly respectable fish, for the sturgeon is one of the most primitive fishes surviving. Nor is there cause for astonishment in the fact that the next age preceding, the Cambrian, offered nothing more advanced than shell-fish; for the shell fish, Mollusca and Arthropoda, represent the two phyla most highly developed before the chordates. I know little of the history of geology and biology, but most of this perfectly elementary information was probably available to Adams at the time of his original bewilderment and was unquestionably available to him at the time of his writing the *Education*. His procedure is to be witty rather than intelligent, and, having established a state of confusion for the sake of the wit, to deduce his spiritual suffering from it: that is the literary process; the original psychological process is less simple, as I have shown. The result is a certain iridescence of emotional surface but precisely nothing of sanity. The bewilderment is imposed on the experience, arbitrarily and at every point. What we get is not a philosophical experience, but an emotional experience: a vision of chaos which is cosmological, chronological, and theological.

He draws from this experience the only moral possible to a man in such a condition, the moral that truth is indecipherable:[21]

As he lay on Wenlock Edge, with the sheep nibbling the grass close about him as they or their betters had nibbled the grass—or whatever was there to nibble—in the Silurian kingdom of *Pteraspis*, he seemed to have fallen on an evolution far more wonderful than that of the fishes. He did not like it; he could not account for it; and he determined to stop it. Never since the day of his *Limulus* ancestry had any of his ascendants thought thus. Their modes of thought might be many, but their thought was one. Out of his mil-

[21] Ibid., pp. 231-2.

lions of millions of ancestors, back to the Cambrian mollusks, every one had probably lived and died in the illusion of Truths which did not amuse him, and which had never changed. Henry Adams was the first in an infinite series to discover and admit to himself that he really did not care whether truth was, or was not, true. He did not even care that it should be proved true, unless the process were new and amusing. He was a Darwinian for fun.

From the beginning of history, this attitude had been branded as criminal—worse than crime—sacrilege! Society punished it ferociously and justly, in self-defense. Mr. Adams the father looked on it as moral weakness; it annoyed him; but it did not annoy him nearly so much as it annoyed his son, who had no need to learn from Hamlet the fatal effect of the pale cast of thought on enterprise great or small.

Adams, in brief, did not care for truth, unless it was amusing; for he was a modern nihilist, and hence a hedonist or nothing. But his predicament nevertheless annoyed him, for it frustrated action, just as it did for Melville's *Pierre,* and Adams was a New Englander, to whom action and the comprehension of his action were constitutionally necessary. The entire perversity, the inconsequence, and the tragedy of Adams' predicament are indicated in this passage. And the Pteraspis, elevated in this manner into a symbol, remains one throughout the rest of the book:[22]

History is a tangled skein that one may take up at any point, and break when one has unravelled enough; but complexity precedes evolution. The pteraspis grins horribly from the closed entrance.

The Pteraspis appears to Adams to grin horribly precisely because the entrance is closed, or because Adams thinks it closed. Adams is not content, even provisionally, to study his world as it is, in the hope of arriving at a working knowledge of it; there is no knowledge, for Adams, unless it is a part of a complete system, deriving from an acceptable definition of the Absolute:[23]

[22] Ibid., p. 302.
[23] Ibid., p. 226.

Ignorance must always begin at the beginning. Adams must inevitably have begun by asking Sir Isaac for an intelligible reason why the apple fell to the ground. He did not know enough to be satisfied with the fact. The Law of Gravitation was so-and-so, but what was Gravitation? and he would have been thrown quite off his base if Sir Isaac had answered that he did not know.

This neurotic and childish impatience, amounting almost to insolence, is the final fruit of the Christian doctrine in New England; the patience and humility of an Aristotle or a Newton are incomprehensible.

This state of mind grew on him with the years. It is obvious above all in his comments upon his later discovery of twentieth century psychology:[24]

Unfortunately, the pursuit of ignorance in silence had, by this time, led the weary pilgrim into such mountains of ignorance that he could no longer see any path whatever, and could not even understand a signpost . . . He gathered from the books that the psychologists had, in a few cases, distinguished several personalities in the same mind, each conscious and constant, individual and exclusive . . . To his mind, the compound Ψυχή took at once the form of a bicycle rider, mechanically balancing himself by inhibiting all his inferior personalities, and sure to fall into the sub-conscious chaos below, if one of his inferior personalities got on top. The only absolute truth was the sub-conscious chaos below, which everyone could feel when he sought it.

Whether the psychologists admitted it or not, mattered little to the student who, by the law of his profession, was engaged in studying his own mind. On him, the effect was surprising. He woke up with a shudder as though he had himself fallen off his bicycle. If his mind were really this sort of magnet, mechanically dispersing its lines of force when it went to sleep, and mechanically orienting them when it woke up—which was normal, the dispersion or the orientation? The mind, like the body, kept its unity unless it happened to lose its balance, and the professor of physics, who slipped on a pavement and hurt himself, knew no more than an idiot what knocked him down, though he did know—what the idiot could hardly do—that his normal condition was idiocy, or want of balance, and that his sanity was unstable artifice. His normal thought was dispersion, sleep, dream, inconsequence; the simultaneous action

[24] Ibid., pp. 433-4-5.

of different thought centers without central control. His artificial balance was acquired habit. He was an acrobat with a dwarf on his back, crossing a chasm on a slack-rope, and commonly breaking his neck.

By that path of newest science, one saw no unity ahead—nothing but a dissolving mind.

One should note, here, the emotional quality of much of the language; the feeling is that of the romantic tradition. The bicycle rider balances himself "mechanically" (that is, by a base and contemptible trick); his balance is "artificial" (the artificial and the mechanical are roughly equivalent in romantic thought); and the balance is acquired "habit" (habit, in romantic terminology, does not refer to a psychological fact, but to a spiritual vice: habit is mechanical and imperceptive behavior). The balance keeps the rider safe from his inferior personalities and from the chaos, and one might deduce from this that the balance is valuable; but this is not true, for since the balance is artificial, and there is really a chaos, the chaos is the only absolute truth, and, one guesses, one might as well immerse oneself in it as soon as possible.

I do not know how foolish it may seem to many of my readers for me to state my objections to these ideas more explicitly still, but my acquaintance with the minds of my literary contemporaries is extensive, and I am sure that many of them derive an important part of their thought from Adams, though many of them do not know it; and to my great regret I have found that many of the most brilliant of them understand simple matters only with the greatest of difficulty.

I should therefore like to add my belief that a balance which is artificial, or which is, in my terms, a habit formed by willed perseverance deriving from rational understanding of the need for it, and which preserves one from madness, is in its own nature a good; for madness is in its own nature and quite obviously an evil. A morality which preserves one from this loss of balance is defensible beyond argument by virtue simply of the fact that it so preserves one; and a morality such as that of Adams is evil, simply by virtue of the fact that it aims at loss

401

of balance. One does not need Divine Revelation to know this; a single look at a psychopathic ward is sufficient. And once one has admitted the initial advantage of being sane, one will be forced to admit the additional advantages of being as sane, or as intelligent as possible; and a good deal of careful scrutiny may enable us to refine a very little upon the rough scheme of our initial morality. If one is conscious when awake and semi conscious when asleep, it is fair to assume that both conditions are normal at their proper times and to refrain from introducing mysteries into a universe which already contains two or three problems which no human ingenuity has been able to solve.

Adams appears to point ahead to such writers as Pound, Joyce, and Eliot, in this passage; to those who have found the dissolving mind the normal mind, and who have sought to exploit it at the expense of the other. He gives the impression here that he would explore this mind because there is nothing else to do; but in a few other places he indicates a belief, whether temporary or permanent, that the passive mind is the best medium for reaching truth: that is, he approximates a statement of Emersonian or Bergsonian mysticism.

In telling of his early life, he discusses his youthful contemplation of the Concord faith with some amusement:[25]

He never reached Concord, and to Concord Church he, like the rest of mankind who accepted a material universe, remained always an insect, or something much lower—a man.

Yet he tells how a little later he came to understand Beethoven[26] by listening to him passively and inattentively in a German music hall, and he appears to draw the moral that this was the best way to arrive at an understanding. And in one of the last chapters, in discussing the development of modern science, he writes[27] an extensive passage which is purely Emersonian, not only in its irrationality and its mysticism, but in its very vocabulary as well:

[25] Ibid., p. 63.
[26] Ibid., p. 80.
[27] Ibid. p. 485.

Very slowly the accretion of these new forces, chemical and mechanical, grew in volume until they acquired sufficient mass to take the place of the old religious science, substituting their attraction for the attractions of the *Civitas Dei,* but the process remained the same. Nature, not mind, did the work that the sun does on the planets. Man depended more and more absolutely on forces other than his own, and on instruments which superseded his senses. Bacon foretold it: "Neither the naked hand nor the understanding, left to itself, can effect much. It is by instruments and helps that the work is done." Once done, the mind resumed its illusion, and society forgot its impotence; but no one better than Bacon knew its tricks, and for his true followers science always meant self-restraint, obedience, sensitiveness to impulse from without. "Non fingendum aut excogitandum sed inveniendum quid Natura faciat aut ferat."

The success of this method staggers belief, and even today can be treated by history only as a miracle of growth, like the sports of nature. Evidently a new kind of mind had appeared. Certain men merely held out their hands—like Newton, watched an apple; like Franklin, flew a kite; like Watt played with a tea-kettle—and great forces of nature stuck to them as if she were playing ball.

The foolishness of this passage is obvious, but I hesitate to leave it undefined. The actions of Newton, Franklin, and Watt bore fruit, I suspect, because of previous thought which illuminated the particular adventures. Franklin, in fact, or so I seem to remember it, was flying a kite to verify a theory; he was not merely flying it for fun. The rapid advance of science in the past two centuries is due to the accumulation of knowledge and the improvement of machinery. The more one knows, the more rapidly one can learn; and the better one's instruments, the better the instruments one can make. The process is cumulative and not in itself mysterious. Bacon was scarcely the prophet of modern science that he is popularly supposed to have been, and had small comprehension of the best scientific thought of his day; but his two statements are harmless enough, the first being a recognition of the need of instruments, the second a recognition of the existence of objective truth.

Explicit statements of this kind are rare and fleeting in the *Education,* and it is possible that I over-estimate the importance

of this fringe of Adams' thought; for certainly it did little to mitigate the desolation of spirit of his later years. He was not an
enthusiast, as was Emerson, and he found in this doctrine no discernible trace of Emersonian beatitude. But in 1909 he wrote in
a letter to Margaret Chanler:[28]

I like best Bergson's frank surrender to the superiority of Instinct
over Intellect. You know how I have preached that principle, and
how I have studied the facts of it. In fact I once wrote a whole
volume—called my *Education*—which no one ever saw, and which
you must some day look into,—borrow William James's copy, in
hopes that he may have marginally noted his contempt for me,—in
order to recall how Education may be shown to consist in following
the intuitions of Instinct. Loeb calls it *Tropism,* I believe; which
means that a mother likes to nurse her own child.

If he came as late as 1909 to feel, however, that in the *Education* he had discovered a way of life, there is small evidence
of such feeling in the book itself, or elsewhere in his writing,
before or after. Nothing was comprehensible; each event and
fact was unique and impenetrable; the universe was a chaos of
meaningless and unrelated data, equivalent to each other in value
because there was no way of evaluating anything. Comprehension, judgment, and choice being nullified, there was no reason
for action, physical or spiritual, and life was mere stagnation:[29]

The outlook lacked hope. The object of travel had become more
and more dim, ever since the gibbering ghost of the Civil Law had
been locked in the dark closet as far back as 1860. Noah's dove had
not searched the earth for resting-places so carefully, or with so little
success. Any spot on land or water satisfies a dove who wants and
finds rest; but no perch suits a dove of sixty years old, alone and
uneducated, who has lost his taste even for olives. To this, also, the
young may be driven, as education, and the lesson fails in humor;
but it may be worth knowing to some of them that the planet offers
hardly a dozen places where an elderly man can pass a week alone
without ennui, and none at all where he can pass a year.

[28] *Letters of Henry Adams,* op. cit., p. 524.
[29] *Education,* op. cit., p. 357.

In his old age, he joined his only political party, the Conservative Christian Anarchists, a party of which the only other member was his young friend Bay Lodge. His last letters, in their despair, malice, and frantic triviality are very painful reading.

I have been tracing the disintegration of a mind. Yet the moral sense persisted, strong as ever, but running amuck for lack of guidance. Adams, as I have shown, was as passionate an allegorist as Mather had been; instead of seeing God's meaning in every event, he saw the meaninglessness of a godless universe, but with a Calvinistic intensity of vision. He had, as he confessed in writing of Henry James the "obsession of idée fixe." And not only had he the passion to see his allegorical vision, but he had the true Calvinist's passion to provide his vision with his own theology. He wrote:[30]

From cradle to grave this problem of running order through chaos, direction through space, discipline through freedom, unity through multiplicity, has always been, and must always be, the task of education.

Yet the problem, though one was bound to endeavor to solve it, could never be solved in fact: the solution must be a delusion:[31]

Chaos was the law of nature; Order was the dream of man.

More than once he thought he saw his solution in permitting himself, as T. S. Eliot would have us do, to be determined by what he took to be his time, by what in fact was casual impulse:[32]

To him, the current of his time was to be his current, lead where it might . . . he insisted on maintaining his absolute standards; on aiming at ultimate Unity.

This Emersonian disguise of his own disintegration, however, was something that he could not consistently maintain: his dis-

[30] Ibid., p. 12.
[31] Ibid., p. 451.
[32] Ibid., p. 232.

integration was not a voyage, governed by absolute standards, on a supernatural current in the direction of Unity; it was merely disintegration. And the only way to find Order in it, was to discover the reason for the disintegration and chart its rate.

He was too good a determinist and too devoutly sorry for himself to seek any part of the reason in himself, and partly because of these facts, and partly because he was committed to an obscurantistic view of history, he failed to seek it in any segment of history definite and limited enough to imply that the difficulty was due to human error that might in some measure be corrected. Like a true Calvinist and a true determinist, he turned at once, for his answer, to the Nature of the Universe, and sought to show that the whole universe, as a single mechanism, was running down. The cosmological scope of the doctrine appears most fully in the volume of essays posthumously published as *The Degradation of the Democratic Dogma;* but in *Mont Saint-Michel and Chartres* and in the *Education* he seeks to illustrate the tendency by defining the difference between two extremes of civilization:[33]

Any schoolboy could see that man as a force must be measured by motion, from a fixed point. Psychology helped here by suggesting a unit—the point of history when man held the highest idea of himself in a unified universe. Eight or ten years of study had led Adams to think he might use the century 1150-1250, expressed in Amiens cathedral and the Works of Thomas Aquinas, as the unit from which he might measure motion down to his own time, without assuming anything as true or untrue, except relation. The movement might be studied at once in philosophy and mechanics. Setting himself to the task, he began a volume which he mentally knew as *Mont Saint-Michel and Chartres: A Study of Thirteenth Century Unity.* From that point he proposed to fix a position for himself which he could label: *The Education of Henry Adams: A Study of Twentieth Century Multiplicity.* With the help of these two points of relation, he hoped to project his lines forward and backward indefinitely, subject to correction from anyone who should know better.

We have seen the manner in which Adams demonstrated twentieth century multiplicity; and as I have already said, it

[33] Ibid., p. 435.

seems to me pointless to invent difficulties in a universe in which irreduceable difficulties flourish. The philosophical problem, as I see it, is to define the various possible mysteries, and where choice is possible, to choose those which eliminate the greatest possible number of the remainder; and to keep as scientific, as Aristotelian, an eye as possible upon the conditions of our life as we actually find ourselves forced to live it, so that we may not make the mistake of choosing a mystery which shall, in proportion as it influences our actions, violate those conditions and lead to disaster. For example, a strictly deterministic philosophy, whether materialistic or pantheistic, and no matter how enticing the cosmology or theology from which it may derive, can lead only toward automatism in action, and automatism is madness. And similarly, a strictly nominalistic view of the universe can lead only to the confusion and paralysis reached by Adams; whereas a certain amount of understanding, small no doubt in the eye of God and of the philosopher, but very useful in itself, is actually possible. If we find that a theory violates our nature, we have then learned something about our nature; and we have learned that there is something wrong with the theory. When Dr. Johnson demonstrated the real existence of the wall by kicking it, he employed a philosophical argument far from subtle but absolutely unanswerable. The philosopher who needs further convincing may try driving his car against the wall, and at as high a rate of speed as he may feel the ingenuity of his philosophy to require: he may, in this manner, learn something of the nature of absolute truth. Adams quotes Poincaré[34] as saying that it is meaningless to ask whether Euclidean geometry is true, but that it will remain more convenient than its rivals. I am no mathematician and can only guess what this means; but I surmise that it means that a bridge built by Euclidean geometry may conceivably stand, whereas one built by a rival system will certainly fall. If this is true, I should be willing to accept the fact as perhaps a Divine Revelation regarding the nature of the physical universe and as a strong recommendation for the study of Euclidean geometry.

[34] Ibid., p. 455.

Some such intention as I have just recommended would appear to have motivated Aristotle and even Aquinas. I myself am not a Christian and I fear that I lack permanently the capacity to become one; but Aquinas's examination of the nature of man appears to me acute and extremely usable, and his disposition of theological difficulties perhaps the best disposition possible. Adams, however, is bent on proving the existence of a unified mind in the 13th century, because he is bent on proving that man has disintegrated since, and his discussion of Aquinas centers wholly in the theological difficulties, for he assumes that the philosophy derives from the theological solutions, whereas in reality the philosophy and the philosophical method derive very largely from Aristotle, who was a scientific observer and analyst and neither a Christian nor a theologian. And since the theological difficulties were real, and since the answers of Aquinas are less satisfactory to Adams than they must have been to Aquinas, Adams asserts that the entire structure, philosophy as well as theology, depends from faith, and "if Faith fails, Heaven is lost." And as we have seen, when Adams says that Heaven is lost, he means that everything is lost.

The unity which Adams finds, therefore, in the 13th century is a unity of faith, which results, he seems to believe, in a unity of social and artistic purpose. He is aware of the diversity of philosophical views, but he does not take it seriously, for philosophy is not a serious matter while there is faith, if indeed it can be shown to be a serious matter at all. Yet the controversy over universals was essentially a controversy over the very existence of the rational faculty itself: had there been no Aquinas to slow the spread of nominalism, to steady the thought of the period with a little of that rarest form of profundity curiously called common sense, it seems highly improbable that the Church as we know it could long have survived, for the Church rests solidly on a recognition, whether explicit or implicit, of the reality of ideas; Faith without intellectual unity can scarcely maintain its own unity or any other for long, as the history of the Reformation seems to indicate. Within the Church itself there was a diversity of views on fundamental subjects, a diversity of the most perilous kind; and the unity of the 13th century Church, in so far as it was achieved, was due far less to the spirit of the age than to the mind of Thomas Aquinas.

And to what extent can one fairly say that the Church provided religious unity for Europe as a whole? As one proceeded downward from the great doctors of the Church, through various intellectual and social levels, the religion became simpler and simpler, and ultimately more and more pagan. If even a small part of the conclusions of the folk-lorists of the past fifty years can be trusted, the Stone Age persisted as a solid sub-stratum but a little below the surface of Christianity. The great Church of the thirteenth century, as we know it in its literary and artistic remains, was the product of a relatively small class, and of a class confined to the centers of culture. Behind the cities lay isolated and small communities, living on the land, and encountering the outside world for the most part only as they were devastated by war. The last great period of the Stone Age, a period of considerable artistic development and of wide and persistent religious beliefs, had lasted perhaps twenty thousand years, and had formed the peasant mind, which is tenacious, whereas Christianity in most of Europe was a matter of a very few hundred years. One can learn something of the extent to which most of the population must have been isolated from the civilization of the time by reading the first six chapters of Adams' own history, or by reading the third chapter of Macaulay. The life of the thirteenth century peasant was probably as primitive in every respect as had been the life of his ancestors in the caves and about the lakes, and was probably more fraught with peril and less provided with animal comforts.

Of political unity there was little. Between the death of Charlemagne and the rise of the centralized monarchies of the Renaissance the system was feudal, which is to say chaotic, irresponsible, and brutal. In what sense can the mass of the feudal lords be called Christian? They called themselves Christian, but their Christianity was that neither of Christ nor of any doctor of the Church. Of the entire class perhaps Richard of England is as high a representative as any, and his ideals were not Christian but chivalric; they were vainglorious and merciless, although heroic in their way and impressive in retrospect. The great literary expression of this group of men is the *Song of Roland*, a beautiful poem, which Adams praises because of its strong simplicity and directness, qualities which he associates rightly with the chivalric ideal; but these qualities are the result less of a masterly understanding of human nature than of the exclusion from consideration of most of what is important in human nature. Even George Herbert is a greater poet than Turoldus, as he is a wiser and more civilized man.

And if Richard and Turoldus came close to realizing even this simple ideal, it is wise to remember that few others did so. The medieval baron or prince was in general brutal and unscrupulous; to compare the great industrialists of our own period to these their predecessors is a very harsh judgment, I suspect, in spite of the crimes of our period. Part of our dissatisfaction with our time is due to one of the few really valuable heirlooms left us by the Romantic movement, our sense of social responsibility. We see the injustices and misfortunes suffered by the poor; we feel that much can and should be done to mitigate them, and although we have done a great deal, we feel that we have not done enough, for we see the evils remaining and are embittered. That we have done a good deal, however, anyone may discover by a moderately attentive reading of such writers as Chaucer, Defoe, and Dickens. Dickens was a reformer, and so may be suspected of overdrawing his picture, but Defoe and Chaucer merely depicted what they saw, with pity, but with no indignation; and if we may trust them, and others like them, the life of most of the lower classes on the land and in the cities equally, and perhaps well into the nineteenth century, beyond all argument in the middle ages and in the Renaissance, was far more terrible than that of any considerable number of persons in North America or in Western Europe during the twentieth century, even at the lowest ebbs of our social and economic life.

I do not ignore the wars of the twentieth century when I say this, and having had no personal experience of them, I may be foolish to speak of them. But if my literary contemporaries would read a few full and leisurely histories, such as those, for example, of Motley, which deal with the wars of the Renaissance or with the wars of the Middle Ages, they might suspect that wars are not much worse than they were: what our ancestors lacked in equipment they made up in thoroughness, and the long protraction of the wars probably caused a suffering greater in proportion to the population of those times than any caused by the wars of our day. In fact the mere figures relating to the increase of population during the past century and a half are proof in themselves that the basic hardships of life have decreased beyond our imagining.

I do not wish to give the impression that I believe our civilization is perfect. We do not enjoy a high degree of civilization, and I believe that probably we never shall; the race is not capable of it. But Adams' view of the Middle Ages, which has been adopted by Eliot and his followers, is merely a version of the Romantic Golden Age; the thirteenth century as they see it never existed, and their conviction that major intellectual and spiritual achievement is possible only in such a Utopia can do nothing but paralyze human effort. Much of the unity and simple strength which Adams so admires in the thirteenth century was merely the result of callous indifference to horrors worse than any the twentieth century has ever known. I have the greatest of respect for the mind of Aquinas, and but little, I fear, for many of the most influential minds of the twentieth century; but I respectfully submit that had Aquinas felt himself determined by the stupidity and confusion of his time, he would probably have accomplished very little. He endeavored to learn as much as possible from the best minds of his time and of the two thousand years, more or less, preceding; and having learned that, he set out to do the best that he could with it. Adams arrived at his view of the middle ages by concentrating on a few great products of literature, thought, and architecture; ignoring everything else, he asserted that these were the thirteenth century. He arrived at his view of the twentieth century by reversing the process. He thus deduced that the world was deteriorating, and so found a justification for his own state of mind.

The Cosmology which expands Adams' view of history to its ultimate generality is to be found in *The Degradation of the Democratic Dogma*. The essays were written during the latter part of Adams' life. In his letters he frequently refers to them as jokes, perpetrated to stir up his slow-witted colleagues; but he also refers to them seriously, and there is every reason to believe that he took them seriously. They merely enlarge upon the theory which we have been examining, and which is stated more briefly in the latter part of the *Education*; and although they are sufficiently astonishing in their irrationality, I do not know that they are much worse in this respect than the two books thus far considered.

The most important of these essays is *A Letter to American Teachers of History*. It begins with the unquestioning acceptance of two theological principles, both the product of the age which he is endeavoring to prove to be one of ultimate confusion: the Law of the Dissipation of Energy, and the assumption that man is governed by physical laws. Whether we regard Adams as the contemner of his own age, or as the apostle of scepticism, this acceptance is sufficiently startling. It can be understood only if we remember that he was the heir of the Puritans and that sooner or later his heritage was certain to overtake him completely. In order to prove the impossibility of absolute truth, he had to start from absolute truth and create what he could believe for the moment to be a comprehensive system.

The Revelation discloses that Energy is being dissipated steadily in a godless universe: the origin of Energy in a godless universe, and the question of how this process, which must end in time, has had no temporal beginning, but has been undergoing a steady process of diminution from all eternity—these difficulties are never met. The end is certain; the beginning does not matter. The principle explains why heat ends in cold, life in death, motion in station. And the principle once established, it follows that each succeeding manifestation of energy is inferior to the last. Man is thus inferior to the early animals, and civilization is a process of decay. The emergence of human reason during this process does not trouble Adams in the least: Reason, as we have seen, leads only to confusion and inaction and is of no help in the attainment of truth; this in spite of the fact that Adams probably believed that he was using his own reason in arriving at the truths which he elucidates. Reason is a degraded form of will:[35]

Reason can be only another phase of the energy earlier known as Instinct or Intuition; and if this be admitted as the stem-history of the Mind as far back as the eocene lemur, it must be admitted for all forms of Vital Energy back to the vegetables and perhaps even to the crystals. In the absence of any definite break in the series, all must be endowed with energy equivalent to will. . . . Already the anthropologists have admitted man to be specialized beyond hope of further variation, so that, as an energy, he must be treated as a weakened Will—an enfeebled vitality—a degraded potential. He cannot himself deny that his highest Will-power, whether individual or social, must have proved itself by his highest variation, which was incontrovertibly his act of transforming himself from a hypothetical eocene lemur,—whatever such a creature may have been,—into men speaking elaborately inflected language. This staggering but self-evident certainty requires many phases of weakening Will-power to intervene in the process of subsidence into the reflective, hesitating, relatively passive stage called Reason; so that in the end, if the biologists insist on imposing their law on the anthropologists, while at the same time refusing to admit a break in the series, the historian will have to define his profession as the science of human degradation.

We thus see that life has proceeded from the energetic form of the rock crystal, to the passive and listless form which it manifests, for example, in the United States in the twentieth century; and since this process is proven a process of degradation, the emergence of the human mind with its various complex creations, is necessarily a symptom of degeneration. Human Reason can scarcely go farther, or so one might think for a moment. But actually there is one further deduction, and Adams makes it in the course of the essay. Life has deteriorated from the energetic form of the rock crystal, through all the forms of vegetation, of animal life, and of civilization, the highest form of civilization

[35] *The Degradation of the Democratic Dogma*, by Henry Adams, Macmillan, 1919, pp. 192-5.

having existed in the thirteenth century; and the energy of the universe must continue to dissipate itself until life will be reduced again to rock-crystals. This is an unbroken process of deterioration; and it provides the cosmological frame for Adams' theory of history.

Man's deterioration thus becomes a matter of cosmology, of Revealed Truth, and there is no help for the matter. The best thing man can do is trust his instincts, for they are worth more than his reason, and they will guide him infallibly along the current of his time to progressively more complex degeneracy. Art is a human function, and will be governed by the general law. Art also is deteriorating, but it must deteriorate to express honestly the general deterioration of man; and we thus arrive at one of the central ideas of T. S. Eliot, which has been one of the most influential of the past twenty years, at least among the more scholarly and intellectual of our poets and critics. At the end of *Mont Saint-Michel and Chartres* we find the matter stated in Adams' own words:[36]

Art had to be confused in order to express confusion; but perhaps it was truest so.

If the chaos of the subconscious is the only reality, and if the subject-matter of art determines the form of the work, then we have arrived at *Finnegans Wake* and the poetry of Pound and Eliot as the finest expression of civilization, that is to say, of degeneracy, although in some way which almost eludes me, we have left that other product of degeneracy, the Reason, a little way behind us in arriving at our goal.

III. THE WRITING OF HISTORY

I have dealt very harshly with the later work of Adams; I have stated my opinion that this work represents the radical disintegration of a mind. The mind, however, had been a great one, though its true greatness is suspected only by professional historians at

[36] *Mont Saint-Michel and Chartres,* by Henry Adams, Houghton Mifflin, p. 375.

the present time and is little more than suspected by most of them. Of the early work, the novels and the life of Randolph are trivial; but the life of Gallatin is still regarded by historians as one of the great works in American biography, and although it is long and heavily documented, and is very different from the bird's-eye views of biography which have been so popular during the past ten or fifteen years, it is a massive and distinguished work of literature. It has never gone into a second edition, I believe, and is very hard to obtain.

Lack of space forbids that I write of more than the history. The *History of the United States During the Administrations of Thomas Jefferson and James Madison*,[37] a work in nine volumes, has been reissued only once to my own inexpert knowledge; it is now out of print. All things considered, I suspect that it is the greatest historical work in English, with the probable exception of *The Decline and Fall of the Roman Empire*, although any such judgment by one who is not an expert scholar in a number of historical fields, as well as something of a critic of literature, must be very tentative.

The relationship of literary quality to historical scholarship in a work of this kind perhaps needs to be briefly considered. The historian such as Gibbon or Macaulay, one is inclined to suppose, examines his material to the best of his ability, and on the basis of that examination forms a fairly definite idea of the characters and actions involved. In this stage of his work, he is comparable to the novelist who has long meditated his characters and outlined his plot. The final literary form of the history represents an evaluation, a moral judgment, of the material which he has held in his mind. Such judgment is inevitable, even though the historian refrain completely from any didacticism: it resides in the very act of writing, and no historian, be he a good stylist or a bad, can escape it. The difference in this respect between a good stylist and a bad is merely that the good stylist knows what he is doing, and if he is a conscientious man, both as a scholar and as a stylist,

<hr>

[37] The latest edition, the one in my possession, and the only one I have seen, was published by Albert and Charles Boni in 1930. It is a great misfortune that the work is not available in some such edition as The Modern Library or The World's Classics.

can take every possible precaution to make his judgment sound; whereas the scholar who suffers from the delusion that he can be perfectly impersonal runs the risk at least of being uncritical of his style, that is of the ultimate and definitive boundary of his judgments. Professor Andrews, I believe, has expressed the theory that the historian should have no style; but by the Grace of God, or through God's just retribution, he has achieved the finest historical style with which I am acquainted this side of Adams—the average scholar is likely to be less fortunate unless he is guided by a more admirable doctrine.

The professional research scholar tends to distrust the historian of literary pretensions, such as Motley or Macaulay. The danger, apparently, is that such an historian runs the risk of devoting more attention to the second function which I have mentioned than to the first, and thus of creating something closer to historical fiction than to history. The danger, of course, is real, and the accusation has been levelled repeatedly at Gibbon, Macaulay, Motley, and Parkman, yet all survive; and the amateur such as myself cannot but wonder whether much of the criticism is not due merely to the fact that these writers have survived and have remained so long the objects of careful reading. That they are guilty of many sins I am sure, and that they suffer from the state of scholarship in their respective times or from the vicissitudes of their private lives is more than likely; but that they are guilty of more errors in proportion to their achievement than are many scholars of no great literary pretensions strikes me as much less certain, especially on those occasions when I have just put in a few hours reading what various scholars have written of each other. Certainly there is something to be said for the theory that the history of civilization can best be recounted by a man who is himself a distinguished product of civilization and who is therefore in a position to understand in some measure what civilization really is.

After examining the work of Adams' later years, one might expect him to be the greatest sinner of all in this particular manner, yet I should not be surprised to discover that he is the least; I have at any rate encountered fewer accusations against him than against the others, although this may be merely the result of his being the latest in time and the least subjected to scrutiny. He gives the impression of adhering very closely to his documents, and of judging them carefully and with a watchful attention to the possibility of his being prejudiced. If there is a constant prejudice in his history, in any wise comparable to the political bias of Hume or of Macaulay, it is a distrust of democratic procedure, a distrust which was to reach a state of violent exasperation in his later years. His fascination with confusion is already apparent, although in the history it is restrained; on the other hand, the confusion in the American government during the period which he treats was assuredly real, and it would be hard to convict him of over-emphasis or of drawing unwarranted conclusions.

In order to understand the literary achievement of this work, one needs, I think, to consider a few of the greatest historians in English preceding Adams: Hume, Robertson, Gibbon, Macaulay, Prescott, Motley, and Parkman will suffice.

Modern historiography in English may probably be said to begin with Hume's *History of England*, though it might well begin with Bacon's *Henry VII*, except for the gap in time between that work and the next important efforts. By modern standards, Hume was far from being a careful scholar, but his prose is remarkable both for its virtues and its defects: Hume adapted the style of eighteenth century prose at its best to the purposes of historiography, and he imposed that style so successfully upon historiographical tradition that its influence persisted longer in history than in any other field of literature. The virtues of the prose are its precision, its structure, and its dignity. Hume, in common with the best stylists of his century, possessed a command of the rhetorical possibilities of grammatical structure which diminished notably among the great writers of the century following. Accumulation, climax, antithesis, the ironical by-thrust; the exact identification of causal, temporal and other relations by means of grammatical form; perfect clarity at every moment in the process of difficult stylistic maneuvers; variety and precision of rhythm: such mastery is the norm of his style; he takes it for granted, as a concert pianist takes for granted the athletic proficiency of his fingers. Such a style is necessarily formal, and scarcely lends itself, except in the guise of the mock heroic, to the familiar narrative of the fictionist: it tends naturally toward the expository form and the ironic comment, and, in narrative, toward the heroic.

Hume's very defects as a scholar assisted him in utilizing the possibilities of this style to the utmost.[38] His scholarship was so deficient that he seems to have been largely unaware of geographical, climatic, racial, religious and other influences on history. He saw man as essentially the same in all times and places, and as a perfectly free and unhampered agent, though in certain times and places guilty of incomprehensible stupidity. The history of nations thus became political history purely and simply, and largely a history of individual men; and individual action was to be understood wholly in moral terms. Any man or action who could not be approved by the enlightened standards of the mid-eighteenth century, was judged immediately and without recourse to the study of social or other historical influences, and thus condemned, or more than likely ridiculed. History was seen in two dimensions, and that which appeared out of focus was merely a proper subject for satire. The result is an heroic style greatly tempered with formal irony. It is a style of great beauty, and in dealing with certain subjects probably comes very close to the truth; but in the main it provides a simplification of its material so extreme that is principal value today resides in its impact on later historians.

Hume's style displays another mark of the eighteenth century, more specifically of the literary tradition affected directly or indirectly by deism.[39] The curious self-righteousness, mild but immovable, the security that all problems had been solved and that all were really very simple, which we meet in the thought of Shaftesbury and his followers, and which they seem to have imposed upon the attitudes of most of the writers of the generation

[38] Much of what follows on Hume, Robertson, and Gibbon is based on the essays of J. B. Black, *The Art of History*, Methuen, London, 1926.

[39] This subject is discussed a little more fully in my essay on Stevens in the present volume.

or so following, had as one of its most obvious results the kind of stylistic stereotype which we have come to consider as more or less characteristic of eighteenth century style: a stereotype both general and genteel, and commonly sentimental in its tendency, and which is used as a regular substitute for exact rendering of the material under discussion. J. B. Black points out a tendency in the work of Hume's contemporary, Robertson, which may do something to increase the inclination to this vice in Gibbon and in his disciple, Prescott: a concern for the dignity of history, which makes it imperative to eliminate the detail taken from vulgar but vivid reality; to eliminate, for example, the king's dagger left sticking in the body of Rizzio, which Robertson found in his original document.

The effect of these men on the monumental genius of Gibbon was very real, or at least the resemblance is real. The style has developed into something that one is tempted to call a prose equivalent of Milton's verse, but it is not that, for it is softer, smoother, and less uncompromising: but it is rich, complex, and massive, and like Milton's verse appears at times to be restricted in its perceptions by its very grandeur: Black quotes Bagehot's complaint that Gibbon cannot say Asia *minor*. Perhaps the following passage will suffice as well as any other to indicate the manner in which Gibbon is frequently constrained by the very nature of his instrument. It is from the portrait of Theodora, and I take the liberty of using my own italics:

> The beauty of Theodora was the subject of *more flattering praise* and the source of more *exquisite* delight. Her features were delicate and regular; her complexion, though somewhat pale, was *tinged with a natural color; every sensation* was instantly expressed by the *vivacity of her eyes; her easy motions displayed the graces of a small but elegant figure;* and *either love or adulation* might proclaim that *painting and poetry were incapable of delineating the matchless excellence of her form. But this form was degraded by the facility with which it was exposed to the public eye and prostituted to licentious desire.* Her *venal charms* were abandoned to *a promiscuous crowd of citizens and strangers* . . . The satirical historian has not *blushed to describe the naked scenes* which Theodora was not ashamed to exhibit in the theatre. After exhausting the arts of sensual pleasure,

419

she most *ungratefully murmured* against the *parsimony of Nature;*
but her murmurs, her pleasures, and her arts must be veiled in the
obscurity of a learned language.

The subject of this passage is a prostitute who became em-
press. The historian's embarrassment is extreme, but the embarrassment is probably as much as anything stylistic and practical. The normal tone of his prose, the entire state of mind established by it, forbids his dealing with this material with much
greater precision.

Prescott, like Gibbon, chose, for his two most famous histories,
themes which in themselves possess extraordinary grandeur.
They have not the chronological and geographical sweep of the
theme of Gibbon, nor are they as important in the development
of western civilization; but what they lack in these respects they
make up by their strangeness, and the fall of an empire such as
that of the Incas, of a civilization such as that of the Mexicans, is
sufficiently impressive. The cadence, whether of sentence, of
paragraph, or of narrative, is similar to that of Gibbon; the
scholarship, within the more limited field, is probably as com-
petent, though on this subject I can merely hazard a guess; the
style displays a similar quality of polite imperception, of decadence, and more consistently and obviously, at the same time that
it is in spite of this defect beautifully controlled and almost invariably interesting. There may be a greater awareness on the
part of Prescott than on that of Gibbon, who in this respect is
closer, though not extremely close, to Hume, of the necessity of
laboring to understand the minds of people of remote times and
cultures. This may account in part for the complete lack of irony
in Prescott, although the lack is no doubt more largely due to a
lack of perception of another kind, to a kind of provincial caution,
placidity, and decorum. Prescott lacks the range and cultivation
of Gibbon's mind, and his prose represents a gentle deterioration
of that of his master. When in his last history, he endeavored,
apparently, to clear his prose of its floridity and magniloquence,
he merely retreated, with no appreciable advantage, toward the

420

kind of prose one can find in the average textbook, as a comparison with parallel passages in Motley will easily show.

If style were a more or less independent organism, living, maturing and dying according to its own principles, this should have been the end of the grand manner of writing history; but the manner was revived and in certain respects very brilliantly revised, by Macaulay and Motley.

Macaulay is a master of the long sentence, but he tends to shorten its units and hasten its movement; and he deliberately employs the short sentence to achieve flexibility and variation. The prose remains heroic, but has ceased to be grandiloquent; the stereotyped phrase is rare; there is no difficulty in rendering the dagger left sticking in the body or the dungheaps beneath the windows of the country gentlemen. These few lines from the account of the execution of Monmouth represent a revolution in the practice of historical prose:

> The head sank down once more. The stroke was repeated again and again; but still the neck was not severed, and the body continued to move. Yells of rage and horror rose from the crowd. Ketch flung down the axe with a curse. "I cannot do it," he said; "my heart fails me." "Take up the axe, man," said the sheriff. "Fling him over the rails," roared the mob. Two more blows extinguished the last remains of life; but a knife was used to separate the head from the shoulders.

This is near the end of one of the greatest pieces of narrative in Macaulay's history, and indeed in English literature, the account of Monmouth's rebellion. The men, the country, the mud, the weather, as well as the blood and disaster, are rendered unforgettably, and this passage is followed immediately by the magnificent meditation on Monmouth's burial, a meditation worthy of Shakespeare. But no detail damages the prose. The prose is quick as well as intricate. It changes pace rapidly, and moves easily from subject to subject, but it never loses its identity. Whatever Macaulay's defects as an historical scholar—and he resembles most scholars in this, that his errors appear to have been many and serious—his contribution to the development of historical prose was one of the greatest. Motley's virtues are similar and perhaps not greatly inferior, although there is a stronger trace in Motley of the heroic stereotype.

Parkman has similar virtues at his best, but even to the end of his career the opportunity of describing a forest scene will demoralize him completely and reduce his style to a cold delirium of academic pseudo-poeticism. And the hardships of his private life, his engrossing and exhausting struggle with blindness, insanity, rheumatism, arthritis and perhaps other disorders, although one cannot but admire him for his strength of character in dealing with them, unquestionably limited both his scholarship and his understanding to the point where he is relatively a minor figure. He was forced to concentrate on the immediate data of his subject: he knew to perfection what the priests had done in the wilderness, but his understanding of the religious mind was that of Hume; he knew how the Iroquois and the Hurons appeared to the priest and how they behaved in war, but he knew nothing of anthropology and seems not to have considered even the lessons to be drawn from Prescott's treatment of the civilized tribes. The Indian and priest in juxtaposition, and in certain kinds of action, as seen from without by a man of heroic temperament and limited understanding, he could depict to perfection. He was at his best in dealing with the simple military man or adventurer, whose qualities he was easily able to comprehend.

But to the best of my knowledge, Parkman is the last distinguished historian of the heroic line.[40] Adams introduces a new style and an entirely new conception of historiography. The Adams who wrote the history was in the full possession of his intellectual powers, but he was the same Adams who was to deteriorate in the particular manner which we have seen. He was not heroic, and he did not see men as heroic, or at least he did not see those as heroic who were close to him in time and civilization. But he had a curiosity about psychological motives and action comparable to that of Henry James; his gift was for high comedy.

[40] I am simply taking it for granted that my reader feels, as I do, that the less said about Carlyle the better.

Gibbon chose for his subject the decline and fall of the Roman Empire; and the other historians whom I have mentioned did their best to rival this selection among the subjects remaining to them. The subjects were all essentially epic. Adams chose as his subject a period of sixteen years in the history of a nation which was, at the period which he examined, of about the same importance as Ecuador or Bolivia in the world of today; and which was, at the time of his writing, in spite of its astonishing growth, in a period of economic, political, and moral confusion which may well have made its future seem doubtful. But it was Adams' own country, and his forbears had helped to make it; so the subject was serious. Yet although it was a subject which called for serious investigation, it could scarcely hope for better than disinterested examination from Adams: if comedy was inherent in the subject, then comedy would certainly result in the literary product.

I have already spoken of Adams' admiration for James's treatment of character; I have quoted Adams on the "pleasure of seeing the lights of his burning glass turned on alternate sides of the same figure." He was fascinated with the manner in which the Jamesian character tends to shift and dissolve and assume new aspects under scrutiny, and he was conscious that he possessed the same kind of sensibility. And his central figure, Thomas Jefferson, probably lent itself better to representation by a man of Adams' talents than any other major American statesman would have done.

The history opens with six chapters of analysis of general conditions, and the last volume closes with a similar analysis. The narrative proper begins with the seventh chapter, which gives a picture of Jefferson's inauguration and an introductory portrait of each of the main figures in the administration, a portrait which is brief, mainly physical, and skillfully suggestive. His final summary of Jefferson's appearance and mannerisms is as follows:[11]

For eight years, this tall, loosely built, somewhat stiff figure, in red waistcoat and yarn stockings, slippers down at the heel, and

[11] Op. cit., Vol. I, p. 187.

clothes that seemed too small for him, may be imagined as Senator Maclay described him, sitting on one hip, with one shoulder high above the other, talking almost without ceasing to his visitors at the White House. His skin was thin, peeling from his face on exposure to the sun, and giving it a tettered appearance. This sandy face, with hazel eyes and sunny aspect; this loose shackling person; this rambling and often brilliant conversation, belonged to the controlling influences of American history, more necessary to the story than three fourths of the official papers, which only hid the truth.

And later, when the narrative has progressed sufficiently for the statement to be comprehensible, he writes:[42]

The contradictions in Jefferson's character have always rendered it a fascinating study. Excepting his rival, Alexander Hamilton, no American has been the object of estimates so widely differing and so difficult to reconcile. Almost every other American statesman might be described in a parenthesis. A few broad strokes of the brush would paint the portraits of all the early Presidents with this exception, and a few more strokes would answer for any member of their cabinets; but Jefferson could be painted only touch by touch, with a fine pencil, and the perfection of the likeness depended upon the shifting and uncertain flicker of its semi-transparent shadows.

To attempt a summary or description of his method of depicting this character would be useless, for he does it only in rendering fully and cautiously the manner in which Jefferson dealt with the many confusing situations encountered in his position; but one can illustrate it on a very small scale by quoting complete his account of a minor incident, the Callender scandal:[43]

James Thompson Callender, a Scotch adventurer compared with whom the Cobbetts, Duanes, Cheethams, and Woods who infested the press were men of moral and pure life, had been an ally of Jefferson during the stormy days of 1798, and had published at Richmond a volume called "The Prospect before Us," which was sufficiently libellous to draw upon him a State prosecution, and a fine and some months imprisonment at the rough hands of Judge Chase. A few years later the Republicans would have applauded the sentence, and

[42] Ibid., p. 277.
[43] Ibid., pp. 322 to 327.

424

regretted only its lightness. In 1800 they were bound to make common cause with the victim. When Jefferson became President, he pardoned Callender, and by a stretch of authority returned to him the amount of his fine. Naturally Callender expected reward. He hastened to Washington, and was referred to Madison. He said that he was in love, and hinted that to win the object of his affections nothing less than the post-office at Richmond was necessary for his social standing. Meeting with a positive refusal, he returned to Richmond in extreme anger, and became editor of a newspaper called "The Recorder," in which he began to wage against Jefferson a war of slander that Cobbett and Cheetham would have shrunk from. He collected every story he could gather, among overseers and scandal-mongers, about Jefferson's past life,—charged him with having a family of negro children by a slave named Sally; with having been turned out of the house of a certain Major Walker for writing a secret love-letter to his wife; with having swindled his creditors by paying debts in worthless currency, and with having privately paid Callender himself to write "The Prospect before Us," besides furnishing materials for the book. Disproof of these charges was impossible. That which concerned Black Sally, as she was called, seems to have rested on a confusion of persons which could not be cleared up; that relating to Mrs. Walker had a foundation of truth, although the parties were afterwards reconciled; that regarding the payment of debt was true in one sense, and false only in the sense which Callender gave it; while that which referred to "The Prospect before Us" was true enough to be serious. All these charges were welcomed by the Federalist press, reprinted even in the New York "Evening Post," and scattered broadcast over New England. There men's minds were ready to welcome any tale of villainy that bore out their theory of Jefferson's character; and at the most critical moment, a mistake made by himself went far to confirm their prejudice.

Jefferson's nature was feminine; he was more refined than many women in the delicacy of his private relations, and even men as shameless as Callender himself winced under attacks of such a sort. He was sensitive, affectionate, and, in his own eyes, heroic. He yearned for love and praise as no other great American ever did. He hated the clergy chiefly because he knew that from them he could expect neither love nor praise, perhaps not even forbearance. He had befriended Callender against his own better judgment, as every party leader befriended party hacks, not because the leaders approved them, but because they were necessary for the press. So far as license was concerned, "The Prospect before Us" was a mild libel, compared with Cobbett's, Coleman's, and Dennie's cataracts of abuse; and at the time it was written, Callender's character was not known and his habits were still decent. In return for kindness and encouragement, Callender attempted an act of dastardly assassination, which the whole Federalist press cheered. That a large part of the community, and the part socially uppermost, should believe this drunken ruffian, and should laugh while he bespattered their president with his filth, was a mortification which cut deep into Jefferson's heart. Hurt and angry, he felt that at bottom it was the old theological hatred in Virginia and New England which sustained this mode of warfare; that as he had flung Paine at them, they were flinging Callender at him. "With the aid of a lying renegade from Republicanism, the Federalists have opened their sluices of calumny," he wrote; and he would have done wisely to say no more. Unluckily for him, he undertook to contradict Callender's assertions.

James Monroe was Governor of Virginia. Some weakness in Monroe's character caused him more than once to mix in scandals which he might better have left untouched. July 7, 1802, he wrote to the President, asking for the facts in regard to Jefferson's relations with Callender. The President's reply confessed the smart of his wound:

"I am really mortified at the base ingratitude of Callender. It presents human nature in a hideous form. It gives me concern because I perceive that relief which was afforded him on mere motives of charity, may be viewed under the aspect of employing him as a writer."

He explained how he had pitied Callender, and repeatedly given him money.

"As to myself," he continued, "no man wished more to see his pen stopped; but I considered him still as a proper object of benevolence. The succeeding year he again wanted money to buy paper for another volume. I made his letter, as before, the occasion of giving him another fifty dollars. He considers these as proofs of my approbation of his writings, when they were mere charities, yielded under a strong conviction that he was injuring us by his writings."

Unfortunately, Jefferson could not find the press-copies of his letters to Callender, and let Monroe send out these apologies without stopping to compare them with his written words. No sooner had the Republican newspapers taken their tone from Monroe, and committed themselves to these assertions of fact, than Callender printed the two letters which Jefferson had written to him, which proved that not only had Jefferson given him at different times some two hundred dollars, but had also supplied information, of a harmless nature, for

"The Prospect before Us," and under an injunction of secrecy had encouraged Callender to write. His words were not to be explained away: "I thank you for the proof-sheets you enclosed me; such papers cannot fail to produce the best effect."

No man who stood within the circle of the President's intimates could be perplexed to understand how this apparent self-contradiction might have occurred. Callender was neither the first nor the last to take advantage of what John Randolph called the "easy credulity" of Jefferson's temper. The nearest approach Jefferson could make toward checking an over-zealous friend was by shades of difference in the strength of his encouragement. To tell Callender that his book could not fail to produce the best effect was a way of hinting that it might do harm; and, however specious such an excuse might seem, this language was in his mind consistent with a secret wish that Callender should not write. More than one such instance of this kindly prevarication, this dislike of whatever might seem harsh or disobliging, could be found in Jefferson's correspondence.

A man's enemies rarely invent specious theories of human nature in order to excuse what they prefer to look upon as falsehood and treason. July 17, 1803, Callender was drowned in some drunken debauch; but the Federalists never forgot his calumnies, or ceased ringing the changes on the President's self-contradictions,—and throughout New England the trio of Jefferson, Paine and Callender were henceforth held in equal abhorrence. That this prejudice did not affect Jefferson's popular vote was true, but it seriously affected his social relations; and it annoyed and mortified him more than coarser men could understand, to feel in the midst of his utmost popularity that large numbers of his worthiest fellow-citizens, whose respect he knew himself to deserve, despised him as they did the vermin they trod upon.

One has in this account the portrait of a man who cannot quite gauge himself or his motives, and who appears extremely ambiguous, perhaps, to many of his observers; but we have a portrait of the man in action, a rich exhibition of his actions, feelings, and beliefs, no less rich than James could have exhibited in comparable space, in spite of the fact that every detail in Adams' account is firmly attached to an historical document. The exhibition of Jefferson's character is not only witty, but is honest and perceptive as well; it was only in Adams' later years that his interest in this aspect of human nature was to degenerate into a shallow mannerism, as we have seen it in the *Education*. The early incidents exhibiting Jefferson's nature in minor situations, suggest the man as we shall find him in the larger plan of the total work, dealing with the major problems of statesmanship.

Jefferson is obviously the character who most fascinates and amuses the historian; and Adams is fortunate that Jefferson's part was actually central. But he accepts his obligation as an historian with no qualms; he neither avoids adequate treatment of men of other types nor tries to remodel them. Burr, Jackson, Harrison, Tecumseh, Napoleon, Madison, Gallatin, and Barlow are only a few of the number portrayed at length: each one exists in his own right and is unforgettable. And each is portrayed as he should be portrayed by a careful historian: through his written words, or the written words of observers, and through his acts, one by one and in interrelation, each act taken carefully and curiously naked from the original document. Whether the subject is the maneuvering of Napoleon and the British ministry, whether it is the incidents leading to the death of Hamilton or those leading to the battle of Tippecanoe and the later death of that moderate and distinguished gentleman, Tecumseh, the story is clear and beautifully illuminated. All generalizations are made from the objective data actually presented, and the generalizations give the effect, at least, of caution and precision. We have human action of the most serious kind, the action of mature men affecting and governing the lives of nations. We have become so conditioned—I think that is the word—to the reading of novels, that we are likely to have the feeling that human nature cannot be depicted with depth or subtlety except as it appears in what we should call the personal adventures of the relatively young, in the private relationships arising in what is relatively the leisure time of the characters. To appreciate fully what Adams has done with his people, one must have, I suppose, a sufficient interest in history as bare fact not to be troubled by it; but the interest at least is adult and I can see no great harm in anyone's having it.

To the reader who habitually assumes that the great historians are necessarily in the heroic tradition, and that the only other historical type is that of the schoolroom text or the professional monograph, Adams' history may at first glance appear disappointing: it employs the method of the learned monograph, in a sense, but it raises the method to a form of art. This is what one should not overlook. The style is expert and flexible; it is never too exalted for its subject, as is sometimes the style of Gibbon; it never carries too much conviction to be convincing, as does sometimes the style of Macaulay or that of Motley. It is a style that can offer a sequence of dates or the summary of a document, without loss either of accuracy or of distinction. It is in the passages dealing with the play of character that the book is most brilliant, but if one reads and rereads it carefully, one discovers that the play of character is comprehensible as a result of the author's careful preparations, and that the style is adequate with respect to everything it touches.

The history is penetrated with precise intelligence in all its parts: it is in this quality, I think, that it surpasses any other historical masterpiece with which I am acquainted. There is greater magnificence in portions of Gibbon, Macaulay, and Motley, but there is seldom the skill of penetration, and there is not the uniformity of success in any of them. And the wit of Adams is invariably the result of understanding instead of the result of its absence.

What may have been the immediate cause of his turning away from the writing of history to the irresponsible activities of his later years, it might be hard to say. The death of his wife will not account for it, for a large part of the history was finished after that event; and the suggestion, which occurs in one of his letters, that the cause was the discouragement of his publishers, need be given but very little weight. Probably it was merely the accumulation of emotion, the result of an ancestral tendency, which finally reached a state where it influenced his action definitively. The letters indicate a regret for his past distinction, however. In 1899 he wrote to Elizabeth Cameron:[44]

So I read on and enjoyed my own history, which I am correcting in case of further editions. As a rule it bores me, and I have to drive myself up to the task, but yesterday I happened on the third volume,

[44] *Letters of Henry Adams,* op. cit., p. 215.

and was greatly amused by it. I was honestly surprised that no one ever mentioned it to me, or spoke of it in the press, so that I had never read it or heard of it before.

And to the same correspondent he wrote even more regretfully about two years later, referring to himself by a name of his own invention which he occasionally employs in his letters:[45]

The trouble is, and always has been, and always will be, with the greed and selfishness and jealousy and ambition of senators. On that subject you can read a now forgotten work written by one of your acquaintances long since dead, one Dordy d'Ullivier d' Angoulême, tedious enough but elaborately supported by historical evidence in nine volumes.

And in the same year he wrote to Henry Osborn Taylor, the eminent medievalist, who had formerly been his pupil:[46]

You have gone so far beyond me, both in horizon and in study, that I feel our situations reversed. You are the professor; I am the student. My role suits me better now, for I was always indolent and have always shirked responsibility. Between the admission that everything is right and everything wrong, I could never see my way to set up a sign-post.

In 1917, he wrote to Charles Milnes Gaskell, in one of his last letters:[47]

There are just three of my contemporaries living on this shore, but we have all lost our minds or our senses and no one thinks it worth while to tell us so. No books come out. I am not aware that there are any writers left, certainly none in my branch, which was extinct five and twenty years ago and more. No one even remembers the name of Lord Macaulay. I once wrote some books myself, but no one has even mentioned the fact to me for more than a generation. I have a vague recollection that once some young person *did* mention an anecdote to me that came from one of my books and that he attributed it to some one else.

[45] Ibid., p. 318
[46] Ibid., p. 331
[47] Ibid., p. 644

WALLACE STEVENS

or The Hedonist's Progress[1]

THOUGH WALLACE STEVENS has published almost nothing in
the way of criticism, he has nevertheless been very clear in stating
his theories of life and of literature, and he may justifiably be
treated, I believe, in a series of essays on literary theorists.

His fundamental ideas are stated in *Sunday Morning*, an early
poem, and in some ways his greatest. The poem consists of eight
stanzas in blank verse, each containing fifteen lines, and it
presents a clear and fairly coherent argument.

The first stanza sets the stage and identifies the protagonist.
We are given a woman, at home on a Sunday morning, meditat-
ing on the meaning of death. The second stanza asks the question
which provides the subject of the poem; it asks what divinity this
woman may be thought to possess as a recompense for her ultimate surrender to death; and having asked the question, it replies
that her divinity, which must live within herself, consists wholly
in her emotions—not in her understanding of the emotions, but
in the emotions as a good in themselves. This answer is not quite
the orthodox romantic answer, which would offer us in the emotions either a true guide to virtue or a more or less mystical experience leading to some kind of union with some kind of deity.
Any philosophy which offers the cultivation of the emotions as
an end in itself, I suppose, is a kind of hedonism. In any event,
that is the kind of philosophy which we find here.

[1] All poems mentioned in this essay, unless otherwise identified, are to be
found in the second edition of *Harmonium*, by Wallace Stevens, published by
Alfred A. Knopf, New York, 1931. The book is small, indexed, and well
known, and page references seem unnecessary.

The third stanza, by means of the allegory of Jove and his human loves, through his union with whom he crossed the heavenly strain upon the human, implies that man has a capacity which may at least figuratively be termed divine; the stanza is a subordinate commentary on the one preceding, and does not really advance the argument.

In the fourth stanza, however, the argument moves forward. The protagonist objects to the concept which has been offered her; she states that the beauties of this life are transient and that she longs to believe in a Paradise beyond them. The remainder of the stanza, and the greater part of it, is the poet's reply: in a passage of great rhetorical power, he denies the possibility of Paradise, at the same time that he communicates through the feeling of his language a deep nostalgic longing to accept the ideas which he is rejecting. In the first two lines of the fifth stanza, the woman repeats her objection, and the poet then replies with an explanation of the function of death: it is our awareness of the imminence of death which heightens our emotions and sharpens· our perceptions; our knowledge of life's transience stimulates our perception of life's beauty.

In the sixth stanza the poet considers an hypothetical paradise, and, since he can imagine it only in terms of a projection of the good life as the hedonist understands the good life, he deduces that paradise would become tedious and insipid: we have in this stanza the first sharp vision of the ennui which is to obsess the later work of the poet and which is ultimately to wreck his talent, an ennui arising from the fact that emotion is not a good in itself, but that if cultivated for itself alone is merely a pleasant diversion so long as the novelty of a given experience endures, at most as long as new experiences can give us the illusion of novel excitement, and then becomes a disease of the spirit, a state of indifferency in which there is neither novelty nor significance.

The seventh stanza presents a vision of a future race of men engaged in a religious ritual, the generating principle of which is their joy in the world as it is given them and their sense of brotherhood as "men that perish." The stanza contains suggestions of a pantheism which goes beyond the bounds of a strict hedonism, but they are merely suggestions and they appear nowhere else. The eighth and last stanza begins by denying the immortality of Jesus, and, by implication, of man; and it places the protagonist finally and irretrievably on a small but beautiful planet, floating like a tropical island in boundless space, "in an old chaos of the sun."

This summary, even as summaries go, is extremely skeletalized. It has been my intention, here, merely to isolate the hedonistic theme for future consideration; the theme is not thus isolated in the poem, but is complicated by its interconnections with other human problems from which not even a hedonist can escape. Whatever the defects of the hedonistic theme, and with the possible but by no means certain exception of a few short poems by Stevens and of two or three poems by E. A. Robinson, *Sunday Morning* is probably the greatest American poem of the twentieth century and is certainly one of the greatest contemplative poems in English: in a blank verse which differs, in its firmness of structure and incalculable sensitivity of detail, from all other blank verse of our time save that of a few poems by Hart Crane which were in some measure modeled upon it, it renders the acute uncertainty of what we are inclined to consider the modern mind, but it does so with no uncertainty of method or of statement; it renders an acute consciousness of the imminence of death, of the sensory and emotional richness of life on this bewildering planet, and of the heroic magnificence of the religious myths which are lost to the poet and to many of the rest of us, except as memories of things long past. If Stevens' career had stopped with this poem, or a few years thereafter, it might seem an unnecessary unkindness to insist upon the limitations of understanding which the poem discloses; but those limitations appear very obviously in a few later poems, and they seem to me to be very clearly related to the rapid and tragic decay of the poet's style. As a poet in early maturity, Stevens brought to this subject a style which was the result of a fine native gift enriched by the study of English blank verse; the subject, once formulated, and accepted as a guide to life and to expression, destroyed the style in less than two decades. In *Sunday Morning* itself, we detect the limitations of the subject only by rational analysis; in the later work we see the effect of those limitations.

We may consider briefly, and perhaps as a kind of footnote to *Sunday Morning,* one of the more obscure poems, called *The Stars at Tallapoosa.* As far as I can penetrate this poem, I judge that it postulates the absolute severance of the intellectual and the emotional: the lines between the stars are the lines of pure intellect; the earth-lines and the sea-lines represent the non-intellectual experience (loosely speaking) of daily human life. Both modes of experience have beauty and should be pursued, but they are disparate and unrelated to each other; and it follows, although this is not stated in the poem, that the intellectual experience, since it bears no relationship to the rest of our life and hence is in no way useful, is valuable simply for the independent emotional excitement which one may derive from it.

If we turn to *A High-Toned Old Christian Woman,* a brief didactic and satirical poem, which is quite clear and unmistakable as regards its theoretic import, we get an additional step in the argument: we learn that the "moral law" is not necessary as a framework for art, but that "the opposing law" will do as well, and that in either event, the artists,

> *Your disaffected flagellants, well-stuffed,*
> *Smacking their muzzy bellies in parade,*
> *Proud of such novelties of the sublime,*
> *Such tink and tank and tunk-a-tunk-tunk,*
> *May, merely may, madame, whip from themselves*
> *A jovial hullabaloo among the spheres.*

Stevens, in becoming thus explicit, states his final doctrine, as do certain other contemporary theorists, in language surprisingly reminiscent of Poe:

"It may be, indeed, that here this sublime end is, now and then, attained in fact. We are often made to feel with a shivering delight,

434

that from an earthly harp are stricken notes which *cannot* have been unfamiliar to the angels." [2]

Poe's statement is made, of course, in the tone of saccharine sentimentality which is Poe's nearest approach to sincerity; Stevens' statement is made ironically, but one should not be misled by this fact. For though Stevens is ridiculing himself and his artists, he is ridiculing his old Christian woman, the representative of the moralistic point of view, even more severely: he is offering his opinion as more nearly tenable than hers, notwithstanding the fact that he cannot offer his opinion with real seriousness. Stevens' self-ridicule is as irrational in its way as Poe's sentimentalism, and like that sentimentalism springs from a doctrine which eliminates the possibility of the rational understanding of experience and of a moral judgment deriving therefrom: since no idea is really tenable and since we cannot judge of the justice of a feeling but can only seek to heighten its intensity, all ideas and all feelings may fairly be, and sooner or later, in the history of a sensitive and witty man, are certain to be, subjected to merciless ridicule; but of this we shall see more interesting evidence later.

It is perhaps not important, but it is at least mildly interesting, to call attention at this point to a poem which has been at least twice misinterpreted by commentators who have not taken the trouble to understand Stevens as a whole. The poem is *Anecdote of the Jar:*

> *I placed a jar in Tennessee,*
> *And round it was, upon a hill.*
> *It made the slovenly wilderness*
> *Surround that hill.*
>
> *The wilderness rose up to it,*
> *And sprawled around, no longer wild.*

[2] From *The Poetic Principle*, page 12 of Vol. I of the three volumes of criticism in Poe's works, the edition of Stedman and Woodberry. Quoted and elucidated in my essay on Poe, in the present volume.

The jar was round upon the ground
And tall and of a port in air.

It took dominion everywhere.
The jar was gray and bare.
It did not give of bird or bush,
Like nothing else in Tennessee.

Stanley P. Chase has written of this poem:

"Very likely the little poem is meant to suggest nothing more than the superiority, to an intensely civilized person, of the simplest bit of handicraft over any extent of unregulated 'nature' . . ."[3]

And Howard Baker writes with the same obtuseness, but with greater elaborateness:

"Similarly a wild and disorderly landscape is transformed into order by the presence of a symmetrical vase. . . . The jar acts in the imagination like one of the poles of the earth, the imaginary order of the lines of latitude and longitude projecting around the pole. The jar itself—simple and symmetrical, a product of the human consciousness and not of nature—is a very fitting symbol for man's dominion over nature . . ."[4]

If the poem ended with the fourth line, there might be an imperfect justification of the interpretation offered by these writers, for in the first four lines the wilderness is not only dominated by the jar—as, in fact, it is dominated throughout the poem,—but it is called slovenly. If we examine the next two lines, however, we see that the phrase, "the slovenly wilderness," is in fact a slovenly ellipsis. The wilderness is slovenly after it has been dominated and not before: it "sprawled around, no longer wild." The jar is the product of the human mind, as the critics remark, and it dominates the wilderness; but it does not give order to the wilder-

[3] *Dionysus in Dismay*, by Stanley P. Chase, in *Humanism and America*, edited by Norman Foerster, Farrar and Rinehart, New York, 1930, page 211.
[4] *Wallace Stevens and Other Poets*, by Howard Baker, The Southern Review, Vol. I, Number 2, Autumn 1935, page 376.

ness—it is vulgar and sterile, and it transforms the wilderness into the semblance of a deserted picnic ground. Its sterility is indicated in the last three lines, and if the jar is to be accepted as symbolic of the human intellect, then the poem is in part another example of the same theme which we found in *The Stars at Tallapoosa*, but expressed this time with disillusionment and a measure of disgust. The poem would appear to be primarily an expression of the corrupting effect of the intellect upon natural beauty, and hence a purely romantic performance. To read any measure of neo-humanism into Stevens is as foolish as to endeavor, in the manner of certain young critics of a few years ago, to read into him a kind of incipient and trembling consciousness of the beauty of Marxism.

I have already pointed out that in the sixth stanza of *Sunday Morning*, the stanza in which Stevens projects into the eternity of paradise the highest good which he can imagine, there appears a weary dissatisfaction with the experience, a hint of the dissatisfaction which might imaginably appear in our present life if the experience were too long protracted. This dissatisfaction is familiar to students of romantic literature under the name of ennui; it is the boredom which eventually overtakes the man who seeks for excitement instead of understanding. In the poem entitled *The Man Whose Pharynx Was Bad* we find a statement of this boredom which is both extreme and explicit. The poem as it appears in *Harmonium* lacks four lines of the original version, lines ten to thirteen inclusive, which appeared in The New Republic for September 14, 1921. Those lines are essential to the poem and to the understanding of Stevens, and I shall quote the entire poem in its original version:

The time of year has grown indifferent.
Mildew of summer and the deepening snow
Are both alike in the routine I know;
I am too dumbly in my being pent.

The wind attendant on the solstices
Blows on the shutters of the metropoles,

Stirring no poet in his sleep, and tolls
The grand ideas of the villages.

The malady of the quotidian . . .
Perhaps if summer ever came to rest
And lengthened, deepened, comforted, caressed
Through days like oceans in obsidian

Horizons, full of night's midsummer blaze;
Perhaps, if winter once could penetrate
Through all its purples to the final slate,
Persisting bleakly in an icy haze;

One might in turn become less diffident,
Out of such mildew plucking neater mould
And spouting new orations of the cold.
One might. One might. But time will not relent.

The poet has progressed in this poem to the point at which the intensity of emotion possible in actual human life has become insipid, and he conceives the possibility of ultimate satisfaction only in some impossible emotional finality of no matter what kind. In fact, the figurative opposites of summer and winter here offered suggest the opposites of the moral and the anti-moral which appear in *A High-Toned Old Christian Woman*.

The situation in which Stevens may here be observed is similar to a difficulty in which Poe found himself. Poe, like Stevens, sought only emotional stimulation in the arts, and hence he considered novelty, and novelty of a fairly crude kind, to be an essential of good art. He wrote:

"Nothing is more clear than this proposition, although denied by the chlorine critics (the grass-green). The desire of the new is an element of the soul. The most exquisite pleasures grow dull in repetition. A strain of music enchants. Heard a second time, it pleases. Heard a tenth it does not displease. We hear it a twentieth, and ask ourselves why we admired. At the fiftieth, it produces ennui, at the hundredth disgust." [5]

[5] Op. cit. Vol. III, p. 107.

Both men are in search of intense feeling; neither is in search of just feeling, of feeling properly motivated. The poem as an exercise in just feeling is an act of moral judgment, as I have repeatedly indicated; and though all such judgments must of necessity be governed by general principles, yet each particular judgment, since it arises from an individual relationship between unique persons and events, will be, if truly just, unique, as individual men are unique, and will have its own inexhaustible fascination as a living entity. But if one does not recognize this principle of justice, then the poem can have no true uniqueness: the poet and the reader alike are bent, as are Poe and Stevens, on a quest for the new, which, in the realm of emotion divorced from understanding or any principle of propriety, can be found only in new degrees of intensity and of strangeness; and as each new degree achieved becomes familiar it is submerged in the monotone of that which is no longer new, so that the search is equally devoid of hope and of significance. Poe never had the wit to perceive the futility of this search; Stevens has the wit not only to see the futility but to be both depressed and ironic in consequence, yet he is unable to think himself out of the situation into which he has wandered.

Unless one change one's entire philosophy, having arrived at this impasse, there can remain open to one only two modes of action: one may renounce one's art and subside into a kind of stoical silence; or one may pursue, not greater intensity of experience, for human language and the human organism alike set a certain limit to progress in that direction, but experience increasingly elusive and incomprehensible. Stevens has considered both of these possibilities, but since he has chosen the latter, we may fairly examine first the mode of action which he has considered and discarded. It so happens, incidentally, that his meditation upon the possibility of renunciation has resulted in his longest single work.

The Comedian as the Letter C (the significance of the title, I regret to say, escapes both my learning and my ingenuity) is a narrative poem in six parts, dealing with a poet who begins with romantic views of the function of his art and who, in reforming them, comes to abandon his art as superfluous. The first part of the poem deals with Crispin's encounter with the sea, that is, with his realization of a universe vast, chaotic, and impersonal beyond his power of formulation or imagination, and rendering him contemptible by contrast. In the second part, Crispin arrives in Yucatan, disillusioned as to his old convictions, but finding a heightened experience and new food for his art in the barbaric violence of the tropical landscape; finding these, that is, until he is overwhelmed by a thunderstorm, of which the symbolic function is similar to that of the sea in the first part, and is driven with the terrified crowd about him into the cathedral. In the third part he returns to North America, intent now, not on the extreme and unnatural excitements of the southern landscape which he has left, but on the discovery of reality:

> He gripped more closely the essential prose
> As being, in a world so falsified,
> The one integrity for him, the one
> Discovery still possible to make,
> To which all poems were incident, unless
> That prose should wear a poem's guise at last.

But he is bent on discovering not the reality of his own nature, but rather the reality of his native country. Man is no longer, as in the first line of the first part, the intelligence of his soil; but the soil, as we note in the first line of the next and fourth section, is man's intelligence. These statements do not have the philosophical lucidity which would delight the present simple paraphraser, but they seem to mean, in their relationship to this poem, that Crispin has been turned away first from the attempt to study himself directly, and second from the attempt to indulge in exotic experiences, and that he has been turned instead to the attempt to master his native environment—to master it, that is, for the purposes of poetry. The nature of this last procedure I do not pretend to understand, and since the words which I have just used are my own and are not quoted from Stevens, it is possible that my confusion is of my own contriving. But in general, I should say that Stevens appears to have slipped here into the Whitmanian form of a romantic error common enough in our literature, but current especially in Stevens' generation and espoused in particular by Stevens' friend W. C. Williams: the fallacy that the poet achieves salvation by being, in some way, intensely of and expressive of his country. A common variant of this notion is the idea that the poet should bear the same relationship to his time, and in fact the two versions are perhaps most commonly combined, as they are in Williams. Felt with sufficient intensity, they become indistinguishable, as in Crane or even in Whitman, from pantheism, and go quite beyond the bounds of hedonism; but the notions in question represent merely a casual subject for meditation in Stevens, a subject which he considers because he is confused but which involves a spiritual quality, a capacity for naively whole-hearted enthusiasm, which is quite foreign to his nature. The ideas are the attempt to justify a kind of extroversion: the poet, cut off from human nature, which is his proper subject-matter, seeks to find a subject in the description, or, as the saying goes, in the expression, of what is round about him. In practice, this results mainly, as in Williams, in a heavy use of the native landscape, sometimes as legitimate symbolism or background, sometimes as the subject of mere description, sometimes as false symbolism:[6] in the first of these three instances, the poet is actually intent on doing something not adequately explained by his theory; in the second he is doing something relatively easy and unimportant; and in the third he is writing badly. Crispin seeks, then, an understanding not of himself but of his native landscape, and his native landscape is a temperate one, which does not offer the flamboyant and succulent excitements of Yucatan:

> *The spring came there in clinking pannicles*
> *Of half-dissolving frost, the summer came,*
> *If ever, whisked and wet, not ripening,*
> *Before the winter's vacancy returned.*

* This whole topic is discussed at length in the essay entitled *The Experimental School in American Poetry* (the section on pseudo-reference) in the present volume.

This landscape is the one which appears in *The Man Whose Pharynx Was Bad,* and which Stevens there uses to symbolize his own frustration. But Crispin, having returned from Yucatan, hopes now to achieve the beatific pleasure reserved for the successful hedonist, not by extravagance of experience, but by honesty and accuracy of experience: by honesty and accuracy, however, so far as we can judge from the poem, merely in describing the scenery which surrounds him, as if, perhaps, there were some ulterior virtue in this process which cannot quite be defined in words. The fourth section of the poem is really an elaboration upon the central ideas of the third, and it scarcely calls for comment at present. In the fifth and sixth parts, Crispin's concentration upon the normal world about him results in his marrying and begetting daughters; and finding that the facts which he had set out to describe with such exemplary honesty are more engrossing than the description of them, he abandons his art, in order, as very young people are sometimes heard to say, to live. This is not surprising, for the honest description which Crispin set out to achieve is in itself a moral experience, though of a very limited kind: honest description renders the feeling appropriate to purely sensory experience, and is hence a kind of judgment of that experience. But if Crispin had realized this, he would have realized the whole moral basis of art, and would have proceeded to more complex subjects; not realizing this, he lost interest in his simplified art, and found the art even in this simplified form to be the last element of confusion remaining in his experience: to achieve intelligent objectivity, Crispin is forced to abandon his description and merely enjoy the subject-matter of his description in the most naked possible of conditions:

> He first, as realist, admitted that
> Whoever hunts a matinal continent
> May, after all, stop short before a plum
> And be content and still be realist.
> The words of things entangle and confuse.

> *The plum survives its poems.....*
> *........it survives in its own form,*
> *Beyond these changes, good fat guzzly fruit.*

We have now the complete argument, I believe, which leads to Crispin's renunciation. The passage in which the renunciation takes place, however, is interesting for another reason; for the quality of the rhetoric employed at this particular juncture helps us profoundly to understand Stevens himself. The passage follows closely upon the lines just quoted and will be found about half-way through the fifth section:

> *Was he to bray this in profoundest brass*
> *Arointing his dreams with fugal requiems?*
> *Was he to company vastest things defunct*
> *With a blubber of tom-toms harrowing the sky?*
> *Scrawl a tragedian's testament? Prolong*
> *His active force in an inactive dirge,*
> *Which, let the tall musicians call and call,*
> *Should merely call him dead? Pronounce amen*
> *Through choirs infolded to the outmost clouds?*
> *Because he built a cabin who once planned*
> *Loquacious columns by the ructive sea?*
> *Because he turned to salad beds again?*

What I wish the reader to note is this: that the passage describes Crispin's taking leave of his art, and describes also his refusal to use his art in the process of leave-taking, because the art is, after all, futile and contemptible. Yet for Stevens himself the entire poem is a kind of tentative leave-taking; he has not the courage to act as his hero acts and be done with it, so he practices the art which he cannot justify and describes it in terms of contempt. Furthermore, the chief instrument of irony in this passage, and throughout the poem, and indeed throughout much of the rest of Stevens, is a curious variant on the self-ridicule, the romantic irony, with which we are familiar from Byron through

443

Laforgue and his modern disciples;[7] the instrument is self-parody, a parody occasionally subtle, often clumsy, of the refined and immutable style of Stevens at his best. To estimate at least a part of the tragedy represented by Stevens' career, the reader can scarcely do better than compare the lines quoted above with the last section of the much earlier *Sunday Morning*:

> *She hears upon that water without sound,*
> *A voice that cries, "The tomb in Palestine*
> *Is not the porch of spirits lingering.*
> *It is the grave of Jesus where he lay."*
> *We live in an old chaos of the sun,*
> *Or old dependency of day and night,*
> *Or island solitude, unsponsored, free,*
> *Of that wide water, inescapable.*
> *Deer walk upon our mountains, and the quail*
> *Whistle about us their spontaneous cries;*
> *Sweet berries ripen in the wilderness;*
> *And, in the isolation of the sky,*
> *At evening, casual flocks of pigeons make*
> *Ambiguous undulations as they sink,*
> *Downward to darkness, on extended wings.*

Since the poet, having arrived at the predicament to which we have traced him, however, is not to abandon his art, there remains only the possibility that he seek variety of experience in the increasingly perverse and strange; that he seek it, moreover, with no feeling of respect toward the art which serves as his only instrument and medium. In the poem entitled *The Revolutionists Stop for Orangeade*, we are given the theory of this type of poetry:

> *Hang a feather by your eye,*
> *Nod and look a little sly.*

[7] This entire subject is discussed in the latter part of my second essay in *Primitivism and Decadence*, already mentioned.

444

> *This must be the vent of pity,*
> *Deeper than a truer ditty*
> *Of the real that wrenches,*
> *Of the quick that's wry.*

And from this point onward there remains little but the sly look and a perverse ingenuity in confusing the statement of essentially simple themes. *The Man with the Blue Guitar*,[8] for example, which is one of his most recent performances, is merely a jingling restatement of the old theme of the severance between the rational understanding and the poetic imagination. But the statement is never quite clear; and since the theme, though unsound, is far from difficult to understand, one is inclined to suspect that the lack of clarity is the result of a deliberate choice, a choice motivated, perhaps, by the hope that some note more moving than the poet has a right to expect may be struck from the obscurity. And if one does not always encounter such wilful semiobscurity in the later poems, one much too commonly encounters the kind of laborious foolishness to be found in the following poem, entitled *The Mechanical Optimist*, published in *New Directions* for 1936:

> *A lady dying of diabetes*
> *Listened to the radio,*
> *Catching the lesser dithyrambs.*
> *So heaven collects its bleating lambs.*
>
> *Her useless bracelets fondly fluttered,*
> *Paddling the melodic swirls,*
> *The idea of God no longer sputtered*
> *At the roots of her indifferent curls.*
>
> *The idea of the Alps grew large,*
> *Not yet, however, a thing to die in.*

[8] *The Man with the Blue Guitar*, by Wallace Stevens, Alfred A. Knopf, N. Y., 1937.

It seemed serener just to die,
To float off on the floweriest barge,

Accompanied by the exegesis
Of familiar things in a cheerful voice,
Like the night before Christmas and all the carols.
Dying lady, rejoice, rejoice!

The generating mood is one of ennui; the style represents an effort, half-bored and half desperate, to achieve originality; the victim of the irony is very small game, and scarcely worthy of the artillery of the author of *Sunday Morning;* the point of view is adolescent. The author of *Sunday Morning* and of *Le Monocle de Mon Oncle,* the heir of Milton and of Jonson, is endeavoring, in his old age, to épater les bourgeois. The poem is the work of a man who twenty or twenty-five years earlier was one of the great poets of the English language.

This is the outline, I believe, of the sequence of ideas and states of mind which have debased the greatest American poetic talent of the twentieth century. The sequence is offered merely as a species of logical sequence; it is only imperfectly chronological. Stevens was a hedonist from the beginning, and the entire complex of ideas and feelings which I have recounted are to be found in his work from the beginning. But although it is possible to find some of his most willful nonsense—*Earthy Anecdote,* let us say, or *Metaphors of a Magnifico*—among his earlier poems, it is likewise true that all of his great poetry is early. *Sunday Morning* is one of the earliest compositions; *The Snow Man, Le Monocle de Mon Oncle, Of the Manner of Addressing Clouds, Of Heaven Considered as a Tomb, The Death of the Soldier* are all of the next few years. All of these poems were written and first published before 1923, the date of the first edition of *Harmonium;* and if there is a later poem as good I do not know it or cannot appreciate it. There are other poems, more or less early, less perfect or of smaller scope but still of considerable beauty, such as *Peter Quince at the Clavier* or *Cortège for Rosenbloom,* and such poems as these one may find equalled occasion-

446

ally, though very rarely, at a later date; but these two surpass anything by the author which I have read in the past decade.

Some of the virtues of *Sunday Morning* I have indicated in very general terms, but one cannot turn from the poem that may be the greatest American work of our century without considering briefly some of its more haunting beauties, if it be only as an act of piety.

I have already quoted the final stanza of the poem, and its beauty should be obvious; yet as removed from its context, the stanza loses much of its complexity. The "water without sound," the "wide water inescapable," is not only an image representing infinite space; it is an image, established in the first stanza, representing a state of mind, a kind of bright and empty beatitude, over which the thought of death may darken suddenly and without warning:

> *She dreams a little, and she feels the dark*
> *Encroachment of that old catastrophe,*
> *As a calm darkens among water-lights.*

The language has the greatest possible dignity and subtlety, combined with perfect precision. The imminence of absolute tragedy is felt and recorded, but the integrity of the feeling mind is maintained. The mind perceives, as by a kind of metaphysical sense, the approach of invading impersonality; yet knowing the invasion to be inevitable and its own identity, while that identity lasts, the only source of any good whatever, maintains that identity in its full calm and clarity, that nothing may be sacrificed without need. This combination of calm and terror, in dealing with this particular theme, will be found in only one other poet in English, in Shakespeare as one finds him in a few of the more metaphysical sonnets.[9] The calm clarity of tone enables the poet to deal with a variety of kinds of feeling which would be impossible were the terror emphasized for a moment at any point, were the complete

[9] I have discussed this attitude of Shakespeare and some of its historical background in Poetry: A Magazine of Verse for February, March, and April, 1939; and have analyzed the 77th sonnet with this attitude in mind on page 49 of the issue for April.

and controlled unity of the experiencing mind for a moment disordered by its own perceptions. The same poem, for example, is able to contain the following lines, of a sweetness and of an illusory simplicity which again are scarcely less than Shakespearean:

> She says, "I am content when wakened birds,
> Before they fly, test the reality
> Of misty fields, by their sweet questionings;
> But when the birds are gone, and their warm fields
> Return no more, where, then, is paradise?"

And out of this passage proceeds the great lament for the lost myths, which I have already mentioned. This passage and others similar, though beautiful in themselves, are a preparation for the descriptive lines in the last stanza, and when we finally come to those lines, they are weighted with meaning and feeling accumulated from all that has gone before. It is difficult for this reason to quote from the poem for the purpose of illustrating its beauty.

One aspect of the poem may perhaps be mentioned, however, with some small profit, and it may best be indicated, I believe, through a brief comparison with Bryant's *Thanatopsis*. Bryant's poem is a great poem and is worthy of the comparison, and its resemblance to Stevens' poem in certain ways is both surprising and illuminating. Both poems are semididactic meditations on death, written in a firm but simplified Miltonic blank verse, the verse of Stevens, possibly, being somewhat smoothed and softened by the intervention of Tennyson. Both poems are pagan in their view: but that of Bryant, the New Englander of the early 19th century, is essentially stoical, whereas that of Stevens, the Pennsylvanian of the 20th century, is Epicurean. Both poems find man, a spiritual being, isolated in a physical universe: but for Bryant that universe is the Earth, hairy, vast, and almost against the eye; for Stevens it is the tropical Pacific of infinity, in which the earth appears as an infinitesimal floating island.

The poems resemble each other more curiously, however, in

that each bears a particular relationship to an antecedent body of more or less decadent poetry.

The deistic philosophy of the 18th century had early generated in its numerous followers a combination of ideas and attitudes which was to mark literary style, and especially poetic style, more strongly, perhaps, than any other philosophy has ever done. Deism was an amateur philosophy, a fact which may account in part for its rapid rise to popularity among men of letters and gentlemen at large: it received its definitive philosophical outline from the third Earl of Shaftesbury and its definitive literary expression from Alexander Pope, in *The Essay on Man.* Roughly speaking, one may say that these writers taught:[10] that the world is ruled by a beneficent mind, that everything is as it must be, that what appears to be evil is actually good as relative to the whole, that because the ruling mind is beneficent man will find happiness in all his benevolent affections and beneficent actions and misery in their opposites. They taught likewise[11] that virtue is natural to man and that the instincts and emotions are more reliable guides to conduct than the reason, though training and cultivation may refine these guides; that, in the words of Robertson,[12] "to be good humored and truly cultivated is to be right in religion and conduct, and consequently happy." The contradictions in this philosophy have been so often recounted that I need scarcely remark upon them here. What I wish to point out is this: that in spite of all contradictions the philosophy represents an attack on the rational faculty and a fairly complete outline of later romanticism; that the attack is made by means of what purport to be the methods of the rational faculty—that is, the attack is composed of a small set of concepts which are supposed to explain all experience, and which are moved about in various pseudo-rational relationships in order that certain philosophical

[10] Shaftesbury's *"Characteristics,"* edited by J. M. Robertson, London, Grant Richards, 1900; editor's introduction pp. xxix and xxx.
[11] Pope, *Essay on Man,* especially Epistle III, more especially section II thereof; e.g., lines 97-8: And Reason raise o'er Instinct as you can,/ In this 'tis God directs, in that 'tis Man.
[12] J. M. Robertson, op. cit., p. xxxi.

conclusions may be reached. The deists appear to have achieved the delusion that they were reasoning with a final and immutable clarity, at the same time that they were attacking with all their small but apparently sufficient intellectual powers the very foundations of reason itself.

Their ideas generated an attitude of smug imperception in at least two ways: they were sure, in the first place, that they had solved all the essential problems of philosophy, history,[13] and morals, with the result that moral ideas and feelings were with increasing regularity expressed in a fixed set of stereotyped expressions or literary counters, which of necessity had for the most part a somewhat sentimental quality; and the general tendency of their philosophy worked to destroy the belief in the value of rational criticism, so that in spite of the composition of a good deal of literary criticism in the period, most of it somewhat superficial, the virtue of these counters long passed unchallenged, and when the challenge came, it came, strangely enough, not in the name of the intellect but in the name of the sensibility. Christian doctrine, and to some extent the best classical philosophy preceding it, had taught man to examine himself according to sound and intricate rules, in order that he might improve himself, and, if a Christian, achieve salvation. Deistic doctrine taught him that he was fairly certain of achieving any salvation that there might be available if he would only refrain from examining himself: "There needs but thinking right [i.e., deistically], and meaning well."[14] The result was the 18th century cliché, the most obvious symptom of the neat and innocent reasoning and perceiving of so many 18th century writers.

The Age of Reason has won that name from its heirs: from those who have agreed with it so completely as to abandon its literary methods, which were merely the methods of the preceding age, and too often unduly simplified.[15] The reasoning of the

---

[13] See *The Art of History*, by J. B. Black, Methuen and Co., Ltd., London, 1926. This book, which I fear is out of print, is one of the most brilliant pieces of criticism of our century, and ought to be more widely available.

[14] Pope, *The Essay on Man*, Epistle IV, l. 32.

[15] The conclusion of *The Dunciad*, though not unduly simplified, is an example of the continuance: it is the natural development of the procedure

Age of Reason was very largely directed toward the destruction of the authority of Reason. Later romantic writers accepted the notion of the essential baseness of Reason with no real argument, and, when they began to see the monotony of 18th century language at its worst, they had recourse to the standard romantic explanation of dullness, that it was caused by excessive intellectualism; and we have as a result the nineteenth century judgment, which still prevails, of eighteenth century poetry, that it is bad because too intellectual, whereas in reality eighteenth century poetry is commonly good and is often great but displays defects which are primarily due to intellectual deficiency. The eighteenth century poetic language had become so well established by the middle of the century that it could dominate men with no respect for the ideas which seem to have generated it: Samuel Johnson had nothing but contempt for deism, yet his style shows the influence of deism; the influence upon his prose was small, for that was the medium which he cultivated most assiduously, but the influence upon his verse was great. The prologues to *Comus* and to *A Word to the Wise*, which are probably his greatest poems, are stereotyped in almost every detail of language, but are poems of extraordinary power because of the conviction and intelligence of the author, which are expressed mainly in the plot and rational outline, and in a certain tragic irony with which the stereotypes are occasionally used: these poems are the work of a great genius employing a decadent language. The Reason, at this time, was tending toward immobility; and in those who accepted the doctrine, the emotions were freed: the natural outcome was to be found in Gray and Collins, men who in a discreet and sophisticated manner cultivated the feelings for their own sake, who generalized about the feelings with facile elegance but with small understanding, and who in varying degrees were the victims of uncomprehended melancholy.

These men and others of less talent but closely related, such as Blair and Macpherson, formed much of the immediate back-

---

established by Gascoigne, Ben Jonson, Greville, Donne, and others, and is one of the greatest passages in English poetry. *The Essay on Man* discloses a related procedure weakened by nonsense and sentimentalism.

ground of Bryant. The influence of Blair is to be seen in the form and matter of *Thanatopsis;* the influence of Ossian has been seen in Bryant's taste for panoramic landscape, though as a matter of fact Gray, Collins, and others of the period might be cited in this connection with equal justice. One of the most obvious relationships to these poets is to be seen in Byrant's early taste for the semi-epigrammatic epithet, which marks Gray's *Elegy* so strongly, a type of phrase which seems to show the breaking down of the Popian epigram in the direction of the standard cliché of the period: Gray's "mute inglorious Miltons" meet their milder descendants in Bryant's "solemn brood of care." The most interesting resemblance of Bryant to these romantic predecessors, however, is to be found in moments of a kind of melancholy, which though in a measure formal and even arbitrarily imposed upon the matter, is deeply felt by the poet.

> . . . . *the vales*
> *Stretching in pensive quietness between . . .*
> *Where thy pale form was laid with many tears. . . .*

These lines are very beautiful in their way, but they are far from specific: a sadness deriving in part from the general theme of the poem, and in part from a traditionally fixed rhetoric and emotional approach, is spread like a fine haze across the whole body of detail. This rhetoric, with its cognate melancholy, which, though formulary, is none the less profoundly a state of mind, is the most obvious characteristic of early romanticism: it is obvious in Gray and Collins and faintly discernible in the early Bryant.

Blake and Wordsworth broke the somewhat narrow frame of this early romanticism by freeing new emotions, mainly the obscurely prophetic; Wordsworth freed himself from the rhetorical forms of the preceding century by scrutinizing with literal exactness not his own human nature but the external nature of landscape, and Blake and Coleridge achieved a comparable freedom by a similar literalness in treating the phantasmagoria of the supernatural. The scope of romantic poetry was thus widened, but it remained essentially romantic poetry: poetry, that is, which sought to free the emotions rather than to understand them. Romantic poetry developed in the nineteenth century in England more or less along the lines indicated by these poets, and with no radical innovations of method after their time: the English romantics sought to free the emotions by writing about them in a more or less emotional manner; Wordsworth, of course, became less consistently Romantic as he matured.

The next step in the development of romantic practice, though it was suggested by Coleridge in the doctrine of organic form, was first indicated more or less fully by Poe, and in the matter of actual poetic practice was perhaps first taken by Poe, though very haltingly. One sees its nature precisely in the great French Symbolists. If it is the business of the poem to "express" emotion, then the form itself of expression should be expressive and if we are rigorously reasonable, as a few of the romantics are, in the pursuit of their unreasonable ends, we shall see that language can best be purely expressive of emotion if it is so used that all except emotional content is as nearly as possible eliminated. Mallarmé was quite clear as to the necessity of eliminating rational content from language[16] and was more brilliant and more elaborate than any other poet has ever been, in his technique of elimination. The later poems especially display extremely obscure symbolism and reference, stated in a syntax so perverse as to be barely and very uncertainly explicable, at the same time that the individual phrases communicate feelings and perceptions more sharp and interesting, when viewed in isolation, than they frequently have a right to communicate when viewed as a part of any deducible whole. The suggestiveness of the details is forced into startling isolation by the difficulty of comprehending the poems as wholes; and this effect appears, at least, to be deliberately sought. The reader who is curious may profitably study the three sonnets beginning respectively *Tout Orgueil fume-t-il du soir*, *Surgi de la croupe et du bond*, and *Une dentelle s'abolit* in the

---

[16] See his *Avant-dire* to René Ghil's *Traité du Verbe*. An extensive quotation from this, with a brief commentary upon it, will be found on page 18 of the present volume.

Fry-Mauron edition.[17] In the last of these, the technique of negation, by which gross matter is eliminated, and feeling, it is hoped,
is preserved, approaches the quality of unintentional parody: "A
lace curtain is effaced in doubt of the supreme Game [the nature
of the supreme Game, one should observe, is more than uncertain]
to display like a blasphemy nothing but the eternal absence of any
bed." The same doctrine is stated, perhaps less clearly, but in
terms approaching those of Stevens in *The Revolutionists Stop
for Orangeade*, by Paul Verlaine, in *Art Poétique:*

> *Il faut aussi que tu n'ailles point*
> *Choisir tes mots sans quelque méprise:*
> *Rien de plus cher que la chanson grise*
> *Où l'Indécis au précis se joint. . . .*
>
> *Car nous voulons la Nuance encor,*
> *Pas la couleur, rien que la Nuance!* [18]

And Rimbaud, in the version of *Bonheur* which appears in *Les
Illuminations*, informs us that the beatitude of which he has
made a magic study has made his speech incomprehensible, has
caused it to take wing and escape; and earlier in the same poem
he states that he has eliminated rational control from his life as
well, for the same beatitude has taken possession of his life, both
body and soul, and dispersed all effort. Just as the first great

[17] Poems by Mallarmé. Translated by Roger Fry, with commentaries by
Charles Mauron. 1936, Chatto & Windus, London.

[18] In spite of this statement Verlaine is more innocent than Mallarmé, and
less capable of intellectual perversity, as he is less capable than Rimbaud of
consistent anti-moral energy and passion. On pages 99 and 100 of this volume I refer to Verlaine as primitive—that is, limited, or minor, but relatively
sound in method—rather than decadent. Such a view is supported by some
of his best poems—*Malines* or *Le piano que baise une main frêle*, for example
—but not by all. The poem beginning *Dans l'interminable* differs not at all
in method from Rimbaud's *Larme;* both employ a description of strange landscape to communicate a feeling; but what is more or less conventionally
obscure melancholy in Verlaine—obscure in the sense that the motive of the
melancholy is nowhere suggested—is pushed to pure hallucination in Rimbaud.
And many other poems by Verlaine use the same method: *C'est l'extase lan-
goureuse*, for example, or *Green*. And it is worth remembering that the title
of his best collection is *Romances Sans Paroles*.

English romantics released the new subject matter, these poets, who were in rebellion against the stylistic looseness of their immediate predecessors in France, released the method which was, essentially, the proper method of romantic poetry. They released it, that is, within the bounds imposed by more or less traditional forms and by their own considerable talents and training: in their less fortunate successors we can observe the rapid progression toward le surréalisme. Mallarmé, like Gray, is a scholarly and sophisticated enemy of Reason; the body of his work, like that of Gray, is small; and similarly its generative power is very great. Mallarmé and his coadjutors seem to have played a part in the career of the young Stevens similar to that of Gray and Collins in the work of the young Bryant.

Mallarmé and Verlaine resemble Gray and Collins in their precise artistry and in their sophisticated melancholy, a melancholy which arises in both generations for much the same reasons, and which is kept within fairly close stylistic bounds in both pairs of poets by comparable sophistication of style. But the Frenchmen surpass the two Englishmen of a century earlier in the elusive fluctuation of their perception; they have come closer to writing not merely about their emotions but with their emotions, and in addition to being in certain ways more sensitive, they are harder to understand. In fact, they seem to exist very close to that precarious boundary beyond which meaning will become so diminished that sensitivity must rapidly diminish with it, since the feeling contained in language is indissolubly connected with the abstract sense of language and must vanish if that abstract sense is wholly destroyed.

It is in relationship to this resemblance and to this difference that it is most interesting to compare *Thanatopsis* to *Sunday Morning*. Both Stevens and Bryant in these poems were influenced perceptibly by the preceding decadent masters; both seem to have recovered from the influence to such an extent that the influence appears as a faint memory, as the supersensitivity of a kind of convalescence, in poets who are even more heavily influenced by antecedent and stronger tradition. But in Byrant this recovery was aided by more than mere literary tradition: he found his support in the skeletalized morality and etherealized theology of Unitarianism. From these he derived concepts over-simplified much as were those of deism, but over-simplified, at least, from something that was originally sound. The best of his later poems, *To a Waterfowl, The Past, The Battlefield,* and *The Tides,* are written on themes which are clear and reasonably sound but which he was able to apprehend only in terms so general as to approach without quite impinging upon vagueness. There is in these poems a good deal of the moral conviction that we find in the best poets of the English Renaissance, along with a remarkable gift for style, but there is very little left of the old moral intelligence, the diversity, the subtlety, and the precision. Bryant had not the intellect requisite to surpass the dominant ideas of his generation in New England and recapture anything of the earlier intelligence, but the ideas at least supported him, and he had enough either of simplicity or of stubbornness not to exchange them for anything worse. But Stevens appears to have been supported at this point in his career by little except literary tradition; like Bryant he accepted one of the current philosophies of his time, but one more beguiling and at the same time more dangerous than that of Bryant, and like Bryant he seems to have accepted it with no trace of scepticism, and with the result that we have seen. His history epitomizes that of four generations of French poets.

But we have done with the outline of Stevens' general history; it is with the moments of dangerous but successful balance in his earlier years that we are now concerned. I have spoken of the elusive fluctuation of perception in Mallarmé and Verlaine, and I have referred to the extraordinary subtlety with which Stevens perceives the impingement of death, as well as other matters, in *Sunday Morning;* and I have compared this quality in Stevens to a similar quality in some of Shakespeare's sonnets. This particular kind of sensitivity is fairly common in modern poetry, but nowhere at so high a level of excellence, I think, except in Valéry, certainly nowhere in English: at a lower level, or in another language and rhetorical tradition, it would probably display nothing that we should think of as Shakespearean.

Le Monocle de Mon Oncle, a work produced a few years later than *Sunday Morning,* endeavors to· treat the subject of love in hedonistic terms and confesses ironically to encountering more than one difficulty. The poem is often obscure, and, perhaps because one cannot easily follow it, appears far less a unit than *Sunday Morning;* it contains extraordinary writing, however. The second stanza may fairly illustrate what I have said:

> *A red bird flies across the golden floor.*
> *It is a red bird that seeks out his choir*
> *Among the choirs of wind and wet and wing.*
> *A torrent will fall from him when he finds.*
> *Shall I uncrumple this much-crumpled thing?*
> *I am a man of fortune greeting heirs;*
> *For it has come that thus I greet the spring.*
> *These choirs of welcome choir for me farewell.*
> *No spring can follow past meridian.*
> *Yet you persist with anecdotal bliss*
> *To make believe a starry connaissance.*

The first four lines are incomprehensible, except as description, and the claim of the fifth line is unjustified; the remainder of the stanza, however, displays a combination of bitterness, irony, and imperturbable elegance not unworthy of Ben Jonson.

Of the Manner of Addressing Clouds deals essentially with the same subject as the passage in which Crispin contemplates the plum, but deals with it in a different mood; that is, the poet sees much the same relationship between his art and his subject as does Crispin, but ·since he sees himself alone in the "old chaos of the sun," "that drifting waste," amid the "mute bare splendors of the sun and moon," he is glad to retain his art as a mitigation of his solitude: what kind of mitigation he does not venture to say, but the mere fact of mitigation suffices him. The opening lines of this poem display a faint suggestion of Stevens' self-parody in one of its most frequent forms, an excess of alliteration which renders the style perversely finical. If one will compare these lines to the opening of *The Come-*

dian as the Letter C, he may readily see how rapidly the method can degenerate into very crude comedy. *Of Heaven Considered as a Tomb* is a vision of death as extinction. These two poems deal with the evaluation of the central theme of *Sunday Morning,* with the irremediable tragedy, and they are free from all in that poem which invites question as well as much that provides richness and variety. The style of both has a cold concentration, related to this purity of motive, which almost surpasses, for me, the beauty of the longer poem. *The Snow Man* and *The Death of the Soldier* deal respectively with life and with death in a universe which is impersonal and devoid of any comfort except that which one may derive from the contemplation of the mute bare splendors. They have great power, but probably less than the other short poems which I have just mentioned, perhaps because of the metrical form."[10]

There appears to be in the best of the early poems, as I have said, a traditional seriousness of attitude and a traditional rhetoric cognate with that attitude and precisely expressive of it. This traditional element in the early work enables Stevens' talent to function at its highest power; but it is not only unjustified and unsupported by Stevens' explicit philosophy, it is at odds with that philosophy. And the conflict between the traditional element and the element encouraged by the philosophy results little by little in the destruction of the traditional element and the degradation of the poet's style. It is extremely important that we understand Stevens for more reasons than one; he has written great poems, and we should know them and know why they are great; and we should know what is bad, and why it is bad, so that we may separate the bad from the good and the more surely preserve the good. But beyond this, he gives us, I believe, the most perfect laboratory of hedonism to be found in literature. He is not like those occasional poets of the Renaissance who appear in some measure to be influenced by a pagan philosophy, but who in reality take it up as a literary

[10] The scansion of free verse and the influence of the meter on the total poetic result may be found discussed at great length on pages 103 to 150 of this volume. The scansion of *The Snow Man* is there marked. That of *The Death of the Soldier* is similar in principle, but simpler in form.

diversion at the same time that they are beneath the surface immovably Christian. Stevens is released from all the restraints of Christianity, and is encouraged by all the modern orthodoxy of Romanticism: his hedonism is so fused with Romanticism as to be merely an elegant variation on that somewhat inelegant System of Thoughtlessness. His ideas have remained essentially unchanged for more than a quarter of a century, and on the whole they have been very clearly expressed, so that there is no real occasion to be in doubt as to their nature; and he began as a great poet, so that when we examine the effect of those ideas upon his work, we are examining something of very great importance.

A Postscript: 1959.

When this essay was written, Stevens had only begun the elucidation of his theory of the Imagination, and its outlines were not clear. They are not clear yet, but one can decipher them. Briefly, Stevens believed that we live in a nominalistic universe made up of unrelated and inscrutable particulars, and that the only order possible in such a universe is that created by the poetic imagination. This notion is discussed most fully, but far from clearly, in his volume of prose, *The Necessary Angel*, and it is discussed or illustrated laboriously in most of his later poems. The best poem dealing with the topic may be *Idea of Order at Key West*, but the subject is thin and the style is largely decorative. The theory is partly an attempt at a philosophic foundation for the hedonism which I describe in my essay and partly an extension of this hedonism. The trouble with the theory is this: that the order in question is imaginary, whereas reality remains incurably nominalistic. In *The Hudson Review* for the spring of 1951, Stevens published a poem entitled *The Course of a Particular*, in which he explicitly renounces the doctrine. This poem was omitted from the *Collected Poems*, but appears in the *Opus Posthumous*. In the latter publication, however, there is an error which ruins the poem: in the next to the last line the word *ear* is changed to *air*, and the alteration renders the poem meaningless. The poem in the correct form is one of the greatest of Stevens' poems, and perhaps the greatest.

T. S. ELIOT

or The Illusion of Reaction

T. S. ELIOT IS PROBABLY the most widely respected literary
figure of our time; he is known primarily as the leader of the
intellectual reaction against the romanticism of which he began his career as a disciple. It is my purpose to show that his
intellectualism and his reactionary position are alike an illusion. It is perhaps needless to say that I use the word *reactionary*
in no emotional or pejorative sense, but in a simple and literal
one; I regard myself as a reactionary.

Eliot is a theorist who has repeatedly contradicted himself
on every important issue that he has touched, and he has dealt
in some fashion with most of the important literary issues of
our time. Between some of his contradictory statements there
is a greater or less lapse of time, and one might account for
them by a change of view if he showed any consciousness of
contradiction; but many of them occur within the same book
or even within the same essay. In this connection, however,
the year 1928 should be held in mind as a crucial one if any
important change is to be demonstrated, for it was in this year,
in his book of essays *For Lancelot Andrewes*, that he announced his conversion to Catholicism and to classicism.

The first aim of this essay will be to demonstrate the existence of these contradictions; the second will be to determine
as far as possible the main tendency in his theories; and the
last will be to show the effect of this tendency upon his poetry
and to indicate the effect upon his disciples.

Eliot's critical discussion deals with a fairly definite number of topics, and in the interests of clarity I shall do my best to treat each topic separately, though a certain amount of overlapping will be inevitable.

I. AUTOTELIC ART

In *The Function of Criticism*[1] Eliot writes:

"No exponent of criticism . . . has, I presume, ever made the preposterous assumption that criticism is an autotelic activity. I do not deny that art may be affirmed to serve ends beyond itself; but art is not required to be aware of these ends, and indeed performs its functions, whatever they may be, according to various theories of value, much better by indifference to them. Criticism, on the other hand, must always profess an end in view, which, roughly speaking, appears to be the elucidation of works of art and the correction of taste."

One is confronted here with several problems. How, for example, can an artist perform a function better for not knowing what it is? Is Eliot assuming an automatic, or unconscious art, an art which is an extreme form of romantic mysticism? Where also is the line between prose which is art and prose which is not art? Are we to assume that there is no art in expository prose, let us say in Johnson's Introduction to his dictionary? Or merely that there is no art in that branch of expository prose which we call literary criticism? And if there is no art in expository prose, then what shall we say about expository verse? What shall we do, let us wonder in passing, with the first of Donne's *Holy Sonnets*, with the *Epistle to Dr. Arbuthnot*, or with much of *The Divine Comedy*? In the same essay he adds:[2]

"I have assumed as axiomatic that a creation, a work of art, is autotelic; and that criticism is about something other than itself."

[1] Selected Essays, by T. S. Eliot. Harcourt, Brace & Co. P. 13. (1932).
[2] Ibid., p. 19.

461

Art, then, is about itself, but this information does not help me to answer my questions, for I do not understand it. What, for example, would Pope or Dante have understood if this statement had been made to them regarding the poems which I have just mentioned? Or what can we understand with regard to these poems? About all we can deduce from such a passage is that the artist does not really know what he is doing; a doctrine which we shall find suggested and elucidated elsewhere, and which leads directly to the plainest kind of determinism.

Yet every poem appears to the unpracticed eye to say something about some aspect of human experience. What are we to make of this? In one of his earliest and most famous essays, Eliot deals with this problem by way of a figure of speech:[a]

"The analogy was that of the catalyst. When the two gases previously mentioned are mixed in the presence of a filament of platinum, they form sulphurous acid. This combination takes place only if the platinum is present; nevertheless the newly formed acid contains no trace of platinum, and the platinum itself is apparently unaffected: has remained inert, neutral, and unchanged. The mind of the poet is the shred of platinum. It may partly or exclusively operate upon the experience of the man himself; but the more perfect the artist, the more completely separate in him will be the man who suffers and the mind which creates; the more perfectly will the mind digest and transmute the passions which are its material.

"The experience, you will notice, the elements which enter the presence of the transforming catalyst, are of two kinds: emotions and feelings. The effect of a work of art upon the person who enjoys it is an experience different in kind from any experience not of art. It may be formed out of one emotion, or may be a combination of several; and various feelings, inhering for the writer in particular words or phrases or images, may be added to compose the final result. Or great poetry may be made without the direct use of any emotion whatever: composed out of feelings solely. Canto XV of the *Inferno* (Brunetto Latini) is a working up of the emotion evident in the situation; but the effect, though single as that of any work of art, is obtained by a considerable complexity of detail. The last quatrain gives an image, a feeling attaching to an image, which 'came,' which

[a] *Tradition and the Individual Talent*, Ibid., p. 7 and thereafter.

did not develop simply out of what precedes, but which was probably in suspension in the poet's mind until the proper combination arrived for it to add itself to. The poet's mind is in fact a receptacle for seizing and storing up numberless feelings, phrases, images, which remain there until all the particles which can unite to form a new compound are present together.

"If you compare several representative passages of the greatest poetry you see how great is the variety of the types of combination, and also how completely any semi-ethical criterion of sublimity misses the mark. For it is not the 'greatness,' the intensity, of the emotions, the components, but the intensity of the artistic process, the pressure, so to speak, under which the fusion takes place, that counts. The episode of Paolo and Francesca employs a definite emotion, but the intensity of the poetry is something quite different from whatever intensity in the supposed experience it may give the impression of . . . the murder of Agamemnon, or the agony of Othello, gives an artistic effect apparently closer to a possible original than the scenes from Dante. In the *Agamemnon,* the artistic emotion approximates to the emotion of an actual spectator; in *Othello* to the emotion of the protagonist himself. But the difference between art and the event is always absolute."

This passage requires a good deal of comment. In the first place, one should note the words *emotion* and *feeling:* the first refers to an emotion, as we commonly use the term, which arises from an experience outside of literature; the second to an emotion stirred by a work or a fragment of literature. Emotion and feeling are the ingredients of literary art; there is no reference to rational understanding. Emotion, moreover, in Eliot's sense of the word, is transformed by the artistic process into something which differs absolutely from that which it was originally, so that semi-ethical criteria are irrelevant to our judgment of the work of art. Art appears to be in this passage, as in Poe, a matter of the novel combination of materials; and there is no question of the artist's understanding what he is saying: the criterion, as in Poe, is one of *effect.* This is interesting, for in reading Eliot, one cannot avoid the conclusion that he has absorbed much from Poe, but through early or fragmentary or otherwise uncritical reading: many of Eliot's theories resemble those of Poe without Eliot's apparently knowing it, and his references to Poe are almost invariably inaccurate.[4]

There is further evidence in this passage that Eliot regards the poet as passive: he refers to him as "inert, neutral, unchanged," during and after the act of creation. Yet the figure is not developed consistently, for later Eliot asserts that it is "the intensity of the artistic process, the pressure, so to speak, under which the fusion takes place that counts." He does not say whether this intensity is a function of the inert mind of the poet or an accident affecting the mind from without. Nor, if we try to interpret the figure, to translate it into plain language, can we determine what is meant either by inertness or by intensity; nor can we guess what occurs when the poet writes: the entire process is a mystery, and if the critic can say no more about it than he has said, he would have done well to employ less and simpler language.

If I may be pardoned for insisting, for a moment, on my own view of these matters, I should like to suggest that it describes more accurately the facts which Eliot appears to have in mind than does the theory of Eliot himself. According to my view, the artistic process is one of moral evaluation of human experience, by means of a technique which renders possible an evaluation more precise than any other. The poet tries to understand his experience in rational terms, to state his understanding, and simultaneously to state, by means of the feelings which we attach to words, the kind and degree of emotion that should properly be motivated by this understanding. The artistic result differs from the crude experience mainly in its refinement of judgment: the difference in really good art is enormous, but the difference is of degree rather than of kind. The "intensity" of the work of art, which is different from the

<hr/>

[4] In the essay on Marvell (Selected Essays, New York, p. 259), for example, Eliot writes: "There is here the element of *surprise*, as when Villon says: Necessité faict gens mesprendre Et faim saillir le loup des bois, the surprise which Poe considered of the highest importance." But it was *originality* not *surprise*, about which Poe theorized, and he conceived it as a more or less arbitrary effect of scenery or meter, not as simple precision of comparison. See my essay on Poe in the present volume.

intensity of the crude experience, lies in this: that what we call intensity in a work of art is a combination of the importance of the original subject and the precision of the judgment; whereas that which we call intensity in life is most often the confused and therefore frightening emotion resulting from a situation which we have not yet had time to meet and understand, and our feeling toward which, as it approaches clarity and control, approaches, though from a considerable distance, the condition of art.

I must ask the reader to bear carefully in mind not only the passage just quoted from Eliot but my statement of my own point of view, while he is considering the following passage from the essay called *The Metaphysical Poets*:[5]

"In the seventeenth century a dissociation of sensibility set in, from which we have never recovered; and this dissociation, as is natural, was aggravated by the two most powerful poets of the century, Milton and Dryden. Each of these men performed certain poetic functions so magnificently well that the magnitude of the effect concealed the absence of others. The language went on and in some respects improved; the best verse of Collins, Gray, Johnson, and even Goldsmith satisfies some of our fastidious demands better than that of Donne or Marvell or King. But while the language became more refined, the feeling became more crude. The feeling, the sensibility, expressed in the *Country Churchyard* (to say nothing of Tennyson and Browning) is cruder than in the *Coy Mistress*."

The significance of this passage is not quite clear, but Eliot returns to the subject and elucidates it in his essay on Marvell:[6]

"When we come to Gray and Collins, the sophistication remains only in the language, and has disappeared from the feeling. Gray and Collins were masters, but they had lost that hold on human values, that firm grasp of human experience, which is a formidable achievement of the Elizabethan and Jacobean poets."

But how does this firm grasp of human values get into an autotelic art, to which ethical criteria are irrelevant? Has Eliot

[5] Op. cit., p. 247.
[6] Ibid., p. 256.

changed his mind radically over a period of years? *The Function of Criticism*, from which the first quotation in this essay is drawn is dated[7] 1923. *Tradition and the Individual Talent*, which provides the second quotation is dated 1917, and first appeared in book-form in *The Sacred Wood*, in 1921. The two other essays, however, are both dated 1921, and the essay on Swinburne, which appears in *The Sacred Wood*, finds Swinburne a poet of very limited value because his poetry was not nourished on human experience, and it ends with the statement:[8]

". . . the language which is more important to us is that which is struggling to digest and express new objects, new feelings, new aspects, as, for instance, the prose of Mr. James Joyce or the earlier Conrad."

How does the language "digest" these subjects, without being "about" them? This passage and the passage from the essay on Marvell, though carelessly put, are comprehensible in my terms but not in the terms of the other essays cited. Eliot has not changed his mind over a given period, for the dates of the essays forbid such a view. The fact of the matter is that at any given time he can speak with equal firmness and dignity on both sides of almost any question, and with no realization of the difficulties in which he is involved.

II. THE THEORY OF THE OBJECTIVE CORRELATIVE

My own view of poetry, which I have already indicated, is a simple one: I believe that the feeling expressed by the work is, or should be, motivated by the artist's comprehension of his subject, which is drawn from human experience; and that the value of the work depends upon the justness of the motivation, in whole and in detail. Eliot sometimes adopts this view, but in the main he prefers to assume the emotion as initial:

[7] Ibid. see list of dates in table of contents.
[8] Ibid., p. 285.

the result is his famous and widely influential theory of the objective correlative. In his essay on Hamlet[9] he writes:

"The only way of expressing emotion in the form of art is by finding an 'objective correlative'; in other words, a set of objects, a situation, a chain of events which shall be the formula for that *particular* emotion; such that when the external facts, which must terminate in sensory experience, are given, the emotion is immediately evoked."

This seems to me, I confess, a reversal of the normal processes of understanding human experience, and a dangerous reversal. Mario Praz traces this concept to Pound:[10]

"Pound's idea of poetry as 'a sort of inspired mathematics which gives us equations, not for abstract figures, triangles, spheres, and the like, but for the human emotions,' may be said to be the starting point for Eliot's theory of the 'Objective correlative.'"

Praz continues:

"That influence is closely connected with Eliot's interpretation of Dante's allegory along the lines suggested by Ezra Pound—as we have seen above. Clear visual images, a concise and luminous language: these are the two qualities of Dante Eliot has in mind. The former is the 'objective correlative' of the emotions they intend to suggest, the latter appeals to the auditory imagination: there is an element of extreme precision and extreme vagueness in both . . . The pattern of images in *Ash Wednesday* seems thus suggested by Dante, but in a peculiar way. It is as if Eliot had been reading Dante without giving much heed to the meaning, but letting himself be impressed by a few clear visual images."

Praz is unquestionably correct in his claims for the extensive influence of Pound upon Eliot's critical theories. Nevertheless, this particular theory is at least as old as Poe and is more than likely older, and Poe states it much more nearly in Eliot's terms. Poe writes in his essay on Hawthorne:[11]

---

[9] Ibid., p. 124.
[10] Southern Review, Vol. II, No. 3, pp. 525-548. The passage from Pound occurs on p. 5, *The Spirit of Romance*.
[11] Stedman and Woodberry edition, p. 31 of the second of the three volumes of Poe's criticism. For further comment see my essay on Poe, already mentioned.

467

". . . having conceived, with deliberate care, a certain unique or single *effect* to be wrought out, he [the skillful literary artist] then invents such incidents—he then combines such events as may best aid him in establishing this preconceived effect."

One will find the same procedure elaborated in *The Philosophy of Composition*.

Eliot, however, is unable to adhere to his position. In the same essay—indeed on the same page—he writes:

"Hamlet is up against the difficulty that his disgust is occasioned by his mother, but that his mother is not an adequate equivalent for it; his disgust envelops and exceeds her. It is thus a feeling which he cannot understand . . ."

And the play as a whole is found at fault in the end for the same reason with relation to Shakespeare: the events of the play are not an adequate equivalent for the disgust which Shakespeare, in Eliot's opinion, was trying to express. Now finding an "objective correlative" for an emotion is not the same thing as understanding it: to understand it we must know and correctly judge its motive. There seems to be a suggestion here that Eliot's theory is inadequate to his feeling about the play. There is a similar suggestion in this passage from the essay on Cyril Tourneur:[12]

"The cynicism, the loathing and disgust of humanity, expressed consummately in *The Revenger's Tragedy*, are immature in the respect that they exceed the object."

And a few years earlier he is even more explicit. In the essay on Lancelot Andrewes, he writes:[13]

"Andrewes' emotion is purely contemplative; it is not personal, it is wholly evoked by the object of contemplation, to which it is adequate; his emotion is wholly contained in and explained by its

[12] Op. cit., p. 166.
[13] Ibid., p. 298. The last three essays mentioned are dated 1919, 1931, and 1926 respectively.

object. But with Donne there is always something else, the 'baffling' of which Mr. Pearsall Smith speaks in his introduction. Donne is a 'personality' in a sense in which Andrewes is not: his sermons, one feels, are a 'means of self-expression.' He is constantly finding an object which shall be adequate to his feelings: Andrewes is wholly absorbed in the object and therefore responds with the adequate emotion. Andrewes has the *goût pour la vie spirituelle,* which is not native to Donne."

Now it is immaterial with respect to my present purposes whether this comparison of the two men is a just one; the point which interests me is this: that Andrewes is praised because he adheres to my principles, whereas Donne is blamed because he adheres to those of Eliot. Eliot does not explain his self-contradiction, nor does he give any evidence that he is aware of it.

III. THOUGHT AND EMOTION IN POETRY

The theory of the "objective correlative" rests, as Eliot says in discussing Andrews, on the assumption that the poet is trying to express an emotion, not on the theory that he is trying to understand it. It is as good a fundamental principle as one is likely to find to serve as a justification for the sort of confused motivation which I have discussed under the name of pseudo-reference in the group of essays called *Primitivism and Decadence.* I should like to reiterate what I shall be able to show in great detail later, that this primacy which Eliot gives to the emotions leads directly to a thorough determinism of the most dangerous sort: if we are bound to express our emotions without understanding them, we obviously have no way of judging or controlling them, but must take them as they come. Eliot deals with the general subject of the relation of thought to emotion in a great many passages, of which I must confine myself to a relatively small number for comment.

In the essay on *Shakespeare and the Stoicism of Seneca*[14] he says:

[14] Ibid., p. 115.

"The poet who 'thinks' is merely the poet who can express the emotional equivalent of thought. But he is not necessarily interested in the thought itself. We talk as if thought was precise and emotion was vague. In reality there is precise emotion and there is vague emotion. To express precise emotion requires as great intellectual power as to express precise thought."

This passage is a startling one. What, for example, is the emotional equivalent of thought, unless it is the emotion motivated by thought? We are not concerned, here, with the objective correlative of an emotion, but with the emotional correlative of a thought, which must then be expressed by means, I presume, of an objective correlative. What is the nature of the extraordinary sequence of relationships here implied? And if the emotion is to be considered as motivated by the thought, what are we to think of the poet who can express such emotion when he is not "interested in the thought itself"? Furthermore, how can such emotion be expressed except in terms of the motivating thought unless we are to falsify it utterly? And how can it be precise unless the motivating thought is precise?

In the same essay and on the next page Eliot writes:

"The difference between Shakespeare and Dante is that Dante had one coherent system of thought behind him; but that was just his luck, and from the point of view of poetry is an irrelevant accident. It happened that at Dante's time thought was orderly and strong and beautiful, and that it was concentrated in one man of the greatest genius; Dante's poetry receives a boost which in a sense it does not merit, from the fact that the thought behind it is the thought of a man as great and lovely as Dante himself: St. Thomas . . . In truth, neither Shakespeare nor Dante did any real thinking—that was not their job; and the relative value of the thought current at their time, the material enforced upon each to use as the vehicle of his feeling, is of no importance."

Now Eliot, as we shall see elsewhere, is usually of the opinion that Shakespeare was the inhabitant of a very inferior intellectual milieu, so that this passage is in effect a comparison of two very great poets one of whom is supposed to have inherited (without much effort) the clearest and most intricate philosophy of all time and the other a ragbag of disparate philosophical fragments. But what, then, is the meaning of the passage? In what sense does Dante's poetry "receive a boost," irrespective of the question of merit? Is Dante's poetry better for the clarity of its thought, or is it not? If it is better, in what sense is the clarity of its thought an irrelevant accident? It is not Dante's personal merit with which we are concerned, but the quality of his poetry. The last sentence, however, is emphatic, and it is emphatically anti-intellectual and deterministic at the same time: "the relative value of the thought current at their time, the material enforced upon each to use as the vehicle of his feeling, is of no importance." We may observe from this that the quality of a writer's thought is at once enforced upon him and is irrelevant to the quality of his work.

Much the same view is expressed more fully a little later:[16]

"What every poet starts from is his own emotions. . . . The great poet, in writing himself, writes his time. Thus Dante, hardly knowing it, became the voice of the thirteenth century; Shakespeare, hardly knowing it, became the representative of the end of the sixteenth century, of a turning point in history. But you can hardly say that Dante believed, or did not believe, the Thomist philosophy: you can hardly say that Shakespeare believed, or did not believe, the mixed and muddled scepticism of the Renaissance. If Shakespeare had written according to a better philosophy, he would have written worse poetry; it was his business to express the greatest emotional intensity of his time, based on whatever his time happened to think. Poetry is not a substitute for philosophy or theology or religion, as Mr. Lewis and Mr. Murry sometimes seem to think; it has its own function. But as this function is not intellectual but emotional, it cannot be defined adequately in intellectual terms. We can say that it provides 'consolation': strange consolation, which is provided equally by writers so different as Dante and Shakespeare. . . .

"I doubt whether belief proper enters into the activity of a great poet, qua poet. That is, Dante, qua poet, did not believe or disbelieve the Thomist cosmology or theory of the soul: he merely made use of it, or a fusion took place between his initial emotional impulses and a theory, for the purpose of making poetry. The poet makes poetry, the metaphysician makes metaphysics, the bee makes honey, the spider secretes a filament; you can hardly say that any of these agents believes: he merely does."

[16] Ibid., p. 117.

This passage also is curious in a great many ways. In the first place we have no authority for Shakespeare's intellectual equipment save Eliot's unsupported impression; and Eliot's impression even of so monumental a subject as this, as we shall ultimately have occasion to see, is not incapable of sudden and unpremeditated reversal; but let us suppose Shakespeare to be what Eliot here says he is. Eliot displays a knowledge of the personal beliefs and motives of two poets of distant ages that can be matched for its clairvoyance, I imagine, only by the perceptions of certain characters of Henry James; and he refines upon this clairvoyance in the case of Dante by distinguishing between Dante *qua* Dante and Dante *qua* poet. Anyone who can take this sort of thing seriously is welcome to do so. These points are all trivial, however, as compared to another; namely a kind of mystical determinism which has seldom been stated with such naive emphasis except by Emerson himself. Eliot writes: "Thus Dante, hardly knowing it, became the voice of the thirteenth century . . ." And Emerson: "Great men have always confided themselves childlike to the genius of their age . . ." And again:

> "The hand that rounded Peter's dome,
> And groined the aisles of Christian Rome,
> Wrought in a sad sincerity;
> Himself from God he could not free."

A passage in which God, the universe, and the period are conceived to be one. And it is worth noting in passing that Eliot's belief that only intellectual matter may be treated by the intellect introduces a new complication, with really extraordinary irradiations, into the practice of philosophy and of criticism.

Eliot is not without his hesitations, however. In writing elsewhere of Dante,[17] he says:

"And clear visual images are given much more intensity by having a meaning—we do not need to know what the meaning is, but in our

[17] Ibid., p. 204.

472

awareness of the image we must be aware that the meaning is there too. Allegory is only one poetic method, but it is a method which has very great advantages.

"Dante's is a *visual* imagination. It is a visual imagination in a different sense from that of a modern painter of still life: it is visual in the sense that he lived in an age in which men still saw visions. It was a psychological habit, the trick of which we have forgotten, but as good as any of our own. We have nothing but dreams, and we have forgotten that seeing visions—a practice now relegated to the aberrant and uneducated—was once a more significant, interesting, and disciplined kind of dreaming. We take it for granted that our dreams spring from below: possibly the quality of our dreams suffers in consequence."

It is possible, of course, as Eliot somewhere else remarks, to admire a poem deeply without wholly understanding it; but such admiration must rest on an understanding at least imperfect, and the idea that this admiration is adequate as compared with that which comes with full understanding is mere nonsense. Dante's visions, with their meaning obscured, are dreams, as Praz points out; though in Dante, at least, and in part by virtue of the meaning which helped Dante to see them, they may be dreams of unusual clarity. If the meaning is important in the creation of the poem, at any rate, it is foolish to suppose that one can dispense with it in reading the poem or that the poet did not take his meaning seriously. Only the frailest barrier exists between the idea of this passage and Poe's theory that the poet should lay claim to a meaning when he is aware of none.

Eliot goes still farther, in his essay on Marvell, in the direct-tion of admitting the importance of thought in the poem, but the passage is merely an undeveloped hint, and one does not really know what he meant by it:[18]

"These verses have the suggestiveness of true poetry; and the verses of Morris, which are nothing if not an attempt to suggest, really suggest nothing; and we are inclined to infer that the suggestiveness is the aura around a bright clear center, that you cannot have the aura alone."

[18] Ibid., p. 259.

And in writing of Dryden, he says likewise:[19]

"Swinburne was also a master of words, but Swinburne's words are all suggestions and no denotation; if they suggest nothing, it is because they suggest too much."

This is a good statement, but there is small reason to believe that Eliot knows what it means. He concludes his essay on the Metaphysical poets, for example,—an essay, which, incidentally, comments with a certain penetration on some of the qualities of metaphysical poetry—with this remarkable judgment:[20]

"It is not a permanent necessity that poets should be interested in philosophy, or in any other subject. We can only say that it appears likely that poets in our civilization, as it exists at present, must be *difficult* . . . The poet must become more and more comprehensive, more allusive, more indirect, in order to force, to dislocate if necessary, language into his meaning . . . Hence we get something which looks very much like the conceit—we get, in fact, a method curiously similar to that of the metaphysical poets . . ."

The idea is illustrated by a passage of fragmentary and weakly allusive French symbolism. This statement by Eliot has been often quoted, and is probably one of the main reasons why so many of the young and decadent romantics of our own period are convinced that they are in the tradition of Donne. If one cannot be profound, it is always fairly easy to be difficult.

Only one deduction is possible from Eliot's many comments upon this subject: namely that he believes that a poet who merely pretends to be saying something may be as successful as one who succeeds in saying something, that, as he said clearly in the passages quoted earlier in this section, the intellectual content of a poem is irrelevant to its value. That the intellectual content of a poem, whether good, bad, or fraudulent is an inseparable part of the poem and is inextricably involved in the emotion, simply by virtue of the fact that the poem is composed of words, he does not seem to consider.

[19] Ibid., p. 273.
[20] Ibid., p. 248.

474

The subject of poetry and belief is little more than a subsidiary topic under the preceding head; for this reason, I shall consider only one passage from Eliot, a characteristic one, and shall try to make a few elementary distinctions of my own. This may seem presumptuous, but the problem of poetry and belief does not seem to me nearly so difficult as more learned authorities than myself have apparently thought it. In writing of Dante, Eliot comments as follows on certain ideas of I. A. Richards:[21]

"We may raise the question whether 'literature' exists; but for certain purposes, such as the purpose of this essay on Dante, we must assume that there is literature and literary appreciation; we must assume that the reader can obtain the full 'literary' or (if you will) 'aesthetic' enjoyment without sharing the beliefs of the author. . .

I deny, in short, that the reader must share the beliefs of the poet in order to enjoy the poetry fully. I have also asserted that we can distinguish between Dante's beliefs as a man and his beliefs as a poet. But we are forced to believe that there is a particular relation between the two, and that the poet 'means what he says.' If we learned, for instance, that *De Rerum Natura* was a Latin exercise which Dante had composed for relaxation after completing *The Divine Comedy,* and published under the name of one Lucretius, I am sure that our capacity for enjoying either poem would be mutilated . . .

And I confess to considerable difficulty in analyzing my own feelings, a difficulty which makes me hesitate to accept Mr. Richards' theories of 'pseudo-statements.' On reading the line which he uses,
Beauty is truth, truth beauty . . .
I am at least inclined to agree with him, because this statement of equivalence means nothing to me. But on rereading the whole ode, this line strikes me as a serious blemish on a beautiful poem; and the reason must be either that I fail to understand it, or that it is a statement which is untrue . . ."

Like Eliot, I find the statement of Keats a blemish, and for the reason given, a reason which, however, Eliot has no right to give, for the general theories which we have been examining will not support it. What "particular relation" can there be between the beliefs of the two Dantes, or how can the poet "mean what he says" if he is "not necessarily interested in the thought itself"? Eliot is not making fine distinctions when he writes thus; he is indulging in unpardonable confusion.

The difficulty in the statement by Keats, however, is not the same difficulty that Dante might be supposed to encounter in Lucretius or Lucretius in Dante; the difficulty is one of simple incomprehensibility. Beauty and Truth are abstract terms with distinct meanings; to say that they are interchangeable without explaining oneself leads to confusion. The non-Christian, however, might easily share a wide community of belief with Dante. The portraits of the damned are portraits of human beings, represented in Hell as they might be seen in life, suffering for sins most of which are acknowledged to be sins by intelligent men, whether Christian or not. As we proceed, however, toward the final vision of beatitude, we find ourselves dealing with concepts which are more and more purely Christian, and it is more than likely that only the convinced Christian can feel the poetry at something like its full value: for the rest of us, the poetry offers a theoretic projection of the imagination, a representation more or less dramatic. Not purely, however: for such poetry will of necessity be colored by feelings, desires, and ideas common to all men, and this alloy renders easier our entrance into the Christian state of feeling.

Let us consider another case. One of the few great poems of the twentieth century in America, I imagine, is *Sunday Morning*, by Wallace Stevens. The poem is a meditative composition, discreetly didactic in form; and its doctrine is one of more or less Paterian hedonism. Now I am not, myself, a hedonist of any variety; my dislike for the philosophy is profound, and I believe that it has, in the long run, done serious damage to the style of Wallace Stevens. But I know that hedonists exist, and the state of mind portrayed in the poem seems proper to them, and moreover it seems beautifully portrayed. It is no more necessary that one be a hedonist in order to enjoy this particular poem than that one be a murderer in order to enjoy Macbeth. Furthermore, in my own case, various subsidiary themes facilitate my entrance into the dominant theme: the theme of twentieth century scepticism, of doubt of immortality, the vision of the world as an infinitesimal island floating in infinite space. These themes, however, might merely increase the difficulty for Dante; but allowing Dante the same opportunity for the historical study of our period that we enjoy in the study of his, we may reasonably guess that he would be able to understand the poem fairly well.

My chief objection to a hedonistic philosophy is not that it contradicts my own view of human experience, but that it offers a very small portion of it in place of the whole, and that the error of mistaking that portion for the whole may prove very serious; that portion, however, may be truly described. On the other hand, Emerson, I believe, contradicts the most elementary and obvious facts of experience, and his poems may offer a problem of considerable difficulty. Emerson believes that all good comes from surrender to instinct and emotion; all evil from the functioning of the rational faculty. Emerson's ideal man would be, it appears to me certain, an automaton, a madman; it is simply impossible to envisage human experience in these terms, for the terms are a negation of everything that we know. When Emerson, therefore, preaches his doctrine directly, in purely didactic terms, and with intentions purely to explain and convince, as in *The Problem*, he achieves a kind of incomprehensibility comparable to that in the passage from Keats. His language is very general, with the result that certain passages, if found in isolation, might be given a significance anything but Emersonian, as, for instance, could this passage about Michael Angelo:

> *The hand that rounded Peter's dome,*
> *And groined the aisles of Christian Rome,*
> *Wrought in a sad sincerity;*
> *Himself from God he could not free.*

Standing alone, these lines offer an impressive portrait of the devout Christian artist. But if we take them in the entire poem, we find that they mean something the reverse of Christian: we find that the God in question is the God of the Pantheist, and that the artist could not free himself from Him, simply because he wrought automatically as a determined and inseparable portion of the whole. If we could force ourselves to see what Emerson meant, and refuse to be misled by the traditional associations of the language when it is considered fragmentarily, then the poem, it seems to me, would be damaged past remedy. Of course we can never quite do this; the traditional associations are there, and they keep the poem alive in a marginal and unsatisfactory way, but nevertheless alive, and this is true of much similar poetry.

And one might find a poem stated throughout in terms so general that alternative interpretations might be possible. Consider, for example, Blake's *Introduction* to the *Songs of Experience*. Blake's philosophy resembles that of Emerson, except that it is not pantheistic; it contradicts the common observation of human nature in much the same fashion. The *Introduction* is, in fact, an invitation to humanity to throw off the shackles of intellect and law, and thus to free the true God, who was overthrown by Lucifer and bound in Hell: it rests on a precise inversion not only of Christian mythology, which perhaps does not matter, but of Christian morality as well. Yet we know this only by examining Blake as a whole; the poem as an isolated invocation might as well be Christian. What then are we to do with such a poem? Are we to read it with an attempt to accept for the moment Blake's full meaning, even if that meaning appears to be nonsense? If we do that, we shall have the same difficulty as in the poem by Emerson. Are we to read it with a resolute determination to give it as much of our own private meaning as the nature of the statement permits, even while realizing that Blake's meaning was the reverse of this? Such a procedure would be justified, so far as it might be possible, I believe, if it were necessary. In this poem, however, the abstract statement is very general: the poem is an invocation to humanity to free itself from evil and to enter the good life; the feeling of the poem is a feeling proper

478

to that very general statement, and we may reasonably take the poem in that condition of generality and not trouble ourselves about the difficulties of Blake's philosophy until we actually trip on them.

These speculations, however, all derive from the conviction that the thought of a poem must be in some sense acceptable; that the thought is of the greatest importance as a part of the poem itself. Eliot, in the last passage quoted, would like, it appears, to make some such admission, but is hampered by the contrary trend of his general theory; and he once more takes refuge in mystery. But the believer in pure poetry will probably demand to know what there will be in pre-romantic poetry for the reader who believes with Emerson. The question in one form or another is constantly raised, and is mildly interesting. One may reply at the outset that the romantic theorist is by his nature either an untalented or an untrained theorist, and is therefore, like Emerson, practically certain to be inconsistent. His inconsistencies will probably rescue a good deal of the poetry in question for him. However, his understanding of such poetry, like Emerson's, is likely to be a very imperfect affair. If we could find a truly consistent Emersonian, it is certain that he would understand nothing of pre-romantic poetry or of anything else; furthermore he would have no particular rights in the matter. One might as well demand poetic rights for those who cannot read or speak, or poetic rights for idiots. Poetry is for the intelligent.

V. TRADITION

Much of what has been thus far discussed verges on the question of tradition. The question is one that has fascinated Eliot from the beginning, and on which he has made some of his most interesting comments. In the early essay, *Tradition and the Individual Talent*, he writes:[22]

> "We dwell with satisfaction upon the poet's difference from his predecessors, especially his immediate predecessors; we endeavor to

[22] Ibid., p. 4.

find something that can be isolated in order to be enjoyed. Whereas if we approach a poet without this prejudice we shall often find that not only the best but the most individual parts of his work may be those in which the dead poets, his ancestors, assert their immortality most vigorously. And I do not mean the impressionable period of adolescence, but the period of full maturity."

This seems to me admirable as far as it goes, but the relation of the individual contribution to the traditional procedure is not made very clear. One may depart from it in almost any direction, and Eliot in regarding Pound as the greatest modern poet in English, seems to depart somewhat curiously: what, precisely, is Pound's relationship to tradition, and why is it superior to that of Bridges, Hardy, or Robinson? And in what does it resemble the relationship of Valéry, whom Eliot apparently judges, as do I, to be the greatest modern in French? On the face of it Pound and Valéry appear to have almost nothing in common save native talent: Pound's relationship to tradition is that of one who has abandoned its method and pillaged its details—he is merely a barbarian on the loose in a museum; Valéry's relationship to tradition is that of a poet who has mastered and used the best of traditional method, and has used that method to deal with original and intelligent matter. Valéry is a living and beautifully functioning mind; Pound is a rich but disordered memory.

Eliot continues in the same essay:

"Yet if the only form of tradition, of handing down, consisted in following the ways of the immediate generation before us in a blind or timid adherence to its successes, 'tradition' should positively be discouraged. We have seen many such simple currents soon lost in the sand; and novelty is better than repetition. Tradition is a matter of much wider significance. It cannot be inherited, and if you want it you must obtain it by great labor. It involves in the first place, the historical sense, which we may call nearly indispensable to anyone who would continue to be a poet beyond his twenty-fifth year; and the historical sense involves a perception not only of the pastness of the past, but of its presence; the historical sense compels a man to write not merely with his own generation in his bones, but with a feeling that the whole of the literature of Europe from Homer and

480

within it the whole of the literature of his own country has a simultaneous existence and composes a simultaneous order. This historical sense, which is a sense of the timeless as well as of the temporal, and of the timeless and of the temporal together, is what makes a writer traditional."

This passage raises much the same questions as the last, and even more emphatically: and these questions become central to the whole question of Eliot's influence when we arrive, as we shall arrive later, at the question of the determining effect upon a writer of his own time. Is Pound, for example, a man who possesses this historical sense, when he writes a formless revery loaded with quotations and literary reminiscences, but having no other discernible relationship to past literature? And is Eliot another such man, when he does almost the same thing with less skill? Or is Valéry such a man, when he brings to bear upon problems of the modern mind and of the modern sensibility a mode of thinking and of writing, an entire moral, literary, and philosophical apparatus descended from Greek antiquity but heavily influenced by the tradition of his own country from the time of its greatest literary period, that of Racine, to the present? Eliot has praised both men in equally high terms, but, though he has pillaged a few lines from Valéry, he has followed the method of Pound. If the view of tradition offered gives no reason for choice between two men so diverse, it is worthless, and if it leads us to choose Pound, it is vicious.

And finally it is interesting to note that Eliot informs us in this essay that tradition can be obtained only by hard labor, whereas in his later and Christian period he offers a less Christian view:[23]

"I hold . . . that a *tradition* is rather a way of feeling and acting which characterizes a group throughout generations; and that it must largely be, or that many of the elements in it must be, unconscious; whereas the maintenance of *orthodoxy* is a matter which calls for the exercise of all our conscious intelligence. . . . Tradition may be conceived as a by-product of right living, not to be aimed at directly. It is of the blood, so to speak, rather than of the brain."

* *After Strange Gods,* Harcourt, Brace, and Co., 1933. Pp. 31-2.

From which we may deduce that tradition is a way of feeling and orthodoxy the corpus of ideas by which we may criticize it. But in the paragraph preceding, the paragraph in which Eliot justifies his own poetry against the criticism of Paul Elmer More, a paragraph which I shall later have occasion to quote, Eliot informs us that tradition, so conceived, cannot be modified by orthodoxy, that the attempt to modify one's feeling as a result of self-criticism can lead to nothing save pious insincerity. Orthodoxy thus becomes a mere intellectual pastime, like chess, with no spiritual value, and one's feelings, from which poetry and character alike appear to be derived, are determined and beyond the power of self-modification.

Eliot's concept of the relation of the artist to tradition may be illustrated by one more characteristic passage:[24]

"I was dealing then with the artist, and the sense of tradition which, it seemed to me, the artist should have; but it was generally a problem of order; and the function of criticism seems to be essentially a problem of order too. I thought of literature then, as I think of it now, of the literature of the world, of the literature of Europe, of the literature of a single country, not as a collection of the writings of individuals, but as 'organic wholes,' as systems in relation to which, and only in relation to which, individual works of literary art, and the works of individual artists, have their significance. There is accordingly something outside of the artist to which he owes allegiance, a devotion to which he must surrender and sacrifice himself in order to earn and obtain his unique position. A common inheritance and a common cause unite artists consciously or unconsciously: it must be admitted that the union is mostly unconscious. Between the true artists of any time there is, I believe, an unconscious community. And as our instincts of tidiness imperatively command us not to leave to the haphazard of unconsciousness what we can attempt to do consciously, we are forced to conclude that what happens unconsciously we could bring about and form into a purpose, if we made a conscious attempt."

Such a phrase as 'organic whole' in this connection has a deterministic flavor almost as extreme as anything to be found in Taine. Further, if we are to indulge our privilege to be particular,

[24] *The Function of Criticism, Selected Essays,* Harcourt, Brace, p. 12.

what is the nature of the organic whole which includes and determines Pound and Valéry, Eliot and Robinson? And is it the function of the conscious intellect merely to accelerate and render efficient that which otherwise would happen unconsciously? If so, we have a determinism, which though perhaps not wholly pure, is surely pure enough.

The best possible comment on this kind of theorizing has been made by Eliot himself. In the *Introduction* to *The Use of Poetry and the Use of Criticism*[25] he has written:

"I hold indeed that in an age in which the use of poetry is something agreed upon you are more likely to get that minute and scrupulous examination of felicity and blemish, line by line, which is conspicuously absent from the criticism of our time, a criticism which seems to demand of poetry, not that it shall be well written, but that it shall be 'representative of its age.'"

But it is primarily Eliot and a small handful of his influential disciples, not the rest of us, who demand that our poetry shall be representative of its age; and they appear to have decided consciously that the unconscious tendency of the age is to produce poetry in the manner of Pound and Eliot, except when one of them by some unaccountable atavism occasionally happens to feel a liking for a poet of some other kind.

VI. DETERMINISM

We have seen that the entire tendency of Eliot's thought is toward a deterministic view of literature. Yet Eliot is very severe in his comments upon deterministic views when he is able to recognize them. In the essay on John Bramhall, he writes as follows:[26]

"Hobbes' philosophy is not so much a philosophy as it is an adumbration of the universe of material atoms regulated by laws of motion which formed the scientific view of the world from Newton to

[25] *The Use of Poetry and the Use of Criticism*, by T. S. Eliot. Faber and Faber, London. P. 25.
[26] *Selected Essays*, p. 303.

Einstein. Hence there is quite naturally no place in Hobbes's universe for the human will; what he failed to see is that there was no place in it for consciousness either, or for human beings. So his only philosophical theory is a theory of sense perception, and his psychology leaves no place in the world for his theory of government. His theory of government has no philosophic basis: it is merely a collection of discrete opinions, prejudices, and genuine reflections upon experience which are given a spurious unity by a shadowy metaphysic.

"The attitude of Hobbes toward moral philosophy has by no means disappeared from human thought; nor has the confusion between moral philosophy and a mechanistic psychology."

In *Catholicism and International Order*[27] he writes:

"The non-Catholic, certainly the non-Christian philosopher, feeling no obligation to alter himself, and therefore no cogent need to understand himself, is apt to be under the sway of his prejudices, his social background, his individual tastes. So, I dare say, are we: but we at least, I hope, admit our duty to try to subdue them."

And on the next page of the same essay:

"Very few people, indeed, want to be better than they are; or, to put it in more consecrated terms, hunger and thirst after righteousness. And what we happen to like as individuals outside of the main current which is the Catholic tradition is apt to be what our own sort of people within a narrow limit of place and time have been happening to like. We are likely to assume as eternal truths things that in fact have only been taken for granted by a small body of people or for a very short period of time."

And in *The Function of Criticism:*[28]

"The critic, one would suppose, if he is to justify his existence, should endeavor to discipline his personal prejudices and crankstares to which we are all subject—and compose his differences with as many of his fellows as possible, in the common pursuit of true judgment."

[27] *Catholicism and International Order*, in *Essays Ancient and Modern*, Harcourt, Brace and Co., N. Y., p. 118.
[28] *Selected Essays*, p. 14.

And three pages farther in the same essay:

"The question is, the first question, *not* what comes natural or what comes *easy* to us, but what is right?"

The general tendency of all these passages is to affirm the power of man to criticize and improve himself, with reference to an absolute norm, and to affirm the necessity of his doing so. With this point of view I am in perfect agreement. It is with reference to this point of view, apparently, that Eliot objects to a passage from Herbert Read. At the end of his volume entitled *After Strange Gods*, Eliot offers an appendix containing four specimens of modern heresy, of which Read's statement is the third:

"Character, in short, is an impersonal ideal which the individual selects and to which he sacrifices all other claims, especially those of the sentiments or emotions. It follows that character must be placed in opposition to personality, which is the general common denominator of our sentiments and emotions. That is, indeed, the opposition I wish to emphasize; and when I have said further that all poetry, in which I wish to include all lyrical impulses whatever, is the product of the personality, and therefore inhibited in a character, I have stated the main theme of my essay."

Briefly, this passage means that poetry is the product of what we are, and that any attempt to remake ourselves according to an ideal will damage the poetry, and Eliot objects to it, I should judge, because it recommends the poet's doing what is natural and easy to him instead of what is right. Yet Eliot, in defending his own poetry, at the end of the first essay in the same volume, uses Read's argument with no apparent realization of the fact:[29]

"From another aspect also I have a personal interest in the clearing up of the use of the terms with which I have been concerned. My friend Dr. Paul Elmer More is not the first critic to call attention to the apparent incoherence between my verse and my critical prose— though he is the first whose perplexity on this account has caused

[29] *After Strange Gods*, p. 30.

485

me any distress. It would appear that while I maintain the most correct opinions in my criticism, I do nothing but violate them in my verse; and thus appear in a double if not double-faced role. I feel no shame in the matter. I am not of course interested by those critics who praise my criticism in order to discredit my verse, or those who praise my verse in order to discredit my opinion in religious or social affairs; I am only interested in answering those critics, who like Dr. More, have paid me the compliment—deserved or not does not matter—of expressing some approval of both. I should say that in one's prose reflections one may be legitimately occupied with ideals, whereas in the writing of verse one can only deal with actuality. Why, I would ask, is most religious verse so bad; and why does so little religious verse reach the highest levels of poetry? Largely, I think, because of a pious insincerity."

Now if we change Eliot's *ideals* to Read's *character* (an ideal concept), and Eliot's *actuality* to Read's *personality*, and the terms in these two passages are certainly interchangeable, we have exactly the same statement in both men, and it is less excusable in Eliot than in Read because Read has at least the virtue of being roughly consistent with himself. In both men the statement means about this: that our individual natures are determined for us, and our actual way of feeling cannot be changed, though it may be a pious and admirable practice to consider the theoretical characteristics of a better kind of nature—it may be a pious and admirable practice to do so, that is, so long as we do not indulge in the pious insincerity of attempting to conform our own nature to this ideal. The pious sincerity which Eliot has derived from his Christianity in the past thirteen or fourteen years would probably baffle the simpler sort of Christian.

And lest the reader think that I have misrepresented Eliot by taking a passage unfairly from its context, let me cite another and briefer passage from earlier in the same essay:[30]

"No sensible author, in the midst of something that he is trying to write, can stop to consider whether it is going to be romantic or the opposite. At the moment when one writes, one is what one is, and the damage of a lifetime, and of having been born into an unsettled society, cannot be repaired at the moment of composition."

[30] Ibid., p. 27.

At the moment when one writes, one is what one is: one has, in other words no power over that moment; one must surrender to one's feelings and one's habits at that moment if one is to achieve sincerity. Yet at what point in a poet's career does this become true? If it were true at the age of sixteen, the poet would develop but little beyond that age; and if the poet at the age of sixteen is to be encouraged to improve his literary habits, why should not the poet at the age of forty-six? Obviously one will not change one's literary habits between moments of composition; one will change them if at all in writing. And if one's conversion to Catholicism and to classicism is worth a flourish of the pen, it is worth risking a few years of unsatisfactory composition in order to form new habits. I am reasonably certain that both Aquinas and Aristotle are on my side in this matter. Eliot's position is one of unmitigated determinism.

The point of view here indicated is, furthermore, related to the Marxist and Fascist view that the individual lacks the private and personal power to achieve goodness in a corrupt society; it is a utopian point of view, not a Christian one. Christianity rests upon the assumption that man can, with God's grace, save himself in a corrupt world; and if Eliot is convinced that the civilization of our period, bad as it may be, offers greater hazards, let us say than the Mediterranean civilization of the time of Augustine, or the British civilization of the time of Bede, he would do well to clarify his opinion.

Eliot appears to have adopted uncritically some such nostalgic historical lyricism as that of the later Henry Adams. Like Adams, he repeatedly contrasts the period of Dante and Aquinas with the twentieth century; and when he refers to the period of Dante and Aquinas, it is obvious that he refers especially to the minds of Dante and Aquinas, not to the vast underworld of sluggishly brutal paganism which surrounded them, as it is obvious that in his references to the twentieth century he has in mind his own confusion, as well as that of such men as John Dewey and Bertrand Russell, and not such minds as those of Gilson, Maillol, and Valéry. It is a difficult if not impossible thing to define the spirit of any age: the age of Pope, the mind of Pope himself, is a scene of complicated conflict; and nearly any other age is more complicated still. The inept deism of *The Essay on Man* was not forced upon Pope by the age: Pope himself, by virtue of his inability to think and his ability to write as if he thought perfectly, did at least as much as Shaftesbury to impose it on the age, and had he possessed as sharp a mind as Samuel Johnson the history of the age might easily have been greatly different from what it was.

The writer bent on finding the spirit of an age is certain to be the victim of impressions of a very limited kind; and seeking the spirit of his own age, in order that he may conform to it and thus be at once sincere and properly determined, he is likely to be the victim of impressions which merely flatter his weakness. In order to illustrate this difficulty, let me cite two passages from Eliot describing the age of Shakespeare. In the essay on John Ford we find the following statement:[31]

"In the work of Shakespeare as a whole, there is to be read the profoundest, and indeed one of the most sombre studies of humanity that has ever been made in poetry; though it is in fact so comprehensive that we cannot qualify it as a whole as either glad or sorry. We recognize the same assumption of permanence in his minor fellows. Dante held it also, and the great Greek dramatists. In periods of unsettlement and change we do not observe this: it was a changing world which met the eyes of Lucian or of Petronius."

And in *Shakespeare and the Stoicism of Seneca*[32] we meet this alternative impression:

"In Elizabethan England we have conditions apparently utterly different from those of Imperial Rome. But it was a period of dissolution and chaos; and in such a period any emotional attitude which seems to give a man something firm, even if it be only the attitude of 'I am myself alone,' is eagerly taken up."

If the second statement is a true one, then we cannot but cite the cases of Jonson and Shakespeare to prove that art need not be chaotic in a period of chaos; if the first statement is a true one, we

[31] *Selected Essays*, p. 179.
[32] Ibid., p. 112.

488

must cope with Webster and Fletcher. The two statements taken together, along with the speculations which they inspire, may reasonably lead us to believe that most periods are varied and full of hazards, that the existence of Gilson and Valéry in our own period may be real and not an illusion, and that any attempt to gauge the spirit of the age by a glance of the eye is likely to result in very casual impressionism.

VII. THE DRAMATIC ELEMENT IN LYRIC POETRY

"It has been said by T. S. Eliot that the best lyric poetry of our time is dramatic, that it is good because it is dramatic." So writes Allen Tate,[33] and though I cannot put my finger on the passage in Eliot in which the statement occurs, there are many passages nearly as explicit.

F. O. Matthiessen writes:[34]

"Perhaps the most important thing that is revealed by applying Eliot's conception of the 'objective correlative' to his own work is the essentially dramatic nature of all his poetry. What is said by one of the speakers in his 'Dialogue on Dramatic Poetry' certainly seems expressive of one of his own most sustained beliefs:

'What great poetry is not dramatic? Even the minor writers of the Greek Anthology, even Martial, are dramatic. Who is more dramatic than Homer or Dante? We are human beings, and in what are we more interested than in human actions and human attitudes? Even when he assaults, and with supreme mastery, the divine mystery, does not Dante engage us in the question of the human attitude toward this mystery—which is dramatic?'

In the terms of such a description the dramatic element in poetry lies simply in its power to communicate a sense of real life, a sense of *the immediate present*—that is, of the full quality of a moment as it is actually felt to consist."

What Eliot means by the dramatic in lyrical poetry, one can only deduce as best one is able: the combination of Homer and

[33] *Reactionary Essays on Poetry and Ideas*, by Allen Tate, Scribners, N. Y. P. 200.
[34] *The Achievement of T. S. Eliot*, by F. O. Matthiessen, Houghton Mifflin, Boston and N. Y. P. 66.

the minor writers of the Greek Anthology, for example, gives one ample opportunity to think at large. The notion, derived by most of his disciples, however, and one of the two upon which they most commonly act, is indicated by the phrase *the immediate present,* which is italicized in Matthiessen's commentary. Poetry is dramatic—and hence good—in so far as it produces the illusion that the experience described is taking place in the immediate present.

Now when Matthiessen suggests that there is any relationship between this concept and the concept of the objective correlative, he is merely indulging in incoherence. The idea of the objective correlative is this: that the poet starts with an emotion and after casting about finds objective data which he believes can be used to embody it; nothing more. Matthiessen's concept seems to place the main emphasis on the data themselves. Matthiessen does not attempt, as I remember, to reconcile this concept of the dramatic with the concept of autotelic art, but it would be well worth his trouble. The idea of an art which is about itself, yet which is successful in so far as it gives a sense of the immediate present in dealing with something other than itself, would provide a worthy foundation for a system of esthetics.

Matthiessen is by no means alone. Theodore Spencer[35] in an essay on Yeats, written more or less in answer to an essay by myself on T. Sturge Moore, has written as follows:

". . . Mr. Yvor Winters has recently compared the poetry of W. B. Yeats with the poetry of T. Sturge Moore . . . In his opinion, Moore is a greater poet than Yeats . . . To say that Moore is a better poet than Yeats seems to me meaningless. . . . Compare, for example, the opening lines of Moore's sonnet, 'Apuleius Meditates,' which Mr. Winters praises very highly, with the opening of Yeats's sonnet on Leda and the Swan."

Spencer then quotes the passages, which the reader may examine if he desires, and proceeds:

[35] *The Later Poetry of W. B. Yeats,* by Theodore Spencer, Hound and Horn, Vol. VII, p. 164, and *Literary Opinion in America,* ed. by M. D. Zabel, Harpers, N. Y. P. 263. My essay on Moore is in the Hound and Horn, Vol. VI, p. 534.

"There is an important distinction illustrated here, a distinction which applies to other poetry than that of Moore and Yeats. It is the distinction between the poetry of revery and the poetry of immediacy."

He elaborates upon this distinction in terms which indicate that his concept of immediacy is essentially similar to that of Matthiessen.

Now I agree with Spencer that the lines from Yeats are better than the lines from Moore: the poem by Yeats is one of his two or three best, perhaps his best, and the lines from Moore, as I pointed out in quoting them, are extremely faulty. Spencer in failing to note my criticism of these lines adhered rigidly to a convention of contemporary literary controversy against which it would ill become a very young writer like myself to protest. But whatever the faults of Moore's poem, it is not a poem of revery; it is, like other and better poems by Moore and other men, a poem of meditation. Pound's *Cantos* are poems of revery and so likewise are most of Eliot's poems: revery proceeds by the random association of daydream, and possesses a minimum of rational coherence; in fact, in the form it takes in the stream-of-consciousness novel, it is frequently defended because of the sense of immediacy it produces, the assumption being that this is the way people really think. Spencer is very revealing when he fails to distinguish between revery and meditation.

For what, after all, is a poem, if we approach it in my own innocent state of mind? It is a statement about an experience, real or imagined. The statement must follow the experience in time: Donne, for example, could not have written *The Ecstasy* while engaged in the experience described. The poem is a commentary upon something that has happened or that has been imagined as having happened; it is an act of meditation. The poem is more valuable than the event by virtue of its being an act of meditation: it is the event plus the understanding of the event. Why then should the poet be required to produce the illusion of the immediate experience without intervention of the understanding? Perhaps the understanding is supposed to occur surreptitiously, while the poet is pretending that something else is occur-

491

ring. But what is the value of such deception? Is it assumed that understanding itself is not a "real" form of experience? The practical effect of the doctrine of dramatic immediacy is to encourage a more or less melodramatic emotionalism: such melodramatic emotionalism is perhaps the worst fault of Yeats, a poet whom Eliot admires, I should judge, little more than do I, but who is admired uncritically by Eliot's most eminent disciples.

Eliot has given rise, however, to another and in some respects different view of the way in which lyrical poetry may be dramatic. Many of his essays are attempts to define the stylistic qualities of one or another of the Elizabethan dramatists; they quote dramatic passages which he analyzes at length, the same passages being requoted and reanalyzed by many younger writers who appear to be more familiar with Eliot's views of the dramatists than with the dramatists themselves; and his own poetic style, even as early as Prufrock, has been heavily influenced by the style of these dramatists. *Gerontion*, for example, which I believe to be his best poem, is written in a more or less Websterian blank verse, has the texture of dramatic monologue, and seems to imply a dramatic context from which it has been excised. But this texture is the wrong texture for a lyric. Such poetry in a play is intended to exhibit the mannerisms of a character, so that Eliot runs the risk of imitating Bosola rather than Webster, which is a serious risk indeed; and such a passage in a play is likely to be full of allusions to matter within the play but without the passage, so that imitation of the style in a short poem is likely to result in incomprehensible irrelevancies. In the second and third essays in the section called *Primitivism and Decadence* I endeavored to analyze some of these particular effects in *Gerontion* itself.

It is worth noting that Shakespeare and Jonson, for example, the two greatest dramatists in English and two of the half dozen or so greatest masters of the English lyric, employed dramatic blank verse only when writing drama, and employed the conventions of the lyric in writing the lyric; and further that one will be hard put to find a passage in any of their plays which, as a passage, and clean of its context, will stand serious comparison with any of a dozen short poems by either man.

No matter how the doctrine of dramatic immediacy is understood, it is a doctrine which leads to illegitimate emotionalism; and understood as it appears in Eliot's practice, it leads to irrelevance and to incoherence as well.

VIII. ELIOT'S POETIC PRACTICE

Before attempting to relate Eliot's poetry to the body of opinion which I have been endeavoring to elucidate, I must summarize very briefly the career of Ezra Pound, who is beyond question the chief influence on Eliot's style. I shall describe the poetry of these men in the most general terms, for I have already dealt with it, and with similar poetry, in greater detail in *Primitivism and Decadence*. In that book I dealt with the types of poetic structure employed by these and allied poets, and sought to show the necessary effect of such structures upon the ultimate value of their work. I am concerned now, not with a detailed description of these structures, which I feel that I may reasonably take for granted, but with some of the principal concepts which generated them.

Ezra Pound, Eliot's master in poetry, began his poetic career as a student of the troubadours and of other early Romance poets, and as a disciple of Swinburne, the pre-Raphaelites, and the early Yeats. If we examine such a poem as his *Canzon: Of Incense,* for example, we see a poem written in a difficult Provençal form, but showing a quality of feeling which appears to derive from the late romantics. It is part of an attempt, extending over some years, by a belated disciple of the nineties, to recreate early Romance poetry in the modern world, and with very little explicit reference to the modern world. The attempt was doomed at the outset: the late romantic influences were unsound, and the early Romance models, though admirable in their kind, represented an elaborate development of a very limited state of mind, the elaboration and the limitation equally being the product of a very special social system and philosophy now dead these many hundred years. One might imitate Dante more successfully than Arnaut Daniel, I imagine, as one might imitate Jonson more successfully than Spenser: Dante and Jonson are timeless stylists; Spenser, and I should judge from what little I know of him, Daniel, display—with great beauty, no doubt—the eccentricities of their times, in spite of the fact that there are apparently important differences between the respective eccentricities. The curious thing about it, however, is this: that it came much closer to succeeding than one would have expected. The Pound of this period is not as good as the best Swinburne, but he is better than Dante Rossetti or the early Yeats, and by a comfortable margin.

About 1912 or a little later, however, Pound appears to have turned from his Provençal models except as he continued at times to translate them; he became a modern. Pound's aim appears now to have been no longer the recreation of a past period, but the exploration of the life of his own time as he might be able to understand it. We have as a result the tentative beginnings to be found in his collection called *Lustra:* satirical thumb-nail sketches of people seen in London, and simple but real fragments of life seen more seriously, though very impressionistically, such as *Fish and the Shadow*. This poetry, whether satirical or not, is notable mainly for the effect it gives of charming fragments, as of something valuable shattered, a quality which I have elsewhere described as essentially primitive: aside from differences of subject matter, it greatly resembles the slight but startling observations to be found in much of the poetry of the American Indian. We have a trained and refined sensibility unsupported by a unifying intellect, and employing the brief and annotative method apparently proper to it.

It was at about this stage in Pound's development that the widow of Ernest Fenollosa appears to have been struck with the idea that Pound was the man to put into final literary form the many literal translations left by her husband. According to the story current, she was impressed by the similarity of Pound's poetry to the Chinese, in spirit if not in form. She may well have been impressed by the translations which Pound had already made from other languages: his version of the Anglo-Saxon *Sea-Farer*, and of a certain Provencal alba, alone, are enough to place him among the very few great translators in English. In any event, Pound got the manuscripts and set to work on them. They apparently provided him with material exactly suited to his talents at that stage of his development: the Chinese poets, like Pound, were primitive in their outlook, and dealt with the more obvious and uncomplicated aspects of experience; but their outlook, though primitive, like Pound's, differed from Pound's in a richness and security of feeling within its limits—their subjects, though simple, were nevertheless more rich than any with which Pound had thus far dealt, and, though this may not seem important at first glance, they lent themselves to the composition of poems longer than most which Pound had thus far attempted, so that he had an opportunity to explore the possibilities of the free verse which he had previously begun to employ.

Whether or not the first *Cantos* were begun before the work on the Fenollosa manuscripts I cannot say; but the first three *Cantos* as they originally appeared in *Poetry: A Magazine of Verse* were awkwardly Browningesque affairs which bear little resemblance to the later *Cantos* or to their own later forms. The *Cantos* in general come after the Chinese translations: in length they quite surpass the Chinese translations, and in meter they show a greater development as well, for whereas the Chinese translations are written in what is really a heavily cadenced prose that continually verges on verse without achieving it, the *Cantos* are written in a slow and heavily accentual verse, which at its best displays an extraordinary suavity and grace of movement.

But in the *Cantos* Pound is thrown back on his own subject matter, and although his style has developed enormously since the poems which preceded the Chinese versions, his general intelligence has remained about where it was. He is no longer at liberty to borrow the technical and more or less intellectual framework of the troubadours, and he has none of his own to offer, yet he is bent on fusing his impressions into some kind of whole, and he seems to desire a whole which shall not falsify them or violate their essential quality: only one convention is plausible, the convention of remembered impressions, or revery. Thus we get the *Cantos*, poems in which a poet remembers his past experience of all kinds, literary, personal, and imaginative, and moves from recollection to recollection purely and simply by means of suggestion. We may observe as a brief and fairly obvious example of the method the passage in the fourth *Canto* which begins in the second paragraph and extends to the passage beginning "Thus the light rains." This section takes us through references to a number of stories, some historical and some mythological, of cannibalism and of transformation, and the two kinds of stories appear solely because both elements appear in a few of them, so that the transition from allusion to allusion is easy. The other transitions in this *Canto* may appear more arbitrary if one merely describes them, but the feeling inherent in the revery is so constant that one is not troubled so long as one resigns oneself to the form of revery and asks for no more.

Pound at maturity, then, sees life primarily as a matter of remembered impressions, and his art is an art of revery: he is a sensibility without a mind, or with as little mind as is well possible. It is this Pound who provides the foundation for the more ambitious work of Eliot.

Eliot's earliest poems display various influences if one regard the detail. The influence of Elizabethan dramatic verse is already evident in *Prufrock,* and the influence of Pound's satirical sketches is to be found in some of the short early poems. The principal influence is probably that of Laforgue, whose poetry Pound had begun to champion at least as early as 1917: the influence is seen not only in translated passages, but in the whole attitude of romantic irony in an urban setting, of which Laforgue is perhaps the most interesting exemplar among the French poets of the late nineteenth century. The longer poems in this book already display the structure of revery which is carried farther in Pound's *Cantos* and in the later Eliot. There follow a few poems in rimed quatrains, which display a trace of the influence of Corbière, a strong influence of Gautier, and very little of Pound, except in so far as Corbière and Gautier are two of Pound's favorite poets. In the same original collection with these appeared *Gerontion,* the first example of Eliot's later manner and matter, and in my own opinion the most considerable of his poems.

Gerontion is the portrait of an individual from whom grace has been withdrawn, and who is dying of spiritual starvation while remembering his past; it is thus a prelude to *The Waste Land*, a portrait of a society from which grace has been withdrawn and which is dying of its own triviality and ugliness. I should like to deal primarily with *The Waste Land,* for its method is that of all the later work and it illustrates very clearly the problems to which I have been leading, and the faults which seriously weaken even a poem of so much strength as *Gerontion*.

The matter of *The Waste Land* is Baudelairian. It is no accident that the last line of the introductory poem of *The Waste Land* is also the last line of the preface of *Les Fleurs du Mal.* That preface details the sins of the modern world as they appeared to Baudelaire, and it names as the most horrible of them all the sin of Ennui. Now Ennui, as it appears in much romantic literature is very much the same sin as the Christian sin of acedia, or spiritual torpor, and it might well be regarded as the most deadly of sins because it leads to all the others and interferes with one's struggling against them: it would be above all other sins the one most likely to appear, if we accept Christian postulates, in a man or a society deprived of grace.

Both poets deal with such a society, and both endeavor to judge it from a more or less Christian position. But there is this difference between them, if no other: that Eliot surrenders his form to his subject, whereas Baudelaire does not do so. Henry Adams, whose influence on Eliot's entire poetic theory is probably greater than has been guessed, worked out in his *Education,* in *Mont Saint Michel and Chartres,* and in certain minor essays the entire theory of modern society and its relationship to the society of the Middle Ages, upon which Eliot's critical theory rests; and near the end of *Mont Saint Michel and Chartres* he offered the now commonplace theory that modern art must be chaotic in order to express chaos[36]—a variant, I suppose, of the earlier romantic doctrine of organic form sponsored by Coleridge; and Eliot was sufficiently moved by him to construct one of the

---

[36] *Mont Saint Michel and Chartres,* by Henry Adams. Houghton Mifflin Co., Boston and N. Y., p. 375: "Art had to be confused in order to express confusion; but perhaps it was truest, so."

better lines of *Gerontion*—"In depraved May, dogwood and chestnut, flowering judas"—from the first paragraph of the eighteenth chapter of the *Education*.

Now if the modern world is demonstrably chaotic in relationship to the world of past periods, and if we accept the postulate that the poet is formed by the society into which he is born, that this age must give him not merely his subject matter but his entire spiritual shape, as it were, so that the form of his art will be determind by the quality of his age, then the formlessness of Pound's *Cantos* is something determined by forces more important than any in Pound's character: the *Cantos* offer the only form available to the poet who would write honestly and sensitively; this in spite, as I have already suggested, of the awkward presence of such writers as Valéry, Robinson, Bridges, and Hardy. Eliot, in dealing with the chaos of this graceless world, found his form ready to use, and he produced *The Waste Land*.

Baudelaire, however, did something very different. Eliot writes of him as follows:[37]

"To say this is only to say that Baudelaire belongs to a definite place in time. Inevitably the offspring of romanticism, and by his nature the first counter-romantic in poetry, he could, like anyone else, only work with the materials which were there. It must not be forgotten that a poet in a romantic age cannot be a 'classical' poet except in tendency. If he is sincere, he must express with individual differences the general state of mind—not as a *duty*, but simply because he cannot help participating in it."

This passage should sound remarkably familiar to the reader who has been so patient as to reach it; it contains an element of truth and a larger element of error. What Baudelaire actually accomplished in his best work was a vision and evaluation of evil as it appeared to him in his own time, that is, in the guise of romantic excess. He was not a rigorous thinker, though his thought was often profound, and his judgment was sometimes beguiled by the romanticism which at other times he judged with appalling lucidity. A poet is conditioned by his time to this extent,

[37] *Selected Essays*, p. 340.

498

that it offers him most of his subject matter; but what he does with that subject matter—let me insist at the risk of excommunication—is very largely the result of his own intelligence and talent. A minor talent, or an imperfect talent, may be grievously damaged through the influence of a bad tradition, such as the tradition represented by Pound and Eliot; but a greater talent need not be. To assume that Shakespeare and Jonson possessed no great intellectual power may occasionally be comforting to us, but a study of either man will not support the assumption. As H. B. Parkes has said in another connection, there is nothing inevitable about stupidity.

The subject matter of *The Waste Land* is in general similar to that of *Les Fleurs du Mal*. Yet if one will compare let us say *Le Jeu* with *A Game of Chess*, one may perhaps note what Eliot overlooked. Eliot, in dealing with debased and stupid material, felt himself obliged to seek his form in his matter: the result is confusion and journalistic reproduction of detail. Baudelaire, in dealing with similar matter, sought to evaluate it in terms of eternal verity: he sought his form and his point of view in tradition, and from that point of view and in that form he judged his material, and the result is a profound evaluation of evil. The difference is the difference between triviality and greatness.

The difference is in part, however, merely the difference between a poet with a great native gift for poetic style and a poet with very little gift. Eliot has written in his essay on Massinger:[38]

"One of the surest of tests is the way in which a poet borrows. Immature poets imitate; mature poets steal; bad poets deface what they take, and good poets make it into something better, or at least something different. The good poet welds his theft into a whole of feeling which is unique, utterly different from that from which it was torn; the bad poet throws it into something which has no cohesion."

Such a statement might easily be used in defense of Pound, who, except for Eliot, borrows more extensively than any other poet of our time: Pound's revery has a discernible consistency at its best, and the borrowed material is either selected or re-

[38] Ibid., p. 182.

499

worked so judiciously that it seems in place. And such a statement might be cited in defense of *Gerontion* and even of some of Eliot's earlier work, frail as it is. But the meter of *The Waste Land* is not the suave meter of *The Cantos* or of *Gerontion:* it is a broken blank verse interspersed with bad free verse and rimed doggerel. And what is one to say of the last eight lines of *The Waste Land,* which are composed, as nearly as I can determine with the aid of the notes, of unaltered passages from seven sources? A sequence of such quotations cannot by any stretch of the imagination achieve unity, and its disunity can be justified on no grounds except the Adams-Eliot doctrine of modern art, of which the less said by this time the better. The method is that of a man who is unable to deal with his subject, and resorts to the rough approximation of quotation; it is the method of the New England farmer who meets every situation in life with a saw from *Poor Richard;* it betokens the death of the mind and of the sensibility alike. The last line, in fact, is a classic of its kind. It reads: "Shantih shantih shantih," and in the note at the end of the poem Eliot tells us that " 'The Peace which passeth understanding' is a feeble translation of the content of this word." Surely there was never another great sentiment expressed with such charming simplicity!

Eliot, in brief, has surrendered to the acedia which Baudelaire was able to judge; Eliot suffers from the delusion that he is judging it when he is merely exhibiting it. He has loosely thrown together a collection of disparate and fragmentary principles which fall roughly into two contradictory groups, the romantic on the one hand and on the other the classical and Christian; and being unaware of his own contradictions, he is able to make a virtue of what appears to be private spiritual laziness; he is able to enjoy at one and the same time the pleasures of indulgence and the dignity of disapproval. He is right in confessing that his later work has not appreciably changed, and Mario Praz is right in finding in it more of the nature of dream than of vision. And he is right again in regarding as heretical, that is, as anti-Christian, the ideas which he has used to justify his failure to change when he meets those ideas expressed by another writer; though it is strange that he should fail to recognize the heresy when he employs it himself. When Eliot announced his conversion to Catholicism and to Classicism in 1927, his modernist followers were astonished, and they have never really forgiven him; but they might well have spared themselves so much devout feeling, for the conversion appears to have been merely nominal; at least, so far as one can judge from what Eliot has written, it really meant nothing at all.

There are scattered essays, especially early essays analyzing qualities of style, which are valuable even when one does not agree with them, and his poems display charming or excellent passages here and there as well, and *Gerontion* in fact deserves much higher praise than this. To this side of Eliot I may appear unfair. The fact of the matter is, however, that it has received far more than its due praise from other hands than mine; and the theory and influence of Eliot, with which I am at present dealing, seem to me the most dangerous and nearly the least defensible of our time. They have grown upon our time with all the benumbing energy of a bad habit, till any attempt to analyze the defects of modern poetry in the light of civilized standards is accepted merely as evidence that the critic is not of the elect, is not a recipient of the grace of the Zeitgeist; till the good poetry written in our time is more commonly than not excluded from consideration and even from publication, because it is regarded as insensitive to the realities of the twentieth century. And when one seeks closely to find the features of the divinity, the primal spirit of the age to whose will surrender is required, one may well be appalled; for behind the shadows thrown by veil after veil of indeterminate prose one will find, if one is patient, the face of Ezra Pound in apotheosis.

JOHN CROWE RANSOM

or Thunder Without God

I. RANSOM'S CONCEPT OF MORALITY IN POETRY

IN DISCUSSING RANSOM'S THEORIES of poetry, I shall concentrate on those theories; I shall not examine his estimates of other critics. But in this respect I shall be forced to make one exception: I must consider in some detail the matter of his objections to my own position, for I am endeavoring to clarify and defend that position, and it is only with respect to that position that I can write intelligibly of Ransom. However, I shall not take the trouble to defend myself against Ransom's objections to incidental details in my criticism, but shall defend merely my essential concepts, the concepts to which he takes the most extreme exception.

Ransom objects primarily to my concept of the morality of poetry, and in order to make myself clear I shall have to restate that concept briefly and then indicate briefly the way in which Ransom misapprehends it. My theory rests on the observation that language, if one disregard for the present its phonetic values, is dual in nature; that each word is both conceptual and evocative, denotative and connotative, and that the feeling, evocation, or connotation is directly the result of the concept and dependent upon the concept for its existence. The word *tree* is conceptual: it refers to a class of objects. The word, or rather the concept, suggests a loose body of perception and feeling, the result of our experience with large numbers of individual trees. What the genetic relationship may be between percept and concept, I am not sufficiently philosophical to say, but when we come to use the language, it is the concept which evokes the feeling. Deprive the sound of its conceptual content, and the sound will evoke nothing in particular. In words which represent qualities, ideas, or states of mind, such as *justice* or *malice*, the content of sensory perception is for most persons negligible; but these words are at least vaguely evocative of emotion, and can be made precisely evocative if properly employed.

Now a poem is composed of words; that is, it is conceptual in its origin, and it cannot escape from its origin. A poem about a tree is composed primarily of abstractions, and secondarily of the feelings aroused by those abstractions: the tree, its leaves, its bark, its greenness, its brownness, its roughness, its smoothness, its strength, its motion, and all its other qualities must be indicated in terms which are primarily conceptual. These terms, however, all suggest certain loose possibilities in the way of perception and feeling; and the poet's business is so to relate them, or others similar to them, that a single and definite idea emerges, in company with a mental image of some aspect of a tree, and in such a way that the feeling is communicated which is appropriate to the total idea-image both as a whole and with respect to each detail as one comes to it in reading.

The poet, then, understands his subject in rational terms, and he so employs language that he communicates simultaneously that understanding and the feeling which it properly motivates. The poet differs in this respect from the writer of theoretical prose, who endeavors as far as may be to use language cleared of all save its rational content. The act of the poet I have described in a number of essays, and I have repeatedly called it an act of moral judgment. The act of moral judgment so considered is far more difficult, is a much fuller experience, than an act of classification; it is a full and definitive account of a human experience.

Ransom's difficulty is that he can understand the idea of morality or of moral judgment only with reference to an act of simple classification, or with reference to an overt action deriving from an act of simple classification. He reads this meaning into my every use of the terms, in spite of all my precautions against such misunderstanding, with the result that most of my criticism, even when he believes that he approves it, is incomprehensible to him. He writes:[1]

. . . for moralism conducts itself very well in prose, and conducts itself all the better in pure or perfect prose. And the good critics who try to regard the poem as a moral discourse do not persuade themselves, and discuss the poem really on quite other grounds.

And again:[2]

It is like according a moral dimension to poetry because there are some poems which not only present their own content but in addition moralize about this content.

From both of these statements we may see that Ransom cannot understand that poetry can have moral content except in the form of didacticism; that is, in the form of purely theoretical statement. The same notion appears in an earlier volume:[3]

And all the poets famous in our tradition, or very nearly all, have been poets of a powerful moral cast.

So I shall try a preliminary definition of the poet's traditional function on behalf of society: he proposed to make virtue delicious. He compounded a moral effect with an aesthetic effect. The total effect was not a pure one, but it was rich, and relished highly. The name of the moral effect was goodness; the name of the aesthetic effect was beauty. Perhaps these did not have to co-exist, but the planners of society saw to it that they should; they called upon the artists to reinforce morality with charm.

This passage rests on the notion that the moral content of poetry can be only didactic; that the content which is not didactic must be aesthetic. My own idea is that the term *aesthetic* has been used primarily to conceal a great deal of inaccurate thinking. This passage is essentially Horatian, and Ransom reverts to the same ideas later, with reference both to Horace and myself:[4]

[1] *The New Criticism*, by John Crowe Ransom, New Directions, Norfolk, Conn., 1941, page 279.
[2] Ibid., p. 283.
[3] *The World's Body*, by John Crowe Ransom, Charles Scribners Sons, New York, 1938, page 57.
[4] *The New Criticism*, pp. 213-14.

Horace decreed that the aim of poetry was *aut prodesse aut delectare*, either to be morally instructive or to be delightful; and presently he decided that it was both; at any rate he kept the rider along with the moral formula. . . . There has risen increasingly in modern times a concern about Horace's rider; a concern as to how a moral discourse which goes to all the trouble of being technical poetry distinguishes itself from a moral discourse in prose. That is the critical problem.

But if that is the critical problem, it is a very simple one, for the poet is more explicitly concerned with communicating the feeling which ought properly to be motivated by the idea than is the writer of prose; and that is the sole distinction. But Ransom continues without break to discuss my own theories, in a passage of remarkable innocence:

Winters believes that ethical interest is the only poetic interest. (If there is a poem without visible ethical content, as a merely descriptive poem for example, I believe he thinks it negligible and off the real line of poetry.)

At this point I must interrupt again to comment. I believe, to be sure, that ethical interest is the only poetic interest, for the reason that all poetry deals with one kind or another of human experience and is valuable in proportion to the justice with which it evaluates that experience; but I do not believe that a descriptive poem is negligible or off the real line of poetry. A descriptive poem deals with a certain kind of experience, an extremely simple kind, but one of real value; namely, the contemplation of some fragment of the sensible universe. This is a moral experience, like any other, and the task of the poet is to evaluate it for what it is worth.

Ransom continues, still writing of myself:

Now I suppose he would not disparage the integrity of a science like mathematics, or physics, by saying that it offers discourse whose intention is some sort of moral perfectionism. It is motivated by an interest in mathematics, or in physics. But if mathematics is for mathematical interest, why is not poetry for poetical interest? A true-blue critic like Eliot would certainly say that it is, though he would be unwilling to explain what he meant. I think I know why all critics do not answer as Eliot would: because criticism, a dilettante and ambiguous study, has not produced the terms in which poetic interest can be stated. Consequently Winters is obliged to think that mathematics is for mathematical interest—or so I suppose he thinks—but that poetry, in order that there may be an interest, must be for ethical interest. And why ethical? Looking around among the stereotyped sorts of interest, he discovers, very likely, that ethical interest is as frequent in poetry as any other one.

This is a curious statement, for Ransom appears to speculate upon my inner psychological life with the same bland impartiality with which he examines that of the lower animals; but it is offered seriously, and I suppose one must reply to it seriously. As I have already said, any scientific or philosophical statement endeavors to employ as far as may be the conceptual content of language and no other. The scientist is interested in ideas, not in the feelings they motivate; his interest is purely conceptual and amoral. Mathematics, I take it, is the one kind of scientific statement which is able to realize this ideal perfectly, for it subsists wholly in a language of its own. I offer this suggestion with some hesitancy, for I really know very little about mathematics, and I have not the ability, which Ransom possesses in an eminent degree, to write algebraic equations for the purpose of illustrating my critical theories. The subject matter of poetry, on the other hand, is human experience; it can therefore be understood only in moral terms. The language of poetry is normal human speech, which was devised for dealing with normal human experience, and I have already indicated the nature of that speech. When Ransom refers to my finding "that ethical interest is as frequent in poetry as any other one," he is again confusing the terms *ethical* and *didactic* and misunderstanding me in his own private fashion.

This misunderstanding accounts for his objections to my remarks upon Baudelaire. Of Baudelaire I wrote:[5]

He was determined by his period only to this extent: that he dealt with the problem of evil in the terms in which he had met it, the

[5] Page 100, the present volume.

terms of the romantic view of life; and it was because of these terms that he was able to embody the universal principles of evil in the experience of his own age and evaluate that experience.

Ransom quotes this passage and writes of it as follows:[6]

> I have no doubt that Baudelaire evaluated his experience of evil. I honor Winters for not being so tender-minded as to shy off from Baudelaire's poetry because its flowers are "flowers of evil." I wish he could say that the logical materials are evil, but that poetic flowers grow out of them; and drop the business of the "moral evaluation" and the "spiritual control." Aesthetic experience is beyond good and evil in a plain temporal sense . . .

I have no wish to be honored for not "shying off" from Baudelaire; and one reason for my not saying what Ransom wishes me to say is that I do not understand it. The "logical materials" of most of Baudelaire are no more evil than the materials of Shakespeare. The topics of both men are bad enough, for both explore human nature rather far; both depict evil as evil and make us know it as evil. Ransom might conceivably understand what I mean if he would compare *Une Martyre*, a poem which deals with a sadistic murder and which treats it fully and richly and for what it is worth, with *Porphyria's Lover*, a poem on a similar topic by Browning, which endeavors to make the topic cosy and domestic.

I should like to mention two secondary objections made by Ransom in passing. He writes:[7]

> I am struck by the fact that the moral evaluations Winters obtains from the poems are so negative in their effect; the poems seem to evaluate experiences by just imagining them, by having them vicariously, so that it becomes unnecessary for the poets and the readers to have them actually. Poetry becomes the survey of experience, reporting it in such a way as to indispose us to it. . . . It is a kind of moral decadence.

I do not know how a poem can evaluate an experience or do anything else with it except by "just imagining" it; for the

---

[6] *The New Criticism*, page 228.
[7] *The New Criticism*, page 233.

poem exists on paper. One cannot commit a murder and write about it at the same time; the two acts are distinct. I can imagine further that both *Une Martyre* and *Macbeth* might indispose us to murder, but I can see neither harm nor decadence in that; I can imagine no good reason why most love poems should indispose us to fall in love or why most descriptive poems should indispose us to take walks in the country.

Ransom appears in this passage, however, in an unfamiliar role, that of a defender of overt action. He himself is on record, as I assuredly am not, as believing the work of art to be valuable as a check to action. The work of art, for Ransom, as we shall presently see, is an act of sensibility, or, as he sometimes puts it, of cognition; it is an objective apprehension of something outside ourselves, with the sole purpose of apprehending the unique object as nearly as possible in its unique and whole form, and with no ulterior, or practical, end in view. In *God without Thunder* Ransom first develops his thesis that overt action is degrading because it is motivated by ideas, that is by incomplete apprehension of the objective world, and because it aims at the satisfaction of practical, or generalized, appetites, such as lust or hunger. Even as late as *The New Criticism*[8] he identifies morality as belonging to the same class of motives:

Morality is for the practical rather than the aesthetic stage; coordinate with greed, or envy, or lust, or whatever appetites and affections it sets itself up in opposition to.

And in *God without Thunder*,[9] he praises the sensibility as follows:

In order to be human, we have to have something which will stop action, and this something cannot possibly be reason in the narrow sense. I would call it sensibility.

Sensibility is offered as a substitute for Babbitt's Inner Check, but, unlike Babbitt's safeguard, functions as a check to all actions instead of to some.

[8] *The New Criticism*, p. 226.
[9] *God without Thunder*, by John Crowe Ransom, Harcourt, Brace and Co., 1930, p. 190.

The other objection by Ransom with which I wish to conclude this section is better founded, for it rests on a careless statement of my own, though if Ransom had read me more carefully and above all if he had read my second volume of essays as well as my first, I believe that he might have understood my intention. In the first essay of *Primitivism and Decadence*[10] I wrote of the poem:

It is composed of an almost fluid complex, if the adjective and the noun are not too nearly contradictory, of relationships between words . . . a relationship involving rational content, cadences, rhymes, juxtapositions, literary and other connotations, inversions, and so on, almost indefinitely. These relationships, it should be obvious, extend the poet's vocabulary incalculably. They partake of the fluidity and unpredictability of experience and so provide a means of treating experience with precision and freedom.

Of this Ransom writes:[11]

The freedom does very well; the freedom is unpredictability, and the unpredictable or free detail cannot be precise in the sense that it was intended, that it unfolds logically according to a plan. To have an unpredictable experience seems quite different from treating experience with precision.

Ransom reverts a number of times to this objection in treating other passages in my criticism. He reads the passage with his own theory of poetic structure in mind. This theory I shall later examine in detail; it will suffice at present to say that Ransom sees the poem as composed of a logical core and a tissue of irrelevancies: I borrow his language, because I do not understand it quite well enough to paraphrase it. He therefore assumes that I see fluidity and unpredictability in the finished poem, whereas I see them rather in the medium of expression.

What I meant to indicate, or should have indicated, is that the poetic medium has a more finely detailed vocabulary than has the medium of prose, and that one never knows exactly how finely detailed the vocabulary may prove in a given poem

[10] Page 19, the present volume.
[11] *The New Criticism*, p. 221.

until one has done one's best to write the poem. Perhaps the main reason for this subtlety of poetic vocabulary is meter, and I shall try to explain it at least in part when I arrive at the discussion of meter. The poem will treat matters that would be lost in the gaps of the relatively rough vocabulary of prose; but the statement, once it is made, is precise. The poet is like a musician who plays an instrument which does not operate on fixed intervals: the musician can play notes not on the keyboard of the piano, but the notes when played are definite notes. That the poet will scarcely envisage every detail of his poem before he has written it seems likely enough, and that his first rough judgment preceding composition will be improved by revision in the course of composition is devoutly to be hoped; in such ways, the writing of a poem involves a good many unpredictable experiences. But if the poet allows himself irrelevancies in any true sense of the word, his poem will be damaged, and if he allows many it will be spoiled. A good many unpredictable experiences will have to be pruned away, and those which are kept should be kept for their accuracy.

II. THE UNIQUE EXPERIENCE

Ransom is a nominalist, at least in intention, and as far as may be by persuasion, although the entire business gives him a good deal of embarrassment. It would be only with hesitation and regret that he would admit that he and I both are men and that the concept *man* is of the first importance if we are to be understood; this in spite of the fact that he and I are able to conduct an argument on what we take to be the same subject, and, when all things are considered, to understand each other fairly well; in spite of the fact that neither one of us, I imagine, would offer occasion for much astonishment either to an anatomist or to a psychologist. It seems fruitless to revive a question that was thoroughly exhausted in the middle ages; it seems especially foolish for a pair of wholly unscholarly amateurs to revive it. The conflict between realism and nominalism, from the standpoint of pure logic, is sufficiently obscure; the empirical fact that the unique and the general both have reality but that neither can be known in and for itself alone is obvious and incontrovertible, and every act of our lives is testimony to it. This is, I suppose, one of the elemental mysteries of theology and of philosophy equally; it can be neither understood nor ignored: it is like the creation or the difference between prescience and predestination. The best way to deal with such questions is that of Aquinas: to accept the solution which provides the best beginning for an understanding of the rest of our experience; to judge the proposition in terms of the relationship between its consequences and the whole of what we know. The Thomistic distinction between prescience and predestination may be hard for the imagination to seize, but it saves one from greater difficulties which follow upon the refusal to make the distinction.

Ransom has written:[12]

Nevertheless, the life of Jesus was remarkable, and so were all the other events I have named—and how can the "short-hand of routine experience" ever explain satisfactorily what is remarkable? It will never cease to be difficult for science, with its naturalistic principles, to account for any remarkable event. Such a particular tends too obviously to exceed its type, too spectacularly to strain against the confinement of its law. *It tends always to exhibit more particularly than type.* It tends, that is, to be *unique,* and to escape from science altogether.

Yet a Christian realist, of an extreme variety, might reply very simply that Ransom does not know the exact limits of the type from which he assumes Jesus to be a variation; that from the realist's standpoint, every man varies from the type, not by overflowing its limits but by failing to fill them, that variation is deficiency or deprivation; that Ransom is drawing conclusions about the true nature of the concept *man* from his own imperfect observation of imperfect individuals; and that precisely the remarkable thing about Jesus as man is this, that he is a perfect realization of the type. And a scientific realist might con-

[12] *God without Thunder,* p. 63.

ceivably make a similar answer, except that he would add that he too does not know the exact limits of the type, and is constantly forced to alter his definition in the hope of improving it. A few pages later[18] Ransom states the same view in more poetic terms:

The myth of an object is its proper name, private, unique, untranslatable, overflowing, of a demonic energy that cannot be reduced to the poverty of the class concept—

a statement which renders the problem more dramatic and perhaps less mysterious than I am inclined to imagine it to be.

I should like to lay the reader's fears at rest, and say that I am prepared to offer no solution to the problem, unless the reader is satisfied with that of Aquinas, which, though not wholly armed against logical attack, is probably more satisfactory than any other. I am willing to grant without argument that as far as common observation goes the particular appears to exist; but I feel sure that we are aware of it only in so far as we are aware of the universal. The *Socratitas* of Socrates will scarcely be evident to the mind wholly unfamiliar with the idea of man.

And I should like to recall another proposition to which I have already alluded and which I shall have to mention again: that one can say nothing about any object, be it unique or not, except in words, that is through the subdivision and interrelation of abstractions; and that any feelings one may try to express about the object will be expressed through the connotations of those words, that is will be motivated by abstractions— not by the object but by our understanding of the object. And it is perhaps fair to add that the extreme Christian realist already mentioned, with the expenditure of only a little ingenuity, could make much of this fact in the defense of his position.

The difficulty with Ransom's position is this: that he knows, finally, that he cannot get rid of abstractions, yet he has an abhorrence of the rational processes which is less related to that of Ockham than to that of the romantics; it is a traditional

[18] Ibid., p. 65.

feeling—I refer to romantic tradition—which makes him abhor words such as *moral, ideal,* or *rational* without troubling really to understand what they mean. As a result, he tries always to theorize about poetry as if he had actually got rid of the general as a vicious delusion, and sometimes he actually does so theorize. But he has not got rid of it, and it makes him a great deal of trouble.

III. HEDONISM

It is natural that a nominalist should be a hedonist, provided he is not, like Ockham, a voluntaristic Christian; and it is natural that he should endeavor to justify a hedonistic philosophy; and it is natural that he should fail in this attempt at justification. For if one cannot understand, one can at least hope to enjoy; it is in human nature to offer a rational defense of one's way of life, real or imagined, even if that way of life is anti-rational, as we can discover to our weariness and confusion by reading almost anywhere in the critical literature of the last three hundred years; and it is impossible to devise a philosophy which will show us how we can enjoy a universe from which all distinctions have been eliminated.

Of the inner life of cattle, we have, I presume, an imperfect knowledge, but Ransom is more or less plausible in assuming that they see greenery, for example, generically and vaguely, as something to be consumed. And yet *generically* would hardly seem to be the word if the cow lacks reason. Ransom writes on this subject:[14]

As an animal merely, man would simply partake of the banquet of nature as he required. As an animal with reason, he would only gorge himself the more greedily upon it and have more of it to gorge upon. But as an animal with sensibility, he becomes fastidious, and makes of his meal a rich, free and delicate aesthetic experience.

And in his second book:[15]

[14] *God without Thunder,* p. 189.
[15] *The World's Body,* pp. 224-5.

An intelligent individual attachment is, therefore, a great luxury, permitted to human animals almost exclusively, because they are the only animals who can afford it with safety. Our trained scientists, marvelously advanced in technique beyond the lower animals, are valuable to us because their labors improve the production and distribution of necessary commodities and also, incidentally, enable us to indulge sentiment without having suicidal mania. But to the extent that they have to stick to their profession and devote themselves only to commodities, they are scapegoats. They are not infants or lower animals, but it is their fixed rule to pursue the general rather than the particular, and that is exactly the animal or infantile practice. To use an adult and human analogy, under this restriction they are like the sailor in port who pursues generic rather than individual woman.

Persons who are idealists by conviction, or on general principles, are simply monsters. (I mean the Platonic ones, the kind of idealists who worship universals, laws, Platonic ideas, reason, the "immaterial.")

From these passages we may observe that man's reason, a gift which the animals lack, makes him more an animal than they, more like them than they are like themselves, or would do so were he not saved from this fate by his sensibility. Now a common, less ingenious, and less contradictory view of the matter would be this: that the animals are guided by a relatively vague and primitive sensibility and may or may not have some rudiments of reason; but that man's sensibility is refined by the intervention of reason, so that he can scarcely dispense with reason or with any part of it without a corresponding loss of sensibility. Ransom appears at times to suspect some such truth as this, as when he writes:[16]

Croce, for example, does not seem to suspect that the pre-logical experience of the child differs from the mature and sometimes desperate adventures of the artist . . .

These adventures must seem to us desperate indeed if they consist in blasting from beneath himself the foundations of the very structure in which he stands.

[16] *The World's Body*, p. 256.

514

And as a matter of fact, Ransom is not able invariably to get along without some kind of idealism:[17]

The formal tradition, as I have said, lays upon the poet evidently a double requirement. One is metrical or mechanical; but the measured speech is part of the logical identity of the poem; it goes into that "character" which it possesses as an ideal creation, out of the order of the actual. The other requirement is the basic one of the make-believe, the drama, the specific anonymity or pseudonymity, which defines the poem as poem . . .

This anonymity is also a kind of idealization, a merging of the individual in the type as represented by the tradition, and the essay on *Lycidas* in the same volume deals primarily with the function of the poet as a kind of ideal and highly generalized spokesman. And in the essay on Edna St. Vincent Millay, he objects to female poets in general because he finds them insufficiently intellectual and too exclusively and sentimentally devoted to objects of sense.

Ransom's hedonistic attitude interests me little in itself, however; little even for the extraordinary social and religious doctrines which he deduces from it, although these last have their own fascination. What interests me is the influence of the hedonism on his theory of poetry. As we shall see presently, Ransom regards, or tries to regard, the work of art as an imitation, purely and simply, of some aspect of objective nature, an imitation made for love of the original object; and he takes elaborate pains to eliminate from the entire process all emotions on the part of the artist except love of the object. Some of the citations bearing in part on this theory will have to be reserved for subsequent sections of this essay, but in *God without Thunder* he writes:[18]

The esthetic attitude is the most objective and the most innocent attitude in which we can look upon the world, and it is possible only when we neither desire the world nor pretend to control it. Our pleas-

[17] *The World's Body*, pp. 40-41.
[18] *God without Thunder*, p. 173.

ure in this attitude probably lies in a feeling of communion or *rapport* with environment which is fundamental in our human requirements —but which is sternly discouraged in the mind that has the scientific habit.

I should say the esthetic attitude is definable with fair accuracy in the simple and almost sentimental terms: the love of nature.

This statement, if taken in the narrowest possible sense, would appear to limit poetry to the description of landscape; but we discover as we read farther in the three books, that this is intended as a formula for the treatment of almost any subject. But how applicable is it to the subject of *Macbeth* or of *Othello?* Were these plays written because of the love which Shakespeare felt, either for their actions as wholes or for any major part of their actions? Did Shakespeare love the spectacle of ambition culminating in murder, or of jealousy culminating in murder? Did he write of Iago because he loved him so sentimentally that he wished to render him in all his aspects? To ask the questions is to render the theory ridiculous.

Shakespeare wrote the plays in order to evaluate the actions truly; and our admiration is for the truth of the evaluations, not for the beauty of the original objects as we see them imitated. And how, one may wonder, can Shakespeare evaluate these actions truly except from the position of a moralist? To evaluate a particular sin, one must understand the nature of sin; and to fix in language the feeling, detailed and total, appropriate to the action portrayed, one must have a profound understanding not only of language, for language cannot be understood without reference to that which it represents, not only of the characters depicted, but of one's own feelings as well; and such understanding will not be cultivated very far without a real grasp of theoretic morality.

The following passage shows how completely Ransom identifies the poem with its subject and our feeling for the poem with our feeling for its subject. He offers a brief definition of the poem, and then comments on his own definition:[19]

[19] *The New Criticism,* p. 54.

A beautiful poem is an objective discourse which we approve, containing objective detail which we like.

This version mixes objective and subjective terms, but goes much further than simply to say that poetry is a form of discourse which enlists our favorable emotions. It tells where the favorable emotions come: in the pleasure of handling the specific detail while we are attending effectively to the whole. It talks about what we like, and I see no overwhelming necessity to do that, for we shall not have poems nor things in poems, unless we like them; liking is interest, and ultimately I suppose it is part of our unarguable biological constitution.

There is a little more of this commentary, but the remainder does not clarify the issues that interest me. The passage refers more or less implicitly to Ransom's favorite structural theory, the theory of the logical core and the texture of irrelevancy, but that matter will have to wait. We see identified explicitly our liking for the poem and our liking for its subject, an identification deriving from Ransom's doctrine of imitation; but the impossibility of such identification I have already shown.

If we like the poem without liking its subject, however, in what sense do we like it? The word *like* requires more explanation than Ransom is willing to give. To identify liking with interest is preposterous. We may be interested in communism, cancer, the European war, or Ransom's theories of poetry without liking any of them. According to Ransom's theories, the scientist does not like, in this sense, the objective universe, but that he is desperately interested in the objective universe there cannot be the slightest doubt. If we like the poem, we like it because of the truth with which it judges its subject, and the judgment is a moral judgment of the kind which I have already described.

Ransom's devout cultivation of sensibility leads him at times to curiously insensitive remarks. In comparing the subject of a poem by Stevens with that of a poem by Tate, he writes:[20]

The deaths of little boys are more exciting than the sea-surfaces—

[20] *The World's Body*, p. 61.

a remark which seems worthy of a perfumed and elderly cannibal. And in a poem of his own, entitled *Bells for John White-
side's Daughter,* a poem which deals with the death of a little
girl, the dead child herself is treated whimsically, as if she were
merely a charming bit of bric-a-brac, and the life of the poem
resides in a memory of the little girl driving geese. The memory,
as a matter of fact, is very fine, but if the little corpse is merely
an occasion for it, the little corpse were better omitted, for once
in the poem it demands more serious treatment: the dead child
becomes a playful joke, and the geese walk off with the poem.

IV. ART AS IMITATION OF THE UNIQUE EXPERIENCE AND ART AS UNIQUE EXPERIENCE

Ransom believes that the arts are essentially one, and that principles true of painting, for example, should be equally true of
literature. In the last paragraph of *The World's Body,*[21] he
writes:.

> Similar considerations hold, I think, for the critique of fiction, or
> of the non-literary arts. I remark this for the benefit of philosophers
> who believe, with propriety, that the arts are fundamentally one.

Such an assumption strikes me as extremely uncritical. If one
can show the arts to be fundamentally one by analyzing each of
the arts separately and arriving at similar conclusions for all, one
can make such a statement with some show of reason; but thus
far the demonstration has not been made. That all the arts have
certain principles in common is perhaps possible; that any two
of them will have certain principles in common seems much
more likely; but that these principles play the same part in any
two or more of the arts appears to me very doubtful. The arts
employ different media and enter the consciousness by different
routes, and there may well be fundamental differences between
them. I should be inclined to inquire, for example, just how

[21] *The World's Body,* p. 349.

Ransom finds a Bach fugue to be an imitation of an unique object in nature.

Ransom definitely regards the work of art as the imitation of an unique object, however, and he employs the word *imitation* in a simple and literal sense, to understand which one need know nothing of the history of criticism; and at the same time he regards the work of art as an unique object in itself; a curious theory, for if the work of art is a true replica, the two are scarcely unique, and if the imitation is not a replica, it is either an imperfect imitation or something other than an imitation. In *God without Thunder*[22] he writes:

If M. Bergson had defended the freedom of inorganic as well as of organic objects, he might readily have become the great champion of the arts, for the freedom of their objects is precisely what they are devoted to. The artistic representation of a particular is itself particular—infinite in its wealth of quality, though doubtless an abridgment of the infinity of the original. Art celebrates the concrete, the richly sensible, and M. Bergson as the exponent of the free will was in a position to expound also the freedom of the artistic object.

Such a position, however, leaves him with some need to justify the existence of art in a world which without its help is already teeming with natural uniqueness; especially as the work of art appears in this passage to be merely an abridgment of the original object. In *The World's Body*[23] he writes:

And as for the painting: it perhaps does not occur to naïve persons that some painter from his window will command permanently his view of the city roofs, and yet be impelled to paint the imitation of it on a canvas beside the window, and to return again and again to the canvas in preference to the window as the occasion of his aesthetic experience. The studied aesthetician will admit to this fact, but will contend perhaps that the painting is better for the purpose than the view from the window, because the painting has suppressed something, or added something, or distorted something; being quite unable to conceive that its superiority may lie in the simple fact that it

---

[22] *God without Thunder*, p. 222.
[23] *The World's Body*, pp. 196-7.

is the imitation of something rather than the original. An imitation is better than its original in one thing only: not being actual, it cannot be used, it can only be known. Art exists for knowledge, but nature is an object both to knowledge and to use; the latter disposition of nature includes that knowledge of it which is peculiarly scientific, and sometimes it is so imperious as to pre-empt all possibility of the former.

The imitation is here justified because it is a check to action, because it eliminates the useful, which in Ransom's terminology is coördinate with the scientific and rational; so that here as throughout Ransom, we see the constant straining to define an art which shall subsist as nearly as possible without rational content, which shall realize as nearly as possible the primary principle in the system of Poe. Ransom employs the analogy of painting still further:[24]

We are sensible of the love behind all the labor that the patient artist has put into his work, and we respond with ours.

I use the term love not too fearfully. The motive for engaging upon the other kind of transcript is glory, according to the metaphysical idealists; duty, according to the moralists; power, according to the practical scientists; and, for the appetites, greed. It is a single series, and as opposite to love at one place as another.

One of the trick questions in aesthetic suggests itself here, with its proper answer in terms of Greek mimesis. Why would not a photograph of the landscape be superior to the painting? The idea is that the photograph would be both fuller and more accurate as presentation. But it is not fuller, strictly speaking; to be particular at all is to be infinitely full of detail, and one infinite is as full as another. And it does not matter about the meticulous accuracy of the representation; the painter's free version may be for the eye the more probable version and the more convincing, by the same reasoning by which Aristotle prefers poetry as an imitation to history. The great difference between the two versions lies elsewhere. The photograph is a mechanical imitation, perhaps, but not a psychological one. It was obtained by the adjustment of the camera and the pressing of the button, actions so characterless that they indicate no attitude necessarily, no love; but the painting reveals the arduous pains of the artist. . . . The pains measure the love.

[24] *The World's Body*, pp. 208-9.

We have seen previously that the painting is preferable to the object painted, because it separates knowledge from usefulness; here we see that the painting is superior to the photograph and the object equally because it is produced with labor which is a proof of love. But is this second difference symbolic or real? That is, if we merely met the finished products with no knowledge of the techniques in question, would we feel this difference? Or is there actually a difference in the finished product, the result in the painting of a living mind having made every detail as a commentary on something else? And if there is any truth in this last possibility, what is the nature of the commentary? Is it merely an assertion of the artist's love for the object? We have seen the difficulties into which this notion leads us in connection with Shakespeare and Iago, and we might well meditate upon the difficulties into which we should wander if we tried so to consider the work of Goya, or even much of the world's great portraiture, for example scores of surviving portrait busts of the Romans, in which we see an interest on the part of the artist which is far other and far more interesting than mere liking or love. Here as elsewhere, Ransom is confused by the difficulty that his imitation is not really an imitation but is something else.

In *The New Criticism*,[25] Ransom develops this theory, or something very like it, in a somewhat new direction. He states that our emotion for the artistic object cannot be the same as our emotion for the original object. "The original emotion blinded us to the texture of the object, but now there is leisure for the texture." In other words, our imitation in retrospect is more complete than was the object imitated, at least as we saw the object, and is no longer an abridgment. This curious variant comes of an attempt to reconcile in some manner Ransom's doctrines with Eliot's doctrine of autotelic art, that is with Eliot's theory that artistic emotion is generically different from the emotion of human life. In this connection, I should like to reiterate the distinction which I made in discussing this theory of Eliot: namely that the emotion created by the original experience is immediate, provisional, and confused; in so far as we succeed in clarifying

[25] *The New Criticism*, pp. 158-9.

our understanding of the situation and in modifying our feelings accordingly, we approach the judgment possible in the poem; but it is only in the poetic form that something close to a final and defensible judgment is possible, for in poetry we have a finer and more flexible language than we can find elsewhere, and in writing the poem we have an opportunity to fix the judgment in preliminary stages, examine it, and revise it.

I discuss the matter in terms of poetry not out of prejudice against the other arts but because I understand their principles insufficiently well. For reasons already given, I refuse to discuss questions of painting or music in any serious fashion, and I refuse to be bound by any apparent analogies between these arts and poetry. But Ransom is bound by his own analogies, and what he has said of painting we may fairly assume that he means of poetry. And when we come to poetry, his doctrine of imitation unmistakably collapses, for poetry is composed of words, which are primarily abstractions. No combination of abstractions, however fine their subdivision or ingenious their arrangement, will reproduce an unique experience, and if we endeavor to violate their nature in using them we shall merely use them badly.

The poem cannot then be an imitation of an unique experience, but it may conceivably be an unique experience in itself, and in a way which Ransom has not taken into consideration. If we can imagine two poets of talents equally sound and essentially similar in scope, and imagine them describing the same tree, or writing of the experience of love, it is very unlikely that we can imagine them writing the same poem. Their past lives will be different; the relevant circumstances of their present lives will be different; with the result that the definition of each will not be a definition of the thing in itself, which is an impossibility, but a definition by each poet of his own relationship to the thing, and the definitions, though different, may be equally valid, and without our having recourse to any relativistic doctrine to justify them; and the feelings motivated will likewise differ accordingly. The whole procedure, however, is fed on ideas and dies without them.

V. ART AS COGNITION

Ransom's doctrine of cognition, as nearly as I can understand it, is merely an aspect of his doctrine of imitation. The work of art is an imitation of an object, undertaken for love of the object and in the effort to understand the object; to understand it, not rationally, but in its uniqueness. The term *cognition* is employed by Ransom also in connection with the rational activities of scientists and philosophers, and when so used is a term of disparagement; as employed in connection with art, its meaning is different and to myself is very obscure.

Ransom says that the work of art is objective: it deals with the object itself, not with the artist's feelings or emotions, except, I suppose, the one emotion of love for the object, yet Ransom repeatedly speaks of the emotions communicated by the poem, and when he endeavors to deal with his theory of cognition he is forced in some manner to account for them. In *The New Criticism*,[26] he reproves I. A. Richards for dealing with poetry as if it consisted of emotion more or less independent of a motivating object:

> He employs a locution which is very modern, and almost fashionable, but nevertheless lazy and thoughtless. He refers to the distinctive emotion of a poem instead of to its distinctive cognitive object.

And a few pages farther he develops this theory at length in terms that seem for a moment closely to resemble my own:[27]

> The specific quality of any emotion is all but indefinable in pure emotive terms, and that seems to be because the distinctness that we think of as attaching to an emotion belongs really to the object toward which we have it. For example, there is hardly an instance of terror-in-general, or of terror-on-principle, but only terror toward a particular object or situation; like a father, or men armed with machine guns, or the day of doom. That is obvious enough. But I have seen too many instances where literary critics, like Mr. Richards above, find the cognitive object of the poem intellectually obscure,

[26] *The New Criticism*, p. 17.
[27] *The New Criticism*, pp. 20-21.

yet claim to discover in the poem an emotion which is brilliantly distinct. I should think there is generally and ideally, no emotion at all until an object has furnished the occasion for one, and that the critic is faking his discovery of the emotion when he cannot make out its object; and that if he should try to describe to us the emotion he would find himself describing it as whatever kind of emotion would be appropriate toward a certain object, and therefore presently, before he realized it, beginning to describe the very object which he had meant to avoid. That seems to me the case history of Richards' commentary on Eliot's poem above. Once I had a friendly critical passage with a good student who insisted that there were cores of value in poetry which were emotional, and not accessible to logic, or were "metalogical," as he liked to phrase it. When I pressed him he wrote a paper in which he chose a poem and showed how from time to time in it the reader grasped perfectly an emotion which did not receive in the text any adequate logical communication. But it seemed to me that in every instance the emotion realized by the reader was simply the one that was perfectly appropriate to the situation objectively established by the text; though it may have been a highly particularized situation, not easy to put in a few words. It was true that the emotion remained mysterious and ineffable in its own terms, and the poet never bothered about that, but it was not without statement in terms of the object. From this incident I concluded again that emotions are correlatives of the cognitive objects, and all but unintelligible for us in their supposed independent purity.

This passage, which exactly reverses Eliot's doctrine of the objective correlative, states that the emotion is motivated by some cause (the object) and that the emotion is appropriate. It implies, however, that if the cognition of the object is sound, the emotion is automatically appropriate; and states further that a sharp emotion cannot be communicated without adequate cognition as a motive. This I doubt profoundly. The second essay in my volume, *Primitivism and Decadence*, lists many kinds of inaccurate motivation; the false motivation in Crane's poem *The Dance*, and the false motivation in many of the poems of H. D. may be taken as examples, if the reader will have the patience to examine what I wrote about them. In these poems an emotion is asserted and in a large degree communicated which is far in excess of any discernible motive.

In actual life, unsound motivation is the commonest thing one meets, but Ransom, I suppose, would say that this results from unsound cognitions, and that it is the business of the poet to make his cognitions, or imitations, genuinely accurate; the impossibility of doing this, however, I have already endeavored to show. What I have already written ought to show further, that it is impossible for the poet to leave the emotions to shift for themselves, for the emotions like the ideas are communicated by the words, and the poet chooses every word. If his choice is based on only one aspect of the language, the emotions are much more likely to go wrong automatically than to go right; and if he does this—that is, bases his choice on purely conceptual content—he is unlikely to please Ransom any more than myself.

Before leaving this topic, I wish to cite further passages which will show more plainly that Ransom holds the doctrine of the automatic accuracy of the emotion. In *The World's Body* he writes:[28]

The primary business of theorists is to direct their analyses of poetry to what is objective in it, or cognitive, and they will always be safe in assuming if they like that behind any external body of knowledge there will have been feeling enough, possibly amounting to passion, to have attended the subject through his whole exercise. Indeed the feeling must have been entirely appropriate to the exercise.

And in *The New Criticism:*[29]

But we must remark once more, no feeling is identified by a metaphor until an objective situation has been identified by it. In short, the one automatic and sure method of identifying a feeling is to furnish an objective situation and say: Now imagine your feeling in this situation. Under these circumstances I do not see why the critic needs to do more than talk about the objective situations. The feelings will be their strict correlatives, and the pursuit of the feelings will be gratuitous.

And a few pages farther:[30]

[28] *The World's Body*, p. 289.
[29] *The New Criticism*, p. 50.
[30] Ibid., p. 58.

The affections are involved by a poem, but the important thing for theory to see is that they attach spontaneously to the items of context. And since they attach spontaneously, they scarcely need to enter into critical discussion. We need only to say that the poem develops its local particularities while it progresses toward its functional completion.

And not only does Ransom believe that the emotions may be neglected by critic and poet alike, because they attach themselves with spontaneous accuracy, but he believes that it is unhealthy to consider them critically:[31]

Nor, under that procedure, do we feel the ignominy of concerning ourselves about our mental "health," when we are occupied healthily and naturally with our external concerns.

Self-knowledge and self-judgment are morbid as well as unnecessary; if we will merely love the objective universe and endeavor to "know" it objectively and fully, our emotions will take care of themselves automatically.

The emotions, however, are not alone in being able to take care of themselves. In a footnote of considerable length Ransom writes:[32]

The artist resorts to the imitation because it is inviolable, and it is inviolable because it is not real. In strict theory it might be said that his purpose is to exhibit the typical along with the characteristic, but in view of his actual occasion it may be said much more simply to be: to exhibit the characteristic. He has no fear that the typical at this late date will be obscured.

Thus we see that the typical, or the rational, will take care of itself, exactly as does the emotion; it is the poet's business to concentrate on the cognition. But what is the cognition, and precisely through what virtue or aspect of language does it materialize? It is neither abstraction nor emotion nor any relation-

[31] Ibid., p. 26
[32] *The World's Body*, p. 198.

ship of these two. If we were to accept seriously the occasional hints in Ransom's criticism that what he wants is a purely descriptive poetry, we might suppose that he desired the poet to use only words denoting classes of concrete objects and to use them with reference primarily to their connotations and more especially with reference to their connotations of remembered sensory impression. If we could write such poetry, it would be an extreme form of imagism; but we could never write it, and there is a preponderance of evidence in Ransom's books to show that he does not really want us to write it. But what does he want? If we are to believe in the existence of his cognition, I fear we shall have to take it on faith. And if the poet is to realize it, or fool himself into thinking that he can realize it, he will have to work out a method of deliberately violating the nature of language; and this is exactly what Ransom recommends.

VI. DELIBERATE OBSCURITY

Ransom's great embarrassment as a theorist is that he knows that the poet cannot dispense with rational statement; that at times he even seems to admire poetry for having a measure of rational content; yet that he does not know what to do with the rational content, how to account for it or evaluate it. In the preface to *The World's Body* he writes:[33]

I had the difficulty of finding a poetry which would not deny what we in our strange generation actually are: men who have aged in these pure intellectual disciplines, and cannot play innocent without feeling very foolish. The expense of poetry is greater than we will pay if it is something to engage in without our faculties. I could not discover that this mortification was required.

And the same general notion is stated at many other points in his criticism.

In the same volume[34] he discusses two poems, one by Wallace

[33] *The World's Body*, Preface, p. viii.
[34] Ibid., pp. 58-61.

Stevens and the other by Allen Tate, in one of the most revealing passages he has ever written:

A good "pure" poem is Wallace Stevens' *Sea Surface Full of
Clouds*—famous, perhaps, but certainly not well known . . . The
subject matter is trifling . . . Poetry of this sort, as it was practiced
by some French poets of the nineteenth century, and as it is practiced
by many British and American poets now, has been called pure
poetry, and the name is accurate. It is nothing but poetry; it is poetry
for poetry's sake, and you cannot get a moral out of it. But it was to be
expected that it would never win the public at large. The impulse
which led readers to the old poetry was at least as much moral as it
was aesthetic, while the new ·poetry cannot count on any customers
except those specializing in strict aesthetic effects. But the modern
poets intend to rate only as poets, and would probably think it mere-
tricious to solicit patronage by making moral overtures.

Now although this is a little aside from my principal interest,
it is perhaps fair to say that the subject of Stevens' poem is not
quite trifling; the subject is a sequence of half-apprehended
glimpses of the supernatural in a seascape and in its observer.
And the subject on the whole is fairly well executed, though
most of the valuable elements in the poem had been employed
by the poet previously in better works; the chief defect in the
poem itself is a fairly large amount of playful and essentially
weak repetition. If the poem were as nearly pure description as
Ransom appears to believe, however, one would still think Ransom committed to admire it for that reason at least, for it would
approximate, if anything were capable of approximating, Ransom's formula of disinterested imitation of the objective universe.
And I again should be forced, as a plausible moralist, to defend
it, if the description were rendered justly and without the im-
portation of foreign emotions, for the reason that the contemplation of the objective universe is a possible human experience and
may be justly evaluated.

Ransom's comments are curious. "You cannot get a moral out
of it," he writes; a statement which indicates once more that he
sees no possibility of there being any morality in poetry except in
the form of a moral. And although he dislikes a moral in his

poetry, he appears to be displeased with this poem because he finds it so wholly free from one. He confuses the moral with the conceptual, and though he dislikes the conceptual, he wants his poem to have conceptual content. The following passage continues without break from the last:

As an example of "obscure" poetry, though not the most extreme one, I cite Allen Tate's *Death of Little Boys*. Here are some of the verses:

> Then you will touch at the bedside, torn in two,
> Gold curls now deftly intricate with gray
> As the windowpane extends a fear to you
> From one peeled aster drenched with the wind all day . . .

> Till all the guests, come in to look, turn down
> Their palms; and delirium assails the cliff
> Of Norway where you ponder, and your little town
> Reels like a sailor drunk in his rotten skiff.

There is evidently a wide difference between Stevens and Tate, as poets. Tate has an important subject, and his poem is a human document, with a contagious fury about it: Stevens, pursuing purity, does not care to risk such a subject. But Tate, as if conscious that he is close to moralizing and sententiousness, builds up deliberately, I imagine, an effect of obscurity; for example, he does not care to explain the private meaning of his windowpane and his Norwegian cliff; or else, by some feat, he permits these bright features to belong to his total image without permitting them to reveal any precise meaning, either for himself or for his reader. Stevens, however, is objective from beginning to end; he completes all his meanings, knowing these will have little or no moral importance.

Before commenting on Ransom's comment, I should like to say a few things about the two stanzas, which seem to me as bad as poetry can often be found and thoroughly characteristic of the bulk, though not of the best, of Tate's work and of all of the work which I have seen by his and Ransom's younger disciples in the Southern School. The phrase "torn in two" is merely a crudely stereotyped assertion of violent emotion. The word *deftly*, a characteristic word among these writers, introduces an element of false precision; deftness is irrelevant to the situation, and the word has the effect of a cheap trick. The fear in the next two lines is not in the least obscure; it is the fear of death and bereavement. But Tate, in motivating it by a peeled aster, whatever that may be, and projecting it through a windowpane, endeavors apparently to achieve a concrete image where a concrete image is improper; the whole effort is made with a very heavy hand. The turning down of the palms in the next stanza is meaningless and slightly ridiculous; it seems again an effort to achieve the concrete at any cost. The Norwegian cliff is far less mysterious than Ransom assumes: it is an image representing the sense of remote isolation in the face of death and in the experience of grief. The reeling, the drunken sailor, and the rotten skiff, are all trite and over-violent; and they are not realized in themselves, any more than is the cliff. These images represent one of the commonest weaknesses of Tate, Ransom, and their school: a fear of the abstract statement in itself, a fear so acute that they will invariably substitute for it a trite, vague, or even badly mixed figure if. they can think of one. Thus in Tate's *Ode to the Confederate Dead,* there occur the fine lines:

> *And in between the ends of distraction*
> *Waits mute speculation, the patient curse.*

But instead of putting a period at the end, Tate does not punctuate and adds two more lines:

> *That stones the eyes, or like the jaguar leaps*
> *For his own image in a jungle pool, his victim.*

Now if anything so immaterial as speculation or a curse is to be represented by a concrete image, there will have to be an exact allegorical propriety in the representation, and the concrete image will have to be good in itself. But the image of a stoner of *eyes* is fantastic in itself, and could be justified only by some close relationship to the idea; the necessity of speculation or a curse *stoning* anything is not clear; and violent action on the part of that which is *patient* is still more perplexing. Nor does one see why a stoner of eyes should leap, like a jaguar, into a pool, nor why the owner of the eyes should not thereby be benefitted. Further, jaguars do not hunt jaguars; a jaguar would not be misled by a reflection in a pool; and cats do not like water. And all of this nonsense appears to have arisen from a doctrinaire conviction that a mere abstract statement cannot be poetry: the statement must trail its clouds of glory. One could illustrate the blunders resulting from this idea and others similar at great length. The lines quoted by Ransom are not obscure, although the poet seems to have tried to make them so; they are trite, pretentious, and clumsy. It is only fair to add that Tate occasionally forgets himself and writes a good poem. *Shadow and Shade* and *The Cross* are two of the great lyrics of our time, though something short of perfection, and there are other poems containing beautiful passages.

But let us turn to Ransom's remarks. Tate "has an important subject, and his poem is a human document," statements which appear to me to derive from some notion of moral importance. His poem has a "contagious fury," but we have been told elsewhere to neglect the emotion which the poem communicates. The windowpane has a meaning, but Tate is praised for keeping it private; from which we can deduce only that the poem is more satisfactory to the reader than to Tate, and this by virtue of a deliberate act of trickery on Tate's part; but a few lines further we are reassured by learning that it may possibly have no meaning for Tate either. Stevens is "objective from beginning to end," thereby fulfilling one of the requirements upon which Ransom commonly insists very strongly, yet on this occasion Stevens is blamed for it. Tate's poem is superior because of its greater moral content, yet this content must be strangled, and a virtue made, somehow, of the unavoidable presence of the corpus delicti.

There follows a paragraph which merely repeats the main ideas which we have seen, and then come two short paragraphs of summary:

To be more technical: it is as if the pure poet presented a subject and declined to make any predication about it or even to start predication; and as if the obscure poet presented a subject in order to play with a great deal of important predication without ever completing any.

Personally, I prefer the rich obscure poetry to the thin pure poetry. The deaths of little boys are more exciting than sea-surfaces.

I do not understand how a subject can be presented in language without predication, although I am familiar with many ways of confusing the predication. It is impossible to present a subject in language without saying something about it, either well or badly. But to make a clear rational statement about a serious subject would be to "moralize"; and Ransom, as I have already pointed out, has an irrational and habitual fear of that word and of all its relatives. Ransom prefers the subject which is humanly more important, that is morally more important; but he cannot justify his preference on moral grounds and finds himself driven to justify it on hedonistic: he finds the death of a little boy more exciting than sea-surfaces. It is my own feeling that the death of a little boy in actual fact is likely to be a very sad affair and to merit honest and serious treatment. I do not believe for a moment that Ransom is personally as unpleasant as he appears in this unfortunate statement—in fact, I have excellent reasons to believe the contrary—but as a scholar and a philosopher, he should have been wiser and more wary than to let himself be forced by his own reasoning into a position where such a statement was inevitable. If we are to take Ransom at face value, he loves the deaths of little boys more than he loves sea-surfaces, but he believes that the poet should only play with predication about them. This is a view from which all principles of rightness of evaluation have been eliminated; it implies that the poet is in search of meaningless excitement.

Yet Ransom complains[35] of Miss Millay's "overwriting," a term which implies a standard of rightness of some kind or other, and he says on the subject:

[35] *The World's Body*, p. 82.

To wish to make a thing look pretty or look smart is to think poorly of it in itself, and to want it more conventional, and to try to improve it is to weaken and perhaps destroy it.

But he has shown that Tate thinks poorly of his subject and has tried to conceal and confuse it. Tate's writing is as bad as Miss Millay's, and for much the same reason.

VII. THE STRUCTURE OF POETRY: THE LOGICAL CORE AND THE TEXTURE OF IRRELEVANCE

We have seen Ransom defending a procedure of deliberate obscurantism in general terms; it remains to examine his theories of the mechanics of poetic structure by which he endeavors to explain this obscurantism. In *The World's Body* he writes:[36]

> A poet is said to be distinguishable in terms of his style. It is a comprehensive word, and probably means: the general character of his irrelevances, or tissues. All his technical devices contribute to it, elaborating or individualizing the universal, the core-object; likewise all his material detail. For each poem even, ideally, there is distinguishable a logical object or universal, but at the same time a tissue of irrelevance from which it does not really emerge.

We may observe here again the characteristic elements of Ransom's critical theory: the concept, inescapable and necessary, but regrettable, and having no definable function, hopelessly entangled in detail which is admirable largely in proportion to its being irrelevant to the concept. As usual, Ransom fails through failing to note the double function of language, the simultaneous communication of connotation and denotation. The rational content of a poem is not a *core* to which irrelevancies are attached in a kind of nimbus; it is something which exists from moment to moment, in every word of the poem, just as does the feeling; and the value of the poem resides precisely in the relationship between these two elements, and not in qualities supposedly attaching to one of the partners in the relationship.

[36] *The World's Body*, p. 348.

Ransom restates this theory many times, and in *The New Criticism* especially, with an emphasis which makes it impossible that one should overlook its implications. The following passage will serve as an example:[37]

What is the value of a structure which (a) is not so tight and precise on its logical side as a scientific or technical prose structure generally is; and (b) imports and carries along a great deal of irrelevant or foreign matter which is clearly not structural but even obstructive? This a- and b-formulation is what we inevitably come to if we take the analysis our best critics offer. We sum it up by saying that the poem is a loose logical structure with an irrelevant local texture.

And earlier in the same book[38] he makes a statement which may be fairly regarded as completing this:

And an almost quantitative rule might be formulated, as one that is suggestive if not binding: the more difficult the final structure, the less rich should be the distraction of the texture; and the richer the texture as we proceed toward the structure, the more generalized and simple may be the structure in the end.

From these passages it is evident that Ransom wants as little rational content as possible, and that he sees texture, or what I should call feeling or emotion, as existing independently of structure and yet in some obscure manner not wholly escaping from its presence. If he were able to see the manner in which denotation and connotation exist simultaneously throughout the poem, and the manner in which connotation is momently dependent upon denotation for its very existence, he would not regard the poem as a constant effort on the part of connotation to escape from denotation in ways wholly inexplicable in terms of the nature of language.

The anti-intellectual tendency of this doctrine is clear enough in the following passage from *The World's Body*:[39]

[37] *The New Criticism*, p. 280.
[38] Ibid., p. 274.
[39] *The World's Body*, p. 130.

The poetic impulse is not free [he means free from entanglement with ideas] yet it holds out stubbornly against science for the enjoyment of its images. It means to reconstitute the world of perceptions. Finally there is suggested some such formula as the following:

Science gratifies a rational or practical impulse and exhibits the minimum of perception. Art gratifies a perceptual impulse and exhibits the minimum of reason.

This is a close approximation of the doctrine held by Poe and Mallarmé to the effect that since plain prose deals with truth, or reason, and poetry is different from plain prose, poetry should, if possible, contain no truth or reason. The difference between plain prose and poetry is real, as I have endeavored to show, and it is closer at hand than these ingenious theorists have imagined: poetry is merely a more complete statement of experience than prose, and is not a form of nominalistic delirium.

The italics in the above passage are Ransom's. The seriousness with which he means them may be seen in a recent commentary on *Finnegans Wake*. He writes:[40]

I do not know to what lengths the race will react, keeping company with its artists; nor whether for a total action such as is implied in our "age of science" there must be an equal and opposite reaction. But I believe that *Finnegans Wake* is the most comprehensive individual reaction we have yet seen to all that we have accomplished with our perverted ideal of perfect action. . . . Joyce exploits at least two prime devices for obfuscating discourse. One is stream-of-consciousness, which is prepared to excrete irrelevances in any situation. The other is the verbal device of going from the relevant meaning of the word to the irrelevant meaning, or from the word to the like-sounding words, and then to the words like the like-words. . . . His book is the most allusive in literature, except for the dictionaries and encyclopedias, and the allusions are rarely used as structural elements, and never kept to their logical and historical identities. . . . I should judge that Joyce's book is not a unit of design, because the sections do not obey it, but have their own disorderly energies; nor are the sections because they have pages; nor the pages because of the sentences; and as for the sentences, the little fragments of discourse dissipate themselves as readily as the great ones, and apparently for the

[40] The Kenyon Review, I-4, pp. 425-8.

535

same reason, in order to obtain a "maximum connotation." The sentences have the words. . . . To the literary critic Joyce suggests some extreme exponent of surrealist or "abstractionist" painting. The painting seems to intend to render genuine fragments of finished objects, but assembles them in confusion as if to say that these pieces of life will never add up to a whole. . . . Long ago Mr. Richards laid down a canon of relevance: Anything is relevant to the total meaning which belongs to the psychological situation. The canon might as well read: Anything is relevant . . . Yet Joyce's book is on the side of the angels, and I do not like to abuse it. For the poets it is sure to become an inexhaustible source of courage. It shows at most places how to escape from conceptual prose, and into the contingent world; a difficulty that most poets seem unable to surmount.

Ransom apparently has faint doubts about the propriety of the method which he is describing, but they are faint indeed; he would prefer the risk of having no conceptual content to the risk of having too much: and quite rightly from his own point of view. If the method here described, however, represents the infinity toward which true poetry should draw as near as possible without ever quite reaching it, and if his concept of poetry rests, as Ransom frequently assures us, upon a study of traditional English poetry and a deep sympathy for it, one cannot but feel that something has gone wrong in the study. I am reminded of Robert Bridges, who, after devoting years to the study of Milton's meter, formulated what he supposed to be the principles of that meter and then wrote *The Testament of Beauty* to demonstrate the proper application of the principles.[41] And one is inclined to wonder at this point what has become of the unique object, of love for the unique object, and imitation of the unique object. The only object left to us now is the universe, and the universe is so chaotic that it can scarcely be called unique with any real sense of security; and the work of art, which in spite of Ransom's having expressed dislike for the theory is a perfect illustration of the doctrine of expressive form, is merely a shapeless conglomeration of supposedly unique fragments. This, however, is what one would expect of a work of art of which the essential

[41] This curious subject is discussed in the last essay in my volume, *Primitivism and Decadence*.

characteristic is described as a tissue of irrelevancies, and of which the function is pure imitation in a nominalistic universe.

So far as traditional poetry is concerned, Ransom discloses two major concepts of the nature of irrelevancy. One of these is very simple, and I think may be simply refuted. He sees the texture of irrelevancies as that which is left over when one has made a formal outline of the theme of the poem. That is, if one should take a narrative poem with a descriptive background, such as *Peter Grimes*, by George Crabbe, a summary of the plot would exclude most of the descriptive detail, along with other material; and it would no doubt be possible to rewrite the poem from the summary, even with the use of the same general setting, in such a way as to fill in with other details. But the details are none the less relevant: they show where and how the action takes place and each contributes in its own particular way to the whole narrative. Another set of details might do as well, but then they would be relevant. On the other hand, it is not quite foolish to assume that there is a basis of selection among all the possible details of the original situation, and that the poem is good at least in part in proportion as the poet approximates the perfect selection.

The other form of irrelevance enters the poem by way of metaphor and simile. This constitutes a considerable subject in itself, and I therefore reserve it for separate discussion.

VIII. METAPHOR AND SIMILE: THE IMPORTATION OF IRRELEVANCE

Ransom regards metaphor and simile as a direct means of introducing irrelevance into the poem: that is, if the poet compares Time to the driver of a winged chariot, then a winged chariot, which is essentially irrelevant to the subject under discussion but pleasant to contemplate for itself, is introduced to dissipate the interest. He speaks of metaphor as "a device for bringing in new and, I think, surely irrelevant content." [42] He says further, [43]

[42] *The New Criticism*, p. 67.
[43] Ibid., p. 85.

employing Richards' term, *vehicle,* to indicate that to which the original subject is compared:

I am not prepared to lay down principles for effectiveness in metaphor. I should feel disposed at the moment to argue for a logical propriety, a specific "point of the analogy," as the occasion for any given metaphor; and then for brilliance and importance in the body of the vehicle in its own right. But it seems scarcely open to question that the vehicle must realize itself independently and go beyond its occasion. (And I think nowhere does Richards say the contrary.) In doing this the vehicle becomes irrelevant to the structure of the argument, and asserts the poetic undertaking to incorporate local texture.

The logical propriety which Ransom demands, however, is little more than a conventional occasion; as we have seen in the preceding section of this essay, he desires as little logical propriety as possible and as much irrelevance as possible. Now metaphor can unquestionably be used in some such fashion as that here indicated, and the technique, if the poet is bent on it, can be carried very far. One of the supreme examples of the technique in the older English poetry is *The Weeper,* by Crashaw.

Crashaw uses the tears of the Magdalen as the occasion of metaphorical excursions in all directions; the poem is constrained only by the necessity of praising the Magdalen's piety, but the constraint is slight enough, I should think, to satisfy even Ransom. The first five stanzas illustrate the method to perfection. The first stanza compares the weeper's eyes to various kinds of springs; the second stanza translates the springs to heaven, the tears being compared to falling stars, the stars to seeds which will raise a harvest of piety on earth. But the third stanza states that this comparison to seeds was an error, that the tears are too precious for us on earth and merely seem to fall but do not fall in reality; and the fourth stanza continues this argument by saying that the eyes weep upward, and the tears, being stars, form the cream of the milky way. This is a sufficiently bold comparison, but one can still trace by somewhat whimsical and devious routes the "logical propriety" of this figure from the initial notion

538

of the weeper's piety. The fifth stanza, however, though its starting point is the idea of the cream, and though it contains the faint flavor of the original piety, is one of the most remarkable triumphs of irrelevance with which I am acquainted:

> Every morn from hence
> A brisk cherub something sippes
> Whose sacred influence
> Adds sweetness to his sweetest Lippes.
> Then to his musick. And his song
> Tasts of this Breakfast all day long.

The cherub, intrinsically, is charming; he is nearly as diverting as the elves of Herrick's *Nightpiece*—

> And the elves also
> Whose little eyes glow—

elves which, however, are in comparison almost scandalously relevant to the subject of Herrick's poem. But if we can reach the cherub by this route, we can surely reach any point by others similar; and Crashaw before he is done reaches a number quite as remote.

Of Crashaw's poem as a whole, one can scarcely avoid the conclusion that it is foolish and displays in an extreme form an error of method. Much of the detail is bad, and some of it is good, though perhaps none is as fine as the cherub; but even if the detail were all perfect, the poem could be nothing but a chaos of irrelevancies not much better organized than a section of *Finnegans Wake*. The theory of the morality of poetry does not break down in the face of such a poem, for if any detail is successful it will communicate the feeling proper to its individual subject. The trouble is that one does not have a poem: one has a conventional occasion for irresponsible excursions, the result being an agglomeration of minor poems very loosely related to each other. This is what is called baroque, or decorative, poetry;

539

and although a man of genius may sometimes engage in it with brilliant if fragmentary results, it is fundamentally frivolous. It realizes Ransom's formula to perfection.

But let us examine another figure, this from a speech of Wolsey in Act III, Scene 2, of Henry VIII:

> I have touched the highest point of all my greatness;
> And from that full meridian of my glory,
> I haste now to my setting: I shall fall
> Like a bright exhalation in the evening,
> And no man see me more.

The question here, as I see it, is this: to what extent do we have the fall of a star which is irrelevant to the fall of Wolsey? Wolsey's fall is human and therefore spiritual; but it is not visible as a literal fall. The fall of the star is visible. The visibility of the fall derives from the star; the grandeur from Wolsey. A mere falling star could not be described in such a way as to move us as this passage moves us, for we have here the tragedy of a man, the end of a great career; yet the star gives a great sweep of visibility to the image, at the same time that it is kept closely related not merely to the human, but to human grief and helplessness, by being named, in the language of the time, not a star, but an exhalation. That there is an element of Ransom's irrelevance in such a figure is possible, and that the star should be, as it is, as well realized in itself as possible is certain, for the star will accomplish nothing toward reinforcing the tragedy of Wolsey unless it lives in its own right; but the star is introduced for its relevance, and the strength of the figure lies in the similarity between the matters compared. The best poets do not seek such occasions as ends in themselves; they use them when they need them and only when they need them, and they keep them pared as close to the point of relevance as the occasion permits. The occasional margin of decoration that may result from such practice may well be afforded by a strong poem; but to seek to transform the whole poem into decoration is aimless debauchery.

540

Marvell's chariot occupies a position somewhat between these two extremes, I imagine, but closer to Shakespeare's star than to Crashaw's cherub:

> But at my back I always hear
> Time's winged chariot hurrying near.

The logical propriety is real, and not merely conventional: the image suggests pursuit by an immediate, persistent, and supernatural enemy; the physical embodiment of the enemy is perhaps arbitrary, the chariot being chosen as much for its picturesque qualities as a chariot as for anything else. It seems to me very doubtful, however, that the chariot has any great vigor in itself and distinct from the idea of Time: if we change the phrase to "A winged chariot," we shall find that the irrelevancies are vaguely realized indeed; and if we examine the third and final section of the poem, we shall find that the images are much vaguer, both as irrelevancies and as functioning parts of the poem—this in spite of the fact that the blurred writing of this section appears to receive the greatest share of Ransom's approval or at least the smallest share of his explicit disapproval. The poem has been overestimated, I believe, largely as a result of Eliot's admiration; Herrick's *Gather ye rosebuds*, on the same subject and with no irrelevancies worth naming, is clearly superior.

Before leaving the subject of Time, however, I should like to cite four lines which are among the greatest in English poetry. They will be found in number CIV of Shakespeare's sonnets:

> Ah! yet doth beauty, like a dial hand,
> Steal from his figure, and no pace perceived:
> So your sweet hue, which methinks still doth stand,
> Hath motion, and mine eye may be deceived.

Here the subject is the change by which we perceive and measure Time, but especially as that change occurs in a human face: the change on the dial is employed to make us realize more strongly that change is occurring momently in the face as well; and the mind is fixed on the change at the moment when it is occurring and when it therefore cannot be perceived. There is a minimum of irrelevance here; it would be hard to say that there is any. The comparison is used to make the fearful judgment absolutely certain and inescapable. It seems to me fairly sure that poetry of this kind is greater than poetry resembling *The Weeper* or *Finnegans Wake;* in addition that poetry in general is great precisely as it approaches this kind of concentration, and not, as Ransom endeavors to convince us, as it departs towards general dispersion.

IX. METER AND THE THEORY OF IRRELEVANCE

I should begin this section by remarking that Ransom possesses a talent sufficiently rare among living critics and poets: he is able, as far as the evidence appears, to mark the scansion of a line of poetry correctly.

But the theory of meter which he erects upon this ability is less admirable than the ability itself. The theory contains two main propositions: the first, that meter is not a means of expressing any part of the meaning or feeling of the poem, but that it offers an independent phonetic pleasure of its own; the second, that such independent activity must interfere with the statement of the meaning as the meaning must interfere with the meter, with the result that irrelevancies are forced upon both in the course of this conflict.

I shall have to quote Ransom's own statements with regard to these doctrines, before discussing the doctrines. He writes:[44]

And finally we must take account of a belief that is all but universal among unphilosophical critics, and flourishes at its rankest with the least philosophical. It is: that the phonetic effect in a poem not only is (a) metrical and (b) euphonious, but preferably, and very often is (c) "expressive;" that is, offers a sort of sound which "resembles" or partly "is" or at least "suggests" the object that it means. It is necessary to say rather flatly that the belief is almost com-

" *The New Criticism*, p. 326.

pletely fallacious; both theoretically, or on the whole, and specifically, or in detail for most of the cases that are cited to prove it.

And in regard to the other part of the theory, he writes:[45]

> At once a question or two should present themselves very vexingly to the nebulous aesthetician: What sort of liberties does the poet take with a discourse when he sets it to meter? And what sort of discourse is prepared to permit those liberties?
>
> An argument which admits of alteration in order that it may receive a meter must be partly indeterminate. The argument cannot be maintained exactly as determined by its own laws, for it is going to be undetermined by the meter.
>
> Conversely, a metrical form must be partly indeterminate if it proposes to embody an argument.

There is no relationship, then, between meter and meaning; the meter, like the meaning, goes its own way, gathering irrelevancies to itself; but the two coöperate to this extent, that in interfering with each other they increase the irrelevancies of the total poem. Ransom at no point explains why we take pleasure in the irrelevancies of meter; he merely states it as axiomatic that we do so. He nowhere suggests the romantic theory that meter is a form of music, arousing the feelings by pure sound: indeed, his theory precludes the possibility of such an idea, for if meter can do this it is expressive of something. Ransom apparently assumes that we take pleasure in metrical irregularities for their own sake, as we might take pleasure (if we were so constituted) in the bumps and holes in a concrete sidewalk. Since the meter has no relationship to any other aspect of the poem, it is easy to see that the writing of regular meter will be merely a mechanical task and beneath the dignity of a true poet, who will take pains to introduce roughness for the mere sake of roughness:[46]

> It is not merely easy for a technician to write in smooth meters: it is perhaps easier than to write in rough ones, after he has once

[45] Ibid., p. 298.
[46] *The World's Body*, p. 12.

started; but when he has written smoothly, and contemplates his work, he is capable, actually, if he is a modern poet, of going over it laboriously and roughening it.

And a few years later:[47]

It is not telling the whole truth to say that Shakespeare and other accomplished poets resort to their variations, which are metrical imperfections, because a determinate meaning has forced them into it. The poet likes the variations regardless of the meanings, finding them essential in the capacity of a sound texture to go with the sound structure. It is in no very late stage of a poet's advancement that his taste rejects a sustained phonetic regularity as something restricted and barren, perhaps ontologically defective. Accordingly he is capable of writing smooth meters and then roughening them on purpose. And it must be added, while we are about it, that he is capable of writing a clean logical argument, and then of roughening that too, by introducing logical violence into it, and perhaps willful obscurity.

Strictly speaking, however, it is impossible to write with perfect metrical regularity, for no two syllables, as far as I can determine, are of exactly the same length or degree of accent, and length and accent do not very often wholly coincide; so that one might write scores of lines which technically would not vary from the iambic norm, no two of which would be alike. The norm is wholly ideal, and one recognizes every line as a particular variant from the norm; it is the idea of the norm that gives the variant precision, but the poet with his wits about him knows that he cannot cleave to the norm and certainly does not regard the variant as an imperfection, even as a desirable imperfection. The constant variation from an ideal norm provides a situation from which the skillful writer can create rhythm, and the importance of rhythm I shall discuss a little later. For the present I should like to call attention to the following line:

Where thy pale form was laid with many tears.

[47] *The New Criticism,* p. 324.

544

The line is perfectly iambic:[48] yet the unaccented syllable of the second foot is more heavily accented than the accented syllable of the first; the first syllable of *many*, which is accented in its foot, is one of the four most lightly accented syllables in the line, and two others of the four, *was* and *with* (both of which are unaccented in their respective feet) are longer than the accented syllable of *many* and are nearly as long as any other syllables in the line. There is great rhythmic strength even in this isolated line.

It is possible, of course, to write meter that sounds monotonous, but the defect is a defect of rhythm and not of roughness: the rough meters of Ransom and of Tate are frequently very monotonous indeed; and a poem which is rhythmically monotonous will be faulty beyond the limits of the meter, for reasons which will presently appear. To assume that the irregularities in Shakespeare's sonnets are of the same kind as the irregularities in the poems of Ransom and of Tate, and that they differ only in degree and because Ransom and Tate found it too easy to write like Shakespeare—and this is precisely Ransom's claim—is a very rash assumption. There is something wrong somewhere.

There are various inconsistencies in Ransom's theory. Ransom objects to relatively regular meter because it is mechanically easy; yet he recommends a mechanical roughening, a roughening which is purely an end in itself. He believes that metrical difficulties force irrelevancies into the logical argument, yet we have seen him admit that Joyce, writing without the aid or obstacle of meter, has achieved greater irrelevancy than any poet he can name. And we are bound to observe in this theory an additional inconsistency with his doctrine of imitation, for a poem which contains a meter which is independent, an end in itself, cannot in any comprehensible sense be called a true imitation of some "object" devoid of meter.

To clear up this whole matter, I think we shall have to start with the assumption that meter, or rather the total phonetic quality of metrical language, is in some way or degree expressive,

---

[48] It is possible to read the first foot as reversed, but, taken in its context, it seems to me iambic.

in spite of the fact that a great deal of illiterate foolishness has been written to defend or illustrate this idea, as Ransom at various times has abundantly demonstrated.

In the first place, music is expressive of emotion. I do not understand the relationship between sound and emotion, but it is unquestionably very real: the devotional feeling of Byrd or of Bach, the wit and gaiety of much of Mozart and Haydn, the disillusioned romantic nostalgia of Franck, these are perfectly real, and it is not profitable to argue the point. The correlation between sound and feeling may have its origin in some historical relationship between music and language, or it may, like the capacity to form ideas, have its origin simply in human nature as that is given us.

Metrical language, as pure sound, is no substitute for music; a poem read aloud in a foreign language will never equal a Mozart concerto. But metrical language has one of the properties of music; namely, rhythm. And it has in the phonetic forms of the original and unmetered language certain minor but usable qualities which music lacks. And metrical language, if we understand the language, is not pure sound; the sound is merely one quality of the total meaning, but it contributes, or can be made to contribute, to the meaning.

If we consider the matter merely in its broad and obvious aspects, this will become reasonably clear. Had Milton chosen the meter of *The Ancient Mariner* as the medium for *Paradise Lost,* he would obviously have written a bad poem. The meter of *Paradise Lost* contributes largely to what I have defined in *Primitivism and Decadence* as the convention of the poem; that is, to the initial and general state of feeling within which the poem shall occur. And it is not merely the blank verse which does this; it is the Miltonic blank verse. The blank verse of the early Fletcher, for example, is almost song-like in comparison, and could never have sustained the gravity of the Miltonic theme. It is a common-place to assert that Miltonic blank verse is one of the greatest metrical inventions in the history of poetry; and no one except Ransom, I imagine, or some one of his disciples, would assert that Milton invented Miltonic blank verse for the

546

sake of Miltonic blank verse. He invented it for the sake of *Paradise Lost;* the poem could not have been written without it, and we may fairly assume that it functions as an instrument for the expression of something essential to the poem. Different metrical forms establish different kinds of feeling; and certain metrical forms, as I have shown in detail in my essay on meter in *Primitivism and Decadence,* are such that they can be used to suggest within a single poem the effects of a variety of other forms, and thus achieve great complexity of feeling.

If the total rhythmic structure can affect the total feeling of the poem, it is only reasonable to suppose that there is a similar relationship within the details. When the contribution of meter to the detail is primarily musical, in the imperfect sense in which this term can be applied to poetry, it is necessarily elusive, and elaborate attempts to describe it will always be clumsy. Within the detail, however, the contribution of the meter is not always purely musical, but at times is in some measure imitative or suggestive. When Herrick writes of

> . . . *the elves also*
> *Whose little eyes glow*

the quick movement of the second line is actually amusing: perhaps in part because of some intrinsic quality of sound, however slight it may be in language; perhaps in part because there is a suggestion of the quick movement of the little creatures who are being described.

I should like to run the risk of quoting a passage from my own poetry. I have the advantage of knowing my intention, and with all due respect to the reader, even if the reader should be Mr. Ransom, I am reasonably sure of my effect. The passage is from a poem called *The Fall of Leaves:*

> *So was the instant blurred;*
> *But as we waited there,*
> *The slow cry of a bird*
> *Built up a scheme of air.*

The meter is iambic trimeter, and the first, second, and fourth lines are similar in general structure, the first foot of each being reversed, but not heavily, the second and third feet being normal. The third line departs strongly from this norm, however, and for a purpose. The accented syllables of this line are all heavy and long, the unaccented light and short, so that the feet are clearly marked. The first foot, however, differs from the first foot of each of the other lines in being iambic, and the second foot differs in being reversed, so that two long and heavy syllables instead of two short and light are brought into juxtaposition, and in such a way as to slow the line so strongly that the inexpert metrist would probably scan *cry* as a monosyllabic foot, and the words following as a trisyllabic foot. Now the words *slow cry* in this context do not imitate any bird-call known to me, but they suggest the slowness of the cry and the emergence of a definite sound from a surrounding context. The sound apart from the meaning would not have this effect; nor would the sound and meaning of these words alone and apart from the total passage or poem; but I am fairly certain that here they have it.

Effects such as those I have just described have little or nothing, I believe, to do with the suggestion of emotional or dramatic speech; yet in dramatic or narrative poetry, this kind of suggestion is sometimes important:

> O lente, lente curite noctis equi:
> *The starres moove stil, time runs, the clocke will strike,*
> *The divel wil come, and Faustus must be damned.*
> *O Ile leap up to my God: who pulls me downe?*
> *See see where Christs blood streames in the firmament.*
> *One drop would save my soule, half a drop, ah my Christ.*

The slow smooth movement of the Latin line, especially as it appears in the context of the English language and a different meter, accentuates the nervous rapidity, suggesting terror, of the next two lines. The extra syllable in the fourth foot of the fifth line prepares the way for the violent aberration of the sixth: in the sixth line there are six feet instead of five, the fourth of these

548

being inverted, and the fifth, although normally accented, having a rhetorical cesura between the unaccented syllable and the accented, so that the latter part of the line is divided into two rhetorical units of a foot and a half apiece. The rhythm of this line is so curious that it quite eludes description; but that it contributes to the expression of agony and terror I should assert without hesitation. In fact, the main power of this entire passage is derived from its sound.

These lines and others in the same speech are extremely violent and obvious as compared to the expressive variations possible within lyric poetry; I have chosen them because they are too obvious to be overlooked. Within the shorter and subtler form of the rhymed lyric, aberrations so extreme would destroy the total form if they occurred; and further, within a short and strongly defined form, finer effects may be obtained by subtler variations. The whole topic, along with others here mentioned, as well as the general laws of metrical effectiveness, I have discussed at length in the last essay of *Primitivism and Decadence*. It is perhaps worth adding, however, that the abuse of the effect of dramatic speech is one of the commonest defects of recent poetry: it is very easy, apparently, to write in meters which simulate the looseness of conversation in the belief that they simulate the effect of dramatic speech; in fact, it is hard sometimes to determine whether the poet is working on this theory or on the theory of arbitrary roughening, for the effect is about the same in either case. Much of Frost and of Yeats displays this looseness, and much also of the work of the Southern School.

The reader familiar with my writing may wonder whether I am not here defending the doctrine which I have called the doctrine of expressive or imitative form, and which I have elsewhere attacked. I can state categorically that I am not. The doctrine of expressive form states that the poet is "expressing" his subject matter, and that the form of expression is determined by the subject matter. My belief, on the contrary, is this: that the poet is expressing his own understanding of his subject matter and the feelings properly motivated by that understanding; that the value of the poem depends upon the quality of the understanding and the justness of the motivation; that the phonetic form of the poem is an important part of the instrument of expression; that any surrender of the poet to his subject, any attempt to imitate the subject with the form, as Joyce attempts to imitate chaos in *Finnegans Wake,* will result in a more or less serious impairment of the poet's own understanding and control; and that writing in all its aspects is governed by principles, which I have endeavored to elucidate in *Primitivism and Decadence,* and which cannot be seriously violated without a total loss of ability to express anything whatever. Herrick succeeds, perhaps, in suggesting the motion of his elves in a single line, not because he has been trying to imitate their movements or Julia's throughout a poem, but because he has established a metrical form with its own musical values, both general and detailed, and is able for an instant to make a slight movement which suggests the movement of a physical being: the movement would not be perceptible except in the frame, and it is so slight as not to disturb the frame.

As to the notion that meter interferes with meaning, and meaning with meter, whether to the advantage or to the disadvantage of the poem, I should like again to object. If the phonetic value of metrical language is expressive of emotion, or better is capable of qualifying the expression of emotion, even though most of the time very slightly, then the value of any word in metrical language will differ from its value in unmetered language; and the value of the same word will never be quite the same in any two metrical passages, for the precise nature of its sound and its relationship to the context of sound will vary with each passage. To this extent, the poet may be said to create his language as he proceeds, though he is far from being a wholly free agent in creating. He is not endeavoring to invent a logical argument, then meter it, then confuse argument and meter in the interests of excitement. He is seeking to state a true moral judgment; he is endeavoring to bring each word as close to a true judgment as possible; and he has it in his power to modify the values of words within certain limits.

But the medium is incalculably difficult, and for that reason there are very few first rate lyrical poems. The language is crowded with poems which in whole or in part give evidence that the poet proceeded hastily or in ignorance. Ransom examines some of these passages in *The New Criticism* and adduces them as evidence in support of his theory of meter; I should cite them as evidence that good poetry is hard to achieve. If one is indifferent to the distinctions between good and bad, one can approach the whole subject of poetry with a kind of scientific impartiality and deduce laws which will have nothing to do with excellence. Ransom is scientific, in this connection, without knowing it, and though I am a moralist, I find myself forced to protest.

It is for this reason that I have spoken of meter as having moral significance. Meter has certain phonetic values of its own, and it clarifies, identifies, and even modifies the phonetic values of unmetered language. And the total phonetic value of metrical language has the power to qualify the expression of feeling through language. Since the expression of feeling is a part of the moral judgment as I have defined it, the meter has moral significance, for it renders possible a refinement in the adjustment of feeling to motive which would not otherwise be possible. This being true, the poet is not likely to find it embarrassingly easy to write in the "smooth" meters of Shakespeare and Jonson: those meters are difficult in proportion to their smoothness, for they achieve a maximum of effect with a minimum of variation. Every movement in such meter is perceptible, and, in the hands of the good poet, makes its contribution to the total poem. In the lurching meter employed for the most part by Tate, Ransom, and their group, the effectiveness of meter is at a minimum; the meter staggers for the sake of staggering. It is quite as difficult to be Shakespeare today as it was in the year 1600.

In *Primitivism and Decadence*, where the whole problem of meter is discussed more fully than I can hope to discuss it here, I wrote:[49]

. . . in traditional verse, each variation, no matter how slight, is exactly perceptible, and as a result can be given exact meaning as an act of moral perception . . .

[49] Page 129 of the present volume.

and Ransom, in quoting this passage,[50] adds the parenthetical comment, "though he means merely exact phonetic value." The fact of the matter is, that I meant what I said.

X. THE TRIVIALITY OF POETRY

Scattered through Ransom's prose one finds a few brief passages which indicate that his faith in the value of poetry is not all that he would like it to be. In *The World's Body* he writes:[51]

> Our arts, certainly our poems, should fill us with pride because they furnish our perfect experiences. But they fill us also with mortification because they are not actual experiences. If we regard them in a certain mood, say when the heat of action is upon us, they look like the exercises of children, showing what might have been. Participating in the show which is poetry, we expel the taint of original sin and restore to our minds freedom and integrity. Very good. But we are forced to note presently, when we go out of the theater, that it was only make-believe, and as we go down the same street by which we came, that we are again the heirs of history, and fallen men.

So we see that Ransom's qualification of the doctrine of imitation, to wit that the imitation expresses the disinterested love of the artist for the object and hence is preferable to the object, does not at all times convince him. Like the Crispin of Wallace Stevens' poem, Ransom prefers the plum to its poem, for the plum is more than the poem, and the poem adds nothing, really, to the plum. The poem was the result of a delusion.

And it is characteristic of Ransom, that in his essay on Aristotle's cathartic principle,[52] he should insist that Aristotle intended us to understand that tragedy is merely a dose for getting rid of our emotions. He adduces in support of this view the fact that Aristotle was a physician; he fails to add that Aristotle, as a disciple of Plato, is comprehensible only within the Platonic con-

[50] *The New Criticism*, p. 267.
[51] *The World's Body*, p. 249.
[52] Ibid., p. 173.

552

text. I myself am incompetent to discuss the question of what Aristotle really meant, but if his meaning was the one that Ransom attributes to him, one can only regret it, for so great a man should have done better; the fact that Ransom can see no possibility of a better interpretation is characteristic of his awkwardness in writing of the function of poetry and of the manner in which his theories render poetry contemptible. There are, it is true, certain remarks about music in the *Politics,* which support Ransom's view very strongly, but the discussion of music, like Aristotle's other discussions of the arts, is brief, incomplete, and extremely contradictory.

And poetry, according to Ransom's theories, is precisely contemptible. Aside from the doctrine of imitation, which is so confused that it will not stand criticism even within the terminology of Ransom's own thought, Ransom offers no principle of rightness in poetry. Poetry is an obscure form of self-indulgence, a search for excitement by ways that Ransom cannot define, in which we proceed from a limited and unsatisfactory rational understanding of our subject to as complete a confusion as we are able to achieve; it is a technique, not of completing rational understanding, but of destroying it and getting nothing in return. The poem is composed of rational understanding, which is there because we cannot quite get rid of it, but of as little as possible; of a conglomeration of irrelevancies of meaning; and of what Eliot would call, I suppose, an autoletic meter, which goes on its secret way, accumulating irrelevancies of its own and helping to force additional irrelevancies into the meaning.

We can see the fruits of these theories in most of the poetry of Tate, of which the lines already quoted are an average sample; and although Ransom's poetry is in general less confused than Tate's, largely, I think, as a result of its being less ambitious, it is quite clearly modeled on its author's doctrines. Ransom is at his best in a few poems on small themes, which, or parts of which, he has handled with real ability: the best of these, as far as my knowledge extends, are *Bells for John Whiteside's Daughter,* in which the memory of the little girl driving the geese is very lovely, and *Piazza Piece*, which, though slight, seems to me wholly successful. *Captain Carpenter*, however, represents what appears to be his aim, or at any rate it is a fair specimen of the quality of most of his work. I quote its final stanzas:

> *God's mercy rest on Captain Carpenter now*
> *I thought him Sirs an honest gentleman*
> *Citizen husband soldier and scholar enow*
> *Let jangling kites eat of him if they can.*
>
> *But God's deep curses follow after those*
> *That shore him of his goodly nose and ears*
> *His legs and strong arms at the two elbows*
> *And eyes that had not watered seventy years.*
>
> *The curse of hell upon the sleek upstart*
> *Who got the Captain finally on his back*
> *And took the red red vitals of his heart*
> *And made the kites to whet their beaks clack clack.*

The poem illustrates the doctrine of irrelevancy much better than the doctrine of imitation, as one can discern upon examining either the kites or the curses; but that is only what one might expect. It displays a kind of ponderous whimsicality, which endeavors to engage in the labor of wit, and an effort to spin out small themes as far as possible in the absence of any better way of dealing with them. It is a marvel of lucidity, however, as compared to many poems by Allen Tate and the younger Southerners.

XI. DETERMINISM

Ransom is not really impelled, as Eliot is impelled, to devise an historical justification of modern poetry, for he does not believe that the poetry needs that kind of justification. His entire philosophy is aimed at showing, not that the more confused moderns are helpless on the current history, but that they are wisely and deliberately working toward a better kind of poetry.

Nevertheless there are a few passages in his work which indicate a deterministic doctrine very much like that of Eliot:[53]

Apostate, illaureate, and doomed to outlawry the modern poets may be. I have the feeling that modernism is an unfortunate road for them to have taken. But it was an inevitable one. It is not hard to defend them from imputations against their honor and their logic. It is probably a question of whether we really know them, and understand their unusual purpose, and the powerful inhibitions they impose upon themselves.

But let us approach the matter from a slightly different angle. Poets have had to become modern because the age is modern. Its modernism envelops them like a sea, or an air. Nothing in their thought can escape it.

And a few pages later:[54]

I suggest that critics and philosophers fix their most loving attention upon certain natural compounds in human experience. But I say so diffidently, and not too hopefully. It will take a long time to change the philosophical set which has come over the practice of the poets. The intellectual climate in which they live will have to be altered first.

These passages are not important in themselves or in connection with the general plan of Ransom's thought; but they indicate the manner in which it is possible for the systems of Ransom and Eliot to support each other in the minds of younger men, such as Blackmur, Tate, and the young Southerners. On the one hand, Ransom defends the sort of poetry these men most admire; and on the other hand, Eliot proves that no other kind of poetry is possible among honest men in a degenerate age. The two systems are not strictly consistent with each other, but, as Eliot would no doubt remind us, consistency is not one of the virtues of our age.

[53] *The World's Body*, p. 62.
[54] Ibid., p. 75.

POST SCRIPTA

I.

I HAVE TRIED in this book, in addition to pursuing my examination of the mere history of American literary theory, to indicate a theory of my own, to complete the discussion undertaken in my first book, *Primitivism and Decadence*, which was mainly a discussion of style, and which had little reference to the ideas generating styles.

I have tried also to select for examination the minds which represent the most influential tendencies in the literary practice of our time, and as far as may be the most influential minds themselves. The influence of Adams and Eliot has been great for years; that of Ransom has more recently become great. The influence of Stevens as a theorist is probably negligible, for I doubt whether many of his admirers understand his theories; but he represents a common attitude, and since he is a man of genius and a writer of unlimited audacity, he represents the effects of that attitude more perfectly than anyone else I can find. I had thought originally to write of Allen Tate and of R. P. Blackmur, but my book has grown too long and I must refrain. I am convinced, besides, that there is nearly nothing in their thought which is not to be found in Eliot and Ransom: a study of their criticism would be valuable largely in connection with the effect of their borrowed ideas upon their critical taste and upon their poetic style. But that will have to wait for another time.

The writers whom I have discussed are all men of some native ability. Adams wrote a great historical work; Stevens has written great poetry; Eliot and Ransom display sufficient poetic talent to be interesting. But they think as badly as possible, and it is curi-

556

ous that men of so much talent should think so badly, as it is likewise curious that they should so often impose their thought on other men of talent. On the other hand, although there are many literary scholars who have done important work and a few who have done great work, I have yet to discover a professor of English, except for a few relatively young men who are also poets, who could judge a new poem accurately.

The antagonism between the poet and the scholar, I suppose, is in part the result of temperamental differences between extreme types in both groups; it is mainly, however, something left us by the romantic movement, and it is still sufficiently strong so that the older literary men who are in the academic profession frequently show but little trace of academic influence. Yet it is only, I believe, in a combination of the talents of the poet with the discipline of scholarship that one can hope to produce a really finished critic. And the literary life of our time, like the academic life, stands in dire need of a handful of critics who not only are sensitive but know more or less what they are talking about. Unless the critics are forthcoming, literature runs the risk of falling into the hands of the barbarians.

I have showed but little respect, I fear, for the four subjects of the long essays in this book. I should like to indicate very briefly the types of mind to which they seem to me to be surrendering literature.

II.

I suppose that many scholars recognize the weakness of Parrington, yet Parrington's[1] history is apparently the text most widely used in the teaching of American literature, so that the number of scholars unaware of the exceptional badness of the text must be appallingly large; it is likewise more influential than any other book in its field, I should judge, upon the Marxist critics of the past ten or fifteen years. The text is wholly dependent upon two very serious errors: namely, that one can write the history of a

---

[1] *Main Currents in American Thought*, by V. L. Parrington, Harcourt, Brace and Co. 3 vols.

culture with reference only to one intellectual tradition, in this case a tradition of very small influence in the first hundred and fifty years, that is, during the formative period; and that one can determine the ideas governing a work of art without making any attempt to understand the art as art. I should like to enlarge upon these points.

Parrington writes as follows in his first chapter:[2]

Unless one keeps in mind the social forces that found it convenient to array themselves in Puritan garb, the clear meaning of it all will be lost in the fogs of biblical disputation, and some of the ablest men the English race has ever bred will be reduced to crabbed theologians involved in tenuous subtleties and disputing endlessly over absurd dogmas. But tenacious disputants though they certainly were, pursuing their subtleties into the last refuge and cranny of logic, these Puritan dogmatists were very far from being vain practitioners of eccentricity. It is the manner and dress and not the matter of their arguments that is strange; and if we will resolutely translate the old phrases into modern equivalents, if we will put aside the theology and fasten attention on the politics and economics of the struggle, we shall have less difficulty in discovering that the new principle for which those old Puritans were groping was the later familiar doctrine of natural rights; and the final end and outcome of their concern for a more equitable relation of the individual to society, was the principle of a democratic commonwealth, established in the conception of political equalitarianism. Here are liberalisms in plenty to reward the search for the inner core of Puritanism.

In other words, if we will resolutely neglect ninety-nine hundredths of what the Puritans wrote during their first century and a half, we shall arrive at a true understanding of what they were trying to stay, and we shall have made a clear and undeceptive beginning to a history of American literature. This is a view of history to which I am unable to subscribe; but it is the view of Parrington, and, whether they realize it or not, of his disciples and admirers. To those who believe with Parrington that we may safely put aside the theology, let me recommend the latest work of Perry Miller;[3] and to those who believe that the Puritans

[2] Ibid., Vol. 1, page 6.
[3] The New England Mind, by Perry Miller. Macmillan, 1939. See also Miller's paper, *Jonathan Edwards to Emerson*, New England Quaterly, XIII-4.

were greatly concerned with the later familiar doctrine of natural rights, the latest work of Professor Andrews.[4] A consideration of these two works alone should make it evident that Parrington and his point of view should be discarded.[5]

Of Parrington's two initial fallacies, however, the one which I have just considered is the less serious. The more serious is to be found clearly stated in the first two sentences of his introduction:[6]

> I have undertaken to give some account of the genesis and development in American letters of certain germinal ideas that have come to be reckoned traditionally American—how they came into being here, how they were opposed, and what influence they have exerted in determining the form and scope of our characteristic ideals and institutions. In pursuing such a task, I have chosen to follow the broad path of our political, economic, and social development, rather than the narrower belletristic; and the main divisions of the study have been fixed by forces that are anterior to schools and movements, creating the body of ideas from which literary culture eventually springs.

The term *belletristic,* here as elsewhere in Parrington, is a term of contempt for any interest in art as art. Parrington assumes that the best way to understand a work of art is to neglect entirely its nature as a work of art, and to deal with its ideas. He believes that we can know what an artist thinks, without knowing what he does. This is almost brutally crude thinking. At an obviously ridiculous level it leads to identifying the theories of Ahab with the theme of *Moby Dick,* or the morality of Iago with the morality of Shakespeare. I suppose that serious scholars no longer do this sort of thing. But it also leads to identifying the paraphrasable content of the poem with the meaning of the poem; to neglecting the quality of feeling with which the paraphrasable con-

---

[4] *The Colonial Period of American History,* by Charles M. Andrews. Yale U. Press, 4 vols., 1934-38.

[5] It would be a pity to stop here, however: The two essays by H. B. Parkes, Hound and Horn. Vol. V, and *The Puritan Mind,* by H. W. Schneider, though less rich in detail, are probably more incisive in defining essentials than is Miller; they deal with other matter than that of Andrews.

[6] Op. cit. Vol. I, p. iii.

tent is stated, to neglecting, that is, the final and irreducible act of judgment which gives the poem its essentially poetic identity. It leads in general to fastening on the idea lying detached before the eye and to neglecting its function in the unified work, to neglecting, that is, what the artist does with the idea; it thus eliminates carefully the possibility of understanding what a writer means when he states a given idea. Parrington's method offers what appears to be a short-cut to history, though unfortunately it is a short-cut which avoids nearly all of the proper subject-matter of the history in question.

Parrington, then, deals with literature only in so far as literature is a matter of fragmentary ideas clearly visible to the innocent eye; furthermore, he deals only with a limited range of ideas, and relegates the rest to the region of illusion. Had Parrington written, as he seems to imply that he meant to write, a history of Jeffersonian liberalism, and neglected all matter irrelevant to his subject, he might have been more or less successful. But he unquestionably did not do so: he wrote what purports to be a history of American literature, but treated wholly in terms of what he conceives to be the development of Jeffersonian liberalism.

The result could easily have been forecast. His frame-work of ideas has no serious relationship to most of the great writers, and, since he thus has no way of understanding them, his treatment of them is almost purely impressionistic. His treatment of Cotton Mather, I should judge, is notorious among specialists in colonial history, and it ought to be equally notorious among men of letters, for Mather was in his way and in his best passages one of the great masters of English prose; his treatment of Poe, or rather his confession that he has no way of treating Poe, that he is literally rendered helpless by his method, is also notorious. But the handling of Melville, Henry James, and Henry Adams, to name only a few of the more obvious failures is almost as bad. The essay on Melville, for example, is merely a pseudo-poetic summary of the sensational and uncritical book by Mr. Raymond Weaver. One coming upon it, with no knowledge of Melville, would receive no clue whatever to the subject-matter or to the form of any of Melville's books, to Melville's own intellectual history, or to the intellectual history of which Melville is in some part the product. The value of the essay, if it has any, lies wholly in the soundness of Parrington's unguided personal impressions (not to mention Weaver's), and in the beauty of his prose; the virtues are purely belletristic. I prefer to leave the praise of this aspect of Parrington to an admirer. William T. Utter has written as follows of Parrington's artistry:[7]

It must have been apparent to all who knew him that Parrington was essentially an artist. To all classes it was shown in the care, almost meticulous, with which he polished his phrases, the search in his interpretation for harmonious balance and proportion, as if it were a structure of stone, rather than of ideas, which he was erecting. Those who knew him intimately were aware of his interest in architecture and painting; that he had studied in these fields during his first European residence; that he had even considered entering them professionally. He had more than ordinary ability as a poet, according to his friends, although his own judgment did not permit of publication. In his writing, this artistic temperament was to be demonstrated not only in his constant effort to attain unity but also in the care with which each phrase was turned—care which brings to mind the artistry of the eighteenth century conversationalist.

We have already observed the methods by which Parrington obtained unity; it is perhaps worth a moment to examine one of the carefully turned sentences, a more or less representative sentence, on the subject of Herman Melville:[8]

The golden dreams of transcendental faith, that buoyed up Emerson and gave hope to Thoreau, turned to ashes in his mouth; the white gleams of mysticism that now and then lighted up his path died out and left him in darkness.

The style has a vulgar floridity throughout which is quite revolting; the mixed metaphor is one of the most ridiculous specimens that have ever come in my way; the sentence purports to

---

[7] *Vernon Louis Parrington,* by William T. Utter; the Marcus W. Jernegan Essays in American Historiography, U. of Chicago Press, p. 306.
[8] Op. cit., Vol. II, p. 258.

discuss Melville and tells us nothing about him. Except for the metaphor, which is a remarkable thing of its kind, the sentence is characteristic and can be matched on many pages; in fact, many essays, that on Melville among others, are composed solidly in this style.

Such are the short-cuts to history and to criticism about equally. One could gather an interesting garland of comments upon Parrington, with very little labor, by specialists in various fields upon which he touched. Michael Kraus, whose estimate of Parrington is far higher than my own, makes this interesting comment:[9]

Historians complain that Parrington did not know enough history, while students of literature often disagree with his estimates of literary figures.

Even within either field, however, the comment is often somewhat as follows:[10]

Parrington's work is noble and in the main admirable, but he is unfortunately very ignorant of my particular subject.

Yet such a comment is unfair and imperceptive. No historian of a literature—or of anything else—can fairly be expected to be a specialist in every subject upon which he touches; Parrington's defect was a defect not in specialized knowledge but in common sense—it was a defect which made it impossible for him to use the work of specialists intelligently. His work is really as obsolete as the work of George Bancroft; in fact, it was so before it was written.

[9] *A History of American History*, by Michael Kraus, Farrar and Rinehart, 1937. P. 480.
[10] Plagiarized, as regards the form of the statement, from a bibliographical note in *The Puritans*, by Perry Miller and T. H. Johnson, American Book Co., p. 805. Of Vol. I these gentlemen write: "A noble work that is still the best comprehensive history of American thought; inspired by a militant liberalism, consequently hostile and unsympathetic to Puritanism; based upon lamentably insufficient familiarity with the sources, and therefore to be read for stimulation, not for fact or accuracy."

III.

The most ambitious piece of more or less recent Marxian criticism with which I am acquainted is Bernard Smith's *Forces in American Criticism.*[11] Its point of view as regards American literature derives from Parrington, although it would be hard to say how Smith reconciles Parrington's longing for a more Jeffersonian world, with Marx's economic determinism. The point of contact—a point of contact is usually sufficient for the modern critic—is of course the interest of both writers in the plight of the lower classes. This provides, however, a purely sentimental and irresponsible approach to literature. Of Parrington, Smith writes:[12]

Parrington's *Main Currents* arrived to supply the most needed things: an account of our literary history which squared with recent works on the history of our people and a realistic technique for analyzing the relationship of a writer to his time and place—in addition to a militantly progressive spirit. Professorial and literary circles had consciously been waiting for such a work, and if the one that did come forth was far more radical than some people cared for, it simply could not be rejected. The author was a professor too; his scholarship defied scrutiny; and his ideas were couched in terms that were native American, most of them having come over shortly after the *Mayflower*.

Smith, like Parrington, sees reality only in ideas which have what is known today as social significance; religion and morality are mere delusions—not only is there no truth in them, but they never really influenced anybody. Of tradition he writes:[13]

Tradition was the accumulation of manners and beliefs which gentlemen had evolved and handed down to their sons and pupils; it was the symbol of order, the promise of social supremacy to those who were its guardians.

We have learned from Parrington that the first Puritans came to Massachusetts to found a democracy, and that their theological

[11] Harcourt, Brace and Co., 1939.
[12] Ibid., p. 331.
[13] Ibid., p. 233.

language was merely a blind; we learn from Smith that the Unitarian heirs of their spirit were concerned only with retaining their wealth, and that their morality was a shallow pretence.

Smith writes at length on Emerson, and with some perspicuity points out many of his worst errors; he then turns about and praises Whitman without reservation. The only real difference between Whitman's doctrines and Emerson's, however, resides in the fact that Whitman expresses a boundless sympathy with the masses, whereas Emerson is pretty sceptical about them. Smith derives his moral doctrines from his Marxist position and excoriates pre-Marxist morality,[14] and it is his moral doctrines which guide him in judging literature—he has great contempt for all impressionism or relativism. He does not say how he justifies Marxism, yet he appears to accept it because he believes it promises greater justice to men than other social doctrines. Yet justice is a moral concept, and one is perplexed to know whether he derives his concept of justice from Marxism or his Marxism from his concept of justice. After insisting that judgments of literature must be based upon the soundness of the author's social views, he yet defends Shakespeare against one of his more enthusiastic colleagues because of "the values in Shakespeare that are permanent for all classes"; yet blames this writer for treating Shakespeare in terms that are ethical instead of materialistic.[15]

IV.

In the Autumn of 1940 The Southern Review and the Kenyon Review published a joint symposium attacking the methods commonly in use of teaching English. The chief complaint of the contributors was this: that the departments of English in the main teach history instead of criticism, whereas they should teach criticism instead of history. This represents a fallacy, I think, almost as serious as that of Parrington: I do not believe, as I have said, that the history of literature can be grasped unless one has a critical understanding of it; but it seems to me equally obvious

[14] Ibid., p. 287.
[15] Ibid., p. 291.

that a critical understanding is frequently quite impossible unless one knows a good deal of history. The critical and the historical understanding are merely aspects of a single process. As to the quarrel which these gentlemen picked with the philologists and the textual critics, it is quite aside from my present concerns, although I believe it to be foolish. There is far more need even yet for good textual criticism even of many standard writers than these critics seemed to realize, and philology has always been and will always remain a subject of fundamental importance for the student of literature. If more poets had studied philology, the quality of our poetry would probably improve.

If we exclude from consideration, however, the philologists and textual critics, and merely think of the scholars who teach what is known as the history of literature, there is, I think, just ground for objection to a very large part of what is being done, especially, perhaps, in the field of American literature. I should like to preface these remarks, however, with the statement that I can feel little moral indignation at the errors of the unfortunate professors. The number of people capable of doing valuable work in literary criticism in any period is very small. A great critic, indeed, is the rarest of all literary geniuses: perhaps the only critic in English who deserves the epithet is Samuel Johnson. And the number of persons required to teach English is remarkably large: further explanation seems unnecessary. So long as the gentlemen of undeniable literary talent insist on indulging themselves in the strange adventures which we have been examining in this book, we can hardly blame the simple and honest professor if he occasionally becomes confused or even sinks into a kind of antiquarian melancholia.

We must not judge him too harshly as moralists; but as critics we are bound to see his work for what it is worth. I should like to indicate briefly some of the commoner types of blunders which might be classified under the heading of unenlightened specialization. And I should like to repeat that much of the moral responsibility for this kind of thing rests on a few of our more brilliant literary critics.

I have talked with a well-known specialist in Emerson, a man who knows in detail, I believe, the whole Emersonian text and very nearly everything that has been written about Emerson, but who at the time of my conversation with him had not read Cooper since childhood, knew only a small part of Hawthorne, and had a vague conviction that Melville was a transcendentalist in oilskins and Miss Dickinson a transcendentalist in dimity. This authority was almost wholly ignorant of Emerson's contemporaries and also of later American literature. I have talked with a well-known specialist in Poe, who shared all of the ignorance listed above and who was wholly unfamiliar with the French symbolists as well: in fact, American specialists in Poe, as a class, exhibit a kind of bucolic innocence which at times simply paralyzes comment; they appear to have not the vaguest idea of the kind of devilment with which they are dealing.

Now I respectfully submit that only a minute portion of what has been written on Poe or Emerson or any other subject has any considerable value, and that a good deal of what has been written and very respectably published is unmitigated twaddle; and further that no man will ever understand either writer who has not read his major contemporaries thoroughly and with comprehension; and further still, that no man will have done his best to understand either writer who has not done his best to understand not only the writers who led up to the subject of study but the writers who developed from him or from the school of writing to which he belonged. To understand Emerson, it is more important to understand both Cotton Mather and Hart Crane than it is to have bibliographical notes on a multitude of monographs. I do not deny that many of the monographs have value, and that one ought to read as many of them as possible. I merely insist on a proper scale of values: it is with the history of literature that we are dealing, not with the history of monographs, and either one by itself is a tremendous subject. In dealing with such a field as the history of eighteenth century literature in England or in France, a field in which there is already available a good deal of reliable historical and critical guidance, the scholar is relatively safe in extreme specialization; but he can never be wholly so.

The antiquarian habit of mind, moreover, if one can judge

from its products, is likely to grow dimmer and dimmer simply of its own inanition. I should like to cite merely a few of the curiosities which have come to my attention in the past few years, and which indicate a blindness to what one would think fairly massive objective data.

The late Ernest Fenollosa died in 1908, a date sufficiently remote to be fairly respectable, and his contribution to Japanese culture was regarded by the Japanese themselves as so great that the emperor had his ashes removed from London to Japan, and, according to the story, in a Japanese battleship; and he had received many extraordinary official honors during his life. These facts have nothing to do with American literature, but they are the sort of thing that might help the scholar to notice Fenollosa, who is in other respects important. Fenollosa is the author of a large two-volume work on Chinese and Japanese art, which was published posthumously, and it was Fenollosa's literal translations from the Chinese poetry and Japanese drama which gave Ezra Pound the original material for his great English versions, versions which about twenty-five years ago initiated a poetic movement of great importance. Yet the name of Fenollosa, to the best of my knowledge, appears nowhere in any history of American literature now available. During the year 1941, while these pages were in process of composition, there appeared a short paragraph on Fenollosa in the *Oxford Companion to American Literature,* compiled by James Hart, this being the only academic recognition of the writer with which I am acquainted.

The Indian bulletins of the Smithsonian Institution have been famous for years. I do not know exactly how many of them there are, but they constitute an imposing library; and they are the most valuable body of information available on the subject of the American Indian. Furthermore, a good many of the anthropologists contributing to this series have translated admirably from the Indian languages; three of them, at least, Washington Matthews, Frances Densmore, and Frank Russell, are among the few really brilliant poetic translators in English. These and other translators of the same kind, moreover, have been famous for years: in 1918 George W. Cronyn published through Boni and

Liveright a collection of Indian poems, drawn mainly from the bulletins, under the title of *The Path on The Rainbow*; the book was widely read and widely discussed, resulted in the publication of other similar collections, and probably left its mark on the poetry of the time. Yet in all the histories of American literature which I have by chance examined, I have noticed only one discussion of Indian poetry, that by the late Mary Austin, in the *Cambridge History of American Literature*: the discussion is uninformative, unintelligent, and in most respects worse than useless. In 1933 the Oxford Press published a book by Albert Keiser called *The Indian in American Literature*, which makes no use of the anthropologists either as scientists or as translators. And in 1938 there appeared in a series of textbooks published by the American Book Company and under the general editorship of Professor Harry Hayden Clark a critical text on Parkman; a text which disposes of the entire subject of Parkman's understanding of the Indian (and Prescott's to boot, as a matter of fact) with no reference to the bulletins and apparently with no knowledge whatever of American anthropology or archaeology.

I happen to have on my shelves at the present writing two fairly recent histories of American literature, of which the authors are Percy Boynton and W. F. Taylor. I will not tire the reader by citing the long list of their most obvious and least discutable sins, but it seems to me interesting that neither mentions the name of Adelaide Crapsey, who died in 1914, who antedates many of the writers discussed, who is certainly an immortal poet, and who has long been one of the most famous poets of our century.

V.

When the argument over Irving Babbitt's New Humanism was active, one of the objections made to the Humanists was this: that even if their philosophy were sound, it would never prove very effective, because it was represented by no social institution and so could never be brought to bear on more than a few scattered lives. Christianity had been represented by the Church, but what had the Humanists?

I do not consider myself one of the Humanists: I disagree with Babbitt on too many counts to do so, though I admire him and have learned a good deal from him; and Babbitt's colleagues have always appeared to me to be worth very little indeed. But the student of literature who takes his profession seriously, who wishes to quicken it and make it important, has an institution nevertheless. That institution, in spite of what I have been saying, is the university.

This statement, I dare say, will amuse the reviewers for the weekly journals. But notwithstanding all the sins of the literary scholars, the popular view of the academic world, as something cloistered and remote from reality, peopled by souls who have failed in the practical struggle, is a product largely of the Romantic Movement and of the colored funny papers. There have been great literary scholars and the race will continue; but questions of literature aside, most of the great minds in science, philosophy, and history will be found in the universities—these are not men who have taken flight from the modern world, but sometimes for better and sometimes for worse they are the men who are making it. The university is the intellectual and spiritual center of our world. It is likewise a national institution; in fact it was, until the New Order appeared in Europe, an international institution, and it will be again. It offers a concrete embodiment, an institutional representation, of the most important ideals of humanity; of the belief in absolute truth; of the importance, in spite of human fallibility, of the perpetual, though necessarily imperfect, effort to approximate truth; of intellectual freedom and integrity; of the dignity of man. Without the fairly explicit recognition of these ideals, the university would collapse. Even the most irresponsible relativist or determinist—the Marxian romantics and their recurring problems of academic freedom come immediately to mind—will invoke these ideals almost automatically if he feels that they have been violated in his particular case. In the entire history of civilization, only one other institution, the Catholic Church, with its national off-shoots, has played a comparable part. The university, within its limits, is less self-conscious and less efficient than the Church, but its limits are far more inclusive, and few of the great men of our time are able to find their way into the Church. I do not wish, as the reader may have suspected, to flatter unduly the faculties of the universities, though I respect them for excellent reasons, even in the bulk. I am speaking of principles, not of persons. Great men are rare. The academic ideals are frequently violated, but they remain as ideals, as standards of judgment, and as the chief cohesive force in our civilization; and the scholar is their professional guardian.

One of the most curious facts about the poets of my own generation and of the generation following—that is, about the poets now, roughly, under fifty years of age—is this: that many of the best of them are teaching in the universities. There has been no comparable unity of profession among able poets since the 17th century, when most of the best poets were members of the clergy.

I should like to list the poems that seem to me perhaps the highest achievement of the writers in question:[16]

By Mark Van Doren: *Man, Report of Angels.*

By John Crowe Ransom: *Piazza Piece, Bells for John White-side's Daughter.*

[16] The poems in this list may be found in the following collections: *Collected Poems,* by Mark Van Doren (Henry Holt: 1939); *Chills and Fever* (Knopf: 1924) and *Two Gentlemen in Bonds* (Knopf: 1927) by J. C. Ransom; *The Keen Edge,* by Maurine Smith (Monroe Wheeler, Evanston, Ill.: published in 1920, but undated); *Dark Summer* (Scribners: 1929) and *The Sleeping Fury* (Scribners: 1937) by Louise Bogan; *The Collected Poems of Hart Crane* (Liveright: 1933); *Selected Poems,* by Allen Tate (Scribners: 1937); Damon's poem, *The Mad Huntsman,* appears in Smoke, a small magazine published at Providence by Damon and his friends, in the issue for May 1931, and the issue for Dec. 1933 contains another remarkable but less perfect poem by Damon, called *Seelig's Confession; A Letter from the Country,* by Howard Baker (New Directions: 1941) and *Twelve Poets of the Pacific,* an anthology (New Directions: 1937); *Verse,* by Clayton Stafford (Alan Swallow, Albuquerque: 1941); *Intellectual Things,* by Stanley J. Kunitz (Doubleday Doran: 1930); *From Jordan's Delight,* by R. P. Blackmur (Arrow Editions: 1937); *In Plato's Garden,* by Lincoln Fitzell (Alan Swallow: 1941); *The Well,* by Barbara Gibbs (Alan Swallow: 1941); *The Helmsman,* by J. V. Cunningham (Colt Press, San Francisco: 1942); *New England Earth,* by Don Stanford (Colt Press: 1941); *Open House,* by Theodore Roethke (Knopf, 1941).

By Maurine Smith: *Muted.*

By Louise Bogan: *The Mark, Simple Autumnal, The Alchemist, Come break with Time, Henceforth from the Mind, Exhortation, Kept, Song for a Lyre.*

By Hart Crane: *Repose of Rivers, Voyages II.*

By Allen Tate: *The Cross, Shadow and Shade;* perhaps *The Subway* and *Ditty.*

By S. Foster Damon: *The Mad Huntsman.*

By Clayton Stafford: *The Swan and the Eagle, Cape Horn, Hyperborean.*

By Stanley J. Kunitz: *The Words of the Preacher, Ambergris.*

By Howard Baker: *Psyche, Pont Neuf,* perhaps *The Quiet Folk.*

By R. P. Blackmur: *Sea-Island Miscellany: V.*

By Lincoln Fitzell: *Gravestone, Erosion.*

By Barbara Gibbs: *For Her Who Wore This Shawl.*

By J. V. Cunningham: *Lector Aere Perennior, The Beacon, Bookplate, Fancy, Moral Poem, The Symposium.*

By Don Stanford: *The Grand Mesa, The Meadowlark, The Bee, The Seagull, Summer Scene, The Thrush.*

By Theodore Roethke: *The Adamant, Reply to Censure.*

By Ann Stanford: *The Book, Ash Wednesday, Bookplate* (Time sets a term).

The exact limits of any such selection as this are hard to define. I have deliberately excluded work that I like in certain respects. Elizabeth Madox Roberts falls within the chronological limits of the group by virtue at least of the period of her composition; but her best poems, the poems of childhood contained in *Under the Tree,* are of a highly specialized sort, and though they will remain, I believe, a classic of a kind, they represent perhaps a less serious effort than the work I have listed. There are a few poems by Pearl Andelson Sherry which I should not like to see forgotten, notably, *Cats* and *Polar Bear,*[17] but Mrs. Sherry has never been able to free herself from certain immature philosophical

[17] These poems may be found in The Forge (Chicago) for Autumn of 1926, and reprinted in the Autumn number for 1927 on pages 43 and 44.

ideas and from a certain egocentric preciosity of style which obsessed the entire group to which she belonged as a very young writer, a group to which Miss Roberts, Glenway Wescott, Maurine Smith, and I myself belonged. Glenway Wescott[18] likewise displayed an interesting poetic gift as a young man, but diffused and lost it in a kind of obscurely ecstatic description. James Agee has written at least one poem, *A Chorale*,[19] which is remarkable. And there are at least two poems by Achilles Holt, *A Valley* and *To Mélanie*,[20] which momentarily seem to me more remarkable than a number of the poems on my list. I have omitted the name of Archibald MacLeish, who may conceivably fall within my limits, because his work, so far as I am concerned, wears thinner and thinner with time. I have omitted John Peale Bishop because his work seems derivative, with no real center of meaning, and extremely coarse in execution. And I have omitted some of the young Southerners whose reputation is at present rising, for more or less similar reasons, though the inclusion of these would strengthen my argument with reference to the academic profession. .

The selection of poems is likewise difficult. Crane, Tate, Damon, Baker, and Blackmur, are almost as remarkable for certain passages in unsatisfactory poems as they are for the poems I have named. Baker, especially, may be at his best, in the conclusion of *The Passing Generation*, and in certain portions of his *Ode to the Sea* and *Destiny*.

Some of the poets whom I have listed are certainly very minor. I think one can say this of Van Doren, Ransom, Maurine Smith (who died at the age of 23, after a life of invalidism, and left a few poems comparable, perhaps, to those of Gladys Cromwell), Fitzell, Barbara Gibbs, and Blackmur; Miss Stanford might be added to this number, but is very young to be classified even tentatively.

[18] Wescott published two books a good many years ago, *The Bitterns* (Monroe Wheeler: 1920), and *Natives of Rock* (Francesco Bianco: New York: 1925), but many of his better things will be found in Poetry and The Dial as late as 1927 or 1928.

[19] *Permit me Voyage*, by James Agee (Yale University Press: 1934).

[20] *Twelve Poets of the Pacific*, op. cit.

On the other hand, a few of these poets seem to me among the major talents of our time: Miss Bogan, Tate, and Baker seem to me surely so; and I should not have to strain my convictions greatly to add Crane, Damon, Stafford and Cunningham, the main difficulty with Stafford and Damon being the scarcity of mature poems on which to form a judgment.[21]

There is always the danger that such a list as I have made may seem nervous and niggling, but if it has called attention to a few poems that might otherwise be overlooked, it is justified; and even if it contains a good many errors of judgment, it nevertheless indicates fairly enough certain general tendencies which I wish to be indicated. If these writers are compared to the outstanding talents of the preceding generation, that is, of the generation immediately subsequent to that of Frost and Robinson, their common characteristics begin to appear. The leading Experimentalists were Wallace Stevens, Adelaide Crapsey, W. C. Williams, Ezra Pound, Marianne Moore, T. S. Eliot, and H. D. If one looks for lesser talents in this tradition, one will have difficulty finding them, for small talents had difficulty surviving in modes so formless; and if one looks to the traditional poets in this generation, such as the Benets, Elinor Wylie, and Miss Millay, one will find them a very unsatisfactory lot of easy rimers. Stevens alone of his generation did great work in the traditional forms, but he did it early, and became more and more an experimenter. The poets whom I have listed, however, are all moving toward traditional practices and not away from them. Most of them display a certain intellectualism in their way of dealing with their subjects, even when the subjects are essentially anti-intellectualistic. Even those who, as critics, argue in favor of anti-intellectual doctrines, endeavor to argue more closely than did Pound, Williams, Miss Moore, and even Eliot: this is true to some extent of Tate; it is true, I think, as regards the intention, of Blackmur; and it is certainly true of Ransom; and the best poems of these men are straining obviously away from their critical theories. There is a

[21] I may as well go on record here that I believe my wife, Janet Lewis, to be one of the best poets of her generation, as well as one of the best fictionists; but I endeavor, on general principles, not to discuss her work.

great deal of confusion of intention in these poets, both individually and collectively, but in general they are trying to recover what the preceding generation had lost; and in some of them, mainly the younger ones, there is a good deal of maturity, not only of style but of mind.

Now out of this group, a large portion are professional scholars and teachers: Van Doren, Ransom, Tate, Damon, Baker, Cunningham, Don Stanford, and Roethke. And the additional number of serious young poets in the profession, whose talents do not seem to me great, but who have, many of them, acquired reputations and who may conceivably prove in the end to be better than I believe them, would if added about double the academic group. The tendency which I have described among all the poets mentioned is striking; the fact that the tendency is most obvious among the younger poets makes it more so. And the presence of eight of them, including some of the very best, and the best of the youngest, on academic faculties, makes it obvious indeed.

It is in the younger poets that the meaning of this change of emphasis is likely to be most evident eventually; it is most evident already, perhaps, in the work of Cunningham, who may prove to be the best of his generation, who is certainly, so far as my personal knowledge extends, the best scholar and critic among the younger Americans, and who of all, older and younger alike, seems to show most clearly an understanding of the implications of his adherence to the academic profession.

It is possible, of course, that the younger poets here named may deteriorate, and that American poetry may start off in another direction. But of this I feel sure: that this movement offers more hope for the invigoration of American literature than does anything else in sight; that it offers the only hope for American criticism; and that it offers an opportunity for the real improvement of the teaching of literature and the practice of literary scholarship. A handful of brilliant poets, even if congenitally minor, scattered judiciously throughout our best universities, might easily begin to turn us a little in the direction of civilization.

The Significance of
The Bridge
by Hart Crane

OR

WHAT ARE WE TO THINK

OF PROFESSOR X?

THE SIGNIFICANCE OF
THE BRIDGE, BY HART CRANE

or What Are We to Think of Professor X?

In speaking of the "significance" of *The Bridge,* I am using the word "significance" in both of its common meanings: I refer to the content which the author apparently wished to communicate and also to the "moral," so to speak, that we as observers and as members of his society may deduce from his effort and from the qualities of its success or failure. It is the second sense of the word that I should like to emphasize if I had time, but before I can begin on it I must deal somehow with the first: What is *The Bridge* about? What did Crane think he was getting at?

Most of Crane's thought, and this is especially true of *The Bridge,* was derived from Whitman. This fact is generally recognized. It is my personal impression likewise, and my personal impression is derived not only from a study of the works of Crane and of Whitman, but also from about four years of frequent and regular correspondence with Crane and from about four long evenings of uninterrupted conversation with him. Crane and I began publishing poems in the same magazines about 1919; I started quarreling with Harriet Monroe about 1925 or 1926 to get Crane's poems into *Poetry: A Magazine of Verse;* Crane and I started corresponding shortly thereafter; I spent a few evenings talking to Crane during the Christmas holidays of 1927; our correspondence ended as a result of my review of *The Bridge* in 1930; and about two or two and a half years later Crane committed suicide.

577

Most of Crane's thought was, as I say, derived from Whitman. In turn, nearly all of Whitman's thought was derived from Emerson, or could easily have been. Whitman professed himself Emerson's disciple, and Emerson offered Whitman his professorial blessing. But Emerson in turn was in no wise original, at least as regards the bare formulae of his thought: his ideas are the commonplace ideas of the romantic movement, from the time of the third Earl of Shaftesbury to the present. In the restating of these ideas, however, Emerson did something which was important, at least in the American context. What were these ideas, and what did Emerson do to them?

The ideas were, briefly, these:

God and his creation are one. God is good. Man, as part of the creation, is part of God, and so is good. Man may therefore trust his impulses, which are the voice of God; through trusting them absolutely and acting upon them without reserve, he becomes one with God. Impulse is thus equated with the protestant concept of conscience, as a divine and supra-rational directive; and surrender to impulse, which unites one with God, becomes equivalent in a sense to the traditional and Catholic concept of the mystical experience. We are confronted here with an illogicality, for our first principles tell us that man is a part of God whether he trusts his impulses or not; but this is merely a part of the illogicality which denies the validity of Reason. For Emerson, as for other Romantics, Reason is the source of all evil, is the adversary of Impulse, and is that which has no part in God in a universe in which everything is a part of God and in which everything is good. In life and in art the automatic man, the unreflective creature of impulse, is the ideal; he is one with God and will achieve the good life and great art.

Let me quote from Emerson on these subjects:

As to the pantheistic doctrine, he writes, for example, in *Nature*:

The knowledge that we traverse the whole scale of being from the center to the poles of nature, and have some stake in every possibility, lends that sublime luster to death, which philosophy and religion have too outwardly striven to express in the popular doctrine of the immortality of the soul. The reality is more excellent than the report. Here is no ruin, no discontinuity, no spent ball. The divine circulations never rest nor linger. Nature is the incarnation of a thought, and turns to a thought again, as ice becomes water and gas. The world is mind precipitated, and the volatile essence is forever escaping again into the state of free thought. Hence the virtue and pungency of the influence on the mind of natural objects, whether inorganic or organized. Man imprisoned, man crystallized, man vegetative, speaks to man impersonated.

In the last sentence, "man imprisoned" is in apposition with "man crystallized" and with "man vegetative," terms which may be translated respectively as "God in the form of a crystal" and as "God in the form of a cabbage"; the expression "man impersonated" may be translated as "God in the form of man," or more simply, as "man." The passage, like many others in Emerson, indicates that man in death remains immortal while losing his identity. The concept is doubtless comprehensible to those who understand it. I once argued this issue with Crane, and when he could not convert me by reason, he said: "Well, if we can't believe it, we'll have to kid ourselves into believing it." Something of the same attitude seems to be implied in a passage in his poem *The Dance* (that section of *The Bridge* which deals most explicitly with this notion) in which he begs his Indian medicine man to "Lie to us! Dance us back the tribal morn!"

There are innumerable passages in Emerson on the divine origin of impulse and on its trustworthiness. In *The Poet* he writes as follows (here as elsewhere the italics are mine):

It is a secret which every intellectual man quickly learns, that beyond the energy of his possessed and conscious intellect he is capable of a new energy (as of an intellect doubled on itself), *by abandonment to the nature of things;* that beside his privacy of power as an individual man, there is a great public power on which he can draw, *by unlocking at all risks his human doors* and suffering the ethereal tides to roll through him. . . .

In *Spiritual Laws* he writes:

A little consideration of what takes place around us every day would show us that a higher law than that of our will regulates events; that our painful labors are very unnecessary and altogether fruitless; that *only in our easy, simple, spontaneous action we are strong, and by contenting ourselves with obedience we become divine.* . . . We need only obey. There is guidance for each of us, and by lowly listening we shall hear the right word. *Why need you choose* so painfully your place, and occupation, and associates, and modes of action, and of entertainment? Certainly there is a possible right for you *that precludes the need of balance and of willful election.* For you there is a fit place and congenial duties. Place yourself in the middle of the stream of power and wisdom which flows into you as life, place yourself in the full center of that flood, then you are *without effort* impelled to truth, to right, and to perfect contentment.

And in *The Oversoul:*

Ineffable is the union of man and God in every act of the soul. The simplest person who in his integrity worships God becomes God. . . . He believes that he cannot escape from his good. The things that are really for thee gravitate to thee. You are running to meet your friend. *Let your feet run, but your mind need not.* If you do not find him, will you not acquiesce that it is best you should not find him? for there is a power, which, as it is in you, is in him also, and could therefore very well bring you together, if it were for the best.

The last three passages all point unmistakably to Emerson's concept of automatism as the equivalent of the mystical experience; and in the last passage quoted the concept is very dramatically expressed—one could hardly ask for anything more explicit. Closely related to this notion is the familiar romantic notion of the beatitude of ignorance and of mediocrity, to say nothing of the beatitude of infancy. We are familiar with Gray's mute inglorious Miltons and with Wordsworth's young child who was a mighty prophet, seer blest. Similarly Emerson writes in *Spiritual Laws:*

580

The intellectual life may be kept clean and healthful, if man will live the life of nature, and not import into his mind difficulties which are none of his. *No man need be perplexed in his speculations.* Let him do and say what strictly belongs to him, and *though very ignorant of books,* his nature shall not yield him any intellectual obstructions and doubts.

A passage such as this one makes very short work of our universities. In *Self-Reliance* Emerson writes:

What pretty oracles nature yields us on this text in the face and behavior of children, babes, and even brutes! That divided and rebel mind, that distrust of a sentiment because our arithmetic has computed the strength and means opposed to our purpose, these have not. Their mind being whole, their eye is as yet unconquered, and when we look in their faces we are disconcerted. Infancy conforms to nobody; all conform to it; so that one babe commonly makes four or five out of the adults who prattle and play to it.

This passage is offered as a kind of vision of social beatitude. Unfortunately for those of us whose curiosity is insatiable, Emerson does not take the next step in his argument: although he tells us what happens when we have one babe (conforming to nobody) and four or five adults (conforming to the babe), he does not say what happens when we have five or six babes (all conforming to nobody): therein lies the crux of the matter.

Emerson was not wholly unaware of the theoretical objections which could be made to his position, but unless we are to assume that he personally was a corrupt and vicious man, which I think we can scarcely do, we are forced to admit that he simply did not know what the objections meant. In *Self-Reliance* he wrote:

I remember an answer which when quite young I was prompted to make to a valued adviser, who was wont to importune me with the dear old doctrines of the church. On my saying, "What have I to do with the sacredness of traditions, if I live wholly from within?" my friend suggested,—"But these impulses may be from below, not from above." I replied, "They do not seem to me to be such; but if I am the Devil's child, I will live then from the Devil." No law can be sacred to me but that of my nature. Good and bad are but names very readily transferable to that or this; the only right is what is after my constitution; the only wrong what is against it.

Emerson's friend, in this passage, offers the traditional objection of the Roman Church to the quietistic schismatic; and Emerson appears to be ignorant of the traditional functions of the Devil and of the viscera. But in the last few statements in this passage we see clearly another consequence of the Emersonian position: its thoroughgoing relativism. That is right for me which is after my constitution; that is right for you which is after yours; the Oversoul will guide us both in the ways which best befit us, if we will both only follow our impulses. My impulse to commit incest may horrify you; your impulse to commit murder and arson may horrify me; but we should ignore each other and proceed.

In *Circles,* Emerson writes to the same purpose, at the same time suggesting a new difficulty, with which, however, he is not impressed. He says:

And thus, O circular philosopher, I hear some reader exclaim, you have arrived at a fine Pyrrhonism, at an equivalence and indifferency of all actions, and would fain teach us that, if we are true, forsooth, our crimes may be lively stones out of which we shall construct the temple of the true God!

I am not careful to justify myself. . . . But lest I should mislead any when I have my own head and obey my whims, let me remind the reader that I am only an experimenter. Do not set the least value on what I do, or the least discredit on what I do not, as if I pretended to settle anything as true or false. I unsettle all things. No facts are to me sacred; none are profane; I simply experiment, an endless seeker, with no past at my back.

Here Emerson suggests the difficulty that he has eliminated values: in teaching that everything is good, he has merely arrived at the conclusion that everything is equal to everything else, for nothing is either good or bad unless there are grounds for distinction. Emerson has arrived at a doctrine of equivalence, a doctrine to the effect that there are no grounds for choice; and he hopes to save himself only through not having to make a choice, through leaving choice wholly to God and to performing, himself, as an automaton. And in the last expression, in which he describes himself as an "endless seeker, with no Past at my back," we see his glorification of change as change; we can find this elsewhere in Emerson; we can find it likewise in Whitman; it is one of the most important ideas of *The Bridge*. It should be observed that the glorification of change as change is a necessary part of a system in which every act is good, in which there is no way to choose between courses of action, in which there is no principle of consistency, and in which there is no conception of a goal other than to be automatically controlled from moment to moment.

It is not surprising that Emerson should regard that art as the best which is the most nearly extemporaneous. He wrote in *Art*:

> But true art is never fixed, but always flowing. The sweetest music is not in the oratorio, but in the human voice when it speaks from its instant life tones of tenderness, truth, or courage. The oratorio has already lost its relation to the morning, to the sun, and to the earth, but that persuading voice is in tune with these. All works of art should not be detached, but extempore performances. A great man is a new statue in every attitude and action. A beautiful woman is a picture which drives all beholders nobly mad. Life may be lyric or epic, as well as a poem or a romance.

This view of art rests on the assumption that man should express what he is at any given moment; not that he should try by all the means at his disposal to arrive at a true understanding of a given subject or to improve his powers of understanding in general. Related to this notion is the principle that if we will only express what we are at any given moment, if we will only record our casual impressions, we may be sure to equal Shakespeare. This is from *Self-Reliance*:

> In every work of genius we recognize our own rejected thoughts; they come back to us with a certain alienated majesty. Great works of art have no more affecting lesson for us than this. They teach us to *abide by our spontaneous impression* with good-humored inflexibility then most when the whole cry of voices is on the other side. Else tomorrow a stranger will say with masterly good sense precisely what

we have thought and felt all the time, and we shall be forced to take with shame our own opinion from another.

And this is from *The Oversoul:*

The great poet makes us feel our own wealth, and then we think less of his compositions. . . . Shakespeare carries us to such a lofty strain of intelligent activity, as to suggest a wealth which beggars his own. . . . The inspiration which uttered itself in *Hamlet* and *Lear* could utter things as good from day to day forever. Why, then, should I make account of *Hamlet* and *Lear,* as if we had not the soul from which they fell as syllables from the tongue?

The natural conclusion from these speculations would be that the most effective writing is automatic writing. In the poem entitled *Merlin,* in which Merlin is viewed as the bard, Emerson writes:

> *Great is the art,*
> *Great be the manners, of the bard.*
> *He shall not his brain encumber*
> *With the coil of rhythm and number;*
> *But leaving rule and pale forethought,*
> *He shall aye climb*
> *For his rime. .*
> *'Pass in, pass in,' the angels say,*
> *'In to the upper doors,*
> *Nor count compartments of the floors,*
> *But mount to Paradise*
> *By the stairway of surprise.'*

In Whitman and his close followers there is occasionally a momentary approach to the kind of automatic writing here suggested; but this ideal was most nearly fulfilled by another line of Romantic writers, and probably reached Crane by way of them, in the main: the line starting with Poe, and proceeding through Verlaine, Mallarmé, Rimbaud, and the lesser Symbolists to such Americans as Pound, Eliot, and Stevens. The concept of automatic writing is an inevitable development from the

584

initial Romantic ideas, and it is bound to appear whenever the ideas long govern literary practice. Crane had almost no French —I spent a couple of hours one evening taking him through various poems by Rimbaud—but his friends had doubtless translated the French poets for him and described them, and he knew the later Americans very thoroughly. He told me once that he often did not understand his poems till after they were written; and I am fairly confident that this kind of experimentation was common in Crane's generation and earlier, and in fact that it is still common in certain quarters. I know that I myself engaged in it with great fascination when I was young, and I know that certain other persons did so. The result is likely to be a poetry which frequently and sometimes wholly eludes paraphrase by at least a margin, but which appears constantly to be suggesting a precise meaning.

Many poets engage in the practice only semi-consciously; in general, one may say that wherever the poet's sensibility to the connotation of language overbalances his awareness of the importance of denotation, something of the kind is beginning: it is this unbalance which distinguishes the Shakespeare of the sonnets, for example, most sharply from his great contemporaries, such as Jonson, Greville, Donne, and even Sidney. But beginning with the notion of organic form, the notion that the subject, or the language, or the oversoul, or something else operates freely through the poet, who is merely a passive medium, the doctrine begins to be explicit. The beginnings, in theory, may be traced perhaps as far back as Edward Young, certainly as far as Coleridge; and *Kubla Khan* is perhaps the first ambitious experiment in actual practice. Emerson states the theory with an explicitness which verges on violence, but does not appear seriously to have practiced it. Poe's concept of poetry as something which deals with certain materials of this life only incidentally, in the hopes that meanings otherwise unattainable may be suggested, begins to describe the kind of poetry which will result when automatic writing is practiced by men of talent: a poetry which appears always to be escaping the comprehension, yet which is always perceptible; a poetry which deals with the fact

585

of nature *dans sa presque disparition vibratoire,* to use a phrase from Mallarmé, "in its vibratory almost-disappearance."

Mallarmé employs this phrase in an essay called *Relativement au vers:* in English, *On the Subject of the Poetic Line.* In this essay he describes the kind of "pure" poetry in which he is interested, the poetry in which feeling is as nearly as possible isolated from all denotation, and near the end he writes the following passage, which I shall render as nearly verbatim as possible, in spite of any awkwardness which may seem to result:

The pure work implies the elocutory disappearance of the poet, who cedes the initiative to the words, mobilized through the shock of their inequality; they light each other with reciprocal reflections like a virtual train of fires upon jewels, replacing the respiration perceptible in the lyric inspiration of former times or the enthusiastic personal direction of the phrase.

And Rimbaud, in his poem *Bonheur,* states that the charm of which he has made a magic study has taken possession of him body and soul, with the result that his language is no longer to be understood, but takes wing and escapes. Verlaine offers a somewhat more cautious statement of the same doctrine in his poem entitled *Art Poétique,* in which he praises the "drunken song," the word exhibiting a content of "error," in which the indecisive is joined to the precise. Rimbaud's poem might easily have been written by Emerson: in fact Rimbaud's *Fêtes de la Faim* resembles Emerson's *Mithridates* very closely in imagery and in symbolism, though it resembles the stylistic quality of Emerson's best verse less closely than does *Bonheur.* And the passage from Mallarmé, if we make allowances for certain personal mannerisms, might well have been written by Emerson. But Rimbaud and Mallarmé put the doctrine into practice, not occasionally but systematically, and the result was a revolution in style, both in verse and in prose. One of the most eminent practitioners of the semi-automatic method in more recent times was the late W. B. Yeats, with his notions of demonic possession and dictation.

The ideas of Emerson were, as I have said, merely the commonplaces of the Romantic movement; but his language was that of the Calvinistic pulpit. He was able to present the anarchic and anti-moral doctrines of European Romancism in a language which for two hundred years had been capable of arousing the most intense and the most obscure emotions of the American people. He could speak of matter as if it were God; of the flesh as if it were spirit; of emotion as if it were Divine Grace; of impulse as if it were conscience; and of automatism as if it were the mystical experience. And he was addressing an audience which, like himself, had been so conditioned by two hundred years of Calvinistic discipline, that the doctrines confused nothing, at the outset, except the mind: Emerson and his contemporaries, in surrendering to what they took for impulse, were governed by New England habit; they mistook second nature for nature. They were moral parasites upon a Christian doctrine which they were endeavoring to destroy. The same may be said of Whitman, Emerson's most influential disciple, except that Whitman came closer to putting the doctrine into practice in the matter of literary form: whereas Emerson, as a poet, imitated the poets of the early 17th century, whose style had been formed in congruence with the doctrines of Aristotle, Aquinas, and Hooker.

I cannot summarize the opinions of Whitman in this essay as fully as I have summarized those of Emerson. I must ask my readers to accept on faith, until they find it convenient to check the matter, the generally accepted view that the main ideas of Whitman are identical with those of Emerson. Whitman believed this; Emerson believed it; and scholarly specialists in both men believe it. I wish to quote a part—only a small part—of Professor Floyd Stovall's summary of Whitman's views.[1] Professor Stovall is a reputable scholar. Every detail which he gives is referred by a footnote to its source in Whitman. I believe that his summary, purely as a summary, is accurate. He writes:

[1] *Walt Whitman: Representative Selections, with Introduction, Bibliography, and Notes,* by Floyd Stovall; American Book Company; 1934. P. xxxvii.

He saw that creation is a continuous organic growth, not a work that is begun or finished, and the creative force is the procreative impulse in nature. *Progress is the infallible consequence* of this creative force in nature, *and though the universe is perfect at any given moment, it is growing constantly toward higher orders of perfection.* If new forms are needed they are produced as surely as if designed from the beginning. "When the materials are all prepared and ready, the architects shall appear." Every moment is a consummation developed from endless past consummations and preparing for endless consummations in the future. . . .

Nature is not only perfect but also divine. Indeed it is perfect because it is divine. There is no division in nature . . . no separate deity looking down from some detached heaven upon a temporal world that his hand created and may destroy at pleasure. That which is at all is of God. . . . *Whatever is is well, and whatever will be will be well.* . . . God is in every object, because every object has an eternal soul and passes eventually into spiritual results. . . .

 . . . The seed of perfection is in each person, but *no matter how far he advances, his desire for further advancement remains insatiable.*

The final purpose of this restlessness of spirit in man and nature is the continuity of life. Nothing is real or valid, not even God, except in relation to this purpose. . . . Something, Whitman perceives, drives man forward along the way to perfection, which passes through birth, life, death, and burial; he does not fully understand what it is, but he knows that it is form, union, plan—that it is happiness and eternal life.

Whitman calls it soul, this mysterious something, strangely linked with the procreative impulse, that gives form and continuity to the life of nature and impels man toward happiness and immortality. . . .

The ignorance both of philosophy and theology exhibited in such ideas as these is sufficient to strike one with terror. But I must limit myself to only a few comments at the present moment. I wish to call attention especially to the passages which I have italicized: (1) "Progress is the infallible consequence," or to put it more briefly, progress is infallible; (2) "though the universe is perfect at any given moment, it is growing constantly toward higher orders of perfection"; (3) "Whatever is is well, and whatever will be will be well"; and (4) "No matter how far man advances, his desire for further advancement remains insatiable."

I wish to insist on this: that it is impossible to speak of higher orders of perfection unless one can define what one means by the highest order and by the lowest order, and this Whitman does not venture to do. Higher and lower, better and worse, have no meaning except in relation to highest and lowest, best and worst. Since Whitman has identified God with the evolving (that is, with the changing) universe, he is unable to locate a concept of best or highest, toward which evolution is moving, for that concept would then be outside of God and would supersede God; it would be, in theological language, God's final cause; and such a concept would be nonsense. Whitman tells us that whatever happens to exist is perfect, but that any change is necessarily toward a "higher" order of perfection. The practical effect of these notions is merely to deify change: change becomes good of necessity. We have no way of determining where we are going, but we should keep moving at all costs and as fast as possible; we have faith in progress. It seems to me unnecessary to dwell upon the dangers of such a concept.

Hart Crane was not born into the New England of Emerson, nor even into the New York of Whitman; he was born in 1899 in Cleveland, Ohio. The social restraints, the products of generations of religious discipline, which operated to minimize the influence of Romantic philosophy in the personal lives of Emerson and of Whitman, were at most only slightly operative in Crane's career. He was unfortunate in having a somewhat violent emotional constitution: his behavior on the whole would seem to indicate a more or less manic-depressive make-up, although this diagnosis is the post-mortem guess of an amateur, and is based on evidence which is largely hearsay. He was certainly homosexual, however, and he became a chronic and extreme alcoholic. I should judge that he cultivated these weaknesses on principle; in any event, it is well known that he cultivated them assiduously; and as an avowed Whitmanian, he would have been justified by his principles in cultivating all of his impulses. I saw Crane during the Christmas week of 1927, when he was approximately 29 years old; his hair was graying, his skin had the dull red color with reticulated grayish traceries which so often goes with advanced alcoholism, and his ears and knuckles were beginning to look a little like those of a pugilist. About a year later he was deported from France as a result of his starting an exceptionally violent commotion in a bar-room and perhaps as a result of other activities. In 1932 he committed suicide by leaping from a steamer into the Caribbean Sea.

The doctrine of Emerson and Whitman, if really put into practice, should naturally lead to suicide: in the first place, if the impulses are indulged systematically and passionately, they can lead only to madness; in the second place, death, according to the doctrine, is not only a release from suffering but is also and inevitably the way to beatitude. There is no question, according to the doctrine, of moral preparation for salvation; death leads automatically to salvation. During the last year and a half of Crane's life, to judge from the accounts of those who were with him in Mexico, he must have been insane or drunk or both almost without interruption; but before this time he must have contemplated the possibilities of suicide. When his friend Harry Crosby committed suicide in one of the eastern cities, I wrote Crane a note of condolence and asked him to express my sympathy to Mrs. Crosby. Crane replied somewhat casually that I need not feel disturbed about the affair, that he was fairly sure Crosby had regarded it as a great adventure.

In the course of my correspondence with Crane, I must somewhere have made a moralizing remark which I have now forgotten but of which Crane disapproved. I remember Crane's answer: he said that he had never in his life done anything of which he had been ashamed, and he said this not in anger but in simple philosophical seriousness. This would be a sufficiently surprising remark from any son of Adam, but as one thinks of it and of Crane in retrospect, one can understand it, I believe, only in one way, as an assertion of religious faith, neither more nor less.

Crane published two volumes of poetry during his life-time, *White Buildings* in 1926, and *The Bridge* in 1930. His collected poems appeared in 1933, including additional work from earlier and later periods. The element of obscurantism in the details of

Crane's writing, some of it probably intentional, makes it difficult to paraphrase him as fully and precisely as one might paraphrase George Herbert or Ben Jonson. Nevertheless, the general drift of *The Bridge* is clear, and most of the detail is clear. I cannot allow myself at present to do more than discuss the skeletal plan of the work; but the skeletal plan will serve my present purpose. *The Bridge* endeavors to deal in some measure with the relationship of the individual American to his country and to God and with the religious significance of America itself. It reaches its first climax in the poem called *The Dance*, which deals with the apotheosis of the individual, and its second in *Atlantis,* which deals with the apotheosis of the nation. *The Bridge* is a loosely joined sequence of lyrics, and some of the individual pieces have only a tenuous connection with the principal themes.

The first poem is the dedicatory piece to the Brooklyn Bridge. Crane regarded the Brooklyn Bridge as the most beautiful artifact in North America, and largely for this reason he chose it as a symbol. The dedicatory poem is mainly descriptive of the literal bridge, but contains hints of the religious symbolism to follow; so far as the total symbolism is concerned, it has something of the nature of an unrestrained pun: Crane's poem is a bridge; it joins the past to the present, the present to the future, life to death, non-being to birth, the old world to the new; the United States is a bridge which joins the two oceans. The next poem, *Ave Maria,* is a monologue spoken by Columbus as he is returning from America and considering his discovery. Columbus appears to be secondarily the unborn soul approaching birth and the man of the past approaching modernity.

The next five poems are grouped under the heading, *Powhatan's Daughter*. Pocahontas, in these poems, is the symbol of the American soil, and the five poems deal more or less clearly with the awakening love of the young protagonist for his country and for the deity with which his country is identified. We have here a characteristically Whitmanian variation on Emerson's pantheism: for Emerson God and the universe were one, but for Whitman the American soil was the part of the universe to be especially worshipped, so that the pantheistic mysticism tends to become a national mysticism; Sandburg carries this delimitation further by insisting on the Mississippi Valley as the region of chief emphasis and creates a kind of regional mysticism; and we get precisely this Sandburgian mysticism in the third poem in the group which I am now discussing, the poem called *The River*: when Crane was writing this poem, he informed me that he was rewriting Sandburg in the way in which he ought to be written. I wish to make myself clear on one point in this connection: I do not object to these poets' feeling a love for their country or for their region; but I believe that nothing save confusion can result from our mistaking the Mississippi Valley for God.

The first poem in this group of five is *The Harbor Dawn*; it deals with the awakening of the protagonist in a room in New York, a room overlooking the harbor; this protagonist had been previously the unborn soul of the *Ave Maria*; the modern man is now born and the woman with him is vaguely identified as Pocahontas. The second poem in the group, *Van Winkle*, is a flashback to the childhood of the protagonist: we see the schoolboy becoming acquainted with the figures of North American mythology, with Cortez and with Captain Smith and with others. The boy is loosely equated with Rip Van Winkle, as one who has awakened after a long time ("400 years and more"), and so is connected with the Columbus of *Ave Maria*. The third poem in the group is *The River*. This poem opens with a vision of the countryside as seen fragmentarily from the window of the Twentieth Century Limited, a symbolic railway train; then the train suddenly moves ahead and leaves the protagonist walking down the tracks in the company of various hoboes. The hoboes are the intercessors: they introduce the adolescent boy to the soil, to Pocahontas, since they are among the few people left who will take the time really to know the land and its old gods. We then see the train again, and the travelers within are separated from the soil and the folk by their wealth, luxury, and speed; they are advised to "lean from the window if the train slows down," and make the acquaintance of the folk; and we then have a vision of the folk flowing in a kind of symbolic river toward the gulf of eternity. This symbolic river is described in the last five stanzas simply as if it were the real Mississippi. Until we get to the last portion of the poem, the section beginning, "And Pullman break-fasters glide glistening steel," the writing is predominantly pretty bad; from there on it is predominantly very powerful and becomes steadily more powerful, with only a few slight lapses, to the end. This is the one deeply impressive passage of any length in *The Bridge*, and along with a few earlier poems is probably the best writing in Crane. Thepantheism is subdued here; the emphasis is on the country and the folk and on the poet's love for them; and the rhetoric is magnificent. The following poem is called *The Dance*. In this piece the protagonist takes a canoe trip down Hudson River, finally leaves his canoe and climbs into the mountains, and at the same time appears to proceed into the remote past. He finally comes to an Indian dance, where a captured warrior is being burned at the stake; the warrior in death is married to Pocahontas, or in other words is united with the American soil. The tone of the poem is nervous and violent; the poem contains some of the most brilliant lines in Crane and some of the most grotesque; and at the end it illustrates very dramatically the difficulty of the pantheistic doctrine. The warrior is united with the soil, which is God; his identity is presumably lost in this union; yet the language in which the union is described is in part the language of the traditional poetry of devotion, but is mainly the language of love poetry: that is, personal extinction is described for the most part as if it were the consummation of a marriage and in some part as if it were a form of personal immortality. There is a violent dislocation here between the motivating theme and the emotion resulting from it; the poem is not merely confused, but it is confused in a manner which is suicidal. As I have said elsewhere, one does not deal adequately with the subject of death and immortality by calling the soil Pocahontas, and by then writing a love poem to an imaginary maiden who bears the name of Pocahontas. The misuse of metaphor here, the excursion by way of metaphor into pure irrelevance, is irresponsible almost to madness. Yet this poem is one of the two major crises in the sequence: in this poem the relationship of the protagonist to the soil, to God, and to eternity, is presumably established. The last poem in the group is called *Indiana*; in this poem a frontier mother bids farewell to her son and begs him to return home eventually. The mother may have been related loosely in Crane's mind to Pocahontas conceived as a mother; it is hard to be sure about this, but if she is not so related, there is no very evident reason for her being here. The poem is weak and sentimental.

The poems thus far have dealt primarily with what one might call the private spiritual experience, or the fate of the individual; those to follow deal primarily with the public spiritual experience, or the fate of the nation. There are qualifications to this statement, of course: *The River,* for example, as we have seen, deals with a vision of the folk, but it deals primarily with the individual's awakening to the folk and his share in their life; there is an element of private experience in a later poem, *Cape Hatteras,* but it is a secondary element; the *Three Songs,* which follow *Cape Hatteras,* deal with private experience, but have no real place in the sequence. It is worth noting that the poems thus far described, with the exception perhaps of *Indiana,* have a certain structural relationship to each other; whereas those which follow, and which deal with the public experience, are thrown together very loosely, and the aspects of the public experience with which they deal are few and appear to be selected almost at haphazard. Although Crane had curious ideas about the individual, he yet had ideas; but he was simply at a loss in dealing with society either in the present or in the historical past, for his ideas of the individual really preclude the possibility of a society.

The first of the later poems is a piece called *Cutty Sark,* a very slight but perversely amusing meditation on the great days of the American clipper ships. The main reason for the inclusion of such a piece is Crane's enthusiasm for everything pertaining to the sea, but the ships represent a heroic portion of the American past and can be made a symbol of the type of adventurousness treated more explicitly in *Cape Hatteras.* Next comes *Cape Hatteras,* which is primarily an invocation to Walt Whitman and an explicit acceptance of his doctrines. The Whitmanian doctrine which Crane emphasizes in this poem is the doctrine of an endless procession of higher and higher states of perfection, or what

594

I have called the doctrine of change for its own sake. Crane re-states Whitman's symbol of the open road in terms of a vision of airplanes traveling farther and farther into remotest space, air-planes which are more or less the successors of the clipper ships of *Cutty Sark:*

> *Years of the modern! Propulsions toward what capes!*

And again:

> *And now as launched in abysmal cupolas of space,*
> *Toward endless terminals, Easters of speeding light—*
> *Vast engines outward veering with seraphic grace*
> *On clarion cylinders pass out of sight*
> *To course that span of consciousness thou'st named*
> *The Open Road—thy vision is reclaimed.*

Cape Hatteras is followed by *Three Songs* which are only loosely, if at all, connected with the central theme. When Crane was putting the sequence into final order, he wrote me that he wanted to include the songs because he liked them, but that he was not sure the inclusion would be justified. The first song is called *Southern Cross:* it is a kind of love poem addressed to the constellation of that name as if the constellation were a woman or a female divinity; the constellation is equated with Eve, Magdalen, Mary, and "simian Venus," as if all conceivable types of love, like all types of woman, were one and were in some way identified with the mystical experience. The next song, *National Winter Garden,* is a vision of love as lust; and the third, *Virginia,* is a very slight and casual vision of sentimental love in the city. The poems obviously have no place in this latter half of the se-quence, and they would probably fit but little better into the first half. And the significance of the trilogy, simply in itself, and as a related group, is not clear, nor, I think, is the significance of any one of the three songs except the second, with its forthright and ugly portrayal of lust. The recognition of ugliness which we get here, in *Quaker Hill*, and in *The Tunnel*, is strictly speaking out of place in an optimistic system or at best can be justified only by Pope's formula:

> *Whatever wrong we call,*
> *May, must be right, as relative to all,*

which is poor consolation when one is in the predicament. Next comes *Quaker Hill*, a poem which compares the past with the present: Crane borrows his procedure from Eliot, and compares a sentimentalized past with a vulgar present; neither past nor present is understood, nor is there any apparent effort to understand either; both are presented impressionistically. The poem contributes nothing which is not better accomplished by *The Tunnel*.

Next come the two concluding poems, which may be regarded as companion pieces. Superficially regarded, *The Tunnel* is a fragmentary description of a ride in the subway, but it is offered as an account of a kind of inferno through which one must proceed to the final vision; into it Crane has crammed as many as possible of the ugliest details of modern urban life. No reason for the necessity of such an inferno, or purgatory, is offered; the account is given because the literal subway exists and perhaps because Crane had his periods of depression; there is obviously no intellectual grasp of the subject: *The Tunnel* is not well written, but this sudden outburst of ugliness has a curious pathos, nevertheless. It is as if the facts of Crane's life had suddenly and for the moment rebelled against his faith. We see the same Crane who in *The Dance* identifies himself with the warrior at the stake and cries out in one of the purest and most moving lines of our time, but with no understanding of his agony:

> *I could not pick the arrows from my side.*

But *The Tunnel* offers a kind of ugliness which is not justified by the Whitmanian theme and so cannot be treated in terms of the theme. It was an ugliness which Crane experienced, in part as a result of his acceptance of the theme and the fallacies of the theme, but to treat it in these terms he would have had to understand the fallacies and what had happened to him as a result of them. He did not understand, and the poem is an assortment of impressions without meaning. He abandons these particular impressions in the final poem, *Atlantis*, but a few years later they or others like them destroyed him.

In the last poem, *Atlantis*, the bridge is seen in apotheosis. The bridge is the United States of the future, reaching from ocean to ocean, from time to eternity; on it are spread cities and farmlands; from it skyscrapers rise to remoter and remoter distances, as the Whitmanian airplanes had risen earlier:

> *Like hails, farewells—up planet-sequined heights*
> *Some trillion whispering hammers glimmer Tyre:*
> *Serenely, sharply up the long anvil cry*
> *Of inchling aeons silence rivets Troy.*

The poem is unfortunately the most obscurely written in the sequence, if one examines it closely and from line to line; and I confess that I find it next to impossible to decipher except in what seem to me its most general intentions. As nearly as I can understand it, it offers a vision of physical splendor as a symbol for some kind of spiritual splendor; but the spiritual state in question remains undefined, and the final vision is without meaning: what we see ultimately is higher and higher skyscrapers, more and more marvelous in appearance, but ascending into heights of which the nature is uncertain. At the end Crane returns to the pantheism of the central poems:

> *O Answerer of all,—Anemone,—*
> *Now while thy petals spend the suns about us, hold—*
> *(O Thou whose radiance doth inherit me)*
> *Atlantis,—hold thy floating singer late!*

A passage which is, I imagine, Crane's equivalent for Whitman's "Look for me under your bootsoles."

I have indicated the main difficulties in *The Bridge* as I

597

have proceeded in my summary; and I have indicated also the main connections with Emerson and Whitman—in fact, the main difficulties and the main connections are identical with each other. The work as a whole is a failure. It builds up to two climaxes, one in *The Dance*, and one in *Atlantis*, both of which are incomprehensible. As a whole it is loosely constructed. The incomprehensibility and the looseness of construction are the natural result of the theme, which is inherited from Whitman and Emerson. The style is at worst careless and pretentious, at second-best skillfully obscure; and in these respects it is religiously of its school; and although it is both sound and powerful at its best, it is seldom at its best. Yet the last fifty-five lines of *The River*, and numerous short passages in *The Dance* and in *Atlantis* and a few short passages elsewhere, take rank, I am certain, among the most magnificent passages of Romantic poetry in our language; and at least two earlier poems, *Repose of Rivers* and the second of the *Voyages*, are quite as fine. The second of the *Voyages*, in fact, seems to me, as it has seemed to others, one of the most powerful and one of the most nearly perfect poems of the past two hundred years.

The difficulties inherent in the Whitmanian theme come out more clearly in Crane than in Whitman or in Emerson because of the more intense religious passion of the man. He is not content to write in a muddling manner about the Way; he is concerned primarily with the End. And in *The Dance* and in *Atlantis* respectively, he goes to the End. But his end is not an end in either case: it is a void. He does not discover this fact himself, but the passion and the linguistic precision with which he endeavors to render his delusion make it impossible, I think, that we should fail to recognize the delusion for what it is. And the same passion, functioning in his life, made him realize both the Way and the End completely, as Emerson and Whitman were incapable of doing. We have, it would seem, a poet of great genius, who ruined his life and his talent by living and writing as the two greatest religious teachers of our nation recommended.

Is it possible to shrug this off?

I would like at this point to consider the case and the arguments of Professor X. Professor X can be met four or five times on the faculty of nearly every university in the country: I have lost count of the avatars in which I have met him. He usually teaches American literature or American history, but he may teach something else. And he admires Emerson and Whitman.

He says that Emerson in any event did not go mad and kill himself; the implication is that Emerson's doctrines do not lead to madness and suicide. But in making this objection, he neglects to restate and defend Emerson's doctrines as such, and he neglects to consider the historical forces which restrained Emerson and which had lost most of their power of restraint in Crane's time and part of the country. He says that insanity is pathological and that a philosophy cannot be blamed for a pathological condition. Insanity, however, can be both induced and cured; any man can go mad under the proper pressure or influence; and although some cases of insanity, like some cases of tuberculosis, are incurable, many cases are dealt with successfully and many medical men are engaged professionally in dealing with them; and the technique of curing such cases is in a large measure a matter of explaining to the patient what is wrong with him and of securing his cooperation in the formation of desirable habits. And as a matter of curious but nevertheless historical fact, we have a rather large number of madmen and near madmen among literary men of established reputation from the middle of the eighteenth century onward and few or none before that time: once the romantic ideas have been generally accepted and the corresponding attitudes ingrained, we begin to observe such men as Smart, Chatterton, Collins, Clare, Blake, and the second James Thomson, to mention no others. The Emersonian doctrine, which is merely the romantic doctrine with a New England emotional coloration, should naturally result in madness if one really lived it; it should result in literary confusion if one really wrote it. Crane accepted it; he lived it; he wrote it; and we have seen what he was and wrote.

Professor X says, or since he is a gentleman and a scholar, he implies, that Crane was merely a fool, that he ought to have known better. But the fact of the matter is, that Crane was not a fool. I knew Crane, as I know Professor X, and I am reasonably certain that Crane was incomparably the more intelligent man. As to Crane's ideas, they were merely those of Professor X, neither better nor worse; and for the rest, he was able to write great poetry. In spite of popular and even academic prejudices to the contrary, it takes a very highly developed intelligence to write great poetry, even a little of it. So far as I am concerned, I would gladly emulate Odysseus, if I could, and go down to the shadows for another hour's conversation with Crane on the subject of poetry; whereas, politeness permitting, I seldom go out of my way to discuss poetry with Professor X.

Professor X, as a sentimentalist, is inclined to speak of the magic of poetry; he uses the term *magic* in a figurative sense which he has probably never endeavored to define. There is something supernatural about poetry, however, in a simple, literal, and theological sense, which Professor X in all likelihood has seldom considered. In poetry one mind acts directly upon another, without regard to "natural" law, the law of chemistry or of physics. Furthermore, the action is not only an action by way of idea, but by way of emotion and moral attitude; it is both complex and elusive. Poetry is a medium by means of which one mind may to a greater or less extent take possession of another, almost in the sense in which the term *possession* is used in demonology. It is a well-known fact, to medieval and to modern psychologists alike, that our emotional prejudices may pervert our rational faculty. If we enter the mind of a Crane, a Whitman, or an Emerson with our emotional faculties activated and our reason in abeyance, these writers may possess us as surely as demons were once supposed to possess the unwary, as surely as Whitman possessed Crane, as surely as Whitman and Emerson were possessed by their predecessors. If we come to these writers with all our faculties intact, however; if we insist on understanding not only what they are but what they are not; we can profit by what they may have to offer and at the same time escape being bemused by their limitations. Crane and Emerson possessed, for example, the gift of style without the gift of thought. They occasionally happen upon subjects, or fringes of subjects, which permit their talents to function with relatively little hindrance from their deficiencies. This happens to Emerson in the *Concord Hymn*, in *Days*, and in various fragments, and to Crane in the poems and passages which I have mentioned. Every such poem or fragment offers a particular critical problem, and some such problems are very curious and difficult; I cannot settle all of them at present in general terms. If we can isolate that which is good, these writers offer us something positive, however little in actual bulk; they offer us limited regions in which they may actually aid us to grow, to come to life.

Aquinas tells us that a demon may be said to be good in so far as he may be said to exist; that he is a demon in so far as his existence is incomplete. This statement is a necessary part of the doctrine of evil as deprivation. But a demon, or a genius, may be almost wholly deprived of being in large areas in which theoretically he ought to exist, and at the same time may have achieved an extraordinary degree of actuality in the regions in which he does exist; and when this happens, his persuasive power, his possessive power, is enormous, and if we fail to understand his limitations he is one of the most dangerous forces in the universe. Our only protection against him is the critical faculty, of which, I fear, we have far too little. The difference here, between Crane and Professor X, is not that Professor X possesses a wider intelligence, for we have seen that he does not, but that he possesses a less intensely active intelligence. The difference, I believe, is this: that Crane was absolutely serious and Professor X is not serious. Professor X is not restrained by the cast-iron habits which held Emerson in position, but he does not need to be; he is a man who conforms easily. He conforms to established usages because he finds life pleasanter and easier for those who do so; and he is able to approve of Emerson because he has never for a moment realized that literature could be more than a charming amenity. He believes that we should not be too critical of literature; that we should try to appreciate as much literature as possible; and that such appreciation will cultivate us. Professor X once reproved me for what he considered my contentiousness by telling me that he himself had yet to see the book that he would be willing to quarrel over. Professor X, in so far as he may be said to have moral motion, moves in the direction indicated by Emerson, but only to the extent of indulging a kind of genteel sentimentality; he is restrained from going the limit by considerations that he cannot or will not formulate philosophically but by which he is willing to profit. His position is that of the dilettante: the nearest thing he has to a positive philosophy is something to which he would never dare commit himself; that which keeps him in order is a set of social proprieties which he neither understands nor approves. In a world of atomic bombs, power politics, and experts in international knavery, he has little to guide him and he offers extremely precarious guidance to others; yet by profession he is a searcher for truth and a guide to the young.

Professor X will defend democracy in Emersonian terms, never stopping to consider that a defense of democracy which derives ultimately from the doctrine of natural goodness, of the wisdom of the untrained and mediocre mind, and of the sanctity of impulse is the worst kind of betrayal. He tells us that Emerson was an "idealist," but he does not tell us what kind. He tells us that Emerson taught self-reliance, but not that Emerson meant reliance on irresponsible impulse. He will cite us a dozen fragments of what might be mistaken for wisdom, and cite Emerson as the source; but he will neither admit what these fragments mean in the Emersonian system nor go to the trouble of setting them in a new system which would give them an acceptable meaning—and which would no longer be Emersonian. If one insists on driving him back to the naked generative formulae, the only terms which give any of his ideas any precision, he is inclined to find one naive, bigoted, or ludicrous, but he will not say precisely why.

Crane, however, had the absolute seriousness which goes with genius and with sanctity; one might describe him as a saint of the wrong religion. He had not the critical intelligence to see what was wrong with his doctrine, but he had the courage of his convictions, the virtue of integrity, and he deserves our respect. He has the value of a thoroughgoing demonstration. He embodies perfectly the concepts which for nearly a century have been generating some of the most cherished principles of our literature, our education, our politics, and our personal morals. If Crane is too strong a dose for us, and we must yet retain the principles which he represents, we may still, of course, look to Professor X as a model. But we shall scarcely get anything better unless we change our principles.

INDEX OF AUTHORS MENTIONED

INDEX OF AUTHORS MENTIONED

Prescott, W. H.: 193, 417, 419, 420, 422, 568
Proust, Marcel: 341

Racine, Jean: 25, 100, 481
Raleigh, Sir Walter: 31
Ransom, J. C.: 104, 361, 502-555, 556, 570, 572
Read, Herbert: 485, 486
Richards, I. A.: 475, 523, 538
Richardson, Dorothy: 341
Rimbaud, Arthur: 7, 36, 42, 56, 60, 83, 99, 253, 268, 454, 584, 585, 586
Roberts, E. M.: 571, 572
Robinson, E. A.: 30, 37, 104, 433, 480, 483, 498
Rochester, Earl of: 24-25
Roethke, Theodore: 570, 571, 574
Rossetti, D. G.: 494
Rousseau, J. J.: 7
Russell, Bertrand: 487
Russell, Frank: 567

Sandburg, Carl: 51, 591, 592
Santayana, George: 6
Schneider, H. W.: 160, 161
Scott, Sir Walter: 336
Shadwell, Thomas: 41
Shaftesbury, 3rd Earl of: 488
Shelley, P. B.: 50, 85, 93, 238, 242, 368, 369
Sherry, Pearl Andelson: 572
Sidney, Sir Phillip: 26, 29, 85, 131, 133, 296, 585
Simms, W. G.: 194
Smart, Christopher: 599
Smith, Bernard: 563-4
Smith, Maurine: 570, 571, 572
Spencer, Theodore: 490-1
Spenser, Edmund: 83, 494
Spiller, Robert: 176, 178-9
Stafford, Clayton: 104, 570, 571, 573
Stanford, Ann: 571, 572
Stanford, Don: 104, 108, 154, 570, 571, 574
Stevens, Wallace: 23, 69, 70, 95, 104, 105, 124, 126, 361, 431-459, 476, 477, 517, 528, 531, 552, 584
Stovall, Floyd: 234, 261, 587
Surrey, Henry Howard, Earl of: 296
Swinburne, A. C.: 85, 461, 466, 493, 494

Symons, Arthur: 85

Tate, Allen: 15-20, 22, 30, 54, 98, 104, 134, 143, 144, 146, 292, 517, 528-533, 545, 551, 554, 555, 556, 570, 571, 572, 573, 574
Taylor, Edward: 262
Taylor, Henry Osborn: 430
Taylor, W. F.: 568
Tennyson, Alfred: 237, 238, 242
Thackeray, W. M.: 37, 38
Thomson, James (the first of that name): 49, 82
Thomson, James (the second of that name): 599
Thoreau, H. D.: 270
Traherne, Thomas: 269, 278
Trollope, Anthony: 336, 337
Tuckerman, F. G.: 262
Turbervile, George: 90, 95
Turoldus: 410

Utter, William T.: 561

Valéry, Paul: 59, 95, 96, 99, 456, 480, 481, 483, 487, 489, 498
Van Doren, Mark: 570, 574
Vaughan, Henry: 281
Vaux, Thomas, Lord: 95, 296
Vergil: 135, 220
Verlaine, Paul: 56, 99, 100, 454, 455, 456
Very, Jones: 158, 169, 244, 262-282, 288, 344, 357
Voltaire: 7, 70, 73

Weaver, Raymond: 229, 560, 561
Webster, John: 107, 489, 492
Wescott, Glenway: 124, 572
Wharton, Edith: 37, 38, 40, 185, 219, 231, 302, 307, 309, 310, 342
Whitman, Walt: 31, 51, 62, 64, 91, 92, 93, 136, 144, 268, 441, 564, 577-603
Whittier, J. G.: 158
Wilde, Oscar: 84
Williams, W. C.: 23, 35, 36, 49, 51, 55, 63, 77-81, 82, 84, 85, 86, 87, 88, 93, 94, 95, 98, 101, 104, 116, 117, 121, 124, 125, 126, 129, 130, 141
Willis, N. P.: 256

LaVergne, TN USA
13 October 2009
160758LV00005B/7/A